ANNUAL REVIEW OF SOCIOLOGY

ANNUAL REVIEW OF SOCIOLOGY

ALEX INKELES, *Editor*
Stanford University

JAMES COLEMAN, *Associate Editor*
University of Chicago

NEIL SMELSER, *Associate Editor*
University of California, Berkeley

VOLUME 1

1975

ANNUAL REVIEWS INC.   4139 EL CAMINO WAY   PALO ALTO, CALIFORNIA 94306

ANNUAL REVIEWS INC.
Palo Alto, California, USA

International Standard Book Number: 0-8243-2201-0
Library of Congress Catalog Card Number: 74-81448

REPRINTS

The conspicuous number aligned in the margin with the title of each article in this
volume is a key for use in ordering reprints. Available reprints are priced at the
uniform rate of $1 each postpaid. Effective January 1, 1975 the minimum acceptable
reprint order is 10 reprints and/or $10.00, prepaid. A quantity discount is available.

PRINTED AND BOUND IN THE UNITED STATES OF AMERICA

PREFACE

The first *Annual Review* was published in 1932. It dealt with biochemistry, and its list of subscribers has grown steadily over the past 43 years. Other *Annual Reviews* covering eighteen additional scientific fields had entered the lists by 1973, and now, in 1975, sociology becomes the twentieth subject to be represented in this distinguished series.

Sociologists sensitive to the subtle indicators that define a discipline's standing in the ubiquitous schemes for ranking scientific prestige may note that their sister discipline, psychology, the fourth in this series, made its first appearance in 1950, and that anthropology, the only other social science in the *Annual Review* series, first appeared in 1972. Those who are of a competitive temperament may take comfort in the fact that sociology was at least "discovered" before energy, which is the subject of a new *Annual Review* to appear early in 1976.

For ourselves, we care not so much whether we are early or late, but rather rejoice in being here. In recent years specialized lines of research have proliferated, as have journals that focus on different topics. Maintaining a broad perspective, and keeping informed about developments over a wide range of activities, has thus become more difficult for every social scientist. The publication of this *Annual Review* provides the sociological community with a special opportunity for taking stock of progress in its various subfields at intervals.

Although we are gratified to serve the need for periodic reviews, we frankly acknowledge other motives. It is our hope that the articles in the *Annual Review of Sociology* will identify critical issues, sort out the research evidence bearing on them, and facilitate the systematic assessment of what we know. And by identifying new areas to review, as well as explicating and evaluating our individual and collective initial efforts, succeeding authors of *Annual Review* articles should contribute to raising the standards of sociological research both in specific fields and in the discipline at large.

Whatever its objectives, a *Review* such as this faces a reasonable expectation that it will "cover the field." There are many ways of dividing the sociological realm. As an initial framework, the Editorial Committee selected ten major headings, and these are reproduced in the list of Chapter Titles by Category. Without committing ourselves to this framework as a permanent core, it is our intention to maintain it at least for a few years. We adopted a broad interpretation of the field, but of course no one system will satisfy all demands. Thus there is no major heading for Socialization, but this is only because we subsumed it under Individual and Society. Although our major headings are tentatively fixed, we plan to maintain maximum flexibility in our selection of the specific topics on which the articles in each *Annual Review of Sociology* will focus. We can vary the subfields, allowing for the passage of time and the accumulation of new work before cycling back to a subject. We may also call the attention of the profession to coherent bodies of work outside the standard categories that conventionally serve to organize our collective enterprise.

(continued on next page)

No matter how coherent our plan for a volume, we are acutely conscious that while the Editorial Committee proposes, it is ultimately the contributing authors who dispose. Judging by those we have approached to date, sociologists live heavily committed lives. Nearly a quarter of the articles initially promised for this volume were unfortunately not ready at the time we were finally obliged to go to press. We hope some of these will appear in subsequent volumes. But inevitably this means that there are some major gaps in what might have been the ideal outline for this first *Review.* This accounts for the fact that Demography, for example, is not represented by even a single article in this first issue, although we had commissioned two.

Gaps aside, however, we are very proud indeed of the high quality of the contributions to this first *Annual Review of Sociology.* We believe it is the first in a long series of consistently excellent volumes that will represent sociology and help to shape its future as a science and an intellectual discipline.

THE EDITORS AND EDITORIAL COMMITTEE

CONTENTS

(See page viii for list of chapter titles by category)

CHAPTER TITLES BY CATEGORY

DIFFERENTIATION AND STRATIFICATION
  Race and Ethnic Relations
  Age Differentiation and the Life Course
  Sex Roles in Transition: A Ten-Year Perspective

POLITICAL SOCIOLOGY
  Community Power
  Political Participation and Public Policy

SOCIAL PROCESSES
  Convergence and Devergence in Development
  Strands of Theory and Research in Collective Behavior

INSTITUTIONS
  The Comparative Study of Health Care Delivery Systems
  Sociology of Science

INDIVIDUAL AND SOCIETY
  Major Developments in the Sociological Study of Deviance
  Alienation Studies
  Voluntary Action and Voluntary Groups

FORMAL ORGANIZATION
  Organizational Structure

URBAN SOCIOLOGY
  The Study of Urban Community and Personality

DEMOGRAPHY
  (Not represented in this volume)

POLICY
  Evaluation Research

THEORY AND METHODS
  Competing Paradigms in Macrosociology

ANNUAL REVIEWS INC. is a nonprofit corporation established to promote the advancement of the sciences. Beginning in 1932 with the *Annual Review of Biochemistry,* the Company has pursued as its principal function the publication of high quality, reasonably priced Annual Review volumes. The volumes are organized by Editors and Editorial Committees who invite qualified authors to contribute critical articles reviewing significant developments within each major discipline.

Annual Reviews Inc. is administered by a Board of Directors whose members serve without compensation.

Annual Reviews are published in the following sciences: Anthropology, Astronomy and Astrophysics, Biochemistry, Biophysics and Bioengineering, Earth and Planetary Sciences, Ecology and Systematics, Entomology, Fluid Mechanics, Genetics, Materials Science, Medicine, Microbiology, Nuclear Science, Pharmacology, Physical Chemistry, Physiology, Phytopathology, Plant Physiology, Psychology, and Sociology. The *Annual Review of Energy* will begin publication in 1976. In addition, two special volumes have been published by Annual Reviews Inc.: *History of Entomology* (1973) and *The Excitement and Fascination of Science* (1965).

ORGANIZATIONAL STRUCTURE

❖10500

W. Richard Scott

Department of Sociology, Stanford University, Stanford, California 94305

While it is difficult to capture with any precision the amoeba-like contours of an intellectual movement, it appears safe to conclude that until the late 1940s formal organizations did not exist as a distinct field of sociological inquiry. Precursors may be identified but each lacked some critical feature. Thus, there was considerable empirical research on organizations by, for example, criminologists who studied prisons, political analysts who examined bureaus and party structure, and industrial sociologists and applied anthropologists who focused on factories; but these investigators rarely attempted to generalize beyond the specific organizational form under investigation. The subject was prisons or parties or factories, not organizations. Industrial psychologists did pursue such general problems as low morale, fatigue, and turnover across several types of organizational settings, but did not raise their level of analysis to systematically conceptualize and compare the characteristics of organizations qua organizations. And while, from early in this century, administrative and management theorists did concentrate on the development of general principles focused on organizations as such, their approach was more often normative than empirical.

The emergence of organizations as a distinctive field of sociological investigation may be dated from the translations into English of Weber's (1946, 1947) and, to a lesser extent, Michels' (1949) statements on bureaucracy together with the efforts of Merton and associates (1952) to outline the boundaries of this new field of inquiry. Equal in importance to these theoretical efforts was the launching, under Merton's general influence, of a series of path-breaking and influential case studies of diverse types of organizations—the Tennessee Valley Authority (Selznick 1949), a gypsum mine and factory (Gouldner 1954), a government employment and a regulatory agency (Blau 1955), and a union (Lipset, Trow & Coleman 1956). For the first time sociologists were engaged in the development and empirical testing of generalizations dealing with the structure and function of organizations as organizations.

MAJOR TRENDS

Viewed in broad perspective, three major trends may be discerned in the work of organizational sociologists from the period 1950 to the present. As will be shown, the trends are not independent but closely interrelated. Each has contributed to shifting attention from an exclusive concern with explaining behavior within organizations to explaining structural differences among organizations.

Structure as a Dependent Variable

Early researchers took the structural features of organizations as given and proceeded to explore their implications for the behavior of participants. That is, organizational structure was viewed as setting or context, within which the variables of interest—worker satisfaction or "informal" (nonprescribed) communication patterns, for example—could be studied. If Weber can be credited with emphasizing the structural features of organizations, he can also be charged with having set back their systematic empirical analysis by his use of the ideal-type model which implied, or was interpreted as implying, that all modern (bureaucratic) organizations were quite similar in their structural characteristics. Udy (1959a) was among the first to suggest that Weber's model could be regarded as identifying a set of structural variables whose interrelations should not be taken as a matter of definition but as a subject for empirical exploration. Using crude measures of the structural properties of production organizations in nonindustrial societies developed from summaries of ethnographic materials assembled in the Human Relations Area Files, Udy proceeded to demonstrate the variability of these features and their interrelations as well as to begin the search for explanations of the different structural patterns found (Udy 1959a, 1959b, 1962). The transition in the theoretical status of structural characteristics of organizations from contextual or, at best, independent variables to dependent variables, whose variation was to be explained, constitutes the first major trend to be described. While slow to begin it has rapidly developed so that much research attention is currently being devoted to the explanation of organizational structure.

From Closed to Open System Models

When organizational structure is viewed as a limited set of factors which together may be arranged or modified to produce desired outcomes, then the logical model employed is that of the closed system. When the structure itself is viewed as something to be explained at least in part by the operation of external forces and as not completely under the control of system participants, then the underlying image is that of the open system.

Several distinct intellectual traditions have converged to produce a gradual shift in organizational analysis from closed to open system models. One of these stretches back to Michels' study in 1911 of the effects of a hostile political environment on the structural characteristics of the German social democratic party (Michels 1949). His approach inspired the subsequent studies by Selznick (1949, 1952), Clark (1958, 1960), and others who have examined the survival tactics of organizations adapting to (typically hostile) environments. A second incorporates the early insights of Barnard (1938), a remarkable telephone company executive, as developed and extended by Simon, March, and Cyert (Simon 1947, March & Simon 1958, Cyert & March 1963). These analysts view organizations as problem-solving mechanisms confronting uncertainty and beset by cognitive limitations in searching for, process-ing, and acting on information. Structural arrangements are viewed as both exacer-bating and alleviating the limitations of individual participants as information processers and decision makers (Allison 1971).

Yet another major impetus in the shift to open system models has come from the work of general systems theorists, an interdisciplinary intellectual movement begin-ning in the 1950s. The general conceptual approach of the founding fathers, includ-ing von Bertalanffy (1951), Wiener (1954), and Ashby (1956), has been applied by a number of analysts, but particularly Katz & Kahn (1966) and Thompson (1967), to the study of organizations. The approach emphasizes the organization's incom-pleteness and dependence on other units for inputs—ranging from raw materials, and socialized personnel to legitimacy—and for the disposition of its outputs, whether these take the form of manufactured products or rehabilitated clients. They view organizational structures as selected and shaped by the actions of and transac-tions with salient environmental units, and insist that any analysis of internal structure that does not take into account environmental factors is likely to be not simply limited, but misleading. General systems theorists also focus on aspects of structure different from those emphasized by closed system analysts. While a closed system model tends to emphasize the conserving, deviation-reducing "morpho-static" processes that act to preserve or maintain a given state of the system, open system theorists stress those "morphogenic" processes that elaborate, differentiate, and transform the structure (Buckley 1967). Further, the open system model places primary importance on those structural arrangements that permit goal-directed behavior by the creation of feedback loops or servomechanisms. These generate information on the condition of the system that can be compared to established standards, providing the input to a decision process that produces action modifying the system condition in a continuously circulating process (Ashby 1956, 1962, Beer 1964).

From Case to Comparative Studies

While the first two trends point to shifts in theoretical attention and models, the third denotes a change in methodology. The early research strategy of reliance on the case study has given way to a modified survey approach in which data are collected on a number of organizations. The case study has come under criticism not only because of the relatively low quality of the data generated (Weick 1969, Zelditch 1962), but also because of the type of data it elicits (Blau & Scott 1962). Case studies of one or a few organizations allow the systematic study of the behavior or attitudes of individual participants or work groups within organizations, but they do not support the testing of propositions in which the properties of the organiza-tions themselves are the variables of interest. The latter requires the systematic collection of information on relevant organizational variables across a number of organizations.

Survey research procedures are the methods traditionally employed by social scientists to gather large volumes of data efficiently, but these procedures required substantial modification before they were suitable for the study of organizational characteristics. Lazarsfeld and his associates pioneered in this area, devising and systematizing procedures for aggregating data on individual respondents to characterize organizational features (Kendall & Lazarsfeld 1950). A widely recognized typology developed by Lazarsfeld & Menzel (1961) suggests the types of measures that may be used to characterize the properties of a "collective," defined simply as any unit, such as an organization, composed of constituent parts, called "members." The properties of collectives may be: (a) "analytical"—based on some summary measure of the characteristics of its constituent members, for example, the average age of participants in an organization; (b) "structural"—based on a summary measure of the relationships among members, for example, the number of departments with a span of control greater than ten; or (c) "global"—based on information *not* derived from the characteristics of the individual members, for example, the assets of a company. Other important innovations occurring at about this same time in sampling techniques allowed investigators to take into account structural locations of respondents in devising their samples (Coleman 1958–1959).

Survey techniques have been supplemented with the increasing use of preexisting statistical records as an important and inexpensive source of information about organizations. More so than many types of complex units, organizations are likely to keep voluminous records concerning their own operations and to furnish such information to others engaged in accounting, regulatory, and coordinative activities. Sociologists are just beginning to exploit these data for their own analytical purposes.

In the light of the other major trends described, it will come as no surprise that the earliest use of these measures of structure—whether based on survey or archival data—was as independent variables, the analyst determining their impact on participants' attitudes and behavior. A number of closely related techniques, variously referred to as "contextual," "structural," and "compositional" analysis, were developed for this purpose and widely employed in early empirical studies (Lazarsfeld & Thielens 1958; Lipset, Trow & Coleman 1956; Blau 1960). Nevertheless, these developments—in measurement techniques, sample design, and analysis procedures —made possible the transition from case studies focusing attention on the explanation of the behavior of individuals within organizations to comparative studies directed toward explaining variation in the structural characteristics of organizations.

EXPLAINING ORGANIZATIONAL STRUCTURE

It is premature to attempt a comprehensive overview of knowledge on organizational structure. As we have seen, this type of research has been under way for only about a decade and a half and, as will be discussed in a concluding section, current research is beset with both theoretical and methodological problems. It is more useful and appropriate at this point in time to illustrate some of the main lines of investigation. We will consider two: studies examining the impact of technology on structure, and research focusing on the relation between size of organizations and selected structural characteristics.

Technology

While some earlier students of industrial and organizational sociology have noted the importance of technical and production features of the work process for worker behavior and work group structure (e.g. Dubin 1958, Sayles 1958, Trist & Bamforth 1951, Whyte 1961), it was the empirical research of Woodward (1958, 1965) that first called attention to technology as a general determinant of organization structure. The theoretical statements of Thompson (Thompson & Bates 1957, Thompson 1967) and Perrow (1965, 1970) served to broaden the definition of technology to include nonproduction organizations, and have emphasized the importance of technological factors for organizational design.

To focus on the technology of an organization is to view the organization as a mechanism for transforming inputs into outputs. Examination of various recent attempts to define and measure technology reveals that technology has been viewed very broadly (or quite differently) to include the characteristics of the *inputs* utilized by the organization, the characteristics of the *transformation processes* employed by the organization, and the characteristics of the *outputs* produced by the organization. In addition to this variation by stage of processing, Hickson, Pugh & Pheysey (1969) suggest that measures of technology vary depending on whether emphasis is placed on the nature of the *materials* on which work is performed, the characteristics of the *operations* or techniques used in carrying out the work, or the state of *knowledge* which attends the transformation process. Combining these two bases of classifying technology allows us to categorize and summarize some of the types of variables that have been employed to characterize the technology of an organization.

Typology of Technology Variables

   I. Materials Technology

      A. Emphasis on Inputs

         Uniformity of inputs (Litwak 1961)

         Hardness of materials (Rushing 1968)

         Variability of the stimuli (Perrow 1970)

      B. Emphasis on Throughputs

         Number of exceptions (Perrow 1970)

         Interchangeability of components (Rackham & Woodward 1970)

      C. Emphasis on Outputs

         Major product changes (Harvey 1968)

         Homogenizing vs individuating settings (Wheeler 1966)

  II. Operations Technology

      A. Emphasis on Inputs

         Extent to which organization can regulate inputs through buffering or leveling processes (Thompson 1967)

    B.   Emphasis on Throughputs

        Complexity of technological processes (Udy 1959b)
        Technical complexity (Woodward 1965)
        Workflow integration (Pugh et al 1969)
        Routineness of work (Hage & Aiken 1969)

    C.   Emphasis on Outputs

        Extent to which organization can regulate outputs through stockpiling
           or leveling of demand (Thompson 1967)
        Value added in manufacture

III. Knowledge Technology

    A.   Emphasis on Inputs

        Predictability (Scott et al 1967)
        Anticipation of fluctuations in supplies (Thompson 1967)

    B.   Emphasis on Throughputs

        Knowledge of cause-effect relations (Thompson 1967)
        Analyzability of search (Perrow 1970)
        Information required to perform task compared to information pos-
           sessed by organization (Galbraith 1973)

    C.   Emphasis on Outputs

        Time span of definitive feedback (Lawrence & Lorsch 1967)
        Anticipation of fluctuations in demand (Thompson 1967)

While there exist instances of all the types of variables suggested by the typology, they are not equally popular. As might be expected, the largest number of variables seems to exist for type IIB—operations technology for the throughput process. This aspect of typology is emphasized in particular by Woodward and by the Aston group; both supply many examples of specific measures (Hickson, Pugh & Pheysey 1969, Pugh et al 1969, Rackham & Woodward 1970). Next most popular are measures of materials technology with emphasis on the characteristics of inputs, type IA. Also widely employed have been type IIIB measures that emphasize knowledge employed in the production process. An emphasis on knowledge as compared to materials or operations marks a shift from an objective to a more subjective conception of technology. The latter takes into account the characteristics of the performer as well as the characteristics of the work to be performed. For example, stimuli that are objectively variable may be more or less predictable to a performer, depending on the state of his knowledge of laws governing the behavior of the stimuli. This possibility raises a whole family of issues that have received relatively little attention to date; namely how much agreement is there among various types of participants on the characteristics of the technology employed. Studies indicate that differences in conceptions of technology may exist among various categories of performers relating to a single task, between administrators and performers, and between performers in different organizations relating to what is ostensibly the same task (Dornbusch & Scott 1975, Scott 1972).

Surprisingly, there are relatively few attempts to develop variables based on measures of organizational outputs. The largest number of measures of this type have been developed by the Aston group but are regarded by them as measures of organizational "charter"—the social functions or goals of the organization—rather than of technology. Many of the specific measures developed, however, refer specifically to characteristics of outputs—multiplicity, type, and degree of customer orientation or customization (Pugh et al 1969: 99–102)

Our summary of the more popular measures of technology suggests that this concept is not simple and that several underlying dimensions, such as variability and complexity, appear to be involved. Not apparent from the typology is another problem besetting much of the work in this area and rendering noncomparable the results of many empirical studies. This second problem involves the unit of analysis: what unit is being characterized by the variable? Hickson, Pugh & Pheysey (1969: 395) note one manifestation of this problem in commenting on Woodward's typology of production systems: "To describe the general technology of a factory as 'mass,' when this characterizes only some departments and other departments are engaged in small batch and process operation, is an oversimplification." In other words, technologies may vary greatly within as well as between organizations. A second instance of this problem is described by Mohr (1971: 446), who notes that some measures focus on the role of the individual worker while others characterize the larger work process. While these levels are not unrelated, it is often the case that greater complexity at the work system level, as in mass production organizations, may not be accompanied by greater complexity at the level of the worker's role. Indeed, the jobs of individual workers may become more simple and routine as the system level work process gains in complexity.

Given the various types of disagreement and confusion in the conception and measurement of technology in organizations, studies relating technology to various facets of organizational structure do not invariably report similar or comparable findings. Nevertheless, the general shape of the relationships is clear: more uniform inputs and routinized workflows tend to be associated with more centralized, formalized, and differentiated structures. For example, Woodward's (1965) earlier studies of 100 firms in South Essex reported that higher levels of technical complexity were directly related to the length of the line of command, the span of control of the chief executive, and the ratios of managers to total personnel and of clerical and administrative staff to manual workers. Hage & Aiken's (1969) research based on 16 social welfare and health organizations reports that more routinized technologies were associated with higher levels of centralization, greater formalization of roles, and less highly trained workers. And Harvey's (1968) study of 43 industrial organizations reported that the fewer the product changes (the higher the level of technical specificity), the greater the number of specialized subunits, the larger the number of levels of authority, the higher the ratios of managers and supervisors to total personnel, and the higher the amount of program specification or formalization. In other studies, for example Hickson, Pugh & Pheysey (1969), and later research by Woodward (1970), these relations were either not confirmed or were only weakly present.

Many of the disparaties in results from empirical studies may be accounted for by careful attention to the type of measures employed or to differences in the unit of analysis. Other more general factors affecting these relations will be described after we examine a series of studies focusing on the effects of size on structure.

Size

There has been a long-standing research interest in the relation between organizational size and selected structural variables, beginning with a great many studies focused on size and bureaucratization, measured by the relative size of the administrative component. Many critics of organizations, for example, Parkinson (1957), have asserted that large organizations are overbureaucratized, devoting too large a proportion of their staff resources to administration. Recent studies have added a third major variable, differentiation, and attempted to assess the relation between size and differentiation and between both these variables and bureaucratization. Data collected over several decades suggest that on the average organizations are larger, more differentiated, and more bureaucratized today than in the past (Bendix 1956, Melman 1951). However these historical trends should not be confused with the present issue of whether larger organizations tend to have disproportionately large administrative staffs or more highly differentiated structures than small ones.

SIZE AND ADMINISTRATIVE COMPONENT   Four early studies limited attention to the relation between size of organization and relative size of administration. Contradictory findings were reported. Melman's (1951) data on American manufacturing concerns revealed an inverse relation between size and proportion of administrative personnel as did Bendix's (1956) data on German industries analyzed by size of firm and ratio of administrators to production workers. By contrast, Baker & Davis (1954), in a study of 211 manufacturing firms in Ohio, found no relation between size of organization and proportion of administrative officials. And Terrien & Mills (1955), in a study of school districts in California, reported a positive relation: the larger the size of district, the larger the proportion of administrators.

Here the matter rested until Anderson & Warkov (1961) carried out their research on 49 Veterans' Administration hospitals. Their overall sample revealed a negative relation between organizational size and size of the administrative component. However, hoping to account for the Terrien and Mills' findings, they introduced a third variable, which they labeled "complexity," referring to differences among organizations in their sample in the complexity of work carried out. Specifically, tuberculosis hospitals, specializing in a single type of disease, were regarded as less complex than general hospitals that handle many types of illness. Anderson and Warkov found that the more complex hospitals were characterized by a higher ratio of administrators. With this finding, these authors speculated about the relations among the three variables. They suggested that simple increases in the number of employees should not require disproportionate increase in administrators; on the contrary, the relative size of the administrative component should decrease as the number of persons performing identical tasks in the same place increases because of economics of scale. By contrast, increases in the number of locations at which work is carried out can pose additional coordination problems and require the services of a larger number of administrators. This argument could account for the positive relation between school district size, which is positively related to number of schools in the district, and size of the administrative component. However, Anderson and Warkov are less clear in relating complexity of work to administrative requirements. Why should the administrative component be affected by increases in the complexity of work, as measured by the number of different types of tasks performed? Anderson & Warkov (1961:27) hint at the reason when they note that number of different tasks performed may also be thought of as increasing specialization and differentiation of work roles. And specialization of work roles, if the tasks performed are interdependent, implies a need for integration and coordination. But it is *administrative* complexity that is at issue here—problems posed for administrators by a differentiated, but interrelated labor force. By the time we come to the work of Rushing, the linkage between (administrative) complexity and differentiation has become quite explicit. Rushing (1967:275) points out that the prediction of disproportionate increases in administrative personnel associated with increases in organizational complexity "is a straightforward deduction from two assumptions: (1) that increases in the division of labor lead to increases in problems of coordination, and (2) that administrative personnel, rather than production personnel, are the ones primarily concerned with problems of coordination." It seems to us important to clearly distinguish between the complexity of work being performed by rank-and-file employees as indicated by, for example, the number of task activities to be carried out and the differentiation of work roles or locations, as measured by such indicators as the number of different types of occupational roles present in an organization. While it is sometimes empirically the case that complex work is handled by a differentiated structure, complexity of work should not be confused with differentiation of roles. The first is an aspect of technology; the second is a facet of structure.

The concept of differentiation has been introduced, but before pursuing it let us complete the discussion of size and the administrative component. This relation rapidly became more complex and interesting when in 1966 Rushing called attention to the fact that the administrative component was not a unitary structural component but, in his terms, a "heterogeneous category" comprised of various classes of participants performing quite different functional roles. In the first of two studies, based on data from the U.S. Census of Manufactures for 30 manufacturing industries for 1947–50 and 34 industries for 1958–60, Rushing developed six ratios of administrative categories to production personnel. In addition to the familiar proportion of total administrative personnel to production workers, five other ratios were distinguished whose numerators were comprised of managers, officials and proprietors; clerical and kindred workers; professional, technical and kindred workers; sales workers; and service workers. Using measures of average firm size for each of the industry groups, Rushing reported marked variation in the relation between size and each of the ratios as measured by rank correlations. In particular, managerial and sales personnel were found to be negatively related to average size of firm; professional and clerical workers, positively correlated; while service personnel showed weak and inconsistent relations with size. Total administrative ratios showed a negative but low correlation with average size of firm, a conclusion that Rushing (1966:106) argued masked a set of quite diverse and inconsistent relations between size and particular administrative components.

A second study based on U.S. Census data on 279 occupations analyzed by industry failed to reveal such inconsistent findings in the relation between size and various components of administration. In this study Rushing (1967) reduced the number of administrative components to four ratios and attempted to provide more substantive interpretations of their possible role. In addition to total administrators, he distinguished between (a) managerial personnel, a category that "exerts its coordinative functions primarily through hierarchical authority and supervision"; (b) professional personnel, participants representing "an elaboration and development of the staff or advisory functions in industry, and an increase in direction and coordination of production activities based on technical knowledge and expertise"; and (c) clerical personnel, participants whose growth indicates "the development of files and the degree to which production activities are regularized and standardized through formal written specifications and communications" (Rushing 1967:278). Results indicated an inverse relation between industry size and the relative number of administrative personnel for all four administrative ratios, the rank order correlations being slightly stronger for total administration and for clerical structure than for managerial hierarchy and professional authority. However, it is difficult to know how to interpret these findings since they are based on measures of industry size rather than average firm size.

As another example of research examining the effects of size on various components of administration, we have Blau & Schoenherr's (1971) examination of 53 state offices of the employment security agency in the U.S. These researchers distinguished between supervisory ratio—the proportion of participants holding line authority, staff ratio—the proportion of total personnel time devoted to staff and technical services, and clerical ratio—the percentage of clerks in the agency. As with Rushing's first study, these ratios relate differently to size. In particular, the supervisory and staff ratios exhibited a fairly strong, negative relation to size (-.34 and -.44, respectively), while there was no association between agency size and the proportion of clerks (.09).

Finally, Kasarda's (1974) analysis of the administrative component of 178 school systems in the state of Colorado reinforces the need to differentiate between various categories of administrative functions. He reports that while the managerial component within schools declined as a function of size, both the "communicative" component, composed of all secretaries and clerical personnel, and the "professional and technical" component, consisting of such staff members as guidance counselors, librarians, and psychologists, increased with system size. Some notion of the magnitude of these changes is indicated by the following percentages: managerial functions decreased from 77 to 28% of the total administrative component in the smallest as compared to the largest school districts, while the communicative component increased from 8 to 45%, and the professional staff functions from 15 to 27% of total administration in small as compared to large districts.

Thus, it appears that Rushing is correct in his assertion that the administrative component is comprised of several types of personnel and that the relative size of these subcategories may relate quite differently to total size of organization. We cannot hope to account for all of these differing variations, but can shed some light on the issues by taking into account a third variable—organizational differentiation.

SIZE AND DIFFERENTIATION   Early research attention was devoted to exploring the connection between size and bureaucratization. Interest in the relation between size and differentiation developed more slowly with some early researchers reporting no association between these variables. For example, as recently as 1967, Rushing noted that "Although it is generally assumed that size and the division of labor are directly related, there is little actual evidence for this" (p. 283). Then he proceeded to report a Spearman rank correlation of .24 between industry size and the Gibbs and Martin D, a measure of the division of labor taking into account the number of occupations within an industry as well as the evenness of distribution of personnel among them (Gibbs & Martin 1962). And in the same year Hall, Haas & Johnson (1967) reported modest positive correlation between size of organization and several indicators of differentiation but interpret their findings as showing no significant associations. They define differentiation as including "the number of separate 'parts' of the organization as reflected by the division of labor, number of hierarchical levels, and the spatial dispersion of the organization" (p. 906). Horizontal differentiation is measured by such indicators as the number of major divisions or departments, hierarchical differentiation by the average number of hierarchical levels, and spatial dispersion by the geographical separation of organizational facilities and personnel. Using data from 75 quite diverse organizations arranged in three size categories, Hall and his associates reported correlations ranging from .23 to .35 with Kendall's Tau C for seven out of the nine indicators for the three types of differentiation. Perhaps because a fourth set of indicators, measuring goal differentiation, was uncorrelated with size of organizations, Hall, Haas & Johnson (1967:912) somewhat surprisingly conclude that their findings relating size to differentiation were "inconsistent" and that in their view "size may be rather irrelevant as a factor in determining organizational structure." Our interpretation of these data leads to the different conclusion that this study indicates a modest but reasonably consistent positive association between organizational size and three dimensions of structural differentiation.

The strongest evidence relating size to differentiation comes from a series of studies conducted by Blau and his associates in several types of organizations. Blau's view of differentiation is quite similar to that of Hall, Haas and Johnson (Blau 1970:203):

The term differentiation refers specifically to the number of structural components that are formally distinguished in terms of any one criterion. . . . A dimension of differentiation is any criterion on the basis of which the members of an organization are formally divided into positions, as illustrated by the division of labor; or into ranks, notably managerial levels; or into subunits, such as local branches, headquarters divisions, or sections within branches or division.

Data relating size to several dimensions of differentiation were collected by Blau and his colleagues in studies of 53 state employment security agencies together with their division headquarters and local branches (Blau & Schoenherr 1971), 194 finance departments in various branches of state and local government (Meyer 1972), and 115 colleges and universities (Blau 1973). Each of these studies finds consistently strong and positive associations between organizational size and various types of differentiation. For example, for the state employment security agencies, Blau and Schoenherr report zero order correlations with size of .94 for number of local offices, .78 for occupational positions, .60 for hierarchical levels, and .38 for functional divisions.

While these and related studies do report consistently positive correlations between size and several aspects of differentiation, they also reveal enough dissimilarity to suggest that, as in the case of the administrative component, we are not dealing with a homogeneous category. Not only does the response pattern to size vary for these different aspects; their organizational significance also varies. For example, one important basis for distinguishing between types of differentiation is whether the process entails the creation of new types of units. Vertical differentiation in which new types of leadership positions are created or horizontal differentiation in which new work specialities are created are both instances of *functional* differentiation. Both entail the creation of new structural units that differ in their functional role from previously existing units. By contrast, the development of new subunits that are a type of "branch office" appears to represent a quite different process that is usefully termed *segmentation* (Durkheim 1947). They represent the proliferation of additional structural units that do not differ qualitatively from existing units. The former process would appear to involve the possible "adaptive upgrading" of structure, to borrow Parsons' phrase (1966), while the latter would seem to represent a simpler form of growth. Moreover, we would expect functional differentiation to make different demands upon the administrative component than segmentation. More generally, we would expect each aspect of differentiation—whether the number of occupational groups, managerial levels, divisions, or branch offices—to generate differing coordination requirements and so to relate differently to the several administrative components. This suggests the need to examine the interrelations among all three types of variables.

SIZE, DIFFERENTIATION, AND ADMINISTRATIVE COMPONENT   As we have seen, at the most general level organizational size appears to set in motion opposing tendencies. In a remarkable series of propositions Blau (1970) has attempted to summarize and resolve these conflicts as follows. Large size is associated with structural differentiation, and differentiation, in turn, enlarges the administrative component. This occurs because differentiation increases the heterogeneity of work among the various subunits and individuals, creating problems of integration and coordination of effort. The administrative component expands to assume these responsibilities. On the other hand, organizational size is associated with increases in the average size of units, within which the work performed can be relatively homogenous. The larger the number of persons engaged in similar work, the smaller the proportion of administrative personnel needed to supervise it. Blau & Schoenherr (1971:91) conclude that "Large size, by promoting differentiation, has the indirect effect of enlarging the managerial component, but the savings in managerial manpower resulting from a large scale of operations outweigh these indirect effects, so that the overall effect of large size is a reduction in the managerial component." Studies conducted by Blau and his associates report findings generally consistent with these interpretations, but longitudinal studies are required to test the causal explanations proposed. Such studies are just beginning to appear (Holdaway & Blowers 1971, Meyer 1972), and results are inconclusive.

Turning from a consideration of the general to the more specific relations between differentiation and administrative components, there are a few studies that allow us to relate a particular aspect of differentiation to a particular component of administration. For example, Rushing (1967) reports that the division of labor in industries, as measured by the number of occupational groups and the evenness with which personnel are distributed among them, was more strongly related to increases in the ratio of clerical and professional personnel than to increases in the managerial ratio. He speculates (Rushing 1967:292): "Thus, relative to managerial authority and supervision formal communication and professional authority may become increasingly important in coordination as industries become increasingly complex." Analyzing data from the study of the state employment security agencies, Blau & Schoenherr (1971) employ standardized regression coefficients to show that while the supervisory ratio at headquarters is affected by three aspects of structural differentiation—levels, divisions, and sections per division—staff ratio is affected primarily by vertical differentiation (levels), while clerical ratio is responsive to the division of labor as measured by number of job titles. Finally, Blau's (1973) university study indicates that both horizontal differentiation into schools and colleges and vertical differentiation into hierarchical levels were associated with a higher ratio of administrators to faculty; by contrast the clerical-faculty ratio was found to be associated only with horizontal differentiation into departments. Blau (1973:72) argues: "This difference suggests that the degree of differentiation into major components of the administrative structure makes demands on senior administrative personnel, whereas further differentiation within these major components makes demands that can be satisfied with less skilled, clerical personnel."

This type of research is obviously in its infancy. In pursuing these issues, our conception of organizational systems which has become somewhat complex must become even more so. Not only do we need to recognize that there are various components of administration, we also must acknowledge that there are other means of coordination that are not reflected in personnel measures. For example, various impersonal control mechanisms such as rules and schedules, performance records, and assembly lines once established can coordinate work in the absence of personal supervision (Blau & Scott 1962). And automation has replaced clerical personnel in some situations and may soon become a threat to middle management and various staff positions. Further, we have suggested that differentiation may take several forms—for example, functional differentiation as compared with segmentation— each of which has differing implications for coordination requirements, but the complexities do not end there. For example, Blau, Heydebrand & Stauffer (1966) have distinguished between *specialized* and *routinized* differentiation. The former refers to an advanced division of labor in combination with professionalization of the work force; the latter to an advanced division of labor in the absence of professionalization. These two situations are characterized by very different administrative arrangements in that the professionalized work force is likely to assume wider responsibilities and more of the burden for coordination rather than relying on the administrative hierarchy to perform this function (Heydebrand 1973, Stinchcombe 1959).

If we go on to ask why some work arrangements involve the use of a specialized and professionalized labor force while others permit routinization, we return full circle to confront technological differences among occupations and organizations. Only tasks that are predictable and for which there exists cause-effect knowledge to guide processing activities can be safely routinized (Dornbusch & Scott 1975). Thus, an important set of predictions relating differentiation to modes of coordination, including the administrative component, would appear to relate more closely to matters of technology than to size.

Postcript: Technology, Size, and Structure

Early in the presentation of findings on the employment security agencies, Blau & Schoenherr (1971:57) summarize the conclusion to which their data point: "Size is the most important condition affecting the structure of organizations." However, it is difficult to accept this sweeping generalization because of the design of the study, as well as others carried out by Blau's research program on comparative research, which focuses on a single type of organization, in this case, employment security agencies. Basing the study on a single type of organization tends to have the effect of not allowing technology to vary meaningfully across organizations that perform the same tasks or functions but on a varying scale. Examining a single type of organization also reduces variation in other important respects such as the political and economic context within which the organization must operate. It is not appropriate to make comparative assertions as to the relative power of classes of variables under circumstances in which certain of them are arbitrarily restricted in variation or excluded from consideration.

The research program carried out by members of the Industrial Administration Unit at the University of Aston seems better designed in this respect. Concerned with the limitations of focusing on one or two selected variables of interest, they have defined and measured a large number of structural and contextual variables and selected a heterogeneous, random sample of 46 work organizations within which to assess the relative importance of each factor (Pugh et al 1963, Pugh et al 1968, Pugh et al 1969). Unfortunately for our purposes the Aston team employed factor analysis to combine their structural measures, themselves based on a combination of various scales, into three large clusters of variables before considering their relation to such "contextual" factors as size and technology of organization. Size is found to exhibit strong and positive correlations with the dimension "structuring of activities," which includes heavy loadings on such variables as differentiation, standardization, and formalization. It is less strongly associated with the other two dimensions, "concentration of authority," which measures degree of centralization and autonomy of the organization in its decision making, and "line control of workflow," which is concerned with line hierarchy and contains heavy loadings on percentage of work flow superordinates and negative loading on subordinate ratio. By contrast, their measure of technology, "workflow integration," exhibited modest correlations with all three dimensions (Pugh et al 1969). And after a more detailed analysis of these data, Hickson, Pugh & Pheysey (1969:388–89) conclude:

> Operations technology as defined here is accounting for but a small proportion of the total variance in structural features. Other variables contribute more. On this sample, the broad 'technological imperative' hypothesis that operations technology is of primary importance to structure is not supported. . . . The present data suggest that operations technology has only a limited specific effect compared to size.

Even given the improved design and sample on which these conclusions are based, they should not be embraced too quickly. Both the conception of technology as "workflow integration" as well as the specific manner in which this variable is operationalized seem to rest on an excessively narrow view of technology. For example, indicators of "operating variability" and "operating diversity," which most analysts would include as measures of technology (Type IC, materials outputs), are treated by the investigators as measures of "charter" and so are excluded as indicators of technology (Pugh et al 1969; Hickson, Pugh & Pheysey 1969). Further, Aldrich (1972) has shown that the specific empirical findings reported by the Aston group may be used to support quite varying interpretations of the relations among size, technology, and structure. By making explicit the types of causal inferences that are implicit in the analysis by the Aston group, Aldrich shows that with different assumptions, the causal pattern can be reversed. Empirical correlations can be interpreted only with the aid of a theoretical model, and in science that model should be stated as carefully and explicitly as possible.

DIFFICULTIES IN EXPLAINING STRUCTURE

While believing that progress has been made in the last two decades in understanding organizational structure, there remains much room for improvement, both in methodology and theory.

On the methodological front, we have much to learn about measuring organization structure. Just how much is demonstrated by a recent study by Pennings (1973) in which data on organizational characteristics are simultaneously gathered using two sets of instruments: expert informants or organizational documents are used to construct what Lazarsfeld & Menzel (1961) would label "global" measures, and survey data are collected from rank and file participants to construct "analytical" measures. Seven measures of centralization and seven measures of formalization were gathered in a sample of ten organizations and scored both for the total organization and for the production department within each organization. The results for the production department, a more homogeneous unit than the entire organization, are quite disturbing: 8 of the 12 correlations between the survey measures and global measures of centralization are negative and two of these are large enough to be statistically significant! None of the positive correlations is large enough to be significant. Pennings (1973:697) points that: "One should realize that in the current literature all these indicators of centralization are considered as sampling aspects of the same property space. It appears, however, that they cannot be viewed as tapping the same latent trait." Measures of formalization fare little better: of the ten measures, four are negative and none is significantly positive. Obviously, more attention needs to be given to improving the validity and reliability of measures in this area than has been the case to date; and measures used in one study need to be replicated in others. More thought and research attention need to be given to the relative advantages of using documentary evidence, single informants, or surveys of rank-and-file members for gathering data. As comparative studies become increasingly popular, it is essential that we move toward the development of criteria or guidelines for determining what types of information can appropriately be gathered from the various sources available.

Also, we need and show signs of beginning to move from reliance on cross–sectional studies to longitudinal studies utilizing panel and time-series data. Inferences made from cross-sectional studies of organizations of varying size on the effects of organizational growth, for example, may prove to be quite misleading. Holdaway & Blowers (1971) report that data on administrative ratios and organization size for 41 urban school systems in western Canada reveal the familiar negative pattern when examined cross–sectionally, but that the administrative ratios do not decline as a function of increasing size in most districts examined over a five-year period. And Freeman & Hannan's (in press) analysis of data from 769 California school districts suggests that different relations obtain between size of organization and administrative component, depending on whether the organization is in a period of growth or a period of decline. Their analysis reveals that the size of the administrative component increases along with the size of the organization during periods of growth, but that during periods of decline the size of the administrative component does not diminish along with total organizational size. This disparity in rates leads Freeman and Hannan to be skeptical about attempts to develop, from cross-sectional studies, generalizations relating size of administrative component and organizational size, since these studies will inevitably combine data from both growing and declining organizations.

Turning to theoretical limitations in studies of organizational structure to date, we have not yet begun to develop adequate modes of explanation for observed relationships. Some students appear to embrace a deterministic orientation in examining causal patterns among structural variables. Thus, some students argue that the technical requirements of the tasks to be performed force certain regularities upon the behavior of participants and on the forms of organizations, a form of technological determinism. Most would not consciously assume such an extreme posture, but all need to be more explicit about the mechanisms that operate to produce observed relationships. Among possible arguments might be that technological requirements place certain constraints on possible relationships; a contingency argument that certain structures are better suited to certain technologies and that over time these are more likely to survive (Lawrence & Lorsch 1967); or an "isomorphy" argument that related systems tend over time to mirror or resemble one another, although the causal process associated with this latter argument is obscure. Similarly, some students appear to see organizational size as forcing certain structural arrangements. In certain limiting cases, this is the correct explanation. For example, as Meyer (1972:434–35) points out: "Ratios of subordinates to supervisors must increase with size given a fixed number of levels of supervision." For most relations involving size, however, arguments similar to those just made for technology would be appropriate and merit exploration. Recent attempts to develop and test causal models are associated with the decided advantage that analysts are forced to make explicit their causal assumptions.

Certainly the most pervasive causal imagery utilized by current students of organizational structure is that of rationality of decision making and behavior. We are asked to assume that participants in organizations will be motivated to devise and establish the most effective and efficient arrangements for task performance. If tasks are uniform then, in the interests of efficiency, work will be standardized. If work is divided then coordination arrangement will be devised in the interests of effectiveness. Thus, Perrow (1970:80) states: "We must assume here that, in the interest of efficiency, organizations wittingly or unwittingly attempt to maximize the congruence between their technology and their structure." And Thompson (1967) prefaces all of his specific propositions predicting various structural arrangements with the illusive phrase: "Under norms of rationality. . . ." It is a virtue of Pondy's (1969) study of organization size and the administrative component that he treats the relative size of administration as a variable subject to managerial discretion rather than as technologically determined. However, managers' decisions are assumed by the model to be governed by such rational criteria as profit maximization.

Such assumptions are widespread even though we have known since the work of Roethlisberger & Dickson (1939), if not long before, that the "logic of efficiency" is not the only logic utilized by organizational participants. Power, status, conflict, commitment—these forces are not foreign to the operation of organizations; and much of the recent research on decision making in organizations emphasizes the limitations and constraints on rationality (March & Simon 1958, Allison 1971). In a review of their employment security agency study, Street (1972:494) criticizes Blau and Schoenherr for failing to "go beyond an excessively straightforward 'management science' " to develop a more realistic theory of decision making to account for structural regularities. Perhaps these comments serve less well as a criticism of past efforts that have produced important new insights than as a challenge for the next generation of studies.

Literature Cited

Aldrich, H. E. 1972. Technology and organizational structure: a reexamination of the findings of the Aston group. *Admin. Sci. Quart.* 17:26–43

Allison, G. T. 1971. *Essence of Decision: Explaining the Cuban Missile Crisis.* Boston: Little, Brown. 338 pp.

Anderson, T. R., Warkov, S. 1961. Organizational size and functional complexity: a study of administration in hospitals. *Am. Sociol. Rev.* 26:23–28

Ashby, W. R. 1956. *An Introduction to Cybernetics.* London: Chapman & Hall

Ashby, W. R. 1962. Principles of the self-organizing system. In *Principles of Self-Organization,* ed. H. von Foerster, G. W. Zopf, 255–78. New York: Pergamon

Baker, A. W., Davis, R. C. 1954. *Ratios of Staff to Line Employees and Stages of Differentiation of Staff Functions.* Columbus: Bur. Bus. Res., Ohio State Univ.

Barnard, C. I. 1938. *The Functions of the Executive.* Cambridge, Mass.: Harvard Univ. 334 pp.

Beer, S. 1964. *Cybernetics and Management.* New York: Wiley. 214 pp.

Bendix, R. 1956. *Work and Authority in Industry.* New York: Wiley. 466 pp.

Blau, P. M. 1955. *The Dynamics of Bureaucracy.* Chicago: Univ. Chicago Press. 269 pp.

Blau, P. M. 1960. Structural effects. *Am. Sociol. Rev.* 25:178–93

Blau, P. M. 1970. A formal theory of differentiation in organizations. *Am. Sociol. Rev.* 35:201–18

Blau, P. M. 1973. *The Organization of Academic Work.* New York: Wiley. 310 pp.

Blau, P. M., Heydebrand, W. V., Stauffer, R. E. 1966. The structure of small bureaucracies. *Am. Sociol. Rev.* 31:179–91

Blau, P. M., Schoenherr, R. A. 1971. *The Structure of Organizations.* New York: Basic Books. 445 pp.

Blau, P. M., Scott, W. R. 1962. *Formal Organizations: A Comparative Approach.* San Francisco: Chandler. 312 pp.

Buckley, W. 1967. *Sociology and Modern Systems Theory.* Englewood Cliffs, NJ: Prentice-Hall. 227 pp.

Clark, B. R. 1958. *Adult Education in Transition.* Berkeley: Univ. Calif. Press. 197 pp.

Clark, B. R. 1960. *The Open Door College.* New York: McGraw-Hill.

Coleman, J. S. 1958–1959. Relational analysis: the study of social structure with survey methods. *Hum. Organ.* 17(4):28–36

Cyert, R. M., March, J. G. 1963. *A Behavioral Theory of the Firm.* Englewood Cliffs, NJ: Prentice-Hall. 332 pp.

Dornbusch, S. M., Scott, W. R. 1975. *Evaluation and the Exercise of Authority.* San Francisco: Jossey-Bass. 374 pp.

Dubin, R. 1958. *The World of Work.* Englewood Cliffs, NJ: Prentice-Hall. 448 pp.

Durkheim, E. 1947. *The Division of Labor in Society.* Glencoe, Ill.: Free Press. 439 pp.

Freeman, J. H., Hannan, M. R. Growth and decline processes in organizations. *Am. Sociol. Rev.* In press

Galbraith, J. 1973. *Designing Complex Organizations.* Reading, Mass.: Addison-Wesley. 150 pp.

Gibbs, J. P., Martin, W. T. 1962. Urbanization, technology, and the division of labor: International patterns. *Am. Sociol. Rev.* 27:667–77

Gouldner, A. W. 1954. *Patterns of Industrial Bureaucracy.* Glencoe, Ill.: Free Press. 282 pp.

Hage, J., Aiken, M. 1969. Routine technology, social structure, and organizational goals. *Admin. Sci. Quart.* 14:366–77

Hall, R. H., Haas, J. E., Johnson, N. J. 1967. Organizational size, complexity, and formalization. *Am. Sociol. Rev.* 32:903–12

Harvey, E. 1968. Technology and the structure of organizations. *Am. Sociol. Rev.* 33:247–59

Heydebrand, W. V. 1973. Autonomy, complexity, and non-bureaucratic coordination in professional organizations. In *Comparative Organizations,* ed. W. V. Heydebrand, 158–89. Englewood Cliffs, NJ: Prentice-Hall. 571 pp.

Hickson, D. J., Pugh, D. S., Pheysey, D. C. 1969. Operations technology and organization structure. *Admin. Sci. Quart.* 14:378–97

Holdaway, E. A., Blowers, T. A. 1971. Administrative ratios and organization size: a longitudinal examination. *Am. Sociol. Rev.* 36:278–86

Kasarda, J. D. 1974. The structural implications of social system size: a three-level analysis. *Am. Sociol. Rev.* 39:19–28

Katz, D., Kahn, R. 1966. *The Social Psychology of Organizations.* New York: Wiley. 498 pp.

Kendall, P. L., Lazarsfeld, P. F. 1950. Problems of survey analysis. In *Continuities in Social Research: Studies in the Scope and Method of "The American Soldier,"* ed. R. K. Merton, P. F. Lazarsfeld, 133–96. Glencoe, Ill.: Free Press. 255 pp.

Lawrence, P. R., Lorsch, J. W. 1967. *Organization and Environment.* Boston: Harvard Univ. 279 pp.

Lazarsfeld, P. F., Menzel, H. 1961. On the relation between individual and collective properties. In *Complex Organizations: A Sociological Reader,* ed. A. Etzioni, 422–40. Glencoe, Ill.: Free Press

Lazarsfeld, P. F., Thielens, W. Jr. 1958. *The Academic Man: Social Scientists in a Time of Crisis.* Glencoe, Ill.: Free Press. 460 pp.

Lipset, S. M., Trow, M. A., Coleman, J. A. 1956. *Union Democracy.* Glencoe, Ill.: Free Press. 455 pp.

Litwak, E. 1961. Models of bureaucracy which permit conflict. *Am. J. Sociol.* 67:177–84

March, J. G., Simon, H. A. 1958. *Organizations.* New York: Wiley. 262 pp.

Melman, S. 1951. The rise of administrative overhead in the manufacturing industries of the United States, 1899–1947. *Oxford Econ. Papers* 3:62–112

Merton, R. K., Gray, A., Hockey, B., Selvin, H. C., Eds. 1952. *Reader in Bureaucracy.* Glencoe, Ill.: Free Press. 464 pp.

Meyer, M. W. 1972. Size and the structure of organizations: a causal analysis. *Am. Sociol. Rev.* 37:434–41

Michels, R. 1949. *Political Parties: A Sociological Study of the Oligarchical Tendencies of Modern Democracy.* New York: Free Press. 434 pp.

Mohr, L. B. 1971. Organizational technology and organizational structure. *Admin. Sci. Quart.* 16:444–59

Parkinson, C. N. 1957. *Parkinson's Law and Other Studies in Administration.* Boston: Houghton, Mifflin

Parsons, T. 1966. *Societies: Evolutionary and Comparative Perspectives.* Englewood Cliffs, NJ: Prentice-Hall. 120 pp.

Pennings J. 1973. Measures of organizational structure: a methodological note. *Am. J. Sociol.* 79:686–704

Perrow, C. 1965. Hospitals: technology, structure, and goals. In *Handbook of Organizations,* ed. J. G. March, 910–71. Chicago: Rand McNally

Perrow, C. 1970. *Organizational Analysis: A Sociological View.* Belmont, Calif.: Wadsworth. 192 pp.

Pondy, L. R. 1969. Effects of size, complexity, and ownership on administra-

tive intensity. *Admin. Sci. Quart.* 14:47–61

Pugh, D. S. et al 1963. A conceptual scheme for organizational analysis. *Admin. Sci. Quart.* 8:289–315

Pugh, D. S., Hickson, D. J., Hinings, C. R., Turner, C. 1968. Dimensions of organization structure. *Admin. Sci. Quart.* 13:65–105

Pugh, D. S., Hickson, D. J., Hinings, C. R., Turner, C. 1969. The context of organization structures. *Admin. Sci. Quart.* 14:91–114

Rackham, J., Woodward, J. 1970. The measurement of technical variables. In *Industrial Organization: Behavior and Control,* ed. J. Woodward, 19–36. London: Oxford Univ. Press

Roethlisberger, F. J., Dickson, W. J. 1939. *Management and the Worker.* Cambridge, Mass: Harvard Univ. Press. 615 pp.

Rushing, W. A. 1966. Organizational size and administration. *Pac. Sociol. Rev.* 9:100–8

Rushing, W. A. 1967. The effects of industry size and division of labor on administration. *Admin. Sci. Quart.* 12:267–95

Rushing, W. A. 1968. Hardness of material as an external constraint on the division of labor in manufacturing industries. *Admin. Sci. Quart.* 13:229–45

Sayles, L. R. 1958. *Behavior of Industrial Work Groups.* New York: Wiley

Scott, W. R. 1972. Professionals in hospitals: technology and the organization of work. In *Organization Research on Health Institutions,* ed. B. S. Georgopoulos, 139–58. Ann Arbor: Inst. Soc. Res., Univ. Michigan

Scott, W. R., Dornbusch, S. M., Busching, B. C., Laing, J. D. 1967. Organizational evaluation and authority. *Admin. Sci. Quart.* 12:93–117

Selznick, P. 1949. *TVA and the Grass Roots.* Berkeley: Univ. Calif. Press. 274 pp.

Selznick, P. 1952. *The Organizational Weapon.* New York: McGraw. 350 pp.

Simon, H. A. 1947. *Administrative Behavior.* New York: Macmillan. 259 pp.

Stinchcombe, A. L. 1959. Bureaucratic and craft administration of production. *Admin. Sci. Quart.* 4:168–87

Street, D. 1972. Review symposium: *The Structure of Organizations. Cont. Sociol.* 1:492–95

Terrien, F. W., Mills, D. L. 1955. The effect of changing size upon the internal structure of organizations. *Am. Sociol. Rev.* 20:11–13

Thompson, J. D. 1967. *Organizations in Action.* New York: McGraw-Hill. 192 pp.

Thompson, J. D., Bates, F. L. 1957. Technology, organization, and administration. *Admin. Sci. Quart.* 2:325–42

Trist, E. L., Bamforth, K. W. 1951. Social and psychological consequences of the longwall method of coal-getting. *Hum. Relat.* 4:3–38

Udy, S. H. Jr. 1959a. "Bureaucracy" and "rationality" in Weber's organization theory. *Am. Sociol. Rev.* 24:791–95

Udy, S. H. Jr. 1959b. *Organization of Work.* New Haven, Conn.: HRAF Press. 182 pp.

Udy, S. H. Jr. 1962. Administrative rationality, social setting, and organizational development. *Am. J. Sociol.* 67:299–308

von Bertalanffy, L. 1951. Problems of general system theory. *Hum. Biol.* 23: 302–12

Weber, M. 1946. *From Max Weber: Essays in Sociology,* ed. H. H. Gerth, C. W. Mills. New York: Oxford Univ. Press. 490 pp.

Weber, M. 1947. *The Theory of Social and Economic Organization,* ed. A. M. Henderson, T. Parsons. Glencoe, Ill.: Free Press. 436 pp.

Weick, K. 1969. *The Social Psychology of Organizing.* Reading, Mass.: Addison-Wesley. 121 pp.

Wheeler, S. 1966. The structure of formally organized socialization settings. *Socialization After Childhood,* ed. O. G. Brim Jr., S. Wheeler, 53–116. New York: Wiley

Whyte, W. F. 1961. *Men at Work.* Homewood, Ill.: Dorsey & Irwin. 593 pp.

Wiener, N. 1954. *The Human Use of Human Beings: Cybernetics and Society.* Garden City, NY: Doubleday Anchor. 199 pp.

Woodward, J. 1958. *Management and Technology.* London: H.M.S.O.

Woodward, J. 1965. *Industrial Organization: Theory and Practice.* London: Oxford Univ. Press

Woodward, J., Ed. 1970. *Industrial Organization: Behavior and Control.* London: Oxford Univ. Press

Zelditch, M. Jr. 1962. Some methodological problems of field studies. *Am. J. Sociol.* 67:566–76

MAJOR DEVELOPMENTS IN THE SOCIOLOGICAL STUDY OF DEVIANCE

❖10501

Jack P. Gibbs and Maynard L. Erickson
Department of Sociology, University of Arizona, Tucson, Arizona 85721

During the past decade there have been four major developments in the sociology of deviance. First, interest in reknowned theories has gradually declined. Second, the predominant research concern is no longer with rates of deviance or deviants but rather with *reactions* to deviance. Third, far more attention is now devoted to criminal law, with a special emphasis on political considerations. Fourth, a new conception of deviance has emerged. This survey concentrates on the new conception, because it now occupies center stage and is closely intertwined with other major developments.

THE NEW CONCEPTION OF DEVIANCE

The idea that some acts are inherently deviant has been alien to sociology for decades. Accordingly, the reactive conception of deviance (i.e. an act is deviant only if "so labeled") may appear conventional.[1] After all, the advocates only argue that deviance is not an inherent property of an act (or an individual) but, rather, a property *conferred* by an audience. The argument appears compatible with a "normative" conception of deviance, because norms pertain to what members of a social unit ostensibly believe conduct ought to be. So an "audience" is implicit in the normative conception of deviance, i.e. an act is deviant if contrary to a norm.

The seeming compatability of the new reactive conception and the older normative conception stems from the ambiguity of "audience." Members of a social unit (be it a family or a country) constitute an audience but not the kind that advocates of the reactive conception evidently have in mind. Specifically, the conception is neither novel nor controversial unless extended to declarations that (*a*) only individuals who react to a particular act are the relevant audience, (*b*) an act (or individual)

---

[1]For statements that suggest a reactive conception of deviance, see Becker (1963:9), Erikson (1962:308), and Kitsuse (1962:253). Schur (1969) and Gibbs (1972a) have written divergent critiques of the conception.

21

is deviant only if "so labeled," and (c) whether an act (or individual) is so labeled depends on the character of particular reactions.[2] Advocates of the reactive conception could deny that their statements amount to those declarations; but, if so, they should clarify their position. In any case, the reactive conception poses no major issues or has no special import unless extended to such declarations.

Issues, Problems, and Questions

Since no definition is right or wrong, the reactive conception of deviance is neither correct nor incorrect. Nonetheless, critics have raised several objections to it.

Whatever the reactions to an act, they do not literally "label" the act as deviant; for that matter, the reactors may not use the word *deviant*. Hence, critics allege that the reactive conception fails to specify the *kinds of reactions* that identify deviance.

Some kinds appear obvious, such as arrest, trial, or imprisonment; but an illustrative list is not a definition. The problem is that a list of specific distinctive reactions (those that identify deviance) is likely to be incomplete and ethnocentric. Moreover, the illustrative list just considered is restricted to legal (official) reactions. Addition of "unofficial" reactions would pose problems, because those reactions are more varied and difficult to describe. For that matter, advocates of the conception have not *emphasized* that both official and unofficial reactions are criteria of deviance, and their apparent emphasis on official reactions accentuates doubts.

If official reaction (e.g. an arrest) is the *only* criterion of criminality, innocent individuals are never arrested and therefore never punished. Moreover, if all kinds of official reactions are taken as criteria of criminality, then reactions by the police, prosecutors, juries, and judges are *not* necessarily congruent criteria in particular cases. For example, when the police charge an individual with a crime but the individual is subsequently found not guilty, those two reactions are not congruent.

The status terms just used (e.g. prosecutors) give rise to another question. Conceivably, both the character of reactions and the characteristics (e.g. status) of the reactors are criteria of criminality or deviance in general. Even if reactions by persons other than officials are relevant, it is not clear whether perpetrators may react to their own acts so as to identify them as criminal or deviant (i.e. whether "self-reaction" is relevant), nor whether the reactions of those allegedly harmed by acts (i.e. victims, complainants) are criteria.

All of the previous criticisms reduce to two questions. First, exactly what kind of reaction is necessary and sufficient for deviance? And, second, what bearing do the characteristics of reactors have on the criterion of deviance? Without answers to both questions, independent investigators are unlikely to agree in identifying particular acts or individuals as deviant; and such agreement is essential for systematic tests of theories.

Another criticism has to do with normative considerations. Those considerations appear alien to the reactive conception but, so criticism of the conception goes, a "deviant label" *is* normative. To illustrate, Scott (1972:12) presents a list of words —nut, queer, weirdo, rascal, pervert, loony—and says: "I employ the generic term

[2]Contemplate Currie's statement (1968:28): "deviance is what officials say it is, and deviants are those so designated by officials."

'deviance' to refer to that property that is conferred upon persons whenever labels such as these are used." Such a list is bound to be incomplete, and Scott skirts a question: Why are those words deviant labels? It is difficult to imagine an answer that ignores normative considerations. Accordingly, while the reactive criterion of deviance appears to be purely behavioral, critics charge that normative considerations enter into it through the back door.

Even from a normative perspective, whether an act is deviant may depend on its "meaning" (e.g. inferred intentions). That consideration is important because advocates of the reactive conception insist that "meaning is problematical." The dictum poses an issue only to the extent that members of a social unit disagree in identification of particular acts as to type (e.g. robbery) and in their evaluation (approval or disapproval) of those types. Critics of the reactive conception argue that reactions to acts are more uniform than idiosyncratic because of socially shared evaluations of conduct; that is, normative qualities of acts determine the reactions to the acts, and hence the reactive conception of deviance puts the cart before the horse.

Still another criticism is that the reactive conception precludes a question: Why does the character of reactions to deviance vary among social units and over time? If deviance is defined in terms of "reaction," then the character of reactions cannot vary. Thus, accepting the idea that an act is deviant only if punished, it is illogical to ask: Why do some deviant acts go unpunished?

Finally, advocates of the reactive conception evidently question the idea that social science investigators can justifiably identify acts as to type in some objective manner, let alone typify them as deviant, for such distinctions depend on the meaning of acts for the actor and/or the audience. But the advocates presume that investigators can typify *reactions to acts* (those that identify acts as deviant and those that do not), which is surely paradoxical.

In Defense of The Reactive Conception: What Sociologists Actually Do

Despite the foregoing criticisms, effective arguments for the reactive conception can be made. Indeed, the conception suffers from inept defenses of it.

Sociologists rarely use data that are consistent with a purely normative conception of deviance. In criminological research the statistics typically pertain to crimes *reported by the police;* and that reliance on a reactive criterion (judgments by officials) extends to most studies of (inter alia) juvenile delinquency, suicide, and mental illness. So the reactive conception appears to be consistent with what research sociologists actually do.

However, the real issue hinges on an assumption. Sociologists who hold to a normative conception of deviance but use "reactive data" assume that the official incidence of deviance is fairly closely *correlated* with true incidence (i.e. violations of norms, officially recorded or not), but that assumption does not resolve the debate. For virtually any type of deviance, true incidence is unknowable; and a strictly reactive conception denies true incidence apart from reactions.

In Defense of The Reactive Conception: Deviants and Deviant Acts

The normative conception of deviance does not directly answer this question: Who is a deviant? If it is any individual who has committed a deviant act, nondeviant adults may not exist. Then consider the "mentally ill," who are commonly thought of as deviants. Surely a mentally ill individual is not simply anyone who has committed an isolated deviant act, let alone that all mentally ill individuals have committed the same deviant acts. Finally, if a criminal is "anyone who has violated a law," then all adults might well qualify.

Such observations pose fewer problems for a reactive conception of deviance. Thus, a mentally ill individual is simply anyone so labeled, and the same is true of "the criminal" or "the juvenile delinquent." There remains the previous arguments that: (a) labels have normative connotations and (b) the notion of being labeled deviant is ambiguous. Nonetheless, the reactive conception is more defensible when contemplating *deviants* rather than deviant acts.

In Defense of The Reactive Conception: Alternative Data on Crime

Inconsistencies in the "labeling" of acts by different legal reactors (police, judges) are just as troublesome for a normative conception as a reactive conception of crime. In using official statistics on crime, sociologists employ a reactive criterion; but there are various kinds of official statistics—those representing decisions of police, those of prosecutors, etc. So which is decisive? The question has been debated inconclusively for decades, one argument (Sellin & Wolfgang 1964) being that crimes reported by the police more nearly correspond to "true" incidence and another (Tappan 1960:35) that only trial outcomes are authoritative.

Advocates of the normative conception of deviance do not escape the problem by arguing for a statutory definition of crime. Criminological investigators rely largely on decisions made by legal officials rather than actually applying statutory definitions, and it would be questionable to do otherwise (even if they could). Decisions by officials are "social facts" and hardly inferior to judgments of social scientists as to criminality. Viewed that way, the reactive conception is "sociological realism," just as legal realism is an alternative to analytical jurisprudence (Gibbs 1972a: 50).

In Defense of The Reactive Conception: Shortcomings of The Alternative

The strongest argument for the reactive conception lies in the shortcomings of the normative conception. However, advocates of the reactive conception have left their rejection of the normative conception and the reasons for it largely implicit.

The previously stated normative conception of deviance poses a difficult question: What is a norm? Homans (1961:46) answers: "A *norm* is a statement made by a number of members of a group, not necessarily by all of them, that the members ought to behave in a certain way in certain circumstances." Two questions survive Homans' definition. First, are the normative statements of all members equally relevant? And, second, what number of members must make or endorse a statement for it to be a norm? Sociologists have yet to confront the first question seriously, and any answer to the second question would be arbitrary.

Even if both questions could be answered satisfactorily, the validity *and* significance of statements about conduct are most debatable. The issue stems from a perennial argument—alleged expressions of attitudes and actual behavior commonly diverge. Hence there is another rationale for the reactive conception of deviance—that "true" evaluations of conduct can be best inferred from actual reactions to acts.

Although norms pertain to the approval or disapproval of acts, individuals rarely evaluate acts or types of acts without regard to "contingencies," such as the social identity of the actor (e.g. male or female, young or old), the social identity of the object of the act, and situational conditions (e.g. time and place). It would be difficult to identify any type of act that most Americans disapprove *categorically,* especially if questioned closely. To illustrate, contemplate a survey question that might be posed to document American norms: Do you approve or disapprove of sexual relations out of wedlock? One problem is meaning, e.g. whether the respondents think of homosexual or heterosexual relations. Careful wording of questions avoids some meaning problems but not contingencies. Observe that the question does not specify marital status, age, and race, and those specifications could alter responses. Arguing that contingencies are properties of acts solves nothing, and no normative question can *fully* specify all *possible* contingencies.

If instances of deviance are identified by reference to reactions, those identifications *could* reflect contingencies in evaluations of acts that might be ignored by a strictly normative criterion. Thus, given an instance of a type of act, X, and given a distinctive reaction to that instance, the reactor disapproved of the act either because of *or* despite situational contingencies (including the characteristics of the alleged actor and object of the act, the time, and the place). Similarly, given another instance of a type X act but no distinctive reaction, either the potential reactors did not disapprove or situational contingencies were such as to alter their evaluations of the act.

Problems with the strategy are not limited to the obvious circular line of reasoning. Without an unambiguous criterion of a distinctive reaction and relevant reactors, the strategy is not feasible. In any case, given no distinctive reaction to an instance of X, there is no basis for inferring the contingencies (if any) that precluded disapproval of the act. Indeed, potential reactors may not have reacted distinctively because they approve of the act regardless of situational considerations; and even if they disapproved of it, the circumstances (e.g. fear of retaliation) may have precluded a distinctive reaction. Still another complication is that statistics and accounts of crimes reported by the police or arrests necessarily exclude instances where contingencies precluded a distinctive reaction. The general point, though, is that a reactive criterion of deviance cannot reveal the contingencies (if any) that were operative in particular cases. Comparisons of reactions to instances of the same type of act might be construed as indicating contingencies, but that approach is not feasible unless advocates of the reactive conception abandon their nominalistic outlook and grant that investigators can justifiably classify acts as to type. Even so, just as all possible contingencies in the evaluation of a type of act cannot be introduced in normative questions about that type, it is difficult to imagine comparisons of actual reactions to instances of that type as revealing all possible contingencies.

In light of the foregoing, it would be misleading to declare that a reactive conception of deviance takes contingencies into account. The declaration is vague and fails to recognize some horrendous problems. Nonetheless, the reactive conception does permit contemplating strategies for dealing with contingencies that would be alien to a normative conception, and for that reason alone the reactive conception deserves a serious hearing.

A normative conception of deviance does not preclude thinking of deviance as a matter of degree, since only a certain proportion of the members of a social unit may voice disapproval of a type of act and normative questions could be worded such that the responses are indicative of the intensity of disapproval. Nonetheless, sociologists commonly speak and perhaps think of norms and deviance as though they assume normative consensus in a social unit. Whatever the shortcomings of the reactive conception of deviance, it clearly avoids that unwarranted assumption. The only problem is that without recognition of some normative character of deviance, in the social or collective sense, the study of deviance will never transcend the unique. In particular, granted that a particular act is deviant only if "so labeled," when can sociologists properly speak of a *type* of act as deviant? Insofar as advocates of the reactive conception are willing to entertain the idea of types of acts, they have not confronted the question.

Prospects For a Resolution

Since both the normative and the reactive conception of deviance are defective, there is a need for a synthesis—one that would retain the merits of each conception but avoid their shortcomings. Unfortunately, the prospects for such a synthesis are remote.

It could be argued that there are two types of deviant acts: 1. those contrary to norms and 2. those that are reacted to distinctively. The two types are not mutually exclusive, but what is *generic* deviance? The question could be answered only as follows: An act is deviant if contrary to a norm *an/or* reacted to distinctively. That generic definition avoids none of the problems with either conception of deviance.

Of course, one can dismiss the foregoing as mere sophistry. Yet it is difficult to see how the problems and issues are artificial; certainly they have preoccupied the sociological study of deviance for several years (see especially Akers 1968, Mankoff 1971, Liazos 1972, Hirschi 1973).

DECLINE OF INTEREST IN REKNOWNED GENERAL THEORIES

For some 25 years sociological thinking about deviance centered around Merton's (1938, 1957) theory of anomie and Sutherland's (1939) theory of differential association. Neither theory has been rejected dramatically, but they now receive far less attention.

No crucial test of either theory was ever conducted, and it appears that they cannot be tested systematically. Two lines of work that might have enhanced testability were not continued, those two being conceptual extensions of Merton's theory (e.g. Harary 1966) and formal restatements of Sutherland's theory (e.g.

DeFleur & Quinney 1966). However, since sociologists readily tolerate untestable theories, the decline of interest in differential association and anomie reflects something else, even something other than the paucity of policy implications in the two theories (Wilson 1974). That something else is that neither theory emphasizes reactions to deviance, either as a criterion of deviance or as an etiological factor.

Systematic data that appear to support Merton's theory are restricted largely to official arrest or apprehension statistics, which indicate much higher rates for certain types of crimes (or delinquencies) in the lower socioeconomic stratum. The *inferred* higher rates are relevant because Merton's theory depicts crime as a manifestation of the disjunction of culturally approved goals and legal means to those goals. Assuming that members of the lower socioeconomic stratum commonly aspire to goals that they cannot achieve legally, the theory predicts a high crime rate for that stratum. However, the relation between arrest statistics and the true crime rate has been questioned for decades, especially in light of self-reported crimes or delinquencies (see Matza's commentary, 1969:96–98, in connection with Merton's theory), and the reactive conception of crime accentuates doubts even more. But Merton's theory pays scant attention to the possibility that official reactions determine the crime rate directly (through police practices) or through deterrence.

The situation is more complicated in assessing Sutherland's theory. The "differential association" part of the theory deals primarily with the process by which individuals supposedly learn criminal behavior (through a greater exposure to "definitions" favorable to crime), but it is not at all clear how one can derive genuine empirical generalizations about variation in the crime rate (e.g. among socioeconomic strata) from that part of the theory. The "differential organization" part is more relevant in contemplating variation in crime rates, but it is so poorly developed that no testable predictions can be derived from it systematically. Accordingly, since Sutherland's theory makes no testable assertions about crime rates, the reliability of official statistics is less an issue than in the case of Merton's theory. Yet Sutherland and his disciples commonly made reference to those statistics in explicating or defending the theory (e.g. Cressey 1960:54–55). In any case, Sutherland's conception of crime was clearly normative, and for that reason alone his theory has no following among sociologists who hold to a reactive conception. Finally, whereas official reactions can be subsumed under "definition unfavorable to crime," Sutherland eschewed the deterrence doctrine.

THEORIES PERTAINING TO JUVENILE DELINQUENCY

Since the early sixties there have been no major developments concerning *theories* of delinquency. As the reactivist perspective[3] emerged, the last few controversial aspects of "subcultural" theories (Cohen 1955), including those that emphasize

[3]The term "reactivist perspective" is used to denote not only the reactive conception of deviance but also the "labeling perspective," which reduces to the idea that official or punitive reactions to deviance tend to generate more deviance.

"differential opportunity" (Cloward & Ohlin 1960), were debated weakly in the wings. So the last decade was transitional with two conspicuous trends.

Negative Evidence

During the 1960s research findings were increasingly recognized as contrary to subcultural theories. Those findings stemmed from surveys of self-reported delinquencies, none of which found, contrary to the theories, marked concentration in the lower socioeconomic strata. Indeed, delinquency is apparently widespread in rural and suburban as well as urban areas, among females as well as males, and among nongang as well as gang members. So the findings indicated that the major theories misplaced the locus of juvenile delinquency. Sherif & Sherif (1964, 1967) and Lerman (1967), for example, accused criminologists in the "Chicago school" of limiting delinquency theory to lower-class-slum-gang juveniles.

In response to the Sherifs, Short (1965:155–56) attributed such criticism to a regrettable byproduct of Thrasher's work and the preoccupation of older Chicago criminologists with the "inner" city. According to Short, they never meant to limit delinquency theory, but he did not deny that its scope had become narrow and hence inconsistent with contemporary findings.

The Emergence of Alternatives

The second trend was the emergence of alternatives to subcultural theories of delinquency, but those alternatives are difficult to describe. Certainly the reactivist perspective now receives a great deal of attention, but it is scarcely a contending *theory;* and in any case it has generated far less systematic research than did subcultural theories. One possible reason is the failure of its advocates to specify the kinds of research findings that would falsify the reactive perspective. No less important, when extended to juvenile delinquency, the reactive conception of deviance supports the subcultural theories. If a juvenile is delinquent only when so labeled officially, then delinquency *is* markedly concentrated in the lower socioeconomic stratum.

Of course, critics of subcultural theories are not limited to advocates of the reactive perspective (Kitsuse & Dietrick 1959, Toby 1961, Bordua 1961, Miller 1958, Sherif & Sherif 1967, Lerman 1967). In particular, Matza (1964, 1969) rejects subcultural theories without advocating the reactive conception, but it is not clear what he offers as an alternative. It is difficult to see how the notion of "drift" leads to any generalization about delinquency rates, official or unofficial; and the one suggested generalization is uninformative. If by "drift" Matza simply means that *no* juvenile is continually and consistently delinquent, he has not contradicted any sociological theory. As for "neutralization" (Sykes & Matza 1957), the assertion that *some* juveniles rationalize their delinquent acts is unfalsifiable. Further, even if it were asserted that *all* juvenile delinquents "neutralize," that assertion would have no bearing on delinquency rates, not even if one posits rationalization prior to actually committing a delinquent act. As for individual etiology, the notion of neutralization generates no testable propositions about the distinguishing characteristics of delinquents. To summarize, it is not clear what empirical questions about delinquency Matza attempted to answer, let alone how his answers could be falsi-fied.[4] So it is hardly surprising that Matza's perspective has generated so little systematic research.

Future Prospects

All of the foregoing reduces to a characterization of the contemporary sociological study of delinquency as a search for a new theoretical orientation.[5] It remains to be seen what the future holds; in particular, whether interest in the reactivist and drift-neutralization perspectives will continue. But the next decade is not likely to be a period of quantitative, empirical work comparable to the era of subcultural theories. That prospect may not alarm many sociologists, but surely it is important to somehow regain the excitement of the subcultural era.

ALTERNATIVES TO OFFICIAL DATA ON CRIME AND DELINQUENCY

Sociologists who use official crime statistics assume a close relation between the behavior of the public at large and responses of officials. More specifically, they assume that (a) some types of acts are crimes, (b) instances of such types are detected, (c) detected instances are reported to the police, and (d) the police correctly record reported instances. To the extent those assumptions are valid, official crime statistics are reliable.

All of the assumptions were questioned long before the reactive conception of crime, but that conception has accentuated issues about official statistics to the point that any use of them in research is now most debatable. However, it is seldom recognized that the very notion of "reliability" scarcely has any place in a strictly reactive conception of crime, for if a certain kind of reaction by a legal official is by definition the only criterion of crime, then official statistics on crime are viewed in a quite different light.

---

[4]It may be that Matza and advocates of the reactivist perspective are not interested in questions pertaining to the distinguishing characteristics of criminals or juvenile delinquents, nor in questions pertaining to rates of deviance. If so, an explicit statement to that effect would clarify issues, for Matza's perspective and the reactivist perspective are commonly construed as alternatives to theories that do treat those questions as central.

[5]What might be considered as conventional research on juvenile delinquency did not come to a halt during the past decade, and the same may be said of research on crime and noncriminal deviance. Due to space limitations this survey has slighted several noteworthy studies and lines of work. However, until the issues raised by the reactivist perspective are resolved, any particular line of research will have all manner of critics. As a case in point, Douglas (1967), one advocate of the reactivist perspective, has raised so many doubts about official suicide statistics that investigators know that they face a hostile audience if they attempt to use such data. Similarly, while the study of Wolfgang et al (1972) of delinquency in a cohort produced some truly original findings, those findings are based on official delinquency records, and hence many critics will be predisposed to reject the study for that reason alone. All in all, then, the eventual consequence of the issues raised by the reactivist perspective may be a decline in the volume of research on deviance.

Had criminologists been using a definition of crime like that suggested by Becker and Erikson they would not have been faced with serious problems of measurement because "official" statistics (at least to the extent that official agencies record those crimes which come to their attention) would have provided a reasonably good measure of crime defined in this way. (Gould 1969:326).

For more than 30 years American sociologists (e.g. Porterfield 1943) have sought alternatives to official statistics on crime and delinquency. There are now two conventional methods for gathering data on allegedly criminal and/or delinquent acts *independently of responses by officials:* 1. surveys of "self-reported" acts (see Doleschal 1970, Erickson 1973, Hardt & Bodine 1965, Reiss 1973), and 2. "victimization" surveys (see Ennis 1967, Doleschal 1970, Reynolds et al 1973). In both kinds of surveys, statements from individuals are solicited through an anonymous questionnaire or an interview as to (*a*) their *own* involvement in delinquent or criminal acts (self-reports) or (*b*) their experience as victims of criminal or delinquent acts (victimization reports).

The findings of self-report and victimization surveys *suggest* that the incidence of crime and delinquency is several times that indicated by official figures, but inferences about true incidence from such unofficial data are scarcely less debatable than inferences from official data.

Observe again that true incidence is controversial, because according to a strictly reactive conception of crime there is no incidence of crimes apart from official reactions. A less extreme version of the conception would admit both official and unofficial reactions as criteria of crime; but it is not clear whether even that version extends to "self-reaction" or "self-labeling." Hence, if only because the reactive conception is ambiguous, the relevance of data on self-reported crime remains disputable.

Apart from issues raised by the reactive conception, there are formidable problems with data on self-reported or victim-reported crimes. However, only recently have such data been subjected to a critical assessment. Reiss (1973) has conducted a very comprehensive examination of the vast "self-reports" literature, but no one has assessed the much more limited victimization literature in such depth.

Both kinds of data are questionable for reasons that transcend technical considerations (e.g. sampling). If the survey questions employ legal labels of crimes (e.g. grand theft), there is no assurance that respondents will conceive of those labels in a manner consistent with legal definitions. Investigators can describe types of acts (e.g. taking an automobile that does not belong to you) and use those descriptions rather than legal labels in posing questions, but the legal definition of some types of crime cannot be reduced readily to a brief description of one act. Moreover, when a respondent reports or fails to report having committed a particular type of act or having been "victimized," the respondent may be deliberately untruthful, or simply not remember correctly.

There are additional problems that are peculiar to victimization reports. Some crimes (e.g. possession of narcotics) have no victim, and hence victimization reports are irrelevant in estimating incidence. Another serious limit is that the victim may not be able to identify the offender, and hence victimization reports cannot be used

to compute incidence rates by (inter alia) age, sex, race. Age is particularly important, for without that information investigators cannot compute separate rates for
juvenile delinquencies and adult crimes.

In recent years elaborate policies for protecting "human subjects" have been
promulgated by governmental agencies and universities, and those policies make
self-reports and victimization surveys more difficult. For one thing, interviews may
have to be abandoned to insure absolute anonymity. Perhaps more serious, when
prospective respondents are informed as to the "legal status" of their responses
(including all possible liabilities), it furthers their already understandable reluctance
to participate. The policies may well be desirable, but if those policies are rigorously
enforced, then surveys of self-reported crimes and perhaps even victimization surveys may well come to an end.

SECONDARY DEVIANCE

The term "labeling perspective" is ambiguous in that it may denote either the
reactive conception of deviance (which is strictly conceptual) or an idea about the
consequences of reactions, one that has come to be known as the "theory" of
secondary deviance. Whereas the major advocates of the reactive conception are
Becker, Erikson, and Kitsuse, the theory of secondary deviance stems largely from
Tannenbaum (1938) and especially Lemert (1972), neither of whom has advocated
a reactive conception of deviance. In any case, there is a distinction between a
conception of deviance and a theory about the consequences of reactions to deviance.

The "theory" of secondary deviance is introduced by one of Lemert's (1972:63)
statements: "Secondary deviation refers to a special class of socially defined responses which people make to problems created by the societal reaction to their
deviance." It is very difficult to translate that statement (or any others by Lemert)
into testable, informative propositions; but he and his followers have described the
process by which reactions to initial deviance (primary) *could* generate subsequent
deviance (secondary).

One theme is that members of a social unit share certain expectations as to the
behavior of particular types of deviants (e.g. drug addicts, homosexuals). Those who
interact with a "labeled" deviant commonly expect him or her to act consistently
with that label, and hence the deviant is shunned, distrusted, or formally excluded
from normal social relations. The postulated effect is that the person labeled comes
to identify himself or herself as deviant and acts accordingly, meaning (inter alia)
more deviant acts. However, notions other than "identity transformation" can be
invoked in explicating the theory. The notion of stigma commonly enters into
descriptions of the genesis of secondary deviance, and hence all of the literature on
stigmatization (e.g. Goffman 1963, Schwartz & Skolnick 1962) is possibly relevant.
Still another relevant notion is that of "role." As a consequence of being labeled
deviant, individuals may come to play that role, and hence engage in subsequent
deviance as a career. Finally, secondary deviance can be construed as adaptive
behavior, meaning that the labeled deviant is confronted by persistent problems and

engages in secondary deviance to alleviate them. The notion of adaptation enriches the theory but at the same time complicates it, especially with a view to tests. To assert that secondary deviance is adaptive scarcely constitutes a testable proposition, for virtually any kind of behavior is adaptive in one sense or another.

Problems in Interpretation

Since the theory of secondary deviance can be expressed in various ways, it is difficult to ascertain exactly what the theory asserts. If construed as a psychological theory, one concerned with "progressive identity transformation," it really makes no assertions about the frequency of deviant acts, primary or secondary. At most it may pertain only to the necessary and/or sufficient conditions for "career" deviance.

The theory of secondary deviance cannot be reduced to testable propositions without confronting numerous problems. It could be that the theory is really only a definition—a deviant act which has occurred because of reactions to previous deviance is *called* secondary deviance. Alternatively, the theory can be construed as asserting one genuine empirical proposition: *Some* individuals commit deviant acts because of reactions to previous deviant behavior. But the proposition cannot be falsified, no more than the assertion that flying saucers exist. Just one instance would verify the proposition, but there are problems beyond demonstrating causation. One demonstration would not be particularly informative, and there is no basis for stipulating a decisive minimal number.

Illustrative Findings and Arguments

Given the diverse ways the theory of secondary deviance has been stated by its advocates, all manner of research findings and arguments could be considered in assessing it. One common argument against the theory is that it overestimates human plasticity; more specifically, it ignores the possibility that many individuals "reject" deviant labels and hence do not come to identify themselves as deviant. A similar but distinct argument is that individuals commonly come to identify themselves as deviant before and therefore independently of reactions to their deviance. Both "identity" arguments have been questioned in critiques of the theory (e.g. Mankoff 1971, Warren & Johnson 1972), but the criticisms are hardly less impressionistic than observations made in support of the theory.

Attempts to bring research findings to bear on the theory are most debatable. To illustrate, Gove (1970) has concluded that the theory is inconsistent with the findings of several studies of mental hospitalization. One finding is that over two thirds of a particular cohort of mental patients had not been rehospitalized within seven years after release. Gove cites the finding as a contradiction of Scheff's theory of mental illness (1966), which is a special case of the theory of secondary deviance. But none of Scheff's propositions asserts that more than two thirds of mental patients are rehospitalized, nor that more than 24% of the relatives of former mental patients feel stigmatized (another finding cited by Gove). However, it does not follow that Gove failed to test the propositions correctly; on the contrary, given the way the propositions are stated, it is not at all clear how they could be falsified in any systematic way.

Scheff (1974) has argued that the findings cited by Gove are not relevant, and he castigates those who have criticized "labeling theory" as being vague. Scheff evidently believes that the meaning of key terms in a theory must be left open; but if the meaning of *some* terms in a theory is not "closed," sterile debates about relevant evidence are inevitable. Further, if the meaning of only some terms is closed, evidence can be brought to bear on the theory *as a whole* only through tests of derived theorems; but Scheff's set of propositions is clearly not a deductive theory.

Another complication is that the reactive conception of deviance and the theory of secondary deviance are readily confused. For example, Williams & Weinberg (1970) compared two groups of self-reported homosexuals, those who had received a less than honorable release from military service and those released honorably. Their responses to questions indicate that the first group engaged in homosexual relations more frequently before induction, more frequently during service, and more frequently with other servicemen. The findings only suggest that individuals who engage in deviant conduct frequently are likely to be detected. However, the findings take on special significance if construed as indicating, contrary to what advocates of the reactive conception persistently suggest, that the probability of being labeled deviant *does have something to do with actual behavior*. But the findings question the reactive conception, not the theory of secondary deviance. Evidence that might bear on the theory would pertain to differences in the homosexual behavior of the two groups after release from service. As for the findings questioning the reactive conception of deviance, its defenders could argue that the men released from service honorably were not homosexuals because they were not "labeled as such."

The foregoing survey is all too brief, but observations on other studies (e.g. Marshall & Purdy 1972, Gould 1969, Foster et al 1972, Fisher 1972, Reiss 1970) lead to the same conclusion. Until the theory of secondary deviance is stated so as to make it subject to systematic tests, appeals to empirical evidence are pointless.

REACTIONS TO DEVIANCE: A MORE INCLUSIVE PERSPECTIVE

The contemporary literature creates the erroneous impression that interest in reactions to deviance stems from the reactivist perspective. The impact of that perspective on the sociology of deviance has been considerable; there is, nonetheless, a tradition of interest in reactions to deviance independent of the perspective.

Social Control

For heuristic purposes theories on crime or deviance can be broadly dichotomized: (*a*) those that emphasize some generative condition (e.g. unemployment) and (*b*) those that emphasize inhibitory conditions (e.g. the deterrent influence of legal punishments). The second category is loosely identified as "social control" theories.

The problem with the notion of social control is that it virtually defies a satisfactory definition. Some conceptualizations extend to any factor or condition that contributes to social order or conformity to norms. So construed, it is difficult to think of any phenomenon that would not qualify as social control in one context or another (e.g. the custom of wearing wedding rings might be conducive to marital fidelity).

Alternatively, social control can be conceptualized in terms of reactions to deviance (Gibbs 1972b). That conceptualization is relevant for present purposes because it facilitates a description of sociological research on the subject. The research includes far more than studies of actual reactions to particular acts. Just as in all social units there are collective evaluations or expectations of conduct, which sociologists identify as norms, there are socially shared beliefs as to what ought to or what will happen when norms are violated. Those beliefs are identified as *reactive norms,* either legal (e.g. pertaining to statutory penalties) or extralegal; and they extend to the identification of appropriate reactors.

Sociological studies of reactions to deviance have been far more extensive in the past decade than ever before in the field's history. Since even a brief commentary on each investigation is precluded, observations on some kinds of research and a few illustrative references must suffice. Sociologists have examined the certainty and severity of imprisonment (see Tittle & Logan's survey, 1973), public opinion as to appropriate legal punishments (Gibbons 1969), discretionary practices by legal officials in the reactive process (Sudnow 1965), racial or social class contingencies in legal reactions to crime (Green 1970), contingencies in normative reactions of the public to the mentally ill (Phillips 1964), and public opinion as to the seriousness of types of crime (Rossi et al 1974).

A Major Shortcoming of Recent Research

Although sociologists are now preoccupied with reactions to deviance, most recent research on the subject has been atheoretical. Indeed, excluding studies pertaining to secondary deviance or the deterrence doctrine, research on reactions has been largely descriptive.

The descriptive character of recent research is puzzling in that an old body of theory has been ignored. It comprises several distinct theories (commencing with Durkheim) about societal differences in the punitive quality of reactions to crime (see Sutherland & Cressey 1970 for a survey). While those theories are restricted to punitiveness, any theoretical orientation for research is better than none at all.

An Instance of Theoretically Oriented Research

Erikson's (1966) research on reactions to deviance in Puritan Massachusetts is not descriptive, because it represents an extension of Durkheim's perspective. Erikson argues that reactions to deviance serve a boundary maintenance function (i.e. they demonstrate the tolerable limits of conduct), and the argument extends to the assertion (1966:23) that "the amount of deviation a community encounters is apt to remain fairly constant over time."

Assessment of Erikson's assertion is difficult because "apt to remain fairly constant over time" is vague. Consequently, whereas Blumenstein & Cohen (1973) have attempted to defend Erikson's argument by characterizing imprisonment rates in Norway and the United States as "stable" over several decades, that characterization is inherently debatable. Yet it is difficult to consider an increase in the official crime rate of an American city from 91 per 1000 standard population in 1930 to 578 in 1954 as anything but substantial (Alix 1969). Erikson could argue that the increase reflected a "boundary crisis," but that term is also very vague,[6] and without further clarification his argument is unfalsifiable.

Although Erikson speaks of the "amount of deviation" as being fairly constant, his data really are for *reactions to deviance* (trials in particular). The distinction is continually blurred in Erikson's arguments, and it takes on added significance when he asserts that officials apply deviant labels (e.g. make arrests) a fairly constant number of times from one period to the next. As a universal generalization, the assertion is most debatable; and even in particular historical periods where it does hold, a fairly constant number of official reactions could reflect nothing more than a fairly constant number of offenses. The observation is conjectural, but no more so than postulating that officials apply deviant labels fairly constantly regardless of offenses. In any case, Erikson's purported evidence raises more questions than it answers. His data indicate that for quinquennial periods over 1651–1680 in Puritan Massachusetts the number of convicted *offenders* per 100 population varied only from 3.50 to 3.64. However, the *offense* rate (number of crimes for which someone was convicted) per 100 population varied from 4.15 to 6.46. The latter number is over 50% greater, and one must surely wonder why such variation is not contrary to Erikson's argument. Even stability in the "offender rate" is questionable, because Erikson elsewhere argues that Puritan Massachusetts underwent boundary crises during 1651–1680. Like the theory of secondary deviance, Erikson's argument deserves further attention; but the most immediate need is a restatement of the argument so that it becomes subject to falsification.

Revival of Interest in The Deterrence Question

Whereas advocates of the reactivist perspective assert that official reactions to crimes generate more crimes, other sociologists entertain the opposite assertion—that official reactions, especially punitive reactions, prevent crimes. The assertion is a condensed version of the deterrence doctrine.

At one time (ca 1930–1955) there was a considerable sociological research on deterrence, but the interest dwindled because the findings suggested that legal punishments do not deter. In the late 1960s several sociologists reconsidered the deterrence question and justified it by alleging that evidence against deterrence

[6]Vagueness is not the only problem. At various points in *Wayward Puritans,* Erikson (1966) concludes from observations pertaining to an increase in deviation that a "boundary crisis" had been reached in Puritan Massachusetts. If deviation is a criterion of a "boundary crisis," then it is misleading to suggest that there is an empirical relation between them.

doctrine was limited largely to 1. research on the statutory death penalty and homicide rates without regard to the certainty of execution (e.g. Sellin 1967), 2. misleading figures on reimprisonment (see Glaser's criticism, 1964), and 3. one well-known investigation of specific deterrence (Caldwell 1944). In any case, since 1965 sociologists have extended deterrence research to the certainty and severity of imprisonment.

Since Tittle & Logan (1973) have recently surveyed the current deterrence literature, a brief commentary will suffice. Several investigators have reported a moderately negative correlation among states between the estimated certainty of imprisonment for a type of crime and the crime rate. Those correlations have been construed as consistent with conventional interpretations of the deterrence doctrine.

Although the findings have been questioned (Chiricos & Waldo 1970), they have revitalized interest in deterrence. Focusing research on actual punishments was desirable, but investigators have stopped short of analyzing such properties of legal punishments as perceived certainty, perceived severity, and public knowledge of statutory penalties. Moreover, from Beccaria and Bentham to the present (some 200 years), the deterrence doctrine has remained a vague idea. Until the doctrine is restated as a systematic theory, purported tests of it will be questionable; and the restatement will be a gargantuan task. The sheer number of *possibly relevant* properties of legal punishments (prescribed or actual) is a problem, and preventive mechanisms other than deterrence should be recognized. Incapacitation is one such mechanism (auto thieves do not thrive in prison), but it has been ignored in purported tests of the deterrence doctrine.

Even if those tests are defensible, two types of deterrence should be distinguished. In the case of *general* deterrence, individuals refrain from crime because of a perceived threat of punishment but without having been punished. If an individual refrains because of a perceived threat of punishment that has been intensified by actual punishment, then the deterrence is *specific.* The distinction is relevant in contemplating divergent ideas about the consequences of reactions to deviance. It may well be that recent findings only reflect general deterrence, and there are no comparable findings to support the specific deterrence argument. The theory of secondary deviance can be construed as completely contrary to that argument, but the theory has no bearing on general deterrence. In any case, the revival of deterrence research provides a focus (other than the reactivist perspective) in the sociological study of reactions to deviance.

Sociology in General

The concern with reactions to deviance bears on two major issues in sociology. First, since reactions are commonly analyzed in terms of punishment and reward, they are especially relevant in contemplating the use of reinforcement theory in sociology (Homans 1961). Second, reactions to deviance are relevant in the perennial debate over social order and maintenance mechanisms (Scott 1971).

Elaborating on the second issue, reactions to deviance are commonly described as sanctions, and an emphasis on sanctions is consistent with the view that social order is based on conflict and coercion rather than, as functionalists suggest, consensus and the internalization of norms. It is significant that some advocates of the labeling perspective (e.g. Scott 1972; Erikson 1962, 1966) adopt a functionalist perspective when relating the study of deviance to general sociological theory, but an emphasis on reactions is consistent with the "conflict" perspective.

THE "NEW" CRIMINOLOGY

Until recently, sociologists commonly took criminal law as given in their preoccupation with attempts to identify (a) characteristics that distinguish criminals from noncriminals or (b) correlates of the crime rate. In the last decade that preoccupation has been questioned as never before. One argument (Turk 1969) is that criminologists have ignored a far-reaching question: In a given social unit, why are particular kinds of behavior labeled as "criminal"? That question redirects attention to criminal law, but it is not posed merely to expand the subject matter of criminology. On the contrary, the question reflects an argument—that efforts to identify the distinguishing characteristics of criminals are misguided. Extending the argument, individuals "become" criminals not because of their behavior but, rather, because they are labeled as such by legal officials. Hence a "behavioral" explanation of criminality is at best incomplete because it ignores the administration of criminal law. Consider two observations: "criminal status may be ascribed to persons because of real or fancied *attributes,* because of what they *are* rather than what they *do*" (Turk 1969:9) and "Persons and behaviors . . . become criminal because of the *formulation* and *application* of criminal definitions. Thus, *crime is created*" (Quinney 1970:15).

Both statements are extensions of the reactive conception of deviance to criminality, but that conception was originally apolitical. The extreme version of the conception asserts that the labeling of deviants has nothing to do with their behavior; however, it does not purport to explain why officials (e.g. the police) label some individuals as criminals but not others.

An explanation comes from a group of sociologists known as the "new" criminologists. They allege that criminal laws are used by an elite or an "establishment" to control those who are exploited and to silence dissidents. So the latest school in criminology makes political considerations paramount. By contrast, early advocates of the reactive conception of deviance did not make political considerations truly central, and one of their critics (Gouldner 1968) described them as "liberals" or "romantics" rather than genuine radicals.

Yet there are divisions among the new criminologists. Whereas Taylor et al (1973:147–49) expressly reject the reactive conception of deviance, Turk and Quinney accept it. The resolution of that difference should be left to the innovators, but observe that they do agree on one point—criminal law is used by the powerful to protect their interests.

Rather than formulate testable theories, the new criminologists speak incessantly of the powerful dictating criminal law and its enforcement with a view to protecting "interests." Such arguments are little more than tautologies. By definition, those who control the enactment of criminal law have power, and who can conceive of a disinterested party enacting criminal laws?

The point is that a theory about crime must extend beyond vague statements pertaining to power, interest, elites, establishments, etc. It must end with potentially falsifiable assertions about (*a*) the distinguishing characteristics of individuals who control the enactments of criminal law, (*b*) the process by which criminal laws are enacted, (*c*) selective enforcement of criminal laws, or (*d*) contrasts in the criminal laws of different economic-political systems. To illustrate, it is one thing to speak of power, interests, elites, etc, but quite another to assert that the legal proscription of armed robbery is peculiar to capitalism. The criticism is not that new criminologists refrain from that particular assertion; rather, they studiously avoid testable assertions. To deserve a serious hearing, they must confront empirical questions, such as: Is the legal proscription of particular types of crime peculiar to particular types of economic-political systems? If so, which types of crimes and which types of systems?

Answers to such questions should be derived from a theory, but new criminologists scarcely contemplate empirical questions. Taylor et al (1973:217) do little more than make an argument for a Marxist theory of crime, but even they recognize that Marx's analysis of crime was grossly incomplete. They do acknowledge that Bonger (1916) attempted a Marxist theory of crime, but it is startling to be informed by Taylor et al (1973:298) that Bonger fell short because of some "totally unMarxist" emphasis.

In comparison to Taylor et al, Quinney has more nearly formulated a theory of crime in the form of six basic propositions. But by his own admission (1970:15) one of the propositions is a definition, and the analytical character of the other propositions is ignored. Consider his third proposition (1970:18): "Criminal definitions are applied by the segments of society that have the power to shape the enforcement and administration of criminal law." How is the "application of criminal definitions" logically distinct from "enforcement and administration of criminal law"? One may as well proclaim that taxidermists stuff animals.

Turk's (1969) theory is different in that it is subject to falsification, at least in principle. The first part of his theory pertains to "normative-legal conflict," which is asserted to be (*a*) a direct function of the congruence of social and cultural norms for both subjects and authorities, (*b*) a direct function of the amount of "organization" among subjects, but (*c*) an inverse function of the "sophistication" of both subjects and authorities. Turk's conceptualization of the dependent variable is extremely vague, and investigators are not likely to realize even approximate agreement in the numerical representation of the independent variables. Those variables are clearly quantitative, but Turk specifies no formulas or procedures; and his comments about requisite kinds of data are excessively general.

The second part of Turk's theory is somewhat different, for his own illustrations indicate that arrest statistics are indicative of "criminalization" (the dependent variable). But again it is doubtful that investigators could realize even approximate agreement in computing values to represent the independent variables: (*a*) congruence of cultural and social norms, (*b*) realism in the "moves" of conflict, and (*c*) the power of enforcers relative to resisters. Turk relies on intuitive applications of those notions in presenting purported evidence to support the theory. For example, in the United States nonwhites presumably have less power than whites and hence, consistent with the theory, their arrest rate is higher for all 22 types of crimes considered by Turk. However, consider the high arrest rates for ages 18–39, a population that Turk initially identifies as more powerful than the young or the old, but only to recant and plunge into a vague reanalysis of power. No less startling, the male arrest rate is higher than the female arrest rate for all but "prostitution-vice," and the differences are enormous. Confronted with those contrasts, Turk abandons the "relative power" argument and asserts that females (*a*) are more likely to agree with legal norms, (*b*) have less opportunity to violate those norms, and (*c*) are less exposed to law enforcement. But Turk cannot bring himself to say that females are perhaps "less exposed" because they commit less acts of particular types, which is to say that criminalization is *not* divorced from what people "do."

CONCLUSION

The previous observations are obviously critical of the labeling perspective, the reactive conception, and "new" criminology. Nonetheless, those three "schools" are a major turning point in the sociological study of deviance.[7] Surely even the most conservative sociologist will admit that something fundamental is missing from the older theories of crime and deviance, and this survey indicates what is missing— a lack of concern with reactions to deviance.

But just as something is missing from older theories, so is there a glaring gap in the reactivist perspective. Advocates of that perspective have not thrown the baby out with the bath; rather, they deny the infant ever existed. That infant is the hardly incredulous belief that being labeled deviant commonly has something to do with behavior prior to and in that sense independently of reactions (legal or extralegal).

The issue can be resolved quickly by two admonitions: 1. normativists, cease presuming that data on deviance can be interpreted independently of reactions to deviance; and 2. reactivists, cease presuming that reactions to deviance have nothing to do with prior behavior. But more than a truce is needed, meaning that the goal should be a new theory. That theory should focus on two variables: Dt, the "true" rate of some type of deviant act (or the "real" perpetrators); and Dr, the officially *reported* rate (or alleged perpetrators). Dt is unknowable, but it is commonly difficult to make sense out of Dr values without postulating Dt (reconsider the low arrest rates for women). In other words, accounting for variation in Dr is *the* problem, but some of the variance is attributable to Dt. Given that assumption, one

[7]The turning point is not one of substantive interest alone. On the contrary, the new perspectives and rejections of older theories undoubtedly reflect an antipathy to positivism in preference for the tradition of phenomenology, ethnomethodology, or political activism. Hence we recognize that demands in this critique for formalized and falsifiable theories may well be alien to the methodology and even the philosophy of the new perspectives. To the extent that is the case, the issues cannot be resolved; but the field would profit from recognizing that many of the current controversies are beyond constructive debate.

part of the theory would comprise assertions (axioms or postulates) about the relation between Dt and so-called etiological factors (e.g. unemployment, participation of women in the labor force). None of those assertions would be directly testable, and they become indirectly testable only when coupled with assertions about the Dr/Dt ratio. Those latter assertions would form another distinct part of the theory.

The two parts of the theory can be illustrated by the logical form of two premises: 1. Dt reaches a maximum under condition X, and 2. the Dr/Dt ratio reaches a maximum under condition Y. Those two premises would generate the major theorem: Dr reaches the maximum under conditions $X-Y$. Observe that advocates of the reactivist perspective and the new criminologists must supply the second premise. Much of their analysis points in that direction; but they cannot supply the premise without recognizing Dt (even if as purely theoretical); and the new criminologists will not make a contribution unless they recognize that exhortations about power, interest, and conflict do not constitute a testable theory.

Literature Cited

Akers, R. L. 1968. Problems in the sociology of deviance: social definitions and behavior. *Soc. Forces* 46:455–65

Alix, E. K. 1969. The functional interdependence of crime and community social structure. *J. Crim. Law Criminol. Police Sci.* 60:332–39

Becker, H. S. 1963. *Outsiders.* New York: Free Press. 179 pp.

Blumenstein, A., Cohen, J. 1973. A theory of the stability of punishment. *J. Crim. Law Criminol.* 64:198–207

Bonger, W. 1916. *Criminality and Economic Conditions.* Boston: Little, Brown. 364 pp.

Bordua, D. J. 1961. Delinquent subcultures: sociological interpretations of gang delinquency. *Ann. Am. Acad. Polit. Soc. Sci.* 338:119–36

Caldwell, R. G. 1944. The deterrent influence of corporal punishment upon prisoners who have been whipped. *Am. Sociol. Rev.* 9:171–77

Chiricos, T. G., Waldo, G. P. 1970. Punishment and crime: an examination of some empirical evidence. *Soc. Probl.* 18:200–17

Cloward, R. A., Ohlin, L. E. 1960. *Delinquency and Opportunity: A Theory of Delinquent Gangs.* Glencoe, Ill.: Free Press. 220 pp.

Cohen, A. K. 1955. *Delinquent Boys: The Culture of The Gang.* New York: Free Press of Glencoe. 198 pp.

Cressey, D. R. 1960. Epidemiology and individual conduct: a case from criminology. *Pac. Sociol. Rev.* 3:47–58

Currie, E. P. 1968. Crimes without criminals: witchcraft and its control in Renaissance Europe. *Law Soc. Rev.* 3:7–32

DeFleur, M. L., Quinney, R. 1966. A reformulation of Sutherland's differential association theory and a strategy for empirical verification. *J. Res. Crime Delinquency* 3:1–22

Doleschal, E. 1970. Hidden crime. *Crime Delinquency Lit.* 2:546–72

Douglas, J. D. 1967. *The Social Meanings of Suicide.* Princeton, N.J.: Princeton Univ. Press

Ennis, P. H. 1967. *Criminal Victimization in The United States: A Report of a National Survey.* Washington, DC: GPO. 111 pp.

Erickson, M. L. 1973. Group violations and official delinquency: the group hazard hypothesis. *Criminology* 11:127–60

Erikson, K. T. 1962. Notes on the sociology of deviance. *Soc. Probl.* 9:307–14

Erikson, K. T. 1966. *Wayward Puritans: A Study in The Sociology of Deviance.* New York: Wiley. 228 pp.

Fisher, S. 1972. Stigma and deviant careers in school. *Soc. Probl.* 20:78–83

Foster, J. D., Dinitz, S., Reckless, W. C. 1972. Perceptions of stigma following public intervention for deviant behavior. *Soc. Probl.* 20:202–9

Gibbons, D. C. 1969. Crime and punishment: a study in social attitudes. *Soc. Forces* 47:391–97

Gibbs, J. P. 1972a. Issues in defining deviant behavior. In *Theoretical Perspectives on Deviance,* ed. R. A. Scott, J. D. Douglas, Chap. 2, 39–68. New York: Basic Books. 373 pp.

Gibbs, J. P. 1972b. Social control. *Warner Modular Publ.,* Module 1:1–17

Glaser, D. 1964. *The Effectiveness of a Prison and Parole System.* Indianapolis, Ind.: Bobbs-Merrill. 592 pp.

Goffman, E. 1963. *Stigma.* Englewood Cliffs, N.J.: Prentice-Hall. 147 pp.

Gould, L. C. 1969. Who defines delinquency: a comparison of self-reported and officially-reported indices of delinquency for three racial groups. *Soc. Probl.* 16:325–36

Gouldner, A. W. 1968. The sociologist as partisan: sociology and the welfare state. *Am. Sociol.* 3:103–16

Gove, W. R. 1970. Societal reaction as an explanation of mental illness: an evaluation. *Am. Sociol. Rev.* 35:873–84

Green, E. 1970. Race, social status, and criminal arrest. *Am. Sociol. Rev.* 35:476–90

Harary, F. 1966. Merton revisited: a new classification for deviant behavior. *Am. Sociol. Rev.* 31:693–97

Hardt, R. H., Bodine, G. E. 1965. *Development of Self-Report Instruments in Delinquency Research.* Mimeographed. Syracuse, N.Y.: Syracuse Univ. Youth Develop. Center. 60 pp.

Hirschi, T. 1973. Procedural rules and the study of deviant behavior. *Soc. Probl.* 21:159–73

Homans, G. C. 1961. *Social Behavior: Its Elementary Forms.* New York: Harcourt, Brace & World. 404 pp.

Kitsuse, J. I. 1962. Societal reaction to deviant behavior: problems of theory and method. *Soc. Probl.* 9:247–56

Kitsuse, J. I., Dietrick, D. C. 1959. Delinquent boys: a critique. *Am. Sociol. Rev.* 24:208–15

Lemert, E. M. 1972. *Human Deviance, Social Problems, and Social Control.* Englewood Cliffs, N.J.: Prentice-Hall. 2nd ed. 277 pp.

Lerman, P. 1967. Gangs, networks, and subcultural delinquency. *Am. J. Sociol.* 73:63–72

Liazos, A. 1972. The poverty of the sociology of deviance: nuts, sluts, and perverts. *Soc. Probl.* 20:103–20

Mankoff, M. 1971. Societal reactions and career deviance: a critical analysis. *Sociol. Quart.* 12:204–18

Marshall, H., Purdy, R. 1972. Hidden deviance and the labelling approach: the case for drinking and driving. *Soc. Probl.* 19:541–53

Matza, D. 1964. *Delinquency and Drift.* New York: Wiley. 199 pp.

Matza, D. 1969. *Becoming Deviant.* Englewood Cliffs, N.J.: Prentice-Hall. 203 pp.

Merton, R. K. 1938. Social structure and anomie. *Am. Sociol. Rev.* 3:672–82

Merton, R. K. 1957. *Social Theory and Social Structure.* New York: Free Press. Rev. ed. 645 pp.

Miller, W. B. 1958. Lower class culture as a generating milieu of gang delinquency. *J. Soc. Issues* 14:5–19

Phillips, D. L. 1964. Rejection of the mentally: the influence of behavior and sex. *Am. Sociol. Rev.* 29:679–87

Porterfield, A. L. 1943. Delinquency and its outcome in court and college. *Am. J. Sociol.* 49:199–208

Quinney, R. 1970. *The Social Reality of Crime.* Boston: Little, Brown. 339 pp.

Reiss, A. J. 1973. *Surveys of Self-Reported Delicts.* Unpublished paper prepared for the Symposium on Studies of Public Experience, Knowledge, and Opinion of Crime and Justice, Washington, DC, March 17–18, revised July 1973. 66 pp.

Reiss, I. L. 1970. Premarital sex as deviant behavior: an application of current approaches to deviance. *Am. Sociol. Rev.* 35:78–87

Reynolds, P. D., Blyth, D. A., Vincent, J. J., Bouchard, T. J. 1973. *Victimization in a Metropolitan Region: Comparison of a Central City Area and a Suburban Community.* Minneapolis: Minn. Center Sociol. Res. Mimeographed. 272 pp.

Rossi, P. H., Waite, E., Bose, C. E., Berk, R. E. 1974. The seriousness of crimes: normative structure and individual differences. *Am. Sociol. Rev.* 39:224–37

Scheff, T. J. 1966. *Being Mentally Ill.* Chicago: Aldine. 210 pp.

Scheff, T. J. 1974. The labeling theory of mental illness. *Am. Sociol. Rev.* 39: 444–52

Schur, E. M. 1969. Reactions to deviance: a critical assessment. *Am. J. Sociol.* 75:309–22

Schwartz, R. D., Skolnick, J. H. 1962. Two studies of legal stigma. *Soc. Probl.* 10:133–42

Scott, J. F. 1971. *Internalization of Norms: A Sociological Theory of Moral Commitment.* Englewood Cliffs, N.J.: Prentice-Hall. 237 pp.

Scott, R. A. 1972. A proposed framework for analyzing deviance as a property of social order. In *Theoretical Perspectives on Deviance,* ed. R. A. Scott, J. D. Douglas, Chap. 1, 9–35. New York: Basic Books. 373 pp.

Sellin, T., Ed. 1967. *Capital Punishment.* New York: Harper & Row. 290 pp.

Sellin, T., Wolfgang, M. E. 1964. *The Measurement of Delinquency.* New York: Wiley. 423 pp.

Sherif, M., Sherif, C. W. 1964. *Reference Groups: Exploration into Conformity and Deviation of Adolescents.* New York: Harper & Row. 370 pp.

Sherif, M., Sherif, C. W. 1967. Group processes and collective interaction in delinquent activities. *J. Res. Crime Delinquency* 4:43–62

Short, J. F. 1965. Social structure and group processes in explanation of gang delinquency. In *Problems of Youth: Transition to Adulthood in a Changing World,* ed. M. Sherif, C. W. Sherif, Chap. 8:155–88. Chicago: Aldine. 336 pp.

Sudnow, D. 1965. Normal crimes: sociological features of the penal code in a public defender office. *Soc. Probl.* 12:255–76

Sutherland, E. H. 1939. *Principles of Criminology.* New York: Lippincott. 3rd ed. 651 pp.

Sutherland, E. H., Cressey, D. R. 1970. *Criminology.* Philadelphia: Lippincott. 8th ed. 659 pp.

Sykes, G. M., Matza, D. 1957. Techniques of neutralization: a theory of delinquency. *Am. Sociol. Rev.* 22:664–70

Tannenbaum, F. 1938. *Crime and The Community.* Boston: Ginn. 487 pp.

Tappan, P. 1960. *Crime, Justice and Correction.* New York: McGraw-Hill. 781 pp.

Taylor, I., Walton, P., Young, J. 1973. *The New Criminology.* New York: Harper. 325 pp.

Tittle, C. R., Logan, C. H. 1973. Sanctions and deviance: evidence and remaining questions. *Law Soc. Rev.* 7:371–92

Toby, J. 1961. Delinquency and opportunity: a critique. *Brit. J. Sociol.* 12:282–89

Turk, A. T. 1969. *Criminality and Legal Order.* Chicago: Rand-McNally. 184 pp.

Warren, C.A.B., Johnson, J. M. 1972. A critique of labeling theory from the phenomenological perspective. In *Theoretical Perspectives on Deviance,* ed. R. A. Scott, J. D. Douglas, Chap. 3, 69–92. New York: Basic Books, 373 pp.

Williams, C. J., Weinberg, M. S. 1970. Being discovered: a study of homosexuals in the military. *Soc. Probl.* 18:217–27

Wilson, J. Q. 1974. Crime and criminologists. *Commentary* 58:47–53

Wolfgang, M. E., Figlio, R. M., Sellin, T. 1972. *Delinquency in a Birth Cohort.* Chicago: Univ. Chicago Press. 327 pp.

THE COMPARATIVE STUDY OF HEALTH CARE DELIVERY SYSTEMS[1]

❖10502

David Mechanic

Department of Sociology, University of Wisconsin, Madison, Wisconsin 53706

It is only in very recent years that there has been significant effort to examine comparatively the organization and performance of health care delivery systems. But even recent efforts have been largely developed within a health services framework and have lacked guidance by any significant theoretical perspectives. The existing data are thus descriptive of particular locations and periods of time, and lack coherence for developing a theoretical paradigm that sharpens important issues from a sociological perspective. This review will be limited by the idiosyncratic data base available. As with comparative research in many other areas, the definition and measurement of comparable units within varying sociocultural and historical circumstances are difficult, and samples of complex entities, such as delivery systems, are only obtained with considerable effort and cost.

One possible level of sociological analysis involves examining the character of the health care delivery system in relation to the structure of society. Glaser (1970b), for example, on the basis of visits to various nations and through interviews and written material available on health care delivery in these countries, posed a number of hypotheses concerning the relationships between the religious, familial, and economic aspects of social organization and the character of hospital organization including such matters as recruitment into hospital occupations and the development and uses of technology. Careful, empirical investigation of these hypotheses would be a task of major proportions. While it is interesting to know to what extent the strength of a religious mandate to help strangers affects motives for employment, the priority of hospital work, and the length of working hours, such propositions, however, do not tell us a great deal about varying dimensions of performance among health care systems within modern industrial societies. Glaser's approach is useful in bringing to our attention the extent to which variabilities in the structure and performance of modern health care systems have been narrowed by industrializa-

[1]Supported in part by the Robert Wood Johnson Foundation.

43

tion, urbanization, secularization, and the growth of technology; and his hypotheses provide useful concepts from which to examine the differences in medical care in developed and underdeveloped nations.

Health care delivery systems have broad social functions not only in treating disease and disability, but also in alleviating tensions and distress and in sustaining persons in the performance of social roles (Mechanic 1968). The health care delivery system frequently deals with conflicts and dilemmas resulting from larger societal demands, and may be either an instrument of social control, a means of social support, a context in which difficult social disputes can be informally managed, or all of these.

The intangible consequences of many health services and their varying social functions make comparative study difficult. Even within more narrow conceptual limits, there is a lack of specification of outputs reasonably expected to be affected by the types of inputs characteristic of medical organization (Donabedian 1973). Levels of investment in health services and variations in organization—as far as we can presently ascertain—have had limited impact on the most readily available output measures, such as infant and adult mortality (Abel-Smith 1967). More subtle indicators are underdeveloped, and it is only very recently that greater effort is being devoted to developing more appropriate measures (Elinson 1973). Thus, sociological researchers have concentrated almost all of their effort on inputs and processes of care in contrast to performance measures. Across nations, such inputs and processes reflect different traditions, cultures, and political and economic processes.

THEORETICAL CONSIDERATIONS

It is commonly agreed at a more general level that the organization and priorities of health care organization reflect the political and economic priorities of its sponsors, and that each health care system has developed within its own historical and sociocultural context affecting many of its more unique qualities. However, such observations are confirmed more by case studies of individual systems than by comparative studies of the economic and political bases of medical care in diverse settings.

At the macro level of analysis, the most sustained and fertile thread derives from Parsons' (1951) conceptualization of the functional role of health services within the larger social system. At the individual level, illness serves as an accepted excuse for relief from ordinary obligations and responsibilities, and may be used to justify behaviors and interventions not ordinarily tolerated by the social system without significant sanctions. At the societal level the definition of illness may be used more or less as a mechanism of social control to contain deviance, to remove misfits from particular social roles, or to encourage continued social functioning and productive activity. Thus, from a sociological standpoint, the locus of control of medical decision making is a key variable in examining the implications of medical care for social life more generally. For the most part, sociologists have not carefully examined varying approaches to regulation in different nations, the extent to which physicians in different countries have extramedical responsibilities, and the resulting implications for society. It is inevitable, however, that with the growing bureaucratization of medicine and increased regulation, sociologists will more and more direct their attention to such issues in the future (Goss et al 1973).

Given the diversity of political contexts among nations, the extent to which most medical care delivery systems have resisted intrusion of larger political interests is in itself a remarkable phenomenon, and reflects in part the immense status and autonomy of medicine as a recognized profession on a worldwide basis.[2] The growth of medical knowledge and technology has had a pervasive influence in shaping the character of health delivery systems to the point that nations with very different ideological preferences have similar forms of medical care systems and face common problems and dilemmas (Mechanic 1974b, Field 1973). Although government sponsorship and control of medical care have in some contexts resulted in radical alterations in the distribution of services (Douglas-Wilson & McLachlan 1973, Horn 1969, Sidel 1971, Stein & Susser 1972), the typical forms of service delivery and professional organization are less varied than might be anticipated on the basis of ideological, political, or economic differences among nations alone.

One consequence of increasing knowledge and technological potential is the growth of specialization and fragmentation in the delivery of services in all modern medical care systems. Although it is difficult to meet ordinary primary care needs with increasing reliance on specialized technologies and an elaborate division of labor, new organizational models for meeting these basic functions have been slow to develop. The slow adaptiveness of social organization to emerging technologies reflects both the economic and political strength of the health professions throughout much of the world and the extraordinary difficulties in developing an adequate accommodation between a rapidly growing knowledge base and sophisticated technology and the expectations, understandings, and preferences of populations (Mechanic 1972a).

A major difficulty in the sociological investigation of comparative medical organization is the inadequacy of traditional concepts describing emerging structural arrangements and ongoing organizational processes. The conceptual approaches that fit centralized, bureaucratized organizations are poorly adapted for studying intraorganizational programming and cooperation, coordination among agencies, and organizational networks. In the American context, for example, we have no adequate sociological paradigm that facilitates the classification and study of such organizational entities as health sciences centers, prepaid group practices, comprehensive medical foundations, hospital mergers, and the like. An examination of any of these organizational devices suggests a wide range of dimensions on which entities having similar designations may differ, but we have yet to develop an adequate set of generic concepts that are meaningful in understanding prevailing forms of organization within single countries, much less on a cross-national level. Most research depends on commonly understood designations such as hospitals, clinics, medical schools, etc.

[2]The current debate concerning the uses of psychiatry in the Soviet Union reflects international sensitivities to the political uses of medical institutions.

Given the meager development of comparative sociological study of national systems of medical care, this review focuses on several types of comparative studies both between and within national systems. The appropriate boundaries of medical care systems are frequently unclear since medical work may be more or less closely related to the delivery of social welfare services. This review emphasizes the health care sector as compared with broader social welfare functions in varying societies. From the point of view of clients, however, varying delivery systems are often alternatives for dealing with similar problems.

After a brief examination of the world system of medical care, a tentative paradigm describing the operation of national health systems will be suggested, followed by more specific models of various components of health delivery systems and their comparative effects on health outcomes. All of these models will be presented in an exploratory way to help define issues for research and to organize disparate efforts in the area. The reader should keep in mind, however, that available comparative data are both limited and frequently flawed, and thus these suggested models primarily direct attention to issues requiring more focused research.

THE INTERNATIONAL KNOWLEDGE, TECHNOLOGY, AND MANPOWER MARKETPLACE

Science and technology transcend national boundaries. With the facility of rapid transmission of information in modern societies, new knowledge or technological innovations may rapidly diffuse throughout the world. The character of medical care is dependent on the degree of established knowledge and technological development at any point in time. Education for medical science and practice derives from the existing base of science and technology. Medicine, in particular, is characterized by intricate and rapid communication networks involving innumerable scientific journals—many of an international character—and abstracting, indexing, and translating services. Moreover, drugs and medical products are produced by industries of considerable size that aggressively market their technologies on a worldwide basis.

Even in less developed countries there is a strong trend toward approaches to medicine characteristic of modern nations, despite the fact that such development may be ill-suited to major population needs or the ability of the country to support it economically on a wide scale. This results, except for some of the socialist countries, in a highly stratified system of medical care, where a well-developed medical capacity characteristic of modern Western nations caters to a tiny minority of the population. The limited affluence of many of these countries and their priorities for development make it unlikely that such services will be offered to a significant proportion of the population.

Medical schools throughout the world tend to emulate those characteristic of modern nations and are part of the worldwide medical community. Medical education thus encourages a pattern of practice that these countries can ill afford to implement widely. This results in limited economic and scientific opportunities for medical practice, and encourages an international migratory pattern of medical and scientific manpower for both education and employment. This migratory pattern is supported by greater available opportunities in modern nations, more prestige, income and autonomy, and political factors. The ability to migrate is influenced by the need for physicians in receiving areas, immigration and licensing requirements, cultural and language similarities, and political orientations consistent with the prevailing medical system in the receiving country. The migratory pattern is one from the less to the more affluent countries which can offer better facilities and social opportunities to practice scientific medicine. The United States is a major recipient of physicians from a variety of countries throughout the world, and foreign-trained physicians constitute a significant proportion of doctors licensed in any year. During the past decade England and Wales lost a significant number of physicians through immigration to the United States, Canada, New Zealand, and Australia, but replaced them with doctors from India and Pakistan (Abel-Smith & Gales 1964). It may be that models describing the flow of populations from areas of lesser to greater opportunities through stages can successfully describe physician migration, but only fragmentary data are available on a worldwide basis, and most of the existing studies have been carried out from an American or British perspective.

PATTERNS OF MORTALITY AND MORBIDITY AND NATIONAL DEVELOPMENT[3]

In this century, patterns of mortality and morbidity in developed nations have shifted significantly from a preponderance of infectious disease problems to a variety of chronic degenerative diseases, accidents, and psychological and behavior problems (Mechanic 1968, McKeown 1965). Underdeveloped countries, however, still show the characteristic pattern of malnutrition, abundant deaths from diarrhea and dysentery, tuberculosis, and a variety of other infectious, intestinal, and respiratory diseases (Bryant 1969). The pattern of disease has a devastating effect on the population, and interacts with malnutrition to produce substantial disability and mortality in the population.

There is no question that patterns of disease and disability in underdeveloped countries have an enormous toll on the capacities of those afflicted. The actual interaction between the health status of the population and national development, however, is much less clear. Most of the data available cannot clearly differentiate such relevant factors as the capacity of workers, underemployment related to economic forces, the effects of increased education, and other changes that often accompany improvements in health status, and the consequences of increased fertility. Measures of health status and economic development vary from one analysis to another and may be an important factor in conflicting data and conclusions. Health, for example, may be defined in terms of mortality rates from specific diseases, life-expectancy rates, man-years of labor available, infant mortality rates, levels of health expenditure, and the like.

[3]I am indebted to Bruce Turetsky for his assistance in reviewing the literature on the role of health in national development.

Much of the literature on health and national development is speculative and written more to convince the reader about the economic value of health investments than to unravel the complex dynamics underlying the relationship. Most empirical efforts have been carried out by economists interested in human capital and those from the public health field (Baldwin & Weisbrod 1974, Barlow 1967, Malenbaum 1970, Scott 1971, Taylor & Hall 1967, Weisbrod et al 1973). These studies have illustrated some of the intervening processes that make it difficult to come to any simple conclusions about the effects of improved health. The studies examine such varied outcomes as the productive capacities of individual workers, entire farms, or regional areas using such measures as per capita gross national product, per capita energy consumption, total acreage under cultivation, production levels of specific crops or products, per capita agricultural output, and the like. Some public health programs, i.e. malarial eradication, have beneficial effects both on human health and reclaiming land for agricultural development, but long term effects are complicated by changes in fertility (Frederikson 1962, Barlow 1967).

Although it is difficult to determine the specific impacts of the delivery of health services on national development, it is clear that in underdeveloped nations preventive health programs, such as those concerned with improved nutrition, sanitation, pure water sources, family planning, and the like, bring far greater benefits than those associated with curative medicine as practiced in modern nations (Benjamin 1965). The application of relatively simple public health measures has an enormous capacity to reduce mortality and increase longevity. From the perspective of national development, however, control of fertility is essential. The translation of medical techniques characteristic of modern nations to underdeveloped countries has relatively little impact in contrast to investments in broader public health measures.

The elaboration of the health care delivery system usually accompanies national development and interacts with improved economic and social conditions. However, the premature application of highly specialized curative medical care often captures resources for the few that can potentially reap greater benefits for the larger population. Countries with greater centralized control over the expenditure of medical resources are developing priorities along these lines, while those more closely allied with a capitalistic ethic tend to develop a curative medical care system to serve those more affluent (Weinerman 1969, Douglas-Wilson & McLachlan 1973, Mechanic 1974b).

HEALTH CARE DELIVERY SYSTEMS IN MODERN NATIONS

Health care delivery systems are shaped by the historical context within which they are embedded. Such factors as economic organization, ideological forces, the available technology, and pre-existing professional organization affect access to medical care, the distribution of health care services, and ultimately the quality of health care. Figure 1 depicts a variety of gross categorizations that can serve as a framework for organizing various studies and helps make apparent how few of the possible areas of investigation concerning national systems have been explored. Beyond an occasional case study there are almost no data on the influence of ideology, eco-

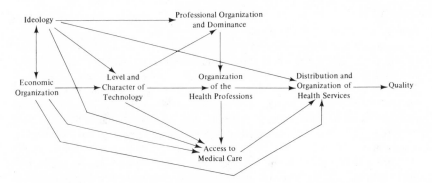

Figure 1   System determinants of the distribution and quality of health services.

nomic organization, and the level and character of technology. Of these areas of concern, most neglected of all is technology and its relationship to either variables describing the social structure of the country or the organization of health care delivery. There are attempts to link economic investment in medical care to health care outcomes as in the study of Abel-Smith (1967), and ideology to the organization of the health occupations (Anderson 1972, Alford 1975, Field 1967), but such analyses are rare, indeed.

Almost all of the research effort among sociologists has dealt with the organization of the health professions and occupations and with access to and distribution of medical care. Most influential among these studies is the work of Freidson (1970a) on medical dominance of physicians over the work of other health professions and his study of professional controls. Physicians throughout the world have been able to control substantially their conditions of work as well as those of other health occupations. Research on access to medical care has focused on economic and sociocultural barriers to utilization (McKinlay 1972, Aday 1972) and only indirectly speaks to larger issues of social organization. The great mass of studies deals with client perceptions, conflicts among health workers, factors affecting demand for medical care, differential reactions to services, and the like (Freeman et al 1972, Donabedian 1973). Thus, for the most part, sociological inquiry in medicine, as well as work in the health services area, contributes relatively little to understanding health care at the institutional level of analysis (Alford 1972).

National ideology, as it pertains to medical care, may be defined in terms of government involvement in the financing, administration, and regulation of the health sector. Government participation may vary in terms of the proportion of medical costs assumed by the public sector, the extent of government intrusion and control over various types of decisions, and the extent to which government itself owns and operates the health care delivery system. Although various historical studies suggest the danger of attempting to understand contemporary developments outside the context in which professional patterns and relationships have developed (Abel-Smith 1964, Stevens 1966, Eckstein 1964), it is possible to order national systems on various criteria describing the relationship between government and the medical sector. Anderson (1972) makes an ambitious attempt to examine inputs and outputs in the United States, England, and Sweden, and to relate this to the larger sociopolitical and historical context. He reaches certain conclusions about equity and the propensity toward innovation in these three countries, but it is not clear on what particular indicators these conclusions rest and whether there is a clear basis for the assessment. Anderson's study and the comparative studies by Stevens (1971) on the United States and England both suggest the complexity of the issues, the intangibility of the criteria, and how difficult it is to unravel organizational features from the unique historical forces that have come to shape the evolution of each system of care.

In general, it appears that in nations in which government assumes the highest proportion of total medical care costs, greater emphasis is given to public health, preventive medicine, and ambulatory medical care. Moreover, in these countries government is more willing to intrude on the professional dominance of medicine in establishing medical care priorities, although they tend not to intrude on clinical professional work. An important intervening factor is the degree of bureaucratic organization of medicine which appears to be related to both government investment and the extent of regulation.

Most of the literature on medical care systems deals with costs and various aspects of administering medical care services. As government investment increases, there are greater incentives to impose various cost controls. Throughout most of the world, government agencies or insurance funds must negotiate with physician groups over payment and service-related matters. An enormous array of devices have been developed around the world to establish appropriate remuneration schedules for different types of health manpower (Glaser 1970a). Among Western nations, medical groups retain considerable influence in these negotiations and generally have sufficient support to determine the mechanism by which they are paid. Different interpretations of this process are offered by Eckstein (1960) and Marmor & Thomas (1971), but they agree that, at least in England, physicians hold considerable bargaining power.

In sum, sociological contributions to understanding the medical care sector as a whole are very limited. Much of the problem involves the failure to specify the aspects of the health care sector of greatest significance to sociology in contrast to health economics or health administration. Moreover, few sociologists have directed themselves to the role of medicine relative to other social institutions and to the larger social and cultural significance of health care institutions. We now turn to such issues.

THE SOCIAL FUNCTIONS OF HEALTH CARE

Throughout the world the growth of the medical domain has accompanied the diminution of the authority of religious conceptions. Various aspects of life, previously under the province of morals and religion, have become increasingly secularized, and the authority of traditional institutions in molding these perspectives has been very much diminished. The extent to which medical conceptions have come to dominate perspectives in other realms of life is a remarkable phenomenon, and the functional domain of medicine has served to more effectively sustain social patterns in a manner consistent with modern economic and social activity.

Although much of social science inquiry is oriented toward analyzing failures in medical care relationships—such as failure or delay in seeking medical care, the client's use of marginal healers, or noncompliance with the physician's advice—the remarkable fact is that the authority of the physician extends as widely as it does. In fact, we take it so for granted that seeking medical care is the rational and natural thing to do when ill that we are frankly surprised at the persistence of folk and religious concepts in what we view as the legitimate province of medicine. As Parsons & Fox (1952) noted, with industrialization, medicine increasingly took over the functions of family care and thus facilitated the smooth persistence of social activities despite sickness and social disability among family members. Hospitals, in particular, have served to insulate society against the problems of coping with the mentally ill, the aged, the retarded, and those with a variety of other problems in functioning. And with increasing secularization and modernization, medicine has filled the vacuum to deal with problems that were once under the authority of the family, religion, or the legal system. The domain of medicine is increasingly encompassing a variety of deviant behaviors, social maladjustments, and difficulties in coping.

Sigerist (1960) and Parsons (1951) alerted sociologists to the importance of health care as a means of relieving social tensions produced by other social institutions, such as the factory or the home, or as a mechanism to control deviance in the society. In an illuminating monograph, Field (1957) illustrated how illness could be manipulated by both clients and the state, each to achieve its own particular goals. The most direct attempt to attack this issue empirically is a study by Shuval (1970) in which she develops measures of different levels of social need among Jews of varying ethnic origins, and relates these to measures of reported utilization of Kupat Holim, the largest health service program in Israel. She found that higher levels of need for catharsis, legitimation of failure, and resolution of the magic-science conflict are associated with higher levels of utilization. Although this study is provocative, Shuval unfortunately had no data from medical records that could validate utilization reports and add depth to the study. Another study in Israel by Mann and colleagues (1970) found that latent social need was influential in the long term pattern of use of health services. Persons who had been in concentration camps showed much higher levels of utilization over a period of years than could be accounted for solely on the basis of morbidity patterns. Cole & Lejeune (1972), in a study of welfare mothers, build a persuasive empirical case to support the contention that reported illness behavior is used to legitimate failure. And a great variety of studies have found a relationship between life change, psychological distress, and help-seeking behavior (Mechanic 1972b, Dohrenwend & Dohrenwend 1975).

Antonovsky (1972) suggests an epidemiological model that attempts to explain variations in physician utilization among populations comparable in morbidity. Host characteristics include latent need, intolerance of ambiguity of symptoms, and an orientation toward the use of professionals; characteristics describing medical institutions include availability of facilities, the ability to be responsive to various latent functions, and the degree of receptivity of physicians to patients; characteristics of the larger sociocultural environment include organizational facilitation in using medical services, absence of stigma for such use, cultural pressures to have problems diagnosed, and the degree of availability of functional alternatives. In contrast, Andersen (1968, Andersen et al 1970, Andersen & Newman 1973) presents a less theoretical approach that has been useful in regression models of medical utilization. He views utilization as a consequence of predisposing, enabling, and illness variables. Predisposing variables include demographic variables (age, sex, marital status, etc), social structural variables (race, education, religion, ethnicity, etc), and beliefs and knowledge about health and medical care. Enabling factors include family income, availability of health insurance, source of care and access to regular source of care, as well as the availability of health services, price of health services, and other community characteristics. Illness variables include disability, symptoms, diagnoses, and the like. Also, a variety of social psychological models have been suggested to describe how persons come to perceive and react to illness or to decide to engage in preventive health behavior (Mechanic 1968, Rosenstock 1969, Zola 1964).

The social psychological models and those suggested by Antonovsky and Shuval are most interesting theoretically, but thus far they have not been particularly powerful in explaining aggregate utilization data. In contrast, the Andersen model appears to account for greater variation, but lacks a theoretical conception of the dynamics of the behavior at issue. Antonovsky's suggested model provides a basis for developing a clearer understanding of variabilities in physician utilization among different national systems. Such variation in visiting physicians is substantial among developed nations. Countries such as the Soviet Union and Israel have a per capita utilization of 9–12 visits; the United States and England average 4–6 visits, and such countries as Sweden fall within the 2–3 visit range. These differences reflect cultural variations, availability and accessibility of services, and social ideologies as well as other factors. The only empirical study with comparative data on physician utilization in varying countries is the International Collaborative Study (Rabin 1972). Bice et al (1972) have examined various predicted relationships in each of twelve study areas in seven countries, using a path model including age, education, income, skepticism of medical care, and the reported tendency to use services, and have found some to be relatively consistent in predicting physician use. Skepticism of medical care significantly predicted lower utilization in eleven of the twelve areas; tendency to adopt the sick role predicted correctly to high utilization in ten areas, but only seven of the relationships reached statistical significance. Sociodemographic variables such as age, education, and income yielded inconsistent relationships or patterns contrary to those predicted.

Although these various approaches raise questions of sociological interest, they face conceptual problems. Social need and psychological distress affect not only medical utilization but also morbidity states. Thus, it is not clear to what extent social and psychological factors influence utilization by modifying morbidity, and the extent to which they help trigger help-seeking behavior (Mechanic 1975). Cur-

Although there is a profound belief that effective maternal and child health care prevents infant mortality and other injuries and defects in the child, there is no clear evidence that this is the case. Birth weight is the single best predictor of infant mortality, and when introduced into a multiple regression analysis, other variables fail to explain any appreciable additional variance. Both infant mortality and birth weight, however, are related to socioeconomic status, color, education of the mother, less than optimal age, high parity, illegitimacy of the child, and so on (Mechanic 1968). These variables, however, are all intercorrelated. While age and parity reflect certain biological risks, the other variables are largely viewed as proxies for such variables as social living conditions, nutrition, mothering skills, and access to medical care. It has been shown that the introduction of medical services into an area without such care results in a reduction in the rate of infant mortality, but has been little evidence that in areas with medical resources, the use of late prenatal and postnatal care results in lower infant mortality. A recent Institute of Medicine 1973) of infant mortality in New York City for 1968, atched birth and death records, examined infant death in relation to socio-c and ethnic differences, medical and social risk, and the use of adequate are as indexed by time of first prenatal visit, number of prenatal visits, and he baby was delivered on a public or private service. The last component on the assumption that those whose babies were delivered on public New York City had poor continuity of care. The results of the study show most every ethnic, social, and medical risk and socioeconomic subcate-rs who had adequate care were less likely to lose their infants than those lesser care.

st other studies that do not include random allocation, the conclusion are affects infant deaths is open to alternative explanations. Given the neonatal deaths are more responsive to socioeconomic factors than medical factors, it would have been expected that good prenatal care a greater effect on neonatal than post-neonatal rates, but the study differential effect. The design leaves open the possibility that the een good care and lower mortality is a result of social selection in fluence of medical care. Certainly it is plausible to suspect that a low education, or a member of any other subgroup with social tion, who obtains adequate prenatal care may be different from up who do not receive comparable care. The lack of information er characteristics of the women makes it difficult to clearly More recently, Slesinger (1973), in analyzing data from a en and their children in Washington, D.C. concerning utiliza-child care, found that a significant amount of variance in e—controlling for socioeconomic status—is attributable to and various attitudes toward health. Mothers who were rmal and formal relationships had lower utilization of pre ilities exist in various studies of the effects of prepaid grou onventional services on such outcomes as prematurity an

rent data suggest that social and psychological stresses can affect utilization directly as well as modify illness states. The role of different types of social stress on illness has received much attention (Dohrenwend & Dohrenwend 1975, Moss 1973, Levine & Scotch 1970). There is considerable controversy as to whether social change itself contributes to illness, irrespective of its positive or negative features, or whether illness and utilization follow only adverse life changes. This issue is further compli-cated by the specific physical or behavioral dysfunctions under consideration (Brown & Birley 1968, Brown 1974). Since these matters take us too far afield from the topic at hand, they will not be further explored.

In sum, the issue of why people seek help and where they choose to bring their problems is one where sociologists can make a distinctive contribution. Illness is not only an event that happens to people, but also an important explanation that can be used to sustain one's social identity and social functioning. Although medical utilization is a common source of help-seeking, it is only one of many alternatives. The processes through which persons come to see themselves as having a problem, the way they come to define the problem as relevant for seeking particular types of assistance, and how they present it is a fertile area for understanding the larger significance of medical care and social services to activities more generally (Kadu-shin 1969, Shuval 1970). We now turn to this issue.

POPULATION SELECTION AND HEALTH CARE

In any population at risk, only some with symptoms and illness will enter the available health care services system. Indeed, the formal helping system in the community may be only part of a much more elaborate system of formal and informal help made available by religious agencies, self-help groups, and kinship networks. The nature of the selection process will depend in part on the sociocul-tural and psychological characteristics of the population and in part on the availabil-ity and character of the formal health services system, its various components, and the broader system of helping services in the community at large. Assuming that individuals perceive a problem and define the problem as worthy of assistance, processes which themselves require sociological illumination, an assessment must be made also of the nature of the problem and to which of various alternative sources to bring it. Decision making is influenced by the processes of attribution of symp-toms and causality, but they depend as well on the scope of helping facilities available, their congruence with cultural beliefs and behavior patterns, ease of access and barriers to use, and the larger network of helping patterns in the community, particularly in relation to the formal helping system.

The process of help-receiving is dependent on the character of the first-contact service and how it is linked with other components of the helping system. While the initial arrival of a person to a first-contact service depends on sociocultural and personal contingencies, decisions concerning further care are more substantially influenced by the organization and interlinking of various components of the help-giving system. First-contact care may be isolated from a larger system of helping services if the person in need of assistance first contacts a religious healer or a chiropractor. While the patient may decide to seek other services simultaneously, or because he becomes dissatisfied, the helper can be said to have limited capacity to generate more elaborate and complex services. If the patient begins his search for care from a rural general practitioner or from a small community hospital, the possibilities for referral and further services suggested by the helper are much greater but considerably less expansive than those characterized by major teaching centers that offer a wide array of technological possibilities and specialized consultants. The data on performance show that the more elaborate facilities generate greater cost and more services, in part reflecting a different case load typical of such institutions but also indicative of the potentialities of the institution. That such services are more than just a costly addition is reflected in a variety of studies that show a higher level of performance characteristic of the teaching institutions (Goss 1970).

Thus, each part of the helping system—whether a physician, a medical group, or a facility such as a community hospital—tends to be related to a larger organizational field which influences the options possible and the types of decisions made. The organizational fields are characterized by varying technological and manpower capacities, different levels of demand for services and the ability to respond to them, and varying propensities to generate certain types of services. Cross-national studies, as well as those concerned with variations within single countries or regions, suggest no clear rational basis for large fluctuations in rates of services generated relative to the likely patterns of morbidity in the community. For example, fluctuations of rates of hospitalization, length of stay, and rates of surgical procedures from one setting to another suggest that the availability of hospital resources is the best single predictor of gross rates, although it is much more difficult to demonstrate that excess capacity results in "unnecessary use" (Donabedian 1973, Wennberg & Gittelsohn 1973, Bunker 1970, Klarman 1965). Existing literature suggests that such services can be significantly reduced as a matter of policy without obvious adverse consequences. The use of hospital beds or any other resource within an organizational service field will in part be a product of the organization of resources, the culture of the practicing professions, the types of regulation, and the incentives characteristic of the system. The outputs of these systems are often intangible, difficult to measure precisely, and highly responsive to explicit and implicit incentives which may be more or less consistent with "ideal practice."

In theory, the organization of delivery systems has an implicit logic. Such systems, as one moves from the points of first contact to secondary and tertiary facilities, are organized to deal with more complex and specialized problems, and it is assumed that the sequence of referral reflects increasing severity or the life-threatening nature of the illness, the complexity of the clinical picture, and the need for more specialized care. In large part such factors are predictive of the flow of work, but a great deal of the variance remains unexplained by such objective variables. However, if one examines each of the components of the delivery system as a minisocial system, it is evident that the flow of patients and decision making in respect to them in part result from sociocultural and psychosocial factors un-

related to the severity of the conditions treated or the objective need (Mechanic 1974a). These include the wishes and manipulations of certain kinds of treatments irrespective of their objective value, nonmedical needs that influence how physicians work, the act able, and the pressures on varying components of the system that many hospitals and clinics are multipurpose institutions education, and research require that they construct their the basis of patient care needs but in terms of existing requ of the institution.

THE COMPARATIVE EFFECTS OF HEAL DELIVERY SYSTEMS

Although there has been in recent years conside medical care on global indices of health and mort is frequently defective. The dependent variable influences related to social technology, level public health, and it is not apparent that m large positive effect. Indeed, to the extent t sustains life among chronically ill persons congenital and other defects, it contribut and disability in the population. Mor summary measures affected by numer can reasonably be expected to have a 1973).

A more appropriate means for e procedure or set of procedures i common to evaluate drug and controlled trials, it is only rec successfully applied to healt dures. Cochrane (1972) rev tions of randomized contr impractical or extremely tical approaches to judg is to offer some impor ation.

In recent years among other reas groups and the f in health servic An implicatio tial was a p American r ineffective mortality among the aged. Careful studies examining outcomes among recipients of services from the Health Insurance Plan of New York in contrast to nonsubscribers with similar sociodemographic characteristics show some advantage in rates of prematurity and mortality for prepaid practice recipients (Shapiro 1967; Shapiro et al 1958, 1960, 1967). These findings have been widely cited as demonstrating the medical advantages of prepayment, and have been used by policy makers to support the enlargement of prepayment programs (Department of Health, Education, and Welfare, 1971). However, even when socioeconomic and other controls are applied, the alternative remains that the better outcomes observed in the prepaid contexts are attributable to social selection. Persons with greater health consciousness and interest in maintaining health, when given a choice, may have been more likely to select prepaid practice. Mechanic & Tessler (1974), studying health selection into a prepaid practice program in Milwaukee, Wisconsin, could find no evidence of significant selection on the basis of health consciousness or preventive health patterns.

Even if we assume that the health outcomes observed are attributable to prepaid group practice and not to social selection, the generalizability of such findings to various other settings remains uncertain. Although an abundant literature has accumulated in recent years on prepayment, it is far from certain that these studies deal with the same types of social organization and service patterns. Prepaid group practices are usually discussed as if they are a common form of practice organization; and to the extent that they offer prepaid services from a group practice setting, they have a distinctive similarity. The fact, however, is that these limited criteria are not adequately descriptive of the social entities under consideration. Very few groups are exclusively based on prepayment, and the degree of prepayment from one group to another varies widely. Most such prepaid groups are small, while a small proportion are very large. Although some are general practice groups, other are primarily multispecialty groups. These groups also may differ quite substantially on each of the following criteria: economic organization and how the physician is paid, the use of ancillary manpower, task allocation and delegation, ownership and other relationships to hospitals, scope of services, and availability of specialized services (Mechanic 1972a). Moreover, in the United States, legislation pertains to the more global entity, "Health Maintenance Organization" (HMO), which refers to both prepaid groups and medical foundations. Thus, generalization on the basis of case studies is hazardous; but no investigator has as yet made a serious effort to define the population of prepaid practices and to systematically sample from them in order to evaluate outcomes in relation to competing practices. This, of course, would be a costly task of considerable difficulty.

This issue of comparability and generalizability is very salient in almost all comparative research on health care systems, and is characteristic of comparative research in general. A national system of care, or a health delivery system such as a prepaid practice, constitutes a single case. There are very few studies involving a large number of units whether they be national health systems, hospitals, clinics, or whatever. When such studies have been undertaken, they usually involve relatively superficial analyses or assess organizational variables on the basis of averaging individual interviews with organizational respondents. Studies that relate to quality of medical care or responsiveness of health personnel tend to involve individual institutions (for some exceptions, see Georgopoulos & Mann 1962, Heydebrand 1973, Roemer & Friedman 1971). It becomes extremely difficult, therefore, to separate effects that are due to organizational characteristics shared in common by other organizations, characteristics idiosyncratic to the structure of the particular organization not shared by similar units, or even idiosyncratic traits of professionals who work in that particular organization. Much research is written up as if professional and other health personnel are randomly distributed among varying organizations. The more realistic assumption, of course, is that each type of organization recruits participants who either select themselves or have been selected on the basis of certain characteristics. The same case can be made for clients of professionals and organizations. Often they have gone through a search in which they have selected certain helpers and facilities because of existing complementarities (Kadushin 1962). Few studies of delivery systems delve sufficiently deep to assess such selective tendencies and what role they might have in explaining observed outcomes.

COMPARATIVE STUDY OF PREPAYMENT AND CAPITATION SYSTEMS

The difficulty of specifying appropriate criteria for defining organizational units such as prepaid group practices has already been noted, and the problem is even more difficult in defining comparable units within different national organizational structures. Whether experience with particular payment mechanisms or devices to ration medical services can be generalized from one setting to another, or whether they are so confounded by the sociocultural context to make generalization impossible, must await repeated studies in different social contexts. Most conclusions from such research, therefore, must remain tentative.

In the United States considerable evidence exists that prepaid practices that have been studied have lower rates of hospital admissions, lower rates of surgical intervention, and thus lower overall costs per capita (Donabedian 1969, Department of Health, Education, and Welfare 1971). These differences persist even when taking into account the composition of patient populations they treat and correcting for the purchase of additional services outside the plan. Generally, the cost advantage of the HMO has been attributed to the removal of the incentive to the physician to provide unnecessary services and the possible addition of a financial incentive to avoid hospitalization. Although it has been argued that such savings are the result of an incentive to keep patients healthy in order to avoid later costs for the health care plan, there is little evidence to support such contentions, and even the theory of the health maintenance function is somewhat tenuous. A plausible alternative explanation for cost savings of prepaid group practices is simply the limited specialty personnel and hospital beds available to the enrolled group. Most of the major prepaid groups depend on a lower proportion of specialists and hospital beds relative to competing facilities in the community, and international variations in rates of admission to hospital and surgical intervention are consistent with the hypothesis that the availability of resources affects the rate of utilization (Bunker 1970, Donabedian 1973, Wennberg & Gittelsohn 1973). In all probability, the rather consistently observed differences between prepaid and other contexts are a product of a variety of influences including patient composition, physician incentive, and the different availability of treatment resources.

A continuing concern in the comparative health literature is the manner in which payment incentives affect the motivation and behavior of the physician and the quality of care he provides. After the most comprehensive review of the effects of remuneration in varying countries around the world, Glaser (1970a) concludes that "Once the procedures and levels of pay suffice, and if the nonpecuniary rewards are protected, doctors will adjust to any system of compensation. In practice, the most familiar system usually arouses the least protest." (p. 289) This conforms with findings on job satisfaction more generally which suggest that although perceived adequate remuneration is an important condition for such satisfaction, once a certain level of remuneration is reached, attention focuses on nonremunerative aspects of work satisfaction such as conditions of work, personal autonomy, and opportunities for self-improvement and actualization (Faich 1969). Mechanic & Faich (1970), in studying a remuneration dispute between general practitioners and the English government, came to the conclusion that other dissatisfactions and status insecurities were expressed through conflicts over remuneration since payment issues were the regularized means for dealing with doctor grievances.

From the policy point of view, Glaser's conclusion is inadequate since it does not provide a basis for understanding how to shift from a familiar remuneration system to one less familiar without undermining the motivation and performance of doctors. Increasingly, for example, the United States is considering types of medical organization that propose to shift physician payment from largely a fee-for-service format to one based on capitation, which the majority of physicians oppose. Although little systematic sociological study of such questions is available, Colombotos' (1969) study of doctors' attitudes prior to and following Medicare is helpful in understanding the larger context. Although prior to the Medicare program physicians were very much opposed, following its implementation physicians became more favorable and overwhelmingly participated in the program. Thus, prior attitudes and responses were not predictive of later behavior following implementation. Medicare, of course, basically maintained the structure of the existing payment system, and thus the program was an economic asset from the physician's point of view. In contrast, Medicaid, a federal-state program, which more seriously regulated physicians' fees and conditions of reimbursement, had more difficulty achieving physician cooperation. It seems reasonably clear from the American and other contexts that cooperation can be achieved in moving from one structure and system of remuneration to another if the terms are generous, but not if the new conditions threaten the economic position of the profession.

The difficulty with attempting to shape physician behavior using payment incentives is that the physician is in a position to easily modify his pattern of work to subvert the incentive system when he is unsympathetic with it. As Glaser (1970a) points out, when the payment system remunerates definable units of work, physicians then manipulate their patterns of work to generate more payable units. This might be achieved through the procedures used to diagnose and treat illness or through the extent to which the physician encourages the patient to return for followup care. Medical activity is highly discretionary and very much under the control of the physician (Fuchs & Kramer 1972). Carelessly developed incentives can induce a variety of undesirable and unintended behaviors on the part of the physician. Both consumer studies and studies of physicians in the American system report that doctors on capitation arrangements appear to be less oriented to satisfying the patient's psychosocial needs, are more inflexible, and are more likely to respond to patients' problems as if they are trivial (Mechanic 1975). It is not fully clear to what extent this is a product of the capitation system itself or the fact that physicians on capitation are more likely to limit their hours of work and thus expose themselves to a more concentrated and demanding case load. The perceived lack of responsiveness of physicians on capitation is probably due to the fact that they work under heavy time pressure, while the fee-for-service physician is more likely to expand his hours of work to deal with increased patient demand and to feel rewarded for this additional effort.

PROFESSIONALISM IN MEDICINE AND THE ORGANIZATION OF ROLES

Throughout the world there has been growing bureaucratization of medical practice, and as physicians more commonly work in organized settings, they are increasingly subjected to conflicting demands and incentives. Physicians tend to have an elaborate role set involving not only patients and colleagues but increasingly managers and administrators, third parties who pay and regulate the services provided, and personnel involved in training and research. Physicians in institutional settings frequently face conflicts between service, research, training, and economic and administrative needs.

A few efforts have been made to describe how conflicts between professional and managerial needs are dealt with in varying contexts. Goss (1963), for example, has dealt with the conflicts between hospital administration and medical decision making, and suggests a pattern of advisory bureaucracy in which accommodation is attempted through tactful suggestion and negotiation in contrast to bureaucratic authority. A growing literature is emerging on service bureaucracies, more generally, describing the greater autonomy and flexibility of roles in service bureaucracies, the extent of role development and institutionalization, and the difficulty of developing bureaucratic standards to control a multipurpose organization with intangible goals (Rushing 1964, Bucher & Stelling 1969, Mechanic 1974b, Georgopoulos 1972). Similarly, a growing literature is emerging to deal with intraorganizational negotiation and cooperation which is an important component of the service sector (Levine & White 1972, Aiken & Hage 1968). Much of existing organizational theory, however, is ill-fitted to effectively conceptualize the emerging complexity and variability characteristic of the service sector and particularly medical practice.

rent data suggest that social and psychological stresses can affect utilization directly as well as modify illness states. The role of different types of social stress on illness has received much attention (Dohrenwend & Dohrenwend 1975, Moss 1973, Levine & Scotch 1970). There is considerable controversy as to whether social change itself contributes to illness, irrespective of its positive or negative features, or whether illness and utilization follow only adverse life changes. This issue is further complicated by the specific physical or behavioral dysfunctions under consideration (Brown & Birley 1968, Brown 1974). Since these matters take us too far afield from the topic at hand, they will not be further explored.

In sum, the issue of why people seek help and where they choose to bring their problems is one where sociologists can make a distinctive contribution. Illness is not only an event that happens to people, but also an important explanation that can be used to sustain one's social identity and social functioning. Although medical utilization is a common source of help-seeking, it is only one of many alternatives. The processes through which persons come to see themselves as having a problem, the way they come to define the problem as relevant for seeking particular types of assistance, and how they present it is a fertile area for understanding the larger significance of medical care and social services to activities more generally (Kadushin 1969, Shuval 1970). We now turn to this issue.

POPULATION SELECTION AND HEALTH CARE

In any population at risk, only some with symptoms and illness will enter the available health care services system. Indeed, the formal helping system in the community may be only part of a much more elaborate system of formal and informal help made available by religious agencies, self-help groups, and kinship networks. The nature of the selection process will depend in part on the sociocultural and psychological characteristics of the population and in part on the availability and character of the formal health services system, its various components, and the broader system of helping services in the community at large. Assuming that individuals perceive a problem and define the problem as worthy of assistance, processes which themselves require sociological illumination, an assessment must be made also of the nature of the problem and to which of various alternative sources to bring it. Decision making is influenced by the processes of attribution of symptoms and causality, but they depend as well on the scope of helping facilities available, their congruence with cultural beliefs and behavior patterns, ease of access and barriers to use, and the larger network of helping patterns in the community, particularly in relation to the formal helping system.

The process of help-receiving is dependent on the character of the first-contact service and how it is linked with other components of the helping system. While the initial arrival of a person to a first-contact service depends on sociocultural and personal contingencies, decisions concerning further care are more substantially influenced by the organization and interlinking of various components of the help-giving system. First-contact care may be isolated from a larger system of helping services if the person in need of assistance first contacts a religious healer or a chiropractor. While the patient may decide to seek other services simultaneously, or because he becomes dissatisfied, the helper can be said to have limited capacity to generate more elaborate and complex services. If the patient begins his search for care from a rural general practitioner or from a small community hospital, the possibilities for referral and further services suggested by the helper are much greater but considerably less expansive than those characterized by major teaching centers that offer a wide array of technological possibilities and specialized consultants. The data on performance show that the more elaborate facilities generate greater cost and more services, in part reflecting a different case load typical of such institutions but also indicative of the potentialities of the institution. That such services are more than just a costly addition is reflected in a variety of studies that show a higher level of performance characteristic of the teaching institutions (Goss 1970).

Thus, each part of the helping system—whether a physician, a medical group, or a facility such as a community hospital—tends to be related to a larger organizational field which influences the options possible and the types of decisions made. The organizational fields are characterized by varying technological and manpower capacities, different levels of demand for services and the ability to respond to them, and varying propensities to generate certain types of services. Cross-national studies, as well as those concerned with variations within single countries or regions, suggest no clear rational basis for large fluctuations in rates of services generated relative to the likely patterns of morbidity in the community. For example, fluctuations of rates of hospitalization, length of stay, and rates of surgical procedures from one setting to another suggest that the availability of hospital resources is the best single predictor of gross rates, although it is much more difficult to demonstrate that excess capacity results in "unnecessary use" (Donabedian 1973, Wennberg & Gittelsohn 1973, Bunker 1970, Klarman 1965). Existing literature suggests that such services can be significantly reduced as a matter of policy without obvious adverse consequences. The use of hospital beds or any other resource within an organizational service field will in part be a product of the organization of resources, the culture of the practicing professions, the types of regulation, and the incentives characteristic of the system. The outputs of these systems are often intangible, difficult to measure precisely, and highly responsive to explicit and implicit incentives which may be more or less consistent with "ideal practice."

In theory, the organization of delivery systems has an implicit logic. Such systems, as one moves from the points of first contact to secondary and tertiary facilities, are organized to deal with more complex and specialized problems, and it is assumed that the sequence of referral reflects increasing severity or the life-threatening nature of the illness, the complexity of the clinical picture, and the need for more specialized care. In large part such factors are predictive of the flow of work, but a great deal of the variance remains unexplained by such objective variables. However, if one examines each of the components of the delivery system as a minisocial system, it is evident that the flow of patients and decision making in respect to them in part result from sociocultural and psychosocial factors unrelated to the severity of the conditions treated or the objective needs of the patients (Mechanic 1974a). These include the wishes and manipulations of patients to receive certain kinds of treatments irrespective of their objective value, the incentives and nonmedical needs that influence how physicians work, the actual resources available, and the pressures on varying components of the system. In addition, the fact that many hospitals and clinics are multipurpose institutions involving patient care, education, and research require that they construct their populations not only on the basis of patient care needs but in terms of existing requirements for varied goals of the institution.

THE COMPARATIVE EFFECTS OF HEALTH CARE DELIVERY SYSTEMS

Although there has been in recent years considerable discussion of the effects of medical care on global indices of health and mortality, the rationale of such analysis is frequently defective. The dependent variables used often reflect a wide range of influences related to social technology, levels and style of living, nutrition, and public health, and it is not apparent that medical care should have a particularly large positive effect. Indeed, to the extent that medical care identifies more illness, sustains life among chronically ill persons, and allows the survival of persons with congenital and other defects, it contributes to higher levels of recognized morbidity and disability in the population. Moreover, global indicators like mortality are summary measures affected by numerous factors, few of which, however important, can reasonably be expected to have a major impact on the gross indicator (Mushkin 1973).

A more appropriate means for evaluating the effectiveness of a particular delivery procedure or set of procedures is through controlled clinical trials. Although it is common to evaluate drug and other medical interventions through randomized controlled trials, it is only recently that this methodology has been more frequently successfully applied to health service patterns in contrast to more specific procedures. Cochrane (1972) reviews both the logic and some of the successful applications of randomized controlled trials, but in most situations randomization remains impractical or extremely difficult, and we continue to depend on multivariate statistical approaches to judge the effectiveness of health services. All that is possible here is to offer some important examples of the possibilities and problems of such evaluation.

In recent years many observers have been critical of health services because, among other reasons, of evidence of large disparities in infant mortality in varying groups and the fact that the United States, despite its affluence and large investment in health services, was in an unfavorable position relative to other developed nations. An implication in much of the criticism was that the large white-nonwhite differential was a product of lack of access to medical services, and that the overall high American rate relative to other countries was in part, if not totally, a product of the ineffective organization of health care in the United States.

Although there is a profound belief that effective maternal and child health care prevents infant mortality and other injuries and defects in the child, there is no clear evidence that this is the case. Birth weight is the single best predictor of infant mortality, and when introduced into a multiple regression analysis, other variables fail to explain any appreciable additional variance. Both infant mortality and birth weight, however, are related to socioeconomic status, color, education of the mother, less than optimal age, high parity, illegitimacy of the child, and so on (Mechanic 1968). These variables, however, are all intercorrelated. While age and parity reflect certain biological risks, the other variables are largely viewed as proxies for such variables as social living conditions, nutrition, mothering skills, and access to medical care. It has been shown that the introduction of medical services into an area without such care results in a reduction in the rate of infant mortality, but there has been little evidence that in areas with medical resources, the use of adequate prenatal and postnatal care results in lower infant mortality. A recent study (Institute of Medicine 1973) of infant mortality in New York City for 1968, using matched birth and death records, examined infant death in relation to socioeconomic and ethnic differences, medical and social risk, and the use of adequate medical care as indexed by time of first prenatal visit, number of prenatal visits, and whether the baby was delivered on a public or private service. The last component was used on the assumption that those whose babies were delivered on public services in New York City had poor continuity of care. The results of the study show that for almost every ethnic, social, and medical risk and socioeconomic subcategory, mothers who had adequate care were less likely to lose their infants than those who received lesser care.

As with most other studies that do not include random allocation, the conclusion that medical care affects infant deaths is open to alternative explanations. Given the fact that post-neonatal deaths are more responsive to socioeconomic factors than they are to biomedical factors, it would have been expected that good prenatal care should have had a greater effect on neonatal than post-neonatal rates, but the study found no such differential effect. The design leaves open the possibility that the relationship between good care and lower mortality is a result of social selection in contrast to the influence of medical care. Certainly it is plausible to suspect that a black woman with low education, or a member of any other subgroup with social risk and low education, who obtains adequate prenatal care may be different from others in the subgroup who do not receive comparable care. The lack of information in the study on other characteristics of the women makes it difficult to clearly interpret the findings. More recently, Slesinger (1973), in analyzing data from a sample of black women and their children in Washington, D.C. concerning utilization of prenatal and child care, found that a significant amount of variance in preventive medical care—controlling for socioeconomic status—is attributable to household composition and various attitudes toward health. Mothers who were more isolated from informal and formal relationships had lower utilization of preventive medical care.

Similar selection possibilities exist in various studies of the effects of prepaid group practice relative to more conventional services on such outcomes as prematurity and

mortality among the aged. Careful studies examining outcomes among recipients of services from the Health Insurance Plan of New York in contrast to nonsubscribers with similar sociodemographic characteristics show some advantage in rates of prematurity and mortality for prepaid practice recipients (Shapiro 1967; Shapiro et al 1958, 1960, 1967). These findings have been widely cited as demonstrating the medical advantages of prepayment, and have been used by policy makers to support the enlargement of prepayment programs (Department of Health, Education, and Welfare, 1971). However, even when socioeconomic and other controls are applied, the alternative remains that the better outcomes observed in the prepaid contexts are attributable to social selection. Persons with greater health consciousness and interest in maintaining health, when given a choice, may have been more likely to select prepaid practice. Mechanic & Tessler (1974), studying health selection into a prepaid practice program in Milwaukee, Wisconsin, could find no evidence of significant selection on the basis of health consciousness or preventive health patterns.

Even if we assume that the health outcomes observed are attributable to prepaid group practice and not to social selection, the generalizability of such findings to various other settings remains uncertain. Although an abundant literature has accumulated in recent years on prepayment, it is far from certain that these studies deal with the same types of social organization and service patterns. Prepaid group practices are usually discussed as if they are a common form of practice organization; and to the extent that they offer prepaid services from a group practice setting, they have a distinctive similarity. The fact, however, is that these limited criteria are not adequately descriptive of the social entities under consideration. Very few groups are exclusively based on prepayment, and the degree of prepayment from one group to another varies widely. Most such prepaid groups are small, while a small proportion are very large. Although some are general practice groups, other are primarily multispecialty groups. These groups also may differ quite substantially on each of the following criteria: economic organization and how the physician is paid, the use of ancillary manpower, task allocation and delegation, ownership and other relationships to hospitals, scope of services, and availability of specialized services (Mechanic 1972a). Moreover, in the United States, legislation pertains to the more global entity, "Health Maintenance Organization" (HMO), which refers to both prepaid groups and medical foundations. Thus, generalization on the basis of case studies is hazardous; but no investigator has as yet made a serious effort to define the population of prepaid practices and to systematically sample from them in order to evaluate outcomes in relation to competing practices. This, of course, would be a costly task of considerable difficulty.

This issue of comparability and generalizability is very salient in almost all comparative research on health care systems, and is characteristic of comparative research in general. A national system of care, or a health delivery system such as a prepaid practice, constitutes a single case. There are very few studies involving a large number of units whether they be national health systems, hospitals, clinics, or whatever. When such studies have been undertaken, they usually involve relatively superficial analyses or assess organizational variables on the basis of averaging

individual interviews with organizational respondents. Studies that relate to quality of medical care or responsiveness of health personnel tend to involve individual institutions (for some exceptions, see Georgopoulos & Mann 1962, Heydebrand 1973, Roemer & Friedman 1971). It becomes extremely difficult, therefore, to separate effects that are due to organizational characteristics shared in common by other organizations, characteristics idiosyncratic to the structure of the particular organization not shared by similar units, or even idiosyncratic traits of professionals who work in that particular organization. Much research is written up as if professional and other health personnel are randomly distributed among varying organizations. The more realistic assumption, of course, is that each type of organization recruits participants who either select themselves or have been selected on the basis of certain characteristics. The same case can be made for clients of professionals and organizations. Often they have gone through a search in which they have selected certain helpers and facilities because of existing complementarities (Kadushin 1962). Few studies of delivery systems delve sufficiently deep to assess such selective tendencies and what role they might have in explaining observed outcomes.

COMPARATIVE STUDY OF PREPAYMENT AND CAPITATION SYSTEMS

The difficulty of specifying appropriate criteria for defining organizational units such as prepaid group practices has already been noted, and the problem is even more difficult in defining comparable units within different national organizational structures. Whether experience with particular payment mechanisms or devices to ration medical services can be generalized from one setting to another, or whether they are so confounded by the sociocultural context to make generalization impossible, must await repeated studies in different social contexts. Most conclusions from such research, therefore, must remain tentative.

In the United States considerable evidence exists that prepaid practices that have been studied have lower rates of hospital admissions, lower rates of surgical intervention, and thus lower overall costs per capita (Donabedian 1969, Department of Health, Education, and Welfare 1971). These differences persist even when taking into account the composition of patient populations they treat and correcting for the purchase of additional services outside the plan. Generally, the cost advantage of the HMO has been attributed to the removal of the incentive to the physician to provide unnecessary services and the possible addition of a financial incentive to avoid hospitalization. Although it has been argued that such savings are the result of an incentive to keep patients healthy in order to avoid later costs for the health care plan, there is little evidence to support such contentions, and even the theory of the health maintenance function is somewhat tenuous. A plausible alternative explanation for cost savings of prepaid group practices is simply the limited specialty personnel and hospital beds available to the enrolled group. Most of the major prepaid groups depend on a lower proportion of specialists and hospital beds relative to competing facilities in the community, and international variations in rates of admission to hospital and surgical intervention are consistent with the hypothesis

that the availability of resources affects the rate of utilization (Bunker 1970, Donabedian 1973, Wennberg & Gittelsohn 1973). In all probability, the rather consistently observed differences between prepaid and other contexts are a product of a variety of influences including patient composition, physician incentive, and the different availability of treatment resources.

A continuing concern in the comparative health literature is the manner in which payment incentives affect the motivation and behavior of the physician and the quality of care he provides. After the most comprehensive review of the effects of remuneration in varying countries around the world, Glaser (1970a) concludes that "Once the procedures and levels of pay suffice, and if the nonpecuniary rewards are protected, doctors will adjust to any system of compensation. In practice, the most familiar system usually arouses the least protest." (p. 289) This conforms with findings on job satisfaction more generally which suggest that although perceived adequate remuneration is an important condition for such satisfaction, once a certain level of remuneration is reached, attention focuses on nonremunerative aspects of work satisfaction such as conditions of work, personal autonomy, and opportunities for self-improvement and actualization (Faich 1969). Mechanic & Faich (1970), in studying a remuneration dispute between general practitioners and the English government, came to the conclusion that other dissatisfactions and status insecurities were expressed through conflicts over remuneration since payment issues were the regularized means for dealing with doctor grievances.

From the policy point of view, Glaser's conclusion is inadequate since it does not provide a basis for understanding how to shift from a familiar remuneration system to one less familiar without undermining the motivation and performance of doctors. Increasingly, for example, the United States is considering types of medical organization that propose to shift physician payment from largely a fee-for-service format to one based on capitation, which the majority of physicians oppose. Although little systematic sociological study of such questions is available, Colombotos' (1969) study of doctors' attitudes prior to and following Medicare is helpful in understanding the larger context. Although prior to the Medicare program physicians were very much opposed, following its implementation physicians became more favorable and overwhelmingly participated in the program. Thus, prior attitudes and responses were not predictive of later behavior following implementation. Medicare, of course, basically maintained the structure of the existing payment system, and thus the program was an economic asset from the physician's point of view. In contrast, Medicaid, a federal-state program, which more seriously regulated physicians' fees and conditions of reimbursement, had more difficulty achieving physician cooperation. It seems reasonably clear from the American and other contexts that cooperation can be achieved in moving from one structure and system of remuneration to another if the terms are generous, but not if the new conditions threaten the economic position of the profession.

The difficulty with attempting to shape physician behavior using payment incentives is that the physician is in a position to easily modify his pattern of work to subvert the incentive system when he is unsympathetic with it. As Glaser (1970a) points out, when the payment system remunerates definable units of work, physi-

cians then manipulate their patterns of work to generate more payable units. This might be achieved through the procedures used to diagnose and treat illness or through the extent to which the physician encourages the patient to return for followup care. Medical activity is highly discretionary and very much under the control of the physician (Fuchs & Kramer 1972). Carelessly developed incentives can induce a variety of undesirable and unintended behaviors on the part of the physician. Both consumer studies and studies of physicians in the American system report that doctors on capitation arrangements appear to be less oriented to satisfying the patient's psychosocial needs, are more inflexible, and are more likely to respond to patients' problems as if they are trivial (Mechanic 1975). It is not fully clear to what extent this is a product of the capitation system itself or the fact that physicians on capitation are more likely to limit their hours of work and thus expose themselves to a more concentrated and demanding case load. The perceived lack of responsiveness of physicians on capitation is probably due to the fact that they work under heavy time pressure, while the fee-for-service physician is more likely to expand his hours of work to deal with increased patient demand and to feel rewarded for this additional effort.

PROFESSIONALISM IN MEDICINE AND THE ORGANIZATION OF ROLES

Throughout the world there has been growing bureaucratization of medical practice, and as physicians more commonly work in organized settings, they are increasingly subjected to conflicting demands and incentives. Physicians tend to have an elaborate role set involving not only patients and colleagues but increasingly managers and administrators, third parties who pay and regulate the services provided, and personnel involved in training and research. Physicians in institutional settings frequently face conflicts between service, research, training, and economic and administrative needs.

A few efforts have been made to describe how conflicts between professional and managerial needs are dealt with in varying contexts. Goss (1963), for example, has dealt with the conflicts between hospital administration and medical decision making, and suggests a pattern of advisory bureaucracy in which accommodation is attempted through tactful suggestion and negotiation in contrast to bureaucratic authority. A growing literature is emerging on service bureaucracies, more generally, describing the greater autonomy and flexibility of roles in service bureaucracies, the extent of role development and institutionalization, and the difficulty of developing bureaucratic standards to control a multipurpose organization with intangible goals (Rushing 1964, Bucher & Stelling 1969, Mechanic 1974b, Georgopoulos 1972). Similarly, a growing literature is emerging to deal with intraorganizational negotiation and cooperation which is an important component of the service sector (Levine & White 1972, Aiken & Hage 1968). Much of existing organizational theory, however, is ill-fitted to effectively conceptualize the emerging complexity and variability characteristic of the service sector and particularly medical practice.

An interesting attempt to examine changing role sets characteristic of the shift from entrepreneurial to organized practice is Freidson's (1960) concepts of client and colleague control and their relative influence in the two settings. Freidson offers some provocative hypotheses concerning how the shift to organizational auspices affects both responsiveness to patients and quality of professional practice; and although there are some data supporting his view, these hypotheses have not been systematically examined in a range of practice situations.

One of the most important and persistent problems in the provision of medical care involves the most effective and economical division of labor among physicians, and between physicians and other health workers. Although physicians are numerically a small minority of all health personnel they dominate the organization and control of health work in most if not all societies. Although many of the poorer countries face a great scarcity of health personnel, and thus must depend on ancillary personnel for basic services, in the developed countries the medical profession has attempted to maintain a monopoly over the organization of medical work. Historically, and at present, the development of specialization and subspecialization follows economic and status needs of the dominant profession as much as the requirements of technology and knowledge or the need for effective performance (Stevens 1971).

This is not to say that medical technology has not significantly advanced in a fashion requiring a more specialized division of labor. But an examination of the substance of specialities and how they developed and how they relate to the organization of work more generally would show that their shape is as much a product of the pursuit of self-interest as it is of the scientific elaboration of medicine. In any case, with a more specialized division of labor and a greatly expanded technology, the needs for coordination and integration are more acutely felt in all developed medical systems. Thus, all developed systems of care appear to be struggling with the common problem of how to make use of the growing sophistication of medical knowledge and still retain basic services for the common needs that people have and the ordinary problems they bring to doctors.

CONVERGENCE OF HEALTH CARE DELIVERY SYSTEMS IN POSTINDUSTRIAL SOCIETY

An examination of the available descriptive materials on health care delivery systems in various countries throughout the world suggests that the demands of medical technology and the growth of the science base of medical activity produce pressures toward common organizational solutions despite strong ideological differences (Field 1971, Mechanic 1974b). One difficulty with this hypothesis is the lack of specification of criteria for convergence and the extent to which they have been met in various national contexts. Recent developments in Chinese medicine, for example, can be viewed as supporting or contradicting the convergence hypothesis depending on which of various features of Chinese developments are emphasized.

Most countries of the world have developed some aspects of modern medicine, if for no other reason than for national pride and to serve its elite. In the poorer countries of the world, a developed scientific structure exists frequently for the rich, and there are more limited and less developed services for the poor. As populations increasingly demand medical care, there is growing concern among nations to provide a minimal level of service to all and to decrease obvious inequalities in care. In order to efficiently and effectively use available technology and knowledge, certain organizational options are most desirable. Thus one finds that there is a general tendency throughout the world to link existing services to defined population groups, to develop new and more economic ways to provide primary services to the population without an overelaboration of technological efforts, to integrate services increasingly fragmented by specialization or a more elaborate division of labor, and to seek ways to improve the output of the delivery system with fixed inputs. Although these concerns to some extent characterize national planning in underdeveloped countries, they particularly describe tendencies among developed nations as they attempt to control the enormous costs possible using available technologies (Mechanic 1974b). Throughout the world there is increasing movement away from medicine as a solitary entrepreneurial activity and more emphasis on the effective development of health delivery systems.

The hypothesis of convergence does not imply that medical systems, which develop out of the particular historical and cultural background of a nation and its dominant ethos, will not continue to have distinct cultural and social characteristics reflecting the ideological orientations and the sociocultural context of a country. But the basic pattern of practice in modern society is increasingly dominated by the imperatives of the emerging technology, the objective pattern of morbidity in the population, and growing public expectations which are a world phenomenon.

Literature Cited

Abel-Smith, B. 1964. *The Hospitals, 1800–1948: A Study in Social Administration in England and Wales.* London: Heineman Med. Books

Abel-Smith, B. 1967. *An International Study of Health Expenditure and Its Relevance for Health Planning.* Geneva: WHO Public Health Paper No. 32

Abel-Smith, B., Gales, K. 1964. *British Doctors at Home and Abroad.* London: Bell

Aday, L. A. 1972. *The Utilization of Health Services: Indices and Correlates.* Washington, DC: Nat. Center for Health Serv. Res. Develop., Dept. HEW Publ. No. HSM 73-3003

Aiken, M., Hage, J. 1968. Organizational interdependence and intraorganizational structure. *Am. Socio. Rev.* 33:912–30

Alford, R. 1972. The political economy of health care: dynamics without change. *Polit. Soc.* 2:127–64

Alford, R. 1975. *Health Care Politics: Interest Group and Ideological Barriers to Reform.* Chicago: Univ. Chicago

Andersen, R. 1968. *A Behavioral Model of Families' Use of Health Services.* Chicago: Center for Health Admin. Stud. Res. Ser. 25

Andersen, R., Newman, J. F. 1973. Societal and individual determinants of medical care utilization in the United States. *Milbank Mem. Fund Quart.* 51:95–124

Andersen, R., Smedby, B., Anderson, O. 1970. *Medical Care Use in Sweden and the United States: A Comparative Analysis of Systems and Behavior.* Chicago: Center for Health Admin. Stud. Res. Ser. 27

Anderson, O. 1972. *Health Care: Can There Be Equity? The United States, Sweden, and England.* New York: Wiley-Interscience

Antonovsky, A. 1972. A model to explain visits to the doctor: with specific reference to the case of Israel. *J. Health Soc. Behav.* 13:446–54

Baldwin, R., Weisbrod, B. 1974. Disease and labor productivity. *Econ. Develop. Cult. Change* 22:414–34

Barlow, R. 1967. The economic effects of malarial eradication. *Am. Econ. Rev.* 57:130–48

Benjamin, B. 1965. *Social and Economic Factors Affecting Mortality.* The Hague: Mouton

Bice, T. et al 1972. International comparisons of medical care: behavioral results. *Milbank Mem. Fund Quart.* 50:57–63

Brown, G. 1974. Social class and psychiatric disturbance among women in an urban population. Dept. Sociol., Bedford College, Univ. London. Unpublished

Brown, G., Birley, J. L. P. 1968. Social change and the onset of schizophrenia. *J. Health Soc. Behav.* 3:203–14

Bryant, J. 1969. *Health and the Developing World.* Ithaca: Cornell Univ.

Bucher, R., Stelling, J. 1969. Characteristics of professional organizations. *J. Health Soc. Behav.* 10:3–15

Bunker, J. 1970. Surgical manpower: a comparison of operations and surgeons in the United States and England and Wales. *N. Engl. J. Med.* 282:135–44

Cochrane, C. 1972. *Effectiveness and Efficiency: Random Reflections on Health Services.* London: Nuffield Prov. Hosp. Trust

Cole, S., Lejeune, R. 1972. Illness and the legitimation of failure. *Am. Sociol. Rev.* 37:347–56

Colombotos, J. 1969. Physicians and Medicare: a before-after study of the effects of legislation on attitudes. *Am. Sociol. Rev.* 34:318–34

Department of Health, Education, and Welfare. 1971. *Toward a Comprehensive Health Policy for the 1970's: A White Paper.* Washington, DC: GPO

Dohrenwend, B., Dohrenwend, B. 1975. *Life Events: Their Nature and Effects.* New York: Wiley-Interscience

Donabedian, A. 1969. An evaluation of prepaid group practice. *Inquiry* 6:3–27

Donabedian, A. 1973. *Aspects of Medical Care Administration: Specifying Requirements for Health Care.* Cambridge: Harvard Univ.

Douglas-Wilson, I., McLachlan, G., Eds. 1973. *Health Service Prospects: An International Survey.* Boston: Little, Brown

Eckstein, H. 1960. *Pressure Group Politics: The Case of the British Medical Association.* Stanford: Stanford Univ.

Eckstein, H. 1964. *The English Health Service: Its Origins, Structure, and Achievements.* Cambridge: Harvard Univ.

Elinson, J. 1973. *Toward sociomedical health indicators.* Presented at Int. Conf. Med. Sociol., Warsaw, Poland

Faich, R. 1969. *Social and structural factors affecting work satisfaction: a case study of general practitioners in the English health service.* PhD thesis. Univ. Wisconsin, Madison

Field, M. 1957. *Doctor and Patient in Soviet Russia.* Cambridge: Harvard Univ.

Field, M. 1967. *Soviet Socialized Medicine.* New York: Free Press

Field, M. 1971. Stability and change in the medical system: medicine in the industrial society. In *Stability and Social Change,* ed. B. Barber, A. Inkeles. Boston: Little, Brown

Field, M. 1973. The concept of the "health system" at the macrosociological level. *Soc. Sci. Med.* 7:763–85

Frederikson, H. 1962. Economic and demographic consequences of malaria control in Ceylon. *Indian J. Malariol.* 16:379–91

Freeman, H. E., Levine, S., Reeder, L. G., Eds. 1972. *Handbook of Medical Sociology.* Englewood Cliffs, NJ: Prentice-Hall. 2nd ed.

Freidson, E. 1960. Client control and medical practice. *Am. J. Sociol.* 65:374–82

Freidson, E. 1970a. *Profession of Medicine: A Study in the Sociology of Applied Knowledge.* New York: Dodd, Mead

Freidson, E. 1970b. *Professional Dominance: The Social Structure of Medical Care.* New York: Atherton

Fuchs, V. R., Kramer, M. J. 1972. *Determinants of Expenditures: For Physicians' Services in the United States 1948–1968.* Washington, DC: Nat. Center for Health Serv. Res. Develop., Dept. HEW Publ. No. HSM 73–3013

Georgopoulos, B. S. 1972. *Organization Research on Health Institutions.* Ann Arbor, Mich.: Inst. Soc. Res.

Georgopoulos, B. S., Mann, F. C. 1962. *The Community General Hospital.* New York: Macmillan

Glaser, W. A. 1970a. *Paying the Doctor: Systems of Remuneration and their Effects.* Baltimore: Johns Hopkins

Glaser, W. A. 1970b. *Social Settings and Medical Organization: A Cross-National Study of the Hospital.* New York: Atherton

Goss, M. 1963. Patterns of bureaucracy among hospital staff physicians. In *The Hospital in Modern Society,* ed. E. Freidson. New York: Free Press

Goss, M. 1970. Organizational goals and quality of medical care: evidence from comparative research on hospitals. *J. Health Soc. Behav.* 11:255–68

Goss, M. et al 1973. *Professional organization and control.* Presented at Ann. Meet. Am. Sociol. Assoc., New York City

Heydebrand, W. V. 1973. *Hospital Bureaucracy: A Comparative Study of Organizations.* New York: Dunellen

Horn, J. 1969. *Away With All Pests.* New York: Monthly Rev. Press

Institute of Medicine. 1973. *Infant Death: An Analysis by Maternal Risk and Health Care.* Washington, DC: Nat. Acad. Sci.

Kadushin, C. 1962. Social distance between client and professional. *Am. J. Sociol.* 67:517–31

Kadushin, C. 1969. *Why People Go to Psychiatrists.* New York: Atherton

Klarman, H. 1965. *The Economics of Health,* 139–41. New York: Columbia Univ.

Levine, S., Scotch, N. 1970. *Social Stress.* Chicago: Aldine

Levine, S., White, P. E. 1972. The community of health organizations. In *Handbook of Medical Sociology,* ed. H. Freeman et al, 359–85. Englewood Cliffs, NJ: Prentice-Hall. 2nd ed.

Malenbaum, W. 1970. Health and productivity in poor areas. In *Empirical Studies in Health Economics,* ed. H. E. Klarman, 31–54. Baltimore: Johns Hopkins

Mann, K. J., Medalie, J. H., Lieber, E., Groen, J. J., Guttman, L. 1970. *Visits to Doctors.* Jerusalem: Jerusalem Acad. Press

Marmor, T., Thomas, D. 1971. The politics of paying physicians: the determinants of government payment methods in England, Sweden, and the United States. *Int. J. Health Serv.* 1:71–78

McKeown, T. 1965. *Medicine in Modern Society: Medical Planning Based on Evaluation of Medical Achievement,* 21–74. London: Allen and Unwin

McKinlay, J. B. 1972. Some approaches and problems in the study of the use of services—an overview. *J. Health Soc. Behav.* 13:115–52

Mechanic, D. 1968. *Medical Sociology: A Selective View.* New York: Free Press

Mechanic, D. 1972a. *Public Expectations and Health Care.* New York: Wiley-Interscience

Mechanic, D. 1972b. Social psychologic factors affecting the presentation of bodily complaints. *N. Engl. J. Med.* 286:1132–39

Mechanic, D. 1974a. Patient behavior and the organization of medical care. In *Ethics of Health Care,* ed. L. R. Tan-

credi, 67–85. Washington, DC: Inst. Med., Nat. Acad. Sci.

Mechanic, D. 1974b. *Politics, Medicine, and Social Science.* New York: Wiley-Interscience

Mechanic, D. 1975. Discussion of research programs on relations between stressful life events and episodes of physical illness. In *Life Events: Their Nature and Effects,* ed. B. Dohrenwend, B. Dohrenwend. New York: Wiley-Interscience

Mechanic, D., Faich, R. 1970. Doctors in revolt: the crisis in the English national health service. *Med. Care* 8:442–55

Mechanic, D., Tessler, R. 1974. Comparison of consumer response to prepaid group practice and alternative insurance plans in Milwaukee County. *Research and Analytic Report Series,* 5–73. Madison: Center for Med. Sociol. and Health Serv. Res., Univ. Wisconsin

Moss, G. E. 1973. *Illness, Immunity and Social Interaction: The Dynamics of Biosocial Resonation.* New York: Wiley-Interscience

Mushkin, S. 1973. Evaluations: use with caution. *Evaluation* 1:30–35

Parsons, T. 1951. *The Social System.* New York: Free Press

Parsons, T., Fox, R. 1952. Illness, therapy and the modern urban American family. *J. Soc. Issues* 8:31–44

Rabin, D., Ed. 1972. International comparisons of medical care. *Milbank Mem. Fund Quart.* 50: Part II

Roemer, M. I., Friedman, J. W. 1971. *Doctors in Hospitals: Medical Staff Organization and Hospital Performance.* Baltimore: Johns Hopkins

Rosenstock, I. M. 1969. Prevention of illness and maintenance of health. In *Poverty and Health: A Sociological Analysis,* ed. J. Kosa, A. Antonovsky, I. K. Zola, 168–90. Cambridge: Harvard Univ.

Rushing, W. 1964. *The Psychiatric Professions: Power, Conflict, and Adaptation in a Psychiatric Hospital Staff.* Chapel Hill: Univ. North Carolina

Scott, W. 1971. Cross-national studies of the impact of levels of living on economic growth: an example. *Int. J. Health Serv.* 1:225–32

Shapiro, S. 1967. End result measurements of quality medical care. *Milbank Mem. Fund Quart.* 45:7–30

Shapiro, S. et al 1967. Patterns of medical use by the indigent aged under two systems of medical care. *Am. J. Publ. Health* 57:784–90

Shapiro, S., Jacobziner, H., Densen, P. M.,
Weiner, L. 1960. Further observations
on prematurity and perinatal mortality
in a general population and in the population of a prepaid group practice medical care plan. *Am. J. Publ. Health*
50:1304–17

Shapiro, S., Weiner, S. L., Densen, P. M.
1958. Comparison of prematurity and
perinatal mortality in a general population and in the population of a prepaid
group practice medical care plan. *Am.
J. Publ. Health* 48:170–87

Shuval, J. 1970. *Social Functions of Medical
Practice.* San Francisco: Jossey-Bass

Sidel, V. 1971. Medicine in the People's
Republic of China. *Proceedings of First
Annual Meeting of the Institute of Medi-
cine.* Washington, DC: Nat. Acad. Sci.

Sigerist, H. E. 1960. The special position of
the sick. In *Henry E. Sigerist on the Sociology of Medicine,* ed. M. I. Roemer.
New York: MD Publ.

Slesinger, D. 1973. *The utilization of preventive medical services by urban black
mothers: a socio-cultural approach.*
PhD thesis. Univ. Wisconsin, Madison

Stein, Z., Susser, M. 1972. The Cuban health
system: a trial of a comprehensive service in a poor country. *Int. J. Health
Serv.* 2:551–66

Stevens, R. 1966. *Medical Practice in Modern
England: The Impact of Specialization
and State Medicine.* New Haven: Yale
Univ.

Stevens, R. 1971. *American Medicine and the
Public Interest.* New Haven: Yale Univ.

Taylor, C. E., Hall, M. 1967. Health, population and economic development.
Science 157:651–57

Weinerman, E. F. 1969. *Social Medicine in
Eastern Europe: The Organization of
Health Services and the Education of
Medical Personnel in Czechoslovakia,
Hungary, and Poland.* Cambridge:
Harvard Univ.

Weisbrod, B., Andreano, R., Baldwin, R.,
Epstein, E., Kelley, A. 1973. *Disease
and Economic Development: The Impact of Parasitic Diseases in St. Lucia.*
Madison: Univ. Wisconsin

Wennberg, J., Gittelsohn, A. 1973. Small
area variations in health care delivery.
Science 182:1102–8

Zola, I. K. 1964. Illness behavior of the working class. In *Blue-Collar World: Studies
of the American Worker,* ed. A. Shos-
tak, W. Gomberg. Englewood Cliffs,
NJ: Prentice-Hall

THE STUDY OF URBAN COMMUNITY AND PERSONALITY

❖10503

Claude S. Fischer

Department of Sociology, University of California, Berkeley, California 94720

Urban sociology is a troubled field, its doleful state epitomized by the common use of its name to cloak the study of multifarious social problems. This symbolic diffusion of identity is but a manifestation of more fundamental difficulties in definition and direction. It is the purpose of this essay to address those difficulties. I deal here with basic theoretical, conceptual, and methodological issues in the study of urban community and personality (see also Fischer 1972, 1974, 1975c).

ISSUES

The social problems burden of the field is partly a heritage of its early years. To the classical sociologists, the city was particularly intriguing because it was bold relief representation of modern society and that society's emerging ways of life. Simmel wrote: "An inquiry into the inner meaning of specifically modern life . . . must seek to solve the equation which structures *like the metropolis* set up between the individual and superindividual contexts of life" (1905:47, italics added). Thus, Park suggested making "of the city a laboratory or clinic in which human nature and social processes may be conveniently and profitably studied" (1916:130). One consequence of defining the city for these studies as a microcosm of modern society was to help confuse the mission of urban sociology. Construed as the study of phenomena which occur *in* cities, unique to urban places or not, rather than as the study of *city* phenomena, urban sociology is indictable as a non-field, as being redundant with general sociology (Gutman & Popenoe 1970, Reissman 1964). This, I shall argue, need not be so; there are significant issues which are particularly the domain of urban sociology.

Historical Background

Sociology evolved centrally around a concern for the consequences of the Great Transformation. The discipline's pivotal question was and largely still is: How can

67

the moral order of society be maintained and the integration of its members achieved within a highly differentiated and technological social structure?—the problem of Community in the New Age (cf Nisbet 1966:47–106). ("Community," when capitalized, is used to mean an integrated social unit, with overtones of "communion." When "community," uncapitalized, is used, it will refer to a physical settlement, such as a town.) Since the city seemingly exemplified modern society (cf Durkheim 1933), its study was viewed as an excellent vehicle for approaching sociology's central question. Thus, the agenda for urban sociology's founding fathers became the empirical investigation of the new society via the study of the city. Such considerations formed the background of Simmel's and Park's statements.

Yet, in the course of these investigations, interest naturally developed in the study of the city qua city. In particular, maps produced by Burgess and his students of the territorial distribution of social phenomena (see Burgess & Bogue 1964) helped generate an ecological school "fundamentally interested in the effect of *position*. . . ." (McKenzie 1925: 64). In 1938, Wirth organized Park's (1916) assumptions and assertions about the unique features of urban behavior into a theory, thereby rendering them explicit and problematic. A sociology of cities had emerged.

This sociology was concerned with the interface of social life on the one side and place, position, habitat, territory—what might be summarized as *settlement pattern* —on the other. Within this broad charter, various subdisciplines, for example urban ecology and geography, arose and appropriated specific topics. In the process, however, it seems that a uniquely sociological focus was lost (which has, in turn, helped produce the identity problem mentioned earlier).

I submit that the proper central issue of urban sociology is that which initially concerned the entire discipline: the nature of the moral order (Community) and of the individual within that order (personality). By assessing the consequences of variations in settlement patterns, urban sociology advances our general understanding of the structural determinants of Community and personality. Indeed, such an urban sociology presents a rare opportunity to rigorously and empirically examine some of the processes thought to comprise the Great Transformation. Changes in settlement patterns, particularly in terms of scale, dynamic density, and differentiation, are considered key elements in the historical transition. By analyzing the relationship of settlement to the theoretically significant consequences of the Great Transformation, individuation, normlessness, and the like, urban sociology informs general sociology's main concern. Note that urban research does so not by providing descriptions of social life in cities, but, rather, by developing an analytical understanding of crucial causal processes.

The question which follows immediately upon this declaration is: What about settlement patterns determines Community and personality?

Orienting Assumptions

To ascertain which, if any, characteristics of settlements affect moral order and individuality, it is necessary to make comparisons among and/or within those settlements. Precedent to any such analysis is the assumption that settlement (or community, small "c") is a meaningful object, a "thing-in-itself" (Arensberg 1961, Reiss 1959b). That is: it can be defined, distinguished from that which is not-settlement; one instance of settlement is separate from another, at least with regard to a given issue; and, settlement is a significant category with regard to that issue. This assumption underlies any comparison of communities, whether the dimensions of comparison are structural (e.g. economic differentiation) or individual (e.g. population traits). A parallel assumption underlies intracommunity comparisons.

This assumption has been questioned in various ways. Some consider settlements to be samples, microcosms, of societal phenomena, with little autonomous significance. Consequently, comparative analysis is unnecessary. However, this approach, exemplified in the community studies tradition, does not avoid the need for inter-community research, since investigators must demonstrate the representativeness of their microcosms (Reiss 1959b, Arensberg 1961). Others consider settlements, particularly in modern society, to be derivative from the national social structure rather than to be individual entities. They are differentiated subunits of society, integrated in functional relationships. From this perspective, "the nation, rather than the city, is the meaningful unit for analysis of urbanization" (Reissman 1964:196, Greer 1962, Pickvance 1974). Still others consider settlements to be epiphenomenal manifestations of organizational and communications technology. "Place" is not a fundamental dimension of social systems, though the structure of places may evidence systemic processes (Webber 1968). The currently most influential view is that, while settlement may be a meaningful category for certain purposes (e.g. political science), it is not significant for social life, particularly if the dimension of comparison is ecological. Because social life is conducted in microscopic personal realms, "the city is not the proper unit of comparison" (Lewis 1965:497, Gans 1962b).

Evaluating the assumption that settlement is a meaningful "thing-in-itself" on an a priori basis is difficult, for, while the precise definition of community is elusive, it is nevertheless the case that communities do have concrete reality, both as environments for individuals and as units in their own right, manifested as political entities, for example.[1] Ultimately, whether one should assume that communities are significantly variable objects must be determined by the empirical utility of that assumption, and with regard to specific phenomena. So, for example, settlements would probably not be useful units in an analysis of oligopolistic industries, but would be in a study of crime victimization risks. The assumption that community is a significant "thing-in-itself" is to be evaluated by its empirical utility.

There are also such empirical grounds for questioning the importance of community as an autonomous variable. As supraindividual contexts, communities' characteristics are unlikely to, and in fact usually do not, explain much of individual variation in behavior relative to that accounted for by personal characteristics (the common standard being increment in explained variance). An easy conclusion is

[1]Analogies may help clarify this comment: While it is difficult to precisely define and distinguish ethnic or occupational groups, these categories often do prove to be sociologically significant.

that community is unimportant.[2] While this conclusion may often be correct, I would caution against a too simple application of these statistical standards to assessment of community. It is to be expected that variables more peculiar and proximate to individuals will correlate more highly with their behavior than will contextual ones. In that sense, a simple comparison of the latter's explanatory power to the former's applies an inappropriate standard of evaluation. Furthermore, even a small contextual effect on individuals in a community may be of great import since it indicates a common pressure on an aggregated population with implications for serious effects at that aggregate level. Finally, communities may have complex, interactive, and contradictory effects on particular subpopulations, effects not revealed easily in standard analyses. That is, communities form different matrices of choices and constraints for the playing-out of individual tendencies, not general "causal forces."

Proceeding on the assumption that settlement, or community, is a "thing-in-itself," the next step is formulating a theory relating one or more attributes of community to one or more aspects of moral order and personality.

THEORIES

The dimensions of moral order and personality which rightfully most concern urban theorists are the classic ones—anomie versus solidarity, estrangement versus integration. The more difficult task is selecting the appropriate dimension(s) of communities. It is the major problem of this discipline that the most influential distinction, rural versus urban, has been increasingly the source of discontent but that no substantial alternative to it has been developed.

The Rural-Urban Continuum

This dimension of communities has a formidable intellectual history, far older than sociology itself, and a virtually universal cross-cultural recognition. Most societies ascribe different ways of life to city and to country (Sorokin et al 1930, White & White 1962). The Chicago School developed out of the intellectual material generated by sociological theories of the Great Transformation, a theory of these rural-urban differences (Wirth 1938, Redfield 1947). This theoretical statement involved two steps: First, proposing an empirical generalization that a number of physical, demographic, social, and psychological attributes of communities and of their residents varied together—the rural-urban continuum; second, an explanation for that covariation. This explanation for the most part transfers processes that the grand sociological theories used to explain modernization from the national to the settlement level: scale, dynamic density, and differentiation produce a new community moral order (see exegesis in Fischer 1972).

Many criticisms of the rural-urban continuum seem to assume that it was asserted as an empirical fact, rather than as a theoretical model. These critiques often take

---

[2]The allusion here is to the debate on the importance of contextual effects, a debate which has largely been conducted on school effects (Hauser 1970, 1971, 1974; Farkas 1974; Nelson 1972).

the form of pointing out exceptions to the general pattern (e.g. Reiss 1955, Duncan 1957). If taken, however, as a theoretical statement, as it should be (Wirth 1956), then the notable facts are not the exceptions to but the frequent confirmations of rural-urban differences.

One variant of this argument is the assertion that urban-rural or size-of-community differences may have once been significant, but that in modern, mass society they have been erased. Durkheim (1933) and Wirth (1956), among others, speculated along such lines. Though certain urban-rural differences have been declining, others, particularly with regard to morality and deviance, persist even in contemporary America (Willitis, et al 1973, Fischer 1975a). In this nation and elsewhere, urban and rural communities continue to evidence consistent differences.

More crucial than occasional exceptions to patterns of rural-urban differences were systematic errors in attributing those differences to urbanism rather than to the frequently associated factors of industrialism and Westernization (cf Sjoberg 1960, Dewey 1960, Kolb 1954, Hauser 1965, Morris 1968). These errors compromise a number of propositions in theories of the rural-urban continuum, but do not nullify the theories themselves. They do underline the necessity for making rural-urban comparisons within specified societies and historical periods.

Another serious difficulty in theories of the rural-urban continuum has been the definition of "urban," or, put alternatively, the selection of which variable among those in the rural-urban configuration is primary (see, for example, Dewey 1960). One standard seems to survive best the long and complex debate: population concentration—size and density, perhaps best of all, "population potential" (Stewart 1948, Carrothers 1956). This variable is essentially the only one which is found in virtually all definitions of "urban." Population concentration can be considered as causally prior or predominant to other variables in the continuum. And, it is also particularly in keeping with the concern for "scale" in classical sociology.[3] Therefore, theories of the rural-urban continuum are best understood as empirical hypotheses about and explanations for the correlates of population concentration.

The most significant critique of the rural-urban continuum is that, as empirical fact, population concentration is unimportant, that "the variables of number, density, and heterogeneity as used by Wirth are not crucial determinants of social life or personality" (Lewis 1965:497). Taking Wirth's (1938) presentation as the most complete synthesis of rural-urban theories, the following conclusions can be drawn:[4] 1. Despite all the urban research of the last nearly forty years, the number of critical tests of the theory has been insufficient to permit drawing any firm conclusion, pro or con (Wirth 1956, Hauser 1965, Fischer 1972). 2. The best assessment of the available evidence is that the Wirthian theory is correct about the demographic and

[3]A persuasive case can be made that interactional density rather than population density best meets these criteria (see, for example, Tilly 1972). However, it is more difficult to specify and measure the former than it is the latter. And, it is probably best to consider interactional density as a consequence of population concentration, one which follows under certain conditions (e.g. intracommunity communication).

[4]I shall not take space here to document these conclusions. The reader is referred to Fischer (1972, 1973, 1974, 1975c).

gross behavioral characteristics associated with urbanism (e.g. structural differentiation, deviance). However, it seems incorrect about the cultural and social psychological processes which mediate those associations. In particular, there is little to support Wirth's (or Simmel's) speculations about psychological effects in the direction of urban alienation, disorganization, or apathy (Fischer, 1972, 1973). 3. Yet, Wirth's presentation remains the most explicit, seminal, and comprehensive theory of the rural-urban continuum, and still provides the preeminent framework for the study of Community and personality. Though "Urbanism as a Way of Life" has been extensively criticized, no other theory comprehending the nature of urban life has been advanced which is as significant, as compelling, and as consonant with both Western thought and classical sociology.

Alternative Constructs

Dissatisfaction with the rural-urban continuum has impelled efforts to develop alternative classifications and dimensions of communities (see discussions by Reiss 1959b, Sjoberg 1965, Reissman 1964, Martindale 1958, Benet 1963, Fischer 1972). The following list is but a sampler of suggestions: classifying communities by cultural criteria—dominant values, "atmosphere," cultural region, degree of "orthogeneticism;" institutional categories—legal charter, political structure, nature of the elite; technology and economics—degree of industrialization, economic rank, economic function, presence of a market, extent of diversification; and characteristics of the resident population—degree of community segmentation, population transiency, "role density," or interactional density.

Some of these constructs are intended to redefine or replace the rural-urban continuum, others to provide a cross-cutting dimension. The difficulty here is that none of these schemes has had any extensive theoretical or empirical development. Often, the formulations lack a direct and unique relevance to the community as a "thing-in-itself" (e.g. typologies based on national values). They usually lack a full and systematic analysis linking characteristics of the community to characteristics of moral order and personality. Compared to the older tradition, they often seem unconnected to major sociological themes. Most crucially, they have yet to generate theories and research of much import. As a reviewer of urban anthropology remarks, critics of the rural-urban continuum "have not yet been able to work out a sufficiently comprehensive substitute model that has equal appeal" (Gulick 1973:985).[5]

Another response to dissatisfaction with the traditional paradigm has been to eschew deductive approaches. Duncan's (1957:45) "general position is that careful inductive classifications of communities are of greater scientific value than hypothetical constructs like the 'rural-urban continuum.' " The major research endeavor along these lines is the factorial classification of cities (e.g. Hadden & Borgotta 1965, Berry 1972). However, as Alford (1972) has pointed out, this procedure leaves the

[5]One contributing factor, no doubt, is that public data are categorized in terms of community size, fostering one of those situations in which theoretical interest follows empirical convenience.

investigator, and his theory, at the mercy of arbitrary lists of communities, lists of variables, statistical conventions, and post hoc interpretations. In any event, this research tradition has yet to produce significant theory or findings about communities and their cultures (a recent attempt to do so is Abrahamson 1974).

Conclusion

Theory in urban sociology is at an impasse. There stands the rural-urban continuum, a conceptually and historically momentous theoretical approach, one which connects sociology's concern with moral order and individuality to equally significant structural dimensions of community. Yet, this approach is increasingly dismissed because of empirical contradictions. It is dismissed, but no alternative approach— save the simple denial of community's importance—is sufficiently developed to replace it as an organizing paradigm. The sources of this predicament appear to be three. One is that theories of the rural-urban continuum have not been adequately, much less exhaustively, tested (more on this below). Second, G. D. Suttles (personal communication) has pointed out that sociologists have tended to either wholly accept or reject the analyses of Wirth et al, instead of capitalizing on the latters' insights by modifying those theories.[6] Third, no extended, comprehensive effort has been made to develop distinctive alternate approaches treating the same central issue: the relationship between settlements and the moral order. These three causes of the field's plight also represent three items for its agenda.

Variation Within Communities: The Neighborhood

In contrast to variability between communities, the topic of variability within communities has a relatively brief intellectual history. Yet, the study of internal differentiation is the best known contribution of the Chicago School. As Burgess (Burgess & Bogue 1964:7) recounts, the early urbanists assumed that "like rural communities, [the city] was composed of natural areas, each having a particular function in the whole economy and life of the city, each area having its distinctive institutions, groups, and personalities. . . . We early decided that the natural areas could be significantly studied in two aspects: First, their spatial pattern. . . . Second, their cultural life." The first aspect has been well developed by urban ecology and geography. The second, restated more generally as the study of subareal "moral orders," has been far less developed theoretically or empirically.

The basic unit of theoretical, though rarely of empirical, concern is the "neighborhood." It is assumed to be a meaningful subdivision of a settlement, a "thing-in-itself," and a unit of potential, if not actual, Community and personality. Arguments similar to those pressed against the use of communities as objects of analysis can be presented against the use of neighborhoods, and with greater force. A distinction is to be made: Construed as a spatially defined environment, neighborhood has a sovereign reality. It is, as is community, a setting of human action (though of briefer portions of most individuals' lives than is the community whole). Confusion arises when a social dimension is presumed to be an inherent element of neighborhood,

[6]This author's effort along such lines appears as Fischer (1975b).

when the definition of neighborhood assumes the existence of a moral order binding its inhabitants. Such a presumption both confounds theoretical analysis and is inherently questionable. Fundamentally, the neighborhood is best understood, in social terms, as an aggregate of proximal residents, whose only necessary moral order, if there is one, is the set of quite meager mutual obligations of proximates (see Keller 1968, Heberle 1960, Fischer 1975c:Ch. 5).

One could on such grounds dismiss the neighborhood as relatively inconsequential. However, as Suttles (1972) has argued, the issue is not whether primordial sentiments and moral cohesion are inherent properties of "natural" neighborhoods, but determining the conditions under which a neighborhood does become a meaningful social group. Some minimal conditions are almost always present: interaction engendered by proximity, a degree of interdependency, and some need to unite against external forces. The question then becomes twofold: 1. What conditions make of a neighborhood a significant social unit, one for which the problem of moral order is relevant? 2. What conditions facilitate or inhibit achieving a cohesive moral order? (The methodological question of how to find and bound neighborhoods is another major one.) Thus, the extent to which the issue of moral order and individuality arises at the level of neighborhoods depends on the importance of the vicinage to its population.[7] When it does, one is presented with questions similar to those posed at the community level.

Theories of Intra-Community Variation

That subareas of a metropolis differ in terms of ways of life, personalities, and moral order seems clear, but the significance and explanation of those differences remain problematic. While the rural-urban continuum provides a dominant framework for organizing and interpreting variations among communities, no equivalent paradigm exists for examining the relationship between intrasettlement variation and moral order.

One approach is to adapt rural-urban theory by using the variable of population density to explain deviance and disorganization. Crowded neighborhoods presumably spawn anomie in a manner similar to that of large communities. There is a recent version of this analysis which draws upon the work done in animal ethology to account for urban "pathologies" by the degree of interpersonal crowding in metropolitan subareas. This literature is as yet so faddish and often of such low quality that it cannot yet be treated as a significant contribution (see discussion below).

An older and more extensive tradition is that dealing with "suburbia." The distinction between metropolitan center and suburb has some historical base (see Donaldson 1969), but its precise definition is even more elusive than that of community. During the last twenty-five years or so, a debate has been conducted on whether

---

[7]So, for example, there may be no evidence of social cohesion in an affluent, "cosmopolitan" neighborhood. But that may be irrelevant for a population so independent of and unconcerned with their locality. On the other hand, for a low-mobile population, local moral order is significant.

residents of suburbia (however that is defined) differ in personality and/or ways of life from residents of the city. Where such differences are observed, the controversy has been over which of suburbia's defining traits, if that is what they are (and here the problem of definition becomes acute), accounts for those differences: housing density, housing type, recency of development, homogeneity, political autonomy, peripheral ecological location, etc (cf Marshall 1973, Fischer & Jackson 1975).

The most influential position currently, best expressed by Gans (1967), is that no such ecological or contextual features determine suburban life style. Rather, city-suburban differences, like other intrasettlement differences, are due to self-selection, for example, the fact that families seek detached houses and single people seek apartments. The significance of ecology is restricted, by this analysis, to shaping the housing market and the trade-offs incurred in given residential choices. In fact, in this view, the city-suburb distinction is useless. While this nonecological position currently prevails, it, no less than theories of the rural-urban continuum, lacks conclusive empirical test.

An inductive, empiricist approach to intracommunity differences is quite consonant with the Gans et al emphasis on population traits (as opposed to ecological variables), because the data which have entered into those inductive analyses have usually been restricted to population characteristics. Social area analysis and factorial ecology have classified subareas largely on the basis of population composition, while giving relatively little attention to linking such compositional variables to prior ecological features (Hawley & Duncan 1957; for one case, see Anderson & Egeland 1961). Neighborhood classifications based on such compositional variables have shown meaningful relationships to the nature of the personal and social life in those neighborhoods (e.g. Greer 1956, Bell & Boat 1957), and thereby suggest that there are contextual influences of neighborhood on individuals. However, it is unclear whether those effects simply reduce to the consequences of *social* context (e.g. the influence on elderly people of residing in a youthful area), or whether there are consequences of local ecological factors.

What is missing in the study of intracommunity variation, even more so than in the study of community variation, are compelling theories which connect settlement pattern, in terms of ecological variables, to Community and personality. Furthermore, the existing partial models lack full empirical tests. As in the study of communities, the study of neighborhoods is hindered by old theories inadequately explored, and the lack of adequate alternatives.

CONCEPTS

This section is addressed to the state of the field's concepts—"the definitions (or prescriptions) of what is to be observed; . . . the variables between which empirical relationships are to be sought" (Merton 1968). In particular, I shall be concerned with concepts used in middle range models which link the large scale structural attributes of communities to individual behavior.

The concept of "city" itself warrants a few comments. The simple definition of an earlier time, when a fortress wall demarcated dense construction from open fields, has succumbed to increasing vagueness. The clean town borders have yielded to the fuzzy shadings of the urban-rural "fringe." "City" is distinguished from "country," if at all, only by a gradual decline in dwellings and density. Consequently, some have sought to abandon the concept of "city" for that of "urban area," "metropolis," "megalopolis," or "urban field" (e.g. Friedmann & Miller 1965). Others have declared that "the city is dead;" it has no meaning and perhaps never did (Martindale 1958). Dead with it, of course, would be the study of cities. However, these attacks which form serious challenges to the validity of an urban sociology assume a far more reified (i.e. bricks and mortar) meaning of the term "city" than did traditional sociological theories. The important concept is "urban"—defined, as argued above, in terms of the population concentrated at a point. "City" is but a convenient term for distinguishing high from low population concentration. (For other purposes, such as political science, it has a more exact meaning.) From this perspective, the plowing-under of city walls by commercial strip-highways is not a great threat to the major concern of urban sociology, the study of population concentration and Community.

Probably the greatest need for clarification lies in the realm of urban social psychology: conceiving the nature of the individual's place in and interaction with the urban structure. Simmel's description of a metropolitan type of person as one who "reacts with his head instead of his heart," and Park's use of "temperament," are unsatisfactory formulations. These loose constructions, combined with Durkheim's explicit rejection of psychology, leave the urban field with an inadequate comprehension of how individuals and individual action are to be integrated with theories of moral order (see Short 1971, Mitchell 1969a). Recent developments in the field seem, wittingly or not, addressed to that problem.

Human Ethology

Currently the rage, more so in the popular than in the professional press, are ideas drawn from animal ethology and applied (often in bastardized form) to human behavior. The introduction of biological metaphors to urban studies is hardly new, but, unlike systemic theories of neighborhood succession, these applications involve models of individuals. Most notable are the concepts of territoriality (with its associated notions of dominance, aggression, withdrawal, etc) and of "wired-in" reactions to population density. These concepts have been inserted into older models of urban life, providing explications of the mediating processes by which urbanism presumably disorganizes personality and social interaction.[8] One consequence of the introduction of these concepts has been a series of studies, ranging from laboratory experiments on crowding (e.g. Stokols et al 1973) to ecological correlational research (e.g. Galle et al 1972), directed toward demonstrating human, and urban, parallels to animal density (a critical review appears in Fischer et al 1974.)

[8]Dramatic applications of these ideas to urban studies include Calhoun (1962), Lorenz (1966), Ardrey (1966), Hall (1966), and Carstairs (1969). More sober treatments include Sommer (1969), Lyman & Scott (1967), Suttles (1972), and Goffman (1971).

The value of these concepts and of these studies has yet to be demonstrated—either in their own terms or in their utility for urban sociology. It is uncertain whether concepts of territoriality or of instinctive population control are usefully applicable to humans (see, for example, Montagu 1973, Martin 1972, Freedman 1973). Further uncertainty rests in the largely unexamined assumption that urban or center-city residence is a valid index of experiences of micro-level density or spatial invasions (see Fischer et al 1974). Until such time as those connections are made, concepts drawn from ethology will serve, if they serve at all, studies of small scale environments rather than of communities.

Information Theory

In 1905, Simmel wrote: "the psychological basis of the metropolitan type of individuality consists in the *intensification of nervous stimulation* which results from the swift and uninterrupted change of outer and inner stimuli . . . Thus the metropolitan type of man . . . develops an organ protecting him against the threatening currents and discrepancies of his external environment which would uproot him" (Simmel 1905:48). This insightful though primitive hypothesis has been recently restated in concepts and terminology borrowed from information and systems theory (Meier 1962, Milgram 1970). The model of man is that of an information-processing system with limited channel capacity. The model of the city is that of an information-generating system with high and largely uncontrollable amounts of output. An individual in the city is subject to sensory inputs at levels which threaten "overload" and system collapse. Consequently, adaptive mechanisms are developed to divert or filter information, mechanisms which amount to metropolitan man's "protective organ," and which estrange him from others.

Though based on electronic rather than organic metaphors, this conceptual approach is similar to the ethological one—in theoretical implications and in difficulties. Though processes in humans analagous to overload can be demonstrated (Miller 1960), the general utility of the model has hardly been explored, nor whether an individual's relationship to his environment is best captured by the image of a passive sensor rather than, for example, the image of an active agent and manipulator. Furthermore, whether, to what degree, and to what import, a city locale is actually more productive of sensations and information-bits is unknown.

Network Analysis

Probably the most promising conceptual tool for joining individual behavior to theories of community is "network analysis." The commonly cited definition of social network is Mitchell's (1969a:2): "a specific set of linkages among a defined set of persons, with the additional property that the characteristics of these linkages as a whole may be used to interpret the social behaviour of the persons involved." In distinction (and complementary) to approaches which emphasize institutional or aggregate phenomena and to those which concern intrapersonal processes, network analysis focuses on relationships among individuals (or, in more abstract versions, roles). Examination of the structures and contents of personal networks is intended to reveal both the processes by which social environments influence people and those by which individuals in turn act upon their social worlds. For urban sociology, it promises to provide the conceptual link between individual and community.

Though its current imagery and advanced mathematical paraphernalia are drawn from graph theory—people are points, relationships are connecting lines—the origins of network analysis are firmly sociological. They are to be found in sociometry, exchange theory, personal influence studies, research on kinship and friendship, the literature on diffusion, and elsewhere. In that sense, conceiving of individuals' relationships as "networks" is hardly novel. What is novel is the recent convergence from many disciplines around a core conceptual scheme, together with a self-conscious effort to elaborate this scheme and to apply it to new topics.[9]

It is relevant to note that the recent impetus to this convergence was provided by anthropologists, particularly Africanists, who confronted the inadequacies of older schemes when they followed their tribes to the cities. Structural and institutional concepts, such as lineage, alone did not capture the complexity of urban life. Networks provided a more accurate representation of actual social ties, and insight into how individuals consciously construct, rather than simply inherit, those ties. Reconsideration of rural communities showed that the utility of network analysis was not confined to the city. The consequences for anthropology of these developments seem to have been two: excellent ethnographies which describe subcommunities using network concepts (e.g. Pons 1969, Roberts 1973), and a series of discursive essays on illustrations, definitions, dimensions, and measurements of networks (cf Mitchell 1969b, Boissevain & Mitchell 1973).

It appears to this outsider that network analysis in anthropology, as represented by these essays, has been mired in a wheel-spinning stage. Debates over proper definitions, sampling procedures, and measurements seem to have largely produced lists of network attributes, rarely related to one another or to meaningful exogenous variables. One anthropologist explains, "most of African network literature seems ... completely bogged down in methodology because it has failed to attack important questions of broader substantive theory" (Leeds 1972:5). However, sociologists have made advances in applying network analysis to various topics (in part by acknowledging and ignoring the complications perplexing anthropologists): how individuals obtain important services (Granovetter 1974, Lee 1968, Wellman et al 1973), diffusion of innovation (Coleman et al 1966), ethnic and occupational differentiation (Laumann 1973), political structure and influence (Laumann & Pappi 1973, Sheingold 1973, Burstein 1973), the structure of the economy (Levine 1972), and others. These studies demonstrate the widespread utility of a network approach.

For the study of community and personality, "a network conception permits fairly rapid movement from aggregate characteristics of the community to features of interpersonal relations on the small scale and back again" (Tilly 1972). The settlement is conceived of as a ramified social network of its residents, some of whom

[9]Introductions to network analysis as understood here are provided by Barnes (1972), Boissevain (1974), Mitchell (1969b), Boissevain & Mitchell (1973), and Whitten & Wolfe (1973).

are not linked, some linked in various ways, some linked to outsiders. Attributes of this network define the community's social order. For example, highly intertwined ("dense") and multidimensional ("multiplex" or "redundant") relationships are characteristic of cohesion; clustering with few cross-cluster ties denotes community schisms. (Extended definitions of community in network terms are provided by Craven & Wellman 1974, Tilly 1972, Southall 1973.)

The major theoretical application of network analysis to urban studies so far has been a more precise and formal restatement of traditional theory. The structural differentiation of urban places is translated, via greater interactional density, into less multiplexity of ties, which is essentially equivalent to Wirth's notion of "segmental" relationships and Park's idea that urbanites are simultaneously members of "widely separate worlds." However, such formulations do not foreclose alternative theories of community and personality constructed from the same conceptual material (e.g. Banton 1973, Fischer 1975b).

While useful in theory-building, network analysis is just as important in clarifying empirical findings. Consider three examples:

1. The experiences of the urban migrant are difficult to interpret from a perspective which views him as an individual transplanted from the familiar and primary corporate units of rural society to the strange, impersonal, secondary ones of cities. He should be isolated and disoriented. But, he is not (Nelson 1969). A network approach sensitizes the observer to the interpersonal links which constitute both rural and urban environments and which connect the two. The migrant moves along these networks, and uses them to find housing, jobs, guidance, and to construct his personal social world (see Tilly & Brown 1967, Girard et al 1966, Roberts 1973, Hanna & Hanna 1971:Ch. 3).

2. Who supports and restrains, both materially and socially, the urban individual? From an institutional perspective, the answers are plainly visible in the small community: physically proximate, nameable, corporate groups (e.g. neighbors, clan, kin, church). In the city, they are not so concretely visible, suggesting their absence, or their supercession by large, formal institutions. However, a network approach depicts all social bonds as invisible lines, extendable and divisible (i.e. specializable) to great degrees. Their greater apparent concreteness in the small community is not a central feature, but an incidental one. Thus, it becomes easier to comprehend how it is that urbanites as well as ruralities possess social supports and restraints (see, for example: Wellman et al 1973, Shulman 1972, Litwak 1960, Litwak & Szlenyi 1969, Granovetter 1974, Philpott 1968).

3. If one comprehends the component elements of social structure as discrete, bounded, categoric, institutional or corporate units (kin, community, etc), the urban social system is puzzling. Kin are dispersed, neighborhoods are nominal groups, and community is amorphous. It would be logical, then, to describe urban society as atomistic, held together only by large scale units such as publics and professions (e.g. Reisman 1950). However, if all social structure is understood to be composed of the network of interconnected personal networks, then a different analysis follows. Individuals can be seen constructing personal social worlds by "recruiting" people from categoric "pools," as in choosing which co-workers or neighbors to befriend

(Whitten & Wolfe 1973, White 1965).[10] These networks ramify into a social structure, in both large and small communities, with differences of degree (perhaps), not of kind (for instance, urban dwellers may have more "pools"). Thus, one need not be bound to the largely inaccurate conception of an atomistic city.

This last example brings us full circle, for these social networks, the internal fabric of the social structure, are, with their associated customs and values, the "social worlds" "which touch but do not interpenetrate" (Park 1916). The worlds, or subcultures, are personal social networks which are linked but do not coalesce. That side of the Chicago School which described the diversity and vitality of small moral orders (a perspective which co-existed with the theories of urban anomie) finds conceptual clarification and elaboration in a network approach.

METHODS

The credibility of any theory of community depends, as do all theories, upon: determining the external manifestations of its concepts, observing the predicted concomitant variation among those phenomena, repeating this observation in different situations, and refuting alternative, third-factor, explanations of the covariation (cf Durkheim 1938). Most theories of community and personality must contend, as do other theories of structural determinism, with particularly difficult "third-factors"—self-selection and contextual effects. Self-selection can inflate or deflate covariation. (An example of inflation is criminal "drift" to cities, which increases the urbanism-crime correlation. An example of deflation is the differential movement to the suburbs of automobile owners, which decreases the association between distance and access.) The latter, deflation, is likely to be more common, reducing the observed effects of environmental factors (see argument in Fischer & Jackson 1975). Contextual effects, particularly "climates of opinion," as likely to accentuate inter- or intra-settlement attitudinal and behavioral differences.

These criteria and problems present great hurdles for those attempting to establish what, if any, effects urban environments have on individuals. An example of the rare study which succeeds rather well is one conducted by Michelson (1973a, b). By interviewing residential movers before and after their moves to new environments (city vs suburb, house vs apartment), Michelson is able to allocate observed differences separately to environment and to individual traits. This quasiexperimental design is unusual (and no doubt difficult and costly). More often, the best that can be done to manage the requirements of theory-testing is to employ standardization techniques, usually drawn from econometrics, to simulate the causal logic and third-factor controls of the classical experiment. Yet even such ersatz procedures are uncommon in the urban research literature.

---

[10]In their shifting from categoric to network perspectives, anthropologists formulated halfway perspectives. Barnes (1954) interpreted networks as the relational residue remaining after considering categories. Others have written of "quasi-groups" (Mayer 1966, Boissevain 1968).

Difficulties in Older Research Procedures

Of the hundreds of published studies relevant to urban Community and personality, relatively few meet to any substantial degree the logical requirements outlined above. While they often contribute excellent data necessary for drawing theoretical conclusions, rarely are they able to deliver those conclusions themselves.

The bulk of urban research is composed of ethnographic studies of single communities. These works provide points of comparison, but no actual comparisons of different communities. There are occasional allusions to ideal-type comparisons or to studies conducted by others. The first is obviously inadequate, the second only slightly less so. Because this research does not examine covariation, it is insufficient for drawing conclusions about urban theories. It is invalid, therefore, to assert as some have done that Wirth has been disproven by notable urban ethnographies (e.g. Gans 1962a, Suttles 1968, Young & Willmott 1957), or to declare that city-suburban differences are negligible on the basis of similar research (e.g. Gans 1967, Berger 1960). These excellent studies are necessary but not sufficient. Similarly, most small surveys done in urban areas are also only single-place studies. Occasionally, inter-neighborhood contrasts are made (e.g. Greer 1956, Bell & Boat 1957), but rarely do they actually provide systematic and representative intrasettlement comparisons. These two research traditions comprise most of the existing literature; yet, neither adequately meets the theory-testing requirements of the comparative method (see also Reiss 1959b).

The great part of the urban Community and personality research also fails to meet the criteria of generalizability. This results to some extent from the predominance of English language work. It also results from an inclination to study nonrepresentative groups. We know, for example, more about Italian-Americans in Northeastern cities than we do about the masses of "middle-American" ribbon clerks and clock punchers, not to mention urbanities in other areas of the world.

Finally, only a small number of the accumulated studies are able to exclude third-factor explanations for their findings, even such important and obvious ones as social class, much less complex ones such as self-selection. When one discovers a few key examples of research which substantially meet these various criteria, they are invariably small scale studies (e.g. Reiss 1959a, Tomeh 1964).

It is for reasons such as this, the dearth of critical tests in the urban literature, that I argued earlier that theories of the rural-urban continuum, while having been severely questioned, have not yet been adequately tested in ways sufficient either to confirm or to discount them. The remainder of this section will concern recent developments in research which promise to fill some of the gaps.

Secondary Survey Analysis

As a matter of course, regional and national surveys code attributes of their respondents' communities. Using these codes to re-analyze the surveys for the study of urban issues is not new (e.g. Haer 1952), but the opportunities for doing so have increased greatly in recent years. The number of large, periodic, and comprehensive national surveys has grown, as have the systems for distributing them to other researchers (Hyman 1972). At the same time, statistical procedures for handling such masses of data, and for simulating third-factor controls, have, together with the computer software technology, grown rapidly in sophistication. The potential for exploiting these data banks is excellent and some urban research based upon them has appeared in recent years (e.g. Nelsen et al 1971, Fischer 1973, Kasarda & Janowitz 1974). This approach does have serious limitations: being at the mercy of others' research problems, sample designs, quality control, interview questions, and coding schemes. In particular, classifications of communities are usually restricted to size of community and center/suburb distinctions. Nevertheless, it is one major and relatively inexpensive way to provide critical tests of urban theories.

Experiments

Increasing interest among experimental social psychologists in urban topics raises the possibility that critical psychological assumptions in theories of urban personality might be rigorously tested (for example, notions of overstimulation, or of differential psychological reactions to strangers). As yet, these possibilities are unrealized, since the experimental literature is currently composed largely of crude efforts to simulate cities in the laboratory. But, a significant research potential exists (see Baldassare & Fischer 1974).

Field experiments, particularly those which establish controlled situations in different communities, have great theory-testing potential. To date, only primitive efforts in this direction have been made (e.g. Milgram 1970, Forbes & Gromoll 1971). Quasiexperimental designs using unbiased assignment of respondents to residential areas or before-after comparisons of the residentially mobile also provide an excellent means of meeting the logical requirements for testing theories of urban lifeways (e.g. Michelson 1973a, b; Berger 1960).

The "New Urban History"

Social science's tidal wave of large scale, quantitative, computer-aided methodology has, in the last decade, forcefully struck the discipline of history (Swiernga 1974). During roughly the same period, American historians have become aware and appreciative of the masses of detailed records available in archives—census schedules, tax lists, marriage certificates, and the like (Thernstrom 1971). These records are in many ways superior to contemporary documents. For instance, it is possible to trace the life histories of specific individuals through a number of American 19th Century census schedules. This confluence of massive data and appropriate methods, encouraged further by European social demography (e.g. Laslett 1972), has presented historians with the capability for writing accounts of mass, social history. It also has produced a particular type of that social history, commonly called the "new urban history" (see, for example, the *Journal of Interdisciplinary History* 1971; Warner 1968, Thernstrom 1973, Thernstrom & Sennett 1969, Knights 1971; in the sociological literature, this work is represented by studies such as Tilly 1974). Though not in truth confined to urban data, this field focuses especially upon the process of urbanization and the description of communities, and it draws heavily from city archives.

The limitations faced by the secondary analyst are exacerbated for the urban historian, dependent as he or she is on the procedures of long-deceased census takers and tax collectors. Yet, the contributions this work makes to the study of urban community are significant. For one, we are provided with greater generalizability (or, alternatively, historical specificity) through replication in different eras. Example: Residential turnover in America during the 19th Century, just as in contemporary times, was roughly equal in urban and rural places (Thernstrcn 1973). It provides a developmental perspecitve on contemporary data. Example: Population turnover in antebellum Boston was probably double that of today (Knights 1971: 60–62). And, it applies a corrective to sociologists' frequently faulty retrospective construction of antecedent conditions. Example: Occupational mobility in Newburyport, Massachusetts, was probably no greater before than during the period studied by Lloyd Warner (Thernstrom 1964). It is for reasons such as these that the "new urban history" is an important (and exciting) field to the urban sociologist.

Urban Anthropology

As peoples of developing nations have increasingly moved to cities, trailing close behind have been the anthropologists. In their descriptions of new urban life ways, investigators have had by necessity to evaluate the effects of urban residence on the peoples whom they studied. As a consequence, the subdiscipline of urban anthropology provides the richest and most theoretically germane source of published data for students of the urban community.

There is a large number of studies of urban populations conducted in the traditional ethnographic manner (e.g. Plotnicov 1967, Cohen 1969, Hannertz 1969, Liebow 1967, Little 1965, Magnin 1967). These studies have greatly expanded the breadth of our information about city peoples. The quantification wave has also reached anthropology, generating a mixed form of ethnography, one which combines intensive on-site observation with mass surveys (e.g. Pons 1969, Roberts 1973, Perlman 1975). And, there is a growing number of comparative ethnographies in which the investigator studies the same group in different community settings, usually the city and the rural village of origin (e.g. Bruner 1972, 1973; Bradfield 1973; Butterworth 1962).

The contributions of this literature (in addition to its elaboration of network analysis) include the documentation in detail of critical facts about urban migrants and the urban poor: that they are not disoriented, drifting, isolated, or anomic, but are actually involved in intimate and binding social relationships; that connections to the home village persist; that kinship and ethnicity continue to be meaningful institutions in the urban setting.

While these contributions and the raw descriptive material itself are important, there also exist major difficulties in urban anthropology. Most studies are not comparative, so that conclusions about the relative status of kinship or other institutions in the city remain largely subjective. There is also the common problem of representativeness, exacerbated here by a general predilection for studying atypical groups, such as the exotic or the severely disadvantaged (Plotnicov 1973, Gulick 1973).

The most serious deficiency lies in theory. Urban anthropologists have been sensitive to the rural-urban model as presented to their discipline by Redfield. This has been simultaneously advantageous and detrimental. It has meant that researchers have addressed, reported, and analyzed phenomena relevant to the theory. But, it has also left them stuck in a single theoretical groove. For example, many research reports are framed as debates with the older formulations: "Research on urban family and kinship has very often been done in conscious reaction to the sociological myth of the 'breakdown of the urban family' " (Gulick 1973:1003). Redfield and Wirth suffer constant refutation; yet no important alternative has been formulated.

Aside from this single, repetitive debate, urban anthropology has tended toward atheoretical empiricism—"non-generalizable, not related to generalizable theory, models, or hypotheses, and hence not generative of broader theory as to cities, urban society, or the social evolution of urbanized societies" (Leeds 1968:31). This critique of the field, by an important practitioner, understates its significant contributions, but does underline its critical problem. One reflection of that problem is a vague unease among anthropologists about the definition and purpose of urban anthropology, a disquiet which manifests itself, for example, in expressed fears that it might become another urban sociology!

Conclusion

None of these "new" methodologies can singly meet the criteria of methodological adequacy for critical theory-testing, whether the theory be Wirthian or any other of inter- and intracommunity differences. Together, however, and combined with improvement of "old" methodologies, they provide masses of novel data and promise advancements in our ability to treat those data in analytical, theory-testing ways. Yet, as the last discussion illustrates, no methodological improvement for unearthing new facts can advance us far in the absence of theoretical statements which direct and make meaningful the discovery of such facts.

SUMMARY

This essay has been an effort to examine critical, underlying difficulties in urban sociology, ones which are manifested in the field's very inability to define itself. Fundamentally, there is a lack of focus; the central issue has been lost. This loss is further exacerbated by challenges to the reality and meaning of "urban," and by common confusions between the study of life in cities and the study of city life. Thus, the field is quite vulnerable to charges that it is actually not a field at all (e.g. Pickvance 1974). However, a central issue need not be constructed, only rediscovered. Urban sociology is differentiated from general sociology, and, for that matter, from other urban studies, by its concern for the relationship of settlement pattern to the moral order and the fate of the individual in that order.

Other significant difficulties perplex the field. Most seriously, urban sociology's thought and research have been dominated by one framework, the rural-urban continuum, and that approach is increasingly discounted. It is discounted, but no satisfactory substitute is available; instead, there is a theoretical vacuum.

Two other major problems were also discussed. One is the absence of a social psychology able to account for the connection between structural factors and individual action. It is likely, however, that recent developments, particularly in network analysis, will provide solutions in this case. Second is the predominance of empirical research which is logically inadequate to answer the field's theoretical questions. Here, as well, recent efforts, particularly in interdisciplinary work, promise major advances.

This litany should not discourage the student of urban community. Instead, making explicit the field's difficulties should make more likely their solution and permit subsequent progress in the study of an important issue, one drawn directly from sociology's focal interests, the relationship between the environments men construct and the social orders which ensue.

ACKNOWLEDGMENTS

This work was supported in part by the Institute of Urban and Regional Development, Berkeley, California. I gratefully acknowledge the helpful comments on an earlier draft by Ann Swidler, Gerald Suttles, and Charles Tilly.

Literature Cited

Abrahamson, M. 1974. The social dimensions of urbanism. *Soc. Forces* 52:376–83

Alford, R. R. 1972. Critical evaluation of the principles of city classification. In *City Classification Handbook*, ed. B. J. L. Berry, 3\1–59. New York: Wiley

Anderson, T. R., Egeland, J. A. 1961. Spatial aspects of social area analysis. *Am. Sociol. Rev.* 26:392–99

Ardrey, R. 1966. *The Territorial Imperative.* New York: Atheneum

Arensberg, C. M. 1961. The community as object and as sample. *Am. Anthropol.* 63:241–64

Baldassare, M., Fischer, C. S. 1974. *The Relevance of Crowding Experiments to Urban Studies.* Presented to West. Psychol. Assoc., San Francisco

Banton, M. 1973. Urbanization and role analysis. In *Urban Anthropology*, ed. A. Southall, 43–70. New York: Oxford

Barnes, J. A. 1954. Class and committees in a Norwegian island parish. *Hum. Relat.* 7(1):39–58

Barnes, J. A. 1972. Social networks. *Addison-Wesley Module in Anthropology*, No. 26

Bell, W., Boat, M. D. 1957. Urban neighborhoods and informal social relations. *Am. J. Sociol.* 62:391–98

Benet, F. 1963. Sociology uncertain: The ideology of the rural-urban continuum. *Comp. Stud. Soc. Hist.* 6:1–23

Berger, B. 1960. *Working-Class Suburb.* Berkeley: Univ. Calif.

Berry, B. J. L., Ed. 1972. *City Classification Handbook.* New York: Wiley

Boissevain, J. 1968. The place of non-groups in the social sciences. *Man* 3(4):542–56

Boissevain, J. 1974. *Friends of Friends.* Oxford: Basil Blackwell

Boissevain, J., Mitchell, J. C. 1973. *Network Analysis: Studies in Human Interaction.* The Hague: Mouton

Bradfield, S. 1973. Selectivity in rural-urban migration: the case of Huaylas, Peru. In *Urban Anthropology*, ed. A. Southall, 351–72. New York: Oxford

Bruner, E. M. 1972. Batak ethnic associations in three Indonesian cities. *Southwest. J. Anthropol.* 28:207–29

Bruner, E. M. 1973. The expression of ethnicity in Indonesia. In *Urban Ethnicity*, ed. A Cohen, 251–80. London: Tavistock

Burgess, E. W., Bogue, D. J. 1964. Research in urban society: A long view. In *Urban Sociology*, 1–15. Chicago: Univ. Chicago. Phoenix Ed.

Burstein, P. 1973. *Politics and Social Structure in Israel.* Ph.D. thesis. Harvard Univ. Unpublished

Butterworth, D. S. 1962. A study of the urbanization process among Mixtec migrants from Tilantongo to Mexico City. *Am. Indigena* 22:257–74

Calhoun, J. B. 1963. Population density and social pathology. In *The Urban Condition*, ed. L. J. Duhl. New York: Clarion

Carrothers, G. A. P. 1956. An historical review of the gravity and potential concepts of human interaction. *J. Am. Inst. Planners* 22:94–102

Carstairs, G. 1969. Overcrowding and human aggression. In *The History of Violence in America*, ed. H. D. Graham, T. R. Gurr, 751–63. New York: Bantam

Cohen, A. 1969. *Custom and Politics in Urban Africa*. Berkeley: Univ. Calif.

Coleman, J. S., Katz, E., Menzel, H. 1966. *Medical Innovation*. Indianapolis: Bobbs-Merrill

Craven, P., Wellman, B. 1974. The network city. *Sociol. Inq.* 43:57–88

Dewey, R. 1960. The rural-urban continuum: real but relatively unimportant. *Am. J. Sociol.* 66:60–66

Donaldson, S. 1969. *The Suburban Myth*. New York: Columbia Univ.

Duncan, O. D. 1957. Community size and the rural-urban continuum. In *Cities and Society*, ed. P. K. Hatt, A. J. Reiss Jr., 35–45. New York: Free Press

Durkheim, E. 1933. *The Division of Labor in Society*. Glencoe, Ill.: Free Press

Durkheim, E. 1938. *The Rules of the Sociological Method*. New York: Free Press. 1964 ed.

Farkas, G. 1974. Specification, residuals and contextual effects. *Soc. Methods Res.* 2:333–64

Fischer, C. S. 1972. Urbanism as a way of life: A review and an agenda. *Soc. Methods Res.* 1:187–242

Fischer, C. S. 1973. On urban alienations and anomie: Powerlessness and social isolation. *Am. Sociol. Rev.* 38:311–26

Fischer, C. S. 1974. The metropolitan experience. In *Metropolitan America: Papers on the State of Knowledge*, ed. A. Hawley, V. Rock, 213–48. Washington, D.C.: Nat. Acad. Sci.

Fischer, C. S. 1975a. The effect of urban life on traditional values. *Soc. Forces* 53: In press

Fischer, C. S. 1975b. Toward a subcultural theory of urbanism. *Am. J. Sociol.* 80: In press

Fischer, C. S. 1975c. *The Urban Experience*. New York: Harcourt Brace Jovanovich. In press

Fischer, C. S., Baldassare, M., Ofshe, R. J. 1974. *Crowding Studies and Urban Life: A Critical Review*. Working Paper No. 241, Inst. Urban and Regional Develop., Berkeley

Fischer, C. S., Jackson, R. M. 1975. Suburbs, networks, and attitudes. In *The Changing Face of the Suburbs*, ed. B. Schwartz. Chicago: Univ. Chicago. In press

Forbes, G. B., Gromoll, F. 1971. The lost-letter technique as a measure of social variables: Some exploratory findings. *Soc. Forces* 50:113–15

Freedman, J. L. 1973. The effects of population density on humans. In *Psychological Perspectives on Population*, ed. J. Fawcett, 209–38. New York: Basic

Friedmann, J., Miller J. 1965. The urban field. *J. Am. Inst. Planners* 21:312–20

Galle, O. R., Gove, W. R., McPherson, J. M. 1972. Population density and pathology: What are the relations for man? *Science* 176:23–30

Gans, H. J. 1962a. *The Urban Villagers*. New York: Free Press

Gans, H. J. 1962b. Urbanism and suburbanism as ways of life: A reevaluation of definitions. In *Human Behavior and Social Processes*, ed. A. M. Rose, 625–48. Boston: Houghton-Mifflin

Gans H. J. 1967. *The Levittowners*. New York: Vintage

Girard, A., Bastide, H., Pourcher, G. 1970 (reprint of 1966 article). Geographic mobility and urban concentration in France. In *Readings in the Sociology of Migration*, ed. C. J. Jansen, 203–55. New York: Pergamon

Goffman, E. 1971. *Relations in Public*. New York: Harper and Row

Granovetter, M. 1974. *Getting a Job*. Cambridge, Mass.: Harvard Univ.

Greer, S. 1956. Urbanism reconsidered: A comparative study of local areas in a metropolis. *Am. Sociol. Rev.* 21:19–25

Greer, S. 1962. *The Emerging City*. New York: Free Press

Gulick, J. 1973. Urban anthropology. In *Handbook of Social and Cultural Anthropology*, ed. J. J. Honigman, 979–1029. Chicago: Rand McNally

Gutman, R., Popenoe, D. 1970. Introduction to *Neighborhood, City, and Metropolis*, 3–24. New York: Random House

Hadden, J. K., Borgotta, E. F. 1965. *American Cities: Their Social Characteristics*. Chicago: Rand McNally

Haer, J. L. 1952. Conservatism-radicalism and the rural-urban continuum. *Rural Sociol.* 17:343–47

Hall, E. 1966. *The Hidden Dimension*. Garden City, NY: Anchor

Hanna, W. J., Hanna, J. L. 1971. *Urban Dynamics in Black Africa*. Chicago: Aldine-Atherton

Hannertz, U. 1969. *Soulside.* New York: Columbia Univ.

Hauser, P. H. 1965. Urbanization: An overview. In *The Study of Urbanization*, ed. P. H. Hauser, L. F. Schnore, 1–48. New York: Wiley

Hauser, R. 1970. Context and consex: A cautionary tale. *Am. J. Sociol.* 73:645–64

Hauser, R. 1971. *Socioeconomic Background and Educational Performance.* Washington, D.C.: Am. Sociol. Assoc.

Hauser, R. 1974. Contextual analysis revisited. *Soc Methods Res.* 2:365–75

Hawley, A. H., Duncan, O. D. 1957. Social area analysis: A critical appraisal. *Land Econ.* 33:337–44

Heberle, R. 1960. The normative element in neighborhood relations. *Pac. Sociol. Rev.* 3:3–11

Hyman, H. 1972. *Secondary Analysis of Sample Surveys.* New York: Wiley

Kasarda, J. D., Janowitz, M. 1974. Community attachment in mass society. *Am. Sociol. Rev.* 39:328–39

Keller, S. 1968. *The Urban Neighborhood.* New York: Random House

Knights, P. R. 1971. *The Plain People of Boston 1830–1860.* New York: Oxford

Kolb, W. L. 1954. The social structure and functions of cities. *Econ. Develop. Cult. Change* 3:30–46

Laslett, P., Ed. 1972. *Household and Family in Past Time.* Cambridge: Cambridge Univ.

Laumann, E. O. 1973. *Bonds of Pluralism.* New York: Wiley

Laumann, E. O., Pappi, F. U. 1973. New directions in the study of community elites. *Am. Sociol. Rev.* 38:212–29

Lee, N. H. 1968. *The Search for an Abortionist.* Chicago: Univ. Chicago

Leeds, A. 1968. The anthropology of cities: Some methodological issues. In *Urban Anthropology: Research Perspectives and Strategies*, ed. E. M. Eddy, 31–47. *S. Anthropol. Soc. Proc. No. 2.* Athens: Univ. Georgia

Leeds, A. 1972. Urban anthropology and urban studies. *Urban Anthropol. Newslett.* 1:4–5

Levine, J. 1972. The sphere of influence. *Am. Sociol. Rev.* 37:14–27

Lewis, O. 1965. Further observations on the folk-urban continuum and urbanization with special reference to Mexico City. In *The Study of Urbanization*, ed. P. H. Hauser, L. F. Schnore, 491–503. New York: Wiley

Liebow, E. 1967. *Tally's Corner.* Boston: Little, Brown

Little, K. 1968 (reprint of 1965 article). The migrant and the urban community. In *Urbanism in World Perspective*, ed. S. F. Fava, 312–32. New York: Crowell

Litwak, E. 1960. Geographical mobility and extended family cohesion. *Am. Sociol. Rev.* 25:385–94

Litwak, E., Szlenyi, I. 1969. Primary group structures and their functions. *Am. Sociol. Rev.* 34:465–81

Lorenz, K. 1966. *On Aggression.* Transl. M. K. Wilson. New York: Bantam

Lyman, S. M., Scott, M. B. 1967. Territoriality. *Soc. Probl.* 15:236–49

Magnin, W. 1967. Squatter settlements. *Sci. Am.* 217:4:21–29

Marshall, H. 1973. Suburban life styles: A contribution to the debate. In *The Urbanization of the Suburbs*, ed. L. H. Masotti, J. K. Hadden, 7:123–47. Beverly Hills: Sage

Martin, R. D. 1972. Concepts of human territoriality. In *Man, Settlement and Urbanism*, ed. P. Ucko, R. Tringham, G. Dimbleby, 427–45. Cambridge, Mass.: Schenckman

Martindale, D. 1958. Prefatory remarks: The theory of the city. In *Max Weber: The City*, ed. D. Martindale, 9–62. New York: Free Press

Mayer, A. C. 1966. The significance of quasi-groups in the study of complex societies. In *The Social Anthropology of Complex Societies*, ed. M. Banton, 97–121. London: Tavistock

McKenzie, R. D. 1925. The ecological approach to the study of the human community. In R. E. Park, E. W. Burgess, R. D. McKenzie, *The City*, 63–79. Chicago: Univ. Chicago. 1967 ed.

Meier, R. L. 1962. *A Communication Theory of Urban Growth.* Cambridge, Mass.: M.I.T.

Merton, R. K. 1968. The bearing of sociological theory on empirical research. In *Social Theory and Social Structure*, 139–55. New York: Free Press

Michelson, W. 1973a. "The reconciliation of 'subjective' and 'objective' data on physical environment in the community." *Sociol. Inq.* 43:147–73

Michelson, W. 1973b. *Environmental Change.* Interim Report. Res. Paper No. 60, Centre for Urban and Community Studies, Univ. Toronto

Milgram, S. 1970. The experience of living in cities. *Science* 167:1461–68

Miller, J. G. 1960. Information input overload and psychopathology. *Am. J. Psychiat.* 116:695–704

Mitchell, J. C. 1969a. The concept and use of social networks. In *Social Networks in Urban Situations,* 1–50. Manchester: Manchester Univ.

Mitchell, J. C., Ed. 1969b. *Social Networks in Urban Situations.* Manchester: Manchester Univ.

Montagu, A., Ed. 1973. *Man and Aggression.* New York: Oxford. 2nd ed.

Morris, R. N. 1968. *Urban Sociology.* New York: Praeger

Nelsen, H. M., Yokley, R. L., Madron, T. W. 1971. Rural-urban differences in religiosity. *Rural Soc.* 36:389–96

Nelson, J. I. 1972. "High school context and college plans. *Am. Sociol. Rev.* 37: 143–48

Nelson, J. M. 1969. *Migrants, Urban Poverty and Instability in Developing Nations.* Occasional papers in International Affairs, No. 22. Cambridge: Harvard Center for Int. Affairs

Nisbet, R. 1966. *The Sociological Tradition.* New York: Basic

Park, R. E. 1969 (reprint of 1916 essay). The city: Suggestions for investigation of human behavior in the urban environment. In *Classic Essays on the Culture of Cities,* ed. R. Sennett, 91–130. New York: Appleton

Perlman, J. E. 1975. *Rio's Favelas: The Myth of Marginality.* Berkeley: Univ. Calif. In press

Philpott, S. B. 1968. Remittance obligations, social networks and choice . . . *Man* 3:465–76

Pickvance, C. G. 1974. On a materialist critique of urban sociology. *Sociol. Rev.* 22:203–20

Plotnicov, L. 1967. *Strangers to the City.* Pittsburgh: Univ. Pittsburgh

Plotnicov, L. 1973. Anthropological fieldwork in modern and local urban contexts. *Urban Anthropol.* 2:248–64

Pons, V. 1969. *Stanleyville.* London: Oxford Univ.

Redfield, R. 1947. The folk society. *Am. J. Sociol.* 52:293–308

Reisman, D. 1950. *The Lonely Crowd.* New Haven: Yale Univ.

Reiss, A. J. Jr. 1955. An analysis of urban phenomena. In *The Metropolis in Modern Life,* ed. R. M. Fisher, 41–51. Garden City, NY: Doubleday

Reiss, A. J. Jr. 1959a. Rural-urban and status differences in interpersonal contacts. *Am. J. Sociol.* 65:182–95

Reiss, A. J. Jr. 1959b. The sociological study of community. *Rural Sociol.* 24:118–30

Reissman, L. 1964. *The Urban Process.* New York: Free Press of Glencoe

Roberts, B. 1973. *Organizing Strangers.* Austin: Univ. Texas

Sheingold, C. A. 1973. Social networks and voting. *Am. Sociol. Rev.* 38:712–20

Short, J. F. Jr., Ed. 1971. *The Social Fabric of the Metropolis.* Chicago: Univ. Chicago

Shulman, N. 1972. *Urban Social Networks.* PhD thesis. Univ. Toronto

Simmel, G. 1969 (reprint of 1905 essay). The metropolis and mental life. In *Classic Essays on the Culture of Cities,* ed. R. Sennett, 47–60. New York: Appleton

Sjoberg, G. 1960. *The Preindustrial City.* New York: Free Press

Sjoberg, G. 1965. Theory and research in urban sociology. In *The Study of Urbanization,* ed. P. H. Hauser, L. F. Schnore, 157–90. New York: Wiley

Sommer, R. 1969. *Personal Space.* Englewood Cliffs, NJ: Prentice-Hall

Sorokin, P. A., Zimmerman, C. C., Galpin, C. J. 1930. *A Systematic Source Book in Rural Sociology.* Minneapolis: Univ. Minnesota

Southall, A. 1973. The density of role-relationships as a universal index of urbanization. In *Urban Anthropology,* ed. A. Southall. New York: Oxford

Stewart, J. Q. 1948. Demographic gravitation: Evidence and applications. *Sociometry* 11:31–58

Stokols, D., Rall, M., Pinner, B., Schopler, J. 1973. Physical, social, and personal determinants of the perception of crowding. *Environ. Behav.* 5:87–115

Suttles, G. D. 1968. *The Social Order of the Slum.* Chicago: Univ. Chicago

Suttles, G. D. 1972. *The Social Construction of Communities.* Chicago: Univ. Chicago

Swiernga, R. P. 1974. Computers and American history. *J. Am. Hist.* 60: 1045–70

Thernstrom, S. 1964. *Poverty and Progress.* Cambridge, Mass.: Harvard Univ.

Thernstrom, S. 1971. Reflections on the new urban history. *Daedalus* 100:359–75

Thernstrom, S. 1973. *The Other Bostonians.* Cambridge, Mass.: Harvard Univ.

Thernstrom, S., Sennett, R., Eds. 1969. *Nineteenth-Century Cities.* New Haven: Yale Univ.

Tilly, C. 1972. *An Interactional Scheme for Analysis of Communities, Cities, and Urbanization.* Mimeo, Univ. Michigan

Tilly, C. 1974. The chaos of the living city. In *An Urban World,* 86–107. Boston: Little, Brown

Tilly, C., Brown, C. H. 1967. On uprooting, kinship, and auspices of migration. *Int. J. Comp. Soc.* 7:139–64

Tomeh, A. K. 1964. Informal group participation and residential patterns. *Am. J. Sociol.* 70:28–35

Warner, S. B. Jr. 1968. *Streetcar Suburbs.* New York: Atheneum

Webber, M. M. 1968. The post-city age. *Daedalus* 97:1091–1110

Wellman, B. et al 1973. Community ties and support systems. In *The Form of Cities in Central Canada,* ed. L. S. Bourne, R. D. MacKinnon, J. W. Simmons. Toronto: Univ. Toronto

White, H. 1965. *Notes on the Constituents of Social Structure.* Mimeo, Harvard Univ.

White, M., White, L. 1962. *The Intellectual Versus The City.* New York: Mentor

Whitten, N. E., Wolfe, A. W. 1973. Network analysis. In *The Handbook of Social and Cultural Anthropology,* ed. J. J. Honigman. Chicago: Rand McNally

Willitis, F. K., Bealer, R. C., Crider, D. M. 1973. Levelling of attitudes in mass society: Rurality and traditional morality in America. *Rural Sociol.* 38:36–45

Wirth, L. 1938. Urbanism as a way of life. *Am. J. Sociol.* 44:3–24

Wirth, L. 1969 (reprint of 1956 essay). Rural-urban differences. In *Classic Essays on the Culture of Cities,* ed. R. Sennett, 165–70. New York: Appleton

Young, M., Willmott, P. 1957. *Family and Kinship in East London.* Baltimore: Penguin

ALIENATION STUDIES   ❖10504

Melvin Seeman

Department of Sociology, University of California, Los Angeles, California 90024

The very existence of this chapter on alienation should be recognized as a confirmation of sorts. Though many have declared the idea of alienation wearied and moribund (its obituary already written, Lee 1972), the evidence compiled here suggests otherwise. There is, in the first place, a strong continuing empirical and theoretical interest in alienation; and second, it is commonplace to find formulations that make no express use of the term itself but that are coordinate with, if not directly indebted to, the classical interest in "alienation." This suggests that the cautions involved work both ways: the enthusiasts make alienation the master concept—conveniently imprecise, empirically omnipresent, and morally irresistible when employed as a critique; while the doubters, with equal convenience, forget that dismissing the word in no way eliminates our dependence upon the root ideas concerning personal control and comprehensible social structures which the alienation tradition embodies.

These introductory remarks correctly imply that intellectual struggle, along with empirical profusion, have characterized the recent history of alienation studies. The intellectual struggle is perhaps best reflected in two major reviews of the alienation literature, by Schacht (1970) and Israel (1971). Schacht, a philosopher, surveys the classical sources (chiefly Hegel and Marx) and the modern literature (Fromm, Horney, the sociologists, and existentialists), documenting two important theses: (*a*) the confusion of meanings that we currently associate with alienation has been there from the beginning (e.g. one finds both "separation" and "surrender" in the Hegelian treatment), and (*b*) an unsteady union of descriptive and prescriptive interests makes steady trouble in the concept's use. Israel's work covers much the same historical ground, and, like Schacht, he gives detailed attention to the predominantly American empirical studies of the past decade. Neither of these writers is very happy with the empirical spirit or product, and on at least two major counts they agree regarding the source of their unhappiness: they find the empiricists overly committed to the conception of alienation as a psychological state of the individual (rather than an attribute of the social system, and as such not necessarily, or even regularly, a matter of awareness), and overly committed as well to a "multidimen-

91

sional" concept of alienation, a view which is, as they see it, neither theoretically grounded nor very clear about the relation that holds, in principle or in fact, among the several varieties of alienation.

These debates, along with the general resurgence of Marxian analysis, have produced a voluminous literature which is not itself empirically oriented yet forms the background of alienation studies. Among the best examples are the English translations of Marx's *Grundrisse* (1971) and of Lukacs' *History and Class Consciousness* (1971); the full scale treatments of Marx's theory of alienation by Ollman (1971) and Mészáros (1970); and, especially for preHegelian writings, Murchland's *The Age of Alienation* (1971). These works, among many others (see the exhaustive bibliography by Geyer 1972), testify to the continuing viability of the idea of alienation, despite the recurring unhappiness which leads some to retreat from its use. Israel (1971), for example, finds "reification" a more useful concept; and Fromm, analyzing *The Anatomy of Human Destructiveness* (1973), needs no "alienation" in his index whereas his earlier work (1955) leaned very heavily on that idea.

The perspective that these general and historical works provide is indispensable. Though a narrower focus characterizes the empirically oriented alienation studies, these studies nonetheless lay claim to a broad intellectual tradition which, comprehendingly or not, they develop, challenge, or alter (and, some would say, distort). In that degree, these studies are inevitably involved in trends and debates that go well beyond their manifest subject matter—for example, debates concerning the "human nature" assumptions which the idea of alienation involves (Roszak 1973, Lukes 1967); its implicit embrace of the idea of a "fall" from previous perfection (or at the very least, the "loss" of some prior valued condition, Yinger 1973); the historical secularization of the idea of alienation—i.e. its successive theological, metaphysical, critical, and scientific usages (Lichtheim 1968); and, indeed, the veritable rediscovery of alienation (roughly, since 1935), to the degree that we now retrospectively read that idea to be an integral element in "the sociological tradition" (Nisbet 1967). These intellectual backgrounds and debates are constantly at issue in the empirical investigations of alienation to which we now turn.

THE VARIETIES OF ALIENATION

The effort to define alienation has not slackened, and the latest book-length treatment in that direction is Johnson's work (1973) which features a multidisciplinary set of contributors. As one might expect, given the variety of interests (psychiatric, philosophic, revolutionary, social accounting, etc) that motivate the quest, very little is settled (in Johnson's work or in general) concerning the meaning of alienation. That need not be too disquieting if the search for the "true inheritance" (of Marx, for example) is subordinated to the awareness of different interests in the different usages, and the difficulties that inhere in each. Touraine (1973:198–202), for example, has made explicit the fact that his version of alienation is situated at a different level of analysis than the social-psychological one (Seeman 1959, 1972a). For him, alienation is (a) an integral aspect of social class relations, (b) whereby the dominated actor adopts orientations and social practices determined by and in the interests of the dominating class, presenting thus (c) a contradiction between behavior that corresponds to his true situation and behavior imposed by the going institutions in the service of the dominant order. Such a position is illustrative of those versions of alienation that minimize, as direct indicators of alienation, either the experience of deprivation (e.g. work on the assembly line) or subjective awareness of such deprivation [cf Touraine's (1973:201) crisp remark: "Alienation, therefore, is not the awareness of deprivation, but the deprivation of awareness"].

Touraine's position also illustrates the feature these varied conceptions of alienation share—namely, the notion of "discrepancy." The differences in definition come down to the question of where that discrepancy is located: it may be a case of false consciousness (as it basically is for Touraine); unfulfilled inherent human needs (Etzioni 1968); objective deprivation at work, in politics, or elsewhere (Mandel & Novack 1970); the analyst's postulated gap between ideal conditions and social or personal reality (Marcuse 1964); or the actor's own sense of loss or frustration based on some previous or preferred state of affairs (Jessor, Jessor & Finney 1973). Even the seemingly more neutral formulations of alienation (conceptions that explicitly avoid the polemics of reform, the postulates concerning "truly human" needs, and the concentration on personal despair) embody in their own way this minimal "discrepancy" aspect. Thus, in Seeman's formulation, the idea of "cultural estrangement" points to the perceived gap between the going values in a society (or subunit thereof) and the individual's own standards; and though the notion of powerlessness conceived in expectancy terms ("a low expectancy that one's own behavior can control the occurrence of personal and social rewards," Seeman 1972a: 473) does not propose to measure a gap between desired and actual control, the measuring instruments which put this version of powerlessness into practice regularly focus upon the absence of control in certain domains rather than others (i.e. in domains where control is possible, traditional, or normatively sanctioned). It is the lack of control over economics, politics, interpersonal relations, education, and the like that is featured in these concrete measures of powerlessness; and the implication surely is that these are the domains in which the respondent *could* exercise significant control and in which the absence of control is likely to be experienced as a discrepancy between potential and actual mastery.

Since the bulk of alienation studies has been carried out within the social psychological framework, employing subjective measures cast variously in terms of attitudes, values, sentiments, or expectancies, that framework is employed here. The following summary sketches developments with respect to the six varieties of alienation identified in Seeman's (1972a) revised categories: (a) powerlessness—the sense of low control vs mastery over events; (b) meaninglessness—the sense of incomprehensibility vs understanding of personal and social affairs; (c) normlessness—high expectancies for (or commitment to) socially unapproved means vs conventional means for the achievement of given goals; (d) cultural estrangement (called "value isolation" in an earlier version, Seeman 1959)—the individual's rejection of commonly held values in the society (or subsector) vs commitment to the going group standards; (e) self-estrangement—the individual's engagement in activities that are not intrinsically rewarding vs involvement in a task or activity for its own sake; and (*f*) social isolation—the sense of exclusion or rejection vs social acceptance.

Powerlessness

The political scientist and psychologist, as well as the sociologist, have a fundamen-tal interest in personal and social control, hence it should come as no surprise that the powerlessness version of alienation has been most extensively examined. In a degree, Rotter's (1966) I-E scale (a forced-choice measure of the individual's gener-alized expectancies for Internal-vs-External control), whose early development and relation to alienation was first reported on in the paper by Rotter, Liverant & Seeman (1962), became as popular as the F (authoritarianism) scale was in the 1950s. Variants and near-relatives of it have been used in a wide range of sociological investigations—e.g. in Coleman's (1966) demonstration that mastery attitudes are associated with school achievement, in Neal & Groat's (1970) and Bullough's (1972) finding that high powerlessness is associated with low success in family planning behavior (see also Bauman & Udry 1972), or in Goodwin's (1972) showing that low confidence in one's own fate control (not degree of commitment to the work ethic) distinguishes black welfare mothers from outer city whites (and that the mothers' relative sense of powerlessness is communicated to their sons).

As with the F scale, this concentration of work on powerlessness and/or internal-external control has demonstrated both the strengths and weaknesses of the scale in question, has generated a series of measurement devices with the same general intention, and has produced a collection of bibliographies (on the I-E scale itself, the most extensive is the annotated bibliography developed by MacDonald 1972), state-of-the-field summaries (Joe 1971; Lystad 1972; Phares 1973; Lefcourt 1972; Hill, Chapman & Wuertzer 1974), and readers (e.g. Marcson 1970, Finifter 1972). The main themes exhibited in this generous empirical output can be summarized as follows:

1. The array of instruments available for measuring control-oriented attitudes is impressive. These range from indicators of generalized powerlessness (Dean 1961; Rotter 1966—the latter translated into various languages, including Chinese; Hsieh, Shybut & Lotsof 1969), to more or less specialized measures in particular domains (for example, the five-item political efficacy scale utilized in recent years at the Michigan Survey Research Institute, Converse 1972, Balch 1974), or in particular organizational settings (Aiken & Hage 1966). There are also a number of well-conceived measures for use with children (Crandall, Katkovsky & Crandall 1965; Mischel, Zeiss & Zeiss 1974).

Nevertheless, there remains a strong tendency to use ad hoc measures consisting of a small number of items, often enough of a very general "alienative" (i.e. un-happy) nature, and not particularly systematic or comparable with any well-known index (Simpson 1970, Rushing 1972, Sheppard & Herrick 1972, Tudor 1972). The literature (e.g. Streuning & Richardson 1965, Lowe & Damankos 1968) also reflects a continuing hope that procedures such as factor analysis or Guttman scaling will produce some definitive, generally acceptable order out of the chaos of vaguely related measurements (and of varying names for obviously related scales), and concerning this effort two conclusions seem warranted: (*a*) the dimensions and scales produced in this way have not been notably successful so far as their adoption to date is concerned; and (*b*) they tend to be dominated by the Srole (1956) or Srole-like (McClosky & Schaar 1965) items, which is to say that typically one of the major axes generated is something akin to alienation conceived as generalized unhappiness, negativism, or despair (rather than, let us say, a narrower powerlessness component).

2. Moore (1970) speaks of the "unity of misery," meaning that, at least in comparison with the diversity of the sources of happiness, there is a unitary nature to human suffering. A similar notion of the unity of alienation has dominated the literature. Though the ground for thinking of the several forms of alienation as quite distinct phenomena (i.e. breaking the "false unity" of that idea, Touraine 1967) has been available for some time now, there remains a considerable tendency to think of the sundry alienations in more or less "packaged" terms,—i.e. to propose hypotheses and explanations that rest upon coherence, upon the view that the several brands of alienation (powerlessness, normlessness, self-estrangement, etc) normally go together. Not surprisingly, the literature supports the contention that they do go together (Keniston 1968, especially pp. 326–42), or that they do not (Jessor et al 1968, Caplan 1970), depending heavily, it seems, on the care that has gone into the conceptualization and measurement, the higher correlations between powerlessness and other alienations being produced where instrument-generated factors encourage the bond (e.g. similarity of items under different names, similarity of item format, etc). In short, the unity of the package depends on how it is empirically put together, and a significant share of the coherence is regularly fictional (in the instrument sense described above).

The importance of making the distinctions in question is nicely illustrated in the view advanced by Gamson (1968) and in the studies that have attempted to implement it (Paige 1971, House & Mason 1974). Gamson argued for a strong distinction between an "input" and "output" dimension of political alienation (as do Olsen 1969 and Finifter 1970), the former referring basically to "powerlessness" (sensed inability to have an influence in political affairs) and the latter to "distrust" (lack of confidence in the government's action in one's behalf). One hypothesis derived from this view holds that political mobilization should be greatest where the two alienations are not unitary but discrepant—where powerlessness is low, but distrust is high. Paige (1971) found support for this hypothesis in a study of riot participation among black males in Newark, but several studies by political scientists have resulted in a negative conclusion regarding its validity (Fraser 1970; Hawkins, Marando & Taylor 1971). Whatever the ultimate status of this particular hypothesis, it suggests that at this juncture it may be more productive to think in terms of the disunities rather than the unity of alienation, the strong distinction between trust and efficacy being quite common and fruitful in the politically oriented literature (Easton & Dennis 1967, Aberbach & Walker 1970, Abramson 1972).

3. The same principle of distinctiveness holds even when we restrict our attention to the powerlessness domain itself. The I-E scale (Rotter 1966) was developed as a measure of quite generalized expectancies for control, with no particular attention

within it to different domains in which control might be exercised (e.g. politics, family, or academic life), to different kinds of experience (e.g. failure vs success experience, Weiner et al 1971), or to the different agencies that might be perceived as blocking personal control (e.g. powerful others or bureaucratic rules vs lack of individual capacity, training, or luck, Lao 1970).

A substantial stimulus to rethinking this supposed generality of powerlessness was produced in the work of Gurin et al (1969), who showed the importance of distinguishing between personal and social control, which, in their factor analysis, meant effectively the difference between items containing an "I" reference as against those focusing on "system blame" (for an earlier distinction going in the same direction, see also Seeman 1967a: 120). The pursuit of these subleties concerning the individual's sense of control has produced a substantial literature, much of it in agreement in showing that people treat these attributions about their world of control with considerable discrimination: they do not confuse self and system, work and politics, achievements and failures, luck and talent, or personal competence and civic competence (Mirels 1970, Abramowitz 1973, Schwartz 1973, Aberbach 1974, Balch 1974, Collins 1974, Renshon 1974, Rosenau 1974).

One specific area in which these distinctions have been implemented—particularly the distinction between the sense of personal inefficacy versus powerlessness as system constraint (the latter sometimes called "control ideology," Forward & Williams 1970)—is in connection with the many studies of militancy, activism, and riot participation. Many have contended (Ransford 1968, Seeman 1972b, Clark 1965, Kerner et al 1968, Crawford & Naditch 1970) that the sense of powerlessness was one of the key elements in the civil disturbances of the late 1960s. But the individual's participation in such activity (his proneness to activism, whether violent or not) can be viewed rather differently. Some time ago, Gore & Rotter (1963) as well as Strickland (1965) proposed and found that low powerlessness (high mastery) correlated with greater social activism—in their case, greater expressed readiness to participate in civil rights activities—the thesis being that greater generalized confidence in the efficacy of one's action would translate into greater readiness to take part in such social action. As McWilliams (1973:66) puts it: " . . . estranged men are not often engaged in political protest; those who feel powerless are more inclined to submit and even to mask their resentments."

A similar view has found considerable support in recent analysis (Caplan 1970, Forward & Williams 1970), with the emphasis being placed on the distinction cited above—i.e. on the activist's combined high personal efficacy but low sense of control over the external system-related forces. The latter (low social control) is presumably the primary element in studies of college students—for example in Silvern & Nakamura's (1971) report that among male undergraduates at UCLA externality (powerlessness) was correlated with protest activity (primarily reflecting the externality of left-wing activists), in Kirby's (1971) study of student activism in the University of California, in Lao's (1970) study among black college students, and in Renshon's (1974:194) finding that "individuals with low personal control are more likely to have reported that they took part in mass demonstrations, physical confrontations, and sit ins." The thrust of all this is that the combination of high sensed powerlessness relative to the system and low personal powerlessness is most likely to breed activism; but a part of the problem in reading this literature is that the distinctions in question have not been very well operationalized as yet, hence it is often difficult to determine which brand of powerlessness (and activism, too, for that matter) is at stake in any given instance (in Renshon's case, for example, the personal control measure is heavily infused with system-oriented items). The four items described by Campbell (1971) are of the general-personal variety (e.g. "Have you usually felt pretty sure your life would work out the way you want it to, or have there been times when you haven't been sure about it?"), and these items do not discriminate very much between blacks and whites (a finding consistent with the import of the data presented in Seeman 1972a: 488), nor do these personal mastery items show much connection with receptiveness to racial hostility. A good sampling of the variety of measures available in this general domain can be found in Robinson & Shaver (1973).

4. There is mounting evidence that the sense of powerlessness is not a volatile or free-floating "mere attitude": it shows reasonable stability, yet it is responsive in predictable ways to the person's experience. Some examples:

(*a*) Given the social conditions of the recent past, one might expect an overall rise in feelings of powerlessness (and distrust) in the past decade; and that result has been documented in a variety of studies (e.g. Converse 1972; House & Mason 1974; Miller, Brown & Raine 1973; Rotter 1971; Wolfe 1974). In their summary of the Detroit area studies over the period from 1953 to 1971, Duncan, Schuman & Duncan (1973:96) conclude that the sensed unresponsiveness of public officials "is really quite startling," their data reflecting " . . . a serious erosion of the citizen's confidence in the intentions of those elected to serve and govern him." A recent Harris poll (1973) reports a similarly impressive erosion (e.g. the statement "What you think doesn't count anymore" drew 37% agreement in 1966, and 61% in 1973).

This erosion took place, it should be added, in the face of an overall gain in average education, a gain which should have worked against such increased alienation. What may be even more impressive, given the stereotypes about alienated youth (as well as minorities and the poor), there is substantial evidence that the erosion in question was not strikingly associated with these special categories. As Harris (1973:40) puts it, " . . . the shadow of alienation now cuts across class lines"; and House & Mason (1974:18) concur: "Changes in alienation during the 1950s and especially in the 1960s were remarkably uniform across the entire American electorate."

(*b*) Longitudinal studies are as scarce in the alienation field as they are elsewhere; but the studies we do have reveal the considerable individual stability that one might expect, along with a predictable responsiveness to experience. Thus, Neal & Groat (1974) report a correlation of .45 for an index of powerlessness taken over the eight year span from 1963 to 1971 (using a sample of 334 married women in the Toledo area); and P. Andrisani & G. Nestel (unpublished) report correlations of .55 (for whites) and .35 (for blacks) in a nationwide study of middle-aged working men (over a two year period, 1969–1971, using an abbreviated I-E scale of the forced-choice variety). They report as well that the changes in I-E scores were significantly related to objective intervening events—e.g. to occupational earnings and advancement, or reentry into the labor force.

In a similar way, several studies have shown decreases in externality among patients who have had successful therapy experiences (Smith 1970, Gillis & Jessor 1970), and increases in powerlessness as a result of involvement in the draft lottery (MacArthur 1970) or in a political defeat (Gorman 1968). And if one considers the nuclear family as a setting in which attitudes of powerlessness or mastery are generated by the family experience, the evidence here, too, is supportive, if limited. Renshon (1974:147), for example, reports a significant gamma of .34 between parental beliefs about personal control and the independently derived scores of his undergraduate respondents; and Goodwin (1972:65) reports correlations of .20 and .43 between mother and son regarding sensed control—these correlations being, respectively, for mothers on long and short term welfare (i.e. "welfare mothers tend to transmit to their sons their own lack of confidence," p. 106). Such findings regarding an association between parents' and children's control attitudes are, however, hardly uniform (Phares 1973:19), and it is entirely likely that the connection depends upon complex and as yet undetermined effects of various child-rearing styles—e.g. dominance or pro-independence behavior by the parent (Niemi 1973). Bronfenbrenner (1972:662), however, makes the point that studies on the importance of peer group influences may be telling us that powerful parental influences are far from guaranteed: " . . . the crux of the problem is that many parents have become powerless as forces in the lives of their children."

5. The range of variables with which the attitude of powerlessness has been correlated is extensive, indeed. Many of these correlates of low mastery are not at all surprising (e.g. powerlessness goes with less political participation of the routine sort, Matthews & Prothro 1966; less planful utilization of health services, Ragan 1973). Some, however, are a little more surprising (e.g. externals seem to acknowledge failure more readily, perhaps because they have a handy self-exculpatory ideology to explain it, Lipp et al 1968), and some are even a bit strange (we are told, for example, that the mastery-oriented subject is more responsive to the disguised humor of a laboratory experiment, Lefcourt 1974). In keeping with the caveats and distinctions already reviewed, a major theme in the pattern of these correlations is specificity. Put otherwise, hypotheses that treat powerlessness as though it were a linear or encompassing phenomenon are not making some crucial distinctions and are probably doomed to disappointment. Again, some examples of this specificity:

(a) People who respond to a plea for political action (the "mobilizable" letter writers) score relatively high in perceived personal competence, but they are not particularly sanguine about the competence of interest groups or of the general public to influence political affairs (Rosneau 1974; see also Verba & Nie 1972).

(b) People with a relatively high sense of control ("internals") ought to work harder and longer (be more task persistent) than externals—but that depends on whether the internality and the instrumental activity concern positive or negative outcomes (Mischel, Zeiss & Zeiss 1974).

(c) People who are high in powerlessness tend to be less oriented to learning and achievement in a variety of settings (Bickford & Neal 1969, Brim et al 1969,

Coleman et al 1966, Holian 1972, Maimon 1970, Phares 1968), but these correlations between powerlessness and learning are regularly quite modest and they typically hold only for control-relevant information (Bullough 1967, Seeman 1967a).

(*d*) It is not very likely, on theoretical grounds, that the presence of alienation alone (whether that means powerlessness or the other varieties of alienation) will yield much prediction about the individual's readiness to support or participate in rebellious activity, and an intriguing sociological experiment (Schwartz 1973) provides evidence to that effect.

(*e*) Even the standard and almost guaranteed differentiators in attitude studies —the status variables of income, occupation, and to some extent education—cannot be counted upon to produce major differences with respect to powerlessness. This lack of differentiation by status tends to become all the more true as the indices of powerlessness capture specific arenas in which the respondent experiences low control, rather than diffuse discontents about it. One would find, therefore, that a specifically political efficacy scale (e.g. the Michigan SRC scale, or variants thereof) or the Rotter I-E scale would show modest social class differences relative to, let us say, the Srole scale (for comparisons in the matter, see for example: Finifter 1970; Fried 1973; Mizruchi 1964; Rushing 1973; Seeman 1972a, b). A related example: Schuman & Gruenberg (1970) found that relatively little variance in their efficacy index was explained by "city differences" (using black and white respondents in 15 cities), though their respondents' evaluations of city officials and services did differ by city. They conclude: "This finding is not very remarkable, but it is nonetheless important: one discovers greatest City effects where there are apt to be real city differences; where there is little reason to expect City to be relevant, it usually is not" (p. 230).

(*f*) The tendency to think that almost any improvement in life circumstances will generate a commensurate improvement in the individual's sense of control (or other alienations) is a generalist viewpoint, and it, too, has been doomed to some disappointment—e.g. improving the character of welfare payments (Department of Health, Education, and Welfare 1969) or of the housing environment (Feagin, Tilly & Williams 1972) is not a guarantee that mastery attitudes will revive (the latter authors write: " . . . the move into a better housing environment had little effect on overall sense of potency," p. 119).

(*g*) High powerlessness among black respondents is associated with antiwhite hostility (Ransford 1968; Seeman, Bishop & Grigsby 1971), but this association is sometimes very modest, indeed (Campbell 1971), and there is evidence that it is stronger for males than for females, as well as stronger for women who work than for those who do not (Crain & Weisman 1973). One interpretation, then, is that the connection is not simply an instrument effect of a generalized personality feature, but a function of the degree to which one's actual life chances are tied in a daily and direct way to the race relations issue.

It may not be immediately apparent that the specificity emphasized above carries some important implications. First, it becomes plain that the literature on alienation need not be conceived to be operating as though social behavior depends upon global and generalized personality characteristics (whether these are called "alienation" or some other name). The concern is not so much for subjective states that are presumed to carry one-to-one correspondence with behavior (e.g. achievement needs that are manifested in achievement behavior), but with response capabilities and outcomes that are bound up with the individual's expectations concerning the consequences of alternative actions in given situations. Second, and not unrelatedly, the unhappiness that has been expressed about interpretations based on constructs like alienation—see, for example, McPhail's (1971) and Snyder & Tilly's (1972) doubts about the effectiveness of relative deprivation as an explanation of violence —reflects to some extent a disease that is common to both the alienation analyst and his critic. The disease involves the notion that alienation alone, or alienation in the grand manner, can explain complex, collective, and historically situated events. In the language and perspective elaborated above, it is not intended to, though that is hardly the same as saying that the sense of powerlessness is not relevant to such events.

Meaninglessness

There is considerably less material available on this version of alienation, in part because interest in its measurement has lagged well behind the interest in powerlessness. Neal & Groat (1970) reported that their meaninglessness measure could be ordered along with measures of normlessness and powerlessness into a scalable overall measure of alienation (which then related to the family's differential efficacy in fertility control), but this scale has not been widely used by others. For the most part, investigators have depended on very rough approximations (a few, or single, items and these rarely subjected to any intensive analysis for reliability or validity).

Thus, the idea of "meaninglessness" plays a part in Middleton's (1963) alienation scale, a six-item index which is intended to canvas each of the varieties of alienation reviewed here (the item for meaninglessness reads: "Things have become so complicated in the world today that I really don't understand just what is going on"). A similar item is contained in the four-item Michigan political efficacy scale ("Sometimes politics and government are so complicated that a person like me can't really understand what's going on"). Though Middleton reported that five of his six items formed a usable Guttman scale (the item for "cultural estrangement" excluded), it seems highly unlikely that this patterning of the varieties of alienation, i.e. this coherence of meaninglessness with powerlessness and with the other alienations, holds over time and over other samples (Converse 1972, Balch 1974, House and Mason 1974, Seeman 1972b).

Coordinate as they may seem, it is possible to separate the idea of powerlessness from that of meaninglessness, even though that separation has not been well accomplished in the empirical work thus far. What is intended by "meaninglessness" varies a good deal, of course, depending upon the concrete measurement that is employed. The well-known Srole anomia scale has a strong meaninglessness component (and a powerlessness component, too, in its item concerning the unresponsiveness of public officials), insofar as one of its hypothesized elements is the individual's perception of the social order as fickle and unpredictable, and a related element involves the individual's sense of the meaninglessness of life itself (item: "It's hardly fair to bring children into the world with the way things look for the future," Srole 1956; see also Miller 1970). In the same way, Dean's (1961) normlessness scale contains elements of meaninglessness, the content being closer to the sense of existential futility or generalized unhappiness than to the comprehensibility of events per se (item: "I often wonder what the meaning of life really is").

These skimpy (and in many ways, cloudy) efforts directed toward empirical treatment of the meaninglessness brand of alienation ought to be surprising, given the importance that is attached to variations on that idea in the sociological literature. That these frequent usages of meaninglessness are typically not cast directly as discussions of "alienation" does not alter the affinity they have with the domain of alienation under discussion here. In the field of collective behavior, for example, the "search for meaning" has played a key role for a long time in interpretations of social movement membership (Cantril 1941, Hoffer 1951), and in the two most prominent contemporary models of collective behavior, by Smelser (1963) and Turner & Killian (1972), that idea remains a modified but central ingredient in the analysis. For Smelser, a key feature is the development of "generalized beliefs" of particular kinds (hostile, hysterical, etc), whose function is to reinterpret the given situation for its participants; for Turner and Killian, a key feature is the development of "emergent norms" that provide a new definition of the actor's circumstances and alternatives. These are, it would seem, simply special cases (in a collective behavior context) of the general process of creating a "definition of the situation" (McHugh 1968, Ball-Rokeach 1973)—i.e. the process of generating social meanings for behavior-in-situations; and, often enough, the assumption is that the actor is caught in a substantially "meaningless" setting whose ambiguity, complexity, and unstructuredness he must somehow manage to make comprehensible for action (see also Becker 1967, Klapp 1972 on "meaning-seeking movements"; and Gusfield 1973 on utopian myths).

In addition to this constant sociological interest in the definition of the situation, and the application of that idea to collective behavior, the idea of meaningless is prominent in another way; namely, in the Durkheimian legacy concerning "anomic" conditions. Though it is now customary (following Merton 1957) to equate this concept with deviant motivation or behavior (with "normlessness"; see below), the unclarity of the norms can be conceptually distinguished from their force; and it is the former—not deviance, but meaninglessness—that frequently captures the analytical interest. This is true both in standard sociological analysis —as in Parsons' (1968) commentary on Durkheim, where anomie is seen as a problem of uncertainty rather than as a problem of unavailable means to established goals—and in the newer ethnomethodological studies (especially as they focus on the manufacture and repair of disorder in social interaction, Garfinkel 1967).

These remarks merely recall that there are more serious stakes in the idea of meaninglessness than we perhaps acknowledge; yet it remains true that those with an avowed interest in alienation have made very little progress in illuminating the dynamics of this variety of alienation. Perhaps the most promising direct conceptual use of the idea of meaninglessness can be found in Allardt's treatment (1972; for an interpretation of Allardt's model, see Israel 1971: 226–33) in which the idea of uncertainty with regard, respectively, to values, norms, role-expectations, and definitions of the situation, identifies the main varieties of alienation. His treatment represents one of the recent efforts to repair the fact that the varieties of alienation treated here constitute simply a set of categories whose theoretical relation remains unspecified.

Normlessness

The transition from meaninglessness to normlessness seems natural enough, given that both of these ideas have roots in the notion of "anomie." It is customary, of course, to insist that anomie, properly defined, is a "structural" fact. It is a property of the social system and not of individuals, that property being identified as the condition in which the norms have lost their regulatory power; hence, anarchy, disorder, instability, excessive competition, and individualism. But two things need to be said: (*a*) consistent with our interest in alienation as a social-psychological phenomenon, normlessness is here conceived from the individual point of view— it refers to expectancies or commitments concerning the observance of established norms for behavior; and (*b*) the structural definition, in any case, remains more a hope (or a guiding orientation) than an empirical accomplishment, since the struggle to develop suitable group-level indicators of anomie has not been crowned with notable success.

Often, indeed, it seems that "structural" anomie simply means a widespread occurrence of individual "disrespect" for the norms (Johnson 1960), a view which is in no way incongruent with the social-psychological one. Some propose to use not attitudes (of disrespect or otherwise) but behavior rates as indicators of structural anomie (e.g. rates of deviance, family instability, collective behavior, or the like; Yinger 1973), one difficulty being that these behaviors are often precisely what the concept of anomie is intended to explain (they are consequences to be predicted, not indicators). And still others (Jessor et al 1968) propose an inherently nonindividual indicator of structural anomie, namely the degree of consensus within the community (or subunit) concerning the behavior that is prescribed, proscribed, or permitted to members. Though these perceptions of group norms are individual responses, the index of anomie rests on the degree of agreement among the respondents: high variance reflects discordant expectations, hence high anomie. The Jessor procedure has not been extensively used, but it is a promising group-oriented index of normlessness, as their own work shows—especially in view of the fact that their study of drinking behavior in a tri-ethnic community (Anglo, Spanish, and Indian) embedded the anomie index in a theoretical framework borrowing heavily from both psychological theory (social learning) and sociological theory (the Mertonian means-ends disjunction).

For the most part, however, despite the brave talk and editorials concerning structure, the measurement of normlessness has relied heavily upon attitude scales of one kind or another. The most popular, of course, has been the Srole (1956) anomia scale, which has the advantage of being short (five items) and (at least with some samples) scalable in the Guttman sense. On the other hand, its mixture of alienative elements (powerlessness and meaninglessness, among others), along with its strong "unhappiness" component, means that it is hardly a clear index of normlessness in any sharply distinguishable sense—certainly not in the sense of expectancies or commitments to deviant means. Still, it ought to be recognized that the Srole scale, and modifications of it, have dominated the literature on normlessness. In principle, there is little difference between the Srole scale and sundry variations on the same theme: e.g. Dean's (1961) normlessness scale (item: "Everything is relative and there just aren't any definite rules to live by"); or McClosky & Schaar's (1965) measure of "anomy" (item: "People were better off in the old days when everyone knew just how he was expected to act"); or, for that matter, similar items under the different names of "personal morale" (Kornhauser 1965), "misanthropy" (Rosenberg 1956), "cynicism" (Lyons 1970), or "alienation" when it is used as it is in the Jessor (1968) work where an alienation index (as distinct from the anomie index described above) is presented and turns out to be quite Srole-like in its content.

All of these scales, whatever their names, are probably best conceived as measures of generalized discontent ("alienation" in some global sense) rather than as indices of any specifiable dimension like normlessness. On the whole, the Srole scale and its cousins show this general character via the correlational pattern they exhibit— e.g. the relatively high associations with education and other social class factors (Nelson 1968, Bullough 1969, Mizruchi 1964, Reimanis 1974). Whatever its limitations as a measure of normlessness (see, for example, Carr 1971), the Srole scale (and its counterparts named above) has provided some valuable clues concerning both expected relationships (e.g the connection between anomie and prejudice, Lutterman & Middleton 1970), and some unexpected ones. The latter, as usual, tend to be more interesting: for example, (a) Wilson's (1971) showing that inner-city black ghetto residents were *less* anomic than residents in surrounding low income neighborhoods undergoing racial transition; (b) Schwartz's (1973) showing that a political alienation measure oriented to attitudes about municipal government does not correlate highly with the generalized Srole items (the correlation was .13; Schwartz's conclusion: " . . . political alienation tends to be more directly associated with evaluations of the polity than with simple extrapolations from social dissatisfactions," p. 47); or (c) Fischer's (1973) showing, through secondary analysis of three large surveys, that the supposed impact of urban living on anomie-like attitudes is, in fact, minimal.

On the whole, it seems more useful to implement less diffuse versions of individual normlessness; and some promising efforts along this line have been made. Neal & Groat's work (1970, 1975) has consistently applied an index of normlessness which taps the expectancy that socially unapproved behavior is necessary for goal attainment; and it is a measure which exhibits both a useful independence of conceptually different alienations and some consistent associations, over various samples, with fertility patterns.

As Groat and Neal note, their measure also has some affinity with the notion of distrust, and that is a second direction in which the normlessness idea has been carried of late. It was noted earlier that the dimension of efficacy (input) has been distinguished from the notion of political trust (output), and this is especially so in the recent work on political attitudes. Finifter's (1970) two dimensions of political alienation are labelled, respectively, "political powerlessness" and "perceived political normlessness," the latter having a substantial trust component (item: "All candidates sound good in their speeches, but you can never tell what they will do after they are elected"). A similar distinction (oriented toward trust and efficacy with respect to the Federal government) has been incorporated in the Michigan studies and has helped to document the recent increase in disaffection nationally (Miller, Brown & Raine 1973; Converse 1972).

A more general (less specific to politics) measure of interpersonal trust has also been developed, and applied in a series of laboratory and field studies (Rotter 1971). Rotter's test consists of 25 trust items and 15 filler items, the scale intending to implement a view of trust as "an expectancy held by an individual or group that the word, promise, verbal or written statement of another individual or group can be relied on" (p. 344). Rotter and his colleagues have found that the scale yields meaningful discriminations: it correlates with sociometric ratings by peers concerning trustworthiness, with trusting behavior in laboratory situations, with trusting views of social events (e.g. attitudes concerning the conspiracy element in the Warren Commission report on the Kennedy assassination), and it helps to document again the significant decline in trust, as well as efficacy, that has occurred in the U.S. over the recent past (Hochreich & Rotter, 1970).

Finally, just as it is necessary to distinguish personal efficacy from politically oriented efficacy (as we have seen, they operate rather differently), it is also the case that political trust and interpersonal trust need to be distinguished. In Aberbach's (1974) analysis of the 1968 election, for example, interpersonal distrust showed very little correlation with casting a vote for George Wallace ($r = .12$ in a southern white sample), but political distrust (and to a lesser extent, political inefficacy) predicted the Wallace vote in considerably greater degree ($r = .42$). The importance of results such as these is that they counter the tendency to assume that trust becomes a more or less unitary personality feature, a thread which binds attitudes toward oneself, toward others, and toward the polity into a generally positive (or negative) orientation. To be sure, efficacy and trust may exhibit some empirical connection; Rotter (1971), for example, reports correlations in the .30s for four large samples. Still, though the conceptual distinctions among efficacy and trust dimensions may be perhaps easier to make than are the empirical implementations, the evidence strongly urges that they are distinctions worth making.

Self-Estrangement

In one sense, this version of alienation is more like the master theme in alienation studies than simply a variety of it, hence the literature that one could encompass under this rubric—alienation taken as the failure of self-realization—is almost inexhaustible. Analysts from Marx to Sartre have sought to identify the ways in which men in society come to experience and adopt inauthentic, self-estranged life styles (O'Neill 1972). This commonality of general focus, however, has hardly made for any substantial coherence in the treatment of self-estrangement. Sometimes it refers to the failure to realize one's human potential (Marcuse 1964), sometimes simply to the individual's level of self-esteem or to a sensed discrepancy between one's preferred qualities and realized qualities (Coopersmith 1967), sometimes to repressed or distorted psychopathologies (Laing & Esterson 1965) or to the "loss of identity" (Rainwater 1970), sometimes to one or another form of "bad faith" with oneself (Sartre 1948), and sometimes to behavior that is more or less ritualized or stereotyped (Seeman 1966), or relatedly, to action which is characterized by a disjunction between behavior and affect (Johnson 1973).

Each of these approaches has its own advantages, its own large troubles and small triumphs. Some of the triumphs come by way of evidence that goes contrary to popular conceptions—e.g. the recent demonstration by Rosenberg & Simmons (1972) that black children do not have significantly lower self-esteem than white children (see also Baughman 1971, Zirkel 1971, Zirkel & Moses 1971). But since this wide range of approaches can neither be covered nor clarified here (and certainly not legislated by definition), our concentration is on the version of self-estrangement proposed earlier—namely, the individual's engagement in activities that are not rewarding in themselves. That meaning of self-estrangement was derived originally (Seeman 1959) from the Marxian depiction of work which has become an instrumentalized means rather than a creative end in itself, though Schacht (1970), among others, has advanced objections to this "subjectivized" derivation from the Marxian view. It ought to be signalled, however, that this construction of self-estrangement (with its emphasis on instrumentalized activity) bears an important resemblance to two aspects of interaction that are regularly identified as alienated styles: (a) complaints are often advanced concerning the treatment of others instrumentally, as objects or abstract means rather than intrinsically as "human" or "whole" persons, such instrumental treatment being one of the signs of alienation; and (b) there is considerable talk about succumbing to the "reification" process, meaning essentially to a distortion of experience wherein interaction and institutions are transformed into objects and commodities—into "things" (rather than experienced in their intrinsic character as socially created relationships). The key point is that these two processes (often called "depersonalization" and "reification") are regularly decried as forms of alienation; but it is not so regularly noted that they have an affinity with the notion of self-estrangement under review here.

It is in the area of work experience that the idea of self-estrangement as nonintrinsic engagement has been most extensively applied (though, of course, that specific language need not figure in the analysis). Concern about the problem of alienated labor has intensified in the recent past, that concern being nicely exemplified in the volume titled *Work in America* (an action-oriented report to the Department of Health, Education and Welfare, 1972), and in the reinspired movement looking toward a radical redesigning of the job and the workplace (Hulin & Blood 1968, Davis & Taylor 1972, Walton, 1972). These newer studies build, of course, on some well-known earlier work that incorporates the idea of intrinsic engagement as an essential feature of acceptable work (e.g. Blauner 1964, Turner & Lawrence 1965, Herzberg 1966, Wilensky 1964). What they tend to share is the conviction that the workplace must provide the worker with (a) tasks that are more self-fulfilling and self-respecting, and (b) a greater latitude for exercising personal control over the work itself. They also tend to share the conviction that these values concerning jobs are becoming more widespread and more intensely held (especially among the younger workers, Aronowitz 1973), and that the absence of these qualities in so important a domain as work has very serious consequences—i.e. that the worker's feelings of disrespect and impotence on the job generalize to (infect, one might say) his self-conception as a whole, his family life, his social experience in the neighborhood, his political participation, and the like (Sheppard & Herrick 1972).

Unhappily, the methods used to make the case for these important propositions are not so persuasive as to let the matter rest, despite any personal commitments one might share respecting the envisioned industrial democracy and work improvement. For example, one of the most engrossing of these recent examinations of attitudes toward work is the volume by Sennett & Cobb (1972) entitled *The Hidden Injuries of Class,* based on 150 in-depth interviews of workers. The volume exhibits the themes described above: there is considerable emphasis on the sense of low control at work, on the denial of self-respect on the job, on the importance of intrinsic satisfaction, and on symbolic rather than material rewards. Yet though the analysis is reasonable and sophisticated, nagging doubts remain concerning how much of that analysis is, so to speak, imposed from without via subtle interpretation —to what degree the profound and encompassing hurts described are, indeed, the workers' troubles. In a different way, but generating similar doubts, it is not rare in this literature to find that the understandable commitment to more humanized work clouds the analyst's vision concerning the requirements of empirical demonstration (both *Work in America* and the Sheppard-Herrick volume share such overcommitment, in my judgment).

It may be that a sizable share of the disagreement arises from the failure to maintain with care some of the necessary distinctions. The idea of alienated labor (self-estrangement in work) identifies two potential sources of trouble, but they are discriminable troubles: (*a*) the absence of intrinsic fulfillment in work, and (*b*) the lack of control at work. It may well be, as Singer (1970) has insisted, that discontent generated in the workplace was crucial in the French explosion of May 1968, but the discontent need not have been so much a matter of fulfillment denied but of control denied (Seeman 1972b). In their study of British workers, Goldthorpe and colleagues (1968) argued that expectations concerning intrinsic rewards were not as important as economic goals in workers' attachment to the job, and that the instrumental (in our terms, alienated) attitude appeared to function reasonably well, on the whole. The subsequent bitter strike at Luton has been cited as counter evidence; but, again, it is not at all clear to what degree intrinsic work vs control aspirations were involved. In the same way, recent strikes at Lordstown (Ohio) and Fiat (Italy), among others, have been cited as evidence for the increasing tilt toward intrinsic demands with respect to work, but it is no more clear in those cases to what degree demands regarding greater control play a primary part. Nor does that tilt gain support from the Detroit longitudinal data (Duncan, Schuman & Duncan 1973:74), from which the authors draw the "inescapable" conclusion that " . . . the instrumental, or even hedonistic, values suggested by high income and short working hours, are gaining at the expense of the values intrinsic to work, most notably the idea that doing the job in itself gives one a sense of accomplishment." It seems, however, an exaggeration to say that "there is not one shred of evidence for the alleged turn from material rewards" (Drucker 1973:90); but it is certainly true that the case has not been well made and that intrinsic rewards and control demands have been regularly confused.

Part of the problem, of course, lies in the fact that these two job features are more difficult to separate empirically than conceptually [DeCharms (1968:328) proposes that in fact the two are intimately tied: to experience personal causation is to be intrinsically motivated]. Thus, in one of the more detailed and careful investigations of the generalization of work effects, Kohn & Schooler (1973) argue that "occupational self-direction," which includes the closeness of supervision, routinization of work, and the complexity of it, is an important influence on self-esteem, leisure use, and other elements of psychological functioning. But there is some mixture here, too, of external control (the supervisor's) and the work itself (its routine or complex character). In any event, two points concerning the demonstration are noteworthy: (a) the relationships obtained are consistent but not powerful by any means, and (b) there is little evidence for the popular notion that "men turn their occupational frustrations loose on the nonoccupational world or try to find compensation in nonoccupational realities for occupational lacks and grievances" (p. 117). In short (and again), the generalization is quite limited.

If the emphasis is on the control element, as it directly is, for example, in Pearlin's (1962) definition of work alienation in a hospital setting, work alienation might more properly be seen as another aspect of the powerlessness component of alienation, since it becomes simply a question of one more domain in which mastery or lack of it is manifested. Thus, the "workers' control" movement (in Yugoslavia, for example), frequently identified with the problem of alienated labor, concentrates on effecting an increased degree of worker management of the enterprise rather than on substantial redirection of the character of the work itself (Hunnuis, Garson & Case 1973). To the degree that this is so, the movement is directed at the problem of powerlessness, is no guarantee of improvement in the workers' attitudes about the nature of the work itself or about life outside the plant (Obradovic 1970, Whitehorn 1974), and is open to the charge that the modest transformation involved simply encourages the workers "to share in their own exploitation" (Aronowitz 1973:426; see also Kaplan, Tausky & Bolaria 1969; Strauss & Rosenstein 1970). The alternative argument is that changes encouraging within-plant decision making are tied to improvement in job characteristics and are regularly accompanied by positive effects on the workers' participation in community-wide affairs, as well as on productivity itself (Department of Health, Education and Welfare 1972:9).

These comments are in no way intended to question the fact that different work settings are associated with different levels of work alienation. As one would surely expect, more highly skilled and specialized workers reflect these advantages in lower alienation scores, i.e. their greater sense of mastery and creative autonomy (Blauner 1964; Shepard 1969, 1973; Fried 1973). Nor is there an intention to question that the improvement of the quality of worklife, either through democratization or job enrichment, is desirable in itself (for a comprehensive bibliography on these matters, see Taylor 1973, and for an earlier review, from the perspective of industrial psychology, see Smith & Cranny 1968). What is at issue is the extent of generalization of the worker's experience, from the job proper to the extra-job milieu. Given the tendency to assume that work is of primary importance in defining the self and in connecting the individual with the larger society, and given the centrality of work in the Marxian sources on alienation, it seems surprising how limited the demonstration has actually been concerning this purported generalization of alienated labor. As late as 1973, Kohn & Schooler (1973) could write about their test of the thesis that occupational experience has a substantial impact on men's psychological functioning (which is, after all, simply a variant of the generalization hypothesis concerning the impact of work experience) that this thesis " . . . has never to our knowledge been empirically appraised" (p. 97).

However, a number of measures looking in that direction have been developed as indices of work alienation. The names and conceptions vary, of course, but they are all variants of the self-estrangement theme applied to work. Dubin (1956) asks whether work is a "central life interest"; Wilensky (1964) asks whether the worker's "prized self-image" is fulfilled at the workplace; Seeman (1967b) and Turner & Lawrence (1965), in their somewhat different ways, ask whether the worker experiences variety, creativity, responsibility, and autonomy on the job, as does Herzberg (1968), for whom these intrinsic motivators are sharply distinguished from the "hygiene" factors (such as fringe benefits and working conditions); and Miller (1967) asks basically about the professional's "pride in work." On the whole, what these measures (and others like them; see Featherman 1971) tend to show is not so much that generalization to non-job responses occurs, but that: (*a*) within limits (see, for example, Form 1972, 1973), given work settings produce the expected worker attitudes (highly bureaucratic work environments yield higher work alienation; mechanized workers are more alienated than craft workers; etc; Parker 1971, Cotgrove 1972); and (*b*) work alienation conceived as intrinsic engagement is not the same thing as job satisfaction, partly because satisfaction with the job stems from such a variety of nonintrinsic factors (including pay, security, and the like; cf Crozier 1971; Deci 1972a,; Kahn 1972; Kaplan & Tausky 1972).

The caution reflected here concerning the encompassing importance of alienated work (what Kaufman, 1965, called the Marxian principle of "the sufficiency of alienated labor" as the basic source of assorted other troubles in capitalist society) should be matched by a caution on the other side. Weakness in demonstrating that principle does not add up to the conclusion that work itself is no problem or that efforts toward improving the quality of worklife are of minor importance. The evidence, including the statistics on absenteeism, strikes, vandalism, and the like (Walton 1972; but note that even here there are qualifications concerning the supposed increment in these troubles; see Wool 1973), is clear enough that a great many people abhor what they do, would change jobs if they could, are hostile to the agents of their unhappiness (supervisor, boss, or co-worker), and feel envious of the relative job advancement of others (Terkel 1974). The evidence of the moment may not tell us that improving worklife will bring an assortment of other democratic virtues in its train, but that hardly means that the improvement is unimportant.

Social Isolation

It is no accident that one of the rallying points in recent times has been expressed in the slogan "community control," for that phrase captures two of the central themes identified with alienation: the claim to control (reviewed above), and the quest for community. Here, again, the potential literature for review is extensive, partly because the meanings assigned to the idea of community are so inclusively vague. They include: (*a*) notions of existential (or socially generated) loneliness ("It is fearful to know that one has been born, for the first lesson is loneliness;" McWilliams 1973:623); (*b*) the sense of identity with a specifiable collectivity [what Rossi (1972:90–92) calls the "commensalistic" social psychological version of community, as against the "symbiotic" and basically ecological version]; (*c*) consensual, normatively integrated behavior, or lack of it—an idea that comes closer, perhaps, to the "normlessness" brand of alienation discussed above [see, for example, Wilson's (1968:27) discussion of the failure of community, meaning not the need for belonging but " . . . a desire for the observance of standards of right and seemly conduct" in public places; (*d*) the availability of neighboring activities, voluntary associations, and friendship networks (Laumann 1973); or (*e*) acceptance or rejection on the basis of the individual's membership in minority-type subgroups (the black, aged, radical, gay, etc).

Like the idea of alienation itself, the idea of community comes to stand for the full collection of troubles (the unity of miseries) that modern society supposedly generates—not simply loneliness and social isolation, but also normlessness (deviance), self-estrangement (detachment from, and instrumental use of, others), and cultural estrangement (loss of common values). Something like such a full complement of troubles is invoked, for example, in Slater's (1970) analysis of "the pursuit of loneliness" in American society. Without necessarily adopting the concept of mass society, many of these broad scale treatments of community make use of one or another version of that idea. The recognizable themes, for example, of bureaucratization, increase in scale, and atomization of relations, play an important part in the fascinating historical account by Barber (1974) depicting "the death of communal liberty" in a Swiss mountain canton. The fascination lies in Barber's detailing of a cantonal history in which the experience of political control and of community were inseparable, allowing the members to evade the "lonely, anxious, competitive emancipation" that characterized other Western societies, and to evade until recently "the social pathologies of alienation" (p. 137). In its smaller scale way, the extensive literature on the once active crisis in the universities heavily employed the same images, the university being seen as simply one more mass society in miniature (for a variety of views on these matters, see Wallerstein & Starr 1971, Westby & Braungart 1970).

These comprehensive and pessimistic analyses persist, however, in the face of studies that specify and qualify by a good deal this pervasive gloom regarding the lack of community. Some examples:

1. In a series of papers based on a study of the network of primary ties among some 800 respondents in Toronto, Wellman (1973:1) "found little to substantiate

the 'myth of the lonely urbanites.' " Though this evidence concerning the persistence of primary ties is hardly new (Greer 1962, Sussman 1972), it is regularly forgotten in the clamor concerning social isolation in the metropolis, as is the substantial evidence concerning neighborliness and networks in urban working class settings (Fried 1973).

2. A case can be made, and has been elegantly made by Granovetter (1973), concerning "the strength of weak ties." Kin and intimates aside, a loosely knit network of mere acquaintances serves a very positive function in support and communication (e.g. getting, keeping, and improving one's job). Put in another way, Milgram and colleagues (Milgram 1967, Travers & Milgram 1969, Korte & Milgram 1970) have documented the relatively high cohesiveness of communication networks in the mass society—that, in truth, "it's a small world."

3. Despite the justified objections that have been mustered concerning the multiversity, there is a good deal of evidence to suggest that the activists' complaints about intra-university matters (including specifically the complaints about loneliness and low community) were not very strongly correlated with participation in the demonstrations and disorders of the late 1960s (Gales 1966, Keniston 1967, Kirby 1971). As Touraine (1974) has well argued, the problems went deeper than that, centering around broader political issues in the society at large and most particularly on the role of the university's socio-technical knowledge in modern society. All this has relatively little to do with the university as a miniature mass society, and, it might be added, not as much to do with the personality characteristics of activists as American researchers seem to have thought, given their concentration on that issue (see, for example, Block, Haan & Smith 1969, 1973, Whittaker & Watts 1969).

4. If we mean by social isolation the absence of membership or friendship (i.e. organizational involvement, integration in an occupational community, or a network of other friends), the evidence is not at all persuasive that these types of social engagement are either (a) in short supply, or (b) of very great significance in producing the alienative consequences often attributed to them. In his recent intensive study of "the bonds of pluralism," Laumann (1973:128) comments that "a substantial majority of urban white men at every class level are involved in interlocking networks" (see also Bell & Held 1969, Curtis 1971, Portes 1971, Kasarda & Janowitz 1974). In his related analysis, Cutler (1973) documents both a relatively high level of organizational participation and minimal effects of membership or lack of it (see also Fischer 1973). Similar inconsequential differences attached to the presence or absence of occupational community have been reported as well (e.g. Form 1972, Seeman, Bishop & Grigsby 1971, for a related study of "black belonging" to organizations, see Ross & Wheeler 1971).

5. What Riesman (1969) calls the "contemporary cult of intimacy" is expressed in many ways: in the pressure for small-group learning experiences within the university, in the popularity of encounter groups, and in the resurgence of interest in communes. Kantor (1973:xi) begins her collection of papers on communes with the remark "Community may be the word of the decade," but it is important to recognize that it is not simply the sense of belonging that is at issue for the participants. Most intentional communities are very mixed expressions of the alienation

motif, capturing the mixture described above in the idea of community itself. There is a strong counter-culture strain; an emphasis on meaningful, intrinsically engaging work; on interpersonal relations that are not instrumental [the "nonmanipulative, immediately involved attitude," says Zablocki (1971) in describing the Bruderhof]; and a concern for re-establishing the sense of individual freedom and control. Given the customary gloom in depicting our situation on these matters, and the promise of the commune on so many counts, the surprise may lie in how few persons are called and how few communes succeed (Pitts 1973).

6. The most striking instances of urban isolation (the Kitty Genovese case, involving passively accepted murder in the city streets, is the favorite citation) have generated their own mystique about urban disengagement; and they have generated as well a series of studies on bystander assistance and urban-town differences in responsiveness (Latané & Darley 1968, Milgram 1970). In commenting on these studies, Milgram remarks that " . . . the absolute level of cooperativeness for urban subjects was found to be quite high, and does not accord with the stereotype of the urbanite as aloof, self-centered and unwilling to help strangers" (p. 1465).

These remarks are not intended to dismiss the importance of social isolation, which is certainly a serious problem for some, the aged, for example (Rosow 1967, Tunstal 1967), or a skid row inhabitant (Caplow, Bahr & Sternberg 1968). The aim is to place the matter in some perspective, and perhaps above all to highlight the fact that the sense of loneliness or belonging is only one aspect of social isolation. Bronfenbrenner (1972:663) puts a different cast on the problem in arguing that the fundamental difficulty lies in the increasing isolation of children from meaningful adult relationships: working mothers, child care specialists, the separation of residence and work, and a host of other "manifestations of progress" operate to decrease the meaningful contact between children and adults. His portrait of breakdown may be overdrawn; in many ways, the recent detailed study in London by Young & Wilmott (1973) on *The Symmetrical Family* is more sanguine on many of the points raised by Bronfenbrenner. But the argument has special merit in focusing attention on a more profound meaning of social isolation than is customarily invoked, and by the same token one that is considerably more crucial and difficult to document (though, interestingly enough, relevant evidence is to be found in the literature on urban population density, Mitchell 1971, Galle & Gove 1974; and on modernization, Inkeles & Smith 1970).

Cultural Estrangement

In a not very well known historical analysis of cultural estrangement, Regin (1969:47) writes that "alienation is the predicament of unresolved alternatives," which is hardly a customary conception, but can be taken as a way of highlighting the value conflict and counter-culture element in the idea of alienation. The rejection of the basic alternatives available in American culture, and the uncommitted withdrawal that went with that rejection, were well described by Keniston (1960) in a work which seemed strangely unprophetic when the quiet of the early 1960s was followed by activism. In his later work, Keniston (1968) analyzed the newer breed of "young radicals," discerning a considerable difference in their alienation. Most particularly, he was impressed by the radical's acceptance of the basic "traditional and creedal American values" (p. 301), an acceptance which cast doubt for Keniston on the very applicability in this instance of the idea of alienation. This fundamental allegiance has been documented by others as well—e.g. in the Yankelovich (1972) survey which found widespread disillusionment with major institutions (with "the system") but basic congruence in social and political values between college youth and their parents.

Still, the title chosen for Friedenberg's (1971) edited volume of essays, *The Anti-American Generation,* has its point even if it is a bit exaggerated. There is a sense in which the uncommitted and the militant, whatever the difference in the source of their alienation or in its expression, share a deep rejection of the values commonly identified with American life. The cultural estrangement of activist youth may not have carried with it the same personal sense of powerlessness, of social disengagement, or of normlessness that typified Keniston's uncommitted or the young bohemians described in excellent detail by Mills (1973). But then, there is no special reason, if the notion of unity is abandoned at the outset, why these dimensions must cluster together to warrant the label alienation, nor any special reason to fail to observe the commonality that Mills' "outsiders" and Keniston's "uncommitted" shared with the activists—namely, a profound rejection of central features in American life having to do with the meaningfulness of work and of economic goals generally, the use of time and leisure, and the significance of expressiveness and spontaneity.

It has never been easy, of course, to distinguish genuine cultural revolt from superficial differences. The outward trappings of change (as revealed in dress, music, and the like) can be treated as important insignia (Reich 1971) or dismissed as just one more "product and commodity orientation . . . a political behaviorism which looks no better when adopted by the left than when employed by orthodoxy" (McWilliams 1973:621). It seems clear, however, that cultural estrangement in a much more fundamental sense characterized a variety of youth movements, activist or not; and that the cultural revolt, superficial in some respects, nevertheless has played an important part in recent social movements [see, for example, Touraine's (1971) description of the Events of May in Paris].

Unfortunately, those who are concerned with the empirical analysis of alienation have not been terribly helpful in unraveling the subtleties concerning cultural estrangement, partly because of the limited attention that has been given to the measurement of it. One of the earliest efforts in this direction was the scale developed by Nettler (1957), which nicely fits the conception of cultural estrangement adopted here (i.e. the individual's denial of commitment to established cultural values). But his measure has not been used with anything like the abandon of (say) the Srole scale or Rotter's I-E scale, and it certainly has serious limitations: it shows its age, and it does not tap the kind of profound estrangement that the youth movements displayed. Nor do many of the socalled political alienation measures tap cultural estrangement in this profound sense: they are indices of political cynicism, distrust, or normlessness, but not of value estrangement. Not surprisingly, therefore, in one of the most recent uses of Nettler's scale, Schwartz (1973:53) reports finding virtually no relation between cultural estrangement and a scale measuring political alienation. Middleton (1963) too, it may be recalled, found that cultural estrangement did not cohere with the other brands of alienation included in his index (see also Taviss 1969, and Knutson 1974).

Two somewhat more complex approaches to the matter should be mentioned, though they are more a matter of promise than of performance at this juncture. In a paper on "The Silent Revolution in Europe," Inglehart (1971) develops an empirically based typology of value priorities, and seeks to demonstrate (by way of survey data obtained in six European countries) that: (*a*) the trend is away from the more traditional "acquisitive" values and toward "post-bourgeois" values (meaning an emphasis on free expression and broad scale participation in political decisions); and (*b*) the individual's adoption of "post-bourgeois" values is correlated with support for a new political order in Europe (i.e. support for student demonstrations and for European integration).

The second noteworthy effort is by Kelman (1969), whose interest lies in examining the nature and correlates of "national involvement." Kelman identifies two sources of loyalty (sentimental and instrumental) and three means of integration (ideological, role, and normative means). An early effort to apply this scheme has been reported (Delamater, Katz & Kelman 1969), but for the moment it is not so much the product but the conception that is of special interest. What the conception shows is a clear affinity with the dimensions of alienation under review here: ideological integration is akin to the dimension of cultural estrangement in that it refers to those who share the values on which the nation is based; while normative integration refers to the individual's "unquestioned adherence to its rules" (i.e. the absence of "normlessness" in the language presented above).

SOME CONTINUING CONCERNS

If the above represents a fair summary of the recent thrust of alienation studies, it barely begins to reflect the thunder and volume of debate. Much of that debate (e.g. the disagreement about the early and the late Marx) is not directly relevant here; but some of it is of considerable importance, and among the more critical, I would cite the following:

1. There are those who find the connection between the classical notion of alienation and the empiricized versions discussed here too tenuous [thus Israel (1971:259) remarks: "I find it difficult to understand why one defines alienation as powerlessness, normlessness, meaninglessness, etc"]. Since this chasm between the term's philosophic origins and its empirical use is no mirage, it is worthwhile examining how a reconciliation can be made, Fischer's (1974) effort in this regard being among the more forthright and sensible. He comes to the conclusion (definition) that "alienation is the state in which the actor fails to perceive a positive interdependence between himself and social relationships or other objectifications" (p. 18). Insofar as the idea of "mutual control" is central to this definition, its interesting features are that (*a*) it has a close affinity, indeed, to much that is discussed in the classical literature (including Israel's discussion of "reification"; and Lukacs' as well, 1971,

especially pp. 86–87); and (*b*) Fischer argues that most of the versions of alienation discussed above (the exception being normlessness-anomie) would comfortably fit under the idea of alienation so defined [see also Archibald's (1974) treatment of the empirical relevance of Marx's theory of alienation].

2. The subjectivist cast of the bulk of the empirical work on alienation draws considerable fire (e.g. Plasek 1974). The heart of the issue, however, is that the objectivism that is espoused involves two further features: (*a*) the explicit union of descriptive and prescriptive interests, and (*b*) unexplicit assumptions about the connection between objective alienation and its subjective counterpart. On the first of these, the marriage of is and ought, Schacht's (1970:252) caution is very well taken: " . . . it is hard to imagine a situation more conducive to confusion than one in which the term is allowed to function in both ways." On the second issue, the meshing of objective and subjective accounts, there is considerable ambivalence among the structuralists as to whether the objective societal condition of alienation has (to use Lukacs' phrase) the "inexorable consequence of the subjective marks of an internal alienation" (1971:xxiv).

The connection between circumstances and sentiments of alienation remains a substantial empirical problem (see, for example, Gurr 1970, Rushing 1972, Coleman 1973, Gutmann 1973). Often enough, it is one that is addressed by those who do not use the word "alienation," but who speak of the matter nonetheless. An example is found in Barker & Schoggen's (1973) finely detailed study of "Midwest" (Oskaloosa, Kansas) and a counterpart in Britain ("Yoredale"; Leyburn). They examine (among other things) the psychological consequences of the greater local autonomy found in "Midwest," arguing that the objective powerfulness of Midwest's citizens is (*a*) reflected in their sense of importance and accomplishment (the "Dalesmen are more apathetic toward those aspects of the town's habitat they disapprove of", p. 402), and (*b*) this relative powerfulness carries the cost in "Midwest" of greater tension and insecurity.

3. Researchers on the psychological side have shifted their interest from cognitive dissonance to attribution theory, and though the students of alienation have not given much attention to this development, they would do well to do so for several reasons. First, as in the work on alienation, in these psychological studies the process of attributing characteristics (of causality, ambiguity, reciprocity, state of mind, etc) to persons and structures is the central topic [on powerlessness and mastery, for example, see Steiner's (1970) review of "perceived freedom"]. Second, considerable primacy is accorded to distinctions very much like those involved in the alienation work—e.g. internal vs external causality, or self vs other attributions. This literature has been developed and surveyed in a masterful way by Kelley (1973) and Jones et al (1972).

4. Alienation studies have remained entirely too dependent upon what is basically the "quick fix"—one-shot survey results, with inadequate measures (one or two items is not rare), and with aspirations that do not match the realized gain (e.g. stressing the hardly new distinction between general alienation measures and context-specific ones, Burbach 1972). These research procedures also encourage a cer-

tain carelessness in naming (hence thinking about) the constructs that are used in the broad domain which includes alienation and its not easily distinguishable cousins: for example, Pettigrew's (1971) index of "relative deprivation" comes directly from the Srole anomia scale, and Armer & Schnaiberg (1972) find it difficult to distinguish measures of "individual modernity" from scores on anomie and alienation. Similar examples could be multiplied, since sociologists have not worked very hard at demonstrating what Campbell & Fiske (1959) call "convergent and discriminant validity."

For those who are made unhappy by this style of research, and who are almost equally unhappy with the restrictions of the laboratory, the possibilities in longitudinal and quasi-experimental studies have become more attractive. The longitudinal side has been encouraged by the recent vigor of the "social indicators" movement (Duncan, Schuman & Duncan 1973 is one example, but see also Weigel & Jessor 1973); while the quasi-experimental method has yet to be exploited in any major way with respect to the alienation problem (but see Campbell 1969, Renshon 1974, and Seeman 1972c). None of this, of course, speaks to the argument (more prominent in recent years) that all of these research styles represent alienated methods— i.e. dehumanized and quantified ways of making objects out of persons, secularized in such a degree that one can contend that "ours is a culture alienated in fact and *in principle*" (Roszak 1973:413; see also Kolakowski 1968, Krimsky 1974).

5. The question of the difference in alienation between the socialist states and Western capitalist societies has been addressed (Israel 1971, Plasek & Moreno 1974). As one might expect, the answer is indeterminate since the argument is heavily freighted ideologically, the evidence is limited, and the two (evidence and argument) are hard to dissociate. An excellent example of this problem is found in the four year study of some 2600 workers, conducted by the Laboratory of Social Research at Leningrad (Zdravomyslov, Rozhin & Iadov 1970), a study which sought to examine "the transformation of labor into a first need of life" (p. 44), and a study in which it is most difficult to disengage the conclusions from the commitments.

6. There is perhaps no better way to conclude this review than by a return to the issue of the unity of the so-called dimensions of alienation, for that issue generates a continuing empirical and theoretical debate. The "empirical cluster or 'alienation syndrome' " described by Keniston (1968:327 ff) includes all the variants discussed above, while others, as we have seen, find the absence, the modesty, and the situational specificity of the interconnections of these alienations impressive. Some of this difference in viewpoint is a direct function of methodological differences, but some of it, too, is a matter of philosophy of science and of theory. Thus, the dimensions discussed above become the instigation of a steady search for a better grounded theory of alienation (e.g. Sévigny 1969, Geyer 1974), one that can rationalize more satisfactorily why these six categories have emerged, what ties them together, and how their sources and consequences should be conceived. Despite Marx and the modern exegesis inherited from his work, such a theory remains only a prospect for the future.

Literature Cited

Aberbach, J. D. 1974. *Alienation and American Voting Behavior: 1968 and Beyond.* Presented at 8th World Congr. Sociol., Toronto

Aberbach, J. D., Walker, J. L. 1970. Political trust and racial ideology. *Am. Polit. Sci. Rev.* 64:1199–1219

Abramowitz, S. J. 1973. Internal-external control and social-political activism. *J Consult. Clin. Psychol.* 40:196–201

Abramson, P. R. 1972. Political efficacy and political trust among black children: two explanations. *J. Polit.* 34:1243–75

Aiken, M., Hage, J. 1966. Organizational alienation: a comparative analysis. *Am. Sociol. Rev.* 31:497–507

Allardt, E. 1972. Types of protests and alienation. In *Alienation and the Social System,* ed. A. W. Finifter, 289–305. New York: Wiley. 367 pp.

Archibald, W. P. 1974. *The Empirical Relevance of Marx's Theory of Alienation.* Presented at 8th World Congr. Sociol., Toronto

Armer, M., Schnaiberg, A. 1972. Measuring individual modernity: a near myth. *Am. Sociol. Rev.* 37:301–16

Aronowitz, S. 1973. *False Promises: The Shaping of American Working Class Consciousness.* New York: McGraw-Hill. 465 pp.

Balch, G. I. 1974. Multiple indicators in survey research: the concept 'sense of political efficacy'. *Polit. Methodol.* 1:1–43

Ball-Rokeach, S. J. 1973. From pervasive ambiguity to a definition of the situation. *Sociometry* 36:378–80

Barber, B. R. 1974. *The Death of Communal Liberty: A History of Freedom in a Swiss Mountain Canton.* Princeton: Princeton Univ. Press. 302 pp.

Barker, R. G., Schoggen, P. 1973. *Qualities of Community Life.* San Francisco: Jossey-Bass. 562 pp.

Baughman, E. E. 1971. *Black Americans: A Psychological Analysis.* New York: Academic. 113 pp.

Bauman, K. E., Udry, J. R. 1972. Powerlessness and regularity of contraception in an urban Negro male sample. *J. Marriage Fam.* 34:112–14

Becker, E. 1967. *Beyond Alienation.* New York: Braziller. 305 pp.

Bell, D., Held, V. 1969. The community revolution. *Public Interest* 16:142–77

Bickford, H. L., Neal, A. G. 1969. Alienation and social learning: a study of students in a vocational training center. *Sociol. Educ.* 42:141–53

Blauner, R. 1964. *Alienation and Freedom: The Factory Worker and His Industry.* Chicago: Univ. Chicago Press. 222 pp.

Block, J. H., Haan, N., Smith, M. B. 1969. Socialization correlates of student activism. *J. Soc. Issues* 25:143–77

Block, J. H., Haan, N., Smith, M. B. 1973. Activism and apathy in contemporary adolescents. In *Understanding Adolescence,* ed. J. F. Adams, 198–231. Boston: Allyn & Bacon. 511 pp.

Brim, O. G. Jr. et al 1969. *American Beliefs and Attitudes About Intelligence.* New York: Russell Sage. 291 pp.

Bronfenbrenner, U. 1972. The roots of alienation. In *Influences on Human Development,* ed. U. Bronfenbrenner, 658–77. Hinsdale, Ill: Dryden. 678 pp.

Bullough, B. L. 1967. Alienation in the ghetto. *Am. J. Sociol.* 70:469–78

Bullough, B. L. 1969. *Social-Psychological Barriers to Housing Desegregation.* Los Angeles: Univ. Calif Press (Special Report #2). 134 pp.

Bullough, B. L. 1972. Poverty, ethnic identity and preventive health care. *J. Health Hum. Behav.* 13:347–59

Burbach, H. J. 1972. The development of a contextual measure of alienation. *Pac. Soc. Rev.* 15:225–33

Campbell, A. 1971. *White Attitudes Toward Black People.* Ann Arbor: Inst. Soc. Res. 177 pp.

Campbell, D. T. 1969. Reforms as experiments. *Am. Psychol.* 24:409–29

Campbell, D. T., Fiske, D. W. 1959. Convergent and discriminant validation by the multi-trait multi-method matrix. *Psychol. Bull.* 56:81–105

Cantril, H. 1941. *The Psychology of Social Movements.* New York: Wiley. 274 pp.

Caplan, N. 1970. The new ghetto man: a review of recent empirical studies. *J. Soc. Issues* 26:59–73

Caplow, T., Bahr, H. M., Sternberg, D. 1968. Homelessness. *Int. Encycl. Soc. Sci.* 6:494–99

Carr, L. G. 1971. The Srole items and acquiescence. *Am. Sociol. Rev.* 36:287–93

Clark, K. 1965. *Dark Ghetto.* New York: Harper & Row. 253 pp.

Coleman, J. S. et al 1966. *Equality of Educational Opportunity.* Washington, DC: GPO. 737 pp.

Coleman, J. S. 1973. Loss of power. *Am. Sociol. Rev.* 38:1–17

Collins, B. 1974. Four separate components of the Rotter I-E scale: belief in a difficult world, a just world, a predictable world, and a politically responsive world. *J. Pers. Soc. Psychol.* 29:381–91

Converse, P. E. 1972. Changes in the American electorate. In *The Human Meaning of Social Change,* ed. A. Campbell, P. E. Converse, 8:263–337. New York: Russell Sage. 547 pp.

Coopersmith, S. 1967. *The Antecedents of Self-Esteem.* San Francisco: Freeman. 283 pp.

Cotgrove, S. 1972. Alienation and automation. *Brit. J. Sociol.* 23:437–51

Crain, R. L., Weisman, C. S. 1973. *Discrimination, Personality and Achievement.* New York: Seminar. 225 pp.

Crandall, V. C., Katkovsky, W., Crandall, V. J. 1965. Children's beliefs in their control of reinforcements in intellectual-academic behavior situations. *Child Develop.* 36:91–109

Crawford, T. J., Naditch, M. 1970. Relative deprivation, powerlessness and militancy: the psychology of social protest. *Psychiatry* 33:208–23

Crozier, M. 1971. *The World of the Office Worker.* Chicago: Univ. Chicago Press. 224 pp.

Curtis, J. 1971. Voluntary association joining: a cross-national comparative note. *Am. Sociol. Rev.* 36:872–80

Cutler, S. J. 1973. Voluntary association membership and the theory of mass society. In *Bonds of Pluralism,* ed. E. O. Laumann, 7:133–59. New York: Wiley. 342 pp.

Davis, L. E., Taylor, J. C., Eds. 1972. *Design of Jobs.* London: Penguin. 479 pp.

Dean, D. 1961. Alienation: its meaning and measurement. *Am. Sociol. Rev.* 26:753–68

DeCharms, R. 1968. *Personal Causation.* New York: Academic. 398 pp.

Deci, E. L. 1972a. The effect of contingent and non-contingent rewards and controls on intrinsic motivation. *Organ. Behav. Hum. Perform.* 8:217–29

Deci, E. L. 1972b. Intrinsic motivation, extrinsic reinforcements and inequity. *J. Pers. Soc. Psychol.* 22:113–20

Delamater, J., Katz, D., Kelman, H. C. 1969. On the nature of national involvement: a preliminary study. *J. Conflict Resolut.* 13:320–57

Department of Health, Education, and Welfare, Social and Rehabilitation Service. 1969. *Welfare Policy and Its Consequences for the Recipient: A Study of the AFDC Program.* 217 pp.

Department of Health, Education, and Welfare. 1972. *Work in America.* Cambridge, Mass.: MIT Press. 262 pp.

Drucker, P. 1973. Hysteria over the work thing. *Psychol. Today* 7:87–92

Dubin, R. 1956. Industrial workers' worlds. *Soc. Probl.* 3:131–42

Duncan, O. D., Schuman, H., Duncan, B. 1973. *Social Change in a Metropolitan Community.* New York: Russell Sage. 126 pp.

Easton, D., Dennis, J. 1967. The child's acquisition of regime norms: political efficacy. *Am. Polit. Sci. Rev.* 61:25–38

Etzioni, A. 1968. *The Active Society.* New York: Free Press. 442 pp.

Feagin, J. R., Tilly, C., Williams, C. W. 1972. *Subsidizing the Poor: A Boston Housing Experiment.* Lexington, Mass.: Lexington Books. 199 pp.

Featherman, D. L. 1971. The socio-economic achievement of white religio-ethnic subgroups: social and psychological explanations. *Am. Sociol. Rev.* 36:207–22

Finifter, A. W. 1970. Dimensions of political alienation. *Am. Polit. Sci. Rev.* 64:389–410

Finifter, A. W. 1972. *Alienation and the Social System.* New York: Wiley. 367 pp.

Fischer, C. S. 1973. On urban alienations and anomie: powerlessness and social isolation. *Am. Sociol. Rev.* 38:311–26

Fischer, C. S. 1974. *Alienation: Trying to Bridge the Chasm.* Presented at 60th Ann. Meet. Am. Sociol. Assoc.

Form, W. H. 1972. Technology and social behavior of workers in four countries: a socio-technical perspective. *Am. Sociol. Rev.* 37:727–38

Form, W. H. 1973. Auto workers and their machines: a study of work, factory and job satisfaction in four countries. *Soc. Forces* 52:1–15

Forward, J. R., Williams, J. R. 1970. Internal-external control and black militancy. *J. Soc. Issues* 26:75–92

Fraser, J. 1970. The mistrustful-efficacious hypothesis and political participation. *J. Polit.* 32:444–49

Fried, M. 1973. *The World of the Urban Working Class.* Cambridge, Mass.: Harvard Univ. Press. 410 pp.

Friedenberg, E. Z., Ed. 1971. *The Anti-American Generation.* New Brunswick, NJ: Transaction. 277 pp.

Fromm, E. 1955. *The Sane Society.* New York: Rinehart. 370 pp.

Fromm, E. 1973. *The Anatomy of Human Destructiveness.* New York: Holt, Rinehart & Winston. 521 pp.

Gales, K. E. 1966. A campus revolution. *Brit. J. Sociol.* 17:1–19

Galle, O. R., Gove, W. R. 1974. *Some Effects of Crowding on Behavior in Urban Areas of the U.S.* Presented at 1st World Congr. Environ. Med. Biol., Paris

Gamson, W. A. 1968. *Power and Discontent.* Homewood, Ill.: Dorsey. 208 pp.

Garfinkel, H. 1967. *Studies in Ethnomethodology.* Englewood Cliffs, NJ: Prentice-Hall. 288 pp.

Geyer, R. F. 1972. *Bibliography: Alienation.* Amsterdam: Netherlands Univ. Joint Soc. Res. Center. 55 pp.

Geyer, R. F. 1974. Alienation and general systems theory. *Sociol. Neer.* 10:18–41

Gillis, J. S., Jessor, R. 1970. Effects of brief psychotherapy on belief in internal control: an exploratory study. *Psychotherapy* 7:135–37

Goldthorpe, J. H., Lockwood, D., Bechhofer, F., Platt, J. 1968 *The Affluent Worker: Industrial Attitudes and Behavior.* London: Cambridge Univ. Press. 206 pp.

Goodwin, L. 1972. *Do the Poor Want to Work? A Social Psychological Study of Work Orientations.* Washington, D.C.: Brookings Inst. 178 pp.

Gore, P., Rotter, J. B. 1963. A personality correlate of social action. *J. Pers.* 31:58–64

Gorman, B. S. 1968. An observation of altered locus of control following political disappointment. *Psychol. Rep.* 23:1094

Granovetter, M. S. 1973. The strength of weak ties. *Am. J. Sociol.* 78:1360–79

Greer, S. 1962. *The Emerging City: Myth and Reality.* New York: Free Press. 232 pp.

Gurin, P., Gurin, G., Lao, R., Beattie, M. 1969. Internal-external control in the motivational dynamics of Negro youth. *J. Soc. Issues* 25:29–53

Gurr, T. R. 1970. *Why Men Rebel.* Princeton: Princeton Univ. Press. 421 pp.

Gusfield, J. R. 1973. *Utopian Myths and Movements in Modern Societies.* Morristown, NJ: General Learning. 33 pp.

Gutmann, D. 1973. The subjective politics of power: the dilemma of post-superego man. *Soc. Res.* 40:570–616

Harris, L. 1973. What America thinks of itself. *Newsweek* 1596:40–48

Hawkins, B. W., Marando, V. L., Taylor, G. A. 1971. Efficacy, mistrust and political participation. *J. Polit.* 33:1130–36

Herzberg, F. 1966. *Work and the Nature of Man.* New York: Harcourt, Brace & World. 203 pp.

Herzberg, F. 1968. One more time: how do you motivate employees? *Harv. Bus. Rev.* 46:53–62

Hill, R. A., Chapman, M. L., Wuertzer, V. I. 1974. *Achievement Competence Training: A Report; Part X: Locus of Control.*

Philadelphia: Res. for Better Schools, Inc. 127 pp.

Hochreich, D. J., Rotter, J. B. 1970. Have college students become less trusting? *J. Pers. Soc. Psychol.* 15:211–14

Hoffer, E. 1951. *The True Believer.* New York: Harper & Row. 176 pp.

Holian, J. Jr. 1972. Alienation and social awareness among college students. *Sociol. Quart.* 13:114–25

House, J. S., Mason, W. M. 1974. *Political Alienation in America: 1952–1968.* Presented at 59th Ann. Meet. Am. Sociol. Assoc., New York

Hulin, C. L., Blood, M. R. 1968. Job enlargement, individual differences and worker responses. *Psychol. Bull.* 69:41–55

Hunnuis, G., Garson, G. P., Case, J., Eds. 1973. *Worker Control: A Reader on Labor and Social Change.* New York: Random. 493 pp.

Hsieh, T. T., Shybut, J., Lotsof, E. J. 1969. Internal vs. external control and ethnic group membership. *J. Consult. Clin. Psychol.* 33:122–24

Inglehart, R. 1971. The silent revolution in Europe: intergenerational change in post-industrial societies. *Am. Polit. Sci. Rev.* 65:991–1017

Inkeles, A., Smith, D. H. 1970. The fate of personal adjustment in the process of modernization. *Int. J. Comp. Sociol.* 11:81–114

Israel, J. 1971. *Alienation: From Marx to Modern Sociology.* Boston: Allyn & Bacon. 358 pp.

Jessor, R., Graves, T., Hanson, R. C., Jessor, S. L. 1968. *Society, Personality and Deviant Behavior.* New York: Holt, Rinehart & Winston. 500 pp.

Jessor, R., Jessor, S. L., Finney, J. 1973. Social psychology of marijuana use: longitudinal studies of high school and college youth. *J. Pers. Soc. Psychol.* 26:1–15

Joe, V. C. 1971. Review of the internal-external control construct as a personality variable. *Psychol. Rep.* 28:619–40

Johnson, F., Ed. 1973. *Alienation: Concept, Term and Meanings.* New York: Seminar. 402 pp.

Johnson, H. M. 1960. *Sociology: A Systematic Introduction.* New York: Harcourt, Brace. 688 pp.

Jones, E. E. et al 1972. *Attribution: Perceiving the Causes of Behavior.* New York: General Learning. 386 pp.

Kahn, R. L. 1972. The meaning of work: Interpretation and proposals for measurement. In *The Human Meaning of Social Change,* ed. A. Campbell, P. E.

Converse, 5:159–203. New York: Russell Sage. 547 pp.

Kantor, R. M., Ed. 1973. *Communes: Creating and Managing the Collective Life.* New York: Harper & Row. 544 pp.

Kaplan, H. R., Tausky, C. 1972. Work and the welfare cadillac: the function of and commitment to work among the hardcore unemployed. *Soc. Probl.* 19: 469–83

Kaplan, H. R., Tausky, C., Bolaria, B. S. 1969. Job enrichment. *Personnel J.* 48:791–98

Kasarda, J. D., Janowitz, M. 1974. Community attachment in mass society. *Am. Sociol. Rev.* 39:328–39

Kaufman, A. S. 1965. On alienation. *Inquiry* 8:141–65

Kelley, H. H. 1973. The processes of causal attribution. *Am. Psychol.* 28:107–28

Kelman, H. C. 1969. Patterns of personal involvement in the national system: a social psychological analysis of political legitimacy. In *International Politics and Foreign Policy,* ed. J. N. Rosenau, 26: 276–88. New York: Free Press. 740 pp.

Keniston, K. 1960. *The Uncommitted: Alienated Youth in American Society.* New York: Harcourt, Brace & World. 500 pp.

Keniston, K. 1967. The sources of student dissent. *J. Soc. Issues* 23:108–37

Keniston, K. 1968. *Young Radicals.* New York: Harcourt, Brace & World. 368 pp.

Kerner, O. et al 1968. *Report of the National Advisory Commission on Civil Disorders.* New York: Bantam. 609 pp.

Kirby, D. 1971. A counter-culture explanation of student activism. *Soc. Probl.* 19:203–16

Klapp, O. E. 1972. *Currents of Unrest: An Introduction to Collective Behavior.* New York: Holt, Rinehart & Winston. 420 pp.

Knutson, J. N. 1974. *Psychological Variables in Political Recruitment: An Analysis of Party Activists.* Berkeley: Wright Inst. 63 pp.

Kohn, M. L., Schooler, C. 1973. Occupational experience and occupational functioning: an assessment of reciprocal effects. *Am. Sociol. Rev.* 38:97–118

Kolakowski, L. 1968. *The Alienation of Reason: A History of Positivist Thought.* Garden City, NY: Anchor. 221 pp.

Kornhauser, A. 1965. *Mental Health of the Industrial Worker.* New York: Wiley. 354 pp.

Korte, C., Milgram, S. 1970. Acquaintance networks between racial groups: application of the small world method. *J. Pers. Soc. Psychol.* 15:101–8

Krimsky, S. 1974. The scientist as alienated man. In *Science, Technology and Freedom,* ed. W. H. Truitt, T. W. Graham Solomons, 169–76. Boston: Houghton Mifflin. 272 pp.

Laing, R. D., Esterson, A. 1965. *Sanity, Madness and the Family.* New York: Basic. 372 pp.

Lao, R. C. 1970. Internal-external control and competent innovative behavior among Negro college students. *J. Pers. Soc. Psychol.* 14:263–70

Latané, B., Darley, J. M. 1968. Group inhibition of bystander intervention in emergencies. *J. Pers. Soc. Psychol.* 10:215–21

Laumann, E. O. 1973. *Bonds of Pluralism: the Form and Substance of Urban Social Networks.* New York: Wiley. 342 pp.

Lee, A. M. 1972. An obituary for alienation. *Soc. Probl.* 20:121–29

Lefcourt, H. M. 1972. Recent developments in the study of locus of control. In *Progress in Experimental Personality Research,* ed. B. Maher, 6:1–39. New York: Academic. 251 pp.

Lefcourt, H. M. 1974. Locus of control and the expression of humor. *J. Pers.* 42:130–43

Lichtheim, G. 1968. Alienation. *Int. Encycl. Soc. Sci.* 1:264–8

Lipp, L., Kalstoe, R., James, W., Randall, H. 1968. Denial of disability and internal control of reinforcements: a study using a perceptual defense paradigm. *J. Consult. Clin. Psychol.* 32:72–75

Lowe, C. M., Damankos, F. J. 1968. Psychological and sociological dimensions of anomie in a psychiatric population. *J. Soc. Psychol.* 74:65–74

Lukacs, G. 1971. *History and Class Consciousness.* Transl. R. Livingstone. Cambridge: MIT Press. 356 pp.

Lukes, S. 1967. Alienation and anomie. In *Philosophy, Politics and Society,* ed. P. Laslett, W. G. Runciman, 134–56. Oxford: Blackwell. 184 pp.

Lutterman, K. G., Middleton, R. 1970. Authoritarianism, anomia and prejudice. *Soc. Forces* 48:485–92

Lyons, S. R. 1970. The political socialization of ghetto children: efficacy and cynicism. *J. Polit.* 32:288–304

Lystad, M. H. 1972. Social alienation: a review of current literature. *Sociol. Quart.* 13:90–113

MacArthur, L. A.1970. Luck is alive and well in New Haven. *J. Pers. Soc. Psychol.* 16:316–18

MacDonald, A. P. Jr. 1972. *Internal-External Control: A Partial Bibliography (II)*. Washington, DC: Am. Psychol. Assoc.

Maimon, Z. 1970. The inner-city impact. *Urban Aff. Quart.* 8:233–48

Mandel, E., Novack, G. 1970. *The Marxist Theory of Alienation.* New York: Pathfinder. 63 pp.

Marcson, S. 1970. *Automation, Alienation and Anomie.* New York: Harper & Row. 479 pp.

Marcuse, H. 1964. *One-Dimensional Man.* Boston: Beacon. 260 pp.

Marx, K. 1971. *The Grundrisse,* ed. and transl. D. McLellan. New York: Harper & Row 156 pp.

Matthews, D. R., Prothro, J. W. 1966. *Negroes and the New Southern Politics.* New York: Harcourt, Brace & World. 551 pp.

McClosky, H., Schaar, J. H. 1965. Psychological dimensions of anomy. *Am. Sociol. Rev.* 30:14–40

McHugh, P. 1968. *Defining the Situation: the Organization of Meaning in Social Interaction.* New York: Bobbs Merrill. 143 pp.

McPhail, C. 1971. Civil disorder participation: a critical examination of recent research. *Am. Sociol. Rev.* 36:1058–73

McWilliams, W. C. 1973. *The Idea of Fraternity in America.* Berkeley: Univ. Calif. Press. 712 pp.

Merton, R. K. 1957. *Social Theory and Social Structure.* Glencoe, Ill.: Free Press. 645 pp.

Mészáros, I. 1970. *Marx's Theory of Alienation.* London: Merlin. 356 pp.

Middleton, R. 1963. Alienation, race and education. *Am. Sociol. Rev.* 22:670–77

Milgram, S. 1967. The small-world problem. *Psychol. Today* 1:61–67

Milgram, S. 1970. The experience of living in cities. *Science* 167:1461–68

Miller, A. H., Brown, T. A., Raine, H. S. 1973. *Social Conflict and Political Estrangement, 1958–1972.* Presented at 31st Ann. Meet. Midwest Polit. Sci. Assoc., Chicago

Miller, D. C., 1970. *Handbook of Research Design and Social Measurement.* New York: David McKay. 432 pp.

Miller, G. A. 1967. Professionals in bureaucracy: alienation among industrial scientists and engineers. *Am. Sociol. Rev.* 32:755–68

Mills, R. 1973. *Young Outsiders: A Study of Alternative Communities.* London: Routledge & Kegan Paul. 208 pp.

Mirels, H. L. 1970. Dimensions of internal vs. external control. *J. Consult. Clin. Psychol.* 34:226–28

Mischel, W., Zeiss, R., Zeiss, A. 1974. Internal-external control and persistence: validation and implications of the Stanford pre-school I-E scale. *J. Pers. Soc. Psychol.* 29:265–78

Mitchell, R. E. 1971. Some social implications of high density housing. *Am. Sociol. Rev.* 36:18–29

Mizruchi, E. H. 1964. *Success and Opportunity: A Study of Anomie.* New York: Free Press. 204 pp.

Moore, B. 1970. *Reflections on the Causes of Human Misery.* Boston: Beacon. 201 pp.

Murchland, B. 1971. *The Age of Alienation.* New York: Random House. 208 pp.

Neal, A. G., Groat, H. T. 1970. Alienation correlates of Catholic fertility. *Am. J. Sociol.* 76:460–73

Neal, A. G., Groat, H. T. 1975. Social class correlates of stability and change in levels of alienation: a longitudinal study. *Sociol. Quart.* In press

Nelson, J. I., 1968. Anomie: comparisons between the old and the new middle class. *Am. J. Sociol.* 74:184–92

Nettler, G. 1957. A measure of alienation. *Am. Sociol. Rev.* 22:670–77

Niemi, R. G. 1973. Political socialization. *Handbook of Political Psychology,* ed. J. N. Knutson, 5:117–38. San Francisco: Jossey-Bass. 542 pp.

Nisbet, R. A. 1967. *The Sociological Tradition.* New York: Basic Books. 349 pp.

Obradovic, J. 1970. Participation and worker attitudes in Yugoslavia. *Ind. Relat.* 9:161–69

Ollman, B. 1971. *Alienation: Marx's Conception of Man in Capitalist Society.* London: Cambridge Univ. Press. 325 pp.

Olsen, M. E. 1969. Two categories of political alienation. *Soc. Forces* 47:288–99

O'Neill, J. 1972. *Sociology as a Skin Trade.* New York: Harper & Row. 274 pp.

Paige, J. M. 1971. Political orientation and riot participation. *Am. Sociol. Rev.* 36:810–20

Parker, S. 1971. *The Future of Work and Leisure.* New York: Praeger. 160 pp.

Parsons, T. 1968. Durkheim. *Int. Encycl. Soc. Sci.* 4:311–20

Pearlin, L. I. 1962. Alienation from work: a study of nursing personnel. *Am. Sociol. Rev.* 27:314–26

Pettigrew, T. F. 1971. *Racially Separate or Together?* New York: McGraw-Hill. 371 pp.

Phares, E. J. 1968. Differential utilization of

information as a function of internal-external control. *J. Pers.* 36:649–62

Phares, E. J. 1973. *Locus of Control: A Personality Determinant of Behavior.* Morristown, NJ: General Learning. 24 pp.

Pitts, J. R. 1973. On communes. *Contemp. Sociol.* 2:351–59

Plasek, J. W. 1974. Marxist and American sociological conceptions of alienation: implications for social problems theory. *Soc. Probl.* 21:316–28

Plasek, J. W., Moreno, M. I. 1974. *Updating Marxist and American Approaches to the Study of Alienation.* Presented at 8th World Congr. Sociol., Toronto

Portes, A. 1971. Political primitivism, differential socialization and lower-class leftist radicalism. *Am. Sociol. Rev.* 36: 820–35

Ragan, P. 1973. Expectancies, values and location in the social structure as factors in the under-utilization of medical services. PhD thesis. Univ. Calif., Los Angeles. 220 pp.

Rainwater, L. 1970. *Behind Ghetto Walls: Black Family Life in a Federal Slum.* Chicago: Aldine. 446 pp.

Ransford, H. E. 1968. Isolation, powerlessness and violence. *Am. J. Sociol.* 73:581–91

Regin, D. 1969. *Sources of Cultural Estrangement.* The Hague: Mouton. 157 pp.

Reich, C. A. 1971. *The Greening of America.* New York: Bantam. 433 pp.

Reimanis, G. 1974. *Alienation and Education.* Presented at 8th World Congr. Sociol., Toronto

Renshon, S. A. 1974. *Psychological Needs and Political Behavior: A Theory of Personality and Political Efficacy.* New York: Free Press. 300 pp.

Riesman, D. 1969. Universities on collision course. *Transaction* 6:3–4

Robinson, J. P., Shaver, P. R. 1973. *Measures of Social Psychological Attitudes.* Ann Arbor: Inst. Soc. Res. 750 pp.

Rosenau, J. N. 1974. *Citizenship between Elections: An Inquiry into the Mobilizable American.* New York: Free Press. 526 pp.

Rosenberg, M. 1956. Misanthropy and political ideology. *Am. Sociol. Rev.* 21: 690–95

Rosenberg, M., Simmons, R. G. 1972. *Black and White Self-Esteem: The Urban School Child.* Washington, DC: Am. Sociol. Assoc. 60 pp.

Rosow, I. 1967. *Social Integration of the Aged.* New York: Free Press. 354 pp.

Ross, J. C., Wheeler, R. H. 1971. *Black Belonging: A study of the Social Correlates of Work Relations among Negroes.* Westport, Conn.: Greenwood. 292 pp.

Rossi, P. H. 1972. Community social indicators. In *The Human Meaning of Social Change,* ed. A. Campbell, P. E. Converse, 3:87–126. New York: Russell Sage. 547 pp.

Roszak, T. 1973. *Where the Wasteland Ends: Politics and Transcendence in Postindustrial Society.* Garden City, NY: Anchor. 451 pp.

Rotter, J. B. 1966. Generalized expectancies for internal vs. external control of reinforcements. *Psychol. Monogr.* 80:1–28 (whole #609)

Rotter, J. B. 1971. Generalized expectancies for interpersonal trust. *Am. Psychol.* 26:443–51

Rotter, J. B., Liverant, S., Seeman, M. 1962. Internal versus external control of reinforcement: a major variable in behavior theory. In *Decisions, Values and Groups,* ed. N. F. Washburne, 2:473–516. London: Pergamon. 521 pp.

Rushing, W. A. 1972. *Class, Culture and Alienation: A Study of Farmers and Farm Workers.* Lexington, Mass.: Heath. 190 pp.

Sartre, J. P. 1948. *Anti-Semite and Jew.* New York: Schocken. 153 pp.

Schacht, R. 1970. *Alienation.* Garden City, NY: Doubleday. 286 pp.

Schuman, H., Gruenberg, B. 1970. The impact of city on racial attitudes. *Am. J. Sociol.* 76:213–61

Schwartz, D. C. 1973. *Political Alienation and Political Behavior.* Chicago: Aldine. 560 pp.

Seeman, M. 1959. On the meaning of alienation. *Am. Sociol. Rev.* 24:783–91

Seeman, M. 1966. Status and identity: the problem if inauthenticity. *Pac. Sociol. Rev.* 9:67–73

Seeman, M. 1967a. Powerlessness and knowledge: a comparative study of alienation and learning. *Sociometry* 30:105–23

Seeman, M. 1967b. On the personal consequences of alienation in work. *Am. Sociol. Rev.* 32:273–85

Seeman, M. 1972a. Alienation and engagement. In *The Human Meaning of Social Change,* ed. A. Campbell, P. E. Converse, 12:467–527. New York: Russell Sage. 547 pp.

Seeman, M. 1972b. The symptoms of '68: alienation in pre-crisis France. *Am. Sociol. Rev.* 37:385–402

Seeman, M. 1972c. Alienation and knowledge-seeking: a note on attitude and action. *Soc. Probl.* 20:3–17

Seeman, M., Bishop, J. W., Grigsby, J. E. 1971. Community and control in a metropolitan setting. In *Race, Change and Urban Society,* ed. P. Orleans, R. Ellis, 423–50. Los Angeles: Sage. 640 pp.

Sennett, R., Cobb, J. 1972. *The Hidden Injuries of Class.* New York: Vintage. 275 pp.

Sévigny, R. 1969. Pour une theorie psychosociologique de l'aliénation. *Sociol. Soc.* 1:193–219

Shepard, J. M. 1969. Functional specialization and work attitudes. *Ind. Relat.* 8:185–94

Shepard, J. M. 1973. Technology, division of labor and alienation. *Pac. Sociol. Rev.* 16:61–88

Sheppard, H. L., Herrick, N. Q. 1972. *Where Have All the Robots Gone: Worker Dissatisfaction in the 70's.* New York: Free Press. 222 pp.

Silvern, L. E., Nakamura, C. Y. 1971. Powerlessness, social-political action, social-political views: their interrelation among college students. *J. Soc. Issues* 27:137–57

Simpson, M. E. 1970. Social mobility, normlessness and powerlessness in two cultural contexts. *Am. Sociol. Rev.* 35:1002–13

Singer, D. 1970. *Prelude to Revolution: France in May 1968.* New York: Hill & Wang. 434 pp.

Slater, P. E. 1970. *The Pursuit of Loneliness: American Culture at the Breaking Point.* Boston: Beacon. 154 pp.

Smelser, N. 1963. *Theory of Collective Behavior.* New York: Free Press. 436 pp.

Smith, P. C., Cranny, C. J. 1968. Psychology of men at work. *Ann. Rev. Psychol.* 19:467–96

Smith, R. E. 1970. Changes in locus of control as a function of life crisis resolution. *J. Abnorm. Psychol.* 75:328–32

Snyder, D., Tilly, C. 1972. Hardship and collective violence in France, 1830 to 1960. *Am. Sociol. Rev.* 37:520–32

Srole, L. 1956. Social integration and certain corollaries: an exploratory study. *Am. Sociol. Rev.* 21:709–16

Steiner, I. D. 1970. Perceived freedom. In *Advances in Experimental Social Psychology,* ed. L. Berkowitz, 187–248. New York: Academic. 392 pp.

Strauss, G., Rosenstein, E. 1970. Workers' participation: a critical view. *Ind. Relat.* 9:197–214

Streuning, E. L., Richardson, A. H. 1965. A factor analytic exploration of the alienation, anomia and authoritarianism domain. *Am. Sociol. Rev.* 30:768–76

Strickland, B. R. 1965. The prediction of social action from a dimension of internal-external control. *J. Soc. Psychol.* 66:353–58

Sussman, M. B. 1972. Family, kinship and bureaucracy. In *The Human Meaning of Social Change,* ed. A. Campbell, P. E. Converse, 4:127–58. New York: Russell Sage. 547 pp.

Taviss, I. 1969. Changes in the form of alienation: the 1900's vs. the 1950's. *Am. Sociol. Rev.* 34:46–57

Taylor, J. C. 1973. *The Quality of Work Life: an Annotated Bibliography, 1957–1972.* Los Angeles: Graduate School of Manage.

Terkel, S. 1974. *Working: People Talk About What They Do All Day and How They Feel About What They Do.* New York: Pantheon. 589 pp.

Touraine, A. 1967. L'aliénation: de l'idéologie à l'analyse. *Soc. Trav.* 9:192–201

Touraine, A. 1971. *The May Movement: Protest and Reform.* New York: Random House. 320 pp.

Touraine, A. 1973. *Production de la Société.* Paris: Editions du Seuil. 543 pp.

Touraine, A. 1974. *The Academic System in American Society.* New York: McGraw-Hill. 319 pp.

Travers, J., Milgram, S. 1969. An exploratory study of the small world problem. *Sociometry* 32:425–43

Tudor, B. 1972. A specification of relationships between job complexity and powerlessness. *Am. Sociol. Rev.* 37:596–604

Tunstall, J. 1967. *Old and Alone.* New York: Humanities. 344 pp.

Turner, R. H., Killian, L. M. 1972. *Collective Behavior.* Englewood Cliffs, NJ: Prentice-Hall. 435 pp.

Turner, R. N., Lawrence, P. R. 1965. *Industrial Jobs and the Worker.* Cambridge, Mass.: Harvard Univ. Press. 177 pp.

Verba, S., Nie, N. H. 1972. *Participation in America: Political Democracy and Social Equality.* New York: Harper & Row. 428 pp.

Wallerstein, I., Starr, P., Eds. 1971. *The University Crisis Reader.* New York: Random House. 515 pp.

Walton, R. 1972. How to counter alienation in the plant. *Harv. Bus. Rev.* 50:70–81

Weigel, R. H., Jessor, R. 1973. Television and adolescent conventionality: an exploratory study. *Public Opin. Quart.* 37:76–90

Weiner, B. et al 1971. *Perceiving the Causes of Success and Failure.* Morristown, NJ: General Learning. 26 pp.

Wellman, B. 1973. *The Network Nature of Future Communities: a Predictive Synthesis.* Presented at 23rd Ann. Meet. Soc. Study Soc. Probl., New York

Westby, D. L., Braungart, R. G. 1970. The alienation of generations and status politics: alternative explanations of student political activism. In *Learning about Politics: A Reader in Political Socialization,* ed. R. S. Sigel, 476–89. New York: Random House. 651 pp.

Whitehorn, A. 1974. *Workers' Self-Management: Socialist Myth or Prognostication?* Presented at 54th Ann. Meet. Am. Polit. Sci. Assoc. Chicago

Whittaker, D., Watts, W. A. 1969. Personality characteristics of a non-conformist youth sub-culture. *J. Soc. Issues* 25:65–89

Wilensky, H. L. 1964. Varieties of work experience. In *Man in a World of Work,* ed. H. Borow, 6:125–54. Boston: Houghton Mifflin. 606 pp.

Wilson, J. Q. 1968. The urban unease. *Public Interest* 12:25–39

Wilson, R. A. 1971. Anomie in the ghetto: a study of neighborhood type, race and anomie. *Am. J. Sociol.* 77:66–88

Wolfe, R. N. 1974. *Trust, Anomia and Locus of Control: Alienation in U.S. College Students in 1964, 1969, and 1974.* Presented at 8th World Congr. Sociol., Toronto

Wool, H. 1973. What's wrong with work in America?—a review essay. *Mon. Labor Rev.* 96:38–44

Yankelovich, D. 1972. *The Changing Values on Campus: Political and Personal Attitudes of Today's College Students.* New York: Washington Square. 175 pp.

Yinger, J. M. 1973. Anomie, alienation and political behavior. In *Handbook of Political Psychology,* ed. J. N. Knutson, 7:171–202. San Francisco: Jossey-Bass. 542 pp.

Young, M., Wilmott, P. 1973. *The Symmetrical Family.* New York: Pantheon. 375 pp.

Zablocki, B. D. 1971. *The Joyful Community.* Baltimore: Penguin. 362 pp.

Zdravomyslov, A. G., Rozhin, V. P., Iadov, V. 1970. Man and his work. *Sov. Sociol.* 9:1–398

Zirkel, P. A. 1971. Self concept and the 'disadvantage' of ethnic group membership and mixture. *Rev. Educ. Res.* 41: 211–25

Zirkel, P. A., Moses, E. G. 1971. Self concept and ethnic group membership among public school students. *Am. Educ. Res. J.* 8:253–64

RACE AND ETHNIC RELATIONS

❖10505

Robin M. Williams, Jr.
Department of Sociology, Cornell University, Ithaca, New York 14850
and the Center for Creative Leadership, Greensboro, North Carolina 27402

I. THE FIELD OF STUDY

1. Scope of This Review

Research on race and ethnic relations deals with many diverse topics and reflects rapid changes in social concerns. Severe selectivity is essential. Accordingly, this chapter omits descriptions and analyses of the culture and internal social structures and processes of racial and ethnic minorities, except where the analysis deals with relations between collectivities. This exclusion rules out most of the large literature on kinship and family, including intermarriage (see Barron 1972, Woods 1972). Excluded also is research on crime and deviant behavior, aside from some work on violence (e.g. Horowitz & G. Schwartz 1974, L. R. Schwartz 1972) and on ethnic networks in organized crime (Ianni 1972, 1974). Space prohibits review of the numerous studies that focus on economic policies and legislation. Other omissions will be glaringly apparent to interested readers.

A topical organization, in terms of major institutions, has been chosen, rather than one using analytical categories of variables. The latter more rigorous scheme is conceptually preferable but seems impracticable in the present state of the literature.

Further, only passing attention can be given to problems of conceptualization, operational definitions, and research design. We must note carefully, however, the complex referents that are variously attached to the concepts "racial" and "ethnic." In their psychological aspects, ethnic relations are characterized by variations in salience, clarity, importance, hostility or positive affect, ambivalence, commitment, identification. In the cultural system, ethnicity may involve language, religious beliefs and practices, institutional norms and values, expressive styles, food preferences, and so on. Ethnic collectivities vary in size, interconnectedness, definiteness and strength of boundaries, degree of social closure, centralization, stratification, control of resources, relationships with allies and enemies, internal interdependence, degree and kind of social control of members.

These complexities exist in the real world and cannot be thought away without destroying the empirical subject matter. Consequently, propositions dealing with

125

ethnic relations *in general* often are highly abstract and may be vacuous. Specification of what is being talked about in particular instances is a necessary safeguard against both vagueness and over generalization.

Although we cannot deal with historical investigations as such, it would be an unnecessary fault to neglect the accumulation of valuable data from new studies in social history—immigrants (Dinnerstein & Jaher 1970), the relationships (1619–1973) of black workers and labor unions (P. S. Foner 1974), the place of Jews in the history of the South (Evans 1973), the persistence of public school segregation in the North (Franklin 1974), minority-group organizations (Parris & Brooks 1971), or the dynamics of colonialism and slavery.

Major revisions of interpretations of both slavery and "colonialism" (a much-confused term) have appeared recently. The idea that legal and religious differences among the colonizing powers resulted in "milder" slavery in Latin than in Anglo-Saxon areas was advanced in the 1940s, and widely endorsed and elaborated subsequently (Elkins 1959, Freyre 1946, Klein 1967, Tannenbaum 1947). Criticisms have mounted, and the whole thesis now has been thrown into doubt (e.g. D. B. Davis 1966, Degler 1971, Greenstein 1973, Harris 1964, Knight 1970; cf E. Williams 1944). Recent studies strongly suggest that other specific factors—demographic, technological, military, ecological, and economic—were crucial: e.g. the profitability of large scale agriculture, or the extent of military resistance by "natives" (Fogel & Engerman 1973a, b, Greenstein 1973). Similarly, revised accounts of U.S. urban history imply that "powerlessness" rather than "race" or "ethnicity" per se may be the primary condition needing further analysis (Lynch 1973).

2. The Problem of Mapping Independent and Dependent Variables

The several hundred books and articles reviewed for this chapter contain an appalling number of ad hoc variables and indicators. More happily, what first seems to be wanton diversity can be reduced appreciably by clustering multiple indicators and labels for the same genotypic variables. A really tight and parsimonious ordering, however, still remains a task for the future.

In most instances, sociological studies have used psychological factors, understandably enough, as dependent or intervening variables. Thus, self-esteem may be treated as an outcome of integrated or segregated schooling (Rosenberg & Simmons 1971); prejudice or "conformity" may be conceived as an intervening factor in discriminatory behavior (Warner & Dennis 1970); stereotypes intervene between interethnic communication and perception of its efficiency (Taylor & Gardner 1970). Ehrlich's (1973) formulations of 22 principles (and 38 corollaries) are rather strictly in psychological terms and give minimal attention to social factors. The work is of interest here primarily for its critiques of methodology and conceptualizations and for its characterizations of dependent variables that sociological analysis may attempt to explain.

The location of variables as proximate or distal depends upon the causal scheme of the investigator; "distance" from the explicandum may be (*a*) in time, (*b*) in space, (*c*) in micro- or macro-level of structure—from dyads to metropolitan ecological patterns (D. M. Betz 1972, Meade 1972) to international systems. That proximate factors always occur in a causal context that filters and shapes them has been convincingly shown in analyses of selective communication and perception regarding ghetto disorders (e.g. Warren 1970).

Of course, careful students of race and ethnic relations are acutely aware that what are independent variables in one setting or problem formulation may become intervening or dependent in another. Thus Spilerman (1970, 1971a) knows that while size of nonwhite population alone is the best independent variable for predicting civil disorders in Northern cities from 1965–1969, it will not serve to explain why collective violence characterized the 1960s rather than the 1950s. Black parents who chose integrated rather thal all-black schools in rural North Carolina in 1968 were high on indices of knowledge, educational expectations, and estimates of physical qualities of integrated schools, and low on indicators of alienation; but by 1975 ideologies of separatism and local control may be more decisive in such choices (Binderman 1972).

Further systematic mapping of the entire range of independent, intervening, and dependent variables is essential for cumulation of research findings in a form suitable for building theories. Many of the inconclusive and contradictory results of past research derive from lack of clear specification of the triad of (*a*) concepts, (*b*) indicators of the conceptualized variables, and (*c*) hypothesized relationships among the selected variables (linear or curvilinear, additive or multiplicative, etc). Specification of concepts requires both clear definitions and locating each in relation to other concepts. A mishmash of unordered ecological, psychological, social, and cultural factors no longer can be allowed to pass muster as the starting point for research. The reason for this dictum is not merely a preference for neatness and conceptual economy, but the imperative of discovering networks of causal relationships.

II. RECENT DEVELOPMENTS IN RESEARCH AND THEORY BUILDING

1. Changes in Amount of Activity and Foci of Interest

The civil rights struggles and the urban disorders of the 1960s stimulated not only specific studies but also many symposia, readers, and more or less integrated compendia of analysis and interpretation. Only a few examples can be noted here (Coser 1972, Geschwender 1971, Grimshaw 1969, Short & Wolfgang 1972, van den Berghe 1972). International scope is attempted in several cases (E. Q. Campbell 1972, Richmond 1972). Interminority relations were reexamined in the wake of urban conflicts (e.g. Berson 1971, Harris & Swanson 1970).

A public rediscovery of ethnicity (perhaps somewhat similar to the rediscovery of poverty in the early 1960s) was evident by 1968 and increasingly conspicuous thereafter. The National Project on Ethnic America ("A Depolarization Program of the American Jewish Committee") was begun in 1968. *The Journal of Black Studies* was announced in 1970. Both the new *Journal of Ethnic Studies* and *Ethnicity* were published initially in the Spring of 1973. In Canada, Vol. I, No. 1 of the *Canadian Review of Studies in Nationalism/Revue Canadienne des Etudes sur le Nationalisme* appeared in Fall/Automne, 1973.

The salience of ethnicity is further illustrated by publication of bibliographic aids (cf Kinton 1972), and by numerous articles in journals in all fields of the social sciences (e.g. Stein & Hill 1973.)

From an earlier focus on assimilation and, then, on integration, the most recent work highlights ethnicity. Thus, analysis of data for Detroit shows that ethnoreligious membership is a persisting structure, not eliminated by assimilation; ethnoreligious categories mark off life styles, patterns of informal social interaction and friendship, and associational participation (Laumann 1973). And a flood of books describe and comment on particular ethnic and racial categories. Aside from the vast literature on Blacks, we note: Arab Americans (Hagopian & Paden 1969); Mexican Americans or Chicanos (Grebler, Moore & Guzman 1970; Heller 1971; Moore & Cuéllar 1970; Wagner & Haug 1971); Puerto Ricans (Fitzpatrick 1971); white Protestants (Anderson 1970); Italian Americans (Iorizzo & Mondello 1971, Lopreato 1970); Chinese Americans (Loewen 1971, Lyman 1974); Japanese Americans (Petersen 1971); Greek Americans (Kourvetaris 1971, Tavuchis 1972, Vlachos 1968); Native Americans (Wax 1971); white Southerners (Killian 1970, Reed 1972a); mestizos (Berry 1972); Jews (Berson 1971, Harris & Swanson 1970, Himmelfarb 1973, Glazer 1972, Liebman 1973, Sklare 1971); Polish Americans (Samuels 1970, Sandberg 1974); and Irish Americans (Greeley 1972). This listing is highly incomplete. Scholarly concern with ethnic phenomena has been substantial recently also in Europe (e.g. Braun 1970, Sedoc-Dahlberg 1971, Steiner 1974, Verwey-Jonker 1971).

The recurrent refrain of studies that report persisting ethnic identities and loyalties (Greeley & McCready 1974, Greeley 1971, Novak 1971) has its counterpoint in analyses that focus upon how situational factors affect assimilation and adaptation, e.g. easier adaptation for Samoans than for American Indians in urban employment is favored by the Samoans' positive self-image, close-knit kinship and community networks, and freedom from dependence on bureaucratic agencies (Ablon 1971).

During the last five years the surge of interest in the relationships between ethnicity and political phenomena has been unmistakable and large. Observe this abbreviated list: Bellush & David 1971, Daniels 1972, Enloe 1973, Feagin & Hahn 1973, Glazer 1971, Greenstone & Peterson 1973, Hunt & Walker 1974, Rabuska & Shepsle 1972, Ugalde 1970, Weed 1973. Clear also is the greater attention given to works by black sociologists and to the history of contributions by nonwhite scholars (Bracey, Meier & Rudwick 1971).

Of course, ethnicity in the U.S. actually has diminished greatly over the long term, as indicated by decreased endogamy, lessened interethnic resentment and exclusion, lessened participation in ethnic voluntary associations, and lessened sharing of a nonAmerican nationality culture. What remains is a sense of ethnic membership that may be intensified by perceived advantages or a sense of frustration, by fraternal deprivation, or perceived threat from any newly militant minorities (Goering 1971). What remains also are networks of informal social relationships (Laumann 1973, Suttles 1968) and the highly consequential clustering of persons of similar ethnic origins in particular ecological niches and in advantaged or disadvantaged portions of political and economic structures (Aldrich 1973, Berson 1971, Corwin 1971). The social significance of ethnicity in many other societies is more closely related to differences in language (Lieberson 1970). The new salience of ethnic labels and ethnic identity clearly has major instrumental-political aspects (Glazer & Moynihan 1974).

2. Major Controversies

The new assertions of "ethnic identity" and "cultural authenticity" have revived interest in long-neglected problems in the study of prejudice. If minorities insist that there are, indeed, distinctive subcultures, what becomes of the concept of stereotyping (Ehrlich 1973)? How do we know to what extent so-called stereotypes are accurate or inaccurate? How do we distinguish stereotypes from valid sociological and psychological generalizations? Recently two assumptions have been challenged: (a) that stereotypes should be *defined* as inaccurate; (b) that stereotypes function only as invalid rationalizations for outgroup antipathy or invidious interests (Mackie 1973).

Ideological overlays have obscured analysis in some discussions of the black family. Emphasis on assumed effects of past conditions upon present families may create the impression that direct transmission (e.g. of stability or instability) has been demonstrated. Thus, "slavery" or "institutional racism" has been cited as a major cause of fatherless households in the central cities of the 1970s. But Duncan (1969) found no relation between a broken home in the prior generation and current marital status among the black population. A 1966 survey of a northern metropolitan sample of black males and females (Heiss 1972) showed little relationship among persons of low socioeconomic status (SES) background between parental broken home and being divorced or separated (although there was a substantial correlation among middle-class males). Prior family history simply was not a good predictor. Furthermore, differences between blacks and whites in the proportions of households headed by females are greatest in lower-income areas of central cities —not in the rural areas of the South where a "heritage of slavery" or a matrifocal "tradition" might be expected to be strongest, if it ever existed. It is likely that the poorer urban black families do not have as great a possibility as their white counterparts of returning to rural areas—either as escape from the city or as a source of reinforcement for traditional cultural patterns (Yancey 1972). Finally, evidence is being reexamined to show that most black families are stable and do not fit the alleged pattern of looseness and disruption (R. B. Hill 1972).

Studies since 1965 of differentials in employment and income between whites and nonwhites have produced a literature too extensive to review in detail (cf Burkey 1971). Problems of methodology, data, and conceptualization still are only partially resolved. Increasingly, however, gross comparisons have been disaggregated, leading to a systematic effort to test causal hypothesis. Two major theoretical approaches now are in contention: a market or labor queue model (Hodge 1973, Thurow 1969) and a power class ("neo-Marxian") formulation (R. C. Hill 1974). Although the crucial issue of the relative importance of market competition versus organized bargaining power remains moot, it seems clear that both worker productivity and collective power importantly affect employment and income of different segments of the potential labor force (see the extensive bibliography in R. C. Hill 1974).

Recent studies illustrate the continuing controversies concerning the weight to be given to external social constraints versus sociocultural characteristics of minority populations themselves. Thus both Petersen (1971) and Light (1972) call attention to "success against odds," whereas their critics argue that situational factors have not been given proper due (cf Ikeda 1973; the several reviews in *Journal of Ethnic Studies,* Winter, 1974).

Debates over major social policies typically elicit research and theory construction related to the controversial issues. The great debate over desegregation and antidiscrimination policies between 1954 and 1974 eventually led to a preoccupation with the issues of equality of opportunity and equality of condition. Research has centered in two broad topics: 1. aggregative differences and similarities between social categories in measured aptitudes or intelligence (Dobzhansky 1973, Herrnstein 1973, Jensen 1972, Scarr-Salapatek 1971); and 2. relationships between educational and occupational outcomes and the characteristics of students, communities, and schools (Coleman 1973, Jencks et al 1972, Porter 1973, Mosteller & Moynihan 1972).

That many measured differences between "ethnic" populations may index "surface" characteristics rather than fundamental structures is suggested by intercorrelational analyses (simplex patterns) of observed differences in cognitive tests scores (DeFries et al 1974). Large mean differences were shown to mask the same simplex pattern of intercorrelations (for five ethnic categories in Israel) or the same coefficients of congruence between factor loadings (for Japanese- and European-origin populations in Hawaii).

Crucial to appraisals of test scores are such social variables as SES, birth order, and family size. Analysis of unique data for nearly 400,000 19-year-old Dutch males (Belmont & Marolla 1973) has shown that IQ scores (Raven) decrease with family size and with birth order and with each when the other is held constant; scores are the lower, the lower the SES of the family; lower scores in larger families are marked among manual workers, less so among nonmanual occupations, not present among farmers; regardless of SES, scores decrease sharply with birth order. At the very least, accordingly, these variables must be used as controls in making racial or ethnic comparisons.

Of course, it is well known that objectively disadvantaged minority children and youths sometimes equal or exceed the norms of performance of the dominant educational system, e.g. the cases of immigrant Jews, Japanese Americans, or some Pakistanis in Britain (J. H. Taylor 1973). Partly for that reason, we are likely to see a continuation of debates about the relative importance for social mobility of properties of individuals versus constraints and opportunities in the relevant social environments (cf Greeley 1973).

Recent conceptualization of ethnicity as primordial—as a basic substratum of social orders—makes it ". . . distinct from all the other multiple and secondary identities people acquire" (Isaacs 1974). This view has been disputed (Hechter 1972,

1973, 1974). The counterview is that it is not useful to regard ethnic solidarity as a primordial sentiment, because such solidarity in complex societies is hypothesized to be primarily a response to structural discrimination. Hechter's data indicate that "status politics" rather than "class politics" seem most prevalent in those parts of Great Britain that have been "relatively poor and culturally subordinate"; from this finding, it is inferred that ethnicity usually becomes politically salient only when lines of cultural distinction coincide with or are used as the basis for social stratification (distribution of resources). But the prior existence of "primordial," even if latent, distinctions does not seem thereby to have been disproved.

A central theoretical issue that crosscuts "integration-consensual" versus "conflict-dominance" conceptions of societies is whether and to what extent common values and beliefs affect power relations or are solely derivative from prior constellations of social power (cf Katznelson 1973a). The issue is an extension of the partial view represented by the treatment of ideology and superstructure in Marxian theory. Extreme polemical positions are still being argued, with only anecdotal empirical materials to support intuitive estimates of causal importance (for an uncritical exposition of this type, see Nikolinakos 1973).

Emerging as a point of controversy, although still not sharply focused, is the claim that "structural factors" rather than popular discontent or "tension" are crucial in accounting for collective violence. Among evidence adduced is a lack of close correspondence in 19th century France between urban growth and either personal crime or collective violence—whereas, it is asserted, collective violence fluctuated in accord with struggles for power at the national level (Lodhi & Tilly 1973; Snyder & Tilly 1972, 1974). But of course, one may still ask why there are such efforts in the first place—and ethnic sentiments and popular discontent certainly do help to produce power struggles over disputed rights (Enloe 1973, Rabushka & Shepsle 1972). Thus far the animated debates concerning the weight of "relative deprivation" (or "expectation-achievement" gap) versus political power struggle as basic sources of collective violence have failed to focus the issues sharply enough in terms of appropriate data, to produce any decisive resolution between incompatible hypotheses (Davies 1974, Snyder & Tilly 1974).

3. Codification and Integration of Findings and Hypotheses

Systematic sociological reviews of research in racial and ethnic relations appeared at fairly frequent intervals prior to 1965, e.g. Berelson & Steiner 1964; Harding et al 1954; Mack & Snyder 1957; Rose 1948; Suchman et al 1958; Williams 1947, 1957, 1964. More recent inventories and critiques have made substantial progress in ordering and connecting the very large accumulation of empirical findings and proto-theories. Examples are: F. Barth 1969, Barth & Noel 1972, Blalock 1970, Ehrlich 1974, Himes 1973, Hunt & Walker 1974, Kinloch 1974, LeVine & Campbell 1972, Schermerhorn 1970, Sherif 1966, van den Berghe 1970, Williams 1970.

Needs for sharp conceptual distinctions appear in a wide sampling of problems. In analyses of stratification and mobility, clarity requires specification of ethnic collectivities and stratification orders as overlapping but conceptually distinct social formations (cf van den Berhe 1970; Verba, Ahmed & Bhatt 1971). In studies of status inconsistency, sorting out the diverse phenomena formerly so subsumed accompanies a renewed search for effective statistical models (H. F. Taylor 1973). Careful distinctions between violence and conflict-as-opposition have been productive in several instances (Berk 1972, Edgerton 1972, Schwartz 1972), and conceptual precision has been shown to be essential for practical diagnosis (J. S. Campbell 1972).

Three quite different major attempts to codify hypotheses and empirical generalizations illustrate the heroic effort required for integrating accumulated findings. One such review (Ehrlich 1974) presents 22 basic principles concerning prejudicial attitudes that the author regards as a summary of all the high quality research findings now available. Although the abstract propositions lack coordinating rules for anchoring them to initial conditions, the ordering provides a basis for needed further work. A critical cross-cultural review of research on ethnocentrism produced some 270 hypotheses and empirical generalizations grouped in 12 major categories, and has stated both the congruities and contradictions in the predictions derived from the main theoretical formulations (LeVine & Campbell 1972). A more structural or macro-social perspective informs the propositions and typologies in Schermerhorn's (1970) comprehensive comparative review.

III. SUBSTANTIVE FINDINGS

1. Family, Stratification, and Mobility

According to some estimates the black "middle class" has increased since 1950 from about 5% to about 25% of the black population (cf Kronus 1971, Pettigrew 1971). Even if one discounts the larger estimates, this is a substantial change to have occurred in the absence of widespread residential desegregation or change of economic institutions. Several different types of analysis have produced similar findings. On a standard index of equality (EI), blacks made substantial movement toward equality between 1940 and the late 1960s in income, education, occupational status, and quality of housing (Palmore & Whittington 1970). Relative to white women, from 1950 to 1960 nonwhite women increased their representation in the more desirable occupational categories, but experienced increased high relative rates of unemployment. The latter effect was due in part to migration to the North and West, where unemployment was higher than in the South, and in part to high rates of total unemployment among teenagers, which probably accentuated racial discrimination (Sorkin 1971).

Age-constant intercohort comparisons of data (for males only) from the Current Population Survey (Hauser & Featherman 1974) show that the decade 1962–1972 brought increasing educational attainment, occupational status, and real income to both whites and blacks. In each aspect the proportional gains were greater for blacks than for whites. But the gains are reported for men and in the experienced civilian labor force and, therefore, are partly spurious because a substantial proportion of black men have dropped out of the labor force (of black men aged 45–55, 14%, as contrasted with 6% of whites). Also, large differentials still exist between those blacks and whites who remain in the labor force, partly because of discrimination.

Although the size of discriminatory effects is unknown, effects associated with race are pervasive; no other factor in Porter's analysis showed so marked a pattern: data for black workers show at least ten departures from the expected path correlations previously observed for whites (Porter 1974).

In the sociological studies reviewed, psychological factors typically appear as intervening variables, e.g. white discrimination and prejudice are assumed to cause certain personality conditions among blacks that in turn affect educational and occupational attainments. Thus Crain & Weisman (1972) relate four personality features ("aggression control," internal control, happiness, self-esteem) to achievement in education, occupation, and income; occupational attainments are higher among persons who have never been arrested, who believe in internal control of personal fate, express happiness, and have high educational attainment.

The model develped by Blau & Duncan (1967) and further utilized by Duncan, Featherman & Duncan (1972) assumes that background variables directly affect education and occupation and also have indirect effects through education on occupation; education and occupation have direct effects on income; income also is determined indirectly by education through occupation, and by background variables through education and occupation.

Project TALENT data were used by Porter (1974) to specify patterns of white and black mobility. It was found that the mobility of blacks is reduced by a set of residual effects, over and above those found among whites, that seem attributable to discrimination. But among blacks original socioeconomic position is less closely related to other variables than among whites. Origin position among whites is directly related to educational attainment; not so among blacks. Further, the school grades of black males are independent of "intelligence" measures and educational attainment. But conformity to "middle-class values" has a stronger effect on educational attainment among blacks than among whites, whereas the reverse is true of indicators of ambition. Additionally, education has a strong effect on black occupational attainment. This combination of findings seems to imply ". . . that the locus of discrimination against black youths is not in the relation of education to occupation, but in the determinants of amount of education" (Porter 1974).

Since 1965 there has been an outpouring of studies of social mobility, based on multivariate analysis of large data bases. Both structural and sociopsychological variables have been used in the various statistical models (Blau & Duncan 1967, Duncan 1968, Featherman 1972, Sewell et al 1970). Studies that have dealt with comparisons of blacks and whites include: Blau & Duncan 1967; Duncan 1968, 1969; Porter 1974; Siegel 1965, 1970; see additional references in Miller & Dreger 1973). These analyses showed how greatly racial status has limited social mobility, and demonstrated that the relations of independent and intervening variables to educational and occupational attainments are different for blacks and whites (Blau & Duncan 1967; Duncan 1968, 1969; Porter 1974; Siegel 1965, 1970). For example, because of past discrimination many social characteristics have been less closely linked to occupation or income among blacks than among whites—e.g. local prestige rank or respectability, or the influence of significant others, or initial level of aspirations. Partly separate systems of stratification have created patterns of black mobility that resemble what Turner has called "sponsored" rather than "contest" mobility. For Blacks, "intelligence" and "conformity" become primary factors leading to educational attainments that can be used as a basis for sponsored entry into desirable occupations (Porter 1974).

2. Education

Although the specific social processes through which education may contribute to occupational and income position of blacks are not known in detail, it is certain that neither knowledge and skills gained nor formal certification nor both together can fully account for outcomes. Additional factors may include access to "contacts" and information about economic opportunities (Crain 1970), sponsorship (Porter 1974), and aspirations and motivation (Gurin 1970).

Since the early 1950s and increasingly since the publication of *Equality of Educational Equality* (the "Coleman Report," 1966), an enormous research effort has gone into studies of racially segregated and nonsegregated schools (cf O'Reilly 1970).

As of 1967–1968, full desegregation in urban public elementary schools would have required a shift of schools by 32% of children in Southern, and 26% in Northern cities (Farley & Taeuber 1974; cf O'Reilly 1970). Teachers typically were assigned to pupils of the same racial category. Most rapid change has occurred recently in the South.

An effective case has been made (Heyns 1974) for the necessity of examining *intra* school patterns of stratification and allocation in order to make valid appraisal of effects of resources (inputs) on achievement differentials among schools and among individuals. Inferences drawn from path-analysis for 48 schools suggest that social class background is mediated within schools primarily by curriculum placement and verbal ability; no evidence of an important direct effect of SES background independent of achievement was found, but curriculum assignment appeared to be a major source of differential access to resources. (Any failure to include indicators of such intraschool differentials necessarily *understates* the effects of inputs on outcomes.)

It seems strange that anyone would expect large scale complex social changes in a diverse society to have uniform results. Nevertheless, there is no avoiding such questions as, "Has desegregation of schools been successful?" The obvious answer is, "Yes and no." For a more sensible answer, one has to ask a more sensible question; "desegregation" involves diverse social settings, characteristics of students and teachers, school organizations, pace, timing, methods, scope, objectives. Further, what outcomes are to be classified as "successful" may be defined in terms of academic achievement, personality development, self-esteem, group solidarity, individual satisfaction, character of peer group relationships, and so on. A brief review of only a few illustrative studies is given here. The voluminous literature has been summarized in part in Miller & Dreger (1973).

Reflecting social changes over the last decade, research attention has shifted to some extent away from conditions making for acceptance of or resistance to school desegregation (but see Bonacich & Goodman 1972) to disorders in the schools

(Ritterband & Silverstein 1973), conflict over community control or busing (Rubin 1972), and the consequences of desegregation (J. S. Coleman 1971, 1973; Weigel, Wiser & Cook 1974).

Analysis of social-distance attitudes of white students at the University of Alabama, where dramatic political resistance to desegregation had been played out in the immediate past, showed that between 1963 and 1969 great increases occurred in acceptance of black students (Muir 1971). Each cohort of entering freshman showed greater acceptance than its predecessor, and each cohort gained even more greatly from year to year while attending the integrated university.

Studies going back to the 1930s have suggested that unpredictability or inconsistency in racial discrimination and segregation produces especially acute frustrations and strains on coping mechanisms. Recent data consistent with this formulation show that high educational and occupational attainments and low "aggression" and high happiness among blacks are most likely among those who attended integrated schools in both elementary and secondary schools, next most likely among those who were consistently segregated, and least among those having inconsistent sequences of integration and segregation (Crain & Weisman 1972).

The findings that, among male 7th and 8th graders in rural South Carolina, both achievement motivation and achievement-related values are lower among blacks than among whites have been attributed to the caste-like occupational structure as it apparently influenced black family socialization (Turner 1972). On the other hand, low achievement value orientations were associated with perceptions of low opportunities for mobility among blacks.

A national study of black students (Epps 1969) showed that *self-concept of academic ability* and *conformity* were among the strongest predictors of academic achievement.

A study of 5th and 6th graders in 18 schools in a large Northern city showed a positive relationship between the percentage of white pupils and achievement scores (St. John & Lewis 1971). With controls for sex, family SES, and school SES, the associations were more consistently significant when the independent variable was cumulative experience rather than current school percentage white. The apparent effect of cumulative experience was greater for white than for black students. There appeared to be a "boundary effect" at around 50% white—important differences appeared only for schools more than 50% white.

A study of seven communities that were passing through desegregation of public schools showed that blacks in the recently desegregated settings had self-esteem scores slightly but not significantly higher than blacks in segregated schools (R. L. Williams & Byars 1969, 1970).

Various "measures" (indicators) of self-concepts have been used in different studies, rendering valid comparisons quite difficult. Nevertheless some findings appear to be reasonably well established and important.

A crucial point in all studies of self-conceptions and self-appraisals, often overlooked or ignored, is the *referent or standard of comparison* used by the individual in anchoring his self-judgments. Thus a male black pupil in a segregated urban school may arrive at self-definitions and self-evaluations by reference, for example, to: 1. either parent, or both parents; 2. siblings, same sex or different sex, or both; 3. other boys and girls in the same classroom or same school; 4. black pupils in other schools, urban and rural; 5. white pupils, as known about either directly, by hearsay, or through mass media; 6. one or more teachers, white or black; 7. one or more other adults, white or black; 8. referents in #3–7 differentiated by socioeconomic level.

Some studies that have found a less positive self-concept among both white and black children in segregated than desegregated schools. Other studies give apparently contradictory findings. Clearly the gross results conceal variations in unmeasured conditions. Overall, however, the effects most often appear to be positive for blacks and inconclusive for whites.

Self-esteem of black youths, in general, may equal or surpass that of whites of comparable SES (Rosenberg & Simmons 1971). The evidence is overwhelming that group identity and individual identity are not coterminous, as J.D.R. Porter (1971) has insisted, and that negative outgroup evaluations do not always (or even typically) override positive ingroup evaluations of either the individual or his collectivity-of-membership.

The relationships of segregation to *both* socioeconomic status and ethnicity must be analyzed if we are to guard against mistaking one for the other. Note, for example, how the form and consequences of "pure SES" segregation in schools in Sweden resemble "racial" segregation in Northern U.S. cities (Swedner 1971).

3. The Economy: Racial Differentials

Many studies continue to describe economic differentials between whites and non-whites, e.g. in economic status and in services afforded to the elderly poor (Sterne, Philips, & Rabushka 1974). A massive compilation of studies on racial discrimination in housing and in employment and income explicates the complexities of market processes and of institutionalized regulation, indicating, for example, that such schemes as "ghetto dispersal" are quite inadequate measures to equalize economic opportunities (von Furstenberg & Horowitz 1974a, b).

Controversy continues concerning the empirical importance of "rational economic behavior" versus racist stereotyping and discrimination, e.g. in the behavior of ghetto merchants (Sturdivant 1973, W. E. Williams 1973).

Cutright (1974) analyzed the civilian earnings (in 1964) of a national probability sample of men given preinduction examinations by the Selective Service in the early 1950s. Most draftees had earnings equal to or below those of nonveterans and the data did not demonstrate that blacks (or whites who were likely to have low earnings) benefited from military service in terms of later employment and income. The findings, however, may be specific to the period studied and do not necessarily apply to the volunteer services in the 1970s (Janowitz & Moskos 1974). Census survey data for 1960 showed that among blacks and Mexican Americans incomes were higher for veterans than for nonveterans (Browning, Lopreato & Poston 1973).

Accounts of interrelations between economic institutions and ethnic relations have not been confined to descriptions of discrimination. A renewed effort to develop causal theory is illustrated by the work of Bonacich (1973), who hypothesizes that "sojourning," an intended temporary stay of a visible minority, is a critical factor in responses of the host society. Stryker (1974) endorses this attention to sojourning but argues that "political setting" is decisive; in citing the lack of hostility toward Parsis as a "marginal trading people" in India, he suggests that locality-group organization of a traditionalized caste society prevented the emergence of collective antagonism.

On the assumption that employment can be regarded as the outcome of competitive queuing for jobs, the unemployment rates for black and white workers are interdependent. Data for standard metropolitan areas (1960) support these propositions (Hodge 1973):

> ... (1) the greater the difference between the two groups on the underlying (objective) determinants of employability, the greater the unemployment differential between them; (2) the less the variability of the disadvantaged group on the characteristics determining employability, the less the employment differential among them; (3) the more depressed the economy, the greater the unemployment differential between advantaged and disadvantaged; and (4) the larger the relative size of the disadvantaged group, the less the unemployment differential.

Assertions concerning the sources of differences between blacks and whites in employment, occupations, and income often have been made on the basis of a priori assumptions. Recent economic studies throw doubt upon several conventional explanations. The easy formula of a "dual market" (labor market segmentation) is inadequate. "Segmentation" must be specified: it can represent caste (hereditary occupation), barriers to geographic mobility, barriers resulting from housing segregation, differentials in educational opportunity (both quantity and quality), on-the-job training, employer discrimination in hiring and promotion, and other factors. Studies summarized by Flanagan (1973a, b) indicate that economic discrimination is not attributable wholly to differences in educational opportunity. But many of the barriers that could operate within the labor market opportunity do not account for the differences. Instead (Flanagan 1973a:272–73):

> ... The major market barrier to racial equality in economic status is lack of access to specific on-the-job training. This places the burden of discrimination within the firm and requires that a dual market theory explain the persistence of barriers to training when competitive forces would normally work to integrate a firm at all occupational levels for which both races could qualify. White prejudice and black work habits are frequently cited and possibly complementary explanations.

A severe limitation upon such inferences from macro-analysis is that specific causal processes may be dismissed simply because they are not detectable in the kinds of data used. For example, the global notions of "prejudice" and "work habits" conceal the well-documented processes whereby discrimination affects both conditions, e.g. discrimination creates and reinforces both vested interests and prejudicial evaluations among whites; at the same time it produces some immediate adaptations among low-income blacks that are destructive of longer term economic advancement (cf Rainwater 1970, Hannerz 1970). Reverse processes likewise have been sketched as pressures from minorities altered both practices and perceptions of reality in some areas of economic life: thus, New York City banks found that many jobs previously thought to require elaborate qualifications could be performed by persons of average ability after relatively little training (Corwin 1971).

The notion of "colonialism" has been used to conceptualize the situation of urban racial minorities in Great Britain (Hechter 1974, Rex 1973a, b) and in the United States (Blauner 1969, 1972; Hurst 1972). With regard to the role of absentee-owned or -managed businesses in black ghettos, studies in Chicago, Boston, and Washington, D.C. show that such firms dominate the volume of economic activity (e.g. employing 76% of employees). But absentee businesses are dominant also in white low-income areas: "colonialism" is only partly "racial." *Local* white owners operate very small establishments. White employers hire white employees in greater proportions than found among residents in the ghettos; almost all black employers hire only blacks. "Local control" or "black capitalism" within the ghettos, however, would not meet employment needs and probably would be counter-productive economically, although it might have important social and political values (Aldrich 1973, Thomas 1971). Furthermore, some of the differentials in economic dealings that may be perceived as ethnic discrimination or "institutionalized racism" are based on market characteristics and the organizations of business firms. Thus, there are marked differentials in food prices between inner city ("ghetto"), outer city, and suburbs among independent stores, but the discrepancies are insignificant among chain stores (Sexton 1973). Aid to black businesses by federal agencies faces serious difficulties, even without problems of discrimination (small size, undercapitalization, location in static sectors, etc) (Andreasen 1972, N. M. Singer 1973).

Although the idea of internal colonialism is useful in directing attention to an evocative analogy, it is clearly an oversimplified and distorted image of the actual intergroup situation in contemporary United States: it ignores or minimizes the extent of common culture and social participation, political access and participation, the voluntary character of some separation, and economic interdependence (Glazer 1971).

4. Housing, Residential Segregation, Effects of Contact

During the 1960s some studies dealt with efforts to stabilize integrated residential areas or to establish "community control" of local institutions. Conclusions from such topical studies need to be put into historical perspective to assess current societal implications. For example, local control was the essential base of the Southern system of school segregation; stable urban neighborhoods probably were never very common in the United States. Chudacoff (1972) shows for Omaha that mobility and change have dominated over neighborhood stability from 1880 on. Shifts in the ethnic and racial composition of the population in various parts of metropolitan areas—"ecological succession"—appear to be more nearly consequences than causes of other social and economic changes (Chudacoff 1972, Hunter 1974, Molotch 1972).

Mobility, of course, does not necessarily lessen segregation. The persistence of urban residential clustering or segregation over the last thirty years has been well-documented for the New York metropolitan area not only for blacks and whites but also for whites of different national origin stocks (Kantrowitz 1973). For the nation as a whole, however, as many as one fifth of all white households live in racially integrated neighborhoods. Nor is newness a necessary condition for areal integration —a 1967 nationwide survey showed that the typical integrated neighborhood has been well established and is not a new development (Bradburn, Sudman & Gockel 1970).

Most studies of racially mixed suburban neighborhoods agree in reporting that characteristics of housing services and physical surrounds were more important to both blacks and whites than whether the area was racially integrated. Among blacks, relatively easy adjustment and high satisfaction have been found for young well-educated, middle-income families moving into suburbs in which whites were in the great majority and did not react to incoming blacks as a threat (Winkel, O'Hanlon & Mussen 1974). However, the sheer fact of moving into housing that is more spacious and of better quality has little effect upon functioning of large low-income families (Weller & Luchterhand 1973). Increasingly specific and theoretically informed analysis has shown basic processes whereby particular kinds of occupants come to inhabit particular kinds of housing and residential areas (Hunter 1974). In this field counterfactual propositions have been widely accepted as popular beliefs, e.g. "white flight" and "panic selling" as major factors in movement of white population from central cities to suburbs. There is now a clearer basis for rejecting the conventional wisdom. In a parsimonious theoretical exercise, Schelling (1971) has shown how a slight positive preference for same-group neighbors, without negative discrimination, can lead over time to a high degree of areal segregation.

Empirical support for this "normal process" view of de facto racial separation, given a dual housing market, comes from a case study of South Shore Chicago (Molotch 1972). Rapid racial turnover occurred without prejudice-related "flight" because normal mobility is high and the real estate market is discriminatory. As the price differential widens, the incentive grows for real estate dealers and individual sellers to sell or rent to blacks, who are willing to pay a premium because of discriminatory barriers elsewhere. The primary factor is the institutionalized system of market discrimination that generates "surges" of black population into the limited "open" areas. Local efforts to halt or reverse these processes will be nullified unless two conditions are created: (a) marked reduction of discrimination in the housing market, (b) availability of substantial supplies of new housing.

Residential segregation has important implications for employment, schools, churches, labor unions, political life. It imposes special restrictions on informal social contacts between persons from different racial or ethnic categories. Research interest in the effects of intergroup contact, accordingly, often is directed to residential arrangements.

But special care is required in interpreting findings that show a positive association between intergroup contact and favorable intergroup attitudes. Among other things it often is not clear whether favorable attitudes lead to contact or vice versa. Certainly negative outcomes do occur when contact either perpetuates or accentuates unfavorable orientations. These outcomes seem to be most likely (a) in competitive contacts, (b) under unpleasant conditions, (c) when there are marked differentials in status and rewards, (*d*) when the interaction is frustrating or damaging, or (*e*) when the participants hold incompatible beliefs and values (cf Amir 1969). We would add that third parties, external reference groups and societal authorities, can have great influence under some crisis conditions.

Although the more recent studies of effects of interracial contact still have only partially specified fine-grained processes and social context, we do have evidence that effects may be different for blacks and for whites. W. S. Ford (1972, 1973) finds that "neighboring" in public housing projects is significantly related to lower prejudice among whites; not among blacks. Earlier studies indicate that there was a time when sheer acceptance by whites of co-dwelling in a nonsegregated housing development was regarded by many blacks as a favorable sign of change. Today, any remaining discrimination or prejudice may increase negative attitudes of blacks toward whites. Similar implications are suggested by the findings of a before-and-after study of public school segregation in two Georgia counties: whites become more favorable to desegregation, blacks felt dissatisfaction because of a gap between aspirations and the actual experience (Bullock & Braxton 1973).

Five factors identified as most important in favoring positive change in attitude as an outcome of intergroup contact have been summarized by Cook as follows: 1. situational equality of status, 2. conditions of contact that encourage or require mutually interdependent relationships, 3. social norms favoring intergroup association and equalitarian attitudes, 4. characteristics of participants that contradict negative stereotypes, 5. a setting that promotes intimate rather than distant or casual association. By ingenious experiments controlling these variables, Cook (1970) was able to produce strong changes in attitudes among a sizable proportion of white college students who were initially anti-Negro and opposed to racial desegregation. The study demonstrates that the effects can be produced even against marked initial resistance. Although the large proportion of the participants who did not change indicates that highly influential factors remained to be accounted for, appreciable recent progress is evident in the disentangling of factors affecting outcomes. Following valuable conceptual analysis and experimental findings (Cohen & Roper, 1972, Cook 1970), increasingly precise results have been obtained (Blanchard, Adelman & Cook 1974; Weigel, Wiser & Cook 1974).

5. Religion

Efforts to demonstrate a specific causal relationship between religious beliefs or participation in religious groups and ethnic attitudes and behavior generally have not been convincing (Bouma 1970). Inadequate data and research designs have prevented all but a few studies from going beyond the demonstration of correlations.

But this unsatisfactory state may not be permanent. A renewed effort is illustrated in the treatment of historical data by multiple regression techniques, suggesting that 19th century revivalism in Ohio had specific effects that directly led to increased antislavery voting (Hammond 1974). The apparent effects of revivalism are not removed by controls for rurality, population growth, denomination, prior political party tradition, or ethnicity; it is inferred that the revivals changed the religious orientations of participants and that the new orientations influenced their voting behavior.

Ethnic and religious identification and involvement have been indexed by many diverse, largely ad hoc, indicators. A recent reclassification brings some needed order and unification into study of religious identity (Lazerwitz 1973), while at the same time specifying complexities in determining consequences of religious-group identity and participation. Ethnic community life and religious involvement are closely linked for Jews, but not for Protestants. Apparently the causal sequences in maintaining religious identity (and their consequences) are different for different major faith groupings.

Among the few studies of attitudes of religious leaders there is evidence that white Protestant ministers are more "liberal" than their congregations on racial issues, but that regional differences (South vs nonSouth) continue, possibly because of selective migration and decentralized organization (Rymph & Hadden 1970).

A common element in the very diverse types of black religious movements and organizations has been a concern with social power on the part of a powerless people; cults, sects, and denominations frequently were the context from which political leadership emerged (Washington 1972). This recent thesis is consistent with the double-faced role of organized religion—as "opiate" or "awakener" earlier noted by many other sociological studies.

Equivalent complexity is evident among Southern white Protestant groupings, where rural-urban and class factors seem more predictive than religious beliefs of racial attitudes (Harrell 1971).

Unanticipated involvement of a complex and heterogenous religious organization in a new social movement can place substantial strains upon initial commitments; maintenance of the organizational commitments then is possible only through multiple processes of reassessment (Wood 1972). Evident in all studies of orientations of religious collectivities to ethnic and racial relations are ambivalencies and instabilities arising both from religious values versus social embeddedness and from incompatibilities within religious orientations themselves (Smith 1972, Stark et al 1971).

6. The Polity: Institutions and Processes

Changes in the positions of ethnic segments in American society usually have followed the sequence typical of the origins of modern class stratification (Eisenstadt 1971). The weakening or abolition of ascriptive prohibitions and legal barriers to political participation and to educational and economic advancement is followed by increased collectivity-awareness and a shift away from demands for "equal access" toward struggles for greater resources, better bargaining positions, and favored niches or special advantage (Van Til 1973). If these struggles result in relatively stable mutual accommodations among ethnic collectivities, the competitive processes of stratification eventually produce "legitimized class politics."

Southern black citizens have voted with extraordinary cohesion, with 90–98% of the vote in cities going to the preferred candidate in national elections. The formation of a black electorate as a united bloc has created the basis, in many localities, for substantial effects on electoral outcomes. The extent to which such potential influence leads to significant outputs in governmental actions will vary with many other factors (Keech 1968). Voting and office holding by blacks in the South show rapid growth since the Congressional actions of 1964 and 1965 (Feagin & Hahn 1970).

Correlations of voting turnout in municipal elections with proportion foreign-born are higher for cities with nonpartisan elections than for those with partisan elections (D. N. Gordon 1970). Also, in 1960 the correlations between high ethnicity and high turnout declined from prior levels in the partisan, but not the nonpartisan cities. Gordon infers that ethnic competitiveness has been partly absorbed into the party system in the large partisan cities, whereas ethnic interests continue to induce high voting turnout in nonpartisan cities and in the smaller partisan cities. If these inferences are correct, the main implications are three: 1. ethnicity continues to induce high voting participation where ethnic interests are not well represented through party organizations; 2. the forms of representation and participation directly affect the impact of ethnic factors upon the electorate; hence, 3. the political salience of ethnicity is inversely related to the incorporation of ethnic-related interests directly into the system of representation and decision making.

But let us beware of unexamined assumptions: is it clear that "ethnic voting" actually serves "ethnic interest"? Strong correlations of voting behavior with ethnic background tell us nothing directly about whether ethnic voting actually brought economic or political successes to those so voting. The assumption that such voting actually had any effect on political policies has been challenged by McCormick (1974). Similar doubts and complexities intrude upon any effort to derive a single set of consequences from the use of a political model of "race" versus "ethnic group" or "class" or "interest group" as a basis for ideology and strategy (Glazer 1971).

In relations among large collectivities in complex societies there necessarily is a certain primacy of political considerations. This is so partly because rules of the game must be established *if* panendemic strife is to be avoided, and relative power typically must be ascertained if mutual agreement upon rules is to be developed.

Analyses in the aftermath of the urban upheavals of the 1960s included a review of the conflicting interests that were expressed and compromised in the responses of police and the courts (Balbus 1973). The variations in political repression of black rebels represented uneven, shifting, and often unstable responses to local, state, and national political systems.

The most recent analyses suggest that the causal role of racial and ethnic relations in urban political processes was often underestimated, relative to class, prior to the 1960s (Greenstone & Peterson 1973). It is evident at any rate that ethnic opposition in any institutional sector (e.g. education) can generate conflict with important political consequence (Ravitch 1974).

Behind "racial and ethnic relations" lie demographic, cultural, and social conditions affecting the interests, beliefs, and values that become politically influential. Thus, the core segregationist voting in eleven Southern states since 1954 consistently has been highest in the more rural areas with the highest proportion of blacks (Black 1974, Feagin 1972).

An intensive case study of black leaders and biracial politics in Houston (Davidson 1972) emphasizes the persistence of barriers to effective black political participation and the slowness of gains therefrom, and seeks to appraise the possibilities of class-based coalitions of blacks and whites.

In the context of the 1960s, black political pressures, aided by white allies, often produced clear outcomes, as in the Congressional acts of 1964 and 1965. In other instances, the effects were greatly attenuated by subsequent processes. For example, between 1966 and 1970, under pressure of legal actions and adverse publicity, the Selective Service System moved from having 1.3% black members of local boards to 6.7% (Murray 1971). By 1970, with little overt opposition, black members had been appointed in many strongholds of white supremacy. Primarily because national regulations narrowly constrained local boards, the change in composition was not related to any obvious change in local practices. The rules and practices were differentially used by white youths to secure deferments or exemptions.

A specific example of the importance of situational as compared with background (personal history; status) variables is supplied by the findings that neither type of prior offense nor the racial category (black or white) of violent offenders was related to aggressive behavior in prisons, whereas the specific prison context was substantially involved in differing rates of intraprison violence (Ellis, Grasmick & Gilman 1974). With similar import, a hypothetical model of consequences of racial differentials in social responses to alcoholism among whites and blacks has been partly tested by Lowe & Hodges (1972). Blacks are underrepresented in treatment programs and overrepresented by incarcerations in jails and prisons; if blacks perceive these differentials, there may develop community defenses against intervention, including medical intervention. High rates of alcohol-related deaths may be due in part to this network of conditions.

Informed appraisals differ concerning the success of integration and the extent of conflict in the Armed Services of the United States (W. S. Gould 1973; Janowitz & Moskos 1974; Moskos 1969, 1971, 1973). Nevertheless, it is unquestionable that massive desegregation was initially accomplished without unmanageable disruptions. Between 1948 and 1955 the military services effectively dismantled an entrenched system of official segregation and discrimination; what remained were the relatively enduring effects of past practices and the effects of persisting tensions generated both in civilian society and in the military. As the proportion of blacks in the Army rose from 8.8% in 1948 to 15.% in 1972, to more than 20% (estimated) in 1974, race relations became a focal concern of military commanders (Janowitz & Moskos 1974, Moskos 1973).

7. The Polity: Collective Action and Social Movements

The 1960s offered a rich field of possibilities for study of social movements, and some of the opportunities were grasped. Detailed narrative description and conceptual analysis is available for civil rights movements (Demerath, Marwell & Aiken 1971; Levy 1968), the Congress of Racial Equality (Meier & Rudwick 1973), a local organization known as the Black Crusaders (Helmreich 1973), the puzzling case of the rise and fall of White Citizens' Councils (McMillen 1971), and for the more transparent failure of American Nazism in the 1930s (Bell 1973, Diamond 1974). The National Urban League has been given a detailed (and sympathetic) historical review (Parris & Brooks 1971). For French Canada, useful description is available on Québécois nationalism (e.g. Reid 1972).

Several synoptic works have included treatment of movements concerned with racial and ethnic relations, e.g. Himes 1973, Kriesberg 1973, Oberschall 1973. A comparative cross-cultural approach has been emphasized by several works (Blalock 1970, Schermerhorn 1970, van den Berghe 1970). It seems to have been consistently observed that each major movement, anywhere in the world, drew upon awareness of similar or related movements elsewhere—note, for example, Pierre Vallieres' *Negres Blancs D'Amerique.*

There has been a growing repudiation among students of collective behavior of the conception that protest movements and rebellions are anomic outbursts among disoriented and uprooted elements of the population. Conflict increasingly is seen as less "irrational" and more instrumental and selective than was the case in traditional "collective behavior" interpretations (Berk & Aldrich 1972, Gamson 1975, Skolnick 1969).

Collective violence has been redefined by several analysts as a continuation of "normal" political behavior—regarded as often effective in mobilizing support, establishing collective identity and organization, and attaining goals (cf Coser 1956, 1967; Gamson 1968, 1975; Oberschall 1973; Tilly 1973).

But, surely, both the expressive and the instrumental images are partial truths. Some collective behavior is, indeed, expressive (and often thereby nonrational in terms of goal attainment), and the same is true of organized, routine politics. But much behavior in protests, demonstrations, rebellions, and revolutions is purposive, selective, instrumental, and effective in goal attainment. The most general polar conceptions, therefore, are too general to be usefully defended or attacked. The productive questions are more specific: *under what conditions* do particular types of collective behavior manifest one or another set of processes and consequences. For example, grievances among blacks in 15 large cities are positively related to objective conditions—but only through processes that differ for different sectors of behavior. Objectionable behavior by ghetto merchants apparently become an issue only when made salient by black leaders; responses to police behavior depended both upon police practices and upon the reputation of the local chief of police (Rossi & Berk 1972:299–308).

The description of how a small organization of Puerto Rican migrants in a Northeastern city attempted to bring pressure upon local government shows the sources of failure in disunity and lack of a power base (Rogler 1972). That consolidation and institutionalized organization of a diffuse set of local social movements does not necessarily reduce militancy or effectiveness is suggested by analysis of "open housing" movements of the 1960s (Saltman 1971).

Longitudinal studies of social movements are greatly desired and rarely produced. Exceptional interest accordingly attaches to an analysis, 1965–1969, of civil rights activists in the 1965 Summer Community Organization and Political Education (SCOPE) (Demerath, Marwell & Aiken 1971). The study shows in detail the highly differentiated responses (radical, reformist, drop-out, disengaged) of these volunteers some four years after their intense experiences in the South at the peak of the black-white civil rights coalition.

A striking case of asymmetrical trust was provided by the participation of whites in the civil rights movements, in which they only gradually learned of the pervasive and deep mistrust with which they were regarded by their black coparticipants (Levy 1968).

In contrast to the "gladiatorial" escalation of militancy among black spokesmen during the Northern urban upheavals of 1964–1968, the Southern civil rights movement developed from general charismatic leadership to a specialized cadre, as long range objectives became more central (Nelson 1971).

Adequate evidence shows that the "unity" of large scale social movements is to a high degree "constructed" symbolically on a base of great heterogeneity of goals, motivations, interests and social positions (cf Elder 1970).

Expressions of acceptance or approval of schemes for geographic separation of whites and blacks (blacks having separate states within the U.S., blacks having a separate country outside the U.S.) were elicited in a 1968 national survey. Only 5–6% of blacks as against over 26% (state) and 36% (country) of whites expressed approval (Feagin 1971). Younger blacks are not more favorable than older blacks to separatism; among whites the younger are less favorable than older persons to separation. White separatism is greatest among Southerners and among persons of low education and low occupational status. (Only small variations in black responses appeared across the various SES and demographic characteristics). White separatism is substantially correlated with antiblack sentiments.

Social movements, among disadvantaged minorities, that emphasize separatism and withdrawal always contain the possibility of subsequent development of more active confrontation, as collective consciousness grows and political demands are articulated. This potential exists even in movements that initially are strongly millenarian and other-worldly (Watson 1973).

8. The Polity: The Generic Roles of Ethnicity

Many examples recently have been adduced in which ethnic or cultural distinctiveness is maintained, or even developed ("ethnogenesis," L. Singer 1962) in complex urban societies, partly because of its effectiveness as a basis of political mobilization (Hecter 1973:341). The degree of political utility that may be derived from ethnic maintenance is highly variable, depending upon: (a) the extent to which existing parties incorporate the ethnic aims and demands (or, the extent to which class or other functionally based coalitions are effective), and (b) the degree to which the ethnic segment has a territorial base for political action (cf the photo-editorial "Let's Keep the Inner City Black," Ebony, January, 1972, p. 108). The end of political colonialism in Africa and Asia has been followed by a vast wave of struggles and conflicts among ethnic groupings within new nations (Das Gupta 1974, Duran 1974, Enloe 1973, Hanna & Hanna 1969, Hunt & Walker 1974, Rabushka & Shepsle 1972, Schermerhorn 1970).

The evaluation of ethnicity as a political base and as a criterion of administrative allocations depends in part upon one's causal analysis. For some "militant" ethnic spokesmen, an avenue to radical change is seen in ethnic organization, community control, and territorial autonomy. But radical critiques of this approach regard it as playing into the hands of the established power structure (Katznelson 1973b:477; see also Greenstone & Peterson 1973).

> The mimetic urban counterrevolt thus seeks to encapsulate and utilize the developing corporate consciousness of subordinates. Ethnicity is used as the basis for the allocation of new urban rewards; where a sense of ethnic consciousness is lacking it is sometimes created to provide authorities with manageable, manipulable constituent links. The response to demands by corporately conscious groups for structural control of key territorial and communal institutions is met by participatory concessions and the creation of parallel, discrete institutions for the discontented.

The weight of evidence and reasoning about ethnic factors in polities, however, is increasingly pointing to the political "rationality" of much ethnic-related behavior (see sections #10 and #11 below).

What remains highly problematic is the extent to which national political systems can remain relatively stable when containing major ethnic cleavages. The only "solutions" that have been viable over considerable periods in Western democracies have been assimilation and pluralism (Switzerland, Mexico, U.S.). In general, ". . . the political integration of minority ethnic groups will be facilitated to the extent that systematic structural differences between such groups are progressively effaced." (Hechter 1973:1177).

There remain in modern societies clear examples of long term coexistence of ethnically distinct local groupings in side-by-side contact. Two villages in the Italian Alps retain differences in language (German and a Romance dialect), culture, social organization, and ideologies. Similarities in adaptation to a severe environment have not reduced divergent political commitments linked to the ethnic identities (Cole & Wolf 1974).

Substantial interest has developed among political sociologists in the special features of ethnicity and politics in plural societies. As defined by van den Berghe (1970:14): "Plural societies are those that are segmented into two or more groups that have distinct and duplicatory sets of institutions, except in the political and economic spheres where the institutions are shared."

Even as Japan is the crucial case on which theories of economic modernization have so often foundered, so South Africa is a decisive riddle for predictive theory of racial and ethnic relations. No "conflict theory" that leaves it out can be regarded as well grounded, for it represents a long-continued oligarchic racist system that seems to have been strengthened rather than weakened by rapid economic development and external pressure. How this unlikely result has been attained (through unified coercion, economic palliatives, political fragmentation of opposition, and other factors) has been analyzed by Adam (1971a, b).

As against the view that no major arrangements or strategies are likely to preserve stable democratic politics in plural societies (Rabushka & Shepsle 1972), other studies imply that not all possible institutional modes have been conceived or put into practice (Enloe 1973). For example, the ethnic-oriented revision of the Constitution of Belgium represents a modern political invention—an extremely complex multilevel system, combining features somewhat analogous to the Ottoman *millet* system with both federalism and bureaucratized parliamentary democracy (Dunn 1974). Whether the new arrangements will diminish conflict is not known, but at least there is something new under the sun.

9. Civil Disorders, Riots, or Rebellions

A separate section is necessary for this topic, because of both its theoretical and social significance.

Of the varied and voluminous literature produced in response to the civil turbulence of the 1960s, only a few works can be mentioned. It does seem useful to note the following: Balbus 1973; Berkowitz 1972; Downes 1970; Feagin & Hahn 1973; Ford & Moore 1970; Geschwender 1971; Geschwender & Singer 1970; Grimshaw 1969; Gurr 1972; Janowitz 1969; Jiobu 1971, 1974; Lieberson & Silverman 1965; Morgan & Clark 1973; Mueller 1971; Ransford 1968; Rule & Tilly 1972; Singer, Osborne & Geschwender 1970; Spilerman 1970, 1971a, b; Wanderer 1969; Williams 1970, 1972.

From the complex and sometimes contradictory data and inferences contained in the post-1967 writings, some conclusions elicited partial but substantial critical consensus. A few examples will suggest the character of the yield.

1. Neither absolute nor relative deprivation is a sufficient condition to produce collective shared discontent.

2. Collectively shared discontent, even if widespread and intense among members of a disadvantaged racial or ethnic minority, is not alone sufficient to produce collective protest or rebellion.

3. When widespread and intense discontent is justified by an accepted ideology and when hope of attainment of change has been raised and then blocked within channels of legitimized authority, collective protest will erupt among massive concentrations of the disaffected populations in large urban centers.

4. When nonviolent protest repeatedly meets with violent resistence that is local and episodic, the dissidents will become increasingly militant and the bystander publics will become increasingly polarized.

5. The conditions that explain the outbreak or frequency of collective violence are not the same as the conditions that best account for intensity, severity, or escalation.

6. Factors that account for *where* disorders occur during a particular period may not be those that account for *when* collective violence occurs.

7. Collective violence requires an assembling process that is much less well predicted by individual predispositions than by ecological settings in combination with communication processes (McPhail & Miller 1973).

Useful critical summaries of studies of riots have been published (Feagin & Hahn 1973; Singer, Osborne & Geschwender 1970). Although the data are fragmentary, and often unsatisfactory, some interpretations at least can be rejected or substantially discounted: riots were not primarily produced by a dislocated *lumpenproletariat* (riff-raff), nor by "radical conspiracy," nor by irrational crowd behavior of frustrated aggressive and alienated masses. Explanations in terms of relative deprivation not only fail to account for the transformation of individual discontent into collective action, but rest on uncertain factual bases (Feagin & Hahn 1973:22–24, Rossi & Berk 1972).

In large ghettos of riot cities, about 12–17% of blacks surveyed in 1968 regarded violence as "the best way for Negroes to gain their rights" (Campbell & Schuman 1968, Feagin & Hahn 1973:276–277). A majority of ghetto residents in riot areas said that riots had a definite aim or purpose (Feagin & Hahn 1973:271). Substantial proportions of "age-eligible" persons participated in riot activities, usually more than 10% and up to 35% (Feagin & Hahn 1973:279–82, Folgelson & Hill 1968).

Absolute size of black population and regional location emerged as the primary factors predictive of the *occurrence* (frequency) of urban revolts of the 1960s (Jiobu 1971; Spilerman 1970, 1971a), whereas a number of potentially significant socioeconomic variables were not predictive of rioting. Spilerman reported that the same pattern held for *severity* (intensity) of rioting (1971b). No community having less than 1000 black inhabitants had a riot during 1961–1968; nearly all large cities had disturbances. A critical level of discontent appears to have been reached in nearly all communities. There is some evidence suggesting that the frequency of specific grievances did not differ systematically between riot and nonriot cities (Rossi & Berk 1972). But analysis of data, for 1967 only, from a subsample of 42 cities (using a definition of racial disorders different from Spilerman's) found grievance levels related to riot *severity*—but in a complex manner that as yet does not have a decisive interpretation (Morgan & Clark 1973).

Although aggregative analysis shows that strictly local conditions were overweighed by conditions common to large cities in accounting for the incidence of mass violence, other data indicate that blacks in large central cities were sensitive, at the level of evaluations and expressed grievances, to certain local conditions (Rossi & Berk 1972).

Reflections on the domestic violence of the 1960s led several students of collective behavior to emphasize the two-sided relationships necessary to collective violence, i.e. the indispensability of both dissidents and their opponents. From a primacy concern with the protesting or rebelling population, attention shifted to the active role of the agents of the established social formations (Feagin & Hahn 1973, cf Skolnick 1969). Furthermore, the conception of the urban civil disorders came to be less of a "reactive hostile outburst" or an "unfocused signal of distress and rage" and more proactive, partly purposive, and certainly selective behavior focused on grievances and demands for change. In short, "riots" came to be seen as "civil tumults" or "revolts" or "insurgency," having some important elements of political protest and collective goals (Fogelson 1971, Skolnick 1969).

Another feature of recent study of violent conflict has been the increased use of complex multivariate models to aid in seeking causal inferences. Both characteristics are exemplified in the work of Spilerman (1970; 1971a, b) Jiobu (1971, 1974), and Downes (1970) on urban civil disorders; of Gurr (1970, Gurr & Duvall 1973) on political disorders and rebellion; and of Jacobson (1973) on a structural theory of intrasocietal conflict. In the field of political theory, Rosenau (1973) has argued that in macro-analyses across-systems theory now has greater explanatory power than within-systems theory.

Different types of conflicts within a particular society are positively intercorrelated. Furthermore, substantial autocorrelations are found: ". . . the level of domestic conflict in one year has an important effect on the level of domestic conflict in the following year" (Wilkenfeld & Zinnes 1973: 335; also Collins, 1973:273).

On the other hand, the idea that other nations are used as scapegoats or as elite-manipulated targets to divert domestic discontent receives little support from the finding that domestic and internal politics of nations are largely independent of one another (Burrowes & Spector 1973:315).

It is important to note that much social conflict is not "collective," e.g. the vast harrassment-and-arrest activity of police in the United States. If accurate estimates could be obtained, it is entirely possible that agents of authority initiate most of the activity that leads to violent conflict in American society.

10. Conditions Associated with Protest and Revolt

Neither social discontent nor intergroup conflict is closely correlated with the extent of objective deprivation. For people to experience a given condition as deprivational except for the case of sheer lack of minimal subsistence requires that the available gratifications be less than at a past time, less than known to exist in a reference population, or less than expected on the basis of past experience. To experience a given condition as deprivational because of the presence and actions of members of a different ethnic, racial, or religious grouping requires still more complex conditions.

The deprivations that are most consequential for intergroup relations are *categorical, relative,* and are regarded as *arbitrary* or *unjust.* The evidence supporting this generalization is massive.

To assume that objectively deprivational or oppressive conditions inevitably lead to discontent is unwarranted. To assume that widespread discontent necessarily leads to protest or rebellion is simplistic and incorrect. For discontent may be diffuse and unorganized and the discontented often are faced with overwhelming coercive capacity in the hands of committed supporters of an existing regime. Especially clear is the crucial importance of the willingness of police, armed services, and para-forces to put down protests and uprisings. Without substantial disaffection within the agencies of political authority, effective rebellion is unlikely, and even large scale attempts will be rare (Russell 1974). Disillusionment among students of ethnic relations concerning the effectiveness of coercion alone as a means of social control of violence can lead to serious underestimation of the effects of highly organized coercive systems operating in conjunction with positive incentives (Adam 1971a).

Not only is much behavior in situations of collective violence selective and self-controlled, but it is also limited and guided by group processes involving evaluation and decision by individuals. In confrontations of very high potential risk, violence may be subject to encapsulating and ritualized processes that reduce both intensity and incidence (Berk 1972). The level of acceptable risk varies enormously in different situations and across culture: some communities and some societies do not control violence effectively and thus experience chronically high levels of severe violence (for tribal societies, see Langness 1972).

Why are overt mass conflicts among groupings based on class or ethnicity so much more frequent than any remotely comparable clashes among groupings based on age?

A systematic comparison would be illuminating. The high degree of systemic inequality across age strata implies a strong potential for divergent and opposing interests and for conflict based on such cleavages, as well as upon differences in beliefs and values. Yet age-based collective conflicts are both comparatively rare and highly variable from one historical period to another. The relative rarity of age-related political conflicts is explicable in part by strong conflict-reducing conditions. Age strata are heavily criss-crossed by other group allegiances, common memberships. Such common participation often results in convergence of orientations and commonality of interests. Furthermore, since aging is inevitable and universal, persons usually are oriented both to stages they have left and to those they will enter. These orientations may either reduce or intensify conflict, depending upon the character of the issues, e.g. the military draft, or retirement provisions. In general conflicts over class-linked issues are less likely to polarize age strata against one another than are conflicts over ideal or moral issues (A. Foner 1974).

11. Strategies and Consequences in Collective Struggles

In contrast to preoccupations with the causes of conflict, comparatively little research attention has been directed to the consequences. Plausible assertions have pointed to urban civil disturbances as a possible source of increases in welfare case loads (Piven & Cloward 1971). An attempt to test this conception with aggregative data for the 43 largest cities did show a pattern of increases in combined state and city expenditures for welfare programs, 1965–1967, in the year following a riot (Betz 1974). Although consistent with other data, the hypothesized relationship still has not been demonstrated clearly nor have its dynamic sequences been specified.

Although consequences of different types of strategy and tactics still await rigorous empirical analysis, hypotheses are plentiful. Killian (1972:41) suggests that coercive and hostile "black power" leadership may:

> ... 1) increase the bargaining power of moderate leaders; 2) provide a corrective to illusions of progress ... 3) identify unresolved issues and define new ones; 4) radicalize a growing segment ... and increase the polarization between the movement and its opposition; 5) focus the attention of the opposition and the bystander public on new issues; and 6) evoke extreme repressive measures from the opposition.

Yet a strategy of threat admittedly appears to have secured gains not previously forthcoming.

One of the few studies to specify a sequential relationship between urban disturbances and responses of municipal authorities was Mueller's (1971) analysis of riot negotiations. Riots in the early 1960s had a prominent dramaturgical or "signaling" character. But later riots tended to be used in political bargaining: by 1967–1968, black representatives were carrying on formal negotiations with local officials in almost half of the cities in which riots occured. Using a four-item Guttman scale of outcomes, Mueller found that the first-order correlation of riot violence with success in negotiation was positive and substantial. Likewise, success in negotiations was strongly related to black militancy, as indexed by the range of grievances articulated as formal demands and requests. But when militancy was controlled, the intensity and violence of rioting showed a significant *negative* association with success. In appears, therefore, that the positive effect of rioting was to "gain attention." If clear and comprehensive demands could be presented by unified black representatives in a context of crisis, there was a high probability of some success. But extreme violence, locally, was counter-productive, especially if blacks did not translate grievances into specified demands and requests. Where a crisis could be presented to officials, short of an outbreak of mass violence, militant demands seem to have been successful. Other studies of local struggles seem consistent with these findings (e.g. Shockley 1974, Chalmers & Cormick 1971).

By the most generous estimate, however, the political and economic gains that could be attributed to the riots were quite limited, thus pointing to the prerequisite for political leverage, also indicated by Mueller's study, for "organizationally sophisticated leaders" to formulate and exert long term pressure for demands for social change (Greenstone & Peterson 1973: 308–9).

For new norms and procedures to become institutionalized in a complex social system, a great deal of both individual and "system" learning must occur. The learning typically is protracted. No exception is found in responses of established organizations to protest and violence. Nevertheless it does appear that there has been some learning, not only of techniques and tactics but also of " . . . an etiquette of (dealing with) disruption and protest, as part of a more general pattern of new etiquettes toward previously labeled antisocial activity" (Coates 1973: 35).

12. Beliefs and Values: The Special Case of Black and White in the United States.

There is much evidence of important similarities of opinions, attitudes, beliefs, values, and overt behavior between whites and blacks in the United States. (See the massive compilation in Miller & Dreger 1973). For example, Rossi et al (1974) find that in a Baltimore sample blacks and whites agree quite closely in their rankings of the seriousness of 140 crimes ($r = .89$).

At the highly generalized level indexed by the Rokeach Value Survey, no important relationships are found between individuals' values and their participation in violence, nor between lower class values and interpersonal violence (Ball-Rokeach 1973). A plausible inference is that for the types of violence indicated in the study, interpersonal interaction and situational factors, rather than intrapersonal predispositions, are decisive.

A complex configuration of similarities and differences between blacks and whites is well-defined by a comparative study in St. Louis, as of 1968 (Kahl & Goering 1971). In samples of stable working and middle-class men, blacks and whites were similar in job aspirations and satisfactions. Both segments of the population shared economic ambition, high hopes for their children, satisfaction with job and advancement, and had a sense of personal security in employment. Blacks and whites differed appreciably, however, in political orientations: blacks were more critical, more favorable to protest and to violence, more likely to accept a need for group militancy. In short, personal satisfaction among blacks did not imply political conservatism.

When socioeconomic status (income and education) is matched, blacks and whites differ in very few values (Rokeach 1973): " . . . the relatively few differences that remain after status is held constant provide virtually no support for a distinctive black culture of poverty. . . . The data . . . show only one big and pervasive value difference . . . Black Americans give *equality* high priority; white Americans place a far lower priority on *equality.*" As Rokeach notes, there nevertheless probably are important differences, not at the level of values ("aspirational culture"), but in those beliefs and valuations that concern situational constraints and opportunities.

IV. ISSUES OF METHODS AND THEORY

Research that aims to replace ignorance by knowledge has a relatively simple task, as over against research that is pitted against entrenched misinformation. To locate methodological pitfalls and to devise ways around them in the study of ethnic relations is accordingly a signal contribution. Recent encouraging examples include Spilerman's (1970; 1971a,b) use of theoretical distributions and partitioning to analyze urban riots; exposure of artifactual findings in studies of stereotypes (Ehrlich 1973); Reed's (1972b) development of an indicator of intergroup violence that takes into account the sizes of aggressor/victim populations; critical reexamination of the validity of doll-choices as indicators of racial attitudes (Hraba 1972, J. D. R. Porter 1971); work on specific subindicators of aspirations and expectations (Lorenz 1972); and, analysis of errors arising from use of cross-sectional correlations to infer longitudinal processes (Lieberson & Hansen 1974).

Problems of inference arise when muptiple indicators are used for the same conceptual variable, e.g, there is no compelling reason why occurrence and severity of "rioting" should correlate highly and, in fact, they do not (Jiobu 1974). Special difficulties of interpretation accompany the use of "surrogate" indicates, e.g. Gurr's 1970) use of level of past strife as an index of cultural justifications, or Spilerman's (1970) resort to percentage change in total and nonwhite population as a surrogate for "social disorganization."

Among recently favored statistical procedures, the general linear model overshadows all. Multiple regression methods are widely used; factor analysis, much less frequently. Path-analysis is the dominant fashion, although, increasingly, reservations and criticisms are being voiced, and alternatives explored (Kohn & Schooler 1973).

Overaggregation of available data is a chronic problem, often unavoidable. Nevertheless, the need to disaggregate such diverse conglomerations as "white population" is evident. Illustration of its importance are provided by 1. evidence that interethnic differences in educational attainment in New York City are greater than white-nonwhite differences (Rosenwaike 1973), and 2. educational attainments of children of southern and northern born blacks in the North are substantially different. Statistical controls for generation (and rural-urban background) appear essential for locating sources of variance within the black population (Lieberson 1973). Misleading inferences are likely with highly aggregated comparisons, e.g. a "rise" in income among blacks in the North might simply reflect a decrease of unskilled immigrants from the South.

Specifying the explicandum involves several dimensions, each critical for some purposes, viz: location in time (when), location in place (where), whether a property of individual persons or of aggregates or collectivities, whether a main or direct vs an indirect or interaction effect. A major conclusion from a recent study (Ellis, Grasmick & Gilman 1974:38) is that " . . . the effects of the same variable are not equally important in different social contexts . . . Theories purporting to explain interpersonal violence in prisons should be explicitly formulated in terms of both main and interaction effects."

Progress in comparative work depends crucially upon access to comparable data, but even that will not help greatly unless "comparative" ceases to mean merely "juxtaposed" or talked about together." More rigorous theoretical specifications must show what units and contexts really are structurally similar or different and what processes and sequences can be meaningfully compared. As one step in this process, a need has been identified for critical study of "exceptional cases" of visible and vulnerable ethnic minorities that have *not* been subjected to organized conflict or political efforts to evict or dislocate (Bonacich 1974, Stryker 1974).

A sense of history and an understanding of societies as complex dynamic systems would discourage such overgeneralized or unfounded assumptions as 1. the notion that "nonWASP ethnics" have been excluded from effective participation in the American polity (Novak 1971), 2. racial and cultural minorities can form a common front as easily on *cultural* as on *interest* bases, 3. greater popular participation will bring greater flexibility and less conflict into local political functioning, or 4. local control of urban schools is a new device that will reduce racial and ethnic conflict (see the contrary evidence in Ravitch 1974).

Theories in this field attempt to explain those complex repeated patterns that we call social processes and social structures. It is logically impossible that the dependent variables of interest can be fully explained by a single variable or explanatory concept (cf Cook 1970: 179–81). Always doomed, therefore, are "theories" that deal solely with equal-status contact, relative deprivation, grievance level, critical mass, frustration-discontent, or power struggle—much less with such global concepts as "racism," neocolonialism, or plural societies.

V. CONCLUSION

The high salience and social importance of ethnic relations often lead to a strong "sense of problem" accompanied by equally insistent demands for "solutions." Not surprisingly, research is called upon to be useful or "practical." Given that many social researchers adhere to democratic and universalistic values and that many identify with disadvantaged or oppressed people, we may be sure that much research on intergroup relations will continue to be guided by applied interests.

Much of the American research of the decade just past clearly has been strongly directed to pressing societal or group concerns.

On the record, there is not much danger that research in this field will become socially irrelevant. The more important question concerns the importance and validity of its pronouncements.

As the research of the decade is reviewed against prior codifications of findings and explanations, the following conclusions concerning progress in empirically based theories seem warranted:

1. Single-factor accounts of causation of intergroup attitudes and behavior definitely have been shown deficient and should no longer be taken seriously as scientific explanations. (They will continue to be of interest as objects of study, e.g. by sociology of knowledge and by political sociology).

2. Multivariate theories that confine their accounting to only one of the main systems of action—personality, culture, or social system—have demonstrated considerable power but fail to account for a large proportion of the variance and are logically deficient in specifying dynamic sequences.

3. The most effective attempts to explain ethnic relations have been both multivariate and systematically theoretical. For example, adequate accounting for intrasocietal collective violence requires specification of: (a) sources of widespread discontent; (b) communicative and organizational resources available to the discontented partisans and to the authorities (Gamson 1968), including locations in social structure; (c) cultural values and beliefs concerning priorities of goals and means, attribution of responsibility and efficacy, legitimacy of power, justifications, social trust, and effectiveness of protest and rebellion; (d) resources and organizational support for incumbent authorities and institutions; (e) resources and organizational support for discontented and protesting opponents of incumbent authorities and regimes; (f) "crucial events" that signal intentions and strength or weakness of opposing social formations and movements.

Much of the contribution of past and current research has been the factual confrontations and logical criticisms that have debunked myths and stereotypes, refuted erroneous assumptions, and challenged superficial explanations. This critical activity is indispensable and must continue. But, in addition, we believe the time has come for greater pressure on work in this field to pose *explanatory* problems and to search for sufficient as well as necessary conditions. This usually means a complex research strategy for coping with multivariate designs (R. M. Williams 1972), but closer approximations to experiments should be sought whenever clear specification of main variables is feasible.

Full hospitality is recommended for data, methods, and concepts from other behavioral and social sciences. "Race and ethnic relations" are not respectful of academic boundaries. Of course, there is a distinctive sociological core, and within it emphasis rightly will remain on variables suggested by concepts of norms, institutions, power, and authority, statuses, social networks, social structures, and the like. The power of such variables in explaining large-scale social movements and conflicts of our time has never been clearer—thanks to some of the work here reviewed.

Literature Cited

Ablon, J. 1971. Retention of cultural values and differential urban adaptation, Samoans and American Indians in a West Coast City. *Soc. Forces* 49:385–93

Adam, H. 1971a. *Modernizing Racial Domination, The Dynamics of South African Politics.* Berkeley: Univ. Calif. Press. 203 pp.

Adam, H., Ed. 1971b. *South Africa: Sociological Perspectives.* London: Oxford Univ. Press. 340 pp.

Aldrich, H. E. 1973. Employment opportunities for blacks in the black ghetto, the role of white-owned businesses. *Am. J. Sociol.* 78:1403–25

Amir, Y. 1969. Contact hypothesis in ethnic relations. *Psychol. Bull.* 71:319–42

Anderson, C. H. 1970. *White Protestant Americans, From National Origins to Religious Group.* Englewood Cliffs, N.J.: Prentice-Hall. 188 pp.

Andreasen, A. R. 1972. *Inner City Business, A Case Study of Buffalo, New York.* London: Pall Mall Press. 238 pp.

Balbus, I. D. 1973. *The Dialectics of Legal Repression, Black Rebels Before the American Criminal Courts.* New York: Russell Sage. 269 pp.

Ball-Rokeach, S. J. 1973. Values and violence, a test of the subculture of violence thesis. *Am. Sociol. Rev.* 38:736–47

Barron, M., Ed. 1972. *The Blending American, Patterns of Intermarriage.* Chicago: Quadrangle Books. 357 pp.

Barth, E. A. T., Noel, D. L. 1972. Conceptual frameworks for the analysis of race relations, an evaluation. *Soc. Forces* 50:333–48

Barth, F., Ed. 1969. *Ethnic Groups and Boundaries, The Social Organization of Culture Differences.* Boston: Little, Brown. 153 pp.

Bell, L. V. 1973. *In Hitler's Shadow, The Anatomy of American Nazism.* Port Washington, N.Y.: Kennikat Press. 135 pp.

Bellush, J., David, S. M., Eds. 1971. *Race and Politics in New York City.* New York: Praeger. 202 pp.

Belmont, L., Marolla, F. A. 1973. Birth order, family size, and intelligence. *Science* 182:1096–1101

Berelson, B., Steiner, G. A. 1964. *Human Behavior.* New York: Harcourt, Brace & World. 712 pp.

Berk, R. A. 1972. The emergence of muted violence in crowd behavior, a case study of an almost riot. In *Collective Violence,* ed. J. F. Short Jr., M. E. Wolfgang,

309–28. Chicago: Aldine-Atherton. 387 pp.

Berk, R. A., Aldrich, H. E. 1972. Patterns of vandalism during civil disorders as an indicator of selection of targets. *Am. Sociol. Rev.* 37:533–47

Berkowitz, L. 1972. Frustrations, comparisons, and other sources of emotional arousal as contributors to social unrest. *J. Soc. Issues* 28:77–91

Berry, B. 1972. America's mestizos. In *The Blending of Races, Marginality and Identity in World Perspective,* ed. N. P. Gist, A. C. Dworkin, 191–212. New York: Wiley-Interscience. 289 pp.

Berson, L. E. 1971. *The Negroes and the Jews.* New York: Random House. 436 pp.

Betz, D. M. 1972. The city as a system generating income in equality. *Soc. Forces* 51:192–98

Betz, M. 1974. Riots and welfare, are they related? *Soc. Probl.* 21:345–55

Binderman, M. B. 1972. The failure of freedom of choice, decision-making in a Southern black community. *Soc. Forces* 50:487–98

Black, E. 1974. The militant segregationist vote in the post-Brown South, a comparative analysis. *Soc. Sci. Quart.* 54:66–84

Blalock, H. M. Jr. 1970. *Toward a Theory of Minority-Group Relations.* New York: Capricorn Books. 227 pp.

Blanchard, F. A., Adelman, L., Cook, S. W. 1975. The effect of group success and failure upon interpersonal attraction in cooperating interracial groups. *J. Pers. Soc. Psychol.* In press

Blau, P. M., Duncan, O. D. 1967. *American Occupational Structure.* New York: Wiley 520 pp.

Blauner, R. 1969. Internal colonialism and ghetto revolt. *Soc. Probl.* 16:393–408

Blauner, R. 1972. *Racial Oppression in America.* New York: Harper & Row. 309 pp.

Bonacich, E. 1973. A theory of middleman minorities. *Am. Sociol. Rev.* 38:583–94

Bonacich, E. 1974. Reply to comment by Stryker. *Am. Sociol. Rev.* 39:282–3

Bonacich, E., Goodman, R. F. 1972. *Deadlock in School Desegregation, A Case Study of Inglewood, California.* New York: Praeger. 118 pp.

Bouma, G. 1970. *Is there a religious factor?* PhD thesis. Cornell Univ.: Ithaca, N.Y. 157 pp.

Bracey, J. H. Jr., Meier, A., Rudwick, E., Eds. 1971. *The Black Sociologists, The*

First Half Century. Belmont, Calif.: Wadsworth. 186 pp.

Bradburn, N. M., Sudman, S., Gockel, G. L., Noll, J. R. 1970. *Racial Integration in American Neighborhoods, A Comparative Survey.* Chicago: Nat. Opinion Res. Center. 599 pp.

Braun, R. 1970. *Soziokulturelle Probleme der Eingliederung italienische Arbeitskrafte in der Schweiz.* Erlenback-Zürich: Eugen Rentsch. 589 pp.

Browning, H. L., Lopreato, S. C., Poston, D. L. Jr. 1973. Income and veterans status, variations among Mexican Americans, Blacks, and Anglos. *Am. Sociol. Rev.* 78:74–85

Bullock, C. S. III, Braxton, M. V. 1973. The coming of school desegregation, a before and after study of black and white student perceptions. *Soc. Sci. Quart.* 54:132–38

Burkey, R. M. 1971. *Racial Discrimination and Public Policy in the United States.* Lexington, Mass.: D. C. Heath. 145 pp.

Burrowes, R., Spector, B. 1973. The strength and direction of relationships. In *Conflict Behavior and Linkage Politics,* ed. J. Wilkenfeld, 294–321. New York: McKay. 388 pp.

Campbell, A., Schuman, H. 1968. *Racial Attitudes in Fifteen American Cities.* Ann Arbor: Inst. Soc. Res. Univ. Michigan. 67 pp.

Campbell, E. Q., Ed. 1972. *Racial Tensions and National Identity.* Nashville: Vanderbilt Univ. Press. 262 pp.

Campbell, J. S. 1972. The usefulness of Commission studies of collective violence. In *Collective Violence,* ed. J. F. Short Jr., M. R. Wolfgang, 370–78. Chicago: Aldine-Atherton. 387 pp.

Chalmers, W. E., Cormick, G. W., Eds. 1971. *Racial Conflict and Negotiations, Perspectives and First Case Studies.* Ann Arbor: Inst. Labor Ind. Relat., and Nat. Center Dispute Settlement. 246 pp.

Chudacoff, H. P. 1972. *Mobile Americans, Residential and Social Mobility in Omaha, 1880–1970.* New York: Oxford Univ. Press. 195 pp.

Coates, J. F. 1973. Urban violence—the pattern of disorder. *The Annals* 405:25–40

Cohen, E., Roper, S. S. 1972. Modifications of interracial interaction disability, an application of status characteristic theory. *Am. Sociol. Rev.* 37:643–57

Cole, J. W., Wolf, E. R. 1974. *The Hidden Frontier, Ecology and Ethnicity in an Alpine Valley.* New York: Academic. 348 pp.

Coleman, J. S. 1971. *Resources for Social Change, Race in the United States.* New York: Wiley-Interscience. 109 pp.

Coleman, J. S. 1973. Equality of opportunity and equality of results. *Harvard Educ. Rev.* 43:129–34

Coleman, J. S. et al 1966. *Equality of Educational Opportunity.* Washington, DC: GPO. 737 pp.

Collins, J. N. 1973. Foreign conflict behavior and domestic disorder in Africa. In *Conflict Behavior and Linkage Politics,* ed. J. Wilkenfeld, 251–93. New York: McKay. 388 pp.

Cook, S. W. 1970. Motives in a conceptual analysis of attitude related behavior. In *1969 Nebraska Symposium on Motivation,* ed. W. J. Arnold, D. Levine, 179–231. Lincoln, Nebraska: Univ. Nebr. Press. 17:334

Corwin, R. D. 1971. *Racial Minorities in Banking, New Workers in the Banking Industry.* New Haven: College & Univ. Press. 128 pp.

Coser, L. A. 1956. *The Functions of Social Conflict.* New York: Free Press. 188 pp.

Coser, L. A. 1967. *Continuities in the Study of Social Conflict.* New York: Free Press. 272 pp.

Coser, L. A., Ed. 1972. Collective violence and civil conflict. *J. Soc. Issues* 28:1–234

Crain, R. L. 1970. School integration and occupational achievement of Negroes. *Am J. Sociol.* 75:593–606

Crain, R. L., Weisman, C. S. 1972. *Discrimination, Personality and Achievement—A Survey of Northern Blacks.* New York: Seminar Press. 225 pp.

Cutright, P. 1974. The civilian earnings of white and black draftees and nonveterans. *Am. Sociol. Rev.* 39:317–27

Daniels, R. 1972. *The Politics of Prejudice.* New York: Atheneum. 165 pp.

Das Gupta, J. 1974. Ethnicity, language demands, and national development. *Ethnicity* 1:65–72

Davidson, C. 1972. *Biracial Politics, Conflict and Coalition in the Metropolitan South.* Baton Rouge: Louisiana State Univ. Press. 301 pp.

Davies, J. C. 1974. The J-curve and power-struggle theories of collective violence. *Am. Sociol. Rev.* 39:607–10

Davis, D. B. 1966. *The Problem of Slavery in Western Culture.* Ithaca, N.Y.: Cornell Univ. Press. 505 pp.

DeFries, J. C., Kuse, A. R., Vandenberg, S. G., McClearn, G. E., Wilson, J. R. 1974. Near identity of cognitive structure in two ethnic groups. *Science* 183:338–39

Degler, C. N. 1971. *Neither Black nor White, Slavery and Race Relations in Brazil & the United States.* New York: Macmillan. 302 pp.

Demerath, N. J. III, Marwell, G., Aiken, M. T. 1971. *Dynamics of Idealism, White Activists in a Black Movement.* San Francisco: Jossey-Bass. 228 pp.

Diamond, S. A. 1974. *The Nazi Movement in the United States, 1924–1941.* Ithaca, N.Y.: Cornell Univ. Press. 380 pp.

Dinnerstein, L., Jaher, F. C., Eds. 1970. *The Aliens, A History of Ethnic Minorities in America.* New York: Appleton. 347 pp.

Dobzhansky, T. 1973. *Genetic Diversity and Human Equality.* New York: Basic Books. 128 pp.

Downes, B. T. 1970. A critical reexamination of the social and political characteristics of riot cities. *Soc. Sci. Quart.* 51:349–60

Duncan, O. D. 1968. Patterns of occupational mobility among Negro men. *Demography* 5:11–22

Duncan, O. D. 1969. Inheritance of poverty or inheritance of race? In *On Understanding Poverty,* ed. D. P. Moynihan, 85–110. New York: Basic Books. 425 pp.

Duncan, O. D., Featherman, D. L., Duncan, B. 1972. *Socioeconomic Background and Achievement.* New York: Seminar Press. 284 pp.

Dunn, J. A. Jr. 1974. The revision of the Constitution in Belgium, a study in the institutionalization of ethnic conflict. *West. Polit. Sci. Quart.* XXVII:143–63

Duran, J. J. 1974. The ecology of ethnic groups from a Kenyan perspective. *Ethnicity* 1:43–64

Edgerton, R. B. 1972. Violence in East African tribal societies. In *Collective Violence,* ed. J. F. Short Jr., M. E. Wolfgang, 159–70. Chicago: Aldine-Atherton. 387 pp.

Ehrlich, H. J. 1973. *The Social Psychology of Prejudice: A Systematic Theoretical Review and Propositional Inventory of the American Social Psychological Study of Prejudice.* New York: Wiley-Interscience. 208 pp.

Eisenstadt, S. N. 1971. Continuities and changes in systems of stratification. In *Stability and Social Change,* ed. B. Barber, A. Inkeles, 61–81. Boston: Little, Brown. 451 pp.

Elder, G. H. Jr. 1970. Group orientations and strategies in racial change. *Soc. Forces* 48:445–61

Elkins, S. M. 1959. *Slavery, A Problem in American Institutional and Intellectual Life.* Chicago: Univ. Chicago Press. 247 pp.

Ellis, D., Grasmick, H. G., Gilman, B. 1974. Violence in prisons, a sociological analysis. *Am. J. Sociol.* 80:16–43

Enloe, C. H. 1973. *Ethnic Conflict and Political Development.* Boston: Little, Brown. 282 pp.

Epps, E. G. 1969. Correlates of academic achievement among Northern and Southern Negro students. *J. Soc. Issues* 25:55–70

Evans, E. N. 1973. *The Provincials, A Personal History of the Jews in the South.* New York: Atheneum. 369 pp.

Farley, R., Taeuber, A. F. 1974. Racial segregation in the public schools. *Am. J. Sociol.* 79:888–905

Feagin, J. R. 1971. White separatists and black separatists, a comparative analysis. *Soc. Probl.* 19:167–80

Feagin, J. R. 1972. Civil rights voting by Southern Congressmen. *J. Polit.* 34:484–99

Feagin, J. R., Hahn, H. 1970. The second Reconstruction: black political strength in the South. *Soc. Sci. Quart.* 51:42–56

Feagin, J. R., Hahn, H. 1973. *Ghetto Riots, The Politics of Violence in American Cities.* New York: Macmillan. 338 pp.

Featherman, D. L. 1972. Achievement orientations and socioeconomic career attainments. *Am. Sociol. Rev.* 37:131–43

Fitzpatrick, J. P. 1971. *Puerto Rican Americans: The Meaning of Migration to the Mainland.* Englewood Cliffs, N.J.: Prentice-Hall. 192 pp.

Flanagan, R. J. 1973a. Segmented market theories and racial discrimination. *Ind. Relat.* 12:253–73

Flanagan, R. J. 1973b. Racial wage discrimination and employment segregation. *J. Hum. Resour.* VIII:456–71

Fogel, R. W., Engerman, S. L. 1973a. *Time on the Cross, The Economics of American Negro Slavery.* Boston: Little, Brown. 286 pp.

Fogel, R. W., Engerman, S. L. 1973b. *Time on the Cross, Evidence and Methods—A Supplement.* Boston: Little, Brown. 267 pp.

Fogelson, R. M. 1971. *Violence as Protest.* Garden City, N.Y.: Doubleday. 265 pp.

Fogelson, R. M., Hill, R. B. 1968. Who riots? A study of participation in the 1967 riots. In *Supplemental Studies for the National Advisory Commission on Civil Disorders.* Washington, D.C.: GPO. 248 pp.

Foner, A. 1974. Age stratification and age conflict in political life. *Am. Sociol. Rev.* 39:187–96

Foner, P. S. 1974. *Organized Labor and the Black Worker, 1619–1973.* New York: Praeger. 489 pp.

Ford, W. F., Moore, J. H. 1970. Additional evidence on the social characteristics of riot cities. *Soc. Sci. Quart.* 51:339–48

Ford, W. S. 1972. *Interracial Public Housing in Border City.* Lexington, Mass.: D.C. Heath. 99 pp.

Ford, W. S. 1973. Interracial public housing in a border city, another look at the contact hypothesis. *Am. J. Sociol.* 78:1426–45

Franklin, V. P. 1974. The persistence of school segregation in the urban North, an historical perspective. *J. Ethnic Stud.* 1:51–68

Freyre, G. 1946. *The Masters and the Slaves.* New York: Knopf. 537 pp.

Gamson, W. A. 1968. *Power and Discontent.* Homewood, Ill.: Dorsey. 208 pp.

Gamson, W. A. 1975. *Strategies of Social Protest.* Homewood, Ill.: Dorsey. 217 pp.

Geschwander, J. A., Ed. 1971. *The Black Revolt—The Civil Rights Movement, Ghetto Uprisings, and Separatism.* Englewood Cliffs, N.J.: Prentice-Hall. 483 pp.

Geschwender, J. A., Singer, B. D. 1970. Deprivation and the Detroit riot. *Soc. Probl.* 17:457–63

Glazer, N. 1971. Blacks and ethnic groups, the difference and the political difference it makes. *Soc. Probl.* 18:444–61

Glazer, N., Moynihan, D. P. 1974. Why ethnicity? *Commentary* 58:33–39

Goering, J. M. 1971. The emergence of ethnic interests: a case of serendipity. *Soc. Forces* 49:379–84

Gordon, D. N. 1970. Immigrants and municipal voting turnout, implications for the changing ethnic impact on urban politics. *Am. Sociol. Rev.* 35:665–81

Gould, W. S. 1973. Racial conflict in the U.S. Army. *Race* XV:1–24

Grebler, L., Moore, J. W., Guzman, R. C., Eds. 1970. *The Mexican-American People, the Nation's Second Largest Minority.* New York: Free Press. 777 pp.

Greeley, A. M. 1971. *Why Can't They Be Like Us?* New York: Dutton. 223 pp.

Greeley, A. M. 1972. *That Most Distressful Nation.* Chicago: Quadrangle Books. 281 pp.

Greeley, A. M. 1973. The "religious factor" and academic careers, another communication. *Am. J. Sociol.* 78:1247–55

Greeley, A. M., McCready, W. C. 1974. Does ethnicity matter? *Ethnicity* 1:91–108

Greenstein, L. J. 1973. Slave and citizen, the South African case. *Race* XV:25–46

Greenstone, J. D., Peterson, P. E. 1973. *Race and Authority in Urban Politics, Community Participation and the War on Poverty.* New York: Russell Sage. 364 pp.

Grimshaw, A. D., Ed. 1969. *Racial Violence in the United States.* Chicago: Aldine. 553 pp.

Gurin, P. 1970. Motivation and aspirations of Southern Negro college youth. *Am. J. Sociol.* 75:607–31

Gurr, T. R. 1970. *Why Men Rebel.* Princeton, N.J.: Princeton Univ. Press. 421 pp.

Gurr, T. R. 1972. The calculus of civil conflict. *J. Soc. Issues.* 28:27–47

Gurr, T. R., Duvall, R. 1973. Civil conflict in the 1960's, a reciprocal theoretical system with parameter estimates. *Comp. Polit. Stud.* 6:135–69

Hagopian, E. C., Paden, A., Eds. 1969. *The Arab-Americans, Studies in Assimilation.* Wilmette, Illinois: Medina Univ. Press Int. 111 pp.

Hammond, J. L. 1974. Revival religion and anti-slavery politics. *Am. Sociol. Rev.* 39:175–86

Hanna, W. J., Hanna, J. L. 1969. *Urban Dynamics in Black Africa.* Washington, D.C.: Center. Res. Soc. Systems, American Univ. 356 pp.

Hannerz, V. 1970. *Soulside.* New York: Columbia Univ. Press. 236 pp.

Harding, J., Kutner, B., Proshansky, H., Chein, I. 1954. Prejudice and ethnic relations. In *Handbook of Social Psychology,* ed. G. Lindzey, 2:1021–61. Cambridge, Mass.: Addison-Wesley. 1226 pp.

Harrell, D. E. Jr. 1971. *White Sects and Black Men in the Recent South.* Nashville: Vanderbilt Univ. Press. 161 pp.

Harris, L., Swanson, B. E. 1970. *Black-Jewish Relations in New York City.* New York: Praeger. 234 pp.

Harris, M. 1964. *Patterns of Race in the Americas.* New York: Walker. 154 pp.

Hauser, R. M., Featherman, D. L. 1974. Socioeconomic achievements of U.S. men, 1962 to 1972. *Science* 185:325–31

Hechter, M. 1972. Industrialization and national development in the British Isles. *J. Develop. Stud.* 8:155–82

Hechter, M. 1973. The persistence of regionalism in the British Isles, 1885–1966. *Am. J. Sociol.* 79:319–42

Hechter, M. 1974. The political economy of ethnic change. *Am. J. Sociol.* 79: 1151–78

Heiss, J. 1972. On the transmission of marital instability in black families. *Am. Sociol. Rev.* 37:82–92

Heller, C. S. 1971. *New Converts to the American Dream, Mobility Aspirations of Young Mexican Americans.* New Haven: College & Univ. Press. 287 pp.

Helmreich, W. B. 1973. *The Black Crusaders, A Case Study of a Black Militant Organization.* New York: Harper & Row. 196 pp.

Herrnstein, R. J. 1973. *I.Q. in the Meritocracy.* Boston: Atlantic-Little, Brown. 235 pp.

Heyns, B. 1974. Social selection and stratification within schools. *Am. J. Sociol.* 79:1434–51

Hill, R. B. 1972. *The Strengths of Black Families.* New York: Emerson Hall. 76 pp.

Hill, R. C. 1974. Unionization and racial income inequality in the metropolis. *Am. Sociol. Rev.* 39:507–22

Himes, J. S. 1973. *Racial Conflict in American Society.* Columbus, Ohio: Merrill. 205 pp.

Himmelfarb, M. 1973. *The Jews of Modernity.* New York: Basic Books. 369 pp.

Hodge, R. W. 1973. Toward a theory of racial differences in employment. *Soc. Forces.* 52:16–31

Horowitz, R., Schwartz, G. 1974. Honor, normative ambiguity and gang violence. *Am. Sociol. Rev.* 39:238–51

Hraba, J. 1972. The doll technique, a measure of racial ethnocentrism? *Soc. Forces.* 50:522–27

Hunt, C. L., Walker, L. 1974. *Ethnic Dynamics, Patterns of Intergroup Relations in Various Societies.* Homewood, Ill.: Dorsey Press. 463 pp.

Hunter, A. 1974. Community change, a stochastic analysis of Chicago's local communities, 1930–60. *Am. J. Sociol.* 79:923–47

Hurst, C. 1972. Race, class and consciousness. *Am. Sociol. Rev.* 37:658–70

Ianni, F. A. J. 1972. *A Family Business.* New York: Russell Sage. 199 pp.

Ianni, F. A. J. 1974. *Black Mafia, Ethnic Succession in Organized Crime.* New York: Simon & Schuster. 381 pp.

Ikeda, K. 1973. *Soc. Forces.* 51:497–99

Iorizzo, L. J., Mondello, S. 1971. *The Italian-Americans.* New York: Tawyne. 273 pp.

Isaacs, H. R. 1974. Basic group identity, the idols of the tribe. *Ethnicity* 1:15–44

Jacobson, A. L. 1973. Intrasocietal conflict, a preliminary test of a structural-level theory. *Comp. Polit. Stud.* 6:62–83

Janowitz, M. 1969. Patterns of collective racial violence. In *Violence in America,* ed. H. D. Graham, T. R. Gurr, 45–84. New York: Bantam Books. 822 pp.

Janowitz, M., Moskos, C. C. Jr. 1974. Racial composition in the all-volunteer force, policy alternatives. *Armed Forces and Society.* 1:109–23

Jencks, C. et al 1972. *Inequality, a Reassessment of the Effect of Family and Schooling in America.* New York: Basic Books. 399 pp.

Jensen, A. R. 1972. *Genetics and Education.* New York: Harper & Row. 378 pp.

Jiobu, R. M. 1971. City characteristics, differential stratification, and the occurrence of interracial violence. *Soc. Sci. Quart.* 52:508–20

Jiobu, R. M. 1974. City characteristics and racial violence. *Soc. Sci. Quart.* 55:52–64

Kahl, J. A., Goering, J. M. 1971. Stable workers, black & white. *Soc. Probl.* 18:306–18

Kantrowitz, N. 1973. *Ethnic and Racial Segregation in the New York Metropolis, Residential Patterns among White Ethnic Groups, Blacks, and Puerto Ricans.* New York: Praeger. 122 pp.

Katznelson, I. 1973a. *Black Men, White Cities, Race, Politics, and Migration in the United States, 1900–30, and Britain, 1948–68.* London: Oxford Univ. Press. 219 pp.

Katznelson, I. 1973b. Participation and political buffers in urban America. *Race* XIV:465–80

Keech, W. R. 1968. *The Impact of Negro Voting, The Role of the Vote in the Quest for Equality.* Chicago: Rand McNally. 113 pp.

Killian, L. M. 1970. *White Southerners.* New York: Random House. 171 pp.

Killian, L. M. 1972. The significance of extremism in the Black revolution. *Soc. Probl.* 20:41–49

Kinloch, G. C. 1974. *The Dynamics of Race Relations.* New York: McGraw-Hill. 305 pp.

Kinton, J. F., Ed. 1972. *American Ethnic Groups, A Sourcebook for the 1970's.* Mount Pleasant, Iowa: Soc. Sci. Sociol. Resour. 113 pp.

Klein, H. S. 1967. *Slavery in the Americas, a Comparative Study of Virginia and Cuba.* Chicago: Univ. Chicago Press. 270 pp.

Knight, F. W. 1970. *Slave Society in Cuba during the Nineteenth Century.* Madison: Univ. Wisconsin Press. 228 pp.

Kohn, M. L., Schooler, C. 1973. Occupational experience and psychological functioning, an assessment of reciprocal effects. *Am. Sociol. Rev.* 38:97–118

Kouvetaris, G. A. 1971. *First and second generation Greeks in Chicago.* Athens, Greece: Nat. Center Soc. Res. 111 pp.

Kriesberg, L. 1973. *The Sociology of Social Conflicts.* Englewood Cliffs, New Jersey: Prentice-Hall. 300 pp.

Kronus, S. 1971. *The Black Middle Class.* Columbus, Ohio: Merrill. 182 pp.

Langness, J. F. 1972. *Collective Violence,* ed. J. F. Short Jr., M. E. Wolfgang, 171–85. Chicago: Aldine-Atherton. 287 pp.

Laumann, E. O. 1973. *Bonds of Pluralism, The Form and Substance of Urban Social Networks.* New York: Wiley. 326 pp.

Lazerwitz, B. 1973. Religious identification and its ethnic correlates, A multivariate model. *Soc. Forces* 52:204–19

LeVine, R. A., Campbell, D. T. 1972. *Ethnocentrism, Theories of Conflict, Ethnic Attitudes and Group Behavior.* New York: Wiley. 310 pp.

Levy, C. J. 1968. *Voluntary Servitude, Whites in the Negro Movement.* New York: Appleton. 125 pp.

Lieberson, S. 1970. *Language and Ethnic Relations in Canada.* New York: Wiley. 264 pp.

Lieberson, S. 1973. Generational differences among blacks in the North. *Am. J. Sociol.* 79:550–65

Lieberson, S., Hansen, L. K. 1974. National development, mother tongue diversity, and the comparative study of nations. *Am. Sociol. Rev.* 39:523–41

Lieberson, S., Silverman, A. R. 1965. The precipitants and underlying conditions of race riots. *Am. Sociol. Rev.* 30:887–98

Liebman, C. S. 1973. *The Ambivalent American Jew.* Philadelphia: Jewish Publ. Soc. Am. 215 pp.

Light, I. H. 1972. *Ethnic Enterprise in America, Business and Welfare among Chinese, Japanese and Blacks.* Berkeley: Univ. Calif. Press. 209 pp.

Lodhi, A. Q., Tilly, C. 1973. Urbanization, crime, and collective violence in 19th century France. *Am. J. Sociol.* 79:296–316

Loewen, J. W. 1971. *The Mississippi Chinese, Between Black and White.* Cambridge: Harvard Univ. Press. 237 pp.

Lopreato, J. 1970. *Italian Americans.* New York: Random House. 204 pp.

Lorenz, G. 1972. Aspirations of low-income blacks and whites, a case of reference group processes. *Am. J. Sociol.* 78:371–98

Lowe, G. D., Hodges, H. E. 1972. Race and the treatment of alcoholism in a Southern state. *Soc. Probl.* 20:240–52

Lyman, S. M. 1974. *Chinese Americans.* New York: Random House. 213 pp.

Lynch, H. R. 1973. *The Black Urban Condition, A Documentary History, 1886–1971.* New York: Crowell. 469 pp.

Mack, R. W., Snyder, R. C. 1957. The analysis of social conflict—toward an overview and synthesis. *J. Conflict Resolut.* 1:212–48

Mackie, M. 1973. Arriving at 'truth' by definition, the case of stereotype inaccuracy. *Soc. Probl.* 20:431–47

McCormick, R. L. 1974. Ethno-cultural interpretations of nineteenth century American voting behavior. *Polit. Sci. Quart.* 89:351–77

McMillen, N. R. 1971. *The Citizens' Council, Organized Resistance to the Second Reconstruction, 1954–64.* Urbana: Univ. Illinois Press. 397 pp.

McPhail, C., Miller, D. L. 1973. The assembling process, a theoretical and empirical examination. *Am. Sociol. Rev.* 38:721–35

Meade, A. 1972. The distribution of segregation in Atlanta. *Soc. Forces* 51:182–92

Meier, A., Rudwick, E. 1973. *CORE, A Study in the Equal Rights Movement, 1942–1968.* New York: Oxford Univ. Press. 563 pp.

Miller, K. S., Dreger, R. M., Eds. 1973. *Comparative Studies of Blacks and Whites in the United States.* New York: Seminar Press. 572 pp.

Molotch, H. 1972. *Managed Integration, Dilemmas of Doing Good in the City.* Berkeley: Univ. Calif. Press. 250 pp.

Moore, J. W., Cuéllar, A. 1970. *Mexican Americans.* Englewood Cliffs, N.J.: Prentice-Hall. 172 pp.

Morgan, W. R., Clark, T. N. 1973. The causes of racial disorders, a grievance-level explanation. *Am. Sociol. Rev.* 38:611–24

Moskos, C. C. Jr. 1969. The Negro and the draft. In *Selective Service and American Society,* ed. R. W. Little, 139–62. New York: Russell Sage. 220 pp.

Moskos, C. C. Jr. 1971. Minority groups in military organizations. In *Handbook of Military Institutions,* ed. R. W. Little,

271–89. Beverly Hills, Calif.: Sage Publications. 607 pp.

Moskos, C. C. Jr. 1973. The American dilemma in uniform, race in the Armed Forces. *The Annals* 406:94–106

Mosteller, F., Moynihan, D. P., Eds. 1972. *On Equality of Educational Opportunity.* New York: Random House. 572 pp.

Mueller, C. 1971. *Riot negotiations, conditions of successful bargaining in the ghetto riots of the 1960's.* PhD thesis. Cornell Univ., Ithaca, N.Y. 307 pp.

Muir, D. E. 1971. The first years of desegregation, patterns of acceptance of black students on a Deep-South campus, 1963–69. *Soc. Forces.* 49:371–78

Murray, P. T. 1971. Local draft board composition and institutional racism. *Soc. Probl.* 19:129–37

Nelson, H. A. 1971. Leadership and change in an evolutionary movement, an analysis of change in the leadership structure of the Southern civil rights movement. *Soc. Forces* 49:353–71

Nikolinakos, M. 1973. Notes on an economic theory of racism. *Race* XIV:365–81

Novak, M. 1971. *The Rise of the Unmeltable Ethnics.* New York: Macmillan. 321 pp.

Oberschall, A. 1973. *Social Conflict and Social Movements.* Englewood Cliffs, New Jersey: Prentice-Hall. 371 pp.

O'Reilly, R. P., Ed. 1970. *Racial and Class Isolation in the Schools, Implications for Educational Policy and Programs.* New York: Praeger. 401 pp.

Palmore, E., Whittington, F. J. 1970. Differential trends toward equality between whites and nonwhites. *Soc. Forces* 49:108–17

Parris, G., Brooks, L. 1971. *Blacks in the City, A History of the National Urban League.* Boston: Little, Brown. 534 pp.

Petersen, W. 1971. *Japanese Americans, Oppression and Success.* New York: Random House. 268 pp.

Pettigrew, T. F. 1971. *Racially Separate or Together?* New York: McGraw-Hill. 371 pp.

Piven, F. F., Cloward, R. A. 1971. *Regulating the Poor, The Functions of Public Welfare.* New York: Pantheon. 389 pp.

Porter, J. 1973. Review of C. Jencks et al. *Cont. Sociol.* 2:463–67

Porter, J. D. R. 1971. *Black Child, White Child, The Development of Racial Attitudes.* Cambridge: Harvard Univ. Press. 278 pp.

Porter, J. N. 1974. Race, socialization and mobility in educational and early occupational attainment. *Am. Sociol. Rev.* 39:303–16

Rabushka, A., Shepsle, K. A. 1972. *Politics in Plural Societies, A Theory of Democratic Instability.* Columbus, Ohio: Merrill. 232 pp.

Rainwater, L. 1970. *Behind Ghetto Walls, Black Families in a Federal Slum.* Chicago: Aldine. 446 pp.

Ransford, E. H. 1968. Isolation, powerlessness, and violence. *Am. J. Sociol.* 73:581–91

Ravitch, D. 1974. *The Great School Wars, New York City, 1805–1973. A History of the Public Schools as a Battlefield of Social Change.* New York: Basic Books. 449 pp.

Reed, J. S. 1972a. *The Enduring South, Subcultural Persistence in Mass Society.* Lexington, Mass.: D. C. Heath. 135 pp.

Reed, J. S. 1972b. Percent black and lynching, a test of Blalock's theory. *Soc. Forces* 50:356–60

Reid, M. 1972. *The Shouting Signpainters, A Literary and Political Account of Quebec Revolutionary Nationalism.* New York: Monthly Rev. Press. 315 pp.

Rex, J. 1973a. Quarterly Forum. *Race* XIV:117–18

Rex, J. 1973b. *Race, Colonialism, and the City.* Boston: Routledge & Kegan Paul. 310 pp.

Richmond, A. H., Ed. 1972. *Readings in Race and Ethnic Relations.* Oxford: Pergamon Press. 340 pp.

Ritterband, P., Silberstein, R. 1973. Group disorders in the public schools. *Am. Sociol. Rev.* 38:461–67

Rogler, L. H. 1972. *Migrant in the City, The Life of a Puerto Rican Action Group.* New York: Basic Books. 251 pp.

Rokeach, M. 1973. *The Nature of Human Values.* New York: Free Press. 438 pp.

Rose, A. 1948. *Studies in Reduction of Prejudice.* Chicago: Am. Counc. Race Relat. 112 pp.

Rosenau, J. N. 1973. Theorizing across systems, linkage politics revisited. *Conflict Behavior and Linkage Politics,* ed. J. Wilkenfeld, 25–56. New York: McKay. 388 pp.

Rosenberg, M., Simmons, R. G. n.d. (ca. 1971). *Black and White Self-Esteem, The Urban School Child.* Washington, D.C.: Am. Sociol. Assoc. 160 pp.

Rosenwaike, I. 1973. Interethnic comparisons of educational attainment, an analysis based on Census data for New York City. *Am. J. Sociol.* 79:68–77

Rossi, P. H., Berk, R. A. 1972. Local political leadership and popular discontent in the ghetto. In *Collective Violence,* ed. J. F. Short Jr., M. E. Wolfgang, 292–308. Chicago: Aldine-Atherton. 387 pp.

Rossi, P. H., Waite, E., Bose, C. E., Berk, R. E. 1974. The seriousness of crimes, normative structure and individual differences. *Am. Sociol. Rev.* 39:224–37

Rubin, L. 1972. *Busing and Backlash: White against White in an Urban School District.* Berkeley: Univ. Calif. Press. 255 pp.

Rule, J., Tilly, C. 1972. 1830 and the unnatural history of revolution. *J. Soc. Issues* 28:49–76

Russell, D. E. H. 1974. *Rebellion, Revolution, and Armed Force.* New York: Academic

Rymph, R. C., Hadden, J. K. 1970. The persistence of regionalism in racial attitudes of Methodist clergy. *Soc. Forces* 49:41–50

Saltman, J. Z. 1971. *Open Housing as a Social Movement.* Lexington, Mass.: D.C. Heath, 213 pp.

Samuels, F. 1970. *The Japanese and the Haoles of Honolulu, Durable Group Interaction.* New Haven: College & Univ. Press. 206 pp.

Sandberg, N. C. 1974. *Ethnic Identity and Assimilation, The Polish American Community.* New York: Praeger. 88 pp.

Scarr-Salapatek, S. 1971. Race, social class, and I.Q. *Science* 174:1285–95

Schelling, T. 1971. On the ecology of micromotives. *Public Interest* 25:59–98

Schermerhorn, R. A. 1970. *Comparative Ethnic Relations, A Framework for Theory and Research.* New York: Random House. 327 pp.

Schwartz, L. R. 1972. Conflict without violence and violence without conflict in a Mexican mestizo village. In *Collective Violence,* ed. J. F. Short Jr., M. E. Wolfgang, 149–58. Chicago: Aldine-Atherton. 387 pp.

Sedoc-Dahlberg, B. N. 1971. *Surinaamse Studenten in Nederland.* Amsterdam: Univ. Amsterdam. 232 pp.

Sewell, W. H., Haller, A. O., Ohlendorf, G. W. 1970. The educational and early occupational status attainment process: replication and revision. *Am. Sociol. Rev.* 35:1014–27

Sexton, D. E. Jr. 1973. *Groceries in the Ghetto.* Lexington, Mass.: D.C. Heath. 141 pp.

Sherif, M. 1966. *In Common Predicament.* Boston: Houghton Mifflin. 192 pp.

Shockley, J. S. 1974. *Chicano Revolt in a*

Texas Town. Notre Dame, Ind.: Univ. Notre Dame. 314 pp.

Short, J. F. Jr., Wolfgang, M. E., Eds. 1972. *Collective Violence.* Chicago: Aldine-Atherton. 387 pp.

Siegel, P. M. 1965. On the cost of being a Negro. *Sociol. Inq.* 35:41–57

Siegel, P. M. 1970. Occupational prestige in the Negro subculture. *Sociol. Inq.* 40:156–71

Singer, B. D., Osborne, R. W., Geschwender, J. A. 1970. *Black Rioters, A Study of Social Factors and Communication in the Detroit Riot.* Lexington, Mass.: D.C. Heath. 117 pp.

Singer, L. 1962. Ethnogenesis and Negro Americans today. *Soc. Res.* 29:419–32

Singer, N. M. 1973. Federal aid to minority business, survey and critique. *Soc. Sci. Quart.* 54:292–305

Sklare, M. 1971. *America's Jews.* New York: Random House. 234 pp.

Skolnick, J. H. 1969. *The Politics of Protest.* New York: Simon & Schuster. 419 pp.

Smith, H. S. 1972. *In His Image, But . . ., Racism in Southern Religion, 1780–1910.* Durham, N.C.: Duke Univ. Press. 318 pp.

Snyder, D., Tilly, C. H. 1972. Hardship and collective violence in France, 1830 to 1960. *Am. Sociol. Rev.* 37:520–32

Snyder, D. R., Tilly, C. H. 1974. On debating and falsifying theories of collective violence. *Am. Sociol. Rev.* 39:610–13

Sorkin, A. L. 1971. Occupational status and unemployment of nonwhite women. *Soc. Forces* 49:393–98

Spilerman, S. 1970. The causes of racial disturbances, a comparison of alternative explanations. *Am. Sociol. Rev.* 35:627–49

Spilerman, S. 1971a. The causes of racial disturbances, tests of an explanation. *Am. Sociol. Rev.* 36:427–42

Spilerman, S. 1971b. *Structural Characteristics of Cities and the Severity of Racial Disorders.* Presented at 66th Ann. Meet. Am. Sociol. Assoc., Denver

Stark, R., Foster, B. D., Glock, C. Y., Quinley, H. E. 1971. *Wayward Shepherds, Prejudice and the Protestant Clergy.* New York: Harper & Row. 122 pp.

Stein, H. F., Hill, R. F. 1973. The new ethnicity and the white ethnic in the United States, an exploration in the psycho-cultural genesis of ethnic irredentism. *Can. Rev. Stud. Nat.* I:81–105

Steiner, J. 1974. *Amicable Agreement versus Majority Rule, Conflict Resolution in Switzerland.* Chapel Hill: Univ. N.C. Press. 312 pp.

Sterne, R. S., Philips, J. E., Rabushka, A. 1974. *The Urban Elderly Poor, Racial and Bureaucratic Conflict.* Lexington, Mass.: D.C. Heath. 145 pp.

St. John, N. H., Lewis, R. 1971. The influence of school racial context on academic achievement. *Soc. Probl.* 19:68–79

Stryker, S. 1974. 'A theory of middleman minorities,' a comment. *Am. Sociol. Rev.* 39:281–82

Sturdivant, F. D. 1973. Rationality and racism in the ghetto marketplace. *Soc. Sci. Quart.* 54:380–83

Suchman, E. A. et al 1958. *Desegregation: Some Propositions and Research Suggestions.* New York: Anti-Defamation League of B'nai B'rith. 128 pp.

Suttles, G. D. 1968. *The Social Order of the Slum, Ethnicity and Territoriality in the Inner City.* Chicago: Univ. Chicago Press. 278 pp.

Swedner, H. 1971. *School Segregation in Malmo.* Chicago: Integrated Educ. Assoc. 51 pp.

Tannenbaum, F. 1947. *Slave and Citizen.* New York: Knopf. 128 pp.

Tavuchis, N. 1972. *Family and Mobility among Second Generation Greek-Americans.* Athens, Greece: Nat. Center Soc. Res. 180 pp.

Taylor, D. M., Gardner, R. C. 1970. The role of stereotypes in communication between ethnic groups in the Philippines. *Soc. Forces* 49:271–83

Taylor, H. F. 1973. Linear models of consistency, some extensions of Blalock's strategy. *Am. J. Sociol.* 78:1192–1215

Taylor, J. H. 1973. Newcastle upon Tyne, Asian pupils do better than whites. *Race* XIV:431–47

Thomas, C. 1971. *Boys No More, A Black Psychologist's View of Community.* Beverly Hills, Calif.: Glencoe Press. 125 pp.

Thurow, L. C. 1969. *Poverty and Discrimination.* Washington, D.C.: Brookings Inst. 214 pp.

Tilly, C. 1973. The chaos of the living city. *Violence as Politics,* ed. H. Hirsch, D. C. Perry. New York: Harper & Row. 262 pp.

Turner, J. H. 1972. Structural conditions of achievement among whites and blacks in the rural South. *Soc. Probl.* 19:496–508

Ugalde, A. 1970. *Power and Conflict in a Mexican Community, A Study of Political Integration.* Alburquerque: Univ. New Mexico Press. 193 pp.

van den Berghe, P. 1970. *Race and Ethnicity, Essays in Comparative Sociology.* New York: Basic Books. 312 pp.

van den Berghe, P., Ed. 1972. *Intergroup Relations, Sociological Perspectives.* New York: Basic Books. 327 pp.

Van Til, J. 1973. Becoming participants, dynamics of access among the welfare poor. *Soc. Sci. Quart.* 54: 345–58

Verba, S., Ahmed, B., Bhatt, A. 1971. *Caste, Race, and Politics, A Comparative Study of India and the United States.* Beverly Hills, Calif.: Sage. 243 pp.

Verwey-Jonker, H., Ed. 1971. *Allochtonen in Nederland.* The Hague: State Publishing House for the Ministry of Culture, Recreation and Social Work. 261 pp.

Vlachos, E. C. 1968. *The Assimilation of Greeks in the United States.* Athens, Greece: Nat. Center Soc. Res. 200 pp.

von Furnstenberg, G., Horowitz, A. R., Eds. 1974a. *Patterns of Racial Discrimination, Vol. I, Housing.* Lexington, Mass.: D. C. Heath

von Furstenberg, G., Horowitz, A. R., Eds. 1974b. *Patterns of Racial Discrimination, Vol. II, Employment and Income.* Lexington, Mass.: D. C. Heath

Wagner, N. N., Haug, M. J., Eds. 1971. *Chicanos, Social and Psychological Perspectives.* St. Louis, Mo.: Mosby. 302 pp.

Wanderer, J. J. 1969. An index of riot severity and some correlates. *Am. J. Sociol.* 74:500–5

Warner, L. G., Dennis, R. M. 1970. Prejudice versus discrimination, an empirical example and theoretical extension. *Soc. Forces* 48:473–84

Warren, D. I. 1970. Suburban isolation and race tension, the Detroit case. *Soc. Probl.* 17:324–29

Washington, J. R. 1972. *Black Sects and Cults, The Power Axis in an Ethnic Ethic.* New York: Doubleday. 176 pp.

Watson, G. L. 1973. Social structure and social movements, the Black Muslims in the U.S.A. and the Ras-Tajarians in Jamaica. *Brit. J. Sociol.* 24: 188–204

Wax, M. 1971. *Indian Americans, Unity and Diversity.* Englewood Cliffs, N.J.: Prentice-Hall. 236 pp.

Weed, P. L. 1973. *The White Ethnic Movement and Ethnic Politics.* New York: Praeger. 243 pp.

Weigel, R. H., Wiser, P. L., Cook, S. W. 1975. The impact of cooperative learning experiences on cross-ethnic relations and attitudes. *J. Soc. Issues.* In press

Weller, L., Luchterhand. 1973. Effects of improved housing on the family functioning of large, low-income black families. *Soc. Probl.* 20: 382–89

Wilkenfeld, J., Ed. 1973. *Conflict Behavior and Linkage Politics.* New York: McKay. 388 pp.

Wilkenfeld, J., Zinnes, D. A. 1973. A linkage model of domestic conflict behavior. In *Conflict Behavior and Linkage Politics,* ed. J. Wilkenfeld, 325–56. New York: McKay. 388 pp.

Williams, E. 1944. *Capitalism and Slavery.* Chapel Hill: Univ. N.C. Press. 285 pp.

Williams, R. L., Byars, H. 1969. Negro self-esteem in a transitional society. *Personnel Guidance J.* 47:120–25

Williams, R. L., Byars, H. 1970. The effect of academic integration on the self-esteem of Southern Negro students. *J. Soc. Psychol.* 80: 183–88

Williams, R. M. Jr. 1947. *The Reduction of Intergroup Tensions.* New York: Soc. Sci. Res. Counc. 153 pp.

Williams, R. M. Jr. 1957. Racial and cultural relations. In *Review of Sociology, Analysis of a Decade,* ed. J. B. Gittler, 423–64. New York: Wiley. 588 pp.

Williams, R. M. Jr. 1970. Social order and social conflict. *Proc. Am. Phil. Soc.* 114:217–25

Williams, R. M. Jr. 1972. Conflict and social order, a research strategy for complex propositions. *J. Soc. Issues* 28:11–26

Williams, R. M. Jr., Dean, J. P., Suchman, E. A. 1964. *Strangers Next Door, Ethnic Relations in American Communities.* Englewood Cliffs, N.J.: Prentice-Hall. 434 pp.

Williams, W. E. 1973. Why the poor pay more, an alternative explanation. *Soc. Sci. Quart.* 54: 375–79

Winkel, G. H., O'Hanlon, T., Mussen, I. 1974. *Black Families in White Neighborhoods, Experiences and Attitudes.* New York: The City Univ. New York Graduate Center. 52 pp.

Wood, J. R. 1972. Unanticipated consequences of organizational coalitions, ecumenical cooperation and civil rights policy. *Soc. Forces* 50:512–21

Woods, (Sister) Jerome. 1972. *Marginality and Identity, A Colored Creole Family Through Ten Generations.* Baton Rouge: Louisiana State Univ. Press. 395 pp.

Yancey, W. L. 1972. Going down home, family structure and the urban trap. *Soc. Sci. Quart.* 52:893–906

AGE DIFFERENTIATION AND THE LIFE COURSE

◆10506

Glen H. Elder, Jr.

Department of Sociology, University of North Carolina at Chapel Hill, Chapel Hill, North Carolina 27514

Age has long been recognized as a basic element in social structure and the life course, but we have only recently achieved some appreciation of its diverse meanings and implications. To interpret the effects or correlates of age and birth year we must specify the variables they represent. The complexity of this task is suggested by the following temporal dimensions and locational properties that are derived from age data: (*a*) the individual life time or life span from birth to death—chronological or developmental age as an approximate index of stage in the aging process; (*b*) the social timetable of the life course (e.g. entry into marriage, retirement), which is defined by age criteria in norms and social roles; and (*c*) historical time in the course of social change—birth year or entry into the system as an index of historical location.[1] The focal point of the lifetime framework is the inevitable and irreversible process of aging; that of social time, age differentiation in the sequential patterning, and configuration of social roles; and that of historical time, cohort membership, differentiation, and succession, with their implications for life histories, aging, and social change.

Each temporal focus is associated with a distinctive tradition of theory and research: lifetime, Bühler (1935), the biological cycle of life as reflected in attitudes toward life (see also Bühler & Massarik 1968); social time, theoretical analyses by Linton (1942) and Parsons (1942), and Eisenstadt's (1956) influential synthesis of ethnographic materials on age differentiation; and historical, Mannheim's (1952, orig. 1928) essay on "The Problem of Generations." Continuities within the social time perspective are illustrated by theoretical formulations of social transitions in the life course, from Cottrell's (1942) propositional inventory on adjustment to age

---

[1] In *Aging and Society* (1972), Riley and associates focus upon two dimensions of time: the life span and historical time. The social timetable is discussed in relation to these temporal dimensions by Neugarten & Datan (1973).

and sex roles to Burr's (1973: Chapter 11) essay on social transitions, Glaser & Strauss' (1971) analysis of status passage, and theoretical models of retirement (Carp 1972). Ideas developed in Mannheim's essay, especially cohort differentiation, the stratification of experience, and social units within cohorts, have influenced current theoretical interpretations of research on youth movements and politics (Braungart 1974, Bengtson & Laufer 1974) and are expressed most notably in the age stratification model outlined by Riley, Johnson & Foner in *Aging and Society* (1972). The incipient trend in contemporary work is toward a more inclusive framework which builds upon all three temporal foci (Goulet & Baltes 1970, Neugarten & Datan 1973, Riley, Johnson & Foner 1972). In combination these perspectives represent the core of a potential sociology of age and the life course.

Compared to the body of literature reviewed by Cain in 1964, the past decade of social turmoil has been relatively prolific in studies of age-related phenomena—of youth movements and groups; age-based segregation, solidarity, and conflict; intergenerational relationships, continuity, and change; cohort differentiation in life experience and orientation; and of socialization, development, and career lines over the life span. At the time of Cain's review, major studies of generational relations had not been carried out [with the exception of Eisenstadt's (1956) analysis of ethnographic materials], and few analysts incorporated age cohorts in the study of age groups. Judging from the *Handbook of Marriage and the Family* (also published in 1964, Christensen), generational linkages or lineages assumed center stage as the principal vehicle of social transmission and change. In over 1000 pages of text, the subject index makes no reference to cohort differentiation or succession, and their relevance for the study of change in the family and life course. Some noteworthy progress has been achieved since the mid 1960s toward greater understanding of age distinctions in society and human lives, but the range of current knowledge is very uneven in scope and depth, as *Aging and Society* (Riley, Johnson & Foner 1972) makes abundantly clear.

In this brief essay, I shall give particular emphasis to issues and research on the relation between social change and the life course. This field of inquiry is informed by a life span perspective (in contrast to age-specific analyses), a cohort-historical approach to the formation of life course patterns, and sociocultural aspects of age patterns in the life course, e.g. normative age divisions and transitions, timetables, social and subjective definitions of age status, and temporal characterizations of the life course. While the imprint of historical change on life patterns has been noted by a number of early theorists (Kuhlen 1940, Mannheim 1952), the full implications of this observation for studies of the life course were not made explicit in theory and method until the 1960s. Especially noteworthy in this regard is Ryder's (1965) influential essay on "The Cohort as a Concept in the Study of Social Change." Methods for disentangling the course of human development or ontogenetic change from historical change were proposed at this time by Schaie (1965). The most thorough treatment of the cohort-historical approach is found in *Aging and Society* (1972). The movement of individuals and cohorts through the life course and history centers attention on process, on matters of conceptualizing process, and on suitable methods of data collection and analysis.

The life span perspective views human development, socialization, and adaptations as lifelong processes within an interage framework (Brim 1966, Clausen 1972). Age differentiation is expressed in the sequence of roles and events, social transitions, and turning points that depict the life course. A number of factors have been instrumental in the development of this perspective: the temporal constructs of cohort, career, life history, and life cycles in sociological analysis; theoretical interest in the study of antecedent-consequent relations that extend beyond specific age categories, and the resources of longitudinal data archives; awareness of the reciprocal nature of socialization and generational relations; and the accumulation of evidence on developmental change throughout the adult years. The growing acceptance of a life span version of developmental psychology reflects some of these developments (Goulet & Baltes 1970).[2] This approach is distinguished by its concern with the description and explanation of age-related behavioral changes from birth to death; explanatory analyses focus on the specification of linkages in antecedent-consequent relations.

The chapter begins with a preliminary overview of theoretical perspectives and issues on age differentiation in the life course, and then reviews selected studies of social change in the life patterns of cohorts and individuals. Despite various limitations, these studies suggest promising lines of analysis for subsequent research on the life course. Of necessity and by choice the literature coverage is highly selective relative to the general field of age differentiation. For comprehensive overviews of theory and research in this area, the reader is referred to Neugarten (1968), Riley, Johnson & Foner (1972), and Baltes & Schaie (1973).

THEORETICAL PERSPECTIVES AND ISSUES

The sociological literature on age is informed by two general theoretical perspectives and their complementary insights on age differentiation in the life course: the sociocultural and cohort-historical. Current examples of these perspectives are found in the work of Neugarten (1968) on age-status systems and age norms and in the age stratification model proposed by Riley and associates (1972).

The sociocultural perspective gives emphasis to the social meaning of age and its contextual variations: birth, puberty, and death are biological facts in the life course, but their meanings in society are social facts or constructions, as seen in the variable formation of age categories, grades, and classes across societies (Eisenstadt 1956, Gulliver 1968).[3] Age distinctions are expressed in normative expectations, privi-

---

[2]Paul Baltes observes that "during the last five years we have witnessed a major movement toward the acceptance of a life-span view of human development. . . . [However], the theoretical and empirical rationale for a life-span view of human development is still vague, and, perhaps even misunderstood" (1973:457).

[3]As Linton noted in the early 1940s, age-sex systems "are sufficiently divorced from physiological considerations to make possible almost any amplification of formal categories and almost any choice of transition points. Only birth and death are universally recognized as transition points and even these do not always set the limits of the individual's social participation" (1942:592).

leges, and rewards. As socially recognized divisions of the life course, whether generalized across society or restricted to institutional domains, age grades are defined by norms that constitute a basis for self-definition and specify appropriate behavior, roles, and time schedules.

The cohort historical perspective employs vital data and age as biological facts and social indicators in the study of the life course, age cohorts, and their corresponding age strata. Chronological age serves as a rough index of life stage and aging, while birth year or entry into a given system (e.g. age at first marriage, high school graduation) locates the individual in historical context as a member of a particular cohort. Unlike normatively defined age divisions, cohorts are not, as a rule, socially recognized or normatively specified categories, although they may be distinguished by a collective mentality and distinctive life pattern.[4] In social research, birth cohorts vary greatly in age span according to data constraints and analytic requirements.

This section reviews issues and selected research in these two conceptual domains, beginning with the cohort-historical approach and problems concerning the interpretation of age data. In combination the two perspectives raise largely unexplored questions concerning the interplay of historical change, cohort differentiation, and prescribed age divisions. Socially defined age divisions have been analyzed within the framework of societal development (Eisenstadt 1956); very little is known about historical events and cycles in the modification of age criteria and categories. Are social expectations and responsibilities common to adulthood extended downward to the young in periods of economic hardship or natural disaster? This change is at least consistent with the observed upward extension of dependency constraints during periods of abundance.

Age Stratification

In *Aging and Society* Riley, Johnson & Foner view age as a basis of stratification in historical experience (the cohort-historical approach) and in the sequence of roles within the life course—age hierarchies in access to life opportunity, power, privilege, and rewards. Each formulation has roots in the literature on age phenomena. The cohort-historical perspective has much in common with Mannheim's (1952) theoretical analysis of the generations (actually age cohorts in currently accepted terminology) and builds upon the work of social demographers in cohort analysis (e.g. Ryder 1965). Some complexities and limitations in the hierarchical formulation were briefly discussed by Linton (1942) in his early essay on age and sex categories.

Cohort differentiation in historical experience is stressed in the following contrast between age and class stratification (*Aging and Society,* 1972:23): "Whereas socioeconomic strata are ranked to form a social hierarchy, age strata are typically

---

[4]Though Mannheim emphasized the emergence of collective mentalities (historical consciousness) in cohorts and subgroups (generation units), a perspective most evident in contemporary theory and research on youth and generational relations (see Bengtson & Laufer 1974), *Aging and Society* tends to stress the social demographic aspects of cohort differentiation and succession.

ordered by time (hence, are more akin to geological strata)." Birth year or date of entry into the system locates the individual in the sociohistorical process; with age peers in the cohort, he is exposed to a particular slice of historical experience as he moves through the sequence of roles in the process of aging. To understand the meaning and implications of birth year and cohort membership, the analyst must specify the historical events, conditions, and trends or change at the time, as well as characteristics of the cohort (size, composition, etc), which are themselves a consequence of historical conditions, economic cycles, wars, mass migration. Cohorts are most sharply differentiated in the course of rapid change, and represent a vehicle of social change to the extent that successive cohorts differ in life patterns. As successive birth cohorts encounter the same historical event, they do so at different points in their life course; the impact of the event is thus contingent on the career stage of the cohort at the point of historical change. For an example, we need only compare the lifetime fertility of women, born shortly before and after 1900, who entered the Great Depression at a different stage relative to childbearing (Cain 1967). Cohort differentiation entails "fresh contact" with the social historical world and a "stratification of experience," to use Mannheim's terms.

The notion of age hierarchies enters the analysis in relation to social roles or status. "Rather than occupation or property ownership, we emphasize age as the criterion for delineating strata. Age strata are distinguished by the fact that their members. . . differ in access to positions which are unequally rewarded by wealth, prestige, or power. The age strata cut across the whole society since all individuals are ranked according to age. . ." (Foner 1973:1). But what is the evidence for and nature of generalized age hierarchies? The prestige order of age categories may well follow their order in the pre-adult years (especially through age grading in the educational system), but in what sense can we use the term hierarchy in reference to a generalized ranking of the young, middle-aged, and elderly, to a curvilinear order? Given the multiple covariates of age, contrasting rankings are conceivable—on educational skills, property ownership, etc. The nature of general age hierarchies in the middle years is especially problematic in view of the wide range of variation among age peers in social roles and accomplishments. Even in the case of documented age grading and status systems in groups and organizations, we know very little about the way in which age criteria operate in determining social rank, a point recently emphasized by Zuckerman & Merton (1972) in their provocative essay on age and social hierarchies in the field of science.

The cohort-historical and hierarchical versions of age stratification are based on the premise that age strata order both people and social roles in society. Chronological age serves the cohort model well as an index of age strata exposed to different aspects of the historical process and as a rough index of the cohort's career stage at points of historical change, but it presents many problems in relation to the concept of social hierarchy. Nevertheless some of the advantages and costs of position in a social hierarchy also pertain to historical location in a specific cohort: compare, for example, the life prospects of small cohorts that come of age in times of prosperity (e.g. the Depression-born cohort) with those of large cohorts of young adults in periods of economic depression. Cohort constraints on life options are illustrated by the "marriage squeeze" in the 1960s (an excess of marriageable women), a development which stemmed from the usual mating gradient (husbands two to three years older than their wives) and the greater readiness of young women born at the peak of the baby boom in the late 1940s to enter marriage than of young men in their cohort (Carter & Glick 1970:81–82). One effect of this demographic change is seen in an older age at first marriage among women. With the decline in birth cohorts since 1957, the opposite effect or an excess of marriageable men will occur in the late 1970s and 1980s.

Aging and Society makes a distinctive contribution to our understanding of the life course and social change through its elaboration of the dynamic, cohort-historical approach, a perspective which yields fresh insights on age phenomena when compared to the more static, normative approach and its neglect of historical forces in economic and population change. Within the broad framework of social continuity and change, socialization and allocation processes serve to articulate people and social roles in the course of aging and cohort succession. Symptomatic of the long term shift in the relative contribution of social agents to socialization—from family to school and age peers—is the conclusion that the concept of cohort is more useful than that of the generations or lineage (from parents to offspring) as an analytic framework for the study of social change in the life course (Ryder 1965:853).

Problems of coordination and phasing relative to socialization and allocation in periods of rapid change (see Riley, Johnson & Foner 1972:556 ff) are most vividly illustrated by the effects of sharp variations in cohort size between the 1930s and 1950s. Young Americans in the 14–24 year category increased by an unparalleled 52% between 1960 and 1970, an increase which was largely absorbed by the schools and military (Presidential Science Advisory Commission, 1973: Chapter 3). Youth in the 1960s thus became a much larger component of the population relative to adults, rapidly overtaxed existing educational facilities, and are currently faced with the constraints of a tight labor market and uncontrolled inflation. This demographic change suggests a number of linkages to youth unrest in the 1960s, a relationship which Moller (1967) has explored more broadly in a survey of historical and comparative materials. Such change is a major factor in Musgrove's (1965) historical analysis of the status of young people in England over the 19th century; the status of the young in social regard and rewards fluctuated according to their relative size in the population. He attributes their status decline between 1870 and 1914 to large birth cohorts and economic and ideological conditions that favored the exclusion of young people from the labor market. Recent evidence supports Musgrove's conclusion that young people in the 1960s, as in the 1970s, are apt to "pay the price of their importance and comparative abundance in the previous twenty years" (p. 81).

Some challenging problems of interpretation and method stem from the fact that age locates individuals in the social structure and in a specific cohort; thus age differences in cross-sectional data may be due to life stage, cohort-historical factors, or both. Related to this dual function of age is the problem of disentangling life stage, cohort, and period or date of measurement effects; each of the three indicators—chronological age, birth year, and date of observation—is completely defined in terms of the other two. Clear interpretation in this case is possible only under certain conditions; in particular, when theory or external evidence enable the analyst to assume that at least one factor has no effect (Riley 1973, Mason et al 1973). These and other problems of interpretation and method concerning data have been examined at length in *Aging and Society* (1972: Chapter 2), and by Riley (1973), Hyman (1972: Chapter 7), Mason et al (1973), Baltes (1968), and Schaie (1970). Sensitivity to matters of interpretation, research design, and analysis stands out as a prominent feature of the recent literature on age-related phenomena.

Problems of interpretation with respect to cross-sectional data are commonplace in research on the generations, a particularly active field of study during the past decade, and especially in studies of three generations which maximize both life course and historical differences. As Hill (1970:30) candidly acknowledged in his pioneering study of three generations, the "extent historical circumstances have affected these three generations will be difficult to disentangle from other influences which come with maturation and aging." Value differences between parents and adult offspring could be attributed to their different life stage or historical experience and socialization. Values are transmitted through socialization but they are also formed in response to the imperatives of life situations; a man who learned the value of job security as a child may have little regard for this issue in adulthood if he has achieved a measure of success and security in his worklife. Value differences in cross-sectional data are thus most troublesome with respect to their interpretation.

This point is underscored by results from Bengtson's three generation study of value continuity and change (Bengtson & Lovejoy 1973; Bengtson, unpublished). The sample was drawn from the Los Angeles area and represents a predominantly working class population in the grandparent generation with pronounced upward mobility across the ascending generations. The average age of the grandparents is 67 in comparison to 19 years in the youngest generation. Two general value dimensions were extracted from a factor analysis of items in each generation: materialism-humanism—valuing of finances and possessions, coupled with low priority on equality, service, etc; and individual-institutional—valuing of skill, excitement, freedom, coupled with low priority on loyalty, patriotism, etc. The data show very low intergenerational agreement on these value dimensions and a high degree of variation within each generation. The parent generation ranked highest on materialism (a reflection of the Depression experience?), while no reliable difference on this value orientation was found between the youngest and oldest generation. As might be expected from the item content, generational differences were most pronounced on individualism; average scores increased from the grandparent to the grandchild generation.

An example of the interpretational bind in this analysis is provided by the relative importance of financial comfort across the generations. Bengtson notes that this item was chosen more frequently by the two older generations than by the youth, and speculates that this may be due to the current life situation of the former—to the grandparents' dependency on meager pensions and the financial responsibilities of the parents. An equally convincing case can be made for an historical explanation. While both life stage and cohort-historical factors are taken into account in the overview, data limitations prevent a clear interpretation of the results.

Historical change in the life course presents a number of problems for the analyst who has longitudinal data on a single cohort. Such data are uniquely suited for the study of life course sequences, but these sequences are a product of both aging and historical conditions that are specific to the cohort (as well as general properties of the cohort itself, such as composition and size). The life course of any particular cohort reflects its distinctive historical experience in hard times and prosperity. Without a comparative cohort, the analyst is unable to place the life course of his cohort in historical context or to assess the effects of general social changes in life patterns. However, the latter point should be qualified by the recognition that social change generates differences within as well as between cohorts; historical events do not impinge uniformly on members of a cohort. In the Great Depression, for example, some children experienced severe economic hardship in their families, while others did not and encountered little, if any, disruption in their accustomed way of life (Elder 1974). These differences in economic deprivation (relative income loss) were found among children who were positioned in both the middle and working class before the 1930s, and had enduring consequences for their life course and values. The assumption of cohort homogeneity and the risks entailed in generalizing about the historical experience of cohort members have much in common with the hazard of "cohort-centrism" (Riley 1973), that of generalizing from a single cohort.

The advantages of comparative longitudinal analysis for yielding insight concerning historical effects in life patterns is countered by an important limitation in research on human development; time of measurement is confounded—it is not possible to obtain identical times of measurement for all ages in the cohorts. Since only two sets of information (age and date) can be used to obtain estimates of three parameters (cohort, age, and time of measurement), a number of strategies have been proposed for excluding one of the factors. Schaie (1970: 487–89) has constructed three two-factorial models for this purpose and recommends that data be collected so that it can be analyzed by at least two of them: cohort-sequential, traditional cohort analysis; time-sequential, two or more ages at two or more periods of observation (cohort confounded); and cross-sequential, the analysis of two or more samples from the same cohort at two or more times of measurement (age confounded). Whatever their limitations (Baltes 1968), Schaie's two-factorial models have been employed extensively in research, and with significant payoff for our understanding of social change in ontogenetic development and the inadequacy of cross-sectional data. Substantial cohort variations have been reported in crystallized intelligence, an increase across successive cohorts which may reflect educational upgrading among other factors (Schaie 1970), and in dimensions of adolescent development (Nesselroade & Baltes 1974). Thus far most of the research has been descriptive in aim rather than explanatory. What are the specific historical conditions that differentiate cohorts, the linkages between such conditions and age-related behavior change, and the variables subsumed under "period of observation?" These questions are likely to be in the forefront of future research on life span development.

Age in Sociocultural Perspective

Three sociocultural aspects of age have particular relevance to studies of the life course: social definitions of age status, normative divisions of the life course and age status systems, and age norms as expressed in timetables for lines of action or careers. Issues concerning the beginning and end of human life are part of the more general question regarding social consensus on age categories and boundaries. What is the lower boundary of old age or middle age; or the upper boundary of childhood and adolescence? While legal norms provide some guidance in separating the young and old from adults in the middle years, they do not reflect the diversity of life patterns and their multiple timetables. Social differentiation in complex societies takes the form of plural age structures and timetables, across institutional spheres, and underscores the utility of a multidimensional concept of the life course, a concept of interdependent life paths which vary in synchronization.

Age categories and distinctions have frequently been proposed or accepted as common knowledge without evidence of their meaning to the individuals involved.[5] At what point, for example, do young people begin to take an adult standpoint and view themselves accordingly? At marriage, full time job, or establishment of an independent domicile? With the expansion of the dependency stage through higher education, "youth" (Keniston 1970) and "studentry" (Parsons & Platt 1972) have been added to the vocabulary of age distinctions in reference to sectors of the age span between adolescence and full adult status. But what evidence do we have of the social or normative meaning of these categories to persons so classified or of "old age" to persons over the age of 60 or 65?

Among young people, some evidence suggests that the significance of this age category in consciousness and identifications varies according to life prospects and degree of integration in society (Eisenstadt 1956:236, Johnstone 1970), conditions which may also apply to the self-definitions of the aged. In a sample of elderly persons, Rosow (1967:274) found a moderate relationship between the number of role losses and the tendency to report an older self-image, but regardless of role losses this self-image was much more prevalent among working class than middle-class persons. A corresponding class difference has been reported by Neugarten & Peterson (1957) in their study of 240 adults (ages 40 to 70). They found that men in the lower strata were likely to perceive a more rapid passage through the major age divisions of life than middle class men; maturity, middle age, and old age come earlier in their life span. This difference seems to reflect class-linked occupational demands and activities. The man who relies upon mental skills in a sedentary

---

[5] Age-based stages of the life course have been studied mainly in terms of the emergence of childhood (Ariès 1965) and adolescence (Eisenstadt 1956, Musgrove 1965) as recognized age divisions. In recent years significant contributions to our historical understanding of the social position and worlds of American children and young people have been made by social historians (Demos & Demos 1969, Kett 1971, Bremner 1970, 1973). Great knowledge of the aged in the American past, as well as of other age categories, is likely to come from the rapidly expanding field of historical research on family life.

occupation foresees a relatively long period of productivity, while the man who works with his hands expects a relatively short span of adulthood and a long period of old age. Perceptions of life stages reflect the diversity of options and resources, role sequences, and activities in the life course.

The prevalence of age segregation, perhaps the most visible manifestation of age differentiation, has raised a number of important research and policy questions concerning its consequences for social integration, subcultural differentiation, social learning, and development, etc. In a study of the aged in Cleveland, Rosow (1967) outlined two alternative perspectives on ways to promote the psychological health and social integration of elder citizens: one argues for age-integrated communities which supposedly enable people of all ages to interact and develop friendships, while the other asserts that communities with large concentrations of the aged are best suited to achieve this outcome—common life experience within age groups establishes a base for mutual understanding and enduring friendships. Rosow's analysis supports the view that older people are more likely to be integrated into groups when they live in areas with large concentrations of age peers than in neighborhoods with a diverse age structure. Though age segregation entails both costs and benefits, interpretations of research on children and youth have tended to emphasize the negative consequences (cf Coleman 1961, Bronfenbrenner 1970). In the absence of substantial adult participation in the direction of peer activities, Bronfenbrenner sees little developmental value associated with a child's heavy involvement in groups of age peers. "If children have contact only with their own age-mates, there is no possibility for learning culturally established patterns of cooperation and mutual concern" (1970:117). An extensive review of issues and evidence on age segregation and its effects on American youth is provided in *Youth: Transition to Adulthood* (1973), a report of the Panel on Youth of the President's Science Advisory Committee.

One of the most basic questions in the normative approach to age concerns the point at which an organism is defined as human. In a pioneering study of this problem, Knutson (1967) found striking variations among public health professionals (advanced graduate students in public health) in the way they define and value a new human life, and that a sizable number held judgments that are not consonant with operational definitions in hospital, legal, and medical codes. One fifth of the professionals assigned full value to the new human life at conception, and approximately two fifths at birth or shortly thereafter. Knutson found that most respondents who placed the beginning of a new human life before birth did not assign full value to it until birth or after birth. As might be expected, religion emerged as a principal source of variation in judgments; compared to the more secular respondents, members of conservative religious groups were more likely to reckon the beginning of a new human life from conception, to assign full value at an earlier point in developmental time, and to emphasize the importance of "infusion of the soul" in making an organism human.

Age-appropriate social roles and activities are aspects of a normative model of the life course which is sanctioned by formal and informal networks of social control (Neugarten & Datan 1973). Marriage and motherhood would be key elements of this model in the lives of girls, with economic independence and stable employment assuming priority in the normative life course of boys. According to theory, age expectations define appropriate times for major life events and transitions: there is an appropriate age for leaving home, for marriage and the bearing of children, for the postparental years and retirement. In moving through the age structure, individuals are made cognizant of being early, on time, or late in role performance and accomplishments by an informal system of rewards and negative sanctions. Such awareness of the relation between age and status has received ample documentation in research on organizational careers (Roth 1963) and worklife. In a study of English managers, Sofer (1970:239) noted that the men were constantly mulling over the relation between age and grade in prospects for attaining senior rank, "showing quite clearly that they had a set of norms in mind as to where they should be by a given age." Neugarten and associates (1965) found a high degree of consensus on age norms (usually over 80% agreement) across some 15 age-related characteristics in samples of middle-class adults. The data show general agreement among men and women on the appropriate age for a woman to marry and support the hypothesis that informal sanctions are associated with early and late marriage. On the basis of qualitative data, they conclude that women are aware of whether they are on time, late, or early with respect to marriage and other major role transitions.

Social prescriptions in the timing of events or role transitions in the life course lead to the hypothesis that adverse outcomes are associated with pronounced deviations from the approved time schedule, with transitions that occur too early or late. While such outcomes are known to be associated with first marriages that are at variance with the average or preferred age (for a review of studies on early marriage, see Bartz & Nye 1970), it is much less clear how these outcomes are related to or are influenced by age norms and sanctions. For example, Bacon (1974) suggests that accelerated entry into wife and mother roles generates a conflicting and confusing array of social roles and age expectations which are likely to be expressed in stress and social pathologies. Using data on a nationwide sample of married women with children, he found the usual inverse relationship between marital age and the incidence of marital instability, poverty, and low educational attainment. However the study does not test the proposed normative linkages between early marriage and these outcomes, and does not evaluate alternative interpretations, e.g. the family and developmental antecedents of differential timing of marriage, the effects of timing on the field of eligible men, etc. In contrast to the common assertion of normative influence, the agenda of future research should include studies that incorporate such factors in empirical analysis.

Hill and associates (1970) have studied the timing of family activities and their synchronization over the family career in three generations. Within each generation they found substantial variation among family units in the achievement of long term goals; some families perceived themselves as being on schedule, others "behind schedule," and still others "ahead of schedule." The relative success and failure of families in achieving their goals on schedule is reflected in aspects of life cycle or career management; effective management entailed the synchronization of transitions and activities in a pattern which enabled the multiple career lines of the family to be mutually supportive of progress toward life style goals. Within a well-defined or prescribed timetable, adjustments to the recognition of "being ahead of or behind schedule" may take the form of shifts in perspective; progress ahead of schedule would likely reinforce a perspective in which evaluations are based on a goal of ultimate potential achievement, with career origins tending to serve as a framework of evaluation for individuals or family units which find themselves behind schedule. Relevant to this hypothesis is a study of managerial mobility orientations (Goldman 1973) which found a relationship between an upward career anchorage and work as a central life interest. Tausky & Dubin's (1965) concept of career anchorage suggests a number of fruitful applications to the full range of career lines and timetables in the life course.

The concept of a normative timetable specifies or implies a preferred sequence of related activities or stages in a line of activity, and thus invites research on the determinants and consequences of deviant sequences or disarrangments, such as entry into the maternal role before marriage (Furstenberg 1969, Rains 1971). The normative significance of disarrangements and the nature of their consequences may well vary according to the point at which they occur in the life course; compare, for example, unwed motherhood in late adolescence with this status in the late 20s or early 30s. Apart from their normative implications, deviant role sequences present an array of challenging problems and complexities for causal analyses of life course events, as in the case of a delayed or interrupted pattern of formal education. The variable order of events is a type of contingency in the life course, in addition to events that occur within a broad span of the life course and do not influence all lives, e.g. military service, migration (Duncan, Featherman & Duncan 1972: Chapter 8).

Up to the present, age norms and timetables have not received the priority they deserve in research on the life course. Some concepts about the proper phasing of the life course may well be "cognitive descriptions or predictions of what will happen" rather than normative or moral prescriptions, as Goode has suggested (1973). To my knowledge no large sample study has provided evidence on normative expectations and sanctions regarding the timing and synchronization of social roles and transitions over the life span. Much more is known about culturally prescribed roles and about the scheduling of daily activities (on time budget research, see Szalai 1972) than about social judgments on the appropriate timing of transitions, correlated sanctions, and informal networks of social control. And with few exceptions (Roth 1963), especially in the area of worklife and education, the process by which age norms or timetables are constructed, transmitted, and learned remains largely unexplored territory.

The timing and synchronization of activities and transitions are essential analytic distinctions in a multidimensional concept of the life course; sequences of roles and activities vary in timing, requirements, and options, and thus in problems of coordination, resource management, and adaptation; these patterned lines of action include the familiar sequence of family roles, worklife stages and the earning cycle from first job to retirement, the phasing of social participation and consumption. Marriage joins two life histories and establishes a set of contingent career lines

(Farber 1961). A number of studies have explored the reciprocal effects of two or more role sequences or cycles: for example, Wilensky's (1961) research on worklife patterns and social integration, the Rapoports' (1969) research on couples in demanding career lines, and Hill's (1970) study of socioeconomic, reproductive, child-rearing, and consumption careers. A vivid example of the long arm of work timetables on the temporal structure of family activity is provided by Young & Willmott's (1973: Chapter 7) analysis of shiftworkers in their survey of families in London, England. Though most of the men claimed that their job interfered with home and family (nearly twice the proportion of other workers), the higher wages of such work countered this disadvantage to some extent by alleviating economic pressures—an "economic squeeze" especially common to the early childbearing and rearing stage in which wives withdraw from the labor force; a disproportionate number of the men had large families of young children to support. Young & Willmott also document a high level of strain or interference between role cycles in families in which the wife is employed in a full time professional career. When both homemaking and gainful employment are combined in time demands, the working woman ranks well below employed men and housewives in nonobligated time according to time-budget surveys in twelve societies (Robinson, Converse, & Szalai 1972:119).

The concept of multiple, interlocking role sequences or cycles orients analysis to the context in which specific social transitions are embedded and to the adaptive process of movement through concurrent or a rapid succession of transitions, a life situation especially characteristic of entry into adult roles. The latter problem is the focal point of the career threshold project, which includes a five-year longitudinal study of young men who were 14 to 24 years old in 1966 (Kohen 1973). Initial results of this study show a high degree of experimentation during the first year in the labor market, with over 70% of the men ending up in a different occupation group from that of their first job in a three-year period. The study has not examined as yet the complex interdependencies among worklife, educational, marriage, and parent roles and transitions. Research by Freedman & Coombs (1966) on a sample of Detroit women suggests that early entry into marriage and parenthood is likely to be a major disadvantage in the economic progress of young men in the career threshold project; early marriage, a short interval between marriage and childbirth (either before or after marriage), and a close spacing of children were especially detrimental to the accumulation of goods and assets. While this life pattern is most common in the working class, entry into parenthood is more likely to be defined as a problem situation in the middle class; limited data on this subject indicate that middle-class couples tend to report more difficulties (Jaccoby 1969). The education, career stage, and perspective of both husband and wife appear to be key elements in the meaning and difficulties of assuming the parental role.

The concept of multiple, concurrent role sequences in the life course is at least implied in psychological research on the adaptive problems and effects of life changes—of marriage, childbirth, divorce, demotions and promotions in worklife, residential change, and the like. Using a rating instrument which scales life events on severity of change, Rahe (1969) has assembled a large body of evidence (mainly from cross-sectional samples and thus subject to the limitations of retrospective reports) which indicates a relationship between situational and health change; the more demanding or severe the life change (as in a clustering of such changes), the greater the likelihood of adverse change in health status. Also relevant to this field of study is an ongoing longitudinal study of transitional stages in the adult life course (Lowenthal & Chiriboga 1973) which is comparing incremental and decremental transitions (marriage and parenthood vs the empty nest, widowhood, retirement) in terms of their effects on adaptive processes, whether growth-promoting or constricting. The conceptual model of this study, on adaptive processes in maintaining, achieving, and restoring equilibrium between aims in life and behavioral patterns, has much in common with W. I. Thomas' early formulation of adaptation to drastic change with its emphasis on the relation between claims and control of outcomes (Volkhart 1951, esp. pp. 215–25).

The diverse life lines or sequences in the life course (worklife, marital, residential, etc) have been described in the literature as careers, subcycles, life paths, and life histories. While no general concept will be satisfactory to specialists in each domain, a minimal definition of career, as a patterned sequence of movements and events, does at least bring out basic features of the life course. By comparison, the conventional family cycle typology has some important limitations which are at least implied in Hill's (1970) three generation study. In view of Hill's significant contributions to the development of this typology, and that of his students (see Rodgers 1973), it is noteworthy that the concepts of multiple career lines, their timetables and synchronization, represent key elements in his characterization of family units through time; an elaborate typology of family stages occupies a very minor role in the analysis and proposed theory. As commonly applied in research, the family cycle typology offers a highly restrictive characterization of family units and individuals through time, and tends to obscure or divert attention from important aspects of the life course, as seen in Hill's (1964) nine-stage version.[6]

This temporal formulation of the family is centered on the reproductive process, both sexual and social, and is applicable in a life span framework to a restricted segment of the population that follows the script of a marriage which endures to old age and produces at least one child; variations in family forms are excluded. The typology does not rule out research on interlocking role cycles or careers since it can be supplemented in studies by histories of each parent's worklife, of income, consumption, and residential change, but it is not well suited to this line of analysis,

---

[6]Establishment—newly married, childless; new parents—infant to three year old; preschool family—child 3 to 6 years and possibly younger siblings; school-age family—oldest child 6 to 12 years, possibly younger siblings; family with adolescent—oldest child 13 to 19 years, possibly younger siblings; family with young adult—oldest child 20 and up to when first child leaves home; family as launching center—from departure of first child to last child; post-parental family—the middle years, after children have left home until father retires; aging family—after retirement of father. The 7th International Seminar on Family Research at Paris (September, 1973) included a number of critical evaluations of the family cycle typology. These and other conference papers are being edited by Jean Cuisenier and will be published in a volume by Mouton, The Hague.

in large part because the various stages do not take into account the differential timing of events in the life course; each category may include a range of parental ages which is too wide for research on the synchronization of multiple career lines. Information on these career lines is generally required for explanations of stage variations in family life and the life course of individual members.

SOCIAL CHANGE IN THE LIFE COURSE

Cohorts represent a link between social change and life course patterns, between historical time and lifetime. This relationship is expressed in two lines of research that differ in focal point and level of analysis: cohorts in the analysis of social change in society, and historical change in the life course and experience of individuals. Social change occurs to the extent that successive cohorts follow different life course patterns; hence, analysis centers on the comparison of life patterns (the differential timing of events, life cycle types, etc) across successive cohorts. In order to draw accurate implications from cohort differences on change in society, both the size and composition of cohorts must be taken into account, as Riley (1973) has pointed out. Data constraints, such as information on a single cohort and its subgroups, and small, unrepresentative samples rule out generalizations on the general course of social change in society, but the data may be sufficient for purposes of tracing the effects of historical change in the lives of individuals. This more limited focus may also apply to cohort studies which employ retrospective life histories since the birth cohorts would be biased by the loss of cases through death and perhaps emigration, as in the ongoing Norwegian study of historical change in the occupational life course of three birth cohorts (see Ramsøy 1973).

Social change in the life course has been viewed from both a cohort and generation perspective; the latter is illustrated by Davis' (1940) early essay on parent-youth conflict and by Eisenstadt's (1956) theoretical formulation of generational conflict. As Heberle (1951), among others, has noted, a generational perspective has severe limitations in the study of social change since persons who share a common generational status in the descent hierarchy do not necessarily share a common location in historical time; in fact, they may represent products of vastly different historical contexts, a difference which, if reflected in life patterns, may be greater than any intergenerational difference. Three generation studies provide the most convincing case for distinguishing between age cohorts and generations, and against the tendency to regard the two concepts as synonomous, a practice that is all too common in the literature [see Troll's (1970) overview of the generational concept]. In Bengtson's (Bengtson & Lovejoy 1973) three generation study, the older generation includes an age span which is too broad for precision in the analysis of historical conditions—approximately 20 years. As if in confirmation of this limitation, the study neither provides adequate information on the historical context of each generation, nor links values to historical events, even though the latter were recognized as important factors in the interpretation of findings. Cohort specification within the grandparent generation (by dividing this age group at the median year, etc) and thus across ascending generations would be one approach to the problem of locating the generations in a concrete historical environment. This procedure is also appropriate for Hill's (1970) analysis of three generations. Despite wide age ranges in each generation (from 41 to 70 in the parent generation), the generations were compared as whole units. Age heterogeneity which obscures the effects of historical change is a common problem in studies of successive birth cohorts, as we shall see in the following review. While data constraints may necessitate 10 or even 20 year cohorts, such decisions will leave their imprint on the findings and, perhaps even more importantly, on what does not emerge from the analysis.

As a field of inquiry, social change in the life course is currently more a domain of rich possibilities than of research accomplishments and established knowledge. However, there are studies of exceptional quality, such as Uhlenberg's (1974; see also 1969) research on the life course patterns of American women, white and non-white, in five birth cohorts from 1890–1894 to 1930–1934. From early adolescence to late middle age, three accomplishments have a normative base in the antici-pated life course of young girls: the expectations of begoming a wife, of having a child, and of achieving a stable or intact marriage. Referring to this type of life course, with survivorship to age 50, as the "preferred pattern," Uhlenberg identified four deviant types from census data and life tables: early death—women who do not survive to age 50; spinster—women who survive to age 50 but never marry; childless—women who marry but do not have at least one child between the ages of 15 and 50; and unstable marriage—women whose first marriage fails, but who have children and survive to age 50. In addition to the wealth of potential types that can be delineated by adding status distinctions and events (such as worklife, commu-nity roles, timing distinctions), this approach makes two highly significant contribu-tions to the study of the life course of cohorts: 1. it includes mortality data—since early death has declined appreciably during this century, a complete picture of cohort change in the life patterns of women must take this variable into account; and 2. the types provide a characterization (though skeletal) of life course patterns, of the relative prevalence of life paths followed by women in the middle years of life across successive cohorts. Significant change in the timetable of events in the cohort life course of American women has been documented by Glick & Parke (1965)—in the timing of marriage, first and last birth, death of husband, but their analysis does not show the configuration of these events in the life course of individu-als. Not all females survive to middle age, marry, have children, and enjoy a stable marriage to late middle age. These contingencies are represented in Uhlen-berg's analysis of the life paths followed by cohorts of women over the past 70 years.

Contrary to popular impressions of rising marital instability, the preferred life course has become increasingly more prevalent across successive cohorts of Ameri-can women who were alive at age 15, though Uhlenberg's analysis shows that in all birth cohorts this life pattern is substantially more common among white than among nonwhite females. Between 1890–1894 and 1930–1934 cohorts, the propor-tion of white females following the "preferred life course" increased by a third to .64, compared to an increase from .18 to .35 for nonwhites (these figures apply to cohorts that include the "early death" category). Clues to the uniformity trend in life patterns and to the white/nonwhite difference are suggested by trends in the deviant patterns. Four trends stand out in the life course of white females. First, there has been a pronounced decline across cohorts in the mortality of females between the ages of 15 and 50, owing largely to the control of infectious diseases through improved nutrition, the development of antibiotics, etc. Secondly, the probability of early death among males has also declined over this time period (and hence reduced prospects for widowhood during the childbearing stage), though less markedly than for females. The increasing rate of marriage (and decline in marital age up to the early 1950s) along with a decline in childlessness are the two other trends that have reduced the proportion of females in the deviant life patterns. The increasing rate of divorce, coupled with the limited impact of expected change in mortality, childlessness, and spinsterhood, led Uhlenberg to conclude that the trend toward a uniform life course among white females has come to an end. In fact, analysis of more recent birth cohorts shows a trend toward later marriage, delayed childbearing, and increased marital instability.

Uhlenberg singles out the much higher level of mortality among nonwhite females—early death in the middle years remains twice the rate among white females (male differences between the two groups are also substantial)—as a major factor in the relatively small number of nonwhite women who marry, bear children, and survive to age 50 with their marriage intact. In contrast to the trend among white females, cohort comparisons show an increasing trend in the proportion of unmarried, nonwhite women who survive to age 50, and in the 1940–1945 cohort, the rate of nonmarriage is twice that of whites. The apparent unpopularity of marriage among the more recent cohorts of nonwhite women and the prevalence of marital instability point to an end to the uniformity trend among nonwhite women and the persistence of a cohort picture which is dominated by life course deviations from the preferred type.

While wars and depressions may alter the proportion of women who follow the preferred or deviant life patterns, through early male death and disability, for example, such events have directly influenced the life decisions and timetables of cohorts in the 20th century. Depressed conditions in the 1930s produced delays in the timing of marriage and led to postponements in childbearing which were most often "made up" by the younger cohorts of women. Ryder (1970) suggests that the "succession of depression and then prosperity" called out adaptive responses which resemble a decision strategy for managing a new situation in the life course: "The response with the least consequences, a change in the timing of marriage, is the first undertaken; that with the greatest consequences, a change in the number of children, is the last undertaken." In a broader framework, Hill (1970) has examined the consequences of rapid historical change for the timing and synchronization of status change in the mutually contingent careers of family members. Timing entails the scheduling of status passage and the sequential ordering and coordination of events and actions over the life course; strategies of family cycle management involve the timing of marriage and parenthood, the spacing of children, the husband's entry into the labor market and job changes, the wife's entry and reentry into the labor force, the timing of residential change, and the acquisition of homes and durables. In periods of rapid change, "each generational cohort encounters at marriage a unique set of historical constraints and incentives which influence the timing of its crucial life decisions, making for marked generational dissimilarities in life cycle career patterns" (Hill 1970: 322).

In Hill's three generation study of couples in the Minneapolis-St. Paul area, the middle generation offers striking documentation of this thesis and underscores the inadequacy of generations as units in the analysis of social change and the life course. Couples in the parent generation ($n=95$) actually represent two cohorts defined by marriage in the 1920s and 1930s. As might be expected, the predepression couples ended up with a larger number of children ($\bar{X} = 4.1$ vs 3.1), and were much more diverse on career timetables (on childbearing, childrearing, consumption etc) than the younger group. The two cohorts were found to be sufficiently different in life course "to constitute samples of different universes," and yet they were treated throughout most of the analysis as one generational cohort (perhaps in response to the limitations of sample size). In any case, the heterogeneity of the parent generation is a dominant feature of the analysis, from family and worklife events to consumption schedules, and may have obscured important insights regarding intergenerational continuity and change.

The greatest generational difference in life course and values occurred between the grandparents in Hill's study (who were married between 1900 and 1915) and the parent generation, a difference that roughly parallels Cain's (1967) hypothesis on the effects of historical change in the life patterns of Americans born shortly before and after the turn of the century. He suggests that an "historical 'hinge' or 'watershed' developed at the end of World War I," which has directed these cohorts down different paths of life. The younger cohort included a smaller proportion of the foreign-born, was exposed to greater educational opportunity, and came of age in a period of liberalization in sexual constraints and rising wages. Women in the younger cohort married earlier, gave birth to fewer children (as a result of conditions in the Depression), and experienced a longer postparental phase of life with their husbands.

Cohort analyses show a pronounced change in the worklife patterns of women—from a life course decline among women born in the last quarter of the 18th century to a consistent rise in labor force participation over the life course among more recent cohorts. Change is most pronounced in the rising participation of young married women and apparent lessening of the traditional constraints of childbearing and rearing (Riley, Johnson, & Foner 1972:56). This trend suggests a decline in the proportion of women whose worklife terminated at marriage or first birth and a relative increase in the dual-track career, but cohort analyses along the lines of Uhlenberg's research are needed to identify diversity and change in life patterns across successive cohorts. According to evidence from a large nationwide sample of women in the childrearing years, a common type of worklife—the early interrupted pattern—is associated with downward mobility (Shea et al 1970:171): women who return to work after childbearing and rearing tend to enter jobs that are lower in status than that of their original jobs.

A cyclical account of change in the worklife patterns of women is briefly outlined by Giele (1973) in a cohort analysis of life history data on graduates of an eastern women's college; periods of economic growth spur labor demand and increase employment opportunities for cohorts of college-educated women entering the productive years of life, especially for members of relatively small cohorts that have their origins in the low birth rate of economic troughs, while economic downturns at this life stage favor noneconomic alternatives. Using a subsample of some 15,000 alumnae in the general survey, Giele found that the worklife of women who graduated from college in 1906–1911 and 1931–1936—not the best of years—compared unfavorably with that of women who graduated in the early 1920s and 1940s; the latter were employed more years, were more likely to be upwardly mobile, and were more prevalent in professional lines of work. Voluntaristic activity and the prevalence of a high status background in educational attainment appeared to follow an inverse pattern relative to the economic cycle.

These findings must be regarded as highly tentative in view of the preliminary stage of analysis and the select nature of the sample, but they do at least pose important issues concerning cyclical factors in the life course, as have studies by Easterlin (1968) and Harris (1969). One such issue concerns historical change in sex-role differentiation. From her data on worklife and marriage, Giele tentatively suggests that downswings in the economy heighten sex-role differentiation, an interpretation that generally corresponds with results from a small, longitudinal study of older children (born 1920–1921 in Oakland, California) in the Great Depression (Elder 1974). Economic hardship shifted households toward a more labor-intensive system which expanded the domestic sphere of girls, and increased pressure on boys to seek gainful employment. Girls from deprived families, especially in the middle class, were more likely than the nondeprived to favor domestic values in the 30s and, as middle-aged women, to prefer family over work, leisure, and community activity.

By following cohorts across periods of social upheaval or change, analysts have traced historical experience and acquired dispositions in one period to the response of individuals and social aggregates to subsequent dislocations. Loewenberg (1972) employed this approach in his psychohistorical study of the traumatic deprivation of German children in World War I and its relation to their susceptibility to the Nazi movement and ideology. The focal point of the analysis is the cohort of young Germans who were born between 1900 and 1915. War deprivations included massive famine, stemming in large measure from the allied blockade, with its severe consequences for child health and nutrition, as well as the widespread absence of mothers (through employment in war industries) and fathers in the military. In a lengthy and subtle analysis, Loewenberg argues that such deprivations weakened the character structure of large numbers of children in the Nazi youth cohort, producing a psychic state distinguished by violent aggressive tendencies, inner rage, defenses of displacement and projection, and a defensive idealization of the absent father. Anxieties aroused by the Depression trauma fostered a reversion to childhood imagery and fixations which enhanced the appeal of Nazi ideology and organizations, paramilitary and political. Since wartime deprivations were not a uniform experience of German children, comparisons of subgroups within the Nazi youth cohort would be an appropriate test of Loewenberg's hypotheses. Some work along this line is underway in a quantitative analysis of Nazi autobiographies in the Theodore Abel collection (see Peter Merkl in Loewenberg 1972: 1500).

Factors which lead us to expect cohort variations in the life outcomes of historical change also imply cohort variations in the processes or mechanisms which link these outcomes to specific modes of change. A key factor in this respect is the career stage of the cohort in general and its members. The career stage of a cohort refers to its status on age-linked roles and resources. As indexed by chronological age, the career stage of a birth cohort provides only a rough estimation of the life stage of its individual members; age similars do not follow the same timetable and sequence of social roles, as evidenced by temporal variations on marital age, completion of education, worklife experience, etc. Nevertheless, social change would have differential consequences for persons of unlike age (e.g. young children, adolescents, the middle-aged) to the extent that age differences are related to variations in social roles, exposure to change, adaptive resources, and options. Whether inferred from age or measured directly, indicators of social position provide clues to the factors which link historical change and life outcomes.

Cohorts in the 1930s were distinctively marked by their career stage at the onset of the Great Depression, according to available evidence, but these data also show variations in impact across socioeconomic groups within each cohort; the economic collapse produced differences in life patterns between and within cohorts. Examples of such differences are provided by a comparison of two studies: Thernstrom's (1973) analysis of Boston men who were born during the first decade of this century (one of five birth cohorts in the study—1850–1859, 1860–1879, 1880–1889, 1900–1909, and 1930); and a small longitudinal study of persons who were born in 1920–1921 and grew up in Oakland, California (Elder 1974). Members of the Oakland cohort occupied a favorable position relative to the Depression when compared to the career stage of older and younger cohorts. They were beyond the early dependency stage of development and its vulnerability to family misfortune, and were too young to enter the adult marketplace of marriage and work when economic conditions were most depressed. In terms of future prospects, mobilization for war occurred at a critical point and served to weaken the negative effects of starting out life with a background of family privation. The data show that economic deprivation (relative income loss between 1929 and 1933) reduced prospects for education beyond high school, through loss of parental support and family burdens, and adversely influenced the educational attainment of boys and girls, especially in the working class. This educational disadvantage was minimized by worklife assets in the life course of boys. Early work experience increased their freedom from family and sensitized them to matters of vocation. This sensitivity took the form of crystallized goals and a stable worklife which effectively countered the educational limitations of family deprivation, even among the sons of working-class parents. In the long run, family hardship did not handicap the occupational attainment of the Oakland men.

A very different picture of both temporary and enduring setbacks emerges from the worklives of Boston men who were born in the first decade of the 20th century, a group which had just entered lines of work and family roles prior to the economic collapse. Compared to the older cohorts, these men were less likely to achieve at least some upward mobility from first to last job; in fact, a disproportionate number made no headway at all over their worklife, a life pattern especially common in the lower strata. The Depression sharply reduced the rate of ascent within the non-manual category and increased the proportion of downwardly mobile men from the lower white collar stratum, though most of the latter regained their former status by the early 1940s. Skilled workers and men who entered the Depression at the top of the occupational ladder were most likely to maintain their position through the 1930s. The darkest side of the Depression shows up in the life course of laborers, the semiskilled and unskilled. More than three fourths of the men who held semi-skilled jobs before the Depression remained in this stratum up to their last job, compared to less than half of their counterparts in the older cohorts. We find little basis in Thernstrom's data for concluding that the 1900–1909 cohort "fared better than any other age group during the Depression" (Cain 1967:92), though any firm conclusions in this regard would require a much broader sampling of successive cohorts.

Thernstrom's study is addressed to the general theoretical issue of structural change in life opportunity over the past century, and represents a noteworthy contribution to our understanding of both worklife and intergenerational change across successive cohorts. However, it is well to keep in mind some data limitations, such as the exclusion of outmigrants. The cohorts are restricted to male residents of the Boston area, and thus represent biased samples of the male population; no information was available on the careers of men who left Boston. Career mobility was assessed by comparing the first job before age 30 on which information was available with the last recorded job after the age of 30; the resulting degree of individual variation is indicated by the range of years between each measurement, from 10 to 40 or so. In addition, a number of the birth cohorts cover a very wide age span; this heterogeneity and widely spaced measurements necessarily restricted prospects for discerning the effects of short-run cyclical change in the economy.

Such change in opportunity is the principal theme in Harris' (1969) cohort analysis of the social origins of American men in leadership careers, a study based primarily on three-year cohorts of men (mainly 19th century) in the Dictionary of American Biography. Harris concludes that the proportion of leaders recruited from ordinary homes has varied according to a recurring and predictable opportunity cycle of approximately two decades, a cycle which is linked to economic fluctuations and related change in population and institutional growth. The phasing of cyclical change in opportunity tends to vary in relation to the timetable and requirements of specific career lines, such as the professions and business. The most elitest cohorts of professionals experienced depressed conditions in late childhood and again during their phase of advanced training in the 20s. By contrast, the most open cohorts launched their college or professional training during the early stage of economic growth and established themselves in their careers during this period of expansion. The data show a very different phasing in the origin of elitest and openly recruited cohorts of businessmen. Prosperity during childhood and formal education favored an unusually heavy recruitment of business leaders from high status families, while men in the most open cohorts launched their careers in times when business oppor-tunities were poor. Harris suggests that depressions have created opportunities for new men in the higher ranks of American business by "pruning out inheritors." Apart from matters of evidence and interpretation (see the critique by Smith 1970), Harris' study is a rich source of hypotheses on cyclical change in the life patterns of cohorts and provides a useful counterpoint to the evolutionary or developmental perspective on social change.

This selection of studies reflects something of the diversity of research on social change in the life course, on approach and focal point, limitations and contributions. While other studies could have been cited (see *Aging and Society,* 1972),[7] it is perhaps most striking how little work has focused on this problem area, and, by implication, how much theoretical and empirical work lies ahead. More often than not, current knowledge of the impact of specific historical events or of long term trends on the life course is based upon one or two studies, and only a small fraction of this research incorporates design requirements that permit generalizations regarding social change in society. With few exceptions, we find little explicit treatment of the process by which social change impinges upon the life course. What are the linkages that connect historical change to aspects of the life course, that provide an explanation of such change? In the analysis of historical change, cohort comparisons are based on the assumption that such change has differential consequences for persons who vary in career stage, which suggests that stage variations are related to variations in the meaning of a situation, in adaptive resources and options, and thus in theoretical linkages between change and the life course. These linkages may also vary among members of a cohort, owing to the usual social heterogeneity of such aggregates. Over the past decade, research developments clearly reflect an increasing analytic sensitivity to the imprint of historical change on the life course of cohorts and individuals, and substantial contributions to this area of investigation are likely from studies in progress. Nevertheless, the contemporary literature provides many examples of an ahistorical orientation which neglects the specific historical context of human biographies.

OVERVIEW

As an emerging field of inquiry, age differentiation and the life course is informed by three traditions of research and their age-based temporal perspectives: lifetime and its focus on the process of aging from birth to death; social time, as expressed in the age patterning of social roles and career lines; and historical time, location of the individual in the historical process through cohort membership. Over the past decade we have witnessed two important trends that have given a distinctive shape to the field: 1. the growing acceptance of a life span framework in studies of human development, socialization, and role or status sequences (in contrast to age specific models); and 2. increasing interest in the relation between historical change and life patterns, as seen in comparative studies of cohorts, coupled with the development

[7]See especially Zuckerman and Merton's essay on "Age, Aging, and Age Structure in Science" (Chapter 8 in *Aging and Society,* 1972). For another important source on social change in the life course, see Beverly Duncan's review of her cohort analysis of educational attainment (1968).

of methods for assessing the effects of such change on human development and the life course. From the vantage point of contemporary work, the dynamic, cohort-historical perspective, with its life span framework, stands out as the single most important contribution in recent years to research on age differentiation in the life course; it is recognized as an essential component of studies on life span development and will most certainly be a major influence in future research on career lines and the life course generally.

The study of social change in the life course, a focal point of this essay, draws mainly upon the cohort-historical and sociocultural perspectives on age. In the former approach, which is most fully outlined by an age stratification model in *Aging and Society* (1972), age locates individuals in historical time by defining their cohort membership and in the social structure by indicating their life or career stage; within the flow and differentiation of cohorts, aging, socialization, and role allocation represent dynamic forces in the age structure. Through its development this perspective has generated greater awareness of the dual function of age (as an index of birth year and career stage), of methodological problems in disentangling life stage, cohort, and period or time of measurement effects (each of the three indicators—age, birth year, and date—is completely defined in terms of the other two), and of age as a surrogate for other variables which need to be specified in explanatory analysis. Beyond the ever present methodological problems in this line of research, the most challenging item on the agenda of future research concerns the specification of variables indexed by age and birth year.

The long established sociocultural perspective on age would seem to have much to offer in this regard—on normative age divisions, prescribed transitions, age expectations and timetables, and temporal characterizations of age patterns in the life course. It is a matter of some irony, however, that so little major empirical work has addressed key issues on the normative base of age patterns in the life course; assumptions and assertions far exceed empirical evidence. Though some theoretical progress has been achieved over the past decade, much additional work is needed in developing temporal, process-oriented constructs which are most appropriate for the study of lives through time. As a final point, we should note that the two perspectives raise a number of important and largely unexplored questions on relations among social change, cohort differentiation, and normative age patterns. In order to explain the impact of historical change on the timing of events in the life course, we must know something of the process by which this effect occurred, such as decision processes in behavioral adaptation or a generalized modification of age norms. Our knowledge of this process is primarily a matter of informed conjecture at present.

ACKNOWLEDGMENTS

Financial support of the National Science Foundation (Grant GS-3523) is gratefully acknowledged. I am indebted to John Clausen and Paul Roman for suggestions concerning an early draft of this essay, and to Donald Kacher for bibliographic assistance.

Literature Cited

Ariès, P. 1965. *Centuries of Childhood.* New York: Vintage

Bacon, L. 1974. Early motherhood, accelerated role transition, and social pathologies. *Soc. Forces* 52:333–41

Baltes, P. B. 1968. Longitudinal and cross-sectional sequences in the study of age and generation effects. *Hum. Develop.* 11:145–71

Baltes, P. B. 1973. Prototypical paradigms and questions in life-span research on development and aging. *Gerontologist* 13:458–67

Baltes, P. B., Schaie, K. W., Eds. 1973. *Life-span Developmental Psychology: Personality and Socialization.* New York: Academic

Bartz, K. W., Nye, F. I. 1970. Early marriage: a propositional formulation. *J. Marriage Fam.* 32:258–68

Bengtson, V. L., Laufer, R. S., Eds. 1974. Youth, generations, and social change. *J. Social Issues* 30 (Nos. 2 & 3)

Bengtson, V. L., Lovejoy, M. C. 1973. Values, personality, and social structure: An intergenerational analysis. *Am. Behav. Sci.* 16:880–912

Braungart, R. 1974. The sociology of generations and politics: A comparison of the functionalist and generational unit models. In *J. Social Issues,* Youth, generations, and social change, ed. V. L. Bengtson, R. S. Laufer, 30(2)

Bremner, R. H., Ed. 1970. *Children and Youth in America: A Documentary History* 1:1600–1865. Cambridge, Mass.: Harvard Univ. Press

Bremner, R. H., Ed. 1973. *Children and Youth in America: A Documentary History* 11:1866–1932. Cambridge, Mass.: Harvard Univ. Press

Brim, O. G. 1966. Socialization through the life cycle. In *Socialization After Childhood: Two Essays,* ed. O. G. Brim, S. Wheeler, 1–7. New York: Wiley

Bronfenbrenner, U. 1970. *Two Worlds of Childhood: U.S. and U.S.S.R.* New York: Russell Sage

Bühler, C. 1935. The curve of life as studied in biographies. *J. Appl. Psychol.* 19:405–9

Bühler, C., Massarik, F., Eds. 1968. *The Course of Human Life.* New York: Springer

Burr, W. R. 1973. *Theory Construction and the Sociology of the Family.* New York: Wiley

Cain, L. D. Jr. 1964. Life course and social structure. In *Handbook of Modern Sociology,* ed. R. E. L. Faris, Chap. 8. Chicago: Rand McNally

Cain, L. D. Jr. 1967. Age status and generational phenomena: the new old people in contemporary America. *Gerontologist* 7:83–92

Carp, F. M., Ed. 1972. *Retirement.* New York: Behavioral Publ.

Carter, H., Glick, P. C. 1970. *Marriage and Divorce.* Cambridge, Mass.: Harvard Univ. Press

Christensen, H. T., Ed. 1964. *Handbook of Marriage and the Family.* Chicago: Rand McNally

Clausen, J. A. 1972. The life course of individuals. In *Aging and Society: A Sociology of Age Stratification,* ed. M. W. Riley, M. Johnson, A. Foner, 3:Chap. 11. New York: Russell Sage

Coleman, J. 1961. *The Adolescent Society.* New York: Free Press of Glencoe

Cottrell, L. S. Jr. 1942. The adjustment of the individual to his age and sex roles. *Am. Sociol. Rev.* 7:617–20

Davis, K. 1940. The sociology of parent-youth conflict. *Am. Sociol. Rev.* 5:523–35

Demos, J., Demos, V. 1969. Adolescence in historical perspective. *J. Marriage Fam.* 31:632–38

Duncan, B. 1968. Trends in output and distribution of schooling. In *Indicators of Social Change,* ed. E. B. Sheldon, W. E. Moore, 601–72. New York: Russell Sage

Duncan, O. D., Featherman, D. L., Duncan, B. 1972. *Socioeconomic Background and Achievement.* New York: Seminar Press

Easterlin, R. A. 1968. *Population, Labor Force, and Long Swings in Economic Growth: The American Experience.* New York: Nat. Bur. Econ. Res.

Eisenstadt, S. N. 1956. *From Generation to Generation: Age Groups and Social Structure.* Glencoe, Ill.: Free Press

Elder, G. H. Jr. 1974. *Children of the Great Depression.* Chicago: Univ. Chicago Press

Farber, B. 1961. The family as a set of mutually contingent careers. In *Household Decision-Making,* ed. N. N. Foote, 276–97. New York: New York Univ. Press

Foner, A. 1973. *A Sociology of Age Stratification: The Relevance of the Stratification Perspective.* Presented at Ann. Meet. So. Sociol. Soc., Atlanta, Georgia

Freedman, R., Coombs, L. 1966. Childspacing and family economic position. *Am. Sociol. Rev.* 31:631–48

Furstenberg, F. F. Jr. 1969. Birth control experience among pregnant adolescents: The process of unplanned parenthood. *Soc. Prob.* 19:192–203

Giele, J. Z. 1973. *Age Cohorts and Change in Women's Roles.* Presented at Am. Sociol. Assoc. Meet., New York

Glick, P. C., Parke, R. Jr. 1965. New approaches in studying the life cycle of the family. *Demography* 2:187–202

Glaser, B. G., Strauss, A. L. 1971. *Theory of Status Passage.* Chicago: Aldine

Goldman, D. R. 1973. Managerial mobility motivations and central life interests. *Am. Sociol. Rev.* 38:119–26

Goode, W. J. 1973. *Discussion of Life Cycle Theory.* Presented at 13th Int. Sem. in Fam. Res., Paris, France

Goulet, L. R., Baltes, P. B., Eds. 1970. *Life-span Developmental Psychology: Research and Theory.* New York: Academic

Gulliver, P. H. 1968. Age differentiation. In *International Encyclopedia of the Social Sciences,* ed. D. L. Sills, 1:157–61. New York: Macmillan and Free Press

Harris, P. M. G. 1969. The social origins of American leaders: The demographic foundations. *Perspect. in Am. Hist.* 3:159–346

Heberle, R. 1951. The problem of political generations. In *Social Movements: An Introduction to Political Sociology,* Chap. 6, 118–27. New York: Appleton

Hill, R. 1964. Methodological issues in family development research. *Fam. Process* 3:186–206

Hill, R. 1970. *Family Development in Three Generations.* Cambridge, Mass.: Schenkman

Hyman, H. H. 1972. *Secondary Analysis of Sample Surveys: Principles, Procedures, and Potentialities.* New York: Wiley

Jaccoby, A. P. 1969. Transition to parenthood: A reassessment. *J. Marriage Fam.* 31:720–27

Johnstone, J. 1970. Age-grade consciousness. *Sociol. Educ.* 43:56–68

Keniston, K. 1970. Youth as a stage of life. *Am. Scholar* 39:631–54

Kett, J. F. 1971. Adolescence and youth in nineteenth century America. *J. Interdisciplin. Hist.* 11:283–98

Knutson, A. L. 1967. The definition and value of a new human life. *Soc. Sci. Med.* 1:7–29

Kohen, A. I. 1973. *Career Thresholds: A Longitudinal Study of the Educational and Labor Market Experience of Youth,*

Vol. 4. Columbus, Ohio: Center Hum. Resour. Res.

Kuhlen, R. G. 1940. Social change: A neglected factor in psychological studies of the life-span. *School Soc.* 52:14–16

Linton, R. 1942. Age and sex categories. *Am. Sociol. Rev.* 7:589–603

Loewenberg, P. 1972. The psychohistorical origins of the Nazi youth cohort. *Am. Hist. Rev.* 76:1457–1502

Lowenthal, M. F., Chiriboga, D. 1973. Social stress and adaptation: Toward a life course perspective. In *The Psychology of Adult Development and Aging,* ed. C. Eisdorfer, M. P. Lawton, 281–310. New York: Am. Psychol. Assoc.

Mannheim, K. 1952 (orig. 1928). The problem of generations. In *Essays on the Sociology of Knowledge.* Transl. P. Kecskemeti. New York: Oxford Univ. Press

Mason, K. O., Winsborough, H. H., Mason, W. M., Poole, K. W. 1973. Some methodological issues in cohort analysis of archival data. *Am. Sociol. Rev.* 38:242–58

Moller, H. 1967. Youth as a force in the modern world. *Comp. Stud. Soc. Hist.* 10:237–60

Musgrove, F. 1965. *Youth and the Social Order.* Bloomington, Ind.: Indiana Univ. Press

Nesselroade, J. R., Baltes, P. B. 1974. Adolescent personality development and historical change: 1970–1972. *Monographs of Soc. for Res. in Child Develop.* 39 (1): Serial No. 154

Neugarten, B. L. 1968. *Middle Age and Aging: A Reader in Social Psychology.* Chicago: Univ. of Chicago Press

Neugarten, B. L., Datan, N. 1973. Sociological perspectives on the life cycle. In *Life-span Developmental Psychology: Personality and Socialization,* ed. P. B. Baltes, K. W. Schaie, 53–69. New York: Academic

Neugarten, B. L., Moore, J. W., Lowe, J. C. 1965. Age norms, age constraints, and adult socialization. *Am. J. Sociol.* 70:710–17

Neugarten, B. L., Peterson, W. A. 1957. A study of the American age-grade system. In *Proc. 4th Congr. Int. Assoc. Gerontol.* 3:497–502

Parsons, T. 1942. Age and sex in the social structure of the United States. *Am. Sociol. Rev.* 7:604–16

Parsons, T., Platt, G. M. 1972. Higher education and changing socialization. In *Aging and Society: A Sociology of Age Stratification,* ed. M. W. Riley, M. E.

Johnson, A. Foner, 3:236–91. New York: Russell Sage

Presidential Science Advisory Commission, Panel on Youth. 1973. *Youth: Transition to Adulthood.* Washington, D.C.: GPO

Rahe, R. H. 1969. Life crisis and health change. In *Psychotrophic Drug Response: Advances in Prediction,* ed. P. May, J. R. Whittenborn, 92–125. Springfield, Ill.: Thomas

Rains, P. M. 1971. *Becoming an Unwed Mother.* Chicago: Aldine

Ramsøy, N. R. 1973. *The Norwegian Occupational Life History Study: Design, Purpose, and a Few Preliminary Results.* Oslo: Inst. Appl. Soc. Res.

Rapoport, R., Rapoport, R. 1969. The dual-career family: a variant pattern and social change. *Hum. Relat.* 22:3–30

Riley, M. W. 1973. Aging and cohort succession: interpretations and misinterpretations. *Pub. Opin. Quart.* 37(1):35–49

Riley, M. W., Johnson, M. E., Foner, A., Eds. 1972. *Aging and Society: A Sociology of Age Stratification,* Vol. 3. New York: Russell Sage

Robinson, J. P., Converse, P. E., Szalai, A. 1972. Everyday life in twelve countries. In *The Use of Time,* ed. A. Szalai, 114–44. The Hague: Mouton

Rodgers, R. H. 1973. *Family Interaction and Transaction: The Developmental Approach.* Englewood Cliffs, NJ: Prentice-Hall

Rosow, I. 1967. *Social Integration of the Aged.* New York: Free Press

Roth, J. A. 1963. *Timetables.* Indianapolis: Bobbs-Merrill

Ryder, N. B. 1965. The cohort as a concept in the study of social change. *Am. Sociol. Rev.* 30:843–61

Ryder, N. B. 1970. The emergence of a modern fertility pattern: United States, 1917–66. In *Fertility and Family Planning,* ed. S. J. Behrman, L. Corsa Jr., R. Freedman, 99–123. Ann Arbor, Mich.: Univ. Michigan

Schaie, K. W. 1965. A general model for the study of developmental problems. *Psychol. Bull.* 64:92–107

Schaie, K. W. 1970. A reinterpretation of age related changes in cognitive structure and functioning. In *Life-span Developmental Psychology: Research and Theory,* ed. L. R. Goulet, P. B. Baltes, 485–507. New York: Academic

Shea, J. R., Spitz, R. S., Zeller, F. A. 1970. *Dual Careers: A Longitudinal Study of Labor Market Experience of Women,* Vol. 1. Columbus, Ohio: Center Hum. Resour. Res.

Smith, D. S. 1970. Cyclical, secular, and structural change in American elite composition. *Perspect. in Am. Hist.* 4:351–74

Sofer, C. 1970. *Men in Mid-Career.* New York: Cambridge Univ. Press

Szalai, A., Ed. 1972. *The Use of Time.* The Hague: Mouton

Tausky, C., Dubin, R. 1965. Career anchorage: managerial mobility motivations. *Am. Sociol. Rev.* 30:725–35

Thernstrom, S. 1973. *The Other Bostonians: Poverty and Progress in the American Metropolis, 1880–1970.* Cambridge, Mass.: Harvard Univ. Press

Troll, L. E. 1970. Issues in the study of generations. *Aging Hum. Develop.* 1:199–218

Uhlenberg, P. R. 1969. A study of cohort life cycles: cohorts of native born Massachusetts women, 1830–1920. *Pop. Stud.* 23(3):407–20

Uhlenberg, P. R. 1974. Cohort variations in family life cycle experiences of U.S. females. *J. Marriage Fam.* 36:284–92

Volkhart, E. H. 1951. *Social Behavior and Personality: Contributions of W. I. Thomas to Theory and Social Research.* New York: Soc. Sci. Res. Counc.

Wilensky, H. L. 1961. Orderly careers and social participation in the middle mass. *Am. Sociol. Rev.* 24:836–45

Young, M., Willmott, P. 1973. *The Symmetrical Family.* New York: Pantheon Books

Zuckerman, H., Merton, R. K. 1972. Age, aging, and age structure in science. In *Aging and Society: Sociology of Age Stratification,* ed. M. W. Riley, M. E. Johnson, A. Foner, 3:292–356. New York: Russell Sage

COMPETING PARADIGMS IN MACROSOCIOLOGY

❖10507

Tom Bottomore

School of Social Sciences, The University of Sussex, Brighton, Sussex, England

During the past decade there has been a remarkable proliferation of new approaches and paradigms in sociology; to such an extent indeed that some writers have referred to a "crisis" affecting the whole discipline, which they may judge either favorably, as a condition of intellectual ferment and renewal, or unfavorably, as a state of affairs in which sociological thought seems to have lost any rational coherence; and many others are uneasy about the exuberant growth of new sociological "schools" and "sects." But it would be wrong to exaggerate the significance of these recent trends. Sociology (and this applies also to other social and human sciences) has always been what one writer has called a *multi-paradigm science,* that is to say, a science in which there are "too many paradigms" (Masterman 1970). And it was not unknown, at earlier times, for discussions about a "crisis" in sociological thought to occur. One such occasion was in the last decade of the 19th century when the "revisionist" controversy developed within Marxism, and in the wider field of social thought there was a general assault upon positivism (Hughes 1958); and another was in the late 1920s and early 1930s, when a writer in the journal of the Austro-Marxists, *Der Kampf,* for example, expressed his satisfaction at finding a coherent exposition of sociological theory in the book he was reviewing, at a time when confusion and a sense of crisis seemed to prevail everywhere (Lauterbach 1933). Very often, in fact, a crisis in sociology seems to be associated with, and perhaps reflect, a sense of intellectual crisis in the wider sphere of cultural and political life; and this may well have been the case during the 1960s.

It is clear, at all events, that sociological thought has developed quite new orientations in the course of the past decade. Some indication of the extent of these changes can be found by looking at a collection of articles from the learned journals of the 1950s (Lipset & Smelser 1961), which was intended to portray the main trends in sociology at that time. The section devoted to theory was somewhat limited in outlook, and more or less confined to a consideration of functionalism; it contained no reference to such theoretical approaches as Marxism, phenomenology, ethnomethodology, and structuralism, which are well known, and in varying degrees influen-

191

tial, in the sociological thinking of a decade later. Social stratification was discussed in the 1950s, it seems, without reference to social classes and property, and there was little attempt to analyze the structure of whole societies, or to deal comprehensively with social change. The editors of the collection singled out as being perhaps its most significant general feature the complete triumph of "scientific sociology," in contrast with a policy-oriented, more social-philosophical kind of sociology, though they recognized that some controversial issues remained, arising mainly from the criticisms of functionalism as an unhistorical, politically conservative theory which neglected, in particular, the elements of change and conflict in social life.

In the space of a few years all this has changed.[1] Functionalism no longer occupies such a prominent place as a sociological paradigm, and it is not now the main center of theoretical controversies, even though some of the alternative paradigms may have developed, in part, from criticisms of the functionalist approach. It should also be noted that the influence of functionalism was always strongest in the U.S.A. In Western Europe, where evolutionist theories, Marxism, a historical sociology inspired by Max Weber, and a more philosophical form of sociology (especially in Germany) were still active, the impact of functionalism was much less evident; while in the U.S.S.R. and Eastern Europe, until the mid-1950s, sociology was regarded with disfavor, and a somewhat crude and dogmatic version of "historical materialism" was established as the officially approved science of society. One of the most significant features of the changes during the past decade is that these geographical boundaries have, to a considerable extent, disappeared; and there is now a more clearly international body of theoretical sociology, and controversy about it. An important turning point in this process of change was the emergence, after 1956, of a New Left movement, both intellectual and political, which revitalized and diversified Marxist thought, emphasized more strongly the sociological aspects of Marx's theory, and by its vigorous criticism of what it saw as "establishment sociology," opened the way for attempts to develop a "radical" or "critical" sociology, which is now one of the main currents of thought in the controversies about sociological theory.

The variety of theoretical and methodological conceptions, and the relatively frequent changes in the main orientations of sociological thought in recent years (reflected in the appearance of many new journals, each of which apparently expresses the outlook of a particular "school"), make it difficult to identify with any great certainty those trends that seem likely to have some lasting significance. Nevertheless, a number of fairly well articulated and established paradigms have emerged or have been reformulated during the past decade, and it is worthwhile to consider how they diverge from each other, what the principal controversies are, and how these controversies have developed.

[1]The change is itself an important sociocultural phenomenon that poses questions about the adequacy of some sociological theories. Thus, for example, we have learned in recent years to think in terms of "scientific revolutions," rather than (or at least alongside) more gradual processes of the advancement of knowledge, and this notion obviously has a wider bearing.

Functionalism, or as it came to be called "structural-functionalism" (because its aim was to analyze the functioning of institutions, or elements of social life, as parts of a definite social system or structure), has lost, as I noted earlier, much of the importance as a paradigm that it once had; but in modified forms it continues to direct a good deal of sociological inquiry. The modifications that were introduced, largely through the work of R. K. Merton (Merton 1957), were intended to meet some of the major criticisms brought against the functionalist approach; in particular, that it postulated an unreal degree of functional unity or integration in every society, that it assumed the functional character of all the cultural items in a given society, and that it asserted the indispensability of every existing institution or cultural form. Merton took account of these criticisms by recognizing that the degree of integration of a given society was an empirical question to be decided by investigation, that cultural items and social institutions might be dysfunctional as well as functional, and that there might be functional alternatives to any existing institutions or cultural practices. Having thus formulated a more flexible version of functionalism, and outlined a paradigm which had the virtue of presenting in a systematic way a large number of important theoretical and empirical questions, Merton went on to qualify and restrict still further the claims of functionalist analysis, by treating it as only one possible approach, or one mode of sociological interpretation. This seems to be the sense in which structural-functionalism continues to guide some kinds of sociological inquiry at the present time; namely, by providing a framework within which it is possible to relate partial activities to a larger whole, and thus, in one sense, acquire a fuller understanding of them.

But functionalism was also criticized on other grounds, from the point of view of the logic of scientific explanation; and the question was raised whether functional analysis could ever provide more than a descriptive classification. Durkheim had distinguished clearly between discovering the function of a particular social fact and discovering its cause (Durkheim 1938), but many later functionalists did not pay too much attention to these problems of sociological explanation and they were inclined to refer more vaguely to "sociological analysis" or "sociological interpretation" (as did Merton himself). One writer, however, specifically contrasted functional and causal analysis (Dore 1961), and the question of the nature of functionalist "explanation" was taken up in other discussions of the logic of the social sciences (Hempel 1959, Peters 1958). The criticisms along these lines, however, have now merged into a much wider debate about "explanation" and "interpretation" in sociology which I shall consider later on.[2]

One consequence of the adoption of a functionalist paradigm is a certain indifference to historical processes and historical explanations. As Merton noted, functionalists tend to concentrate upon the static aspects of society and upon social equilibrium; and his own formulation of a broader and more flexible functionalist approach was intended to remove this limitation, among others, by introducing the concept of "dysfunction" ". . . which implies the concept of strain, stress and tension

[2]There is a useful collection of essays expounding and criticizing functionalism from various aspects in Demerath & Peterson 1967.

on the structural level, [and] provides an analytical approach to the study of dynamics and change" (Demerath & Peterson 1967). Even with such modifications, however, the functionalist paradigm did not really encourage, or give any prominence to, historical conceptions of social life, and in recent years it has been abandoned, to a considerable extent, in favor of models that are based more directly upon the idea of historical change.

The revival of interest in a historical sociology has clearly been influenced not only by theoretical controversies about the adequacy of a method that largely excluded history, but also by more general social and cultural factors: by the accelerating progress of science and technology, the sustained postwar economic growth in the industrial countries and its ramifying consequences, the problems of "underdevelopment" and "development" in the Third World, and the reemergence on a large scale, especially in the decade of the 1960s, of radical and revolutionary social movements. This renewed attempt to construct an historical model of society has taken a number of different forms. On one side there has been a distinct revival of evolutionist views, often starting out from 19th century theories that had once been regarded as thoroughly discredited. Thus, Herbert Spencer's sociological ideas have attracted attention again (Peel 1971), and there have been some more general studies of evolutionist conceptions (Burrow 1966). Talcott Parsons, who was at one time a principal architect of the structural-functionalist model, has turned his attention to problems of social evolution and has reintroduced one of Spencer's basic ideas, that the evolution of societies consists above all in a process of increasing internal differentiation (Parsons 1966).

One of the principal characteristics of the evolutionist paradigm is the attempt to comprehend the whole historical development of societies from their earliest to their latest forms. But within this general framework there are quite diverse views. If social development is conceived mainly in terms of increasing differentiation, then the process may well be regarded as being continuous, gradual, and cumulative, without any sharp breaks. An alternative view, however, sees social development as discontinuous, and is more concerned with distinguishing particular stages of evolution, and types of society corresponding with these stages. Hence it provokes a new interest in the analysis of types of social structure, and although this has not yet spread very widely it has given rise to studies of "industrial society" (Aron 1967) and of "post industrial society" (Touraine 1971, Bell 1973), while among Marxist thinkers it has led to a reconsideration of "precapitalist economic formations" (Hobsbawm 1964) and to some interesting attempts to define and classify systems of production (Godelier 1972). The discontinuous conception of social development also poses other important questions, concerning particularly the nature and causes of the transition from one kind of society to another, and in particular brings out the contrast between evolutionary and revolutionary types of social change.

But evolutionist conceptions are not the only form of historical sociology that has begun to flourish again. Gellner has clearly depicted an alternative by contrasting what he calls "evolutionist" and "episodic" views of the historical development of societies, the latter being based upon the idea that man's social history is marked by a single overwhelmingly important transformation, so that this history can be most usefully divided into two periods—before and after the transformation (Gellner 1964). It is evident that many historical-sociological interpretations conform quite closely with this episodic scheme. Weber's analysis of the rise of capitalism treats this transformation as a uniquely significant event in Western social history, and even Marx's theory, though it rests upon a broad evolutionary scheme, attributes a special historical importance to the emergence and development of capitalism. However, the episodic view has appeared most clearly in the extensive recent discussions of "development," "industrialization," and "modernization," most of which make use of the notion of two contrasting forms of society (e.g. traditional/modern, underdeveloped/industrial), and concentrate their attention upon the "great transformation" which occurs between one and the other.

This "episodic" version of historical sociology can well be criticized for its excessive simplification of history. It may lead to a serious neglect of the different levels of development in those societies that are classed together as "preindustrial" or "traditional," and on the other side it does not allow for future transformations. Thus, for example, it is already difficult to fit into this scheme the notion of another profound change occurring in the present age, which has been represented by some recent writers as a movement toward a "postindustrial" or "technological" society. Another type of criticism concerns the criteria for selection of the great transformation itself. The concepts of industrialization and modernization define a different kind of transition, and different forms of society at the beginning and end of the process, from those that are represented in a conception of historical development that deals with the transition from feudalism to capitalism, and then perhaps to socialism. It becomes necessary, therefore, to look more closely at the way in which the basic or crucial features of a type of society are characterized in these different conceptions, in order to judge the usefulness of the rival schemes. This does not mean, however, that there cannot also be some fruitful combination of elements from different schemes of historical interpretation. A study such as that by Barrington Moore begins with the notion of modernization, but then goes on to consider three main alternative "routes to the modern world," through bourgeois revolutions, revolutions from above, and peasant revolutions, which are explained in terms of the class relations within each society, in an analysis which clearly derives from Marxist theory (Moore 1967).

Barrington Moore's study illustrates well the reemergence of Marxism as an important sociological theory. Undoubtedly, the general reawakening of interest in historical interpretations of society, and in the particular problems of social development in the second half of the twentieth century, has contributed greatly to this intellectual revival of Marxism, though many other factors, including changes in the world political situation, have also played a part. At the same time, it has to be recognized that recent Marxist thought has developed in very diverse ways. A good deal of it has involved the rediscovery of earlier Marxist thinkers, among them Lukács, Gramsci, and Korsch, whose work had been somewhat neglected or was known only within a relatively narrow circle; or it has been concerned with the analysis and interpretation of the lesser known writings of Marx himself, especially the *Economic and Philosophical Manuscripts* and the *Grundrisse*. Nevertheless, these scholarly preoccupations have resulted in a very definite change in theoretical outlook; namely, to a view of Marxism which emphasizes much more strongly the role of cultural and intellectual factors—of "consciousness"—in the reproduction and transformation of social life, and in that sense can be regarded as formulating a "voluntaristic" theory of action rather than a theory of "economic determinism."

Besides this general, but far from universally accepted, modification of the Marxist paradigm, there have emerged two more definite versions of Marxist theory that may be regarded as forming distinctive schools of thought. One of these, associated with the work of Althusser, I shall refer to later in discussing modern structuralism. The other is that of the Frankfurt School, and it has become widely known under the name of "critical theory." This term was used much earlier by the Frankfurt Marxists, and notably by Max Horkheimer in a series of articles published in the 1930s and recently reprinted (Horkheimer 1968), to distinguish their form of Marxist thought from the economic determinism and evolutionism of official Marxism, to emphasize the significance of cultural factors (and of theoretical criticism itself) in the development of society, and to mark their affinity with a philosophical, rather than a social-scientific (and more especially positivist) formulation of Marxism. The meaning of critical theory was, in fact, close to that of "critical philosophy" in the sense of Hegel and the Young Hegelians (among them Marx himself), and it has been expounded in these terms by another member of the Frankfurt School, Herbert Marcuse (Marcuse 1941, 1964).

But whereas the Frankfurt thinkers in the 1930s still remained quite close to the main preoccupations of classical Marxism—the economic contradictions of capitalism, the conflict between classes, the crucial social role of the working class—those who formed the postwar generation of the School (and notably Habermas and Wellmer) have concerned themselves with such different questions, and have criticized so extensively Marx's theoretical system, that critical theory in the form in which it is now influential has to be regarded as an independent body of social thought. The "critical theorists" concentrate their attention upon scientific-technological society rather than capitalism (Habermas 1970), reject the idea of a process of social and political liberation based mainly upon the transformation of the economic system, and the preeminent role of the working class in that process (Wellmer 1971), and are especially concerned to criticize the positivism of the social sciences, which they see as having a necessary connection with a technological system of domination. In its assault upon positivism, critical theory has some affinities with the modern philosophy of language and meaning, and with phenomenology; at the same time it revives methodological issues that were articulated very comprehensively in the 19th century by Dilthey and continued to be discussed in diverse controversies about the method of *verstehen* and the interpretation of cultural phenomena. The likely outcome of these renewed methodological debates is far from clear, but it is evident that critical theory occupies an important place in what is now a very widespread movement to give an entirely different meaning to the activity of the social sciences.

Aside from these methodological questions, is it possible to define more precisely the character of critical theory? Its principal content is the analysis of the modern industrial, technological societies, and in this sense its concerns are close to those of other present-day sociological theories that seek to interpret the structure and development of industrial or postindustrial societies. In another way, too, there are similarities, for critical theory also assigns to knowledge and the production of knowledge a preeminent influence in the formation and transformation of modern societies, and tends to regard the principal conflicts within them as cultural and intellectual struggles rather than as clashes of economic interest or class conflicts. But critical theory also inherits from Marxism, and especially from Marx's earlier ideas, a concern with a long term process of human liberation, and in this sense it aims to construct a new philosophy of history as a general framework for empirical investigations.

This feature of critical theory associates it closely with the various attempts in recent years to develop a "radical sociology." But the latter does not yet exist in a coherent, integrated form as a new paradigm directing sociological thought; it is rather a collection of loosely related ideas drawn from Marxism (and more broadly from a variety of socialist and anarchist doctrines), from the work of the later Frankfurt School, from the radical thought of C. Wright Mills, and to some extent from the social movements of the 1960s. One formulation of the desire for such a sociology (Gouldner 1970) mainly portrays the present intellectual uncertainties, but also reveals two general features in the move toward a new paradigm: 1. the concern that sociology, and other social sciences, should resume their task of examining *critically* the institutions and processes in present-day societies (whatever their regimes), instead of serving largely to facilitate their perpetuation; and 2. a commitment to a methodological view which asserts the significance, and relative freedom, of human action, as against any conception of social determinism that would imply either the immutability of a given social order, or some inescapable future state of society. These themes have also been examined, with reference to particular social theorists and schools, in two other recent books (Clecak 1973, Gombin 1971).

Although, as I have argued, one important movement in recent sociological thought has been the revival, in one form or another, of historical conceptions of society, this is by no means the only trend, and two other attempts to give a new orientation to sociology are profoundly unhistorical, if not antihistorical, in their general outlook. The first of these is structuralism. In a broad sense structuralism may be regarded as a long-established approach in the social sciences (Piaget 1970), but the new structuralism, which has been much more influential in social anthropology than in sociology up to the present time, has some particular characteristics that justify treating it as a distinctive paradigm. In the first place it has a close association with linguistics. The structural anthropology of Lévi-Strauss had its principal source in structural linguistics (Lévi-Strauss 1967), and a great deal of the work of structuralists, chiefly in social anthropology, consists in the analysis of cultural phenomena on the model of an analysis of language (Culler 1973). This is the case particularly with Lévi-Strauss' own studies of myth, with a study such as that by Mary Douglas on pollution (Douglas 1966), and with Michel Foucault's work on the history of science in which he attempts to establish the "fundamental codes of a culture" (Foucault 1970). In all these cases the aim is to disclose a structure of meaning, similar to the structure of a language. It is evident that these preoccupations also relate structuralism in certain ways to modern linguistic philosophy, so that it can be said that there is a convergence of work in a number of different fields in the development of the structuralist paradigm.

Another important feature of structuralism, again inspired by structural linguistics, is the preoccupation with what is called "deep structure." A distinction is made between the immediately observable, surface aspects of social and cultural phenomena, and a more profound inner structure which has to be disclosed (or constructed) by analysis—a distinction between "code" and "message"—and it is often suggested, though I think erroneously, that while the new structuralists investigate this deep structure the conceptions of structure held by earlier social scientists remained at the surface level. In Lévi-Strauss' work this concern with deep structure seems to lead from the social or cultural to the psychological sphere, in the aim to relate cultural phenomena to the fundamental structure of the human mind, and the possibility is held out of a further reduction to physiological or physical structures.

It is in this sense, especially, that structuralism is unhistorical; what it attempts to establish is the universal character of cultural codes, over the whole range of human societies and historical periods. And in Lévi-Strauss' writing it takes on occasionally an antihistorical significance, as in the discussion of analytical and dialectical reason in the final chapter of *The Savage Mind* (Lévi-Strauss 1966). As I have noted, structuralism has not yet established itself as a major influence in sociological theory, and seems to be confined to a fairly small circle that has developed around the work of H. C. White, which began with an attempt to construct mathematical models of kinship structures, starting out from Lévi-Strauss' analysis of kinship (White 1963). Nevertheless, structuralism has affinities with other work in sociology, notably with mathematical model building, and with what is called "network" analysis (Mitchell 1969, Barnes 1971), so that there is a diffuse kind of influence. More broadly, structuralism has affected Marxist thought, through the work of Althusser and his followers, and there has grown up a fairly clear opposition between an "historical" and a "structuralist" version of the Marxist theory of society. The structuralists assert that Marx's major scientific work consisted in an analysis of the "deep structure" of modern capitalist society (notably in *Capital*), and that the focus of Marx's thought was this kind of structural analysis rather than the depiction and interpretation of a process of historical development.

The principal value of these ideas seems to be that they have concentrated attention on defining "systems of production," and more broadly "types of society," through structural analysis, and thus contribute to the efforts to resolve one of the most important theoretical problems in sociology. But this structuralist paradigm within Marxist thought has a certain ambiguity, and various weaknesses. It is not the intention of these thinkers, presumably, to establish, in the manner of Lévi-Strauss, fundamental and timeless structures of society. As Marxists, they are concerned with historical social structures, of which modern capitalism is one instance, and one direction for renewed investigation, that has already begun to be followed, would be the structural study of "precapitalist economic formations." This still leaves open a major question; that of the transformation of one structure into another, and in this sphere the contribution of the Marxist structuralists has not been impressive. The problem involves some conception of an historical process, and may well require the reintroduction of notions taken from an historical version of the Marxist theory, in which the development of social movements, changes in consciousness, and purposive human action are seen as crucial elements.

The second major development in sociological theory that has a markedly unhistorical character can be referred to broadly as phenomenological sociology. Its principal source has been the work of Alfred Schutz, especially since this became available in English translations from the early 1960s (Schutz 1962, 1964, 1966, 1967); and Schutz' own conceptions resulted from an application of some of Husserl's ideas to the social world, together with the adoption of the method of *verstehen,* or "understanding social action," outlined by Max Weber. But the phenomenological sociologists, although they borrow very heavily from Schutz, have also been influenced by other thinkers, notably Merleau-Ponty (1962), and some of their views, especially their opposition to positivism, have affinities with the more general themes of both existentialism and linguistic philosophy. The chief point of resemblance is to be found in their concentration upon the understanding of "meaning" as the only valid approach in the study of social life. This coincides precisely, for example, with the conception of social science formulated by a philosophical follower of Wittgenstein (Winch 1963). It may appear also that phenomenological sociology has some affinity with structuralism in its primary concern with meanings, but in this case there is a clear dividing line between the structuralist interest in the formal structure of relations between meanings which are largely taken for granted, and the phenomenological interest in the interpretation of meanings themselves.

The general influence of philosophical phenomenology upon the social sciences may be quite varied, as we can see by contrasting Schutz' use of its ideas with the social theory elaborated by Sartre in an amalgam of existentialism and Marxism, in which the notion of historical development has a crucial place (Sartre 1963). What seems to be common to most phenomenological social theory is a particular conception of the proper method of studying social and cultural phenomena; and a good deal of the work of the phenomenological school consists in methodological clarification and argument, rather than in working out a general theory.

There is, however, one recent school of mainly sociological thought, derived very largely from phenomenology, which is quite clearly attempting to construct a new paradigm—namely, ethnomethodology. The main characteristic of this school is its concentration upon the study of "everyday life" or "common sense experience," or in the case of Garfinkel (who may be regarded as the founder of the school), more especially upon "everyday rationality" (Garfinkel 1967). At first sight this may not appear a very remarkable new departure. Most sociologists would agree that the depiction and interpretation of men's activities in the ordinary affairs of life constitutes an important sphere of research. The distinctiveness of ethnomethodology lies rather in the particular way that it conceives such studies; first, that what is being observed and recorded is conscious "rule-following" activity, not any kind of causal process or outcome of structural arrangements, and second, that in understanding the rationality of everyday life we already comprehend a theory (or theories) of society, without any need to superimpose upon it a "sociological" theory that we construct ourselves.

The first of these views, insofar as it governs the general orientation of ethnomethodological research, presents a sharp contrast with a structuralist approach, for it could be said that ethnomethodology concentrates precisely upon the surface phenomena of social life that structuralism considers to be relatively unimportant and even misleading for scientific inquiry. The second view has a strong resemblance to the doctrine of linguistic philosophy in its heyday, for just as these philosophers took as their subject matter "ordinary language" and did not conceive the business of philosophical discourse as being to reform or go beyond such language, so the ethnomethodologists take everyday life or commonsense experience (and, by implication, ordinary language) as their subject of investigation, and do not propose to correct or supplant the theories of society that already guide everyday life with a superior sociological theory. In this sense we might say that the "Narodniks of north Oxford," as Gellner (1959) once described the linguistic philosophers, have found a new lease of life as the "Narodniks of Southern California."

The paradigms that I have discussed represent some of the principal trends in sociological theory at the present time, but they are far from comprehending all the different tendencies that now exist. There are very diverse conceptions of the main subject matter and problems of sociological theory even within the various schools of thought that I have mentioned, as well as disagreements about the research strategies implied by these conceptions, and about the relation of sociological theory to policy making and to political commitment or action. Nevertheless, I think it is possible, even in the face of this diversity, to distinguish some broad lines of agreement and of contestation.

First, it may be noted that all the paradigms considered here conceive sociological theory in a very broad way, as a general social theory which draws, as the case may be, upon historical studies, philosophical ideas, and the work of economists and social anthropologists, as well as paying attention to those thinkers who have been primarily concerned with elaborating political doctrines (and becoming involved in political struggles), rather than confining themselves to a sphere of "pure" theoretical sociology. The notion of sociological theory as a highly specific and specialized branch of thought seems now to be distinctly out of fashion, and on the other hand, the wider social theory that is sought has come to be regarded, by many sociologists, as closely bound up with practical social and political conflicts. In some respects, therefore, it could be said that sociological thought is realizing an earlier ambition to provide a comprehensive framework within which all the general "problems of the age" are formulated and discussed; though, of course, it does this very imperfectly insofar as it offers so many more or less incompatible and competing schemes of interpretation.

A second general feature of recent paradigms is that they are all elaborated in the context of a broader concern with the logic of the social sciences. The theoretical controversies in sociology over the past decade or so have revived, while introducing some new elements, the *Methodenstreit* of the end of the 19th century and the early 20th century. As in those earlier methodological disputes, two of the principal features are an attack on positivism, and controversy about the place of value judgments in social science, especially those value judgments that are an important ingredient in political doctrines. The main tendency of recent sociological thought has certainly been antipositivist, and there has been a renewal of interest in what can be called broadly a "hermeneutic" method which goes back at least to Dilthey.[3]

The main difficulty with this hermeneutic approach is that it does not seem able to establish any definite criteria for deciding among the various subjective interpretations of social events, processes, or forms of life. If this approach can be characterized, in the words of Isaiah Berlin (1969), as producing the kind of knowledge that is involved " . . . .when a work of the imagination or of social diagnosis, or a work of criticism or scholarship or history is described not as correct or incorrect, skilful or inept, a success or a failure, but as profound or shallow, realistic or unrealistic, perceptive or stupid, alive or dead. . . . ," then it seems to depend much more upon the creative powers, or the quality of mind, of the individual interpreter of social life than upon any accumulated body of sociological theory or rules concerning the testing of propositions by reference to some kind of empirical reality. Its achievements appear in the form of works of art rather than contributions to a systematic social science, and there may emerge (perhaps has emerged) a variety of interpretations among which it is impossible to choose according to any general criteria of validity or truth.

Very often, indeed, the preference for an interpretation seems to be influenced predominantly by a commitment to values of a general cultural, or more narrowly political, kind; and it is not surprising, therefore, that the debate about social science and value judgments has also been resumed very vigorously in recent theoretical writings. Many of the competing paradigms in sociological theory (and this is particularly true of critical theory and of the various forms of radical sociology) include as an important element some formulation of the relation between theoretical models and research on one side, and political action and policy making on the other. It can hardly be said that this debate has yet advanced much beyond the earlier discussions; for the most part, it still revolves uneasily around the themes of Max Weber's essay on "objectivity" and of Marxist conceptions of "ideology," without finding any significant new expression in a form as substantial as Weber's essay. At least, however, the issue has been clearly defined again, and it seems likely that no paradigm will prove generally acceptable or persuasive that does not include among its basic statements or suppositions some reference to the specific nature of the involvement of sociological theory—and of all social theory—with the historical process of social life from which the thinker cannot, any more than other men, extricate himself.

Literature Cited

Aron, R. 1967. *18 Lectures on Industrial Society.* London: Weidenfeld & Nicolson

Barnes, J. A. 1971. *Three Styles in the Study of Kinship.* London: Tavistock

Bell, D. 1973. *The Coming of Post-Industrial Society.* New York: Basic. 507 pp.

Berlin, I. 1969. A note on Vico's concept of knowledge. *New York Rev. Books* 12(8)

Burrow, J. W. 1966. *Evolution and Society: A Study in Victorian Social Theory.* Cambridge: Cambridge Univ. Press. 295 pp.

Clecak, P. 1973. *Radical Paradoxes.* New York: Harper & Row. 358 pp.

Culler, J. 1973. The linguistic basis of structuralism. In *Structuralism: An Intro-*

[3]For some general discussion of these issues see Louch 1966, Wellmer 1971, Giddens 1974, Outhwaite 1974.

duction, ed. D. Robey, 20–36. Oxford: Clarendon

Demerath, N. J., Peterson, R. A. 1967. *System, Change and Conflict: A Reader on Contemporary Sociological Theory and the Debate over Functionalism.* New York: Free Press. 533 pp.

Dore, R. P. 1961. Function and cause. *Am. Sociol. Rev.* 26(6):843–53

Douglas, M. 1966. *Purity and Danger.* London: Routledge & Kegan Paul. 188 pp.

Durkheim, E. 1938. *The Rules of Sociological Method.* Glencoe: Free Press

Foucault, M. 1970. *The Order of Things.* London: Tavistock

Garfinkel, H. 1967. *Studies in Ethnomethodology.* Englewood Cliffs, NJ: Prentice-Hall

Gellner, E. 1959. *Words and Things.* London: Victor Gollancz. 270 pp.

Gellner, E. 1964. *Thought and Change.* London: Weidenfeld & Nicolson. 224 pp.

Giddens, A., Ed. 1974. *Positivism and Sociology.* London: Heinemann

Godelier, M. 1972. *Rationality and Irrationality in Economics.* London: New Left

Gombin, R. 1971. *Les origines du gauchisme.* Paris: Editions du Seuil. 187 pp.

Gouldner, A. W. 1970. *The Coming Crisis of Western Sociology.* New York: Basic. 528 pp.

Habermas, J. 1970. *Toward a Rational Society.* Boston: Beacon. 132 pp.

Hempel, C. J. 1959. The logic of functional analysis. In *Symposium on Sociological Theory,* ed. L. Gross, 271–303. Evanston, Ill: Row, Peterson

Hobsbawm, E. J. 1964. Introduction to Karl Marx. In *Pre-Capitalist Economic Formations,* 9–65. London: Lawrence & Wishart

Horkheimer, M. 1968. *Kritische Theorie.* Frankfurt: S. Fischer. 2 Vols. 734 pp.

Hughes, H. S. 1958. *Consciousness and Society.* New York: Oxford Univ. Press. 433 pp.

Lauterbach, A. 1933. Review in *Der Kampf* 26(12)

Lévi-Strauss, C. 1966. *The Savage Mind.* Chicago: Univ. Chicago Press. 290 pp.

Lévi-Strauss, C. 1967. *Structural Anthropology.* Garden City, NY: Doubleday

Lipset, S. M., Smelser, N. J. 1961. *Sociology: The Progress of a Decade.* Englewood Cliffs, NJ: Prentice-Hall. 635 pp.

Louch, A. R. 1966. *Explanation and Human Action.* Oxford: Basil Blackwell. 243 pp.

Marcuse, H. 1941. *Reason and Revolution: Hegel and the Rise of Social Theory.* New York: Oxford Univ. Press. 431 pp.

Marcuse, H. 1964. *One-Dimensional Man.* Boston: Beacon. 260 pp.

Masterman, M. 1970. The nature of a paradigm. In *Criticism and the Growth of Knowledge,* ed. I. Lakatos, A. Musgrave, 58–89. Cambridge: Cambridge Univ. Press

Merleau-Ponty, M. 1962. *Phenomenology of Perception.* New York: Humanities Press

Merton, R. K. 1957. *Social Theory and Social Structure.* Glencoe: Free Press. 2nd rev. ed.

Mitchell, J. C. 1969. *Social Networks in Urban Situations.* Manchester: Manchester Univ. Press

Moore, B. 1967. *Social Origins of Dictatorship and Democracy.* Boston: Beacon. 559 pp.

Outhwaite, R. W. 1974. *Understanding Social Life: The Method Called Verstehen.* London: Allen & Unwin. 123 pp.

Parsons, T. 1966. *Societies: Evolutionary and Comparative Perspectives.* Englewood Cliffs, NJ: Prentice-Hall. 120 pp.

Peel, J. D. Y. 1971. *Herbert Spencer: The Evolution of a Sociologist.* London: Heinemann

Peters, R. S. 1958. *The Concept of Motivation.* London: Routledge & Kegan Paul. 166 pp.

Piaget, J. 1970. *Structuralism.* New York: Basic

Sartre, J. P. 1963. *Search for a Method.* New York: Knopf. 181 pp.

Schutz, A. 1962, 1964, 1966. *Collected Papers.* The Hague: Martinus Nijhoff. 3 Vols. 852 pp.

Schutz, A. 1967. *The Phenomenology of the Social World.* Evanston, Ill: Northwestern Univ. Press

Touraine, A. 1971. *The Post-Industrial Society.* New York: Random House. 244 pp.

Wellmer, A. 1971. *Critical Theory of Society.* New York: Herder & Herder. 139 pp.

White, H. C. 1963. *An Anatomy of Kinship: Mathematical Models for Structures of Cumulated Roles.* Englewood Cliffs, NJ: Prentice-Hall. 180 pp.

Winch, P. 1963. *The Idea of a Social Science.* London: Routledge & Kegan Paul. 143 pp.

SOCIOLOGY OF SCIENCE ❖10508

Joseph Ben-David[1]
Department of Sociology, Hebrew University, Jerusalem, Israel, and Department of
Sociology, University of Chicago, Chicago, Illinois 60637

Teresa A. Sullivan
Department of Sociology, University of Texas, Austin, Texas 78712

INTRODUCTION

Sociology of science deals with the social conditions and effects of science, and with
the social structures and processes of scientific activity. Science is a cultural tradition, preserved and transmitted from generation to generation partly because it is
valued in its own right, and partly because of its wide technological applications.
Its most distinguishing characteristic is that the primary purpose of its cultivators,
the scientists, is to change the tradition through discoveries. This bears some similarity to the purpose of modern artists and writers. But innovations in art and
literature are accompanied by dissension and conflict, because there are no explicit
criteria and accepted procedures to determine whether an innovation is an improvement or deterioration of existing tradition. Although scientific criteria and procedures are neither perfectly unequivocal nor entirely stable, they are still far superior
to criteria used in the evaluation of other cultural products. The relatively objective,
consensual evaluation of discoveries makes science an extreme case of institutionally
regulated cultural change.

  Sociologists of science have concentrated on this characteristic of science as a
tradition and as an institution. The questions they deal with are: How did this
unique tradition of modern science emerge and become institutionalized? How is it
maintained and controlled? How is research organized? What determines changes
in scientific organization, and how are these changes related to research?

  These are wide-ranging problems, difficult to delimit. Our task of setting limits
to this survey has been further complicated by the fact that the sociology of science,
as of other cultural fields, is the common interest of several different disciplines. In
our selection we concentrate on issues in which important work has been done
during the last five years, but we also include earlier work to the extent that this
is necessary as background for current developments. Relevant work done by non-
sociologists is included more or less on the same basis as that of sociologists.

[1]This work was aided by a grant from the Ford Foundation.

THE INSTITUTIONAL ORIGINS OF MODERN SCIENCE

The question of the emergence and institutionalization of modern science derives from Max Weber's approach to the study of modern society.

It concerns the conditions under which inquiry into the laws of nature becomes an intellectual end in its own right, in contrast to earlier times when such inquiry was subservient to technological and moral-religious ends. Merton's (1938) investigations show the case to be parallel to the rise of modern ("capitalist") economy in that a religious element played an important role in the process (cf Tenbruck 1974).

Many founders of the 17th century English scientific movement were motivated by personal religious beliefs and values. The Puritan life style fostered or selected a personality type capable of the rational, methodical conduct presupposed by scientific inquiry. And Calvinist doctrine, which foreclosed certainty of salvation and satisfaction of the religious yearning to be near to God, suggested the search of God through a rational understanding of creation.

The literature stimulated by Merton's book has concentrated primarily on the assumed link between Puritanism and science. Doubts were raised about Merton's interpretation of religious predisposition and motivation as a positive influence on science (Merton 1957a, Westfall 1958). Although some Puritanic circles supported science, and many scientists came from Calvinistic backgrounds, official Puritanism was not favorable to science. In 17th century Scotland and Geneva, where Calvinistic sects actually held power, there was as much opposition to the autonomy of scientific thought as in places ruled by other denominations. It seems that the positive relationship between Puritanism and science existed only where the Calvinistic clergy lost its control over intellectual life, but where personal religion was still widespread and strong. Then, scientifically inclined people could use the relative freedom of personal interpretation of the Scriptures to justify their intellectual devotion to science, and even to pursue their scientific inquiries with religious enthusiasm. This reinterpretation of the Merton hypothesis (Ben-David 1971) seems to be consistent both with the English case, where the movement started as a reaction to a stalemate in the religious controversy between the various sects, and with the upswing of scientific spirit in 18th century Scotland and Geneva and late 19th century United States.

An obscured point in this controversy is the distinction between science as a private pursuit and as a publicly recognized activity, freed from the control of Church or State. Criticism of Merton's use of personal documents, which were not representative of all scientists, particularly outside of England, obscured Merton's principal concern with the movement leading to the foundation of the Royal Society. This institutional development, which had no precedents or parallels of equal importance outside of England, could not have been explained unless a significant group of people attached to scientific inquiry a moral importance beyond the satisfaction of curiosity. Perhaps some of the controversy could have been avoided by a distinction between the rise of modern science as a new kind of scientific theory and the emergence of its institutional foundations.

There seems to be some justification for exploring the question parallel to that asked about Weber's hypothesis on capitalism, namely whether the emergence of the institutions of modern science in the 17th century was really as discontinuous an event with the past as implied in this whole inquiry. This question has not been asked because the innovations of Copernicus, Galileo, Kepler, and above all, Newton, underlie one of the great myths of modern historical consciousness. It is taken for granted that these events constituted a Scientific Revolution which did away with the past, and created an entirely new era in science. As a result there is a dearth of studies of the social forms of science in earlier societies (see however, Goody 1974).

Explanation of the institutional origins of modern science led to attempts at a detailed description of the characteristics of science as an institution regulated by norms (Storer 1966). Norms implicit in the public conduct of scientists include universalism, emotional neutrality, rationality, individualism, communality, and disinterestedness.

The obvious application of these characteristics was exploring the fit between the norms of science and those of other institutions, in different societies. Attempts were made to see how the norms of science fitted the institutional arrangements of liberal, socialist, and fascist societies. But there was no evidence that incongruity between the norms of science and of other social institutions had a deleterious effect on research.

These attempts faltered on the unfounded assumption that the relationship between the different institutional norms had to be direct and linear, such as "the greater the congruence between the norms of science and those of other institutions, the greater the likelihood that science will thrive in a society." But institutional insulation can compensate for incongruence of institutional norms. This is particularly likely to occur in scientific research, which involves only a small fraction of the population and is by its own norms relatively "value neutral." Furthermore, normative congruence is not a simple variable, for there may be overt or covert disagreement about norms.

An investigation of the changes in the relative standing of different countries in world science has yielded more positive results (Ben-David 1971). At question was the rise of support for science in England during the second half of the 17th century and in France during the second half of the 18th century, and the relative decline following these periods in both countries. The common element present was scientistic movements oriented to political and social reform. For these movements, science was a model for attaining progress, objectivity, and consensus in general. Throughout most of the period, these movements opposed autocratic regimes intent on the preservation of religious and political traditions incongruent with the norms of science. For pragmatic reasons, autocratic rulers were willing to adopt the recommendations of the scientistic groups to the extent of supporting academies and individual scientists. Thus natural science was supported, although on different grounds, both by the rulers and by their opponents. This conferred on science a prestige unequalled by any other intellectual endeavor. But following the revolutions in both countries, the scientistic opposition gained power, and the enthusiasm for science waned. Intellectuals became more interested in practical reforms, technological applications, and literary and artistic culture (Robert Fox 1973). Thus science received relatively more support in a situation in which its norms were partially incongruent with the prevailing social norms than in situations of complete congruence.

This explanation is consistent with the support given to science by authoritarian regimes of this century. The relative ability of science to insulate itself from political and ideological issues, and the regime's need for scientific advice and know-how, confer on scientists in these countries a degree of freedom denied others. This tends to make science a particularly attractive occupation in such societies.

INSTITUTIONAL FUNCTIONS: THE REWARD SYSTEM OF SCIENCE[2]

The most important result of the description of science in terms of moral norms is the investigation of the reward system. Merton (1957b) noted the apparent contradiction between the norm of communality which requires scientists to publish their results and regard them as the property of mankind, and their sensitivity and frequent selfishness concerning priority in discoveries. He suggested that the proper recognition of discovery is a necessary condition for the maintenance of communality, since without recognition scientists could not defend their intellectual property. There would be no incentive to publish and science would not be maintained as an institutionalized public activity.

This hypothesis created a theoretically meaningful basis for the empirical study of the allocation of rewards. If the process of allocation has the importance attached to it by the hypothesis, one would expect the functioning of the reward system to play a central role in the life of science.

This suggestion was followed in a series of investigations using either questionnaires or citation counts. The latter method considers the frequency of citation of a scientist's papers as the amount of recognition given to him.[3] The *Science Citation*

---

[2]The word "reward" is somewhat misleading, since it may imply that the purpose of scientific activity is to obtain honors and material rewards. No such implication is intended here. Scientists have a variety of motives, and most of them are genuinely interested in research and discovery. But their behavior is inevitably influenced by the mechanisms of social reward. In particular, the possibility that someone else may get the credit due to himself is as unacceptable to a scientist as to anyone else. For a critique of the emphasis of reward, see Gustin 1973.

[3]Perfunctory citing is discussed in Michael J. Moravcsik and Poovanalingam Murugesan, "Studies of the Nature of Citation Measures. I: Some Results on the Function and Quality of Citation" and Poovanalingam Murugesan and Michael J. Moravcsik, "Studies of the Nature of Citation Measures II: Variation in the Nature of Citation from Journal to Journal," unpublished manuscripts from the Institute of Theoretical Sciences, University of Oregon, Eugene, Oregon, 1974. The validity of citation as a quality index is investigated in Naomi Cohen-Shanin, "Innovation and Citation," unpublished manuscript, The National Council for Research and Development, Prime Minister's Office, and the Department of Sociology, Hebrew University, Jerusalem, November 1974.

Index makes possible the study of citation counts for whole populations across disciplines.

The first questions investigated within this context were competitiveness and concern with priority among scientists. Competitiveness is most prevalent when widespread consensus exists among scientists about the importance of problems and when large numbers of scientists work simultaneously on the same problems, as in physics, experimental biology, and chemistry. There is some variation among disciplines in the manifestation of competition, which is related to productivity in research (Hagstrom 1967, Collins 1968).

Another question derived from the hypothesis about the importance of reward in science is the extent to which the system operates in accordance with the norms of science. In a series of studies summarized by Cole & Cole (1973), they conclude that for the physical sciences, the evaluation of research closely approaches the universalistic ideal. Almost no work of consequence escapes publication, and high quality work is recognized regardless of the author's extrascientific characteristics. But lower quality work receives more attention if it is authored by a noted scientist. Essentially similar findings are reported for Britain by Gaston (1973) for high energy physicists, and by Blume & Sinclair (1973) for chemists. These empirical findings conclusively contradict the criticism of these norms as idealizations of the behavior of scientists (Barnes & Dolby 1970, Dolby 1971, King 1971, Mulkay & Williams 1971, Brush 1974). The critics fail to distinguish institutional norms from personal behavior. Mitroff (1974) attempts to take this distinction into account, and to interpret apparently deviant behavior as the result of "counternorms." But apart from the logical inacceptability of the concept "counternorm," the fact that scientists are committed to their theories and defend them against evidence so long as the evidence is only plausible but not clinching, is no contradiction to the effectiveness of the norms. The mechanisms of social control in science work on the whole according to the institutional norms in spite of individual deviations.

Thus there is a logical continuity between the historical studies of the institutionalization of modern science in the 17th century, the descriptions of the institutionalized norms of science, and the study of reward systems in present day science.

While the institutional hypothesis has been used in all this work, it has not necessarily guided the work. The questions asked by sociologists have often been determined by changing public issues and not by theoretical problems. Such questions as how Nazi ideology would affect science, discussed in the early 1940s, and whether there is sexual, racial, or class discrimination in science today are prominent in the literature more for their topical than for their theoretical importance (Cole & Cole 1973, Zuckerman & Cole 1975).

On the other hand, a theoretically central question in the early investigation of Cole & Cole (1967, 1968), the relation of reward to the quality and quantity of research, has not been consistently pursued. This question can be investigated through differences among disciplines. Hagstrom (1965) suggested that the absence of an effective reward system in the highly theoretical and specialized field of mathematics is apt to create loss of morale and loss of direction ("anomie") in this field. Zuckerman & Merton (1971), in a discussion of the institutionalization of journal editing and refereeing, note that the position of referee is a form of reward. They analyzed the archives of *Physical Review* and found that the referees tend to be of a higher rank than the authors, at least partly because expertise is correlated with prestige. The work of high-ranking authors is more likely to be evaluated by the editor alone. An interesting difference they note is the much higher rejection rates in more humanistically oriented journals. Presumably this is due to a lower level of consensus in these disciplines. Also the reward system may be more diffuse in some areas. For example, Klima (1972) and Ben-David (1974) point out that discontinuity in social science research is due to the fact that social scientists also write for a broad public, and so they move from subject to subject according to the swings of public opinion and not to the internal logic of their own inquiry. The reward system may also vary by countries; Krantz (1970, 1971a) shows that there are serious barriers to international communication in psychology.

THE ORGANIZATION OF SCIENCE: FORMAL ORGANIZATION

Formal scientific organization ranges from laboratories, departments, and institutions to central national or international scientific agencies. Informal organization includes teams, research groups ("invisible colleges"), disciplinary and interdisciplinary elites, and, on a most comprehensive level, the whole scientific community. Ongoing research has not crystallized around the study of different organizational structures, but around a variety of substantive problems. These include the function of the academies in 17th and 18th century science and of the universities in the 19th century, the emergence and support of a system of research organizations in the 20th century, and the social structure of networks and groups involved in the rise of new specialities. We shall follow these substantive clusters of literature and try to group them under broad categories of organizational structure, starting with historical and comparative studies of formal organization.

The first group of studies to be considered deal with 17th and 18th century scientific academies. Many studies provide information on the social characteristics of the members, on the motivation of the founders and supporters, and on the way the academies functioned. Hahn (1971) uses explicit sociological categories to study the social functions of science in the academies. His most important finding is that the major organizational function of the Paris Academy of Sciences was evaluating and publishing individual contributions, somewhat analogously to present day refereeing. Research had few uses or resources and no "research programs" encouraged sustained coordination and cooperation. On the other hand, many irreconcilable theories and doctrines threatened the unity of the scientific enterprise. In performing its function of supreme arbiter in scientific matters with restraint and neutrality towards untestable doctrines, the Paris Academy of Sciences maintained a measure of consensus concerning scientific procedure and a sense of distributive justice.

The academies did not organize scientific work—it remained individualistic and unorganized. Their function was facilitating scientific communication and administering the reward system of science. Therefore, their functional equivalents in subsequent ages were not universities and research institutes, but scientific journals and meetings.

The determinants of differences in the structure and the functions of the academies of different countries, or those of the metropoles in contrast to those in the provinces, and the effect these differences had on the kind and style of scientific research in various countries remain to be explored.

Due to the increasing importance of university research, the rise of broadly based societies for the advancement of science or of disciplines, and the emergence of specialized and general scientific journals, no central institution can serve as the focus for the study of science organization in the 19th century. However, the development of scientific higher education and the professionalization of research are central themes for such study.

The cost of research until the last decades of the century was relatively low. Provided that it was believed that professionals should receive up-to-date scientific training, research could be charged as overhead for training professionals, especially in medicine, chemistry, and even high school teaching. Given this belief, competent scientists were needed as teachers at the universities which trained professionals. Therefore, the question of how organization affected research in the 19th century can usually be reduced to the question of how the teaching of science was organized, and its effect on the growth of professional research.

There have been a number of studies of the development of scientific education and professionalization in different countries (Morrell 1972a, b; Sanderson 1972, Crosland 1975). These are mainly historical case studies designed to reconstruct the events leading to the institution of courses of scientific study and/or the emergence of training and career opportunities for scientists.

Attempts to explore the sociological regularities in these developments suggest that competition for reputation among universities or government education agencies creates both a rising demand for and supply of researchers. This competition enables scientific societies, or lobbies of scientists, such as the *Gesselschaft deutscher Naturforscher und Arzte,* to persuade governments to establish new chairs and recognize new fields (Pfetsch & Zloczower 1973). Higher education departments of governments in the German states, and university presidents in the United States, were particularly inclined to accept scientific reputation as a criterion for appointing professors and evaluating institutions. Reputation was a relatively objective, almost measurable yardstick of excellence (Ben-David 1972). Contrary to accepted views, academic self-government was not favorable to the research emphasis as a criterion for appointments, because self-governing groups of academics tended to be influenced by local loyalties and by the congeniality of the candidates (Turner 1971).

International competition was probably the major force behind the successive reforms of higher education and the establishment of facilities for training researchers in England and France (von Gizycki 1973). But competition had its greatest effect in decentralized systems, including the German and American systems of higher education. It is probably due to this internal competition that these two systems have succeeded each other as centers of world science (Ben-David 1971).

The development of scientific journals, societies, and congresses in late 18th and 19th century science has received only sporadic attention (Thackray 1971, Shapin 1972, Pfetsch 1974). More systematic attention has been paid to the relationships between science and industry, agriculture, and medicine, and the support of research (MacLeod 1970, 1971, Miller 1970, Rosenberg 1971, Morrell 1973). But the large scale support of research apart from teaching, and often serving some practical purpose, only began in the last decades of the 19th century, and became an important aspect of the social structure of science only in the 20th century.

New structures and mechanisms arose for the support of research at the end of the 19th century, including research grants to individual university scientists and to the universities themselves; special research institutions both outside and inside universities; and research laboratories in industrial firms, hospitals, or government departments. This expansion and diversification, though based on the assumption that research benefitted industrial technology, has not led to the transfer of research to the relevant industries, for only a few firms could afford the risk of financing unpredictable long range research operations. In most countries, the majority of research and development is financed by governments or foundations.

Consequently, science is supported, mainly in the expectation of economic benefits, by a financial and organizational complex of government and other nonprofit agencies. Economic research indicates that there are such benefits, but it is difficult to determine how these benefits accrue from research and how cost-benefit ratios vary with different levels of investment and in different industries (National Science Foundation 1971).

One question investigated by social scientists is the relationship between scientific discoveries and technological inventions. These studies (Jewkes, Sawers & Stillerman 1969; National Science Foundation 1969, 1973) suggest that basic discoveries rarely lead to technological inventions. Inventions occur in response to economic demand (Schmookler 1966). The inventors may utilize available scientific knowledge, or occasionally turn to researchers for the solution to certain scientific problems. Thus industry judges the effectiveness of science organization by the ease and frequency of communication between managers and scientists, and not necessarily by any particular type of formal organization (Katz & Ben-David 1975). These studies conclude that science and technology are distinct processes, each developing according to its own rationale and mutually influencing each other in various ways. D. S. Price's (1965) comparison of scientific and technological publications and citations shows that while scientific publications are a more or less complete reflection of the work of scientists, this is not at all the case in technology.

This leaves unanswered the question of how science and technology influence each other. Current studies have concentrated on the effect of science on technology, but a theoretically significant investigation would have to consider influences in both directions[4] (see also Mansfield 1968, Thackray, 1970, Cardwell 1972).

[4]There is a more balanced treatment among sociological historians of science; see Rossi (1970), Musson & Robinson (1969).

Despite the difficulty in conceptualizing how science contributes to technology, research is supported for its potential practical uses, presumably on the assumption that the consequences of withdrawing support would probably be more deleterious than continuing it on a trial and error basis. As a result, social scientists of science face the dilemma of trying to interpret and make recommendations on a situation which they can only partially understand, or of refraining from dealing with the problem altogether.

Attempts at interpreting such a situation are limited to establishing criteria for choosing between alternatives. Thus most of the literature in this field is normative, dealing with such questions as how to determine the proper level of support for science in general, or for different fields and kinds (basic vs applied) of science (Shils 1968, Dobrow 1970, Krauch 1970b, Price 1971; Kroeber & Steiner 1974, Rabkine 1974).

The question is the extent to which it is possible to go beyond analyses of policy decisions to a theoretical understanding of the place and the functioning of science in contemporary society. There is a small, but growing volume of largely historical literature relevant to this subject (Gilpin 1968, Orlans 1968, Pfetsch 1970, Schroeder-Gudehus 1972, Forman 1974).

International organizations including the Organization for Economic Cooperation and Development (OECD) and UNESCO have undertaken comprehensive surveys and studies of the science organization and policies in different countries. There has been only a single attempt to use this information for a comparative study of the present-day organization of science in Western Europe (OECD 1972, 1973). The findings are preliminary but indicate that in the course of this century there emerged in all of these countries a set of typical institutions for the support of research. In each country, individual grants from central agencies supplement university research budgets, and government research institutes engage in nondirected research. Some of them, such as France and Germany, also have a considerable number of nonuniversity research institutes in pure science, and there are differences in the extent to which governments engage in industrial research in addition to research done in particular firms.

The existence of a system of pure research institutes parallel to the universities seems to be the result of inefficient functioning of the universities. Both the French and German university systems tend to be politicized and resist innovations, thus providing an inhospitable environment for researchers. In Britain and the smaller Western European nations, universities provide a more congenial atmosphere for researchers, making institutes for pure research unnecessary.

Governments would seem to take up research tasks where industry contacts with universities are ineffective or where the industrial firms are too small to organize research themselves, but are of sufficient number and size to utilize it. The results of these direct interventions of governments in research are still to be evaluated.

There is a tendency to think of research, and to support it, as a distinct sector of the economy; nevertheless it is difficult to maintain organizations, or even careers, devoted to full time research. On the whole the most successful organizations have been the universities. In applied research some very large industrial laboratories, or small specialized firms in a few science-based industries (Shimshoni 1970), are successful. Organizations engaged solely in research have a tendency to become obsolete, and are apt to lose touch both with the developments in science and with industrial demands. Innovation is difficult to organize or to engage in full time.

But university research is only possible in relatively few institutions with adequate funds and students capable of participating in research. In many countries the universities are mass institutions whose teachers, many of whom are not competent to do research, teach students, most of whom are unable to benefit from training in advanced research. Besides this, it is too expensive to promote research in such systems on an egalitarian basis. In these countries pure research has to move out from the universities to special research institutes.

Similarly, in most countries there are no firms with the organizational capability of conducting effective applied research, especially in some small scale industries as agriculture. As a result, applied research tends to be organized in separate research institutes which, as has been pointed out, are difficult to maintain on a high level of effectiveness (see also Brooks 1973, Robinson 1973, Townes 1973).

The study of research laboratories and research teams began with the question of the optimal organization of research work.

High levels of motivation were found among technical people who were given considerable responsibility for a project, but who also received information, encouragement, and support from their supervisors. To the extent that a project director superior may be considered a "leader," these findings tended to confirm the hypothesis of Lippitt & White (1943) about styles of leadership.

In science, however, "leadership" might mean merely the administration of the laboratory, or it might include detailed problem-setting and technical direction. The latter threatens individual autonomy, especially among PhD scientists and in basic research settings. Pelz & Andrews (1966) separated these concepts in a study of 1131 scientists and engineers in 11 government, university, and industrial laboratories. They identified as variables individual autonomy and coordination of the laboratory group.

In loosely coordinated laboratories, high individual motivation or stimulation were necessary for achievement. But high autonomy did not necessarily indicate high motivation or stimulation; on the contrary, it might indicate isolation and narrow specialization. In fact, highly autonomous scientists in loosely coordinated settings performed below average. On the other hand, high autonomy and tight coordination were also unsatisfactory, possibly because the rigidities of tight coordination frustrate autonomous scientists. High autonomy scientists performed best, with broader interests, in middle-range coordination settings. Frequent communication among researchers and even "intellectual tension" may compensate for the isolating effects of high autonomy when coordination is loose.

Another explanation for the difference between university, government, and industrial laboratories may be that they engage in different kinds of work. That done in research institutes and industry may involve large scale work which requires more coordination, but differences in the need for coordination may also exist within each type of organization (Weinberg 1967, Hetzler 1970, Krauch 1970a, Swatez 1970).

Recent studies of laboratory teams have concentrated on the division of labor and patterns of interaction within teams as identified by sociometric techniques. The studies of the reward system in science suggest that highly productive scientists should have high status within their work group, and the two-step theory of communication suggests that high status persons should also be communication leaders. In a study of two research and development organizations, Allen & Cohen (1969) asked questions about social relations and the flow of technical information within the laboratory. Those chosen most frequently for technical discussions had more exposure to technical sources outside the laboratory, held significantly more patents, and published significantly more papers than their colleagues.

It is difficult to determine from these findings alone whether the gatekeepers received more information from the outside because they were more productive, or whether they were more productive because they were up-to-date on developments outside their own laboratories. Earlier work with a contradictory finding (Allen 1966) had shown that the performance of government and industry scientists was inversely related to the number of personal contacts made outside the laboratory. The explanation suggested is that the average or poor scientists seek information because their work is not going well, while productive scientists both seek and receive information required for their work and are sought out by others interested in their results. This hypothesis (Allen & Cohen 1969) needs testing.

Another group of studies deals with the effects of organization on job satisfaction. The hypothesis guiding most of these studies has been that the ideal work organization for scientists is that which allows them freedom and discretion in choosing research topics, executing the research, and publishing the results. The preference of scientists for academic work where such conditions prevail, and for similar conditions in industry, is interpreted as evidence supporting the hypothesis. However, this interpretation is difficult to reconcile with Pelz and Andrews' findings that high individual autonomy is not always the optimal condition for productivity in research. It is unlikely that conditions conducive to satisfaction differ from those conducive to productivity, but the differences in satisfaction may result from differences between universities and industry in the rank and level of work.

Furthermore, few researchers engage only in research. Academic scientists also teach, industrial scientists may also be engaged in production, and all may be doing administrative work. The question, as shown by Parsons & Platt (1973), is what determines the preferences for, and what are the results of, different types of role combinations. This question has been widely discussed concerning academics (Halsey & Trow 1971, Bock 1972, Light 1974), but much less concerning industrial scientists (Kaplan 1965). Studies done in England (Cotgrove & Box 1970, Duncan 1972) have shown that dissatisfaction among industrial scientists may not be due primarily to the restrictions imposed on the scientists by the nature and the goals of industrial research, but by inadequate staff-line relationships within industrial firms.

The last aspect of the formal organization of science to be reviewed is the scientific career. The determinants of career mobility of scientists have been studied recently by Crane (1970), Hargens & Hagstrom (1967), Hargens (1969), and Hargens & Farr (1973).

Eminent scientists tend to have earned their degrees in distinguished departments. Among Nobel Prize winners, a large number were the students of earlier laureates (Zuckerman 1970). Rank of doctoral department is correlated with rank of department of the first job and of the current job (Hargens & Hagstrom 1967; Cole & Cole 1973).

The question is whether this career pattern is due to the advantage of a good start at first class institutions, or to merit reflected in the quality of work. The bulk of the evidence indicates that the main condition is merit (Gaston 1969, Hagstrom 1971). It has been suggested that institutional inequalities in resources amplify the inequalities of talent (Allison & Stewart 1974), but the evidence for this is equivocal. The term "cumulative advantage," currently much in use, is misleading, given the absence of satisfactory measures of the "initial advantages." This would be a significant finding only if applied to scientists of equal ability. A study of a relatively nonhierarchical university system—for example, that of Germany—would provide an interesting comparison.

Of course, the theoretically important question for a sociology of science is not whether the scientific career fits some model of social equality, but the question of how different types of career structures are related to scientific productivity and innovation (see also Clark 1968, Mulkay 1972). Zloczower (1973) has shown that the chair system of the 19th century German universities encouraged attempts at founding new disciplines, and that the existence of a hierarchy of universities competing for excellence created opportunities for mobile people to obtain recognition for their speciality as a separate discipline. Clark's (1973) work describing the system of academic patronage prevailing in France during the same time shows how such a system, structurally inimical to innovation, could under certain conditions be used in launching and institutionalizing a disciplinary innovation.

THE INFORMAL ORGANIZATION OF SCIENCE

Informal communication, cooperation, and competition play an important role in scientific work. Sociological study in recent years has concentrated on the study of specialty groups and networks ("invisible colleges"). One model hypothesizes that the number of scientists in a field is a function of the number of remaining discoveries in the field (Holton 1962, D. S. Price 1963, Crane 1972). This suggests that every subfield exhibits a typical pattern of growth and decline. The early influential scientists in the field accelerate the rate of growth by providing resources and training for students. As successful ideas dwindle, or become difficult to test, fewer scientists are recruited to the field and other members leave it. Thus, the demography of the field is linked to its intellectual potential. New discoveries originate subfields, but the reason why such discoveries lead to the splitting off of new groups rather than to continuous growth of existing fields is that when the personnel of a field grows beyond a certain limit, communication among them becomes increasingly ineffective—hence the need to split into subspecialties (see also Mulkay 1972, Toulmin 1972).

A second model tries to explain the occurrence of innovations. It considers the rise of new fields as deliberate creations based on views and ideas inconsistent with the traditions existing within a field. This is particularly the case when the discoveries giving rise to the new specialty are fundamental innovations. This model has been derived from Kuhn's (1970) influential book on scientific revolutions, which asserts that revolutionary changes in science are accompanied by upheavals of the scientific community, namely crises, conflicts, and alienation and the emergence of new groups representing the new ideas. According to this theory, "fundamental innovations" requiring conceptual reorganization of a field would occur similarly to religious or political revolutions, namely through the emergence of ideologically united, intensively solidary groups, presumably with charismatic leadership.[5]

The empirical investigation of these hypothesized group phenomena proceeded in three different ways. Historical case studies of innovations (not necessarily revolutionary ones) have paid increasing attention to the personal and social characteristics of the innovators and of the innovating group. One apparently frequent type of innovation is due to "role hybridization," (Ben-David & Collins 1966) the moving of one or several innovators from a technically and theoretically move to a less advanced field, such as chemists into biology (Kohler 1971) or physicists into biochemistry (Law 1973). Another frequent type of innovation is serendipity, when a researcher stumbles on an important discovery by accident (Mulkay & Edge 1972). Pathbreaking discoveries which occur, as hypothesized by Kuhn, in response to search for the solution to outstanding problems of great significance seem to be quite rare. Even where there are such situations, the actual discovery may occur by serendipity.

However, there is no evidence even in these cases that the discovery is preceded by acute crisis, alienation, and conflict. The only significant case of such symptoms is the history of quantum theory in the 1920s, but Forman (1971) has shown that the much advertised crisis of physics was a response by some physicists to the general malaise of those times in Germany, and not to the internal state of physics. Nor is there evidence of irresoluble conflicts attending fundamental innovations. Scientists jealously defend their views, and are willing to stretch the evidence in their own favor as far as possible (Brush 1974), but there is a point when all agree that the evidence is unequivocal (Forman 1971).

The next step in the development of new fields, the emergence of a network of people identifying themselves with it and deliberately cultivating it, is a lengthy process. It requires the emergence of a fruitful and sufficiently challenging example of doing research, but this does not seem to be a sufficient condition. There has to be in addition a motivation to identify with, and persevere in, the new field. This may be due to lack of career opportunities in the established fields (Zloczower 1973);

[5]These sociological implications are only suggested by Kuhn. They have been spelled out explicitly by Griffith & Mullins (1972).

to a perception that the new field contains greater intellectual opportunities than the ones from which its members originate (Ben-David & Collins 1966); to an intuitive belief that the new kind of research will lead to some strikingly great discovery, such as understanding of the mechanism of heredity by the use of protein-crystallography (Law 1973), or obtaining a new picture of the universe through radio astronomy (Mulkay & Edge 1972); or to the striking practical utility of an innovation, such as was the case with bacteriology (Ben-David 1960).

A sufficiently challenging and promising technique, which can be effectively transmitted in training and applied to potentially important phenomena,[6] seems to be necessary for the emergence of a viable specialty. This supports the general view that scientific innovations tend to become the basis of self-perpetuating traditions of groups. But it contradicts the hypothesis that these traditions are the result of basic ("revolutionary") conceptual reorganizations. In fact, in most of our cases the emergence of a specialty group has preceded, not followed the basic conceptual innovation. This stands to reason, because able people will be more attracted to a promising field in which conceptual innovations are still to be made than to one in which these innovations have already been made (for a particularly interesting case, see Fisher 1973).[7]

These studies of the rise of new research groups need to be distinguished from explorations of the internal structure and function of these groups. The intellectual influence within these groups has been charted in two ways: by patterns of social interaction and by citation patterns.

Sociometric choices made by scientists in rural sociology (Crane 1972) and sleep and dream researchers (Crawford 1971) show that researchers outside the area received over half of the choices, and in finite mathematics, about one third (Crane, 1972). So "invisible colleges" are not closed in the sense of being impervious to outside influence. Within the invisible college, the rate of interaction is much more intense, but not every researcher is in personal contact with every other researcher in the same area, and influence is mediated by written work and not necessarily through personal contact. These studies indicate that specialty groups are not closed solidary groups but networks with many outside ties and with shifting membership.

This is confirmed by the study of patterns of citation. Measures of cross-citation among journals have been used to chart a hierarchy of journals within a field and the journals which serve as "nodes of interchange" between disciplines (Narin, Carpenter & Berlt 1972). Certain journals, such as *Physical Review,* are preeminent influences upon their disciplines, and there are journals which connect several fields.

A different method, co-citation, or the joint citation of several papers, has been used to identify the seminal papers which originate a subfield (Small 1973, Small & Griffith 1974). There may be a lag in exploiting the initial papers, but once the

---

[6]This is part of Kuhn's concept of "paradigm," but that also included many other things (Kuhn 1970, postscript).

[7]The attempt of Griffith and Mullins (1972) to find "revolutionary" specialty groups has only one case, that of operant conditioning in psychology (Krantz, 1971b), which seems to fit the revolutionary description. But even here the case is not entirely clear.

specialty is growing, the rate of citation and co-citation may be used as a measure of the relative activity of the area. These co-citation studies provide a means to trace the emergence of the specialty, its initial growth into a relatively closed network of papers, and its opening up and eventual dissolution in the broader field.

That interpersonal networks tend to be rather loose and that citation networks analyzed by co-citation show more closure are not contradictory. Once a subject is very narrowly defined, the number of papers dealing with it becomes limited. This is not to say that the actual scientific contacts of those active in the field are similarly restricted. No sociological interpretation can be given to the co-citation studies at this point. Such interpretation will be possible only when these citation studies are directly related to the study of actual personal contacts.

THE POLITICS AND THE SOCIAL
RESPONSIBILITIES OF SCIENCE

The large scale support and the widespread use of science for military and industrial purposes have made scientific matters into frequently debated and fought over political issues. D. K. Price (1965) discussed the difficulty of including science in the system of political checks and balances. The relative inaccessibility of scientific knowledge and the contradiction between the claim of the scientific community for autonomy and its reliance on public funds for support (see also Orlans 1968) form part of the problem. His conclusion is that the checks and balances have actually worked, and are likely to work in the future as long as scientists pursue their own goals, and do not claim (or are not given) authority in political matters.

In the last few years many social scientists have tended to believe that as a matter of fact scientists have been influenced in their work by extraneous political interests (Ravetz 1971, Salomon 1973). However, the identification of scientists with ruling political, industrial, and military interests, based on anecdotal evidence, finds no support in empirical investigations of the political behavior of scientists. These investigations have been concerned mainly with academic scientists in the USA and Britain. They show academic scientists (Bidwell 1970, Halsey & Trow 1971, Lipset 1972, Lipset & Ladd 1972, Ladd & Lipset 1972) to be politically left of the center, and generally critical of government, a tendency more marked among elite scientists than among the rank and file but varying considerably from field to field (see also Friedrich 1970).

An aspect of the behavior of scientists which may be relevant to scientists' social responsibilities has been investigated in studies of medical experiments with humans. These studies are important in that they deal with actual behavior, and not only with attitudes. These studies do not indicate that scientists subordinate their medical responsibility to their scientific interests, but they show an awareness of the problem, attempt to involve the patients in the experiments, and usually adherence to ethical standards (Barber et al 1973, Renee Fox & Swazey 1974).

Of particular interest are the findings of Barber et al that the experimenters least successful as scientists are the ones most prone to unethical behavior towards human subjects. Although these findings cannot be generalized to researchers who are not medical doctors and to conflicts involving other than medical responsibilities, they show how the problems raised by the literature on the social responsibility of scientists can be investigated empirically.

CONCLUSION

The growth of the sociology of science has been very rapid in the last few years, particularly in Europe where the field had been practically nonexistent before. Mulkay's (1975) survey of the field in Britain includes 16 references for the period 1950–1968 as compared to 47 references for 1969–1973, and one in West Germany has 76 items for the period 1900–1968 and 70 items for 1969–1974 (Klima & Viehoff 1975; see also Mikulinski 1974).

However, these figures exaggerate the real growth by including a great deal of polemical literature on the validity, objectivity, and the morality of science. The literature stating and restating the opposing views cannot be counted as a contribution to scholarship. But even if these polemics are discounted, there still has been a growth of the field. Some empirical investigations, such as those intended to test whether scientists act according to their institutionalized norms, whether scientific controversies were decided by evidence or by prejudice, or whether scientists have conservative or liberal views, were actually suggested or stimulated by the controversy.

Both negative and positive attitudes have stimulated the growth of the sociology of science. The decisive factor has been widespread interest in contrast to apathy toward science.

Literature Cited

Allen, T. J. 1966. Performance of communication channels in the transfer of technology. *Ind. Manage. Rev.* 8:87–98
Allen, T., Cohen, S. 1969. Information flow in research and development laboratories. *Admin. Sci. Quart.* 14(1):12–20
Allison, P., Stewart, J. 1974. Productivity differences among scientists: Evidence for accumulative advantage. *Am. Sociol. Rev.* 39(4):596–606
Barber, B., Lally, J., Makarushka, J., Sullivan, D. 1973. *Research on Human Subjects.* New York: Russell Sage. 263 pp.
Barnes, S. B., Dolby, R. G. A. 1970. The scientific ethos: A deviant viewpoint. *Eur. J. Sociol.* 11: 3–25
Ben-David, J. 1960. Roles and innovations in medicine. *Am. J. Sociol.* 65(6):557–68
Ben-David, J. 1971. *The Scientist's Role in Society.* Englewood Cliffs, N.J.: Prentice-Hall, 207 pp.
Ben-David, J. 1972. *American Higher Education.* New York: McGraw-Hill. 137 pp.
Ben-David, J. 1974. *Innovations, Fashions, the and Reward System in Social Sciences.* Duke Conf. Innov. Soc. Sci.,

March 29–30. Durham, S. C.: Duke Univ.
Ben-David, J., Collins, R. 1966. Social factors in the origins of a new science: The case of psychology. *Am. Sociol. Rev.* 31(4):451–65
Bidwell, C. E. 1970. Faculty response to student activism: Some preliminary findings from a survey of American professors. *Seventh World Congr. Sociol.* 25 pp.
Blume, S. S., Sinclair, R. 1973. Chemists in british universities: A study of the reward system in science. *Am. Sociol. Rev.* 38:126–38
Bock, K. 1972. *Strukturgeschichte der Assistentur. Personalgefüge, Wert- und Zielvorstellungen in der deutschen Universität des 19. und 20. Jahrhunderts.* Düsseldorf: Bertelsmann. 232 pp.
Brooks, H. 1973. Knowledge and action: the dilemma of science policy in the '70's. *Daedalus* 102(2):125–43
Brush, S. 1974. Should the history of science be rated X? *Science.* 183: 1164–72

Cardwell, D. S. L. 1972. *Turning Points in Western Technology: A Study of Technology, Science, and History.* New York: Hist. Publ. 244 pp.

Clark, T. 1968. Institutionalization of innovations in higher education: Four conceptual models. *Admin. Sci. Quart.* 13(1):1–25

Clark, T. 1973. *Prophets & Patrons: The French University and the Emergence of the Social Sciences.* Cambridge: Harvard Univ. Press. 282 pp.

Cole, S., Cole, J. R. 1973. *Social Stratification in Science.* Chicago: Univ. Chicago Press. 283 pp.

Cole, S., Cole, J. R. 1967. Scientific output and recognition: A study in the operation of the reward system in science. *Am. Sociol. Rev.* 32:377–90

Cole, S., Cole, J. R. 1968. Visibility and the structural bases of awareness of scientific research. *Am. Sociol. Rev.* 33: 397–413

Collins, R. 1968. Competition and social control in science. *Sociol. Educ.* 41:123–40

Cotgrove, S., Box, S. 1970. *Science, Industry and Society.* New York: Barnes & Noble. 211 pp.

Crane, D. 1970. The academic marketplace revisited. *Am. J. Sociol.* 75:953–64

Crane, D. 1972. *Invisible Colleges.* Chicago: Univ. Chicago Press. 213 pp.

Crawford, S. 1971. Informal communication among scientists in sleep research. *J. Am. Soc. Inform. Sci.* 22:301–10

Crosland, M. 1975. The development of a professional career in science in France. *Minerva* 13(1):38–57

Dobrow, G. M. 1970. *Aktuelle Probleme der Wissenschaftswissenschaft.* Berlin: Dietz. 83 pp.

Dolby, R. G. 1971. Sociology of knowledge in natural science. *Sci. Stud.* 1:3–21

Duncan, P. 1972. From scientist to manager. *Sociol. Rev. Monogr.* No. 18

Fisher, C. S. 1973. Some social characteristics of mathematicians and their work. *Am. J. Sociol.* 78(5):1094–1118

Forman, P. 1971. Weimar culture, causality, and quantum theory, 1918–1927. *Hist. Stud. Phys. Sci.* 3:1–116

Forman, P. 1974. The financial support and political alignment of physicists in Weimar Germany. *Minerva* 12:39–65

Fox, Renee, Swazey, J. 1974. *The Courage to Fail: A Social View of Organ Transplants and Dialysis.* Chicago: Univ. Chicago Press. 395 pp.

Fox, Robert. 1973. Scientific enterprise and the patronage in France 1800–70. *Minerva* 11 (4):442–73

Friedrich, H. 1970. *Staatliche Verwaltung und Wissenschaft.* Frankfurt/Main: Europäische Verlagsanstalt. 476 pp.

Gaston, J. 1969. Big science in Britain: A sociological study of the high energy physics community. PhD thesis. Yale Univ.

Gaston, J. 1973. *Originality and Competition in Science.* Chicago: Univ. Chicago Press. 210 pp.

Gilpin, R. 1968. *France in the Age of the Scientific State.* Princeton: Princeton Univ. Press. 474 pp.

Goody, J. 1974. *Literacy, Criticism, and Growth of Knowledge.* Van Leer Found. Conf., Jerusalem

Griffith, B., Mullins, N. 1972. Coherent social groups in scientific change. *Science.* 177:959–64

Gustin, B. H. 1973. Charisma, recognition, and the motivation of scientists. *Am. J. Sociol.* 78(5):1118–34

Hagstrom, W. O. 1965. *The Scientific Community.* New York: Basic Books. 304 pp.

Hagstrom, W. O. 1967. *Competition and Framework in Science.* Madison, Wisconsin: Nat. Sci. Found.

Hagstrom, W. O. 1971. Inputs, outputs, and the prestige of American university departments. *Sociol. Educ.* 44:374–97

Hahn, R. 1971. *The Anatomy of a Scientific Revolution: The Paris Academy of Sciences, 1666–1803.* Berkeley, Los Angeles: Univ. Calif. Press. 433 pp.

Halsey, A., Trow, M. 1971. *The British Academics.* Cambridge: Harvard Univ. Press. 560 pp.

Hargens, L. 1969. Patterns of mobility of new Ph.D.'s among American academic institutions. *Sociol. Educ.* 42: 18–37

Hargens, L., Farr, G. 1973. An examination of recent hypotheses about institutional inbreeding. *Am. J. Sociol.* 78 (6):1381–1402

Hargens, L., Hagstrom, W. 1967. Sponsored and contest mobility of American academic scientists. *Sociol. Educ.* 40:24–38

Hetzler, H. 1970. *Soziale Strukturen der organisierten Forschung.* Düsseldorf: Bertelsmann. 208 pp.

Holton, G. 1962. Scientific research and scholarship: Notes toward the design of proper scales. *Daedalus* 91(2):362–99

Jewkes, J., Sawers, D., Stillerman, R. 1969. *The Sources of Invention.* New York: Norton. 372 pp.

Kaplan, N. 1965. Professional scientists in industry. *Soc. Prob.* 13:88–97

Katz, S., Ben-David, J. 1975. The role of scientific research in agricultural innovation in Israel. *Minerva.* In press

King, M. D. 1971. Reason, tradition and the progressiveness of science. *Hist. Theory: Stud. Phil. Hist.* 10:3–32

Klima, R. 1972. Theoretical pluralism, methodological dissension, and the role of the sociologist: The West German case. *Soc. Sci. Inform.* 11 (3/4): 69–108

Klima, R., Viehoff, L. 1975. The sociology of science in West Germany and Austria. In *Sociology of Science in Europe,* ed. R. Merton, A. Podgorecki, J. Gaston. Carbondale, Ill.: Southern Illinois Univ. Press

Kohler, R. 1971. The background to Edward Buchner's discovery of cell-free fermentation. *J. Hist. Biol.* 4(1):35–61

Krantz, D. 1970. Do you know what your neighbors are doing? A study of scientific communication in Europe. *Int. J. Psych.* 5(3):221–26

Krantz, D. 1971. The changing worlds of European psychology: Impressions and dilemmas. *Int. J. Psych.* 6(2):179–84

Krantz, D. 1971b. The separate worlds of operant and non-operant psychology. *J. App. Behav. Anal.* 4(1):61–70

Krauch, H. 1970a. *Die Organisiserte Forschung.* Neuwied and Berlin: Luchterhand. 287 pp.

Krauch, H. 1970b. *Prioritäten in der Forschungspolitik.* München: Carl Hanser. 102 pp.

Kroeber, G., Steiner, H., Eds. 1974. *Wissenschaft und Forschung im Sozialismus,* Vol. 3. Berlin: Akad. Verlag.

Kuhn, T. 1970. *The Structure of Scientific Revolutions.* Chicago: Univ. Chicago Press. 2nd ed. 210 pp.

Ladd, E., Lipset, S. 1972. Politics of academic natural scientists and engineers. *Science.* 176:1091–1100

Law, J. 1973. The development of specialities in science: The case of X-ray protein crystallography. *Sci. Stud.* 3:275–303

Light, D. 1974. Introduction: The structure of the academic professions. *Sociol. Educ.* 47(1):2–28

Lippitt, R., White, R. 1943. The social climate of children's groups. In Barker, B. *Child Behavior and Development,* 485–508. New York: McGraw-Hill

Lipset, S. 1972. *Academia and Politics in America,* 211–89. Carnegie Comm. Higher Educ. Reprint Ser.

Lipset, S., Ladd, E. 1972. *The Politics of American Sociologists.* Carnegie Comm. Higher Educ. Reprint Ser. 104 pp.

MacLeod, R. M. 1970. The X-Club: a scientific network in late-Victorian England. *Notes Rec. Roy. Soc.* xxiv:305–22

MacLeod, R. M. 1971. The support of Victorian science: Endowment of research movement in Great Britain 1868–1900. *Minerva* 9: 197–230

Mansfield, E. 1968. *Industrial Research and Technological Innovation.* New York: Norton. 235 pp.

Merton, R. 1938. *Science, Technology and Society in Seventeenth Century England,* 4(2):360–632. Bruges, Belgium: Saint Catherine Press

Merton, R. 1957. Bibliographical postscript. In *Social Theory and Social Structure,* 595–605. Glencoe, Ill.: Free Press. Revised ed.

Merton, R. 1957b. Priorities in scientific discovery. *Am. Sociol. Rev.* 22(6):635–59; later reprinted in Merton, R. 1973. *Sociology of Science.* Chicago: Univ. Chicago Press. 605 pp.

Mikulinski, S. 1974. La science de la science: Problèmes et recherches des anées 1970. In *Science Policy Studies,* ed. J. Salomon, I. Spiegel-Rosing, 186–201. Tokyo: Int. Comm. Sci. Policy Stud.

Miller, H. 1970. *Dollars for Research: Science and Its Patrons in Nineteenth Century America.* Seattle: Univ. Washington Press. 258 pp.

Mitroff, I. 1974. Norms and counter-norms in a select group of the Apollo moon scientists. *Am. Sociol. Rev.* 39 (4): 579–95

Morrell, J. B. 1972a. The chemist breeders: The research schools of Liebig and Thomas Thomson. *Ambix* 19:1–46

Morrell, J. B. 1972b. Science and Scottish University reform: Edinburgh in 1826. *Brit. J. Hist. Sci.* 6:39–56

Morrell, J. B. 1973. The patronage of mid-Victorian science in the University of Edinburgh. *Sci. Stud.* 3:353–88

Mulkay, M. 1972. *The Social Process of Innovation.* London: Macmillan. 64 pp.

Mulkay, M. 1975. The sociology of science in Britain. In *The Sociology of Science in Europe,* ed. R. Merton, A. Podgórecki, J. Gaston. Carbondale, Ill.: Southern Illinois Univ. Press. In press.

Mulkay, M., Edge, D. 1972. Cognitive, technical and social factors in the growth of radio astronomy. *Soc. Sci. Inform.* 12 (6):25–61

Mulkay, M., Williams, A. T. 1971. A sociological study of a physics department. *Brit. J. Sociol.* 22 (1):68–72

Musson, A., Robinson, E. 1969. *Science and Technology in the Industrial Revolution.* Manchester: Manchester Univ. Press. 534 pp.

Narin, F., Carpenter, M., Berlt, N. C. Interrelationships of scientific journals. *J. Am. Soc. Inform. Sci.* 23 (5):323–31

National Science Foundation (Meyers, S., Marquis, D.) 1969. *Successful Industrial Innovations.* Washington, DC: GPO. 119 pp.

National Science Foundation. 1971. *Research and Development and Economic Growth/Productivity.* Washington, DC: GPO. 79 pp.

National Science Foundation. 1973. *Interactions of Science and Technology in the Innovative Process: Some Case Studies.* Columbus, Battelle

Organization for Economic Cooperation and Development. 1972. *The Research* System, 1:199–258. Paris: OECD. 258 pp.

Organization for Economic Cooperation and Development. 1973. *The Research* System, 2:117–60. Paris: OECD. 195 pp.

Orlans, H., Ed. 1968. *Science Policy and the University.* Washington, DC: Brookings Inst. 352 pp.

Parsons, T., Platt, G. 1973. *The American University.* Cambridge: Harvard Univ. Press. 463 pp.

Pelz, D., Andrews, F. 1966. *Scientists in Organizations.* New York: Wiley. 318 pp.

Pfetsch, F. 1970. Scientific organization and science policy in imperial Germany 1871–1914: The foundation of the Imperial Institute of Physics and Technology. *Minerva* 8 (4):568–80

Pfetsch, F. 1974. *Zur Entwicklung der Wissenschaftspolitik in Deutschland, 1750–1914.* Berlin: Duncker & Humblot. 359 pp.

Pfetsch, F. Zloczower, A. 1973. *Innovation und Widerstände in der Wissenschaft.* Düsseldorf: Bertelsmann. 151 pp.

Price, D. K. 1965. *The Scientific Estate.* Cambridge: Harvard Univ. Press. 323 pp.

Price, D. S. 1963. *Little Science, Big Science.* New York: Columbia Univ. Press. 119 pp.

Price, D. S. 1965. Is technology historically independent of science? A study in statistical historiography. *Tech. Culture* 6:553–68

Price, D. S. 1971. Principles for projecting funding of academic science in the 1970's. *Sci. Stud.* 1 (1):85–94

Rabkine, Y. 1974. Origines et developpements de la recherche sur la recherche en Union Sovietique. *Progr. Sci.* 170: 39–51

Ravetz, J. 1971. *Scientific Knowledge and Its Social Problems.* Oxford: Clarendon. 449 pp.

Robinson, D. Z. 1973. Will the university decline as the center for scientific research? *Daedalus* 102(2):101–10

Rosenberg, C. E. 1971. Science, technology, and economic growth: The case of the agricultural experiment station scientist, 1875–1914. *Agric. Hist.* 45 (1):1–20

Rossi, P. 1970. *Philosophy, Technology, and the Arts in the Early Modern Era.* New York: Harper & Row. 194 pp.

Salomon, J. J. 1973. *Science and Politics.* Transl. N. Lindsay. London: Macmillan. 277 pp.

Sanderson, M. 1972. *The Universities and British Industry: 1850–1970.* London: Routledge & Kegan. 436 pp.

Schmookler, J. 1966. *Invention and Economic Growth.* Cambridge: Harvard Univ. Press. 332 pp.

Schroeder-Gudehus, B. 1972. The argument for the self-government and public support of science in Weimar Germany. *Minerva* 10 (4):537–70

Shapin, S. A. 1972. The pottery philosophical society, 1819–1835: An examination of the cultural uses of provincial science. *Sci. Stud.* 2 (4):311–36

Shils, E., Ed. 1968. *Criteria for Scientific Development.* Cambridge: MIT Press. 207 pp.

Shimshoni, D. 1970. The mobile scientist in the American instrument industry. *Minerva* 8(1):59–89

Small, H. 1973. Co-citation in the scientific literature: a new measure of the relationship between two documents *Am. Soc. Inform. Sci. J.* 24(4):265–69

Small, H., Griffith, B. 1974. The structure of scientific literature: identifying and graphing specialities. *Sci. Stud.* 4:17–40

Storer, N. 1966. *The Social System of Science.* New York: Holt, Rinehart and Winston. 180 pp.

Swatez, G. 1970. The social organization of a university laboratory. *Minerva* 8(1): 36–58

Tenbruck, F. 1974. Science as a vocation-revisited. In *Standorde im Zeitstrom,* ed. E. Forsthoff, R. Hörstel, 351–64. Frankfurt/Main: Athenáum

Thackray, A. 1970. Science and technology in the Industrial Revolution. *Hist. Sci.* 9:76–89

Thackray, A. 1971. Medicine, manufacturers, and Manchester men: The origins of a scientific society. *Proc. 12th Int. Congr. Hist. Sci., Moscow*

Toulmin, S. 1972. *Human Understanding.* Princeton: Princeton Univ. Press. 520 pp.

Townes, C. H. 1973. Differentiation and competition between universities and other research laboratories in the United States. *Daedalus* 102(2):153–65

Turner, R. S. 1971. The growth of professorial research in Prussia, 1818 to 1848 —causes and context. *Hist. Stud. Phys. Sci.* 3:137–82

von Gizycki, R. 1973. Centre and periphery in the international scientific community: Germany, France, and Great Britain in the 19th century. *Minerva* 11 (4): 474–94

Weinberg, A. M. 1967. *Reflections on Big Science.* Cambridge: MIT Press. 182 pp.

Westfall, R. S. 1958. *Science and Religion in Seventeenth Century England.* New Haven: Yale Univ. Press. 235 pp.

Zloczower, A. 1973. Konjunktur in der Forschung. In *Innovation und Widerstände in der Wissenschaft,* ed. F. Pfetsch, A. Zloczower, 91–150. Düsseldorf: Bertelsmann

Zuckerman, H. 1970. Stratification in American Science. *Sociol. Inq.* 40:235–57

Zuckerman, H., Cole, J. R. 1975. Women in American science. *Minerva* 13(1):82–102

Zuckerman, H., Merton, R. 1971. Patterns of evaluation in science: Institutionalization, structure and functions of the referee system. *Minerva* 9:66–100

CONVERGENCE AND DIVERGENCE IN DEVELOPMENT

❖10509

John W. Meyer, John Boli-Bennett, and Christopher Chase-Dunn[1]
Department of Sociology, Stanford University, Stanford, California 94305

INTRODUCTION

After World War II there arose the intellectual question of whether or not the two blocs of developed societies, and the many less developed ones, would evolve in a common direction. Some argued for convergence around the requirements of the modern economy. Others argued for divergence along lines set by political and cultural factors (for reviews, see Weinberg 1969, Meyer 1970, Kerr et al 1971, Millar 1972, Deutsch 1973, and Hollingsworth 1973).

Recent work has transformed the issue. First, much systematic evidence, reviewed here, shows that most societies are rapidly shifting to modern institutional arrangements.[2] Second, the increasing uniformity of, and exchange between, societies brought awareness that they may diverge or converge with respect to equality of development as well as in organizational modernity. Current disputes center on the rise or decline in international economic equality.

Third, and most important, convergence and divergence are now seen as resulting from the evolution of world society, more than from the independent evolution of separate societies (Hopkins & Wallerstein 1967). The world market and society produce convergence by subjecting all societies to the same forces; they produce divergence by creating different roles for different societies in the world stratification system. Focusing on societal development within a (capitalist) world industrial structure creates at the global level of analysis a repetition of the original post-Marx debate about the homogenizing versus the stratifying effects of industrial society on individuals and classes. The current discussion is almost as politicized as the original

[1]This article was prepared with support from the National Science Foundation (Grant NSF-GS 32065) to John W. Meyer and Michael T. Hannan Jr. We are indebted to Michael Hannan, Richard Rubinson, Albert Bergesen, and Jacques Delacroix for their advice and help.

[2]Widespread agreement prevails concerning the institutional patterns denoted by such terms as "modern" and "developed." We use them for convenience despite their biased and imprecise character.

223

one. Elite representatives stress convergence on personal freedom and economic growth, while representatives of the masses emphasize divergencies in wealth and power.

The introduction of new levels of analysis and new dependent variables has generated arguments more complex than the original debate. We summarize them as follows:

A   Independent Evolution of Distinct Societies

Convergence: 1. (Economic Determinism) Societies converge as they strive toward industrial efficiency and create other institutions adapted to the industrial economy (Inkeles & Rossi 1956, Moore 1963, Kerr et al 1960).

Divergence: 2. (Political and Cultural Determinism) Societies diverge in social institutions as increasing economic resources permit diverse development along lines determined by politics and culture (Odum 1971, Feldman & Moore 1969, Hollander 1973).

B   Diffusion of Modern Institutions Among Societies

Convergence: 3. (Unregulated Diffusion) Societies converge as they copy the social and economic goals and structural means employed in dominant systems (Hoselitz 1972).

Divergence: 4. (State-Directed Diffusion) Societies converge in economic organization but diverge politically; late-industrializing systems employ forced mobilization and state action for development (Horowitz 1966). Strategies for catching up differ from those initially employed.

5. (Diffusion of Rising Expectations) In copying the culture and aspirations of development, less developed societies overload their economies, producing either slow growth or repressive, state-dominated development (Portes 1973).

C   Societal Development in a Capitalist World Structure

Convergence: 6. (Economic Penetration) Expanding world economic and social forces produce convergence by penetrating many societies (Marx in Avineri 1969, Parsons 1971).

7. (Dominance of Nation-States) The fact that neither a system of empires nor a regulating world state dominates politically enhances the take-over of less developed societies by strongly legitimated nation-states that organize development and arrogate powers to pursue it. These states frequently organize activity in terms of capitalist interests that cut across state boundaries to coordinate production in the larger world economy (Wallerstein 1974).

Divergence: 8. (Roles in a World System) Distinct economic roles are allocated to different societies, creating "underdevelopment" or unequal and restricted development in peripheral societies (Baran 1956, Frank 1969, Galtung 1971).

9. (Reactive State Mobilization) Societies react differently to their roles in the world system. Peripheral and middle-level societies react with state-directed mobilization to try to obtain greater equality (Young 1970, Wallerstein 1972a).

This list of main propositions broadens the original issue: it extends the range of independent variables beyond political, cultural, and economic forces at the national level, and it augments the variety of dependent variables to include properties of nation-states and aspects of international equality.

To order this complexity, we review the research in this field in terms of four sets of dependent variables created by the intersection of two simple distinctions. One, the institutional focus of attention may emphasize economic and social modernization, or it may emphasize development of the state and forms of political participation. Two, one can focus on convergence or divergence in societal development, or on the degree of equality among societies created by this development. These two distinctions create four sets of dependent variables:

Institutional Emphasis

		Economic and Social Organizational	Political Organization
Dimension of Attention	Societal Development	1. Rationalized social & economic organization	3. Construction of the modern state
	Intersocietal Equality	2. International socio-economic equality	4. International political equality

Three of these four types of variables are fairly clear in meaning. "The construction of the modern state" is, however, unclear, since there is only limited agreement on the nature of political modernization, or on the forms on which modern states might converge. There is agreement that modern states are stronger: their power, jurisdiction, and functions increase. Increased participation by individuals and subgroups is also generally seen as a component of political modernization. The question is how much this participation represents the interests of the individuals and subgroups in contrast with the interests of the state and its dominant elites. Does modernized political participation increase the political freedom of individuals and subgroups, or do increased state power and mobilized participation repress individual and subgroup freedom? Given these problems, our consideration of convergent or divergent political development must allow for three disparate variables: state power, political participation, and political freedom.

We review evidence, and some theoretical issues, on each of these four sets of dependent variables in turn.

1 RATIONALIZED SOCIAL AND ECONOMIC ORGANIZATION

Originally, two main proposals for divergence seemed plausible: First, that underdeveloped countries, freed from the directives of colonialism, would stagnate socially and economically. Second, that the Socialist countries, dominated by centralist regimes (as well as by terror), would develop economically but stagnate socially. The data and events of the last quarter-century have destroyed these possibilities, producing consensus on what would, in 1950, have been considered convergence theories.

Table 1 shows some of the findings from now well-institutionalized international data-gathering systems. The table shows the overall mean development, on various modernization indicators, of countries for the period from 1950 to 1970. It also shows the mean for richer and poorer countries (grouped in terms of Gross National Product per capita).

Countries have risen substantially on every indicator of social and economic modernization since 1950. Measures of all of the following have increased for both richer and poorer countries: 1. economic production, 2. economic structure, 3. density of communications networks, 4. formal education (see also Coombs 1968), 5. urbanization, and 6. scientific medical organization.

The information presented in Table 1 does not represent a biased selection of indicators. Every general indicator of economic and social modernization on which longitudinal data are available shows similar changes. Differentiated, rationalized social organization is epidemic, and the idea that large categories of countries might regress in these respects is now in disrepute.

The same processes occur in other institutions. 7. Family and demographic modernization proceeds rapidly. Birth and death rates fall in almost all countries (Population Council 1974), and the latter fall more rapidly the later modernization begins (Arriaga 1970). Neolocal nuclear families become more common, though this may not be as necessary to achieve modernization as had been thought (Goode 1966).

8. Stratification systems converge on modern structures. The original convergence debated was in part fueled by a paper by Inkeles & Rossi (1956) showing great similarity in occupational prestige among countries. More recent evidence (Hodge, Treiman & Rossi 1966, Lane 1971) and a major study by Treiman (1975) confirm the point (but not all analysts agree: Goldthorpe 1966). To be precise, however, no one has shown convergence—social change in a common direction—occurring. Perhaps the imperatives of industrial society create uniformity (Inkeles & Rossi 1956); but perhaps almost any society with occupational roles comparable to those in other countries will allocate prestige in roughly the same way the others do, even though that society is not highly industrialized.

Whether or not the prestige rankings of occupations converge, the structure of occupational specialization certainly does. With development, more and more people are shifted into occupations that are essential to the modern system, and on which status rankings are highly uniform among countries. Recent decades have seen a great decline in the number of traditional occupational roles that are parochial to particular cultures and that do not have counterparts carrying similar prestige values in most other societies.

The same points hold for social mobility. Rates are similar in different modern societies (Miller 1960), in part because changing occupational distributions imply a good deal of mobility. Data over time are rare, and it is uncertain whether mobility rates are becoming more similar. How much contemporary societies differ from traditional ones in overall mobility rates is also in dispute (Kelley 1971).

Structurally, however, mobility systems converge. Mobility and status allocation are increasingly processed by educational systems that have greatly expanded; edu-

Table 1 Indicators of national social and economic development

Dimension	Indicator	Sample	Cases	1950 Mean	1950 SD	1955 Mean	1955 SD	1960 Mean	1960 SD	1965 Mean	1965 SD	1970 Mean	1970 SD	Source
1. Economic Production	gross national product/capita 1964 ($ US)	all	129	329	423			441	577			753	907	IBRD 1971, 1973
		rich[a]	64	562				753				1319		
		poor	65	95				129				195		
	electricity ($\log_{10}$) consumed/capita (kW-hr)	all	95	1.87	0.94			2.35	0.79	2.53	0.77			UN Stat. Yearb. 1950
		rich	56	2.45				2.82		2.98				
		poor	33	1.14				1.73		1.93				
2. Economic Structure	male labor force not in agriculture (%)	all	138	38.2	25.9			43.4	26.9					ILO 1971
		rich	63	60.4				66.9						
		poor	65	20.0				24.4						
	gross domestic product-in manufacturing (%)	all	88			20.4	13.2			22.4	14.1			IBRD 1971
		rich	55			25.1				26.6				
		poor	33			12.7				15.6				
3. Communication Density	telephones/1000 population	all	96			36.4	63.9			55.2	96.3			Taylor & Hudson 1971
	radios/1000 population	all	104	67.6	97.1					144.54	156.6			
4. Educational Expansion	primary students/appropriate age group population	all	117	58	40			71	34			83	32	UNESCO 1950
		rich	51	90				98				102		
		poor	56	37				53				72		
	secondary students/appropriate age group population	all	102	12.7	16.3			21.5	22.1			30.5	23.8	
		rich	49	21.3				35.8				46.4		
		poor	46	5.3				9.4				17.0		
	tertiary students/appropriate age group population	all	109	1.4	0.97			2.8	3.8			5.3	6.4	
		rich	46	2.6				5.2				9.2		
		poor	55	0.6				1.2				2.6		
5. Urbanization	population in cities over 100,000 pop. (%)	all	133	13	16			17	17					Davis 1969
		rich	61	22				28						
		poor	64	6				9						
6. Scientific Health Organization	physicians per million population	all	106			508	500			541	576			Taylor & Hudson 1971

[a] Throughout the table, rich countries are defined as those above median 1950 GNP/capita ($172 in 1964 US dollars).

cation has become the dominant processing element in all societies that have been studied. Ascriptive rules may affect mobility patterns as strongly in modern societies as in others; but their role in the organization of the mobility process diminishes with modernization.

9. There has been extraordinary convergence in recent decades in central cultural elements, though quantitative longitudinal data are usually not available.

Western scientific-technical conceptions of reality have penetrated almost everywhere. Rapidly expanding education systems universally promote science, technology, and mathematics (UNESCO 1971), implicitly advancing a conception of natural reality as law-like, strictly causally ordered, and manipulable. This conception is also built into institutions of scientific research, national planning, and national industrialization.

Descriptions of transcendental authority also become more uniform. Universalistic and unitary conceptions of God (or, equivalently, of history) prevail. Indigenous, localized religious systems applying only to particular groups die out or are transformed to resemble more widespread systems (Singer 1966).

Finally, descriptions of the nature of man and society converge. Individuals are seen as both malleable and as possessing many economic and social rights that are remarkably similar, in the abstract, from country to country. Obligations to maintain economic progress and social justice are defined in uniform terms. To a remarkable degree, every sort of state defines for itself uniform long-run economic and social goals (Waterston 1965).

Modern and convergent conceptions of society, man, and the world also become part of the social values and personal perceptions of individuals; perhaps the most striking data appear here. No longitudinal studies exist, but cross-sectional research finds similar syndromes of modern individual orientation penetrating different societies. Inkeles & Smith (1974) find that a number of dimensions of individual modernity (openness to change, tolerance, faith in science and technical methods, efficacy, and so on) are related in much the same way in six developing societies. In each society, their overall modernity scale heavily reflects the impact of education and factory experience, both of which are becoming much more common in the modern world (cf Form 1972, on the factory environment). This strongly suggests that large convergent changes occur in such measures during the current period.

Theories

In the face of the evidence, the claim that divergence would result from diverse political and cultural choices has fallen by the wayside. It should be noted, however, that current research reflects a context of world economic expansion. A period of contraction—along the lines of, say, the 1930s—would engender different events and different theories. At present, however, the problem is to explain the sudden and widespread economic growth and modernization.

(a) It seems unlikely that the process results from the independent evolution of societies toward more efficient structures, given the suddenness and rapidity of the changes. (b) Diffusion processes clearly operate. "Demonstration effects" lead less developed societies to adopt the goals of economic development, the technical means employed in developed societies, and the general culture of modernization. Diffusion imagery offers a possible explanation of the intensification of the whole process in recent decades in the familiar S-curve that the adoption of innovations often follows (Rogers 1962; see also Inkeles 1973). (c) Conceptions emphasizing the integration of world society add two other explanations. First, through dominant economic powers, the world economy increasingly subjects societies to the pressures of the rationalized market (Sahlins & Service 1960, p. 115 ff). Second, the world political system heightens the pressure. In the absence of a world state, the breakdown of direct political imperialism after World War II redefined many nations which were previously dependent and insulated as independent societies. Exposure of these societies directly to the world market confers on them, as states, the political status and responsibilities of "citizenship" in the world. These newly empowered agencies find themselves under great external and internal pressure. From the outside, the world market and world society threaten to subjugate them, while offering opportunities to engage in economic and social status competition. From inside, the political demands of a suddenly created citizenry also rise. In response, they take aggressive action to establish positions in the emerging world system, and in the process they incorporate many of its institutions (Chase-Dunn et al 1974, Young 1970, Wallerstein 1974).

Thus, economic and political changes in the world, which move developing societies from indirectly linked peripheral positions closer to the center of action, may be important explanatory factors.

In any event, it is clear that Western, Socialist, and developing societies converge on modern institutions. Our initial Proposition 2 (Political and Cultural Determinism) fails in the present period. Whether the appropriate explanation lies in the evolution of the modern economy (Proposition 1), diffusion of modernity (Proposition 3), or penetration of the world economy (Proposition 6) into independent states (Proposition 7) is not clear.

2   INTERNATIONAL SOCIO-ECONOMIC EQUALITY

Much of the intellectual discussion of convergence has shifted to the question of inequality among societies: given that similar values and institutions predominate, stratification along these shared dimensions commands attention. Divergence proponents assert that inequalities among societies are increasing.

Theories

Most analysts concur on the convergence or divergence effects that various development mechanisms have with regard to economic success, but they disagree about which mechanisms are dominant, and thus on the likely outcomes. Prevailing theories include the following: (a) Conceptions of societies as independently evolving toward social modernization leave open the possibility that less successful societies are more committed to traditional institutions and thus continue to grow and modernize less rapidly (Smelser 1963). (b) Diffusion theory argues that poorer countries will gradually achieve equality as they copy the technology of (and acquire capital from) technically more successful social forms. These ideas further suggest that advanced societies may overspecialize and overinvest in outdated economic and social structures, thereby falling behind by this well-known evolutionary process. In particular, once the outlines of economic and social modernization have been established through the slow, haphazard, unplanned processes of development in the West, societies developing later can adopt purposive policies of forced mobilization which lead more quickly to the same ends. Thus the "demonstration effect" makes possible more rapid development among societies the later they begin the modernization process (Feldman & Moore 1969).

Another line of thought in the same vein foresees contrary results. If the main engines of diffusion are the collective goals and techniques of development, demonstration effects should make late but accelerated development possible. Some argue, however, that diffusion of the culture of modernity, in terms of popular social and political aspirations, is more rapid and significant in the contemporary world than diffusion of the technology of modernization. This "revolution of rising expectations" (Theobald 1960) places so many social demands, controls, and constraints on production that it inhibits economic growth in initially lagging societies, thus producing cumulative economic inequalities among societies. This perspective is pessimistic about the possibilities for rapid modernization under democratic regimes, because such regimes presumably represent social demands that the interests of economic growth must suppress. More authoritarian political structures can successfully restrict these demands, pursue forced modernization, and plan rapid growth (Sahlins & Service 1960).

(c) Theories that invoke features of global society suggest increasing inequality of modernization. First, less developed societies face increasingly severe external competition, in contrast to less restricted opportunities in early Western development (Kuznets 1971). Second, currently developing societies, given the complexities of contemporary economic and technical requirements, rely heavily on capital from more developed societies. The profits from such investments can be "skimmed off," thereby inhibiting the growth of dependent societies (Frank 1969, Chase-Dunn 1974). Third, in the world structure the less developed societies are pushed into specialized roles that contain fewer possibilities for growth (e.g. agriculture, extractive industries, low-wage production) (Galtung 1971, Pinto & Knakal 1973). Finally, because an egalitarian world state has not arisen, they encounter a situation —analogous to the unbridled capitalist state—in which the political possibilities for economic defense or redistribution are very limited. This contrasts sharply with the dominant political position held by the currently more developed societies when they went through the same process.

A final theoretical point from this perspective: regardless of the actual changes in world economic and social equality, the increasing integration of local systems into world society and modernization of social structures in many societies greatly increase consciousness of inequality and inequity among societies. Integration transforms societies that once were distinct and noncomparable social units into similar units competing in the same stratification system (Lagos 1963). Just as the social integration and standardization engendered by the industrial revolution created awareness of inequality and inequity, current changes in world society make class consciousness of international inequity (with states as units) a major issue.

Evidence

A simple methodological artifact obscures comprehension of the evidence on changes in international equality. Given a world in which modernization is epidemic (i.e. in which every general indicator of modernization is rising), it follows from reasonable assumptions that absolute inequalities will increase: if countries are initially very unequal, and are all modernizing at about the same rate, then the absolute differences (inequalities) between given pairs or groups of countries on any measure will increase at the common rate of growth. If overall growth rates are high, even a situation in which low-ranking countries are growing more rapidly than high-ranking ones will usually produce increasing absolute differences in the system (which statistically appear as increasing variance).

The evidence shows this process in full force. The standard deviation of almost every indicator of modernization in Table 1 substantially increases over the period. The only exception is the primary education ratio; its absolute variation among countries declines simply because more and more countries reach the primary enrollment ceiling: all children are in school. But results produced by artifacts of measurement do not reflect the main substantive finding: absolute inequalities increase greatly as the system as a whole modernizes and grows.

Data that show increasing absolute inequalities between rich nations and poor nations are used by increasingly powerful egalitarian political forces, but they do not relate directly to the intellectual issue of inequality as it is usually formulated.

In assessing inequality in the distribution of resources that are themselves changing, it is conventional to consider the proportion of the total resources held by, say, the 10% of the population that has the most resources, or the 20% that has the fewest resources.[3] This approach treats two systems as having identical levels of inequality if, for example, each income group of one system has the same proportion of total income as the equivalent income group in the other system—even though one system might have twice the per capita income of the other, and thus twice the absolute income differences among groups.

Some data are presented in Table 2. The table shows the degree of concentration of a series of indicators of economic and social modernization in 1950, 1960, and 1970. We present four measures of concentration: the proportion of each resource in the countries constituting that fifth of the world's population highest in that resource; the proportion of the resource in the countries constituting that fifth of the world's population lowest in the resource; and the proportion of the resource going to the 60% of the world's population that is between the other two groups. In addition the proportion of the resource going to the United States (which is in the highest group for every indicator) and the proportion going to the Socialist bloc are shown.

[3]Such distributions can be subjected to an overall index of inequality, using the same general conception. The GINI index is the most common one (Alker & Russett 1966).

Table 2 Concentration of resources among nations in the world system[a]

	Percentages		
Economic Production The proportion of Gross World Product going to:	1950	1960	1970
the countries highest on GNP per capita with 20% of world population	73.8	69.0	69.2
the middle countries on GNP per capita with 60% of world population	23.4	27.8	28.6
the countries lowest on GNP per capita with 20% of world population	2.8	3.2	2.2
the United States	41.9	35.8	30.4
13 Socialist nations	12.4	18.1	23.2
	129 cases (IBRD 1971, 1973)		
The proportion of world electrical energy consumed by:	1950	1960	1970
the countries highest on KWH per capita with 20% of world population	66.5	64.9	58.9
the middle countries on KWH per capita with 60% of world population	32.9	34.4	39.3
the countries lowest on KWH per capita with 20% of world population	.6	.7	.8
the United States	42.0	38.5	30.4
9 Socialist nations	15.0	19.1	21.8
	75 cases (UN Statistical Yearbook 1950)		
Economic Structure Proportion of the world nonagricultural labor force living in:	1950	1960	
the countries highest on % nonagricultural work force with 20% of world population	44.3	40.0	
the middle countries on % nonagricultural work force with 60% of world population	48.4	50.5	
the countries lowest on % nonagricultural work force with 20% of world population	7.3	9.5	
the United States	15.2	13.6	
14 Socialist nations	22.4	28.5	
	138 cases (ILO 1971)		
Educational Enrollments Proportion of world primary students enrolled in:	1950	1960	1970
countries highest on % primary students enrolled with 20% world population	27.0	23.1	23.4
middle countries on % primary students enrolled with 60% world population	63.9	65.5	62.4
countries lowest on % primary students enrolled with 20% world population	9.1	11.4	14.2
the United States	15.9	14.7	12.1
13 Socialist nations	37.3	42.7	40.0
	91 cases (UNESCO 1950)		
Proportion of world secondary students enrolled in:	1950	1960	1970
countries highest on % secondary students enrolled with 20% world population	53.6	44.0	41.4
middle countries on % secondary students enrolled with 60% world population	42.6	50.4	51.3
countries lowest on % secondary students enrolled with 20% world population	3.8	5.6	8.3
the United States	20.3	18.0	21.1
9 Socialist states	13.4	11.5	14.3
	91 cases (UNESCO 1950)		
Proportion of world tertiary students enrolled in:	1950	1960	1970
countries highest on % tertiary students enrolled with 20% world population	58.0	54.3	53.7
middle countries on % tertiary students enrolled with 60% world population	38.9	42.8	42.8
countries lowest on % tertiary students enrolled with 20% world population	2.1	2.9	3.5
the United States	38.8	34.8	34.9
8 Socialist nations	26.6	28.8	24.5
	83 cases (UNESCO 1950)		
Urbanization Proportion of world city-dwellers living in:	1950	1960	
countries highest on % urbanization with 20% world population	50.0	46.3	
middle countries on % urbanization with 60% world population	44.7	47.8	
countries lowest on % urbanization with 20% world population	5.3	5.9	
the United States	16.7	15.7	
14 Socialist nations	23.9	25.5	
	133 cases (Davis 1969)		

[a] Data are reported only for countries with data at all time points. The totals are calculated similarly. Because some countries are excluded from the total, the absolute numbers cannot be taken seriously: comparisons over time, however, are appropriate.

Several caveats are in order: 1. The table has been prepared so that only countries on which data are available for all of the three dates are included in the analysis of each measure. Each group, however, may include different countries at different times, because countries rise and fall between groups over the 20-year period. 2. On some indicators, data are missing for many countries. This means that comparisons of concentration across indicators are inappropriate. It could also mean that the structure of findings would be greatly changed with the inclusion of more data, although close examination of the problem assures us that this is very unlikely. 3. The data do not show inequalities among individuals in the world, but inequality among countries, with each country weighted by its population.

The data reveal striking trends, which we summarize as follows:

First, those indicators that reflect the possession and penetration of specific modern structures—education, electricity consumption, urbanization, and nonagricultural labor force—show marked equalization. They reveal the operation of a substantively significant "floor effect": the indicators reflect institutions created by and concentrated in a few countries several decades ago that have since spread to nearly all countries. Many other indicators of structural modernization would certainly show this pattern as particular institutions have proliferated. Second, the most general indicator of modern development available, GNP per capita, shows a different pattern. The wealthiest countries, especially the United States, obtain a decreasing proportion of gross world product (GWP) over time. But so do the poorest countries.[4] Detailed analysis shows that the countries in the top 30% of the income distribution, but below the top 10%, achieve the largest proportionate gains. Strikingly, the Socialist countries fall into this category, showing even higher percentage gains than the group as a whole. This and other findings suggest that Socialist countries play a role in the world system like that of the bourgeois class (viz, the Protestants) in capitalist societies: they organize strongly around "achievement" and in a number of respects withdraw structurally and restrict internal opposition in pursuit of this end.[5]

The GWP data show results different from the other indicators because they are the data most sensitive to the changing nature of the global economic and social structure. Increasingly modernized and integrated, it constantly generates at its centers new institutions of modernity that are initially highly concentrated but gradually diffuse through the system in increasingly equal fashion. Still newer institutions appear in turn, constituting new forms of control over resources, ex-

[4]The gross world product data overstate the decline in the relative position of central countries, and understate the relative losses of the periphery. Transnational corporations, controlled in central countries, generate profit in peripheral countries and retain at least part of it there. The inclusion of this profit in the product of peripheral societies produces inaccuracies in the data.

[5]Wallerstein's (1972) argument that "semi-peripheral" societies (especially Socialist states) adopt highly centralist policies to achieve upward mobility in the world structure suggests this line of reasoning.

change, and value, and serving as new sources of power, inequality, and integration. These new institutions, as fundamental sources of differential productivity in the changing system, are captured more clearly by GWP indices than by other, more specific, measures.

This argument represents another instance of the parallel between the development of world society and that of individual industrial societies. Many kinds of measures (e.g. voting rights, education enrollments) show increasing equality among classes within industrial societies, but much less equalization occurs in total wealth controlled by classes. This happens because equalization of particular rights does not make up for the increasing integration, and new forms of concentration in power, that continually characterize industrial societies. So it may be with world industrial (or post-industrial) society.

We know of no quantitative evidence on the question of perceptions of world inequity, which theoretically should be rising. Certainly worldwide public discussion of inequalities and inequities among countries within a single world system is rising quite rapidly, replacing an earlier discussion in which these differences were seen as results of the independent evolution of separate bounded societies (and which, therefore, failed to raise the question of equity at all).

Last, we note that the kind of worldwide data reviewed above is a recent phenomenon; such data cover most countries only since World War II. This has been a period of continuous world economic expansion. Many of these findings would likely be altered during a phase of economic contraction of the sort that has periodically recurred in recent centuries. Such a contraction would produce sharply increased inequalities on a number of dimensions as "lesser producers" were squeezed out of the global economic system.

3 CONSTRUCTION OF THE MODERN STATE

Disagreement about political convergence masks ambiguity in the concept of political development. The modern state is both corporate and representative: both the state and subgroups increase their power and participation in society (Almond & Powell 1966). The question is, whose interests are reflected in this expanded power and participation? Some foresee in the East and in the developing world changes toward political participation representing the interests of individuals and subgroups (McCord 1965, Kassof 1968), and thus an expansion in political freedom. Others foresee a general rise in state power employed in the pursuit of the independent ends of the state or its controlling elites, and thus perhaps increased repression of the political freedom of individuals and subgroups (Huntington 1968).

There is general agreement that political participation rises as part of modern development. The speculation that authoritarian states might restrict participation in the push toward modernization has died with events [though some revivals have surfaced in response to recent nonparticipatory military regimes (Linz 1970)]. The real issue now is not participation, but its form, and the interests around which it is organized. Will societies converge on political freedom—participation structured to award peripheral groups access to state power—or on mobilized participation organized by and for states that repress a wide range of interests arising among individuals and subgroups in society? Or, as a third alternative, does modern political development integrate the interests of the state with those found in society and thus dissolve the problem of freedom and authority?[6]

Theories

We review theories and evidence on three properties of the modern state: its power and authority, the extent of political participation it constructs, and political freedom—or the degree to which the modern state legitimates a wide range of individual and group interests in society.

(a) Theories viewing societies as independently evolving units produce two ideas. First, political forms may reflect historical forces that are distinctive to each society, and which the resources of economic development augment. Self-reinforcing divergencies in state power, political participation, and political freedom result (Hollander 1973, Feldman & Moore 1969). Second, the economic and social structures of modernization may impose convergent state forms (Apter 1965). Most theorists accept this formulation with respect to political participation, which is understood to increase by this process. What forms of state power result is less clear, for the degree of centralization required by an economically complex society is not known. This issue has produced a large literature in economics about the crucial pricing and investment allocation decisions in society, and their implications for state power (Millar 1972). In considering Socialist states, this literature generally assumes that decentralization in economic decision-making is a component or correlate of political freedom [but see the early discussion of Schumpeter (1950) for a view which takes more possibilities into account]. Only a few economists, on the other hand, regard the increasing centralization of basic economic allocation decisions in the West as an automatic indicator of the loss of political freedom.

A major debate centers on the possible convergence of market and planned economies to a common, hybrid form (Heilbroner 1962, Galbraith 1964). Proponents of this view claim that a given level of industrialization requires a specific, technically most appropriate structure (which societies may copy from each other). Opponents argue that functional alternatives are available (Cole 1973), and that industrial societies frequently do not employ the most efficient structures. The issue stands unresolved.

(b) Diffusion theory adds two possibilities: First, peripheral states copy central ones. If the latter converge, so will the former. Second, peripheral states may adopt largely state-directed organization through a process of forced mobilization in response to the demonstration effects generated by central states (Horowitz 1966). If the goal of economic development dominates most societies, those that are the last to initiate development will employ state power most fully. In such states, political

---

[6]In the long run, these alternatives are not genuine ones: many theorists obviate them in stressing the idea of "nationbuilding"—the conjunction of private interests with public ones through socialization and social control as well as participatory democracy (Bendix 1964, Rokkan 1970).

participation will presumably be organized around the purposes of the state rather than the traditional interests held by individuals and subgroups, and political freedom will thus be limited. This line of reasoning apparently lies behind the common idea that peripheral societies, facing the urgent problems of development, cannot afford democracy. Similar states operating in earlier eras with less modernizing pressure from demonstration effects would presumably have been able to afford a greater degree of political freedom.

(c) Theorists stressing the structure of world society add several ideas: First, the structure contributes to convergence by forcing its state "citizens" to assume new powers, while the failure of a sovereign world state to arise concentrates legitimate authority in nation-states (Ness & Ness 1972). The world culture of modernity emphasizes the primacy of individuals and the goals of economic and social development, adding pressures for the extension of state action (Chase-Dunn et al 1974). Further, the rise of transnational organizations, which some consider destructive of nation states, may in fact reinforce their powers because of the explicitness of the external forces which such organizations represent. They provide a much more urgent call to action than the pressures of an amorphous world market (Huntington 1973); compare Marx's argument about the impact of the capitalist factory system on the consciousness of the proletariat). These ideas all argue for the expansion of state power and probably of political participation; their bearing on the rise or fall of individual political freedom is unclear.

Second, however, the same unregulated world economy subjects each society— especially peripheral ones—to strong exogenous forces that may make the creation of a powerful state impossible (Frank 1972, Galtung 1971), thus creating divergence. The implication is that state power, political participation, and probably political freedom would not expand, at least in peripheral societies.

Third, the world order leads different interests to dominate different societies. Dominant systems can adopt open, decentralized, representative polities involving high levels of participation and political freedom, whereas more peripheral ones try to resist penetration by closing boundaries and attempting forced mobilization, with increases in state power and decreases in political freedom. An elaborated version of this argument has it that only the more successful peripheral societies (the semi-periphery) can adopt this strategy, while truly peripheral ones, dominated by export agriculture or extractive industries, are weakened and subservient to exogenous interests mediated by a few local elites (Wallerstein 1972a,b). This line of reasoning implies tripolar divergence: representative states with fairly high state power and free participation arise in the centers; strongly mobilized states with limited freedom arise in parts of the semi-periphery; and weak states with little participation and rather less political freedom develop in the peripheries. One of the strengths of this argument is the light it sheds on the mobilized and boundary-maintaining features of Socialist bloc states as a result of their "mobility" efforts in the world stratification system. Their internal restrictions on political freedom are seen as analogous to the internal psychological and moral restrictions that went along with the rise of the early capitalist classes in the first industrializing countries.

Theorists thus generally agree that both political participation and state power rise. They disagree sharply about the extent to which state power rises in peripheral societies. They concur in the view that if state power rises, it does so while incorporating freer political participation in central states, and more mobilized (or less free) forms that transcend the aggregate interests of subgroups in semi-peripheral and peripheral states. There is, however, little agreement on overall trends in political freedom, or the coincidence between state and subgroup or individual purposes. The general spread of modern world culture carries with it the norms of expanded and free participation, and presumably some of its cultural forms. But the spread of the goals of economic progress and the pressures created by the intensification of the world system create more and more urgent demands on states to restrict internal freedom in the interests of collective purposes.

A note on "primordial groups": To some theorists, the ubiquitous rise in state power and in political and social nationalism appears reactive, or even reactionary, and likely to lead to divergence because different societies emphasize different cultural values (Geertz 1963). Such revitalization activity in fact represents part of the process by which national subgroups adopt modern world culture. These movements emphasize boundaries, but the actual contents within the bounded units homogenize. States and other groups form around (or create) primordial boundaries, but they do so in attempts to use these boundaries as bases for effective action in the modern system. This accounts for the sudden surge in modernization that has accompanied the breakdown of the colonial system in the last three decades.

Hechter (1973) similarly argues that the resurgence of ethnic movements in many modern societies is a mechanism by which groups adapt more effectively to their positions in the modernizing structure.

Evidence on Participation

Whether as a result of state or of subgroup mobilization, political participation rises, according to the following indicators:

(a) The most obvious indicator of this process is the extension of citizenship to include most or all members of society. The constitutional documents of all states include strong definitions of citizenship (Peaslee 1965). The breakdown of colonialism and spread of world culture, resulting in the creation of modern state forms, have fashioned a world in which the vast majority of persons have an explicitly defined set of rights and obligations vis-a-vis one, and only one, state.

(b) As another result of the breakdown of colonialism, the proportion of persons in the world with the right to vote has greatly increased (Europa 1948–1973).

(c) Similarly, the expansion of education noted in Table 1 ordinarily occurs under the direct jurisdiction of the state (UNESCO 1955–1968). Such expansion represents another form of individual participation in the structure of the state.

(d) The same points apply concerning the extension of a variety of welfare, family allowance, and social security programs by states. The latter in particular have expanded very rapidly and include an increasing proportion of states (U.S. Department of Health, Education & Welfare 1961, 1967).

(*e*) Cutright & Wiley (1969–1970) constructed a measure of formal political representation, indicating high representativeness when a polity has an elected head of government, an elected multiparty parliament, and universal franchise. Calculated for five-year intervals, the mean of the measure shows steady increases from 13.0 for 1946–1950 to 15.5 for the 1961–1965 period, based on 55 non-Socialist and noncolony cases (maximum value on the scale is 25).

(*f*) Adelman & Morris (1971) created a more direct measure of the amount of political participation in 74 generally less developed countries, using case study materials as well as statistical sources. The mean value of their index for the 1957–1962 period was 8.6; for 1963–1968 it had increased to 9.6. Unfortunately, this study also excluded Socialist countries.

In short, all of these different indicators show increases during the recent period. The evidence that in some ways is most convincing, however, is indirect. Several studies have surveyed individuals in a number of countries with respect to political information, involvement, and participatory attitudes and behavior. The most well known are those by Almond & Verba (1963), who studied five relatively more developed societies, and Inkeles & Smith (1974), who studied six relatively less developed societies. In these and other studies, education is the one demographic variable that most affects participatory attitudes and actual participation. As the UNESCO data in Table 1 show that education is expanding very rapidly, one can hardly deny that participation is very much on the rise, although the amount of participation accompanying a given amount of education may decline as aggregate education expands. How much of this increase in political participation results from the interests of citizens, how much of it is mobilized by states, and how much represents overlapping interests, is problematic.

Evidence on the Extension of State Power

Rare is the indicator that measures the power of states as collective entities in contrast to their representative activity; contemporary states almost always claim to represent their citizens. Nevertheless, a few indicators appear in the literature:

(*a*) One general indicator is the total revenue of the central government as a percentage of GNP. Data for 59 non-Socialist countries have been assembled by the World Bank (IBRD 1971). The mean value for the 1951–1960 period was 20.5%; by 1968–1969 it had risen to 23.7%. The figure rose for both the richer 43 nations (from 22.2% to 26.1%) and the poorer 16 nations (from 16.0% to 17.3%). State power clearly rises at both the top and the bottom of the world stratification system. The evidence is especially striking because during this period, the GNP of most countries rose sharply; states are taking a larger proportion of a larger product. Accounting differences exclude the Socialist states from such an analysis, but their exclusion does not vitiate the point.

(*b*) Similar data on the taxing power of the central government, which overlaps a good deal with total revenue, show the same trends (IBRD 1971).

(*c*) Granted that states acquire more funds from the production system, how much effort do they expend to control this system? Extraordinary results are found in a chronology of state adoption of economic and social planning (Waterston 1965).

Before 1945, only 8 nations had ever engaged in national planning. In successive five-year periods, 49, 30, 27, and 43 new political units assumed this function; by 1965, 136 sovereign states had established national planning agencies. State action in this area is now routine.

(*d*) The research of Black (1966) provides more indirect evidence on this point. In classifying countries on their "political modernity," he finds it possible to sort countries essentially by the time at which their respective political elites became committed to economic and social modernization. He finds little evidence that elites abandon such commitment.

(*e*) We also have evidence of the extension of state power into arenas of social life. As noted above regarding participation, state-controlled educational and welfare systems have greatly expanded. A more general indicator of this process is the size of each government's Cabinet, since Cabinet officers are usually appointed to monitor important social functions (see *The Statesman's Yearbook* 1970–1971), not simply to represent important groups. The average Cabinet size reported by Banks (1971) for 72 countries increased from 14 in 1950 to 18 in 1965. For 25 poorer countries, it increased from 13 to 20; for 46 richer countries, it rose from 14 to 17.

(*f*) One obtains another indicator of the same general variable by inspecting national statistical yearbooks. These state documents, especially since 1950, have greatly expanded the number of social arenas in which they collect and report data, though no one has yet formally surveyed them.

Altogether, these measures establish convincingly that state power is increasing in most societies, both rich and poor. If there is convergence in the degree of state power, it is in the direction of central planning and state-controlled or -regulated economy. This does not, of course, answer the ultimate question of whose interests are being represented. State power can in theory benefit citizens greatly and be exercised explicitly at their behest and interest. Whatever interests are ultimately represented, the evidence suggests that states have become more corporate—that is, organized around more centralized purposes, power, and authority—during the recent period. The increased integration of the world as an economic system, the absence of a world state, and rising social demands have shifted a great many powers to nation-states and legitimated their exercise of them.

Evidence on Political Freedom

There is little evidence on convergence or divergence in political freedom, defined here as the degree to which states legitimate a wide range of individual and subgroup interests in society. Some writers have interpreted the general rise in political participation as an increase in freedom, but this seems unwise in the absence of evidence on the interests in terms of which participation is organized. In the literature the issue arose out of speculations that the Socialist bloc states might inevitably shift from more corporate, totalitarian, and mobilized structures to those legitimating a wider range of social interests.

To this particular issue the events of the past two decades have provided a partial resolution. Students of the Socialist bloc states almost uniformly describe shifts toward the representation of a broader range of social interests in these states and a decline in the employment of the most extreme forms of repression (Korbonski 1974, Triska & Johnson 1973, Hollander 1973, especially pp. 98–108). Most scholars describing these shifts hesitate to suppose that they reflect long-run or inevitable trends, and a number of their critics focus attention on the restrictions of further liberalization that may be anticipated (e.g. Croan 1974, Griffith 1974).

Parallel observations or changes in political freedom in the third world provide practically no evidence. The literature on changes in political freedom in the West is highly polemic and no formal evidence has been developed. Recent events, especially in the United States, have shown that the expansion of world political and economic systems creates state powers and state purposes independent of those individuals and subgroups, which may restrict liberty. At the same time, the state's intensified obligation to provide welfare services—perhaps also a consequence of the world system—may increase individual and subgroup rights. No overall conclusion can be reached.

In general, it seems clear that the assumption by states of external functions, and of responsibility for economic development, has acted to restrict internal political freedom. But amplified state powers also enlarge citizenship rights—in part in response to the larger world system—thereby increasing freedom. We can expect a continuing debate on the overall outcome of these conflicting processes. The debate may well never be resolved because of fundamental ambiguities in the conception of political freedom. No matter how the political rules of states change, the present world structure fuels growing expectations for human rights in more and more aspects of life. Thus, constantly expanding societies—and social conceptions of society—continue to create new social perceptions of given political systems as unequal, unjust, and unfree. Enlarged conceptions of society and of individual and subgroup rights raise new issues of political freedom.

4   INTERNATIONAL POLITICAL EQUALITY

We have found little direct discussion of convergence in political equality, apparently because most writers assume that it corresponds directly to changes in economic equality. As in the parallel literature on equality within industrial societies, to make this assumption is to oversimplify.

Because one can only with difficulty contemplate measuring the political equality of individuals in the world, the literature is restricted to a consideration of states.

Theories

Over and above effects carried by economic processes, which are considered above, we discuss only those theories which identify factors affecting political equality.

Independent-evolution and diffusion theories offer very little insight. Conceptions of societal development in a world system are more fertile. First, political inequality diminishes relative to economic inequality. This occurs because as peripheral nations attempt to modernize in emulation of world development, or as they attempt to construct political defenses against economic dominance and penetration, their state power increases. Additionally, the boundary formation occurring in the Socialist semi-periphery pluralizes the international political system and allows increased maneuverability for the "Third World" (Parsons 1961).

A second line of reasoning leads to the same conclusion. As world culture penetrates peripheral societies, perceptions of internal and external inequities arise, provoking social demands for, and legitimation of, increased state action. Applying a twist to conform to contemporary sociological reasoning by incorporating "status-inconsistency" ideas, one version of this line suggests that economically low status countries experience deprivation relative to their expectations for equality; they compensate by taking political action (see Lagos 1963 for a discussion).

Theories in this area resemble early discussions of capitalist society: the ideology of political equality arises as a component of the bourgeois culture of individualism and as a technique employed by subordinate groups to convince the state to reduce the enormous economic inequalities they face.

Evidence

There is strong evidence that national boundary formation, the legitimation of states, and the entry of states into the world as formally equal citizens have been widespread:

(a) The number of formally independent states has increased from 93 in 1950 to 145 in 1970 (*The Statesman's Yearbook* 1950, 1970–1971). Almost no formal colonies remain.

(b) Most of these independent states are full members of the United Nations, having one vote each (except for an anachronistic Security Council provision providing veto power for certain center states). The number of members has gone from 60 in 1960 to 127 in 1970 (UN 1950, 1970).

(c) Most states enjoy high levels of legitimation from other states; only a few lack universal diplomatic recognition. Further, recognition is on a basis of formal equality: one study, which attempted to measure stratification of states in the world by examining the status rank of the diplomatic representatives sent by major powers to various countries, found that by 1919 these powers sent formally equal ambassadors to almost all other countries (Singer & Small 1966).

(d) Just as deTocqueville noticed the spread of a network of voluntary ties in individualistic American society, a similar network spreads among states. The number of multilateral treaties and agreements deposited with the UN jumped from 52 in 1950 to 141 in 1970 (UN 1949, 1970). The number of multilateral treaties and agreements to which the United States is a party rose from 301 in 1955 to 450 in 1970 (U.S. Dept. of State 1955, 1970).

(e) Although the force of "world opinion" as an influence on internal affairs may take on more importance, actual legitimate authority to take action within a territory, and the responsibility to do so, concentrate in states. Formal internal intervention by an external state is illegitimate; intervention assumes an informal, covert form.

Thus the boundaries and formally equal status of states become highly institutionalized. The degree of equalization among states in actual political power is much less clear (though legitimacy acts in any event as one critical source of power), as the following points suggest.

1. If political power derives from economic resources, the data above on changing economic concentration are ambiguous enough to provide few clues.

2. Research on military power shows the percentage of world military expenditures spent by the militarily "richest" nations (representing approximately the top 30% of the world's population on this variable) declining from 91.1% in 1961 to 85.5% in 1971 (U.S. Arms Control & Disarmament Agency 1972).

3. States increasingly engage in collective action to protect their economic and political interests. We noted above the increase in numbers of mutilateral treaties; similarly it appears that specialized associations of national producers (e.g. OPEC) and even consumers in various commodity markets are becoming more common. These differ sharply from corporately integrating associations among countries (COMECON, LAFTA); they reflect the adaptation of states to their specialized roles in the world system.

To summarize: Formal political equality of states has increased; with increasing integration of the world system, and increasing consciousness of this integration, perceptions of political inequality as inequity will continue to increase, no matter what the course of "actual" levels of equality (again, compare similar assertions about class consciousness within industrial societies). There is no evidence that formal political equality and accompanying concern about inequity provide resources to effectively moderate other pressures in the world system toward greater inequality.

CONCLUSIONS

The research on convergence and divergence in social systems has produced remarkably consistent results in the recent period:

1. Almost all societies grow and modernize economically, rapidly extending modernization to many aspects of social structure.

2. The distribution of specific modernized institutional structures among countries becomes absolutely more unequal, but relatively more equal, as the whole system develops.

3. Relative equality of economic resources changes less than that of structures; some evidence of a decrease in the proportion of resources held by the richest and the poorest countries appears. Mobilized Socialist societies improve their relative position in the world economy.

4. Both political participation and state power rise in most societies. The extent to which they are creatures of the state as opposed to creatures of individuals and subgroups in society is unclear. Whether changes in the disjunction of interests between state and society take place is unknown.

5. Formal political equality among societies greatly increases. Its effectiveness in reducing economic inequality is unclear.

Certain theoretical issues are of central importance and may transform both the way the problem of convergence is formulated and the empirical results which appear in coming years:

1. The body of recent research and data collection we have reviewed reflects events of the last quarter century, a period of rapid expansion of the world structure. If expansion gives way to a period of world economic contraction, both data and theoretical sensibilities may change greatly. Many arguments presented above implicitly suggest that a period of contraction would increase both diversity and inequality among societies.

2. The original convergence-divergence issue was formulated as if societies were independent units; but societies are part of—and may be greatly affected by—a larger world system with which they must cope. The emergent properties of this system are vitally important in explaining such transparent divergencies as the inclination of some semi-peripheral countries (particularly Socialist ones) to form sharp boundaries as they mobilize around economic development, or the inclination of many peripheral societies to engage in forced mobilization around comprehensive socioeconomic development. Divergencies, where they are found, may be less a result of history and culture than of the division of labor, and reactions to it, in the larger world system.

3. More fundamentally, the economic centrality of multinational corporations, and the proliferation and increasing strength of transnational associations and organizations, threaten to render the entire debate irrelevant as they call attention to issues of differentiation and inequality at a new level of analysis.

4. Even assuming continued convergence in development and reduction in international inequality, global integration and increasing structural similarity of subunits should further heighten consciousness of inequality and inequity. Conflict can be expected to increase: it may take violent forms, or it may be contained within the solidarities of the larger division of labor and find outlet in rancorous economic and political competition.

Literature Cited

Adelman, I., Morris, C. T. 1971. *A Conceptualization and Analysis of Political Participation in Underdeveloped Countries,* Res. Rep. No. csd-2236. US Agency for Int. Develop.

Alker, H. R. Jr., Russett, B. M. 1966. Indices for comparing inequality. In *Comparing Nations,* ed. R. L. Merritt, S. Rokkan, 349–72. New Haven: Yale Univ. Press

Almond, G. A., Powell, G. B. Jr. 1966. *Comparative Politics: A Developmental Approach.* Boston: Little, Brown

Almond, G. A., Verba, S. 1963. *The Civic Culture.* Princeton, NJ: Princeton Univ. Press

Apter, D. E. 1965. *The Politics of Modernization.* Chicago: Univ. Chicago Press

Arriaga, E. 1970. *Mortality Decline and its Demographic Effects in Latin America.* Berkeley: Univ. Calif. Inst. Int. Stud. Population Monogr. Ser. No. 6

Avineri, S. 1969. *Karl Marx on Colonialism & Modernization.* Garden City, NY: Anchor Books

Banks, A. S. 1971. *Cross-Polity Time-Series Data.* Cambridge: MIT Press

Baran, P. 1956. *The Political Economy of Growth.* New York: Monthly Rev. Press

Bendix, R. 1964. *Nation-Building and Citizenship.* New York: Wiley

Black, C. E. 1966. *The Dynamics of Modernization.* New York: Harper & Row

Chase-Dunn, C. 1974. *The Effects of International Economic Dependence on Development and Inequality,* Presented at Ann. Meet. Am. Soc. Assoc., Montreal, Aug. 29

Chase-Dunn, C., Boli-Bennett, J., Meyer, J. W. 1974. *Some Effects of the Contemporary World Structure on Nation-states and Other Subunits.* Presented at Ann.

Meet. Pac. Sociol. Assoc., San Jose, Calif., March 28–30

Cole, R. 1973. Functional alternatives and economic development. *Am. Sociol. Rev.* 38:424–38

Coombs, P. H. 1968. *The World Educational Crisis: A System Analysis.* New York: Oxford Univ. Press

Croan, M. 1974. Some constraints on change in Eastern Europe. *Slavic Rev.* 33:240–45

Cutright, P., Wiley, J. A. 1969–1970. Modernization and political representation: 1927–1966. *Stud. Comp. Int. Develop.* 5:23–41

Davis, K. 1969. *World Urbanization 1950–1970.* Berkeley: Univ. Calif. Population Monogr. Ser. No. 4

Deutsch, K. W. 1973. Social and political convergence in industrializing countries—some concepts and the evidence. In *Social Science and the New Societies,* ed. N. Hammond. East Lansing, Mich.: Soc. Sci. Res. Bur.

Europa Yearbook. 1948–1973. London: Europa

Feldman, A. S., Moore, W. E. 1969. Industrialization and industrialism: convergence and differentiation, In *Comparative Perspectives on Industrial Society,* ed. William A. Faunce. Boston: Little Brown

Form, W. H. 1972. Technology and social behavior of workers in four countries: a sociotechnical perspective. *Am. Sociol. Rev.* 37:727–38

Frank, A. G. 1969. *Latin America: Underdevelopment or Revolution.* New York: Monthly Rev. Press

Frank, A. G. 1972. *Lumpenbourgeoisie and Lumpendevelopment.* New York: Monthly Rev. Press

Galbraith, J. K. 1964. *The New Industrial State.* New York: The New American Library

Galtung, J. 1971. A structural theory of imperialism. *J. Peace Res.* No. 2:81–117

Geertz, C. 1963. The integrative revolution: primordial sentiments and civic politics in the new states. In *Old Societies and New States,* ed. C. Geertz. New York: Free Press

Goldthorpe, J. H. 1966. Social stratification in industrial society. In *Class, Status and Power.* ed. R. Bendix, S. M. Lipset. New York: Free Press

Goode, W. J. 1966. *World Revolution and Family Patterns.* New York: Free Press

Griffith, W. E. 1974. The pitfalls of the theory of modernization. *Slavic Rev.* 33: 246–52

Hechter, M. 1973. The persistence of regionalism in the British Isles, 1885–1966. *Am. J. Sociol.* 79:319–342

Heilbroner, R. L. 1962. *The Making of Economic Society.* Englewood Cliffs, NJ: Prentice-Hall

Hodge, R. W., Treiman, D. J., Rossi, P. H. 1966. A comparative study of occupational prestige. In *Class, Status and Power,* ed. R. Bendix, S. M. Lipset, 309–21. New York: Free Press

Hollander, P. 1973. *Soviet and American Society: A Comparison.* New York: Oxford Univ. Press

Hollingsworth, J. R. 1973. Perspectives on industrializing societies. *Am. Behav. Sci.* 16:715–39

Hopkins, T. K., Wallerstein, I. 1967. The comparative study of national societies. *Soc. Sci. Inf.* 6:25–58

Horowitz, I. L. 1966. *Three Worlds of Development.* New York: Oxford Univ. Press

Hoselitz, B. F. 1972. Development and the theory of social systems. In *Social Development,* ed. M. Stanley. New York: Basic Books

Huntington, S. P. 1968. *Political Order in Changing Societies* New Haven: Yale Univ. Press

Huntington, S. P. 1973. Transnational organizations in world politics. *World Polit.* 25:333–68

Int. Bank Reconstruct. Develop. Econ. Program Dept. Socioeconomic Data Div. 1971. *World Tables.* Washington DC: IBRD

Int. Bank Reconstruct. Develop. 1973. *World Bank Atlas.* Washington DC: IBRD

Int. Labour Organ. 1971. *Labour Force Projections,* Parts 1–5. Geneva: ILO

Inkeles, A. 1973. *The Emerging Social Structure of the World.* Presented to Ann. Meet. Int. Polit. Sci. Assoc., Montreal, August 1973

Inkeles, A., Rossi, P. H. 1956. National comparisons of occupational prestige. *Am. J. Sociol.* 61:329–39

Inkeles, A., Smith, D. H. 1974. *Becoming Modern.* Cambridge, Mass.: Harvard Univ. Press

Kassof, A. 1968. *Prospects for Soviet Society.* New York: Praeger

Kelley, J. 1971. *Social mobility in traditional society: the Toro of Uganda.* PhD thesis. Dept. Sociol. Columbia Univ., New York

Kerr, C., Dunlop, J. T., Harbison, F. H., Myers, C. A. 1960. *Industrialism and Industrial Man.* New York: Oxford Univ. Press

Kerr, C., Dunlop, J. T., Harbison, F. H., Myers, C. A. 1971. industrialism and industrial Man (postscript). *Int. Labor Rev.* 103:519–40

Korbonski, A. 1974. The prospects for change in Eastern Europe. *Slavic Rev.* 33:219–39

Kuznets, S. 1971. *Economic Growth of Nations,* Cambridge: Harvard Univ. Press

Lagos, G. 1963. *International Stratification and Underdeveloped Countries.* Chapel Hill, NC: Univ. North Carolina Press

Lane, D. 1971. *The End of Inequality?* Baltimore: Penguin

Linz, J. J. 1970. An authoritarian regime: Spain. In *Mass Politics: Studies in Political Sociology,* ed. E. Allardt, and S. Rokkan, 251–83, 374–81. New York: Free Press

McCord, W. 1965. *The Springtime of Freedom: Evolution of Developing Societies.* New York: Oxford Univ. Press

Meyer, A. G. 1970. Theories of convergence. In *Change in Communist Systems,* ed. C. Johnson. Stanford: Stanford Univ. Press

Millar, J. R. 1972. On the theory and measurement of economic convergence. *Quart. Rev. Econ. Bus.* 12:77–93, 302–6

Miller, S. M. 1960. Comparative social mobility. *Current Sociol.* 9:1–89

Moore, W. 1963. Industrialization and social change. In *Industrialization and Society,* ed. B. F. Hoselitz, W. E. Moore. Paris: UNESCO

Ness, G. D., Ness, J. R. *Metropolitan Power and Demise of Overseas Colonial Empires.* Presented at the 67th Ann. Meet. Am. Sociol. Assoc., August 28–31, 1972

Odum, H. T. 1971. *Environment, Power, and Society.* New York: Wiley

Parsons, T. 1961. Polarization and the problem of international order. *Berkeley J. Sociol.* 6:115–34

Parsons, T. 1971. *The System of Modern Societies.* Englewood Cliffs, NJ: Prentice-Hall

Paxton, J., Ed. 1970–1971. *The Statesman's Yearbook 1970–71.* London: Macmillan

Peaslee, A. J. 1965. *Constitutions of Nations.* The Hague: Martinus Nijhoff

Pinto, A., Knakal, J. 1973. The centre-periphery system 20 years later. *Soc. Econ. Stud.* 22:34–89

Population Council. 1974. *World Population: Status Report 1974.* Reports on Population/Family Planning No. 15. New York: Population Council

Portes, A. 1973. Modernity and development: a critique. *Stud. Comp. Int. Develop.* 8:247–79

Rogers, E. 1962. *The Diffusion of Innovations.* New York: Free Press

Rokkan, S. 1970. *Citizens, Elections, Parties.* New York: McKay

Sahlins, M. D., Service, E. R. 1960. *Evolution and Culture.* Ann Arbor, Mich.: Univ. Michigan Press

Schumpeter, J. A. 1950. *Capitalism, Socialism and Democracy.* New York: Harper and Row

Singer, J. D., Small, M. 1966. The composition and status ordering of the international system: 1815–1940. *World Polit.* 18:236–84

Singer, M. 1966. The Modernization of religious beliefs. In *Modernization: the Dynamics of Growth,* ed. M. Weiner, 55–67. New York: Basic Books

Smelser, N. 1963. Mechanisms of change and adjustment to change. In *Industrialization and Society,* ed. B. F. Hoselitz, W. E. Moore. Paris: UNESCO

Steinberg, S. H., Ed. 1950 *The Statesman's Yearbook 1950.* New York: Macmillan

Taylor, C. L., Hudson, M. C. 1971. *World Handbook of Political and Social Indicators II.* Ann Arbor, Michigan: Interuniv. Consortium for Polit. Res., Univ. Michigan

Theobald, R. 1960. *The Rich and the Poor.* New York: Potter

Treiman, D. J. 1975. *Occupational Prestige in Comparative Perspective.* New York: Seminar Press. In press

Triska, J. F., Johnson, P. M. 1973. *Political Development and Political Change in Eastern Europe: A Comparative Study.* Unpublished paper, Stanford Univ.

United Nations. 1949. *Signatures, Ratifications, Acceptances, Accessions etc. concerning the Multilateral Conventions and Agreements in respect of which the Secretary General Acts as Depository.* Lake Success, NY: UN

United Nations Dept. Econ. Soc. Affairs. *Statistical Yearbook.* 1950. New York: UN

United Nations. 1950, 1970. *Yearbook of the United Nations.* New York: UN Office of Public Inf.

United Nations. 1970. *Multilateral Treaties in Respect of which the Secretary-General Performs Depository Functions.* New York: UN

UNESCO. 1955–1968. *World Survey of Education.* Vols. 1–5. Louvain, Belgium: UNESCO

UNESCO. 1950. *Statistical Yearbook.* Louvain, Belgium: UNESCO

US Arms Control and Disarmament Agency, 1971, 1972. *World Military Expenditures.* Washington DC: US ACDA

US Dept. HEW. 1961, 1967. Soc. Secur. Admin. *Social Security Systems Throughout the World.* Washington DC: GPO

US Dept. State. 1955, 1970. *Treaties In Force.* Washington DC: GPO

Wallerstein, I. 1972a. *The Rise and Future Demise of the World Capitalist System.* Presented to Ann. Meet. Am. Sociol. Assoc., August 28–31

Wallerstein, I. 1972b. Three paths of national development in sixteenth-century Europe. *Stud. Comp. Int. Develop.* 7:95–101

Wallerstein, I. 1974. *The Modern World-System.* New York: Academic

Waterston, A. 1965. *Development Planning: Lessons of Experience.* Baltimore: Johns Hopkins Press

Weinberg, I. 1969. The problem of the convergence of industrial societies: a critical look at the state of a theory. *Comp. Stud. Soc. Hist.* 11:1–15

Young, F. 1970. Reactive subsystems. *Am. Sociol. Rev.* 35:297–307

VOLUNTARY ACTION AND VOLUNTARY GROUPS

❖10510

David Horton Smith
Department of Sociology, Boston College, Chestnut Hill, Massachusetts 02167

INTRODUCTION

A key problem in the study of voluntary action (voluntary participation, citizen participation, discretionary participation, social participation, common interest activity, citizen involvement—all approximate synonyms as used here) is definition. While the struggle for greater definitional clarity as an important step toward developing adequate theories of voluntary action has brought about some agreement on what the definitional issues are, there has been little agreement on how to resolve them (e.g. Pennock & Chapman 1969; Smith, Reddy & Baldwin 1972: Part One; Meister 1972). The approach used here follows the line of Smith, Reddy & Baldwin (1972).

Voluntary action is the action of individuals, collectivities, or settlements insofar as it is characterized primarily by the seeking of psychic benefits (e.g. belongingness, esteem, self-actualization) and by being discretionary in nature [not determined primarily by biosocial factors (physiological compulsions in their socialized forms), coercive factors (sociopolitical compulsions backed by a threat of force), or direct remuneration (direct, high-probability payment or benefits of an economic sort)].

This definition is rooted in the motivational theory of Maslow (1954), conforms fairly well to common sociological usage, is broad but not all-inclusive of human social behavior, defines voluntary action positively as well as negatively, is applicable at all major levels of system reference (shifting from individual motivation to a concern for goals as aggregated motivational intents at collectivity and settlement levels), applies fairly well across the usual disciplinary boundaries and intradisciplinary compartments, is broadly connotative and analytical rather than narrowly denotative, is a matter of degree, not a qualitative distinction, and is not rooted in a particular limiting common sense paradigm of a single kind of voluntary action (e.g. "cult," "movement").

The behavior of any actor (individual, collectivity, settlement) can be described in terms of the relative *extent* to which it is rooted in voluntary intentions (motivations or goals), biosocial factors, coercive factors, and direct remuneration. Nearly

247

all behavior tends to have at least some minimal voluntary component, but the other three components often predominate. When the voluntary component predominates (which is an empirical question) in explanatory importance, the behavior involved is central to the study of VA. When other factors predominate, the behavior involved is peripheral or even irrelevant to the study of VA.

The definition of Kelly (1972) and the empirical studies of Bull (1971) lend support to viewing VA at the individual level as leisure behavior, which in turn includes a wide range of behaviors that are not directly related to work or physical needs and that generally involve a high degree of discretion. The degree of discretion characterizing behavior corresponds roughly to its greater inter-individual variability in duration and its lesser predictability by the individual. Other empirical measures of the "discretionary" or "voluntary" component of individual behavior would be useful additions to our understanding of VA and leisure behavior.

At the individual level our focus in this chapter, however, will be confined to individual participation in conventional voluntary associations and in social movement- or social protest-related formal voluntary groups, leaving other chapters in this or subsequent volumes to deal with some aspects of individual VA (e.g. political behavior, collective behavior, much of religious behavior and labor union behavior, and conventional recreational behavior), while other sources (e.g. the forthcoming *Voluntary Action Research: 1975* review volume, edited by the author and Jacqueline Macaulay) will deal with some aspects.

At the collectivity level, we shall be concerned only with formal voluntary groups, associations, and organizations (cf the definitions of Smith 1972, and of Smith, Reddy & Baldwin 1972: Ch. 10), leaving informal and very noninstitutionalized collective behavior to another chapter. However, some other chapters in the present and subsequent volumes will also presumably deal in part with certain types of voluntary associations (e.g. political parties and pressure groups, social movements as collective behavior, voluntary associations as a subtype of formal organizations, churches and religious groups, and labor unions and industrial relations as part of the sociology of occupations).

At the settlement level ("territorial groups," "communities," or "communal groups") we shall be concerned here mainly with the rates of individual or group VA aggregated at some territorial settlement level (from local community to nation-states) and to a lesser extent with the activity of communes or intentional communities. Again, we assume that other chapters will deal with the role of voluntary groups in community decision making, as important institutions in the sociology of community, and as elements in the total political process of settlements.

Abbreviations we shall use in discussing the three subrealms of VA include VAP (individual voluntary association participation) and FVG (a formal voluntary group, association, or organization).

Having sketched some crucial conceptual aspects of VA, let us now turn to examine selected empirical studies dealing with four basic issues of VA relevant at each system reference level (VAP, FVG, settlement VA). 1. What is the sociography of VA, that is, what is the distribution and what are the rates of VA? 2. What are the roots or determinants of VA? 3. What are the forms and processes of FVGs?

4. What are the outcomes or impacts of VA? Other recent general reviews of the literature on VA should also be consulted by the interested reader (Smith & Freedman 1972; Smith, Reddy & Baldwin 1972; Smith 1973c, 1974b; Tomeh 1973; Zeldin 1974).

THE SOCIOGRAPHY OF VOLUNTARY ACTION

The "sociography" of VA refers to the descriptive, empirically derived "vital statistics" of VA population size, birth and death rates, average life spans, merger rates, and spatial distribution of VA (cf Meister 1975: Chap. 2). An alternative term might be the "demography of VA" within a broader field of the "demography of social organization."

Voluntary Association Participation Frequencies

First, how frequent is voluntary association membership and participation? Most studies focus only on adults (aged 20+ usually), though a few studies of educational institutions show the association participation of youthful school attendees (in school clubs, teams, student government groups, etc) to be very substantial (e.g. Barker & Gump 1964: Chap. 5; Fichter 1964: Part 2; Smith 1973a). Among adults, the results depend upon how one defines VAP. For customary and basically non-theoretically justifiable reasons, church participation is usually omitted from consideration, arguing that membership is ascriptive and involuntary. But this is only true for the very young. Adolescents and adults in contemporary society are generally free to change their religious affiliations and often do so (cf Bibby & Brinkerhoff 1974, Stark & Glock 1968), and religious organizations themselves are clearly FVGs (see Scherer 1972).

Moreover, actual participation in religious activities (worship, church committees, etc), rather than mere stated affiliation, is even more clearly VA, whether one maintains or changes from the religious affiliation of one's parents. Smith (1972) has argued that at least some minimal level of participation ("provision of services") is a defining element of "analytical membership" in an organization (as contrasted with "official membership" or self-reported membership). This approach to defining FVG membership and participation provides a solution to the common problem of differential tendencies of groups or individuals to claim a known false "official membership" for reasons of prestige, ideology, self-justification, etc.

Depending on the level of participation used as a minimum criterion (e.g. at least once per week, month, or year), recent surveys show that substantial portions of the adult population of advanced Western nations report frequent church attendance, and the large majority participate at least sometimes in formal religious ceremonies (cf Stark & Glock 1968, Alston 1971, 1973, Blaikie 1972). Still higher proportions report membership in one or another religion.

There is also controversy surrounding the inclusion or exclusion of industrial labor unions, with some noting that in closed-shop unions the member is required to join as a condition of employment or that the motives involved are purely economic. This situation is clearly more compulsory and economically motivated than in many other forms of VAP, but, on analysis, does not disqualify union participation as VAP, since VA is a matter of degree in any event. Most importantly, *participation* in union activities is rarely compulsory or directly economic but rather discretionary. Hence, there may be a high frequency of "official" union membership that, for lack of actual participation, does not constitute "analytical" membership (Smith 1972, Verba & Nie 1972: 42, Van de Vall 1970: 154–55).

When union memberships are excluded, national sample surveys of VAP in industrial nations show an average of 10% lower rates of VAP than when unions are included (Curtis 1971). Less industrialized nations would probably show smaller differentials if adequate data were available, because of a smaller portion of the labor force in manufacturing jobs.

Another important factor affecting reported levels of VAP is the type of item used. Some important studies (cf Hyman & Wright 1971) have used a global, open-ended question with one or two probes, while others (cf Curtis 1971) have used a more detailed question or series of questions on a variety of VAP types. Although no study known to the author simultaneously compares the reliability and validity of these two types of items, studies using the second, more detailed approach have shown higher average VAP rates even at comparable time periods in U.S. national sample surveys (cf Hyman & Wright 1971: 195 for 1962 data vs Curtis 1971: 874 for 1960 data). While sampling variations or other factors might account for such a difference, other research on methods of eliciting self-reports of activity suggests that the more detailed ("aided-recall") version of the question will give more accurate results on VAP as for other topics.

With these cautions in mind let us look briefly at recent national sample survey research on VAP rates including union participation (but not church participation because it is not reported by the researchers). National sample survey data (Hallenstvedt 1974, Curtis 1971, Verba & Nie 1972: 176) make it clear that the long-quoted remark of de Tocqueville about the U.S. being distinctively a nation of "joiners," however true it may have been early last century, is no longer true. Several advanced Western nations (especially Scandinavian nations) have VAP rates as high as or higher than the U.S. For instance, Hallenstvedt (1974: 217) reports that 79% of Swedish adults report FVG membership, whereas Verba & Nie (1972:41) report that only 62% of U.S. adults report such memberships, as contrasted with 25% of Mexican adults (Curtis 1971:874). When multiple memberships are considered (two or more affiliations), the results are even more striking in proportionate differences among countries, ranging from 39% for the U.S. (cf Verba & Nie 1972: 176) to only 2% for Mexico (Curtis 1971: 875). It would be most interesting to have comparable data on Eastern European socialist-communist countries and on very underdeveloped Third World countries (though relevant noncomparable data can be found in various chapters of Smith 1974b).

Unfortunately, only Verba and Nie give careful attention to actual activity rates (and hence, to analytical vs nominal memberships) in their national sample data. They report (1972: 176) that only 40% of U.S. adults indicate activity in VAP (vs 62% reporting membership). (See also Olsen 1974.) We may expect reported memberships in general, therefore, to be an overestimate (perhaps by half) of actual VAP in the U.S. if a strict criterion of activity is used (self-report as "active"). On the other hand, longitudinal analysis of a random sample of U.S. adults from a Midwestern state (Babchuk & Booth 1969) indicated that, although the average VAP rate did not change over a four-year interval, about 4% of the sample who were not members at time one became members by time two, balanced by an equivalent dropout rate from among previous participants at time one. Hence, measuring VAP at any one point in time somewhat underestimates life span VAP probabilities. If an adequate longitudinal study were done over the full life span, it is quite possible that virtually everyone might be involved in VAP at one time or another in advanced industrial nations. Existing longitudinal data gathered for other purposes but including VAP data might be reanalyzed in order to test this hypothesis.

Other measures of VAP for national populations that have been studied recently included time budgets, computation of imputed value of contributed time, and computation of total number of memberships (cf Smith & Baldwin 1974a). And Verba & Nie (1972: 42) open an important line of research by indicating the marked differences in average VAP rates among different types of FVGs.

Formal Voluntary Group Frequencies

Although long concerned with the frequency of individual VAP, sociologists have shown relatively little interest in the incidence and prevalence of voluntary associations as groups. There is a voluminous literature of case studies on the formation, growth, and decline of particular types of associations, and even many comparative analyses of several associations of a given kind. Quantitative comparative studies of the incidence or prevalence of associations are, however, rare for any territorial level of settlement.

Two volumes of the *Voluntary Action Research* annual series (Smith 1973c: Part One, 1974b) have attempted to deal with this problem in a modest way, as have studies by Vondracek (1972), Nall (1967), Feld (1971), and Skjelsbaek (1973), all of which are concerned with cross-sectional or time series data on national or international FVG incidence-prevalence. Although the data on involvement of nations in international FVGs and on FVGs connected with educational institutions are generally complete, it is striking that at other levels the published data are generally poor. There are directories of national associations for several countries, but in no country, apparently, are there adequate data on all kinds and levels of FVGs for the nation as a whole or states (or equivalent) within it.

One very general finding of the research studies cited above is that there are very wide variations in FVG prevalence among nations and within particular nations over time, leaving much variance to be explained. Also, there seem to be numerous FVGs of a variety of types in *every* contemporary nation studied (including the U.S.S.R. and Communist China—cf Swanson 1974, Fisher 1974) plus evidence of significant FVG prevalence for various societies in earlier times (cf Bradfield 1973, Anderson 1973, Peterson & Peterson 1973, Ross 1973, Brown 1973).

At the local level, numerous community studies have been performed over the past four decades and in recent years that include FVG prevalence data (e.g. Drake 1972, Traunstein & Steinman 1973, Meister 1974: Chap. 2). Yet there have been few attempts to collate the results of this research in terms of its quantitative implications for voluntary association prevalence. When such collation and synthesis has been attempted (cf Meister 1974: 36, Smith & Baldwin 1974a), the relative narrowness of the range of variation (roughly from 5 to 100 FVGs per 1000 persons, or somewhat more than one order of magnitude) in FVG prevalence per 1000 population is notable, in spite of great differences in research methods, community settings, and even definitions of FVGs. This suggests that common powerful social processes may underlie FVG incidence-prevalence in most developed nations, perhaps even in lesser developed countries (cf Drake 1972, Fisher 1974: 4).

Much more rigorously comparative studies of FVG prevalence at all territorial levels are urgently required if this newly opening area of VA research is to be adequately pursued. Much more careful attempts must be made to assess the comparability of methods and definitions and to synthesize the results of different prior studies than have so far been done, and highly varied samples of communities, states, and nations must be studied quantitatively and longitudinally in the future using common definitions, methods, and analytic approaches.

THE ROOTS OF VOLUNTARY ACTION

The Roots of Individual Voluntary Association Participation

There are by now probably a few thousand empirical studies of different aspects of individual VA, and at least a thousand dealing specifically with VAP. Much of this literature has been reviewed by Smith & Freedman (1972: Ch. 6), by various authors in the volume edited by Smith, Reddy & Baldwin (1972: Part Two), and by Tomeh (1973). Hence, we shall confine the present review to discussing the general implications of recent research here, and pointing out major gaps and extensions beyond the usual U.S. or North American research settings.

Recent research too extensive even to mention corroborates and expands our knowledge of how VAP is affected by social background factors (cf Payne et al 1972, Tomeh 1973). Several generalizations from prior research (largely performed in the U.S.) have received cross-cultural confirmation for other Western industrial nations in recent years. In addition, some simple generalizations have been shown to be more complex when examined carefully in multivariate analyses. Some examples are the following generalizations.

Males have higher overall FVG membership rates than females (Verba & Nie 1972:181, Curtis 1971, Kellerhals 1974, Hallenstvedt 1974), but such differences narrow or even vanish when actual FVG activity levels are taken into account (Verba & Nie 1972:181, Booth 1972), when union memberships are omitted (Curtis 1971:874), or when church membership and participation are included (Alston 1971). Still, the less industrialized and developed the country (and hence the greater the sex role inequalities), the more clearly the original generalization holds (Curtis 1971).

Persons of the middle-age range (roughly 35–55 years) have higher VAP rates than younger or older persons (Verba & Nie 1972:181, Curtis 1971:877, Hallenstvedt 1974). The decline in VAP with the approach of old age and retirement, however, is far more pronounced for instrumental (e.g. occupation-related) FVGs than for expressive ones (Bultena & Wood 1970).

Married persons have somewhat higher VAP in terms of multiple FVG memberships (for several countries, Curtis 1971), but the generalization that married persons have higher VAP, derived basically from U.S. and Canadian studies, does not seem to hold up consistently for various other nations when membership in one or more FVGs is the VAP measure (Curtis 1971), and unions are excluded.

More educated persons tend to have higher overall VAP rates in all countries studied (Curtis 1971, Verba & Nie 1972:181, Hyman & Wright 1971, Hallenstvedt 1974). But Waisenen & Kumata (1972), using data from several nations, show that because of functional illiteracy at very low levels of education in developing countries, there is a curvilinear, usually flat initially but then ascending, positive (log curve) relationship between education and VAP.

Persons with higher occupational status and income have higher VAP rates in various countries studied (Van Es & Whittenbarger 1970, Hodge & Trieman 1968, Kellerhals 1974, Hallenstvedt 1974, Hyman & Wright 1971). Moreover, Hodge (1970) has shown that combined indices of socio-economic status (SES) used to explain VAP are likely to mask important differences among the components of the SES index (e.g. income, occupational status, education).

Social mobility (changes in SES) affects VAP, but not in the complex way suggested by Durkheim's social isolation logic and by research that fails to control for both initial and present status levels (e.g. Stern & Noe 1973, Vrga 1971). Socially mobile people tend to adapt themselves more or less to the status level at which they arrive. Their VAP in such circumstances is usually an additive function of their status of origin and their current status. There seem generally to be no fancy interactions or status inconsistency effects here, just a basic socialization/adjustment to the appropriate VAP style of a new status level (cf Vorwaller 1970, Bruce 1971, Jackson & Curtis 1972, Mirande 1973).

Ethno-religious roles affect VAP, but only recently have there been studies of this relationship that adequately control for other important variables like occupational status and education (Laumann & Segal 1971, Greeley 1974). The problem here is that there is little internal evidence to indicate why certain ethno-religious roles (e.g. Scandinavian, Irish-Catholic) tend to have consistently higher VAP rates than other roles (e.g. French Catholic) in the USA.

Racial-ethnic roles also affect VAP, but recent research has exploded the stereotype of blacks as more passive and unorganized than whites. When SES is not controlled, blacks tend to have lower VAP rates in the U.S. than whites (Hyman & Wright 1971). But when the powerful SES variables are controlled for, blacks show higher VAP rates (Olsen 1970, Ross & Wheeler 1971, Williams et al 1973) than whites. Olsen (1970:692) suggests, with some support from his data, that higher identification with the black ethnic community is associated with higher VAP. Relating such ethnic, racial, and religious role identification variations among individuals to VAP variations would seem to be a fruitful line for future research, as an addition to and elaboration of the usual nominal category analyses presented here.

Individual VAP rates are affected by various "contextual" factors (community size, heterogeneity, etc) that will be referred to later under the category of "situational" factors.

Nearly all of the foregoing kinds of studies relating social background characteristics to VAP tend to suffer from the same major defect in one degree or another: They tend to be more concerned with the empirical demonstration of predictability rather than with theoretically grounded explanation using quantitative empirical data. Theoretical explanations tend to be thrown in as afterthoughts, rather than actually tested. All such social background characteristics need to be better integrated into theories or paradigms regarding *why* they are important for explaining VAP. One important attempt to provide a general paradigm relating to social background characteristics is made by Lemon, Palisi & Jacobson (1972).

Lemon, Palisi & Jacobson (1972:32) define a "dominant status position" as "that category on a social dimension which is commonly accorded the highest amount of value in relation to other categories by the members of a group or society." This means that the most valued category on a given social dimension may vary through time and among groups or societies. Although some social dimensions are seen as more important than others for a given reference population, an individual's dominant-subordinate position on all relevant dimensions is viewed as being directly and cumulatively related to social participation (e.g. VAP) in that population. This explains why VAP in U.S. society is correlated with higher Socioeconomic status (SES), being middle aged, male, married, a Protestant, and living in an urban area —all these categories are examples of the dominant status on their respective social dimensions. The authors go on to demonstrate the empirical utility of this theory in explaining the VAP of a sample of college students on vs off campus.

This theory or paradigm seems to be both simple and powerful, having widespread relevance to all VA research, particularly VAP research. What is lacking in the initial formulation is adequate specification of how to operationalize the notion of "most valued category." For this first attempt to use the paradigm, the dominant status categories were named inductively and a priori. Subsequent studies should actually measure the degree of consensus within a defined population on what is the most valued status. Variations in consensus may be important modifiers of how strongly a given dominant status category and social dimension predict participation.

A second needed elaboration of the Lemon, Palisi, and Jacobson paradigm is specification of the range of VA for which it holds. There may well be types of VA (e.g. revolutionary and protest activity) with which the dominant status category (relative to the total population) is negatively related to higher participation. In any event, the suggested paradigm deserves widespread attention and many further attempts at testing or modification.

Another important theoretical approach that merits more attention here is to show how specific social background and role characteristics in a given society are associated with particular attitude, personality, and situational variables, which in turn are conducive to individual VAP. This approach lends itself to the use of path analysis statistical techniques. Unpublished research analyses by the author (to be reported in *The Roots of Voluntary Action*) confirm that apparently powerful social background and role characteristics lose much or most of their direct explanatory power when intervening attitude, personality and situational variables (which have direct explanatory power) are controlled statistically.

One final kind of social background characteristic that deserves more attention is the whole set of parental characteristics during early life. This concern is already present in studies of the effect of (intergenerational) social mobility in VAP. But almost nothing has been done relating general parental VAP to one's own VAP. The Hodge & Trieman (1968) study, demonstrating an independent effect of parental VAP on own VAP even while controlling for SES factors (own and parents'), has only been subsequently replicated in two completed studies (Reddy 1974, Smith & Baldwin 1974b) to our knowledge (although numerous studies document the strong influence of parental political party and religious affiliation upon own VAP in these areas). This notable gap in a promising research area needs to be filled as soon as possible, especially in view of the proven powerful effects of parental socialization in other areas.

There continues to be a dearth of studies relating individual VAP to personal health and physical abilities or impairments (cf Smith 1973a: 74, Cutler 1972). The health factor is worthy of much greater research attention, especially when severe or chronic illnesses or impairments are involved. Since most random area probability samples omit the institutionalized portion of the population (including hospitalized, rest home, and clinic residents), since poor health is probably one important factor in refusal to be interviewed among the noninstitutionalized population, and since many samples of the adult population have upper age limits that exclude older (e.g. age 65+) people more likely to be in poor health, nearly all studies of individual VAP involve sampling systematically biased toward the healthy. This greatly attenuates any impact of health factors even if they are examined, though inclusion of any but psychosomatic symptoms in VAP studies is very rare.

The whole range of psychophysiological capacities as possible determinants of VAP has also been almost totally neglected. No published studies dealing with this kind of relationship have been discovered in the present review of materials appearing over the past five years or so. There is every reason to believe, on the basis of socialization, social exchange, and intelligence theories (plus a few pieces of prior research such as Gough 1952, Bronfenbrenner 1960), that greater individual VAP is associated with greater capacities, especially verbal and relational capacities. This relationship may be expected to be stronger for instrumental than expressive VAP. But adequate measures of interpersonal skills (e.g. ability to communicate through nonverbal, expressive movements) would probably be significantly associated with expressive VAP.

A small amount of research has been done recently on the relation of individual VAP to personality characteristics (broad, relatively transituational dispositions) and to attitudes (narrower, more situationally specific dispositions), though both areas remain underdeveloped. Miscellaneous samples (mainly students at various levels, plus businessmen and service volunteer program participants) have been studied to relate VAP to various personality measures such as

1. A composite social conformity factor based on the Omnibus Personality Inventory (for sorority members vs sorority dropouts, Rose & Elton 1971).
2. Rotter's internal-external control scale (for Women's Liberation movement members and controls, Sanger & Alker 1972; and for levels of social service, protest and political activity among undergraduates, Silvern & Nakamura 1971).
3. The Tennessee Self Concept Scale, Schutz's FIRO-B, and the concept domain questionnaire (for matched groups of high and low risk service volunteers and nonvolunteers, Horn 1973).
4. Kohlberg's Moral Judgment Interview and teacher-peer ratings of leadership and popularity (for levels of student social organization participation) (Keasey 1971).
5. The Edward's Personal Preference Schedule need affiliation scale (for levels of high school student extra-curricular activities, Query & Query 1973).
6. Indices of psychological adjustment, interpersonal attitudes, social desirability, and internal-external control (for levels of nonuniversity VAP among college students, Townsend 1973).

Although highly variable in methodology and analytic approach, most of the results of these studies tend to be consistent with the psychological model of individual VAP suggested by Smith (1966). That model suggests that higher VAP will be associated with higher scores on "personality" variables, such as social conformity, efficacy (internal control), self-confidence, assertiveness, sociability, affiliation needs, personal adjustment, etc, as these characteristics in combination portray the hypothetical "ideal participant" in FVGs and VA. The principal exception among the foregoing studies is that the internal/external control factor seems to have two separable components that operate differently for conventional vs protest forms of VAP (Sanger & Alker 1972, Silvern & Nakamura 1971).

These results can be readily absorbed by the Smith model, adjusting the "ideal personality" of high participation to specify higher personal internal control feelings mainly in more conventional kinds of VAP, while predicting higher personal and especially sociopolitical external control feelings mainly in more protest and social advocacy forms of VA or VAP. The latter adaptation of the model is a theoretical recognition (not mere ad hoc adjustment) that most protest forms of VA involve striking out against real or imagined relative deprivations seen as imposed by external forces.

A few pieces of research have recently delved into the relations of overall VAP to various kinds of individual perceptions, attitudes, beliefs, and interests. Studies that relate attitudes to VAP in general are uncommon (cf Mulford & Klonglan 1972) but a few have been performed in recent years.

Young & Larson (1970), for instance, found that greater village and community identification (attitudes) were associated with greater VAP for people in a rural New York state community and its surroundings. Eitzen (1970) found lower Srole anomie scores to predict higher VAP among middle-class, midwestern, urban women. Kasarda & Janowitz (1974) found higher VAP among English adults with more community interest. In view of these and earlier results, it is somewhat surprising that Hoerner (1973) found perceived seriousness of community problems *not* to be significantly related to number of FVG memberships when social class, community size, and age were controlled (although multicollinearity effects may be part of the problem here).

An even broader range of attitudinal measures was included by Townsend (1973) in his study of VAP among freshmen university students. He found that higher overall participation in nonuniversity-based FVGs was significantly related to indices of more positive attitudes toward voluntary organizations, a higher sense of political efficacy, a greater sense of general citizen responsibility, and more perceived efficacy in the voting process. The first two of the foregoing indices were especially significant even after controls for SES and other variables were introduced. Similar results, using a broad range of attitude measures, have been obtained for other kinds of samples by Reddy (1974), Rogers (1971), and Smith (unpublished research on *The Roots of Voluntary Action*). These studies generally confirm the "attitudinal-fit" model suggested by Smith (1966), who argues that a variety of general and specific attitudes characterize the "ideal participant" in FVGs and are therefore conducive to individual VAP.

Several studies also relate VAP in particular *kinds* of groups to attitudes and personality dispositions. (The distinction between the two opposite poles of the transituational dispositions continuum becomes hard to maintain in the middle ground, where we find rather general attitudes or narrow personality traits such as dogmatism, authoritarianism, alienation, anomie, etc.) Among randomly selected Minnesota small businessmen, authoritarianism, alienation, and anomie are related to membership in sectarian churches and authoritarian organizations (Photiadis & Schweiker 1970). For samples of peace group members (in groups of varying degrees of radicalism) and random nonmember townspeople, joining any peace group and joining a particular peace group (varying in terms of radicalism levels) were related to indices of political attitudes, foreign-policy attitudes, powerlessness, meaninglessness, normlessness, isolation, and perception of social explanation for problems (Bolton 1972). Students at a black Florida university were more likely to be involved in VAP (a "passive" civil rights activity index) if they anticipated relative deprivation for blacks in general, felt less deprived (i.e. better off) relative to all blacks, and perceived more blocked opportunities for themselves (Geschwender & Geschwender 1973).

With data from a statewide sample of Wisconsin farm operators who were rank and file (nonleader) farm organization members, Warner & Rogers (1971) found participation in group activities to be related to perceived personal influence on the group, and to the ratio between perceived personal control and control by the president and executive committee. Among Latin American university students from six nations, Smith (1973a) found participation in various kinds of voluntary groups related to such attitudes as sociopolitical radicalism, lack of acquiescent-traditionalism, intellectualism, and political activity interests. And Marsland & Perry (1973) found members of four different types of youth groups in an area of London to be highly differentiable in terms of such variables as teenage ethnocentrism, restrictiveness ("moral liberalism"), rejection of older people, Srole's anomie, and self-esteem, even when various social background variables are controlled. Bailey (1973) found participants in conventional voluntary associations to be very different from participants in a militant Alinsky-type group, in terms of several attitudes relating to the utility of conventional political processes for the expression of power and influence, dissatisfaction with local officials, community orientation, and commitment to civil liberties.

These studies suggest several conclusions: Individual VAP is in general quite predictable on the basis of attitudes, especially if members of very different groups are compared. The most fruitful research of this type has used members from a purposive sample of two or more associations of a distinctive theoretical type or, better, corresponding to different points on a theoretical continuum of organizational structure, process, or composition (e.g. organizational radicalism, authoritarianism, structuredness, etc). This permits explaining why individuals with certain kinds of attitudes are more likely to be found in some corresponding kinds of VAP rather than others. The fit of individual personality-attitude dimensions with the organizational role demands for FVG members/participants may be seen as the underlying root paradigm of this kind of research (cf Smith 1966), even though this paradigm is not often made theoretically explicit by the researchers involved. The best examples of this kind of research relating VAP to attitudes include as a control group either a matched sample of nonmembers or a cross-sectional sample of the general nonmember population (e.g. Bolton 1972, Smith 1973a).

The differential prediction/explanation of VAP *among* different types of FVGs is complementary to the more general prediction/explanation of overall VAP using attitudes and personality dispositions as predictors. But in the latter case there is some evidence for the utility of a *general* personal system model of the "active participant" in *most* kinds of VAP, while in the former case this model needs to be modified by more careful attention to role requirements for participants in the *particular* theoretical kinds of groups. And when this specific type of VAP is sufficiently different from the conventional kind (e.g. for high protest-oriented or otherwise deviant groups), elements of the *general* attitudinal and personality model of "ideal FVG participant" require substantial modification or elimination, not mere elaboration by inclusion of more specific group-relevant attitudes (cf Geschwender & Geschwender 1973 and Bolton 1972 vs Smith 1966). When nonassociational forms of VA are considered, even greater modification of the general model tends to be necessary though common elements remain (cf Geschwender & Geschwender 1973).

What is greatly needed now is a series of large sample studies of individuals in the general population focusing simultaneously on the problems of explaining (*a*) overall levels of VAP, (*b*) choice between formal (VAP) and more informal forms of VA (protest, interpersonal visiting, helping behavior, etc), (*c*) choice among the major types of VAP in terms of common goal types (e.g. environmental VAP, health service VAP, political VAP, etc), (*d*) choice among major structural and process types of VAP within a given goal type category (e.g. within environmental VAP), (*e*) choice of a specific voluntary association from within broader type categories (*c* and *d*), and (*f*) choice among role types of activity (e.g. meeting attendance,

committee work, elective office, protest, service projects) within a given association
—all in relation to attitude-personality variables in addition to the usual social
background characteristics. Very few existing studies have tried to explain more
than one of these levels of variation in VAP.

One great flaw in all research so far relating VAP to attitude-personality dimensions is that there have been no adequate longitudinal panel surveys. An equally
good case can often be made for selection *and* socialization effects with regard to
attitude and personality measures, and both processes probably operate for most
VAP. As a result, whether attitudes and personality dispositions will be seen as
causes or consequences of VAP varies with investigator theoretical preferences in
cross-sectional research, and the basic issue of causation remains unresolved.

The final major class of variables that have been related to VAP consists of current
situational influences—contexts, stimuli, perceptions, and resources (Smith &
Reddy 1972). VAP has been found to be greater where a person has more friends
at work (Ross & Wheeler 1971, Dulz 1973), works in a company that encourages
community VAP by employees (Fenn 1971), has been influenced by co-workers to
engage in VAP (Van de Vall 1970:Ch. 4), and has been influenced by a spouse,
friends or other personal contacts to engage in VAP (Jennings & Niemi 1971, Booth
& Babchuk 1969, Welton 1971, Reddy 1974:165, Lounsbury 1973, Hagburg 1968,
Althoff & Brady 1972).

Such studies are all consistent with the broader theory of "significant others" or
reference persons as influences on individual behavior. What is needed now is more
research on *who* significant others are for a given individual and *why* they are
important for VAP decisions. The only study we have found dealing with this issue
is that by Evans & Ehrlich (1973). They find that willingness to volunteer in writing
for participation in various civil rights activities is positively related to being influenced over a longer period by a significant other who has more of such characteristics as importance, visibility, centrality, legitimacy, and control.

VAP has also recently been found to be greater in winter than summer (for
middle-class, married women with children in Canada, Michelson 1971), and
greater for those who have access to personal transportation (among older people
in a small midwestern U.S. college community, Cutler 1972), those who reside in
more SES-homogeneous neighborhoods (for blacks and whites in Detroit, Warren
1974), those who have resided for a long time in their community (among English
adults, Kasarda & Janowitz 1974), those who reside in single family homes rather
than mobile homes (Edwards et al 1973), and those who live in towns of under
50,000 population (for national samples in four of five countries, Curtis 1971).

This kind of situational approach is very much neglected in the literature, and
where present tends to be inadequate in specifying and measuring the intervening
theoretical variables of perception (e.g. who is a "significant other" for the individual) that mediate the effects of external social and physical processes upon VAP.
It will also be important to specify theoretically in more detail the full range of
situational "opportunity" variables and "personal influence process" variables that
may affect VAP as constraints and facilitators. This area of research holds much
promise.

How can all these general classes of factors be fit together to explain VAP in a coherent manner? To begin with, attempting this is very rare. The great majority of VAP studies are content to demonstrate the existence/nonexistence of certain effects, with little care for the total reduction in error variance in VAP. Second, few studies combine two or more (especially three or four) types of explanatory variables (background, health and capacities, attitudes, personality, situation) in the same study. Third, there are very few studies that present and test any kind of relatively comprehensive theory or model of VAP with quantitative empirical data. Because of these facts, the following studies are exceptional on one or more of these grounds: Grupp & Newman 1973, Townsend 1973, Crigler 1973, Smith 1973a, Reddy 1974, and Rogers 1971.

Some tentative conclusions to be seen as hypotheses for future research may be drawn from these studies, although the basis for making them is shaky owing to a lack of comparability of methods, samples, and measures. 1. More variance (60–70% or more) tends to be accounted for in purposive samples that involve group members who are very different from one another (e.g. very active vs. inactive group members, members of groups representing two political extremes) than in broader cross-sections of people in the community or in an educational institution (where 20–40% explained variance is more common). This is largely an artifact of the sampling. 2. When other realms are included as predictors along with social background variables, the latter decline sharply in direct explanatory power, indicating that attitude, personality, and situational factors tend to mediate the usually observed relationships between VAP and social background variables. 3. About 10–30% more variance tends to be accounted for when (a) more different realms of relevant predictors are included in the study, especially the nondemographic realms, and (b) *appropriate* personality and attitude variables are included, based on an analysis of the role demands of the kind of VAP being studied, whether overall VAP or a specific kind. 4. When both specific and general attitudes toward voluntary associations are included in the same study, specific attitudes tend to be more powerful in explaining VAP (specific attitudes tend to focus on perceptions of a particular VAP setting, including some of its situational characteristics).

Although there are some consistencies across types of VAP, samples, and countries in how particular predictors affect VAP, there are even more inconsistencies. Both the consistencies and inconsistencies are often understandable in terms of "dominant status" theory (for social background variables—see Lemon, Palisi & Jacobson 1972) and "personal system-role demand compatibility" or "personal system fit" theory (for personality, attitudes, and situational variables—see Smith 1966).

Some of the multivariate studies cited earlier as well as a series of other studies indicate that a significant proportion of the variance in VAP is associated with other forms of VA such as mass media consumption, recreation, adult education, church participation, political participation, social protest, etc (Townsend 1973; Crigler 1973; Smith 1973a; Hagburg 1968; Grupp & Newman 1973; Verba & Nie 1972: 193; Kasarda & Janowitz 1974; Blaikie 1972; Von Eschen, Kirk & Pinard 1971; Bronfman 1974; Olsen 1972, 1974). Indeed there seems to be a general correlation of different kinds of VA with each other, leading to a common factor which Smith (1969) has termed the "general activity syndrome." In a direct way, the existence of this syndrome can be viewed as evidence for the utility of a broad definition of VA in the first place. VA as defined here refers to a series of individual activity types that are empirically interrelated in a positive way in addition to being conceptually distinguishable.

If there is such a general activity syndrome, and a corresponding set of personality and attitude variables that underlie it (see the author's forthcoming monograph on *The Roots of Voluntary Action*), then one *component* of the explanation of any specific kind of VAP is likely to be the influence of this broader syndrome and its underlying personal system determinants. This component will still have to be supplemented by explanations of general VAP and of specific forms of VAP, as suggested earlier. An analysis-of-variance-components statistical model of explanation would be appropriate to test the relevance of these different theoretical component levels of the roots of VAP. Research to test this intriguing possibility is urgently needed.

The Roots of Voluntary Groups

Though far less well studied than determinants of individual VAP, voluntary group formation, growth and demise have been the subject of many studies in recent years. The great majority of this research, though empirical, has been nonquantitative in nature, generally a theoretical description based on single or multiple case studies using historical and social anthropological methods.

The best studies using "qualitative" empirical methods are distinguished by virtue of systematically applying to, or else deriving from, the descriptive data some conceptual model or generalizations. This permits some reasonable generalizations from what otherwise tend to be merely interesting descriptions. The value of these more consciously analytical studies is greatly enhanced additionally when they involve a comparison of results from case studies on several groups, rather than only one or two, and when the groups are studied over a substantial period of time (e.g. Manzer 1969, Gerlach & Hine 1968, Van de Vall 1970, Schmidt & Babchuk 1973).

We could find only one quantitative empirical study of FVG formation/demise in recent years, studying churches in Missouri in 1952 and 1967 (Hassinger & Holik 1970). It would be most useful if a large cross-section of case studies of FVG formation/demise were carefully categorized and later coded in terms of relevant conceptual schemes, as are research data on primitive and peasant societies in the Human Relations Area Files. Such a highly comparative data base could then be used in secondary analysis by numerous scholars to make quasiquantitative tests of their own and others' models more rigorously and systematically while still using qualitative primary data. Divising an adequate sampling strategy for inclusion of case studies would be among the most difficult methodological aspects of creating the data base.

We found two quantitative empirical studies of another aspect of group VA— average participation in different FVGs (Wicker, McGrath & Armstrong 1973; Betz 1973). Both show FVG attendance levels or rates to be significantly predictable from internal characteristics (e.g. FVG size and meeting place capacity) or external characteristics (e.g. neighborhood SES) of the groups. In view of the known wide variation in group participation rates (cf Verba & Nie 1972: 42), it is strange that more attention has not been given to exploring these FVG variations. Virtually all empirical studies seem to have focused on the roots of individual VAP. The solid findings about individual VAP cannot be generalized to the collectivity level of system reference without committing the "Synechdochic Fallacy" (Berry & Martin 1974).

The Roots of Settlement Voluntary Action

The determinants of settlement VA might be investigated at several levels, *all* of which have been seriously neglected. First there is the level of purposive or intentional communities (communes, utopias, residential collectives, etc). Although there are many recent descriptive and some analytic case study materials (e.g. Kanter 1972a, Treece 1971), there is very little in the way of quantitative analytical research on the origins, growth, and decline of such "voluntary communities." Stephan & Stephan (1974) use recorded material on all U.S. utopian communities existing in the period between 1776 and 1900 to show that the average life span of religious communes is much greater than that of nonreligious communes. Their study is an excellent model of what might be done in the way of explanatory, quasiquantitative, comparative, settlement VA research based on qualitative case study materials.

Second, there is a small amount of research on the roots of FVG incidence-prevalence or the mobilization of participation in towns or neighborhoods (Apte 1974, Bridgeland 1973, Brown 1973). One of the best of these finds local mobilization for environmental action to be significantly related to several variables of community structure and process (Bridgeland 1973), but suffers from having to use data from only six key informants in each of the 124 towns studied. Ideally, more reliable data collection methods can be used for each locality in the sample and more precise and comprehensive conceptual models can be devised to synthesize past results and guide future research.

At higher territorial levels of settlement (i.e. nations or their major subunits), much of the empirical research again consists of descriptive, historical, or social anthropological case studies, leavened by a few analytical and comparative studies that attempt not only to describe but also to explain generally the emergence/prevalence/demise of all or certain kinds of voluntary groups within a society (cf Eisenstadt 1972, Anderson 1973, Bradfield 1973, Smith & Fisher 1971, Smith 1973b, Brown 1973, Baldwin 1973). Several of these studies lend support to a theory of FVG incidence-prevalence suggested by Smith (1973b) and rooted in the intercommunication network development, goal differentiation, and collective action orientations of a settlement.

Baldwin (1973) reviews various earlier studies of voluntary associations and formal organization prevalence and theories of their emergence, concluding that the social structural convergence models, such as that of Smith (1973b) need to be tempered by use of the "historical specificity" model that argues for the relevance of unique social structural and cultural factors in determining associational incidence/prevalence rates. The conceptual scheme of Smith & Fisher (1971) attempts such an integration, illustrating its relevance with a variety of historical and contemporary examples.

A major inadequacy of all of this comparative analytical research on prevalence is that adequate quantitative measures of the important independent and dependent variables have not been generally available from records and existing data sources. New and extremely costly survey and sociohistorical research on many societies, past and contemporary, will be needed if appropriate tests of the convergence and historical specificity models (or their hybrids) are to be made. As suggested elsewhere, it would be useful here to develop a large Human Relations Area File-like data base on the incidence-prevalence of associations in many societies at different time periods, together with data on social structural, cultural, population composition, and environmental characteristics of each society. Then researchers might systematically code the historical data in different ways to test particular theories and hypotheses regarding voluntary association prevalence, with each new set of codes becoming part of the data base. Such quasiquantitative research usually using qualitative primary data will need to be supplemented by massive comparative survey research projects. Such cross-national survey projects will need to obtain adequate comparable survey data on associational incidence-prevalence rates and average individual VAP rates, together with data on explanatory variables relevant to the various suggested models. To some extent, existing national sample poll data may serve as a stopgap until sufficient resources can be mobilized to perform such studies.

FORMS AND PROCESSES OF VOLUNTARY GROUPS

The literature on FVG structure and process is far too extensive even to cite selectively, let alone to deal with adequately in the space available for this chapter given other priorities. Hopefully, some of the relevant literature will be covered in the chapter on formal organizations or in the next chapter on VA in this series. Also, certain key aspects of FVG structure have already been touched on in earlier sections. The most we can do here now is to indicate the approximate relative magnitudes of the recent empirical research literature on different topics.

By far the greatest number of studies are global case studies of particular FVGs or small sets of similar FVGs, with some being analytical and more broadly comparative. Perhaps next most frequent are leadership studies and internal efficiency/effectiveness studies of FVG actions and their roots, FVG relations with other groups, FVG structure and its roots, and FVG socialization. In each of these topical areas there tend to be a few really good quantitative pieces of research, and numerous quasiquantitative or qualitative ones. Moreover, there is a tremendous amount of time spent on development of typologies, concepts, and models—some empirically grounded and linked, many not.

THE IMPACT OF VOLUNTARY ACTION

Like the previous section, the present topic is far too large and complex to cover in available space.

Voluntary Action Impact on the Social System

The best examples of VA systemic impact research use some quantitative index of change in a settlement characteristic (at some territorial level) and relate this impact measure to the presence or prevalence of VA across a sample of settlements, controlling other factors statistically. For instance, door-to-door political canvassing of voters by volunteer party workers can have demonstrably significant effects on subsequent aggregate voter turnout and candidate margin within voting precincts, controlling other factors (Price & Lupfer 1973). The presence of community-wide voluntary associations in large U.S. cities tends to have demonstrably positive effects on the existence of hospital councils (Turk 1973), while the presence of national FVG headquarters tends to have a positive effect on federal poverty program activity in large U.S. cities (Turk 1970). Labor unions can have moderate to strong effects on the wage levels of members vs nonmembers (Robinson 1973). And the presence of a volunteer blood donor system in a country is associated with higher average quality of blood used for medical purposes (Titmuss 1971).

Quantitative research of this sort is quite rare, on the whole, but promises to be of increasing importance in the future. Its major flaw, as for other areas, is the usual lack of time series data. On the whole, however, such studies support the conclusion that VA can have a variety of significant systemic impacts in settlements of various territorial levels.

Voluntary Association Participation Impact upon Participants

A lengthy review of this area of research was published recently (Smith & Reddy 1973). Its conclusions have not been greatly altered by more recent research. There is still very little methodologically adequate research done on any kind of VAP impact.

Several pieces of recent research demonstrate that overall VAP has a powerful predictive effect on conventional political participation (cf Bronfman 1974; Olsen 1972, 1974; Sallach, Babchuk & Booth 1972; Sproule-Jones & Hart 1973). However, none of these studies involve time series data that could be used to demonstrate causal linkages, so the hypothesized "impact" of VAP is still in doubt. Nearly all of the findings could in principle be explained away as spurious owing to the joint determination of both individual political participation and VAP (as components of the "general activity syndrome"—Smith 1969) by underlying personality, attitude, and background variables. Thus, the additional findings of Trela (1972; and to a lesser extent Useem 1972) are especially important in that they provide some longitudinal evidence of actual individual changes as a result of VAP, though more in political ideology than in political action. There is still great need, however, for a broader sample panel survey of the possible VAP impacts on individual political participation and ideology.

Recent studies of the impact of service volunteer programs upon their participants show weak or mixed results (Ritzman 1972, Townsend 1973, and Koopman 1973 find no effects, while King, Walder & Pavey 1970 and Sager 1973 find some significant self-image changes in before-and-after studies).

Finally, there are still mainly illustrative case studies of the impact of socialization/conversion in religious sects (Kanter 1972b, Lebra 1972) and in deviant self-help groups like Alcoholics Anonymous (Petrunik 1972, Jones 1970), rather than longitudinal quantitative studies. Yet these kinds of VAP are precisely the ones where both common observation and theory would suggest the greatest individual impacts of VAP are to be found.

DIRECTIONS FOR FUTURE RESEARCH

Since numerous specific suggestions for future research have been made throughout this chapter, no attempt will be made here to restate them. Instead, there are three important general points we would like to make about future research.

First, whatever future research on VA is done, a significant proportion of it needs must be both quantitative *and* longitudinal if real progress is to be made. Many of the assumed causal relationships we find in cross-sectional studies may be over-turned by appropriate longitudinal analyses (as Meyer 1972 shows for the relation of size and organizational structure in work organizations).

Second, voluntary action research is not and should not be the exclusive province of sociologists if we are really to understand VA in all of its modes and ramifications. Thus, scholars concerned about VA research should consciously seek out cross-disciplinary inputs, both in terms of literature and other scholarly consultation/collaboration/communication. The recently formed Association of Voluntary Action Scholars[1] provides one means for facilitation of such interdisciplinary activity.

Third, many recent attempts have been made to spell out in greater or lesser detail the areas of needed research on VA, especially with regard to VAP and FVGs. This has been done for a few special topical areas such as international organizations (Judge & Skjelsbaek 1972), VA and socioeconomic development (Parvey 1972), court-related volunteer service programs (Peters 1973), and citizen involvement in local decision making (Ball 1973). There have also been several broader attempts to spell out research needs (Smith & Reddy 1971, Smith 1974a), including a large collaborative and interdisciplinary project attempting to define VA *policy* research needs (Smith et al 1974). These sources should be consulted in conjunction with this chapter to get an adequate overview of what we think we need to know about voluntary action.

ACKNOWLEDGMENTS

This chapter represents a great deal of literature searching over a period of many months by several people in addition to the author. I wish to thank especially Eugene D. White, Burt R. Baldwin, and Barbara MacLaury, as well as Margaret Barth, Nancy Casper, Maureen Kiernan, Joanne Kilsdonk, Pat Simmons, Janice Singer, and Marianne Venezia for their dedicated efforts to make this chapter as good as we all could make it.

[1]This Association publishes the *Journal of Voluntary Action Research* and holds an annual convention as well as co-sponsoring sessions at annual meetings of other disciplines and fields of study. Its current address is Box G-55, Boston College, Chestnut Hill, Mass. 02167.

Literature Cited

Alston, J. P. 1971. Social variables associated with church attendance, 1965 and 1969: evidence from national polls. *J. Sci. Study Relig.* 10:233–36

Alston, J. P. 1973. Review of the polls. *J. Sci. Study Relig.* 12:453–55

Althoff, P., Brady, D. 1972. Toward a causal model of the recruitment and activities of grass roots political activists. *Soc. Sci. Quart.* 53:598–605

Anderson, R. T. 1973. Voluntary associations in history: from paleolithic to present times. In *Voluntary Action Research: 1973,* ed. D. H. Smith, Lexington, Mass.: Lexington Books, D.C. Heath

Apte, M. L. 1974. Voluntary associations and problems of fusion and fission in a minority community in South India. *J. Volun. Action Res.* 3:43–48

Babchuk, N., Booth, A. 1969. Voluntary association membership: a longitudinal analysis. *Am. Sociol. Rev.* 34:31–45

Bailey, R. 1973. Militants and conventionals: role behavior and neighborhood participation. *J. Volun. Action Res.* 2:102–11

Baldwin, B. R. 1973. Formal Volunteer Organization Prevalence Among Nations. In *Voluntary Action Research: 1973,* ed. D. H. Smith. Lexington, Mass.: Lexington Books, D. C. Heath

Ball, G. H. 1973. *Research Needs in Citizen Involvement.* Menlo Park, Calif.: Stanford Res. Inst.

Barker, R. G., Gump, P. V. 1964. *Big School, Small School: High School Size and Student Behavior.* Stanford, Calif: Stanford Univ. Press

Berry, K. J., Martin, T. 1974. The synecdochic fallacy: a challenge to recent research and theory building in sociology. *Pac. Sociol. Rev.* 17:139–66

Betz, M. 1973. Neighborhood status and membership in locality based instrumental associations. *Sociol. Focus* 6:61–73

Bibby, R. W., Brinkerhoff, M. B. 1974. The circulation of the saints: a study of people who join conservative churches. *J. Sci. Study Relig.* 13:273–83

Blaikie, N. W. H. 1972. What motivates church participation? Review, replication and theoretical reorientation in New Zealand. *Sociol. Rev.* 20:39–58

Bolton, C. D. 1972. Alienation and action: a study of peace-group members. *Am. J. Sociol.* 78:537–61

Booth, A. 1972. Sex and social participation. *Am. Sociol. Rev.* 37:183–92

Booth, A., Babchuk, N. 1969. Personal influence networks and voluntary association affiliation. *Sociol. Inq.* 39:179–88

Bradfield, R. M. 1973. *A Natural History of Associations.* London: Duckworth. 2 vols.

Bridgeland, W. 1973. *Community structure, environmental issue-specificity and the level of citizen mobilization for environmental quality.* PhD thesis. Univ. Illinois, Urbana-Champaign

Bronfenbrenner, U. 1960. Personality and participation: the case of the vanishing variables. *J. Soc. Issues* 16:54–63

Bronfman, B. H. 1974. *Participation in community life: a comparative study of three nations.* PhD thesis. Univ. Oregon, Eugene

Brown, R. D. 1973. The emergence of voluntary associations in Mass., 1760–1830. *J. Volun. Action. Res.* 2:64–73

Bruce, J. M. 1971. Intergenerational occupational mobility and participation in formal associations. *Sociol. Quart.* 12: 46–55

Bull, C. N. 1971. One measure for defining leisure activity. *J. Leis. Res.* 3:120–26

Bultena, G., Wood, V. 1970. Leisure orientation and recreational activities of retirement community residents. *J. Leis. Res.* 2:3–15

Crigler, P. W. 1973. *Significant variables indicative of commitment to the women's movement.* PhD thesis. Northwestern Univ., Evanston

Curtis, J. 1971. Voluntary association joining: a cross-national comparative note. *Am. Sociol. Rev.* 36:872–80

Cutler, S. J. 1972. *The Availability of Personal Transportation, Residential Location, and Voluntary Association Participation among the Aged.* Presented at the Annual Meeting of the Gerontological Society, San Juan

Drake, G. F. 1972. Social class and organizational dynamics: a study of voluntary associations in a Colombian city. *J. Volun. Action Res.* 1,3:46–52

Dulz, N. L. 1973. *The effect of job and primary interaction experiences on voluntary organization membership: A study of automobile workers in four nations.* PhD thesis. Michigan State Univ., East Lansing

Edwards, J. N., Klemmack, D. L., Hatos, L. 1973. Social participation patterns among mobile-home and single-family dwellers. *Soc. Forces* 51:485–89

Eisenstadt, S. N. 1972. The social conditions of the development of voluntary associations—a case study of Israel. *J. Volun. Action Res.* 1,3:2–13

Eitzen, D. S. 1970. A study of voluntary association memberships among middle-class women. *Rural Sociol.* 35:84–91

Evans, W. L., Ehrlich, H. J. 1973. The relative influence of reference others with regard to civil rights activism. *Sociol. Focus* 6:1–13

Feld, W. 1971. Nongovernmental entities and the international system: a preliminary quantitative overview. *Orbis* 15:879–922

Fenn, D. H. 1971. Executives as community volunteers. *Harvard Bus. Rev.* Mar–Apr: 4–19

Fichter, J. H. 1964. *Parochial School: A Sociological Study.* New York: Anchor Books

Fisher, A. 1974. Associational life in the people's republic of China. In *Voluntary Action Research: 1974,* ed. D. H. Smith. Lexington, Mass.: Lexington Books, D. C. Heath

Gerlach, L. P., Hine, V. H. 1968. Five factors crucial to the growth and spread of a modern religious movement. *J. Sci. Study Relig.* 7:23–40

Geschwender, B. N., Geschwender, J. A. 1973. Relative deprivation and participation in the civil rights movement. *Soc. Sci. Quart.* 54:403–11

Gough, H. G. 1952. Predicting social participation. *J. Soc. Psych.* 35:227–33

Greeley, A. M. 1974. Political participation among ethnic groups in the U.S. *Am. J. Sociol.* 80:170–204

Grupp, F. W., Newman, W. M. 1973. Political ideology and religious preference: the John Birch Society and the Americans for Democratic Action. *J. Sci. Study Relig.* 12:401–13

Hagburg, E. C. 1968. Influence of primary groups on participation in the unions. *Rev. Ciencias Soc.* 12:365–75

Hallenstvedt, A., 1974. Formal voluntary associations in Norway. In *Voluntary Action Research: 1974,* ed. D. H. Smith. Lexington, Mass.: Lexington Books, D. C. Heath

Hassinger, E. W., Holik, J. S. 1970. Changes in the number of rural churches in Missouri, 1952–67. *Rural Sociol.* 354–66

Hodge, R. W. 1970. Social integration, psychological well-being, and their socioeconomic correlates. *Sociol. Inq.* 40:182–206

Hodge, R. W., Trieman, D. J. 1968. Social participation and social status. *Am. Sociol. Rev.* 33:722–40

Hoerner, J. V. 1973. *Voluntary Organization Affiliation and Perceived Seriousness of Community Problems.* PhD thesis. Washington State Univ., Pullman

Horn, J. C. 1973. *Personality Characteristics of Direct Service Volunteers.* PhD thesis. U.S. International Univ., San Diego, Calif.

Hunt, G. J., Butler, E. W. 1972. Migration, participation and alienation. *Sociol. Soc. Res.* 56:440–52

Hyman, H., Wright, C. 1971. Trends in voluntary association memberships of American adults: replication based on secondary analysis of national sample surveys. *Am. Sociol. Rev.* 36:191–206

Jackson, E., Curtis, R. 1972. Effects of vertical mobility and status inconsistency: a body of negative evidence. *Am. Sociol. Rev.* 37:701–13

Jennings, M. K., Niemi, R. 1971. The division of political labor between mothers and fathers. *Am. Polit. Sci. Rev.* 65:69–82

Jones, K. 1970. Alcoholics anonymous: a new revivalism? *New Soc.* 16:102–3

Judge, A. J. N., Skjelsbaek, K. 1972. Transnational Association Networks (TANs). *Int. Assoc.* 10:481–85

Kanter, R. M. 1972a. *Commitment and Community.* Cambridge, Mass.: Harvard Univ. Press

Kanter, R. M. 1972b. Commitment and the internal organization of millenial movements. *Am. Behav. Sci.* 16:219–43

Kasarda, J. D., Janowitz, M. 1974. Community attachment in mass society. *Am. Sociol. Rev.* 39:328–39

Keasey, C. B. 1971. Social participation as a factor in the moral development of preadolescents. *Develop. Psychol.* 5:216–20

Kellerhals, J. 1974. Voluntary associations in Switzerland. In *Voluntary Action Research: 1974,* ed. D. H. Smith, Lexington, Mass.: Lexington Books, D. C. Heath

Kelly, J. R. 1972. Work and leisure: a simplified paradigm. *J. Leis. Res.* 4:50–62

King, M., Walder, L. O., Pavey, S. 1970. Personality change as a function of volunteer experience in a psychiatric hospital. *J. Consult. Clin. Psych.* 35:423–25

Koopman, E. J. 1973. *Identity formation processes in volunteer and nonvolunteer university students.* PhD thesis. Univ. Maryland, College Park

Laumann, E. O., Segal, D. R. 1971. Status inconsistency and ethno-religious group membership as determinants of social participation and political attitudes. *Am. J. Sociol.* 77:36–61

Lebra, T. S. 1972. Millenarian movements and resocialization. *Am. Behav. Sci.* 16:195–217

Lemon, M., Palisi, B. J., Jacobson, P. E. 1972. Dominant statuses and involvement in formal voluntary associations. *J. Volun. Action Res.* 1,2:30–42

Lounsbury, J. W. 1973. *A community experiment in dissemination models for citizen environmental action.* PhD thesis. Michigan State Univ., East Lansing, Michigan

Manzer, R. 1969. Selective inducements and the development of pressure groups. *Canad. J. Polit. Sci.* 2:103–17

Marsland, D., Perry, M. 1973. Variations in 'adolescent societies'—exploratory analysis of the orientations of young people. *Youth Soc.* 5:61–83

Maslow, A. H. 1954. *Motivation and Personality.* New York: Harper

Meister, A. 1972. *Toward a Sociology of Associations.* Paris: Les Editions Ouvrieres

Meister, A. 1974. *Participation in Associations.* Paris: Les Editions Ouvriers

Meyer, M. W. 1972. Size and the structure of organizations: a causal analysis. *Am. Sociol. Rev.* 37:434–40

Michelson, W. 1971. Some like it hot: social participation and environmental use as functions of the season. *Am. J. Sociol.* 76:1072–83

Mirande, A. M. 1973. Social mobility and participation: the dissociative and socialization hypothesis. *Sociol. Quart.* 14:19–31

Mulford, C. L., Klonglan, G. E. 1972. Attitude determinants of individual participation in organized voluntary action. In *Voluntary Action Research: 1972,* ed. D. H. Smith, R. Reddy, B. Baldwin. Lexington, Mass: Lexington Books, D. C. Heath

Nall, F. C., Jackson, J. 1967. *The Emergent American Society,* ed. W. L. Warner, Ch. 8. New Haven: Yale Univ. Press

Olsen, M. E. 1970. Social and political participation of blacks. *Am. Sociol. Rev.* 35:682–96

Olsen, M. E. 1972. Social participation and voting turnout: a multivariate analysis. *Am. Sociol. Rev.* 37:317–33

Olsen, M. E. 1974. Interest association participation and political activity in the United States and Sweden. *J. Volun. Action Res.* 3,3:17–33

Parvey, C. F. 1972. The role of voluntary associations in third world develop-ment: some questions for exploration. *J. Volun. Action Res.* 1,2:2–7

Payne, R., Payne, B. P., Reddy, R. D. 1972. Social background and role determinants of individual participation in organized voluntary action. In *Voluntary Action Research: 1972,* ed. D. H. Smith, R. Reddy, B. Baldwin. Lexington, Mass: Lexington Books, D. C. Heath

Pennock, J. R., Chapman, J. W., Eds. 1969. *Voluntary Associations.* New York: Atherton

Peters, C. 1973. Research in the field of volunteers in courts and corrections: What exists and what is needed? *J. Volun. Action Res.* 2:121–34

Peterson, S., Peterson, V. A. 1973. Voluntary associations in ancient Greece. *J. Volun. Action Res.* 2(1):2–15

Petrunik, M. G. 1972. Seeing the light: a study of conversion to Alcoholics Anonymous. *J. Volun. Action Res.* 1:30–38

Photiadis, J., Schweiker, W. 1970. Attitudes toward joining authoritarian organizations and sectarian churches. *J. Sci. Study Relig.* 9:227–34

Price, D. E., Lupfer, M. 1973. Volunteers for Gore: the impact of a precinct-level canvass in three Tennessee cities. *J. Polit.* 35:410–38

Query, W. T., Query, J. M. 1973. Birth order: urban-rural effects on need affiliation and school activity participation among high school male students. *J. Soc. Psych.* 90:317–20

Reddy, R. D. 1974. *Personal factors and individual participation in formal volunteer groups.* PhD thesis. Boston College, Chestnut Hill, Mass.

Ritzman, E. R. 1972. *Identity formation and effects of volunteer work experiences in community college students: An exploratory study with implications for counseling and education.* EdD thesis. Rutgers Univ., New Brunswick, NJ.

Robinson, J. F. 1973. *The development and economics of firefighter and police unionism: A comparative study.* PhD thesis. Univ. Illinois, Urbana-Champaign

Rogers, D. L. 1971. Contrasts between behavioral and affective involvement in voluntary associations: an exploratory analysis. *Rural Sociol.* 36:340–58

Rogers, D. L., Heffernan, W. D., Warner, W. K. 1972. Benefits and role performance in voluntary organizations: an exploration of social exchange. *Sociol. Quart.* 13:183–96

Rose, H. A., Elton, C. F. 1971. Sorority dropout. *J. Coll. Student Pers.* 12:460–64

Ross, J. 1973. Voluntary associations in ancient societies. In *Voluntary Action Research: 1973,* ed. D. H. Smith. Lexington, Mass: Lexington Books, D. C. Heath

Ross, J. C., Wheeler, R. H. 1971. *Black Belonging.* Westport, Conn.: Greenwood

Sager, W. G. 1973. *A study of changes in attitudes, values, and self concepts of senior high youth while working as fulltime volunteers with institutionalized mentally retarded people.* EdD thesis. Univ. South Dakota, Vermillan, S. D.

Sallach, D. L., Babchuk, N., Booth, A. 1972. Social involvement and political activity: another view. *Social Sci. Quart.* 52:879–92

Sanger, S. P., Alker, H. A. 1972. Dimensions of internal-external locus of control and the Women's Liberation Movement. *J. Soc. Issues* 28:115–29

Scherer, R. 1972. The church as a formal voluntary organization. In *Voluntary Action Research: 1972* ed. D. H. Smith, R. Reddy, B. Baldwin. Lexington, Mass: Lexington Books, D. C. Heath

Schmidt, A., Babchuk, N. 1973. Trends in U.S. Fraternal Organizations in the Twentieth Century. In *Voluntary Action Research: 1973,* ed. D. H. Smith. Lexington, Mass.: Lexington Books, D. C. Heath

Silvern, L. E., Nakamura, C. Y. 1971. Powerlessness, social-political action, social-political views: their interrelation among college students. *J. Soc. Issues* 27:137–57

Skjelsbaek, K. 1973. The growth of international nongovernmental organizations in the twentieth century. In *Voluntary Action Research: 1973,* ed. D. H. Smith. Lexington, Mass.: Lexington Books, D. C. Heath

Smith, C., Freedman, A. 1972. *Voluntary Associations: Perspectives on the Literature.* Cambridge, Mass.: Harvard Univ. Press

Smith, D. H. 1966. A psychological model of individual participation in formal voluntary organizations: application to some Chilean data." *Am. J. Sociol.* 72:249–66

Smith, D. H. 1969. Evidence for a general activity syndrome: A survey of townspeople in eight Massachusetts cities and towns. *Proceedings, 77th Ann. Conv., Am. Psychol. Assoc.*

Smith, D. H. 1972. Organizational boundaries and organizational affiliates. *Sociol. Soc. Res.* 56:494–512

Smith, D. H. 1973a. *Latin American Student Activism.* Lexington, Mass.: Lexington Books, D. C. Heath

Smith, D. H. 1973b. Modernization and the emergence of volunteer organizations. In *Voluntary Action Research: 1973,* ed. D. H. Smith. Lexington, Mass.: Lexington Books, D. C. Heath

Smith, D. H., Ed. 1973c. *Voluntary Action Research: 1973.* Lexington, Mass.: Lexington Books, D. C. Heath

Smith, D. H. 1974a. *Research and Communication Needs in Voluntary Action.* In *Volunteerism: An Emerging Profession,* J. Cull, R. Hardy. Springfield, Ill.: Thomas

Smith, D. H., Ed. 1974b. *Voluntary Action Research: 1974.* Lexington, Mass.: Lexington Books, D. C. Heath

Smith, D. H., Baldwin, B. R. 1974a. Voluntary associations and volunteering in the U.S. In *Voluntary Action Research: 1974,* ed. D. H. Smith. Lexington, Mass.: Lexington Books, D. C. Heath

Smith, D. H., Baldwin, B. 1974b. Parental socialization, socio-economic status and volunteer organization participation. *J. Volun. Action Res.* 3,4:59–66

Smith, D. H., Fisher A. 1971. *Toward a Comparative Theory of the Incidence-Prevalence of Voluntary Associations in Territorial Social Systems.* Presented at the Ann. Conv., Assoc. for Asian Studies, Washington, DC

Smith, D. H., Reddy, R. D. 1971. Voluntary action and social problems. *J. Volun. Action Res.* Monograph #2

Smith, D. H., Reddy, R. 1972. Contextual and organizational determinants of individual participation in organized voluntary action. In *Voluntary Action Research: 1972,* ed. D. H. Smith, R. Reddy, B. Baldwin. Lexington, Mass: Lexington Books, D. C. Heath

Smith, D. H., Reddy, R. D. 1973. The impact of voluntary action upon the volunteer participant. In *Voluntary Action Research: 1973,* ed. D. H. Smith. Lexington, Mass.: Lexington Books, D. C. Heath

Smith, D. H., Reddy, R. D., Baldwin, B. R., Eds. 1972. *Voluntary Action Research: 1972.* Lexington, Mass.: Lexington Books, D. C. Heath

Smith, D. H. et al 1974. *Voluntary Sector Policy Research Needs.* Washington, DC: Center for a Voluntary Society

Sproule-Jones, M., Hart, K. 1973. A public-choice model of political participation. *Canad. J. Polit. Sci.* 6:175–94

Stark, R., Glock, C. Y. 1968. *American Piety.* Berkeley: Univ. Calif. Press

Stephan, K. H., Stephan, G. E. 1974. Religion and the survival of utopian communities. *J. Sci. Study Relig.* 13:89–98

Stern, S. E., Noe, F. P. 1973. Affiliation-participation in voluntary associations: a factor in organized leisure activity. *Sociol. & Soc. Res.* 57:473–81

Swanson, J. M. 1974. Non-governmental organizations in the U.S.S.R. 1958–73. In *Voluntary Action Research: 1974,* ed. D. H. Smith. Lexington, Mass: Lexington Books, D. C. Heath

Titmuss, R. M. 1971. *The Gift Relationship: From Human Blood to Social Policy.* New York: Pantheon Books

Tomeh, A. K. 1973. Formal voluntary organizations: participation, correlates, and interrelationships. *Sociol Inq.* 43:89–122

Townsend, E. J. 1973. An examination of participants in organizational, political, informational and interpersonal activities. *J. Volun. Action Res.* 2:200–11

Traunstein, D. M., Steinman, R. 1973. Voluntary self-help organizations: an exploratory study. *J. Volun. Action Res.* 2:230–39

Treece, W. J. 1971. Theories of religious communal development. *Soc. Compass.* 18:85–100

Trela, J. E. 1972. Age structure of voluntary associations and political self-interest among the aged. *Sociol. Quart.* 13:244–52

Turk, H. 1970. Interorganizational networks in urban society: initial perspectives and comparative research. *Am. Sociol. Rev.* 35:1–18

Turk, H. 1973. Comparative urban structure from an interorganizational perspective. *Admin. Sci. Quart.* 18:37–55

Useem, M. 1972. Ideological and interpersonal change in the radical protest movement. *Soc. Probl.* 19:451–69

Van de Vall, M. 1970. *Labor Organizations.* Cambridge: Cambridge Univ. Press

Van Es, J. C., Whittenbarger, R.L. 1970. Farm ownership, political participation and other social participation in Central Brazil. *Rural Soc.* 35:15–25

Verba, S., Nie, N. H. 1972. *Participation in America: Political Democracy and Social Equality.* New York: Harper & Row

Vondracek, F. 1972. The rise of fraternal organizations in the U.S., 1868–1900. *Soc. Sci.* 47:26–33

Von Eschen, D., Kirk, J., Pinard, M. 1971. The organizational substructure of disorderly politics. *Soc. Forces* 49:529–44

Vorwaller, D. J. 1970. Social mobility and membership in voluntary associations. *Am. J. Sociol.* 75:481–95

Vrga, D. J. 1971. Differential associational involvement of successive ethnic immigrations. *Soc. Forces* 50(2):239–48

Waisenen, F. B., Kumata, H. 1972. Education, functional literacy and participation in development. *Int. J. Comp. Soc.* 13:21–35

Warner, W. K., Rogers, D. L. 1971. Some correlates of control in voluntary farm organizations. *Rural Sociol.* 36:326–39

Warren, D. I. 1974. The linkage between neighborhood and voluntary association patterns: a comparison of black and white urban populations. *J. Volun. Action Res.* 3,1:1–17

Welton, R. F. 1971. *Relationship of student characteristics and program policies to participation in FFA.* PhD thesis. Ohio State Univ., Columbus, Ohio

Wicker, A. W., McGrath, J. E., Armstrong, G. 1973. Organization size and behavior setting capacity as determinants of member participation. *Behav. Sci.* 17:499–513

Williams, J. A., Babchuk, N., Johnson, D. R. 1973. Voluntary associations and minority status: a comparative analysis of Anglo, Black, and Mexican-Americans. *Am. Sociol. Rev.* 38:637–46

Young, R. C., Larson, O. F. 1970. The social ecology of a rural community. *Rural Sociol.* 35:337–53

Zeldin, D. 1974. Voluntary action in Britain. In *Voluntary Action Research: 1974,* ed. D. H. Smith. Lexington, Mass.: Lexington Books, D. C. Heath

COMMUNITY POWER ❖10511

Terry Nichols Clark[1]

Department of Sociology, University of Chicago, Chicago, Illinois 60637

BACKGROUND

This paper complements other recent reviews, especially Friedman (1970), Kirlin & Erie (1972), Hawley & Svara (1972), Fried (1973), Walton (1973), Leif & Clark (1973), Clark (1973d), and Scheuch (1973). We focus on recent developments, some with roots further back, but most taking place in about the last five years.

The debate of "elitists" and "pluralists" in the early 1960s seems almost ancient —in good part from redefinition of research problems. This theoretical redefinition has been accompanied by changes in research design. Prior to the mid-1960s, practically all community power research consisted of case studies of individual cities. F. Hunter, in his influential study of Atlanta, essentially asked the question: Who constitutes the power elite? He sought to identify a "community power structure" and portray relations among its members. Much research throughout the 1950s followed Hunter's lead. Then in his study of New Haven, Dahl (1961) argued against Hunter's elitist approach. Studying specific decisions, he found that leading actors differed across issues—a pattern he labeled pluralistic.

Both Hunter and Dahl asked different versions of the question, Who governs? By the mid-1960s, contrasting results from dozens of case studies had become available. Comparative studies of two or more communities also began, which documented clear differences across cities. Such results helped relativize Hunter's and Dahl's questions, simultaneously underscoring the necessity for a more comprehensive conceptual framework. The framework gradually emerged by extension of the range of research questions beyond the traditional question: Who governs?

Most current research starts from a series of four interrelated questions: *Who governs?*—what is the nature of community leadership; *Where?*—in what kinds of communities; *When?*—under what conditions; and *With what effects?*—how do decisions affect policy outputs and impacts? These basic questions, and their answers, have helped shape a conceptual framework encompassing most recent work. Specific formulations vary, but many converge on basically similar portrayals (e.g.

[1]Support is gratefully acknowledged from NSF, GS-1904, GS-3162, and PHS, NICHD, HD08916-01. This is research report No. 55 of the Comparative Study of Community Decision-Making.

271

Aiken & Mott 1970, Fried 1973, Clark 1973d, Laumann & Pappi 1973, Hawley & Wirt 1974). Figure 1 outlines a framework of basic variables; equations 1–3 portray the same basic structure:

$$L_i = a_i + b_{i1}I_a + b_{i2}CC_c + e_i \qquad\qquad 1.$$

$$PO_j = a_j + b_{j1}I_a + b_{j2}CC_c + b_{j3}L_i + e_j \qquad\qquad 2.$$

$$PI_k = a_k + b_{k1}I_a + b_{k2}CC_c + b_{k3}L_i + b_{k4}PO_j + e_k \qquad\qquad 3.$$

where L_i = leadership processes, PO_j = policy outputs, PI_k = policy impacts, I_a = inputs to the local community, CC_c = community characteristics, a_i, a_j, a_k = constants, b_{i1} to b_{k4} = coefficients to be estimated, and e_i, e_j, e_k = error terms. Verbally, inputs to the local community (such as federal grants) and community characteristics (demographic, economic, etc) influence leadership processes. These three sets of variables in turn generate policy outputs (e.g. municipal expenditures). Then the four variable sets structure policy impacts, or changes in earlier variables resulting from the policy outputs. Obviously more statistical sophistication could be brought to this recursive model by introducing feedback loops, simultaneous equations inside blocks of variables, etc. Current work is moving in this direction.

Six types of methodological approaches may be distinguished, as shown in Table 1. Historically first were case studies of individual communities (generally municipalities in the US). Immediate access, convenience for participant observation, and relatively low cost have long encouraged case studies. They have provided some of our richest portrayals of the dynamics of community processes. Despite the development of more complex methods, case studies continue to perform important func-

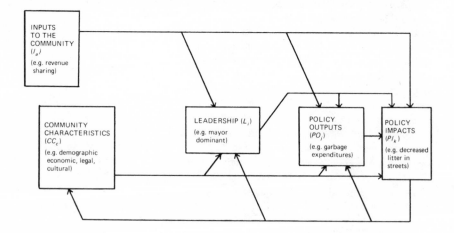

Figure 1 A basic framework of variables.

Table 1 Six methodological approaches to community power research

Original Data Collected and Analyzed	1. Case studies of individual communities (e.g. Dahl 1961)	3. Small n comparative studies (e.g. Agger, Goldrich & Swanson 1964)	5. Large n comparative studies (e.g. Clark 1973b)
Secondary Analysis of Data from Varied Sources	2. Small n impressionistic comparisons of case studies (using type no. 1 data) (e.g. Rossi 1960)	4. Large n coding and quantitative analysis (of type no. 1 and 3 data) (e.g. Walton in Aiken & Mott 1970: 443–63)	6. Large n secondary analysis (of type no. 5 data) (e.g. Williams 1973)

tions in community research. But these "city biographies" suffer the disadvantage of all biographies: the generality of their findings is never clear.

By the mid-1960s, case studies of over 150 individual communities had been completed. Many reported disparate results. Efforts to resolve these disparities began: comparisons (often impressionistic) of results from a few case studies conducted by different persons were made, and explanations for the cross-community differences were sought. Explanations in such "small n comparisons" gradually moved toward the framework in Figure 1 (e.g. Rossi 1960). But incomplete data and noncomparable results soon frustrated such efforts.

A third approach is comparison of results from two to four communities, but using data collected by a single researcher or team, following standardized methods. This logical extension of the case study has been used several times (e.g. Agger, Goldrich & Swanson 1964). But if the approach permits clear documentation of differences across communities, the small n precludes quantitative analysis.

A fourth approach made possible quantitative analysis without the expense of original data collection: coding and comparison of published case study results. J. Walton, C. Gilbert, M. Aiken, T. N. Clark, and others pursued this approach in the late 1960s (Clark 1973d: Chapter 6). But the disparate case studies were hard to code, as indicated in low explained variance in the quantitative analyses. A great deal of measurement error was clearly involved; the approach was not continued. Recently, Nelson (1974) has further documented difficulties with comparing case studies. He wrote to the original authors of studies of 43 communities, asking them to classify their results with the coding categories of later research analysts. The outcome was quite shocking: "there is at best a fifty-fifty chance of the analyst correctly identifying the power structure the author claims to have found" (Nelson, 1974: 535). Perhaps even worse, three of four pairs of co-authors disagreed as well!

A fifth approach clearly solved many of the above problems: it involved collecting directly comparable data for large numbers of communities using standardized procedures. The value of this approach was recognized for some time, but so was its major disadvantage: high costs. Only in the late 1960s did funding for such work become adequate. Several large n comparative studies were then launched in the US and abroad, as discussed below.

In the early 1970s, a sixth approach became widespread as the generous funding of the late 1960s receded: secondary analysis of data collected earlier (mainly

following the fifth approach). The richness of available materials has encouraged
activities for simple and inexpensive distribution of data sets through interrelated
professional committees and data banks (Aiken 1973, Clark 1973d:77–80).

Results from all six approaches are considered below. The discussion proceeds in
terms of the framework in Figure 1: community characteristics, leadership, policy
outputs, policy impacts, and local autonomy.

LEADERSHIP

Before other variables were appended to the framework (in Figure 1), leadership
processes (L_i) were the major focus of attention. If the range of research questions
has been extended, the issue of who governs is still a concern of most studies. Table
2 distinguishes three types of answers: base resources, power, and influence. It is
important to hold these answers separate, if only because of past confusion. Debates
developed in earlier years when researchers analyzed the data for different cells of
Table 2, some arguing that their cells were "superior" to others. But to be compared,
methods or findings must be conceived as alternatives to the same end—otherwise
they are merely "different." An alternative can stand as "superior" only when a
common standard is applied. But as Table 2 makes explicit, different standards are
often in question. Still, the threefold (or fifteenfold) distinctions in Table 2 have
emerged only recently. If anticipated by many years of research, they appear here
for the first time in this manner.

Probably the best known debate of earlier years involved Hunter, Dahl, and their
respective followers. Reputational and decisional methods were viewed as conflicting means to the same end: answering the question of who governs? (On these and
related debates, see Aiken & Mott 1970.) With time, however, the fact that they were
studying distinct phenomena has become clearer. Hunter's basic concern was *power,*
conceived as the potential for influence. Dahl's concern was *influence,* conceived as
the making of explicit decisions among alternatives. Hunter's reputational method,
inquiring of the potential import of various actors, operationalized power. Dahl's
decisional method, focusing on particular actors in reaching specific decisions,
operationalized influence. Similarly, a *power structure,* as the patterned distribution
of power, may be distinguished from a *decision-making structure,* or the patterned
distribution of influence in a social system.

Third, and distinct from power and influence, is *base resources.* (The adjective
"base" is added to distinguish base resources from some definitions of power.) Base
resources are the actor's properties or facilities that may be converted into power
or influence. Some obvious examples are money, high social status, and verbal skills.
Appropriate measures vary for different base resources. However an important class
of base resources consists of those deriving from occupancy of a particular social
status—mayor, city councilman, bank president, etc. One simple procedure for
gauging such base resources has been termed the positional method: it generates a
listing of statuses occupied by leading individuals in a community.

The three concepts of base resources, power, and influence appear in separate
rows of Table 2. Data generated by operationalizing them may be aggregated to

Table 2 Dimensions of leadership: base resources, power, and influence

General Concept	Operational Measure	Individual Properties and Individual Actors	Sectoral (Coalitional) Properties	Community Properties
1. Base resources	2. Positional method; Questions about resources posed to expert informants	3. Base resources of individual or status; e.g. the bank president controls $10 million in loan funds	4. Base resources of sector; e.g. the downtown businessmen own $30 million in real property	5. Distributional measures of base resources; e.g. $\frac{1}{4}$ of community real property is controlled by $\frac{1}{10}$ of the residents
6. Power	7. Reputational methods, including issue-specific and other variations (open ended, closed ended, etc)	8. Power of individual; e.g. the bank president is scored powerful for urban renewal	9. Power of sector; e.g. the downtown businessmen are scored medium for urban renewal	10. Properties of community power structure; e.g. the community power structure is centralized, and includes two basic coalitions, centering on the downtown businessmen and the Democratic Party
11. Influence	12. Decisional methods, including ersatz decisional and other reconstructions of decisions	13. Influence of the individual; e.g. the bank president did not participate in the urban renewal issue	14. Influence of the sector; e.g. the downtown businessmen were moderately involved in urban renewal	15. Properties of community decisionmaking structure; e.g. the decisionmaking structure is highly decentralized, and includes 14 separate coalitions

various levels: individual actor, sector, or community. All three are combined in the literature, and although some studies focus on just one or two cells, most encompass several. A few examples illustrate analyses in different cells.

One aspect of base resources was studied by Fried (1974). Limited to existing source data like most of those involved in historical work, he sought at least some leadership measure for several dozen cities in Germany, Switzerland, and Austria, from the interwar years to the present. He used a positional method. Specifically, he classified elected political leaders in the cities according to party affiliation (as in cell 3 of Table 2). Going a step beyond most positional-based research, he then used party affiliation (and other variables) to explain policy outputs.

Two studies that complement Fried's in operationalizing base resources are those of Nuttall & Bolan (1973) and Laumann & Pappi (1974, in press). Both presented expert informants with lists of resources, and had them score leading actors on continuous scales representing such resources as money, verbal skills, etc (as in cell 3). Both studies also aggregated resources available to coalitions on opposing sides of community issues (cell 4).

Bassand (1974: 293) studied power using a classical reputational item: "In general, it is said that in a commune a relatively limited number of persons positively or negatively influence the evolution of social life and public affairs. Could you tell me who presently in (this town) is important in public affairs, even if they do not hold public office or reside in the commune." His sample included 136 Swiss communes, as well as two suburbs of Geneva studied in depth. From the questionnaire data, he constructed power scores for both individuals (cell 8) and leading sectors, including public officials, the press, churches, etc (cell 9).

Bassand's project is a partial replication of the study of 51 American cities (e.g. Clark 1972b, 1973a) which included (issue-specific) reputational items as well as an ersatz decisional series for four decisions. The ersatz decisional series inquired essentially:

1. Who initiated a decision?
2. Who supported the decision?
3. Who opposed the decision?
4. Who mediated among conflicting actors on the decision?
5. Who prevailed in the decision?

Influence scores for four decisions were computed for individual statuses, such as the mayor (cell 13), by dividing the number of mentions of involvement of the status in such a decision by the number of mentions for all other statuses. Several procedures were used to aggregate such influence scores into sector scores (cell 14). Then individual and sector scores were in turn aggregated into measures of centralization of decision making for the community (cell 15).

For some studies, a single measure from one of the many cells of Table 2 can suffice. For example, Fried (1974) and others concerned primarily with explaining policy output levels have been less concerned with interrelations among cells of

Table 2. Other research has focused primarily on such interrelations. For example, the Laumann and Pappi, Bassand, and Clark studies all included measures of base resources, power, and influence. Two general questions concerning interrelations are these: through what processes can (community actors or researchers) move (*a*) horizontally to the right and (*b*) vertically down to the bottom in Table 2?

One mode of moving horizontally to the right is by building coalitions. Under what conditions do separate individuals join one another to form sectors (or coalitions)? And under what conditions do sectors remain distinct or consolidate in community-wide movements? Coalition theory suggests answers to these questions in terms of the values of individuals and sectors, their resources, and the types of issues. One idea, for example, is that *the more the inputs at the disposal of a potential coalition member are complementary to those at the disposal of other coalition members, the more likely he is to join the coalition.* This proposition assumes that a combination of resources is essential to the coalition. For example, if money and votes are both necessary for the success of an issue, actors with money are likely to seek out others with votes. Coalitions also vary with the type of issue. One typology of issues is based on the degree to which the issues resemble public or separable goods. Pure public goods are those which must be provided to everyone equally, and from which no one can be excluded. For example, polluted air is polluted equally for everyone in the area; no one (outdoors) is excluded. A patronage job, by contrast, is a nearly perfect separable good in that it can be allocated to a single person; it is not shared, and people can be excluded from it. Whether issues are more public or more separable influences in turn the types of coalitions that emerge. For example, *when outputs approximate public goods, the more the outputs desired by a coalition member are similar to those desired by other members, the more likely he is to join a coalition.* This follows, because if the output must be shared by all community members, an individual is led to support the coalition only when its members favor what he wants. But this simple logic changes for separable goods: *the more outputs approximate separable goods, the less important the preferences of coalition members are to the potential coalition member.* For example, if the output is patronage jobs, some of which may go to members of the winning coalition, particular preferences of coalition members should matter little to the potential coalition member. Both propositions, of course, assume other things to be equal, including the implications of joining different coalitions for different issues. These particular propositions are developed in Clark (1972b) and used to specify conditions under which newspapers and businessmen act together. A more general review of coalition theory is found in de Swaan (1973).

The concept of coalition implies explicit agreement among a cluster of persons to act in concerted manner. Some community actors resemble coalitions; many others are less coherent. Indeed, one may conceive of a continuum of clusters, varying in such attributes as cohesion, distinctiveness, and value consensus. Analysis of such dimensions helps classify clusters from left to right in Table 2. A recent methodological development known as network analysis has contributed to such efforts. A basic datum for network analysis is a choice matrix for members of a population: Who chooses whom? or Who knows or socializes or acts in conjunction with whom? Such raw data—deriving from interviews, participant observation, or self-administered questionnaires—may be arrayed in matrixes with all members of the population $(1...n)$ listed on both x and y axes. Choices are indicated in cells of the matrix. Choice matrixes may be multiplied or divided by other column vectors or matrixes, such as value patterns or social background characteristics; or one may seek to explain the frequency of social choices using values or social background characteristics. These data may be analyzed to isolate clusters using a variety of procedures—matrix algebra, factor analysis, multidimensional scaling, etc. Originating as a simple mathematical procedure to study small groups, network analysis has been applied to community leaders by Laumann & Pappi (1974, in press) in studies of one town in Germany and two in Illinois, all under 100,000. They express reservations about applying the technique to larger cities. Miller (1975) was bolder: he used interviews with, supplemented by questionnaires mailed to, leaders in Boston, New York, Philadelphia, Baltimore, and Washington, DC to collect social choice data, which he analyzed using a related network approach. Network analysis clearly has advantages in terms of its precision and statistical manipulability; it portrays dimensions of social clusters more graphically than traditional fieldwork procedures. A major disadvantage, at least to date, is the necessity for extensive researcher-collected data about community leaders. Because of this, the approach is expensive to apply to numerous cities in comparative manner. Although much network analysis has focused more on power than on influence, Laumann & Pappi (1974) regressed the results of decisional outcomes on the base resources of actors favoring and opposing the decisions. They interpreted their results as weights for conversion of different base resources into influence.

This brings us to the theoretical question of how to move *down* the columns of Table 2. Several approaches exist. Many deterministic theories, more common in the nineteenth century but still with us, posited the preeminent role of a single resource or class of resources for most decisions. Racial, military, legal, and economic determinists each held that their class of variables was most essential. The beauty of such deterministic theories is that they obviate the need to consider why base resources are converted into power and in turn into influence: without the base resource-power-influence distinctions, they simply are, almost by definition.

Dahl (1961) reacted strongly against this mode of thinking, and by helping to replace terms like "constitutional framework" or "economic substructure" with the more general "resources," thus emphasized their similarity to one another by virtue of their mere potentiality for influence. He introduced such terms as "pyramiding" of resources and "slack" to capture the degree to which members of a social system simultaneously converted their resources into influence. But why, when, and in what manner did such pyramiding take place? Where Dahl left off, others have continued.

An approach developed by Clark (1968: Chapter 3), Stinchcombe (1968: 191 ff.) and Coleman (1971) considers the properties of resources in relation to each other and in relation to requisites for influence in particular issue areas. Matrixes were thus constructed indicating the "prices" at which various resources could be converted into one another in "wholesale" manner, or the outcomes of decisions "bought" in "retail" transactions. But if this general approach assumed enough comparability of resources across individuals and situations to create matrixes with even rough "prices," it still considered transaction costs significant—enough so to be summarized in matrixes. This helped direct attention to the import of complementary resources for building coalitions. But the assumption of nontrivial transaction costs prevented direct articulation with classical economic theory.

Coleman (1973a) introduced further simplifying assumptions, including zero transaction costs for conversion of resources. Assuming a set of rational actors with limited stocks of resources and fixed interests, he examines conditions under which equilibria can be reached. His moving force is the intensity of preference (or amount of "interest") of each actor in a given decision, compared with that of others in the system. The general model conceives of actors as parliamentarians; it is extended by considering logrolling, committee memberships, and relations with constituents. By using more consistent formalization, and including even a simulation program for modeling alternative results, Coleman has set new standards of mathematical elegance in this area. The great question underlying the analysis, however, is how applicable its results are to various empirical situations—given that its assumptions are more restrictive than most of classical economics. Still, in providing a model of coherent theory, and several precise results, the study points to crucial processes and conditions that others may well address in a less strict theoretical frame or in empirical work.

This direction is taken by Coleman (e.g. 1973b) and others (e.g. Burt 1974) in analyzing "corporate actors," rather than isolated individuals, as in Coleman (1973a). The corporate actors concept is similar to "sector" or "coalition" in involving clusters of individuals. But it goes further in specifying that they form agreements which assign some control over their individual resources to agents who may then act for the collectivity. The approach is promising; it has yet to yield many specific results.

Coleman's (1973a) model deals with activation of resources (or moving down the columns of Table 2) by placing the analytical burden on the interest structure of discrete individuals: the greater an individual's interest in an issue, the greater his concentration of resources in it. Useful as far as it goes, this approach still ignores most social structural conditions. In contrast, Clark (1973d) focuses on the dependence of resource activation on certain structural properties. *The greater the internal differentiation of a sector, the less the activation of its members' resources.* This is an idea that again builds on the assumption of nontrivial transaction costs. Whether one considers members of an ethnic group, or a city ward, or firms in an industry, the more differentiated they are from one another, the higher are the transaction costs which must be overcome to achieve collective action. For example, a city with a diversified economic base is likely to have less political participation by its businessmen than a company town. Similarly, *the higher an actor's input and output transactions involving other community actors, the greater his activation of resources for community decisions.* For example, a newspaper that obtains its news and sells its papers locally is more likely to activate its resources in local matters than an assembly plant which borrows money, sets wages, and sells its product in national markets. Doubtless an actor (or sector) is likely to have greater interests in local affairs if he (it) has more important local transactions. But local transactions also build communication channels and local solidarities likely to involve him in local affairs. These general propositions, developed in unpublished work on the 51 cities, subsume a number of more specific propositions and findings about coalitions and the public involvement of newspapers, businessmen, and political leaders.

Such ideas as those above on resource activation, networks, and coalitions suggest new lines for analysis of community leadership. Many recent studies of leadership configurations across cities generally report results in terms of the relative involvement of mayors, business actors, newspapers, and civic leaders [e.g. Kirby et al (1973) for 91 American cities, Clark (1973b) for 51 American cities, Aiken & Depre (1974) for 196 Belgian cities, Jambrek (1974) for 16 Yugoslav communes, Morlock (1974) for 91 American cities, and Rossi, Berk & Eidson (1974) for 15 American cities]. The results, as presented by their authors, are important. Many of these data are also available for secondary analysis, and may thus be used to elaborate and test new theories of leadership.

COMMUNITY CHARACTERISTICS

What one could see as a comparative perspective began to emerge in certain case studies of community power. As case studies mounted in number, many with differing results, researchers began to comment on possible sources of variation. For example, an author might suggest that centralization of power was due to the small population size of the city studied, or to its lack of economic diversification.

Gradually, in this way, researchers sought to identify community characteristics (CC_c in Figure 1) which could explain variations in leadership patterns across communities. Ad hoc hypotheses were gradually supplanted by efforts to codify propositions about the most important community characteristics, leading toward the sort of framework shown in Figure 1. For example, in Clark (1968: Chapter 5) a series of 38 propositions was developed, such as the following: *the more diverse the economic structures within a community, the more decentralized the decision-making structure.* These and related efforts (e.g. Aiken & Mott 1970) helped advance earlier work by identifying a series of community characteristics which could affect other variables in the model. They alerted the researcher to specific variables for specifying equations like 1 and 2 above.

As community power studies began to incorporate comparative thinking, researchers drew on developments from adjoining fields where community characteristics had long been a central concern. A handbook synthesizing such efforts is Berry (1972), which brought together several traditions of "city classification," "factorial ecology," etc. With comparative data being generated on a large scale, and data banks taking shape, hundreds of variables could serve to operationalize propositions involving community characteristics. Faced with this wealth of data, many researchers followed factor analytic procedures as summarized in Berry (1972).

Their basic idea was to create data matrixes from scores for many (often hundreds) of variables for large numbers of cities. The data matrix was then reduced, generally to less than 10 factors, through factor analysis and related procedures. The resulting factors were often entered in contingency tables or regression equations (resembling 1 and 2 above). Examples: Bassand (1974), Bonjean (1971), Eberts, Eby & Kluess (1969), International Studies of Values in Politics (1971), Pusic (1974), Roig, Mingasson & Kukawka (1970). Three basic factors recur in numerous samples and national settings, associated with socio-economic status, life cycle (exemplified by suburbs with young couples), and ethnic or racial differentiation. Although additional factors have often been extracted, they generally grow increasingly diffi-cult to interpret. Strengths of this general approach include its data-reduction ability and the generation of nearly uncorrelated sets of community characteristics, which nicely eliminate problems of multicollinearity in equation estimation. The major weaknesses concern interpretation. "Factor ambiguity" troubles virtually every factor, as factors are a weighted composite of many different variables. As a (sub-stantively) arbitrary statistical algorithm generates specific weights for each vari-able, their interpretation is often ambiguous, or, at worst, meaningless. When several ambiguous factors combine in statistical models (like regression equations), "model muddling" results: regression coefficients are distorted by the measurement error from ambiguous factors. Factor-based models are compared with their analogues estimated from individual variables in Clark (1972a), and further problems are discussed.

Problems of interpretation have plagued many census-derived variables in com-munity research, even without the complications brought by factor analysis. A leading case is the MPO ratio. Before original comparative data were collected on leadership patterns, A. Hawley (1963) sought to create a measure of power centrali-zation from US Census data. Starting from numbers of persons by job classification, he computed the ratio of managers, proprietors, and officials (MPO) to the total employed civilian labor force in each of many cities. A lower ratio, he suggested, implied greater concentration of power. The ease of computation led many to follow in his footsteps (e.g. Aiken & Alford 1974). But nagging doubts led to several probes of the MPO ratio's validity. Three separate studies applied overlapping methods. Aiken classified 31 case studies of community power along a four-point scale from pyramidal to dispersed (Aiken & Mott 1970: 487–525). Comparing these results with Hawley's MPO ratios, he found a negative relation, the opposite of what Hawley had hypothesized. Williams (1973) pursued a similar analysis using 44 case study communities coded by Walton, and 17 communities where the Bonjean two-step reputational approach was employed. Correlating MPO ratios with these data, he found (as did Aiken) a negative relation for the sample of 44, but a weak positive relation for the sample of 17. Williams (1973), Aiken & Alford (1974), and Dodge (1972) followed nearly identical approaches. All three correlated MPO ratios with an Index of Decentralization computed from NORC interviews in 51 cities (re-ported in Bonjean, Clark & Lineberry 1971: 297). They found $r = -.46$, supporting the earlier results that revealed that the MPO ratio indicated the opposite of what Hawley had intended. Williams concludes: "anyone interested in measuring power through the use of census data would do well to scrap the MPO."

A broader question asks: What do census data (on community characteristics) measure? Income, occupation, education, national background, and other basic variables can be viewed as measures of base resources, in which case the MPO ratio taps a concept different from that tapped by reputational or decisional studies. Census variables have also been increasingly conceived as measures of values. But this interpretation is best considered in discussing policy outputs and impacts.

POLICY OUTPUTS

Just as a comparative perspective pushed research back one analytical step from leadership to community characteristics, so it helped move it forward to policy outputs. Policy outputs were treated in many case studies (e.g. Dahl 1961) as the logical outcome of decision-making in the community. Occasional passages might express concern about specific interpretations. Still the general message was clear: policy outputs quite simply followed from decisions made by decision makers. Stated thus, the matter seems almost sorrowfully trite. It takes on interest, however, when the researcher has at hand information not only about decision-making processes but also about community characteristics for numerous communities. One research question then immediately arises: how much variance in policy outputs is explained by decision-making variables in contrast to community characteristics? The portion of Figure 1 summarized in equation 2 structures the same basic question.

We note in passing that concern for explaining policy outputs developed almost simultaneously in studies of counties, states, and national governments (cf Sharkansky 1970, Heclo 1972). These were often self-conscious efforts by political scientists to assess the explanatory power of "political" versus "environmental" variables, where environmental included roughly everything other than the political process. Numerous studies emphasized the limited variance explained by the available political variables (often party affiliation of leaders and competition in legislatures or city councils). Far more important were community characteristics—demographic, economic, etc. These results generated several reactions.

First was a chastening sensitivity to constraints on political leaders, especially at the city level. The great pressures on American local leaders, punctuated by violence in the late 1960s, led many mayors and observers to despair at their limited alternatives (e.g. Lupsha 1974, Kotter & Lawrence 1974).

A second reaction was to reexamine the leadership implications of certain socioeconomic characteristics of cities earlier dismissed as "environmental." For example, the startling findings that the percentage of Roman Catholics and particularly Irish residents were more important than most other variables in explaining expenditure levels (Clark 1975) suggest that they may be as "political" as the legal form of government. Why? Because, it seems, in many American cities the Irish played a central role in creating strong (mainly Democratic) parties, obtaining patronage positions in city agencies, and enlisting the support of other Catholics in important primaries and bond referenda. The result: increased public spending. Several studies have used "foreign born" and other variables highly correlated with Catholics and Irish without considering the implications of such results on local leadership. The specific pattern seems limited to the US, however; the percentage of Catholics even in Canadian cities does not increase expenditures (Fowler & Lineberry 1972). No doubt other community characteristics have similar, if less dramatic, impacts on policy outputs. They too demand more careful examination.

A third reaction was an increased interest in "spatial models" of collective decision making, building on work by economists Anthony Downs, Otto Davis, and others (cf Riker & Ordeshook 1973 and the journal *Public Choice*). From some basic assumptions of classical economics, they derived a conclusion of dramatic simplicity: given pure competition for votes among political leaders, citizen values will be transformed into policy outputs as if by an invisible politician. Politicians become invisible as they compete with one another to maximize policy preferences of the median voter; if one politician wavers, he will be replaced. In the process, logically, L_i disappears from the analysis. This is not an appealing conclusion to those professionally concerned with the policy-making process—i.e. most researchers concerned with community power, among others. But if the logic was troublesome, it became harder to dismiss it outright as results mounted showing the limited impact of L_i variables. Fried (1973) and Hawkins (1971) review a number of empirical studies that, if not explicitly concerned with spatial models, are nevertheless "socio-political" in orientation. That is, an archetypical study provides estimates for equation 2 above, although sometimes deleting I_a.

As work on the problem has increased, the initial hypothesis of convergence to the median has been modified. Recent analyses, even within the spatial modeling tradition, have recognized the oversimplification of initial results. The mediating role of parties and leaders in converting citizen values into policies has been stressed. Considered as actors with their own logic, parties can be analyzed as taking positions reflecting compromises among their own members (Coleman 1972). Analogously, candidates will shift their strategies with varying goals of plurality or policy or vote maximation, and with varying attitudes toward risk (cf Aranson, Hinich & Ordeshook 1974). And leaders will pay special attention to sources of political profit (Frohlich, Oppenheimer & Young 1971). The earlier simplicity vanishes once such complications are introduced. But they do help articulate spatial modeling efforts with the community power tradition.

In particular, they stress the necessity to be quite careful in positing linkages between citizens and leaders before comparing their specific policy preferences. Most empirical studies of this sort compare rankings of "important problems" without systematically considering predictions from alternative models of the spatial modeling approach (cf Verba & Nie 1972, Nix & Seerley 1972). Pappi & Laumann (1974) move a step ahead to distinguish policy preferences of separate community sectors and to link them to different leaders.

Spatial modeling focuses attention on the value implications of community characteristics "external" to the political process, and their linkages to "internal" political process variables. This populist conception of government is countered by "incrementalism." If an extreme "external" approach would neglect L_i variables, uncompromising incrementalists neglect CC_c variables; for them L_i variables far outweigh the rest. The approach derives from the theories of public administration and national policy making of H. Simon, C. E. Lindbloom, A. Wildavsky, and others, adapted to municipal budgeting by Crecine (1969) and Meltsner (1971).

Crecine formulated a simulation model of the budgetary process, based on fieldwork and budgetary data from Cleveland, Detroit, and Pittsburgh. Meltsner investigated budget-making processes in Oakland, California. Both stressed the heads of government agencies as reflecting a general bureaucratic mentality—captured in a process of "incremental" change, e.g. a 5% increase for all agencies over last year's budget. The dynamic element of the model thus becomes the (internal) agency's budget request, not (external) citizen preferences. And agency requests are basically trimmed a bit and then implemented by mayors, city managers, and city councils —in the incrementalist models. In support of these models, incrementalists generally analyze time series for reasonably limited periods: Crecine and Meltsner consider about a decade. And they compare each city only with its past, not with other cities. By contrast, the spatial models, and "socio-political" empirical studies, have generally analyzed cross-sectional rather than time-series data.

Linkages are needed to articulate spatial and incrementalist theories, and other work on collective decisions. A first step toward such convergence is found in Jackson's (1972 and unpublished) work on Cleveland and Boston. In both cities he used time series, but for as long as 20 years. Instead of actual socio-political data, he focused on the major external-internal linkage point: the mayor. Including a dummy variable for the term of the mayor, he found incremental-inspired variables to work well during the terms of most mayors, but that changes in mayors could bring substantial changes in budgetary outputs. Further studies employing combined cross-sectional and time-series data are needed to chart the empirical terrain and help link the complementary theories.

More careful classifications of policy outputs are also called for to suggest alternative functional forms and patterns of coefficients for equations like 2 above. For example, for years the impact of centralized decision-making on policy outputs has been debated. Two traditions have emerged. One tradition, from V. O. Key, and continued by I. Sharkansky, T. R. Dye, and R. I. Hofferbert, investigated the hypothesis that decentralized decision-making (often operationalized as competition among parties) *increases* public expenditures, especially for welfare-type activities. Empirical results have been weak or inconsistent (e.g. Sharkansky 1970).

A second tradition, from E. Banfield, A. Hawley, and D. Rogers, among others, maintained essentially the opposite (e.g. Kirby et al 1973). They suggested in case studies of Chicago and New York, and comparative studies of school integration and fluoridation, that uncoordinated, fragmented (decentralized) decision-making prevented the minimal cohesion necessary for reaching decisions, thus *decreasing* policy outputs. A basically similar proposition summarizes recent work on "interorganizational relations" by Turk (1973), Aiken & Alford (1974), and Warren, Rose & Bergunder (1974). They suggest that cities with more developed horizontal ties, linking (primarily civic) organizations to one another, are more likely to mobilize the support necessary to increase policy outputs, and especially to obtain federal grants-in-aid (OEO, Model Cities, etc). Rephrased: centralization increases policy outputs.

These conflicting traditions demand reconciliation. One solution is to distinguish *types* of policy outputs differentially linked to centralization (Clark 1973b, Ostrom 1974). If one considers policy outputs in terms of a continuum ranging from highly public goods (e.g. fluoridation) to highly separable goods (e.g. patronage jobs), then the two traditions may be reconciled in a single statement: *centralization encourages public goods, but decentralization generates separable goods.* That is, centralized coordination ensures the agreement necessary for enacting public goods like school integration or fluoridation. But decentralized decision-making patterns, by forcing leaders to respond to numerous and competing citizen demands, lead to higher outputs of separable goods, like policy patrols or patronage jobs. (Note that this proposition articulates directly with those above concerning coalitions and policy outputs.) Even if centralization "explains" less variance in policy outputs than many community characteristics, as an L_i variable it is more open to change and thus of greater policy interest.

The proposition nicely subsumes numerous earlier findings, but almost no work has been designed to test or extend it. This suggests a strategic research site.

An aspect of policy output receiving much popular attention, and some research, is service delivery patterns. The norm of equality has been considered violated if public services were provided differentially to social or geographic sectors of cities; many lawsuits have been filed on these grounds.

One of few studies probing implications of differentiated service delivery is Buchanan (1971). He presents a tightly reasoned deductive model and uses it to consider implications of alternative policies of service delivery. Rigorously equal service delivery, he points out, may hurt the poor most of all. This sharply counterintuitive result flows from reasonably unrestrictive assumptions: that local taxes finance most local services, that the more affluent pay higher taxes, and that they can move, to suburbs or elsewhere. He then demonstrates that if city political leaders are concerned with the welfare of the poor, and are rational, they should provide a differntiated tax/service bundle to separate neighborhoods in amounts which (for the rich) are competitive with suburbs. Such differentiation, of necessity, violates the norm of equal service provision. But if a differentiated policy is not followed, the economic incentives for the more affluent to leave will simply increase. Empirically, of course, the more affluent have been emigrating for several decades from many central cities in the US. More probing examination of alternative policies, like that of Buchanan, seems inevitable if any meaningful change is to occur.

Presently available data for measuring inter- or especially intracity service delivery are very scanty. Weaknesses of budgetary data are clear: they include unstandardized categories, noncomparable costs, unrecorded transfer payments, and varying relations to performance levels (Clark 1973c, 1974a, Baldwin 1974). Performance, performance/cost, or citizen satisfaction measures all have advantages, in principle, over simple expenditures; but they in turn pose problems, to which we turn. At present, for comparing output levels across many cities, budgetary allocations probably remain the least insufficient measure. Important work toward developing more adequate performance measures is underway at the Urban Institute, by E. Ostrom and her co-workers, and others. [Cf the articles by Hatry on productivity measures, Young on education vouchers, and Ostrom & Whitaker on police services, all in Hawley & Rodgers (1974); Lineberry & Welch's list of output measures, Fisk & Winnie's discussion of inspector ratings, and Liebert's analysis of "functional inclusiveness," all in Bonjean 1974.]

POLICY IMPACTS

Impacts, in Figure 1, are feedbacks to other variables from each policy output. Several distinct PI_k's could be indicated, in particular more than one for each PO_j. But if an almost limitless number of PI_k's could be shown, those considered more seriously are normally defined by the goals of the agency providing a given policy output, or by other officials or outside agencies evaluating effects of a program. Indeed, the basic problem in assessing impacts resembles that of evaluation research: What difference did the program make? The similarity of these two areas does not yet seem to have been recognized, nor experiences from each area compared. The analogy suggests the import of systematic monitoring of socio-economic characteristics of cities to assess their changes. This of course is a major rationale for urban social indicators. Several lists and categorizations of indicators have been prepared (e.g. Moynihan 1967, Rossi 1972) which encompass varied urban phenomena. Collecting and reporting data on them constitutes a basically descriptive use of social indicators.

More ambitious is data collection for indicators interrelated in models (ideally mathematical) so that impacts can be measured and explained with the variables in the models (Clark 1973c). Equation 3 indicates one basic structure for such models. For example, how much does fire damage (PI_1) decrease with changes in the number of firemen (PO_1); with fire fighting technology—such as types of fire engines (PO_2) and hoses (PO_3); with response time (PO_4); with having a Democratic mayor (L_1); with the fact of being in a city that has low population density (CC_1), numerous heavy industries (CC_2), and considerable local autonomy (I_1), but little revenue sharing (I_2)? The regression weights ($b_{k1} \ldots b_{kn}$) generated by estimating such equations (pace the standard caveats) provide the policy maker with information as to how much effect on fire damage should result from changes in variables in the model. This estimate of the benefits of a given policy (e.g. a 10% increase in the number of firemen) can then be assessed against its costs, fiscal and other, by community decision makers. As the example makes clear, however, assessing the impact of most variables presupposes data on them in numerous communities. Although community characteristic measures are readily available, practically no systematic data are reported for performance-type policy outputs (like response time). Some individual cities (e.g. New York and Chicago) collect such data in great detail—down to the man hours and cost of returning lost dogs. But an individual city does not provide enough internal variation on most basic variables to permit estimation of their importance. Significant research in this area thus awaits more comparable data. Individual cities could benefit, but have difficulty mounting the effort without national coordination. The pressures of citizen demands for increased service, without increased taxes, may encourage federal agencies or national organizations of cities to begin the task. Several European countries already collect such data.

New programs, it seems, are often mounted under pressure of crisis; so, often, are large research efforts. Several major studies were launched under the cloud of riots in the late 1960s. One was a survey of 4300 citizens in 10 cities, sponsored by the

Urban Observatory Program of the National League of Cities–US Conference of Mayors, with both federal and local support. Questions were posed to citizens about their preferences concerning various urban services—police, fire, education, welfare, etc. They were also asked which services they would be willing to support with higher taxes, and what form the taxes should take. Basic marginal tabulations were interesting (reported in Wilburn & Williams 1971) and led to some immediate consequences: the mayor of Boston, for example, learning that citizens were favorable to more stringent enforcement of housing codes, immediately increased housing inspections. But many items were so interrelated with other variables that policy makers were often reluctant to act rapidly. Several analyses in progress link the data with various explanatory models.

Another large scale effort was mandated by the National Advisory Commission on Civil Disorders (1968). The major variable in this study of 15 cities was citizen satisfaction with urban services—especially police, welfare, and education. Schuman & Gruenberg (1970, 1972) sought to explain citizen satisfaction using socioeconomic characteristics of the respondent and his neighbors, social phenomena like crime rates, and public service levels. They estimated the variance explained by each of these classes of variables, separately for black and white citizens. They documented more thoroughly than ever before how much citizen satisfaction varied by city, but also how more variance seemed to be explained by characteristics of respondents and their neighbors than by urban service levels.

The urban service measures available to Schuman & Grunberg were crude. The same citizen satisfaction data were analyzed by Rossi, Berk & Eidson (1974); they were complemented, however, by probably the most comprehensive set of measures to date of urban service delivery. Detailed interviews were conducted with persons providing four major services to poor blacks: policemen, social workers, school teachers, and small merchants. Information was gathered on numerous institutional practices (enforcement of regulations by police, use of "sharp" business practices by small merchants, etc). Several L_i variables were also collected for each city, including the power of different leading actors and the political involvement of blacks. Generally, as in equations 2 and 3, these three levels (city, service-neighborhood, individual) of rich data were analyzed where the major PI_k's were citizen satisfaction with each service (PO_j's). Compared to Schuman & Grunberg, however, and virtually all other research to date, Rossi, Berk & Edison could provide more adequate estimates of the variance accounted for by each variable class in their model: not just crime rates, but also police practices; business power at the municipal level, but also business practices of merchants in local neighborhoods, and characteristics of other persons residing there. Several other studies of citizen values and related matters are underway; it is unclear how many will confront such complex issues with the same thoroughness.

As research sophistication mounts, so does our critical appreciation of what else can be done, and of where weakness remains. Given the amount of research in progress in this area, it is useful to typologize the basic variables, disaggregating them further than in most work to date. We start from two basic dimensions, shown in Table 3. First are public policy characteristics, of four types from 1 to 4. If 3 could

Table 3 Dimensions of public policy and citizen attitudes [from Clark (1947b)]

		Citizen Attitudinal Characteristics			
		(a) Isolated citizen preferences	(b) Preferences of citizen in his socioeconomic context	(c) Perceptions of citizen	(d) Evaluations of citizen
Public Policy Characteristics	1. Fiscal policy outputs (e.g. refuse collection budget per year)	1	2	3	4
	2. Performance policy outputs (e.g. tons of refuse collected per year)	5	6	7	8
	3. Socioeconomic conditions and consequences (e.g. amount of refuse generated)	9	10	11	12
	4. Policy impacts (e.g. decrease in amount of refuse in streets)	13	14	15	16

exist without 2, then $4 = 3 - 2$. But to follow the example shown, no city can permit much time to pass without collecting refuse. Hence, referring to the other dimension, citizens seldom appreciate what is routine. Across the top, four types of citizen attitudinal characteristics are distinguished. Isolated preferences a are those the individual holds apart from his immediate context; these shift to b when he responds in terms of his surroundings. Further, b is structured by c: how he perceives these surroundings. For example, he may consider that his garbage collectors do a good job (box 6). But if he perceives (in box 11) that poor people generate more refuse than others, and he lives in a poor neighborhood, he may conclude logically that streets in his neighborhood should normally show more refuse (box 16) than those in other neighborhoods.

Such a simple accounting scheme makes explicit the difficulties in interpreting a standard Likert scale item like "How satisfied are you with garbage collection in your neighborhood?" Without measures of other variables affecting the response, a policy output's "impact" will be misestimated.

A complex but related issue is how to obtain data on citizen preferences, and then analyze and interpret them. The issue takes on new significance for community decision making as surveys of citizen preferences assume a more central role in certain cities. "Revealed preference" measures include voting in referenda and elections; but party loyalty, blurring of candidates with numerous issues, and low turnout rates complicate ecological analyses and pose formidable problems of interpretation. Interview surveys are thus more generally trusted. Yet these vary dramatically. Simple "polls" requesting yes-no answers are very common, but provide no measure of respondents' intensity of preference. Continuous (often Likert-type) scales assess intensity, but they normally do not impose a "budget constraint" —respondents can state, for example, that they want more spent on all city services, without being forced to recognize fiscal limitations. The "budget pie" format was designed to confront these problems. It exists in several variations (cf Hoinville

1971, Beardsley, in press)—including pegs on a board, poker-type chips, and lines drawn on a circle—but the recurring idea is to have the respondent divide a budget "pie" into pieces representing basic service areas (police, fire, etc). Still, if budget pies answer some analytical problems, they raise others in turn. How to convert fiscal measures to performance measures to attitudinal measures (or "utility")? How to avoid or minimize strategic behavior? How to measure multidimensional attitudes, construct ordinal or cardinal scales, and make interpersonal comparisons? How to handle attitude change and opinion leaders? And how to aggregate preferences and define sectors? Clark (1974b) attempted to provide as reliable answers to these questions as are available. Social scientists must nevertheless remain circumspect about introducing readily misunderstood research tools into policy-making situations. E. Allardt, A. Barton, E. Ostrom, D. Scott, and others have important work in progress on these issues [cf also Hanna (1974)].

FEDERALISM, DECENTRALIZATION, AND LOCAL AUTONOMY

The growing urban role of the US federal government, and increased study of comparable patterns in other countries, have heightened our sensitivity to inputs to the local community. No community is a closed system. Nevertheless, until recently most urban research has assumed an autonomous community. This is doubtless justifiable for some purposes. But as grants-in-aid increase, as legal constraints are more stringently enforced, and as higher administrators grow in number and local involvement, such inputs become fundamental elements of community life.

There has simultaneously been increased questioning of appropriate legal structures. Popular demands for decentralization and community control in the 1960s were complemented by analytical efforts to formulate criteria for assignment of functions to different governmental levels. Dahl's (1967) analysis emphasized the trade off, as governmental units increase in size, between (a) the involvement of a single individual in a collective decision and (b) the importance of that decision. His and other writings on decentralization were criticized in Clark (1970, 1973d: 36–39) and a citizen preference approach suggested. The citizen preference approach has subsequently been developed much further by Rothenberg (1970) and Mueller (1971). This approach underlies a relativistic normative position on decentralization: the "best" level of aggregation varies both with citizen preferences and technical characteristics of public services. It starts, in economists' terms, from a utility function for each individual. This includes not only Dahl's preferences for participation and control, but also all things the individual desires. Each preference is weighted in intensity, and a budget constraint limits the individual's total consumption. Summing preferences across individuals generates a collective demand function for different services. The costs of supplying services in turn vary with the factors producing them; some increase continually with population size, others show economies of scale. The intersection of such demand and supply functions generates, in terms of this framework, optimal levels of decentralization for different public services.

A more positive and less normative approach is to inquire how much autonomy exists in various communities, and why. These questions have been stressed, among others, by observers of non-American communities concerned with explaining cross-national variations. Kesselman & Rosenthal (1974) pursue this avenue, and suggest that the literature on comparative political development can illuminate local processes, just as local results can bring more perspective to (national) comparative politics. An extreme formulation (approximated in Anton 1974) is that in some situations local autonomy is so limited that local politics becomes national politics, *en petit*. This reasoning can lead to study of national party affiliation and social backgrounds of local officials (e.g. Kesselman 1974, Tarrow 1974). The impact of national economic structures on local processes has also been emphasized in France (e.g. Birnbaum 1973, Castells & Godard 1974, Birnbaum et al 1974) and in Latin America (e.g. Walton & Portes, in press). Methodological issues in cross-national comparison are pursued in Hirschi (1973), Miller (1973), and Ostrowski & Teune (1974).

Often, however, local autonomy is better conceived as a continuum than a dichotomy. One is then led to ask what characteristics, of both national systems and local communities, enhance local autonomy? Several recent works bear on these questions. Westerstahl (1974) compares values of leaders and citizens in 36 Swedish communes: in smaller, rural towns, citizens' and leaders' values are closer to each other than in more urban areas. This indicates, he suggests, greater cultural and political autonomy in the smaller communes. Jambrek (1974), studying 16 Yugoslav communes, asked informants to assess the impact of different actors on decisions of their communal assembly. The state (or republican) government, he found, was the leading actor. But in analyzing correlates of state involvement, he discovered the opposite pattern from Westerstahl: smaller, less economically developed, more agricultural communes were *less* autonomous. He interprets this as deriving from state policies providing such communes with larger subsidies; these in turn bring greater supervision. Bassand & Fragnière (1974) interviewed 389 leaders in 9 Swiss communes about perceived and desired local autonomy. They found older leaders who had worked and resided longer in the commune, and members of center or conservative political parties, to perceive greater communal autonomy than leaders with the opposite characteristics. This indicates, they suggest, that the older, more established leaders had created more extensive personal linkages with higher officials. As such linkages enhance their control over the fates of their communes, they perceive and desire less (legal) autonomy than leaders with fewer linkages. Emphasis on linkages with the national government recurs in work by Roig, Mingasson & Kukawka (1970 and unpublished) and Becquart (1974), who found that French mayors with stronger linkage patterns obtained more public works for their towns. Jacob (1974) presents related findings for 120 communities in Poland, India, Yugoslavia, and the US. Responses to an autonomy question show Yugoslav and US leaders to perceive the most autonomy, Polish and Indian leaders the least. But although a second item concerning desired autonomy correlated with other value items—such as greater personal political efficacy and higher standards for public office—it was not related to several local policy outputs.

A number of case studies, evaluations of federal programs, and other reports have been completed on federal-local relations in American cities (e.g. Sundquist 1969, Pressman & Wildavsky 1973). But these seldom articulate their results with community power work.

Clark (1974c:21–54) formulates a series of 48 propositions which subsume findings in this area by linking local autonomy to characteristics of the national society and of the community. A few examples: National centralization of administrative and party structures should decrease local autonomy, as should increases in the (absolute) number of communities and coincidence of social cleavages at local and national levels. Within countries, local communities with greater natural, economic, and social resources should have greater autonomy, as should those with more institutions supporting localism (newspapers, churches, schools, etc). Political power deriving from cohesive electorates, strong party structures, longer terms of office for local officials, and similar base resources should also encourage more local autonomy.

In brief, over the past five years, a concern for local autonomy has significantly entered the community power tradition. Several case studies, some cross-community comparisons, and a few cross-national works have addressed the matter. But if such results have been tentatively codified, the work of relating local autonomy to other community variables in an empirically grounded model largely remains a task for the future.

CONCLUSION

Three recent trends are encouraging, and promise to continue. First, much more ambitious efforts at data collection than in earlier years permit measurement of numerous variables whose interrelations and relative import can be estimated empirically. Second, increasing theoretical sophistication is generating systematic and often formal models that structure analysis of the new data. Third, flowing directly from these two trends is a dramatic increase in immediate policy implications. Emerging research can provide quite specific answers to such questions as the following: How many votes will change if garbage trucks are shifted into an area? How should a federal agency adapt health service organizations to different kinds of cities? How can citizens' groups have the greatest impact on different types of city agencies? To respond to such questions has long been a goal of researchers in this area. The answers improve each year.

*Literature Cited**

Agger, R. E., Goldrich, D., Swanson, B. E. 1964. *The Rulers and the Ruled.* New York: Wiley. 789 pp.

Aiken, M. 1973. Comparative cross-national research on subnational units in Western Europe: problems, data sources, and a proposal. *J. Comp. Admin.* 4: 437–72

Aiken, M., Alford, R. R. 1974. Community structure and innovation: public housing, urban renewal, and the war on poverty. See Clark 1974: 231–88

Aiken, M., Depre, R. 1974. *Politics and Policy Outputs: a Study of City Expenditures Among 196 Belgian Cities.* Presented to Comm. Community Res., 8th World Congr., Int. Sociol. Assoc., Toronto

Aiken, M., Mott, P. E., Eds. 1970. *The Structure of Community Power.* New York: Random House. 540 pp.

Anton, T. J. 1974. The pursuit of efficiency: values and structure in the changing politics of Swedish municipalities. See Clark 1974c: 87–110

Aranson, P. H., Hinich, M. J., Ordeshook, P. C. 1974. Election goals and strategies. *Am. Pol. Sci. Rev.* 68:135–52

Baldwin, T. E. 1974. *Community Structure and the Adaptation of Municipal Finance.* Presented to Comm. Community Res., 8th World Congr., Int. Sociol. Assoc., Toronto

Bassand, M. 1974. *Urbanisation et pouvoir politique.* Geneva: Libr. Univ. Georg. 311 pp.

Bassand, M., Fragnière, J. P. 1974. *Autonomie Communale en Suisse: Analyse des Pratiques et des Représentations.* Presented to Comm. Community Res., 8th World Congr., Int. Sociol. Assoc., Toronto

Beardsley, P. L. *Measuring public opinion on priorities.* Sage Professional Papers in American Politics, 04–014. Beverly Hills & London: Sage. Unpublished

Becquart, J. L. 1974. *French Mayors and Policy Outputs.* Presented to Comm. Community Res., 8th World Congr., Int. Sociol. Assoc., Toronto

Berry, B. J. L., Ed. 1972. *City Classification Handbook.* New York: Wiley-Interscience. 394 pp.

Birnbaum, P. 1973. Le pouvoir local: de la décision au système. *Rev. Fr. Sociol.* 14:336–51

Birnbaum, P., Castells, M., Du Boisberranger, G., Clark, T. N. 1974. Controverse sur le pouvoir local. *Rev. Fr. Sociol.* 15:237–62

Bonjean, C. M. 1971. The community as research site and object of inquiry. See Bonjean, Clark & Lineberry 1971: 5–15

Bonjean, C. M., Ed. 1974. A symposium: measuring urban agency output and performance. *Soc. Sci. Quart.* 54:691–764

Bonjean, C. M., Clark, T. N., Lineberry, R. L., Eds. 1971. *Community Politics.* New York: Free Press. 403 pp.

Buchanan, J. M. 1971. Principles of urban fiscal strategy. *Public Choice* 11:1–17

Burt, R. S. 1974. *Power in a Social Structure.* Presented to Comm. Community Res., 8th World Congr., Int. Sociol. Assoc., Toronto

Castells, M., Godard, F. 1974. *Monopolville.* Paris: Mouton. 475 pp.

Clark, T. N., Ed. 1968. *Community Structure and Decision-Making: Comparative Analyses.* New York: Intext-Chandler. 489 pp.

Clark, T. N. 1970. On decentralization. *Polity* 2:508–14

Clark, T. N. 1972a. Urban typologies and political outputs: causal models using discrete variables and orthogonal factors, or precise distortion versus model muddling. See Berry 1972:152–78

Clark, T. N. 1972b. Structural functionalism, exchange theory, and the new political economy. *Sociol. Inq.* 42:275–311

Clark, T. N. 1973a. The structure of community influence. See Hahn 1972:283–314

Clark, T. N. 1973b. Citizen values, power, and policy outputs: a model of community decision-making. *J. Comp. Admin.* 4:385–427

Clark, T. N. 1973c. Community social indicators: from analytical models to pol-

*Several papers cited were presented at three sessions of the Committee on Community Research of the International Sociological Association at the ISA's 8th World Congress in Toronto, September 1974. Discussions during the paper sessions and a Roundtable were recorded and will be published in *Comparative Urban Research,* which should include a list of addresses of the authors. An address list is also available from T. N. Clark, Dept. of Sociology, Univ. of Chicago, 1126 E. 59th St., Chicago, Ill. 60637.

icy applications. *Urban Aff. Quart.* 9:3–36

Clark, T. N. 1973d. *Community Power and Policy Outputs.* Beverly Hills & London: Sage. 98 pp.

Clark, T. N. 1974a. Theories of policy outputs, and assessing measurement error: comments on Liebert. *Soc. Sci. Quart.* 3(2):787–91

Clark, T. N. 1974b. Can you cut a budget pie? *Policy and Polit.* 3:3–32

Clark, T. N. Ed. 1974c. *Comparative Community Politics.* Beverly Hills & London: Sage. 415 pp.

Clark, T. N. The Irish ethic and the spirit of patronage. *Ethnicity.* In press

Coleman, J. S. 1971. *Resources for Social Change.* New York: Wiley-Interscience. 119 pp.

Coleman, J. S. 1972. The position of political parties in elections. In *Probability Models of Collective Decision-Making.* ed. R. G. Niemi, H. F. Weisberg, 332–57. Columbus, Ohio: Merrill

Coleman, J. S. 1973a. *The Mathematics of Collective Action.* Chicago: Aldine; London: Heinemann. 191 pp.

Coleman, J. S. 1973b. *Power and the Structure of Society.* New York: Norton. 114 pp.

Crecine, J. P. 1969. *Governmental Problem Solving: A Computer Simulation of Municipal Budgeting.* Chicago: Rand McNally. 338 pp.

Dahl, R. A. 1961. *Who Governs?* New Haven: Yale Univ. Press. 355 pp.

Dahl, R. A. 1967. The city in the future of democracy. *Am. Polit. Sci. Rev.* 61:953–70

de Swaan, A. 1973. *Coalition Theories and Cabinet Formations.* San Francisco: Jossey-Bass; Amsterdam: Elsevier. 347 pp.

Dodge, L. B. 1972. *A human ecological approach to the study of power distribution in local communities.* PhD thesis. Brown Univ., Providence, Rhode Island

Eberts, P. R., Eby, J. W., Kluess, P. 1969. *Community structure and poverty. Reg. Develop. Stud. No. 4, Dept. Rural Sociol.* New York: Cornell Univ.

Fowler, E. P., Lineberry, R. L. 1972. The comparative analysis of urban policy: Canada and the U.S. See H. Hahn 1972:345–68

Fried, R. C. 1973. Comparative urban performance. Working paper no. 1, European urban research, UCLA. In *Handbook of Political Science,* ed. F. I. Greenstein,

N. W. Polsby, Vol. 8: Chap. 6. Reading, Mass: Addison-Wesley

Fried, R. C. 1974. Politics, economics, and federalism: aspects of urban government in Austria, Germany, and Switzerland. See Clark 1974c:313–52

Friedman, P. 1970. Community decision-making in the United States: a review of recent research. *New Atlantis* 1:133–42

Frohlich, N., Oppenheimer, J. A. & Young, O. R. 1971. *Political Leadership and Collective Goods.* Princeton: Princeton Univ. Press. 161 pp.

Hahn, H., Ed. 1972. *People and Politics in Urban Society. Urban Affairs Annual Reviews,* Vol. 6. Beverly Hills & London: Sage. 635 pp.

Hanna, W. J. 1974. *Policy Outputs, Symbolic Politics, and Subjective Life Qualities.* Presented to Comm. on Community Res., 8th World Cong., Int. Sociol. Assoc., Toronto

Hawkins, B. W. 1971. *Politics and Urban Policies.* Indianapolis: Bobbs-Merrill. 127 pp.

Hawley, A. H. 1963. Community power and urban renewal success. *Am. J. Sociol.* 68:422–31

Hawley, W. D., Rodgers, D., Eds. 1974. *Improving the Quality of the Urban Environment, Urban Affairs Annual Reviews,* Vol. 8. Beverly Hills & London: Sage. 639 pp.

Hawley, W. D., Svara, J. H. 1972. *The Study of Community Power: A Bibliographic Review.* Santa Barbara, Calif: ABC-Clio. 123 pp.

Hawley, W. D., Wirt, F. M., Eds. 1974. *The Search for Community Power.* Englewood Cliffs, NJ: Prentice-Hall. 390 pp. 2nd ed.

Heclo, H. 1972. Policy analysis. *Brit. J. Polit. Sci.* 2:83–108

Hirschi, T. 1973. On the methodology of comparative urban politics. *J. Comp. Admin.* 4:499–513

Hoinville, G. 1971. Evaluating community preferences. *Environ. & Plann.* 3:33–50

International Studies of Values in Politics. 1971. In *Values and the Active Community.* New York: Free Press. 416 pp.

Jackson, J. E. 1972. Politics and the budgetary process. *Soc. Sci. Res.* 1:35–60

Jacob, P. E. 1974. *Autonomy and Political Responsibility.* Presented to Comm. Community Res., 8th World Congr., Int. Sociol. Assoc., Toronto

Jambrek, P. 1974. Socio-economic change and political development: decision-making in sixteen Yugoslav communes. See Clark 1974c: 163–78

Kesselman, M. 1974. Political parties and local government in France: differentiation and opposition. See Clark 1974c: 111–40

Kesselman, M., Rosenthal, D. B. 1974. Local power and comparative politics: notes toward the study of comparative local politics. See Hawley & Wirt 1974: 371–89

Kirby, D. J., Harris, T. R., Crain, R. L., Rossell, C. H. 1973. *Political Strategies in Northern School Desegregation.* Lexington, Mass: Heath. 262 pp.

Kirlin, J. J., Erie, S. P. 1972. The study of city governance and public policy making: a critical appraisal. *Public Admin. Rev.* 32:173–82

Kotter, J. P., Lawrence, P. R. 1974. *Mayors in Action.* New York: Wiley-Interscience

Laumann, E. O., Pappi, F. U. 1973. New directions in the study of community elites. *Am. Sociol. Rev.* 34:182–97

Laumann, E. O., Pappi, F. U. 1974. *The Resource Bases of Community Influence.* Presented to Comm. Community Res., 8th World Congr. Int. Sociol. Assoc., Toronto

Laumann, E. O. *New Directions in the Study of Community Power Systems* (tentative title). In press

Leif, I. P., Clark, T. N. 1973. *Community Power and Decision-Making: A Trend Report and Bibliography. Current Sociology,* Vol. 20. The Hague: Mouton. 138 pp.

Lupsha, P. 1974. Constraints on urban leadership, or why cities cannot be creatively governed. See Hawley & Rodgers 1974:607–24

Meltsner, A. J. 1971. *The Politics of City Revenue.* Berkeley: Univ. Calif. Press. 303 pp.

Miller, D. C. 1973. Design strategies for comparative international studies of community power. *Soc. Forces* 51:261–74

Miller, D. C. 1975. *Leadership and Power in the Bos-Wash Megalopolis.* New York: Wiley-Interscience.

Morlock, L. L. 1974. Business interests, countervailing groups and the balance of influence in 91 cities. See Hawley & Wirt 1974:309–28

Moynihan, D. P. 1967. Urban conditions: general. In *Social Goals and Indicators for American Society,* ed. B. M. Gross, 159–77. *Annals.,* Vol. 1

Mueller, D. C. 1971. Fiscal federalism in a constitutional democracy. *Public Policy* 19:567–93

National Advisory Commission on Civil Disorders. 1968. *Supplemental Studies.* Washington DC: GPO. 248 pp.

Nelson, M. D. 1974. The validity of secondary analyses of community power studies. *Soc. Forces* 52:531–37

Nix, H. L., Seerley, N. R. 1972. *Community social analysis of DeKalb County, Georgia, Community Soc. Anal. Ser.* Vol. 7. Dept. Sociol. Univ. Georgia. 169 pp.

Nuttall, R. L., Bolan, R. S. 1973. A model of community planning and decision-making, *Final Report to Public Health Service, Dept. HEW.* Washington DC. 554 pp.

Ostrom, E. 1974. Exclusion, choice and divisibility: factors affecting the measurement of urban agency output and impact. *Soc. Sci. Quart.* 54:691–99

Ostrowski, K., Teune, H. 1974. Local political systems and general social processes. See Clark 1974c:395–406

Pappi, F. U., Laumann, E. O. 1974. Gesellschaftliche wertorientierungen und politisches Verhalten. *Z. Soziologie* 2:157–88

Pressman, J. L., Wildavsky, A. 1973. *Implementation.* Berkeley: Univ. Calif. Press. 182 pp.

Pusić, E. 1974. Diversity and integration in the Yugoslav commune. See Clark 1974d:289–312

Riker, W. H., Ordeshook, P. 1973. *An Introduction to Positive Political Theory.* Englewood Cliffs, NJ: Prentice-Hall. 387 pp.

Roig, C., Mingasson, C., Kukawka, P. 1970. Social structure and local power structure in urban areas, analysis of 17 French townships. *New Atlantis* 1:65–84

Rossi, P. H. 1960. Power and community structure. *Midwest J. Polit. Sci.,* 390–401

Rossi, P. H. 1972. Community social indicators. In *The Human Meaning of Social Change,* ed. A. Campbell, P. E. Converse, 87–126. New York: Russell Sage. 547 pp.

Rossi, P. H., Berk, R. A., Eidson, B. K. 1974. *The Roots of Urban Discontent.* New York: Wiley-Interscience. 499 pp.

Rothenberg, J. 1970. Local decentralization and the theory of optimal government. In *The Analysis of Public Output,* ed. J. Margolis, 31–68. New York: Columbia Univ. Press. 409 pp.

Scheuch, E. K. 1973. Soziologie der macht. Schriften des Vereins für Sozialpolitik, Gesellschaft für Wirtschafts- und Sozialwissenschaften, *Macht und ökonomisches Gesetz*, 74/II:989–1042. Berlin: Duncker & Humblot. Neue Folge

Schuman, H., Gruenberg, B. 1970. The impact of city on racial attitudes. *Am. J. Sociol.* 76:213–61

Schuman, H. 1972. Dissatisfaction with city services: is race an important factor? See Hahn 1972:369–92

Sharkansky, I., Ed. 1970. *Policy Analysis in Political Science.* Chicago: Markham. 476 pp.

Stinchcombe, A. L. 1968. *Constructing Social Theories.* New York: Harcourt, Brace & World. 301 pp.

Sundquist, J. L. 1969. *Making Federalism Work.* Washington DC: Brookings Inst. 293 pp.

Tarrow, S. 1974. *Partisanship and political exchange in French and Italian local politics.* Sage Professional Papers in Contemporary Political Sociology, 06–004. Beverly Hills/London: Sage. 54 pp.

Turk, H. 1973. Comparative urban structure from an interorganizational perspective. *Admin. Sci. Quart.* 18:37–55

Verba, S., Nie, N. H. 1972. *Participation in America.* New York. Harper & Row. 428 pp.

Walton, J. 1973. The structural bases of political change in urban communities. *Sociol. Inq.* 43:174–208

Walton, J., Portes, A. *Power and Poverty in Latin America* (tentative title). Austin: Univ. Texas Press. Unpublished

Warren, R. L., Rose, S. M., Bergunder, A. F. 1974. *The Structure of Urban Reform.* Lexington, Mass: Heath. 221 pp.

Westerstahl, J. 1974. Decision-making systems in thirty-six Swedish communes. See Clark 1974c:141–62

Wilburn, Y., Williams, L. A. 1971. City taxes and services: citizens speak out. *Nation's Cities.* 9:9–24, 37–52

Williams, J. M. 1973. The ecological approach in measuring community power concentration: an analysis of Hawley's MPO ratio. *Am. Sociol. Rev.* 38:230–42

SEX ROLES IN TRANSITION: ❖10512
A Ten-Year Perspective

Jean Lipman-Blumen and Ann. R. Tickamyer
National Institute of Education, Washington DC 20208

INTRODUCTION

Myth vs Reality of Status of Women

Popular treatments of the changing role of women continue to belabor the myth that the status of women has enjoyed uninterrupted progress in modern history. To the contrary, closer scrutiny suggests that women in the seventh decade of the twentieth century still are striving to regain the relatively independent economic and individual status they enjoyed before the disruption caused by the Industrial Revolution (Myrdal & Klein 1956, Smelser 1959, Goode 1963, Knudsen 1969, Blake 1974).[1]

Sparked largely by the Women's Movement, the social sciences have witnessed a recent rekindling of interest in sex roles. With some notable exceptions, the spate of recent studies regrettably focuses almost exclusively upon the female role and neglects the masculine side of the sex role equation. Within the field of sociology, at least one critical review (Hochschild 1973), several research bibliographies (Aldous & Hill 1967, Cisler 1971, Jacobs 1971, Astin, Suniewick & Dweck 1971, Astin, Parelman & Fisher 1974), and research agendas (Epstein 1973a; A. Daniels, forthcoming) have signaled the renewed concern with sex roles.

Demographic Background and Social Role Changes

In the United States, this burgeoning research interest is most properly set against the background of demographic changes in the profile of women. First, women's longevity has increased dramatically since the turn of the century.[2] Women are

---

[1]In more recent history, women in the academic world, as graduate students and professionals, experienced a brief peak during the 1930s, which dropped dramatically over the next several decades until a recent resurgence in the late sixties (Bernard 1964, Ginzberg et al 1966, Simon et al 1967, Jencks & Riesman 1968, Mooney 1968, Astin 1969, Parrish 1962, Rossi & Calderwood 1973.)

[2]A female child born in the US in 1966 can expect to live, on the average, approximately 74 years, compared to a female born in 1900 whose life expectancy was 48 years (US Dept. of Labor 1969).

297

marrying somewhat later, planning and having smaller families, and delaying their families (US Dept. of Labor 1969). More women are choosing to remain childless, and legal abortions are depressing the overall, and particularly the illegitimate, fertility rate (Sklar & Berkov 1974).[3]

The last decade has witnessed an impressive increase in the number of female-headed families, partly a reflection of the rising divorce rate. In 1972, 14% of all families with children had a female head, an increase of 40% since 1960 (Ross & Sawhill 1975.) Female-headed families with children under 18 are relatively poor, with a median annual income of $4000.

Women's labor market participation continues to grow. By 1975, 45.6% of all women of working age (16 and over) were in the labor force, and women represented 39% of all workers (US Dept. of Labor). In 1973, 42% of married women with husbands present worked, and almost 39% of widowed, divorced, or separated women were in the labor force (US Dept. of Labor 1973). Among women workers with husbands present, 50% had children ages 6 to 17, and, by 1975, 37% had children under 6.

Despite continuous increases in their labor force participation, women remain within a very narrow band of occupations, with more than one third in clerical roles and less than 25% in professional or technical occupations (mostly in teaching, nursing, and social work).

The educational picture for women reveals comparable trends. Whereas boys and girls enter primary school in approximately equal numbers, an attrition of female students begins in early adolescence. Female attrition is reflected in census reports which indicate that the proportion of females enrolled from the total population in school at each level from 14–24 is less than that of men (Coleman 1973). The Carnegie Commission reports that, since 1900, women are less likely than men to enter college, despite the fact that they are more likely than men to complete secondary school.

Studies of human capital have shown that the rate of return for white women from a college education is less than that for white males, but that the reverse is true for nonwhites. Mincer (1970) suggests that women have weaker incentives to invest in forms of human capital, including education, because they spend only a limited period of their lives in the labor market. Mincer's economic analysis is no longer valid in view of recent figures which reflect lengthening periods in the labor force over the life spans of both married and single women (US Dept. of Labor 1969). But even when women make the human capital investment, remaining in school as long as men and developing work experience, their annual median earnings as full-time workers are only 80% those of men.[4]

[3]The drop in fertility rate of women 18–29 also is affected by the increase in the age of first marriage, educational attainment, labor force status, and metropolitan/nonmetropolitan residence (US Dept. of Commerce 1972).

[4]For the majority of women who lack equal educational and occupational background, as full-time workers, they earn only 59% the annual median earnings of their male counterparts in the labor force.

The resurgence of the Women's Movement in the late 1960s has challenged the social sciences to address the central issues underlying these demographic changes. The present paper represents an attempt to review selectively, rather than exhaustively, much of the resulting research (although some important work reviewed here predates this period).

Since the demand for such research has created a proliferating supply, we have had to set limits in terms of the substantive areas we would review. Consequently we have chosen to focus primarily upon the contributions within the field of sociology, and secondarily psychology, with less attention on anthropology, political science, economics, and history.

In addition, we have designated certain areas, many of which deserve major reviews in their own right, to be beyond the scope of this paper. These generally excluded areas are female deviance, status attainment, small group behavior, volunteer work roles, education, sexual behavior, endocrinology, aging, and non-black minority research. In attempting to consolidate the literature of sex roles, we have divided the field into eight substantive areas: sex differences, gender roles, sex roles, sex role socialization, women as an out-group, the feminist critique, sex as a differentiating variable, and sex as a stratification variable. (These are not rigid divisions, only guidelines, which give way on occasion to overlap.)

Finally, we propose a set of research strategies designed to help build, in a systematic fashion, the knowledge still lacking in various areas.

OVERVIEW OF EXISTING APPROACHES

Neglect of Male Roles

Until very recently, sex role research has been dominated by work on women and the family. In the past few years, however, the topic has expanded to include women's roles in the educational, occupational, legal, and economic systems. Reasons for this trend are the following: recognition of previous scholarly neglect of women's participation in these institutions; increase of this participation as a result of the demographic and social changes cited above; impact of the Women's Liberation Movement on actual patterns of role choice, role allocation, and attitudinal correlates; and expansion of social scientists' awareness of the restricted situation of women. However, with few exceptions (e.g. Parsons 1942, Aldous 1969, Dahlstrom 1967, Turner 1970, Benson 1968, Grønseth 1971–1972, Tresemer & Pleck 1972, Weiss 1973, Bart 1970) male family roles have been ignored. Until recently, much of the focus has been on how male external roles impinge on the family and vice versa (Heer 1958, Blood & Wolfe 1960). Ironically, those topics that are subsumed under sex roles when dealing with women, are classified as substantive subfields of sociology when concerned with men.

Classificatory Schemes

A survey of literature reviews reveals a number of different classificatory schemes. The majority are organized implicitly or explicitly by discipline and/or substantive category. Perhaps the most widely known general review is Hochschild's (1973), which divides the literature into four categories: sex differences, sex roles, women as a minority group, and the politics of caste. Others look at women as portrayed in psychology, anthropology, sociology, political science, and economics, and still others classify research by women's roles in the various sectors of society—family, economy, and polity (Holter 1970, Andreas 1971, Epstein 1971a, Reeves 1971, Sullerot 1971, Chafetz 1974, Yorburg 1974). A cross-cultural perspective is added by Zelditch (1964a), Sullerot (1971), and Yorburg (1974), and numerous readers and collections gather articles from a variety of sources and perspectives (Dahlstrom 1967, Christensen 1964, Roszak & Roszak 1969, Gornick & Moran 1971, Bardwick 1971, Mednick & Tangri 1972, Safilios-Rothschild 1972, Huber 1973).

Bernard (1973) takes a somewhat different approach to the literature. She examines its treatment within various theoretical schools in sociology, looking in turn at functionalism, interactionism, socialization, and exchange theory, and noting their distinctive weaknesses. Functionalism, as epitomized by Parsons (1949, 1959), supports the status quo in sex role allocation, differentiation, and reward. Bernard suggests that interactionism neglects power relations between the sexes.

The socialization literature is useful for explaining women's role adoption and adaptation to role requisites; therefore it has been employed by sociologists attempting to deal with sex roles. Its very utility in this respect, however, has other dysfunctions for understanding women's position, namely by redirecting interest from the power bases entailed in role allocation. Exchange theory, the last theoretical school Bernard considers, suffers from being limited largely to mate selection and family relations.

A somewhat different approach recognizes that the ideal of a "value-free" science is little more than an ideal—and that all social research can be seen as predicated on certain "domain" assumptions that originate largely in the researcher's location in social reality (Gouldner 1970). Eichler (1974) categorizes sex role research on the basis of implied assumptions of sexual equality.

Still another approach focuses on differing methodologies. Bernard (1973) suggests the importance of this task when she underscores the relationship between types of research methods, underlying assumptions, questions posed, and presence of sexist bias. One might add to this both theoretical framework and conclusions.

RESEARCH ON SEX DIFFERENCES

Research Findings

This area draws largely on the literature from biology, psychology, anthropology, and sexology. Within these disciplines there are different theoretical orientations (e.g. developmental, psycholoanalytic, learning theory, and neurophysiology), all recognizing certain gross anatomical, physiological, and hormonal differences between males and females.

In addition, numerous differences in secondary physical characteristics, emotional, intellectual, and cultural traits, and need dispositions have been noted (Oetzel

1966, Maccoby 1966a, Garai & Scheinfeld 1968). For example, physically compared to men, women generally are smaller, muscularly weaker, but healthier, with a longer life span and less serious morbidity (Montagu 1970).

On an interpersonal level, women are reported to be more emotional and expressive, nonagressive, dependent, and concerned with interpersonal relationships (Montagu 1970, Carlson 1971, Bardwick & Douvan 1971). On a cognitive level, women variously are seen as more or less intelligent, depending upon age and task (Maccoby 1966b), but as suffering from high test anxiety (Horner 1968). They are reported to be field dependent, in contrast to the masculine tendency to be field independent (Witkin 1972, Oltman et al 1973).

In terms of need dispositions, women have been reported to have differential achievement motivation (Crandall 1962, Crandall et al 1964, Lesser 1973), and a (now disputed) fear of success and motive to fail (Horner 1968, 1970, Alper 1974, Puryear & Mednick 1974, Tresemer 1974). Women perform differently on projective tests, and their dreams are reported as very different in content from those of men, even in cross-cultural terms (D'Andrade 1966). On a cultural level, women speak and write differently than men (Warshay 1972), perform different work across all cultures (D'Andrade 1966, Galenson 1973), and allegedly exhibit different social organization (Tiger 1970).

Sexually, women and men are reported to have differential arousal patterns and levels (Schmidt & Sigusch 1973), different sexual behavior (Kinsey et al 1953), and different performance capacity (Masters & Johnson 1966). On a quasi-metaphysical level, the sexes have been characterized as having differing life-force orientations polarized around "inner space-outer space" (Erikson 1964), agency-communion (Bakan 1966), instrumentality-expressiveness (Parsons & Bales 1955), and field dependence-field independence (Witkin 1973, Oltman et al 1973).

The plentiful and varied sources documenting sex differences lead to a number of problems. Research findings involve different disciplines, different methodologies, different questions and assumptions, all applied to different portions of reality. Almost any given result may be contradicted by other studies and models. [One example is the debate about whether there is (Warshay 1972) or is not (Battle-Sister 1971) an unique female culture.] Researchers also often ignore the greater within-group than between-group variance that characterizes the sexes.

Interpretation of Research Findings

Little definitive knowledge exists regarding the causes of sex differences. They may be the result of a genetic imperative or of selection processes; and selection processes may be biological, environmental, or social. In many cases of documented differences, unsubstantiated invidious comparisons are made, explicitly or implicitly.

Even starting with the same assumptions, different researchers often arrive at different conclusions. For example, Bardwick (1971) and Rossi (1973a) would agree about the importance of physiological differences between males and females. Both have expressed interest in what Rossi (1973a, p. 151) calls "the interstices between the biological and social sciences"; however, Rossi's (1964) vision of the possibility of androgynous sex roles contrasts sharply with Bardwick's acceptance of biological determinism.

Problems of methodology arise. A major methodological difficulty is the tendency to note only differences, disregarding similarities. A problem endemic to social science as a whole (Morrison & Henkel 1970), it becomes particularly acute in such a subject as this, where the pursuit of differences may obscure the actual ratio of differences to similarities (Lipman-Blumen 1974b, Maccoby & Jacklin 1974). Comparability presents another problem. How do laboratory results compare with field observations or with survey research findings? How does one control for the myriad of factors present in any social situation, to determine what is a true biological difference and what an artifact?

When one realizes that it is not even always clear what is male and what is female, and that recent research demonstrates that sex and gender are the result of a multiplicity of interacting neurophysiological, hormonal, psychological, social, and cultural factors (Stoller 1968), the simple Freudian dictum "anatomy is destiny" becomes part of a complex and controversial debate.

GENDER ROLES

The topic of gender roles is of relatively recent interest and has a somewhat confusing status. Different writers use the term differently, and it is necessary to distinguish among sex, sex identity, sex role, gender, gender identity, and gender role. These distinctions cannot always be made clearly; there is, however, heuristic value in attempting to clarify the conceptual boundaries.

The most common usage for gender involves reference to one's awareness of self as a sexual being. Following Stoller (1968), Bernard (1971) states that "sex is a biological fact; gender, though based on biology, is a socio-cultural-sociological-psychological fact. Gender consists of gender identity and gender role; the first a social and psychological phenomenon; the second a cultural and sociological and interactional one." (Bernard 1971, p. 16.) Gender identity which sometimes is used interchangeably with sexual identity (Green 1974), simply refers to whether one considers oneself a male or a female. Green (1974, p. xv) defines gender identity as encompassing three components: "(1) . . . (a) basic conviction of being male or female; (2) . . . behavior which is culturally associated with males or females (masculinity and femininity); and (3) . . . preference for male and female sexual partners."

Chafetz (1974), however, uses gender (roles) to refer to the physiological, genital domain, and sex (roles) to refer to the social dimension. Neither Chafetz nor Green distinguishes clearly between identity and role; both often use them interchangeably. If one views the second part of Green's definition as pertaining to role performance, and if one realizes that Chafetz' distinction between gender role and sex role really comes closer to a distinction between gender identity and sex role, some of the confusion is dispelled.

Additional problems arise in trying to distinguish between gender role and sex role. Many of the behaviors attributable to gender role could be considered part of sex role, and vice versa; and there sometimes appears to be little consistency to the assignment process. Typical "feminine" behavior, such as maternalism or passivity, may be identified as basic to a woman's identification as a sexual female, or it may be considered socially prescribed behavior for women in a particular time and place.

Bernard (1971) suggests that Mead's (1935) well-known study of sex and temperament was really dealing with the "cultural contents of gender, which she labeled temperament" (p. 21). Mead found that traits considered typically feminine in one society were typically masculine in another. Mead concludes that these traits are culturally defined and conditioned. [Cross-culturally, however, there is considerable regularity in gender roles (D'Andrade 1966).]

To understand the nature of gender roles, it is useful to view them as mediating factors between gender identity and sex role. Via gender roles, which develop out of gender identity, males and females are funneled into what is societally defined as sex-appropriate behavior.

Much of the impetus for the interest in gender roles comes from the study of intersexual disorders, such as transsexualism (Green & Money 1969, Stoller 1968, Green 1974) and homosexuality (Gagnon & Simon 1967). Although, here as elsewhere, it has not been possible to isolate the causative agents from the multitude of biological and environmental factors in gender identity and role (Money, Hampson & Hampson 1955), the attempt to do so provides suggestive material for ultimately understanding the nature of sex roles. The difficulties encountered in correlating specific biological, psycho-environmental, or socio-cultural factors with cross-sex preferences highlights the complex nature of sex role preference in "normal" cases, not to mention so-called deviant cases.

SEX ROLES

Analyses of sex roles emerge primarily from the social-psychological and sociological literature. The study of sex roles concerns roles within all structured settings, the norms and rules governing role performance in these settings, the correlates of role location and performance, the special situation of deviant roles and those who occupy them, and the mechanics of role change.

Before attempting to review this area, it is necessary to clarify the status of the term *sex role* within the context of sociology. [The general role literature suffers from conflicting usage and definitions that, in turn, distort the sex role literature (Sarbin 1954, Turner 1956, Gross et al 1958, Biddle & Thomas 1966, Angrist 1969, Komarovsky 1973b).] At various times, sex roles are used to denote observable behavior, behavioral expectations, behavioral norms, or some combination of these (Angrist 1969). Sex role performance may be viewed as taking place in various types of settings (Angrist 1969) and may vary in degree of institutionalization (Komarovsky 1946).

Three core uses of the term sex role occur in the literature: *position,* referring to normatively appropriate expectations for males and females; *behavior,* referring to what males and females are and do; and *relationships,* detailing the process of role taking. These varying definitions correspond to the variability of role content. To handle this problem, Angrist (1969) suggests that sex roles be viewed as dealing with four distinct elements: label, behavior, expectations, and location. Clearly, any given actor performs in a multiplicity of roles, and the relationship among these roles is an important element in role analysis (Merton 1957).

Although sex role differentiation varies in form and degree over time, place, and group, it appears to be an universal social fact. The socialization process of sex role learning apparently begins early—at birth—and is well articulated at a very early age (Hartley 1959–1960, 1964, Hartley et al 1962, Hartley & Hardesty 1964). Sex role learning is marked by strong cross-cultural stability (Block 1972).

SEX ROLE SOCIALIZATION

Childhood

Sex role learning covers childhood, adolescent, and adult socialization. Socialization is inculcated by "significant others," institutional and organizational contexts, and mass media. Infants are treated differently according to sex from the very beginning (Kagan & Moss 1962, Moss 1967). Girls are talked to and cuddled more; they are jostled less than boys. Initially, boys are handled more often and more roughly than girls, but the amount of handling diminishes with age. In addition to being played with more roughly, boys are discouraged from clinging (Lewis 1972).

As children grow older, these differences are accentuated. By the time a child enters kindergarten, not only are sex role stereotypes well developed, but also the male role is given higher value (Kohlberg 1966). Early on, there is greater pressure for boys to develop masculine identities than for girls to develop feminine ones (Vroegh 1971). Brown (1957) administered to kindergarteners through fifth graders a masculine-feminine scale for children. At all levels, boys were more masculine than girls were feminine, although by fifth grade the girls demonstrated a clear-cut preference for the feminine role. Summaries of the research on sex role learning among children are found in Maccoby (1966a), Lynn (1962, 1969), and Goslin (1969), and include articles from social-learning (Mischel 1966) and cognitive-developmental (Kohlberg 1966) perspectives.

Socialization is a process that continues throughout the life of the individual (Brim 1968, Inkeles 1968). In later childhood, school, peer, and media influences are added to the pressures parents create for sex-typed behavior. Counseling and testing procedures have been shown to be sex-biased (Pietrofesa & Schlossberg 1972) and to perpetuate sex-linked behavior.

Studies of children's books and school texts show characters in highly stereotyped sex role behavior, a preponderance of male images, and an emphasis on variety and creativity in male portrayals not found in female characterizations (Weitzman et al 1972, Frazier & Sadker 1973, Saario et al 1973). Chafetz (1974) reports numerous studies done by students demonstrating extreme sex role stereotyping in everything from Sears Roebuck catalogs to television shows.

Adolescence

Adolescence is marked by singularly acute pressures. Males receive more positive and consistent reinforcement for approximating male role attributes, and there appears to be a connection between role performance and self-esteem (Connell &

Johnson 1970). [The relationship between self-esteem and role performance does not persist among boys who are the youngest children in families with all female siblings (Rosenberg 1956).]

Females are increasingly directed away from external achievement roles, and become more cognizant of impending sex-marriage-family roles that involve role conflict (Komarovsky 1946). Coleman's (1961) account of the double bind faced by bright girls is typical. Because intellectuality is negatively associated with popularity, a structured conflict arises between girls' attempts to conform to expectations both for high academic performance and for popularity. The result is that bright girls tend to do well, but avoid doing their best in an effort to avert negative social consequences (Komarovsky 1946).

Some of the studies on adolescent development contain questionable assumptions and methodologies. Douvan & Adelson (1966), for example, accept traditional sex role stereotypes as "normal" and proceed to use these to construct a femininity-masculinity scale. Women who do not exhibit an interest in "women's" affairs (i.e. family, marriage, children, and domestic tasks), or who are oriented toward "masculine" activities (i.e. occupations), are considered masculine, maladjusted, and immature. Girls who reject marriage are considered "antifeminine," psychologically deviant, and subject to pathology.

Adulthood

Adult socialization continues throughout adulthood. Pressure from the media is not reserved simply for children. Traditional differentiation of sex roles has been reported in American marriage manuals (Gordon & Shankweiler 1971), women's magazines (Friedan 1963), and even medical school texts (Scully & Bart 1973). Furthermore, similar patterns are evident in cross-cultural studies (Michel 1960, Liljestrφm 1966).

Influences in adult socialization stem from complex sources and have varying effects. New roles and statuses in education, family, and community are among the many factors relevant to adult sex role socialization (Brim 1968). One consistency exists from childhood through maturity: males are socialized by prescription, females by proscription.

SOME RESULTS FOR WOMEN

Limitation of Role Choice

One of the main foci of the literature on sex roles has been the detailing of socialization processes by which women are "cooled out" of pursuing external, instrumental, direct achievement roles, and channeled into internal, expressive, vicarious achievement roles (Lipman-Blumen 1973a). These processes subsume both internal and external barriers. Internalized barriers are learned as part of the very definition of femininity and include noncompetitiveness, passivity, and other elements of sex role ideology (Lipman-Blumen 1972). External or structural barriers involve discriminatory policies, sex-typing of jobs, lack of role models, operation of protégé systems, and the stag effect (Epstein 1971a, Roby 1972, Rossi 1972). Theodore (1971) presents a comprehensive, but uneven, collection of readings on the processes involved in career choice, maintenance, and functioning for professional women.

The actual roles that women eventually occupy are limited, and the literature reflects this limitation. Women's family roles heavily dominate earlier research, most of which is colored by a functionalist orientation. Parsons & Bale's (1955) division of family functions into instrumental and expressive roles is a perspective perhaps inappropriately extrapolated from small group research, as the family differs in significant ways from laboratory small groups.

The dichotomy of instrumental and expressive roles, performed respectively by male and female role players has influenced much subsequent work. From Goode (1963, 1964) to Scanzoni (1972), research on the family is largely oriented toward expanding and modifying this approach (Zelditch 1955, Johnson 1963). At its worst, this reinforces sex role stereotyping (Ehrlich 1971). At its best, this instrumental-expressive dichotomy provides many useful insights, but still frequently fails to perceive the dysfunctional aspects of the traditional order into which men and women are socialized.

Marital Roles

Another line of family research, also influenced by this tradition, is an exchange perspective that attempts to assess the relative power of husband and wife. This approach has stirred considerable debate (Blood & Wolfe 1960, Bernard 1968, Gillespie 1971, Scanzoni 1972); nevertheless, it appears that women always are disadvantaged in the "exchange." Results of this research show that a woman's power within the family grows as her access to external resources, such as employment and income, increases (Heer 1958, Hoffman 1963, Holmstrom 1972, Rapoport & Rapoport 1972).

This leads to another set of research concerns that revolve around working wives. Research has been conducted on the effect of mothers' employment on children (Nye & Hoffman 1963, Siegel & Haas 1963) and on marital happiness (Orden & Bradburn 1969).

Of great interest recently is the dual career family where both husband and wife have a career. In one British study, such marriages are faced with at least five areas of stress—overload dilemmas, personal norm dilemmas, dilemmas of identity, social network dilemmas, and role cycling dilemmas—all of which require devising mechanisms for adjustment and stress reduction (Fogarty et al 1972). Although these British couples emphasized egalitarian family relationships, when tension points occurred, many husbands "undercut" their wives (Rapoport & Rapoport 1972, Fogarty et al 1972).

Studies of American dual career families make it obvious that even in the vast majority of cases, men and men's needs dominate the marriages. In Holmstrom's study (1972), whose sample departed from typical middle class sex role differentiation patterns, when problems arose it generally was the wife's interests that were sacrificed. Although the wife's time, interests, and career were highly valued, the husband's were considered still more important. Another study (Poloma 1972) of role conflict in married professional women describes similar results.

Garland's (1972) study of such families found that a wife's status as a professional does not, in itself, affect family structures. Income, however, does have this effect, particularly if the wife earns more than the husband. Despite egalitarian attitudes in some areas, these couples also maintained traditional orientations. For example, in no instance did the wife desire to be more successful than her husband.

Unfortunately, many of these dual-career studies are based on case method or very limited samples, making it difficult to generalize from the findings. The important point, however, is that even among "modern," "egalitarian" couples, remnants of traditionalism affect behavior.

Another marriage pattern that has recently evoked interest is the two-person career, as opposed to the two-career family (Papanek 1973). The two-person career describes the common Western syndrome of using the wife as an unpaid, unacknowledged adjunct to the husband's position. The wife's contribution is seen as an important and necessary contribution to the husband's success. This pattern is closely tied to vicarious achievement patterns among women.

Reviewing the evidence on marital patterns and family roles, it appears that there are two main factors that affect the division of labor, sex-typing of roles, and decision making arrangements: economic resources of the wife and the sex role ideology of both members. As noted below, there is a definite relationship between the wife's economic resources and her position in the family. Nevertheless, there is a gap which cannot be explained completely by economics. Here the importance of sex role ideology suggests itself.

Sex role ideology emerges again as an important predictor in other areas of women's interests and aspirations (Lipman-Blumen 1972). This is supported by cross-cultural evidence (Block 1972). For example, studies have shown that despite the official egalitarian sex role ideology of kibbutz life, there has been a recent increase in sex role differentiation and stratification (Spiro 1956, Talmon 1965, Mednick, 1975). Although economic and demographic shifts are partially responsible for this change, prior traditional sex role ideology presumably also contributes to this pattern.

Occupational Roles of Women

Besides the research on familial roles, there is a large literature on women's education and work. These two are considered together because so frequently they are complementary roles. Barriers to occupational attainment are found within educational institutions, and discouragement from educational goals is often based upon assessments of occupational barriers. Numerous recent studies concerning women in the professions document the difficulties in attaining and maintaining professional status (Bernard 1964, White 1970, Epstein 1971a, 1973b, Fidell & DeLamater 1971, Theodore 1971, Rossi 1972, Rossi & Calderwood 1973, Roby 1972, Silver 1973). Many of the processes discussed above under socialization factors serve to keep women out of high status positions.

Even when women successfully enter so-called deviant occupations they tend to be contained within those specialties which pay most poorly, are least prestigious, and are for various reasons considered "feminine" or compatible with feminine skills (Safilios-Rothschild 1972). Women lawyers go into real estate, trusts, and domestic relations. As doctors, women become pediatricians and psychiatrists. Women architects specialize in residential design, and female engineers enter industrial engineering. The tendency for specialization by sex is cross-cultural, although the specific areas vary from country to country (Kreps 1971, Sullerot 1971, Safilios-Rothschild 1972, Galenson 1973). Epstein has suggested patterns whereby women are actually rewarded for dropping out of professional roles (1971b).

The vast majority of women never approaches professional roles (Sassower 1970, Bernard 1971). Large numbers of women with career aspirations enter the female occupational ghetto of the semiprofessions (Etzioni 1969, Toren 1972). The female occupational ghetto includes social work, nursing, and elementary school teaching—occupations perceived as traditionally female and therefore accorded "semi-professional" status (Harrington 1974). Much of the literature dealing with these positions is directed toward demonstrating why the positions do not qualify as genuine professions.

There are only sporadic examples of other roles women may enter. For instance, women in the armed forces (Goldman 1973), women as faculty wives (Hughes 1973, Weissman et al 1973), women as widows (Lopata 1973), and women as prostitutes (James 1973) represent the limited array of alternative role patterns studied. Several astute studies examine women's changing roles as they move through the life cycle (Neugarten 1963, Lopata 1966, Brim 1968, Mead 1967, Riley et al 1969).

There are major gaps in the literature on women's extra-familial roles. Service and clerical roles, in which the majority of the female labor force works, are largely ignored. Although there is a growing literature on black women and families (Frazier 1949, 1962, Rosen 1959, Reiss 1964, Pavela 1964, Bernard 1966, Haden et al 1971, Carroll 1973), serious gaps remain. The black professional woman has been described as gaining greater access to the occupational structure through the "double negative" of being both black and female (Epstein 1973b). Other studies (Treiman & Terrell 1973) report that, in general, black women more closely resemble black men than white women resemble white men. Black women, however, still are reported to receive less pay than black men, even when they have comparable education, role tasks, experience, and working hours.

Other work on black women examines their attitudes toward the Women's Movement (Hare & Hare 1970) and the myth of the black matriarchy (Mack 1971). The motive to avoid success has been compared in black and white women (Weston & Mednick 1970), as well as in groups of black women varying in their levels of black militancy (Puryear & Mednick 1974). In general, black women are reported to have less motive to avoid success than white women; however, "fear of success" has been associated with black militancy, particularly among women who do not report a permanent relationship with a man. Earlier exaggerated interest in the social deviance, dating patterns, and sexual behavior of black women seems to have diminished in very recent years.

The studies of other minority and working class women (Rainwater et al 1959, Komarovsky 1962) need to be supplemented, as does the recent work on male roles (see above). Much of the literature on men focuses on role conflict (Etkowitz 1971, Komarovsky 1973a) or is embedded in ethnic observational studies, as in *Tally's Corner* (Liebow 1967) and *The Urban Villagers* (Gans 1962). Another area of interest is the subject of the correlates of sex roles. Under this rubric may be sheltered sex roles and politics (Amundsen 1971, Haavio-Mannila 1972) and sex roles and mental health (Bart 1971, Chesler 1971, 1972, Broverman et al 1972, Gove & Tudor 1973, Pearlin 1974).

Perhaps the most common component of *all* roles women perform is what Bernard (1971) calls women's "stroking" function. This function characterizes the universally supportive role women are supposed to take. Many roles considered appropriate for women, both in the family and in the world of work, are characterized by their supportive, enabling, facilitating, and vicarious features (Papanek 1973, Lipman-Blumen 1973a).

WOMEN AS AN OUT-GROUP

Besides examining the roles women play, it is necessary to understand their status as well. Women have long been recognized as constituting an oppressed group; however, the specific nature of this oppression has been a matter of debate. We defer discussion of theories of sexual stratification until later. Here we examine the controversy on the status of women that focuses on women as a caste, class, or minority group.

The caste argument was suggested most notably by Myrdal (1944). In a now-famous appendix to his work on race in the US, Myrdal discussed the similarities between women and blacks. Although Myrdal never specifically calls women a caste, his discussion of the similarities between the positions of women and blacks implies that they share the same status. The caste perspective emphasizes ascriptive recruitment into ranked roles that form a closed, immobile system. Because of the high social visibility of women and blacks, and the rigidity of the caste line, both groups are unable to transcend caste barriers (except in the rare case of the individual who can "pass" as a member of the dominant group). According to Myrdal, the caste situation of women and blacks arises from similar historical contexts (i.e. the application of paternalistic law). Both groups have visible ascribed attributes, rationalizations of status, coping mechanisms, and actual discriminatory experiences.

Present day writers have seized upon this formulation to explain how social roles are determined not by achievement, but by birth—specifically by sex (Andreas 1971). Without denying the importance of these parallels, both Hacker (1951) and Eichler (1973) indicate several ways in which the situation of women diverges from that of blacks and renders the use of the classic definition of caste invalid.

Specifically, sex stratification is not as rigid as the caste formulation requires (some women are more privileged than some men), and therefore women may experience "status inconsistency" (see below). In addition, women's "culture" is not comparable to a caste-culture because of women's constant participation and interaction with men (Rossi 1964, Eichler 1973). Women traditionally associate with men more than with other women and are clearly exogamous, contrary to caste formulations. One of the strongest contemporary supporters of the caste formulation (Andreas 1971) discusses at length the agents of social control which keep the system rigidly stratified. However, Andreas's own emphasis on propaganda factors (popular psychology, advice, etc) raises serious questions about this view. Presumably the rigidity of a caste system would obviate such supports. If nothing else, however, there is considerable evidence of at least some mobility on the part of women (see below).

The second position, a class formulation, originated with Engels (1942) and has numerous recent adherents. Two variations have been advanced by Lenski (1966) and Benston (1969). Lenski states that women constitute a class partly because of low status. He suggests that women have an alternative route to rewards through the marriage market, rather than through the usual male occupational-economic routes. Eichler (1973) rightly criticizes Lenski's formulation by noting the large numbers of women who compete in both markets, and the differences in the two forms of competition. Furthermore, Lenski tends to overemphasize the rewards of marriage, particularly in terms of more recent years when sexual and economic gratification are more freely available outside the confines of marriage.

Benston (1969) explains women's class status in terms of their nonparticipation in the economic market place. She follows the Marxian definition of class, by positing that women have a different relationship to the means of production. Their secondary status results from their participation in the production of "simple use values" rather than "exchange values." In other words, Benston's formulation is based on the fact of women's participation in unpaid, undervalued household labor. This explanation fails to take into account that many women do participate in the money economy (see below).

The third type of analysis commonly advanced is the minority group theory. Hacker (1951) demonstrates that women show most of the structural and psychological characteristics typical of oppressed minority groups. Independent support comes from empirical studies that suggest women themselves may introject the negative stereotype projected by the majority group and project this self-disdain in the form of prejudice against other women (Goldberg 1968, Pheterson et al 1971). Although there are obvious similarities between the situations of women and other minority groups, the minority group perspective fails to account for the power relationship (at least until recently) between men and women and the lack of group consciousness among women.

THE FEMINIST CRITIQUE

Much of the recent literature on sex roles has been prompted by renewed awareness of the problems of sexual inequality, combined with increased interest in the Women's Movement. With few exceptions (e.g. Myrdal 1944, Hacker 1951, Rossi 1964), sociologists were not among the first to evince interest in the problems of sexual inequality; however, the writing of Movement advocates and ideologues has greatly influenced subsequent sociological perspectives.

It was in popular literature and essays that the position of women in contemporary society was first critiqued. The works of de Beauvoir (1953) and Friedan (1963) were among the most significant early treatments, stimulating discussion and providing inspiration for the revitalization of feminism. Subsequently Bird (1968), Millet (1970), Greer (1971), and Firestone (1970), among others, elaborated on these themes. Numerous articles, blueprints, and manifestos have followed, many of them found in collections such as Roszak & Roszak (1969), Morgan (1970), Altbach (1971), Gaskof (1971), Gornick & Moran (1971), and Reeves (1971).

There are many variations in the feminist critique; however, the basic argument suggests that male-oriented social, legal, and economic structures have inhibited women in their development as multifaceted human beings. Feminist writers stress the covert psychological barriers inculcated in women, as well as the more overt structured forms of discrimination. More explicitly, in addition to concrete job discrimination, legal inequities, and the like, there is the vast arena of sex role stereotyping and socialization that narrowly defines womanhood.

These patterns effectively block major lines of development for all but a few women. Frequently, the feminist critics stress the psychic and economic benefits men derive from these patterns. Crucial to most feminist writings is the realization that the problems generated by the inequities of women's position are not open to individual solutions. They reflect the situation of women as a group and require group based solutions.

The oppression of women becomes a political problem entailing the question of power relations with men (see below). The feminist literature calls for adjustment of the situation and emergence of a new social order. It should be stressed that writers vary greatly in their specific treatment of the situation. Degrees of radicalism also vary, both in terms of analysis and of proposed solutions.

The influence of ideas stemming from the Movement is apparent in subsequent social science research. Only a handful of sociologists actively anticipated or coincided with the popular rise of the Movement. Hacker's (1951) article comparing women to oppressed minority groups and Rossi's (1964), calling for an end to sex inequality, are classics in the field.

It was a journalist (Friedan 1963), however, who carillonned the political content and oppressive potential of numerous influential social science theories. Friedan's criticism of Freud and Parsons was a precursor of a more general reevaluation of the treatment of women in psychoanalytic and functionalist theories. This is not to deny her social science predecessors. Earlier, Horney (1969) had attacked several sexist Freudian concepts. Parsons had come under attack from a number of scientific quarters. Friedan's work, nonetheless, explicated the sexist assumptions underlying numerous important social theories.

The rapid spread of ideas generated by the Movement has prompted analysis of the Movement itself as an example of the sociological phenomenon of social movements. A rash of recent studies have investigated the Movement's ideological foundations, recruitment and support, leadership, and influence on public policy (Degler 1964, Bernard 1971, Dixon 1971–1972, Hole & Levine 1971, Freeman 1973, Carden 1974, Safilios-Rothschild 1974).

One historical analysis (Degler 1964) examines the roots of early feminism in the US, noting the conditions that provided fertile ground for its initial growth. These include the Industrial Revolution, the Frontier, and, more recently, World War I. The lack of a strong ideology is identified as a major reason for the eclipse of the Movement after the attainment of women's suffrage.

Rossi (1964) similarly addresses the issue of the earlier Movement's decline. More recently a number of books examining the subject have appeared, including Flexner (1959), Kraditor (1971), O'Neill (1971), and Carden (1974). Collections of writings by early feminist activists have also appeared (i.e. Rossi 1973b, Sochen 1972). Much of the more recent work focuses on the similarities in the causes, conditions, and development of the early and later phases of the Movement, with implications for the study of social movements in general.

SEX AS A DIFFERENTIATING VARIABLE

Social differentiation, of which sex role differentiation is a subform, has been a concern of philosophers and social scientists from Plato's *Republic* to the present day. Durkheim (1933) made a now-classic distinction between mechanical and organic solidarity in society, the former based upon similarity of individuals and groups, the latter upon specialization of tasks and division of labor. Durkheim used the relationship of the sexes within the family as an example of organic solidarity. Linton (1942) and Parsons (1942) have pointed to the universality and extreme elaboration of the system of norms that pertain to gender.

Eisenstadt (1971) suggests that social differentiation "usually refers to (1) the situation that exists in every social unit, large or small, by virtue of the fact that people with different characteristics perform different tasks and occupy different roles, and (2) the fact that these tasks and roles are closely interrelated in several ways." Mayer & Buckley define social differentiation as the "division of social roles and tasks, based upon inherited and socially acquired individual differences" (Mayer & Buckley 1970:4).

Differentiation also has been defined as "a systematic way of distributing tasks, scarce resources, privileges and burdens among the members of a society or a group" (Holter 1970:19). Such distributive systems are perpetuated by the interaction of ideology, including norms and values, with economic, social, and psychological power relations created by the distribution (Holter 1970:19).

According to Eisenstadt (1971: 7–8), for any social system to remain differentiated it must meet two requirements: it must create the conditions for (a) "differential allocation of people to positions and roles," and (b) "the socialization—that is education in the broadest sense—of people for the performance of these roles." The allocation of people to roles requires the use of reasonably stable criteria regarding the characteristics of role occupants and task performance. Theoretically, sanctions should be available to enforce compliance, but socialization is used to ensure voluntary compliance with role assignment and with expected levels of performance (Eisenstadt 1971: 10–11).

This distribution of roles and tasks, as well as of rewards and responsibilities, may be made on the basis of either ascribed or achieved characteristics, a distinction clearly articulated by Linton (1942). Sex differentiation is a system whereby roles and tasks are distributed on the basis of the ascribed characteristics of sex. Unlike distributive systems based upon achievement, ascriptive systems do not require the motivation of individuals to enter and remain in the roles into which they have been preselected on the basis of an inborn characteristic and from which there is no escape. Such is the case with sex and race.

Nonetheless, while most social scientists clearly recognize the differentiation of sex roles, they tend to limit their analyses to the confines of the family system (Holter 1970). They often fail to note that "the norms pertinent to the roles and statuses of the two sexes penetrate every sector of social life" (Holter 1970: 10).

For American sociologists, this limitation of analysis of sex differentiation to the family may be related, in part, to the mythical "creed of classlessness" (Hodges & Lane 1968) which permeates the ideological underpinnings of all American institutions outside of the family.[5]

The neglect and implicit denial of sex differentiation throughout the fabric of society is all the more astonishing in view of the universal nature of differentiation by sex in all known societies. But the very absence of societies that are sex *un*differentiated may be another factor that discourages social scientists who are thereby unable to test hypotheses regarding the causes of such differentiation. In addition, the intricate and sometimes confusing relationship between sex differentiation and sex stratification may lead social scientists to explore less troubled waters.

SEX AS A STRATIFICATION VARIABLE

In sex differentiated societies, although there may be within-group mobility (i.e. a woman may be born into a working-class family, but marry a middle-class husband), between-group mobility is impossible (i.e. except in the extreme case of transsexual surgery). Sex differentiation involves the distribution of roles and tasks, as well as rewards and sanctions, between two groups according to sex.

Almost invariably, as social units are differentiated, differential values are placed upon the groups involved, which give rise to a rank ordering of groups. Such a rank ordering, when institutionalized, is usually referred to as "social stratification." This rank ordering leads to an intrinsic institutionalized social inequality among groups (Heller 1969), an ubiquitous and ancient feature of social systems (Tumin 1953).

Theories of Sex Stratification

CLASS   The direction of the rank ordering of sex roles is itself noteworthy. Perhaps one of the most theoretically interesting (and existentially frustrating) aspects of sex

[5]The creed of classlessness has stood in contradiction to reality from earliest American history, and this denial of a class segregated society was noted as an almost uniquely American phenomenon by de Tocqueville (1947).

differentiation is its constancy and its invariant rank ordering: the male role is always more highly valued than the female role. In contradistinction to the Davis-Moore (1942) theory of stratification, which claims that certain roles are more functionally important to the survival of a system than others and are therefore more highly rewarded, all roles and associated tasks carried out by males in any society become more highly valued. Thus, roles held by women and consequently lowly valued in one society, may be performed by men and be more highly valued in another society (Reiss 1960).

Social stratification always involves the notion of a hierarchy of positions, with differential rewards and access to power. These hierarchies of role categories may be conceptualized as classes, with associated levels of power.

Although he was not directly addressing the question of sexual stratification, Weber's notions of class are relevant here.[6] Weber suggested that a class was constituted of a number of people whose life chances were similarly determined by a specific causal component "represented exclusively by economic interests in the possession of goods and opportunities for income and . . . represented under the conditions of the commodity or labor markets" (Weber 1946: 181). Weber saw a "class situation" as the "typical chance for a supply of goods, external living conditions, and personal life experiences, in so far as this chance is determined by the amount and kind of power or lack of such, to dispose of goods or skills for the sake of income in a given economic order" (Gerth & Mills 1946: 181).

The Weberian formulation also recognizes that class situations are further differentiated by "the kind of property that is useable for returns . . . and the kind of services that can be offered in the market" (Weber 1946: 182). Although Weber does not do so, this distinction may be applied to the system of sex stratification where male power is based upon property and female power upon services (Engels 1942). However, the services of women have been used primarily within the family and without remuneration.

OCCUPATION   Even when women's services have been utilized in the larger economy, they have been segregated to certain low level occupations, or to the lowest levels within higher ranking occupations, a pattern that has considerable cross-national stability (Goode 1963, Baude & Holmberg 1967, Oppenheimer 1968, Holter 1970, Epstein 1970, Collins 1971, Galenson 1973, Blake 1974). Persistent sexual segregation of traditionally feminine occupations has been documented in American society (Gross 1968, Nixon 1973) and cross-nationally (Sullerot 1971, Galenson 1973), with the notable possible exceptions of the Soviet Union, China, and Israel (Dodge 1966).

Predominantly male occupations may undergo a "tipping phenomenon" in which the entrance of a critical proportion of women triggers rapid departure of remaining males. Thus, fresh sexual segregation of women comes about within a new occupational role (Gross 1968). Featherman & Hauser (1974) have analyzed the movement

[6]Weber's conceptualization of class was an attempt to extend Marx's formulation in which class was the relationship to the means of production (Marx 1959).

of women between 1962 and 1972 into low-level, declining occupations as men leave these jobs for higher-level occupations.

The fact that women's status does not necessarily improve with greater economic development has been demonstrated by Boserup (1970). In an anthropological analysis of underdeveloped countries, Boserup shows that advanced, technologically based economic development may have a depressive effect upon women's occupational status. She argues that "economic progress benefits men as wage earners in the modern sector, while the position of women is left unchanged and even deteriorates" (Boserup 1970: 139). The modern sector eliminates enterprises usually conducted by women, who then are squeezed down into unskilled, low-wage jobs.

The equality of privileges and responsibilities for American adults is "seriously modified by the asymmetrical relation of the sexes to the occupational structure" (Parsons 1942: 219). Both adolescence, with its differentiated youth culture, and marriage, with its relinquishment by both sexes of the "glamorous" element of youth, contribute to the eventual differentiation of sex roles in American society.

Parsons (1942) sees the occupational role of the adult male as "fundamental to his social status in general" (p. 222), whereas the adult female's status derives from the husband's occupational position. The fact that the husband is usually the sole occupant of an occupational role is underscored as a principal source of strain in the sex role structure of American society, because it "deprives the wife of her role as partner in a joint enterprise" (p. 223).

Parsons characterizes the housewife role as a "pseudo occupation." However, the logical alternative of married women entering the labor market in positions comparable to their husbands' occupations is dismissed by Parsons as untenable because of the competitive strain it would introduce into the marital relationship. In essence, Parsons argues that sex stratification of the labor market is necessary to maintain the sex stratification and equilibrium within the conjugal family. Lenski's (1966) class analysis of the sexual stratification system turns the argument around and proposes that limiting female competition to the marriage market protects women from the allegedly greater risks of striving for success in economic and political spheres.

In a discussion of social stratification, Parsons (1949: 164–86) cites the segregation of married women from the occupational world as an important mechanism "for alleviating invidious comparisons" between the sexes, a means of articulating a distinct separation of adult roles to avoid competition. Subsequent increases in the proportion of married women in the labor market have failed to corroborate this view, and several studies of the effect of the wife's working on the marital relationship have indicated an equalizing effect (Blood & Hamlin 1958, Heer 1958, Hoffman 1963, Scanzoni 1972).

CONFLICT AND BARGAINING   Weber's conception of stratification involves conflict, whereby individuals vie for dominance through the use of resources. As resource distribution changes, so do power and domination. Ideology is used to justify the stratification system and to create solidarity within the differentiated groups (Weber 1968). This type of model at first appears (and is probably meant) to describe competition solely among males; but it clearly has implications for male-female dominance patterns, within the family and in other areas. As we discuss below, women have a range of resources that they may use legitimately or illegitimately in the dominance equation in the family, the economy, and the political world.

A conflict theory of sexual stratification, built upon Weberian and Freudian perspectives, is developed by Collins (1971) who sees present-day employment discrimination against women as the product of a sexual stratification system. Collins posits a sexual stratification system based upon male physical dominance, female vulnerability resulting from childbearing and childrearing, and human sexual and aggressive drives. Following Levi-Strauss (1949), Collins cites the institution of sexual property as the basic characteristic of the sexual stratification system. Sexual property is a mechanism whereby males (and sometimes females) can claim exclusive sexual rights over another individual. Variations in the sexual stratification system stem from two independent factors: (*a*) "forms of social organization affecting the use of force and" (*b*) "those affecting the market positions of men and women" (Collins 1971: 9).

When force is not regulated by the state, differential power among males determines the sexual stratification system, and women have no resources with which to bargain. When the use of force is limited to the state, a market for individual sex qualities, along with other personal resources, emerges.

RESOURCE THEORY   Collins related four ideal types of social structure (i.e. low technology tribal societies, fortified households in stratified societies, private households in a market economy, and advanced market economy) to different types of resources available to females and males. The four levels of social structure, with specific patterns of male-female relations, reflect changes in women's bargaining power as well as their participation in the market place.

Family relatives and friends may be counted as part of the total resources of the family. Using this approach, Bott (1957) studied the impact of the family's entire social network (including relatives, friends, and social contacts) upon task division within the family. Families whose networks are limited cannot look to relatives or friends to help with family responsibilities. As a result, husband and wives in small nuclear families tend to be more isolated and are more likely to forego traditional role differentiation than couples with extended social networks.

In general, women's independent income, education, and occupational positions serve to increase their bargaining position and make it theoretically possible to reduce the use of sexuality as an exchange medium. However, because women, even with the same education and occupational experience as men, can hope to receive only a proportion of male economic rewards (Fuchs 1971, Sullerot 1971, Sawhill 1974), sexuality remains an important adjunct resource (Elder 1969). Nonetheless, within marriage, women develop increased bargaining power as their earning capacity reaches a significant level (Fougeyrollas 1951, Wolfe 1959, Heer 1958, Hoffman 1963, Zelditch 1964b, Scanzoni 1972, Rapoport & Rapoport 1972, Holmstrom 1972).

Some writers have suggested that with increased economic power women can follow the male example of demanding increased sexual attractiveness and youth in the men they choose for marriage partners (Walster et al 1966, Collins 1971, Safilios-Rothschild 1971, 1972, 1974).

There is, however, at least one limiting factor to married women's accretion of resources through labor market participation. The married woman's ability to utilize occupational opportunities may be at least partially dependent upon the cooperation (or acquiescence) of her husband (Weil 1961, Holter 1970) who may wish to enforce her leisure as a symbol of his affluence (Veblen 1899).

Numerous studies have documented the negative effect of fertility on working patterns of women. Cross-national studies bear out the inverse relationship between the number of children a woman has and her attachment to the labor market (Kiser & Whelpton 1949–1954, Freedman, Baumert & Bolte 1959, Freedman, Whelpton & Campbell 1959, Acsadi 1961, Whelpton, Campbell & Patterson 1966, Glass 1968, Weller 1968, US Dept. of Commerce 1971a,b, Pinnelli 1971).

Actual total resources, both material and nonmaterial, available in any given society may influence the sexual stratification system. An abundance of educational and occupational positions, as well as an increase in inventions and technology, tends to favor a breakdown in sex differentiation. This is particularly so outside the confines of the family, although a noticeable time lag may exist before women's access to resources actually increases (Oppenheimer 1973). When the market constricts, sex differentiation may increase sharply (Holter 1970). Nonetheless, crises (see below) have a serious and predictable effect upon sex role differentiation.

The ideology of the Women's Liberation Movement emphasizes egalitarian relationships between men and women and the debunking of the concept of women as sex objects. This ideology is most logically linked to the social structure of an advanced market economy, with its increased bargaining resources and possibilities for women.

THE MARXIST ANALYSIS   Marx & Engels (1956), building on Fourier's (1841) notions of women's emancipation and sexual freedom, interpreted the position of women as a measure of general societal advance. In his later writings, Marx (1970) moved from this abstract approach to women's status to an analysis of women's roles embedded in the context of the family.

After Marx's death, Engels more systematically formulated several of the perspectives articulated in Marx's work. Engels, basing his analysis on questionable historical data, traced the modern stratified husband-wife relationship to the period in unrecorded history when the herds of cattle (i.e. the means of developing surplus labor) passed from common tribal possession to ownership by the individual male head of the family. This resulted in "a revolution within the family" (Engels 1942).

Despite the uncertain empirical basis of Engels's treatise, he correctly noted that women's domestic labor was an "unimportant extra," and it has remained that way until the present time. Only very recently have economists begun to consider including women's domestic work in indices of gross national product (Kreps 1971,

Sawhill 1974, Morgan et al 1966). Engels's vision was that the equalization of women depended upon their emancipation from private domestic labor and their participation in production "on a large, social scale."[7]

Engels and Marx saw the first "class opposition" in the monogamous family relationship between the sexes, and this perspective spawned numerous analyses. In her brilliant analysis of the status of women throughout history, de Beauvoir (1953) integrates the reproductive and economic constraints developed by earlier analysts through a psychological perspective.

Mitchell (1966) suggests that "women's condition" cannot be understood by derivation from economic, general societal, or reproductive issues. She concludes that women's condition must be differentiated into four separate components: production, reproduction, sex and socialization of children. These components must be analyzed simultaneously as one integrated structure if they are to lead to the emancipation of women.

Benston (1969), using a Marxian model, suggests that when society industrializes housework, the "material basis for discrimination against women will be gone" (p. 22). Although many housework functions have been industrialized, this has resulted only in a moderate improvement in the status of women. For example, industrialization of housework in Israel has not led to unequivocal equality of the sexes. And time budget studies have shown repeatedly the increased amount of time spent on housework since the advent of technological devices (Girard & Bastide 1959, Szalai 1966, 1968). Further, the industrialization of housework does not address the issue of why sex segregation persists in the labor market. The question of the differential relations the two sexes have to the occupational structure remains unanswered by this approach.

Moving beyond a Marxian approach, Eichler (1973) notes that whereas men have a single status ranking based upon their position in the occupational world, women are subject to a double ranking system. First, women are ranked in terms of their derived status from their husbands' occupational role; second, they are ranked in terms of their independent status from their own occupational position. Women can move in and out of both marriage and employment; however, their derived status is supposed to be above or equal to their independent status.

Housewives who do not work outside of the home represent a more complicated problem. Eichler suggests that the only fact that unites all housewives is their economic dependence on a single individual—usually their husbands—which places them in a position of a *personal dependent*. A personal dependent is defined as any individual who is "economically, socially, and/or legally tied to another person who has authority over him/her as a personal dependent." The individual who has authority over the personal dependent is the personal master. Personal dependents identify with their masters, rather than with each other, thereby eliminating the

---

[7]Engels also points to the change from mother-right to father-right as a serious "historical defeat of the female sex." By linking the inheritance of children to the male line of descent, men gradually increased their wealth and control over the means of production, as well as their authority within the family.

possibility of group consciousness. Customarily, asymmetrical affective relationships are established between personal dependents and their masters, in which the personal dependents offset the master's power through appeal or emotional manipulation. The master, on the other hand, is expected to exercise benevolent paternalism.

One difficulty with this perspective is its failure to take into account the master's dependence upon the personal dependent, except in those cases where the master has multiple replaceable dependents. The threat of economic independence on the part of the personal dependent can lead to subtle and not-so-subtle shifts in the master-dependent relationship. This framework has limited utility, since it applies only to women who are unemployed and who lack other sources of income. Finally, the term personal dependent is not comparable to caste or class in that it applies to the interactional, rather than the structural, level.

Areas of Stratification

POLITICAL SYSTEM   The complex relationship of dependence, dominance, and power is central to the political aspect of sexual relationships (Millet 1970). Historically, males have had virtually total control over the formal and material manifestations of power, whereas the feminine power domain has been largely informal, psychological, and interpersonal.

In all political (i.e. power structured) relationships, one group or individual attempts to dominate and control another. Females, like most politically subordinate groups, have had little representation in political structures. Their subordination in every sector deters their organized opposition and stablizes their widespread oppression. Millet suggests that Western society is organized as a patriarchy in which males control all sources of power. Even the act of coitus, "set so deeply within the larger context of human affairs . . . serves as a charged microcosm of the variety of attitudes and values to which culture subscribes . . . (and) a model of sexual politics on an individual and personal plane" (Millet 1970:23).

LEGAL SYSTEM   The subordinate position of women in every segment of the sexual stratification system is graphically reflected in most legal systems. Tradition is embodied, as well as reinforced, by the legal structure (Schulder 1970, *Valparaiso Law Review* 1971). Kanowitz's (1969), excellent statement of women's legal situation describes the long-reaching effects of concepts embedded in English common law, the doctrine upon which much of the American legal system is based.

The doctrine of coverture, for example, states that upon entering marriage, a woman is deprived of her legal status as an independent individual. She may no longer hold property, keep her original surname, or enter into contracts. The Married Women's Property Acts, enacted in Britain in the nineteenth century, voided many of these prohibitions. However, no comparable comprehensive legislation, to date, has been enacted in the United States; thus, many of these statutes remain on the books in certain states within this country (Kanowitz 1969).

Women's legal status as a subordinate is not limited to family law. Criminal and civil law are replete with examples of women being treated as minors or irresponsible individuals (Chafetz 1974). Many laws, originally designed to protect women from exploitation within the labor market, today act to bar women from desirable jobs. The Civil Rights Act of 1964 did much to alleviate some of these inequities, but the Equal Rights Amendment to the Constitution of the United States remains to be ratified in at least a handful of states. The difficulty involved in attempting to change the legal status of women is mirrored in the fact that this amendment has been introduced into every session of Congress since 1923, and did not receive approval by both Houses until 1972. Even if ratified, this amendment, which would do for women what the 14th Amendment did for blacks 100 years ago, will not be in effect until after 1975 (Chafetz 1974). Much research remains to be done on the impact of legal changes upon the many facets of women's roles.

Ideology and Stratification by Sex

Ideology, as we have suggested above, is a major underpinning of social structure, sometimes even preceding new structural changes (Myrdal & Klein 1956, Goode 1963, Geertz 1964, Holter 1970, Safilios-Rothschild 1972). Divergent ideologies that separate and sustain subgroups within a society may be linked to different types of social structure (Myrdal 1944, Lipman-Blumen 1974b).

Political, economic, and family structures are inevitably buttressed by ideology. Ideology, ingrained by socialization practices, serves as a powerful alternative to enforcing compliance through brute force (Rossi 1969). It may serve as a significant soporific against the harsh realities of living.

A patriarchal social structure rests upon the ideology of male superiority, which has been knit into the major religious systems throughout history.[8] Myrdal (1944) has described in detail the contribution made to the "American Dilemma" by the ideology of male superiority and female (as well as black) inferiority. The core institution of patriarchy is the family, which reflects the larger society in its structure as well as in its ideology. The family, with its ideologically supported male dominance, both links the individual to, and controls the individual for, society (Goode 1964).

Political and religious ideology have impact both upon sex roles within the family, as well as upon sex roles as they are articulated with the economy and other aspects of society. Official and unofficial ideology hold sway in different sectors and under different conditions. In a cross-national analysis, Wilensky attempts to link egalitarian ideology (only crudely defined) regarding women's roles, with societal economic level and women's position in the labor force. Wilensky points to the disparity between official and unofficial ideology; he emphasizes the importance of unofficial ideology and norms in barring women from advancement at different stages in their occupational development. Wilensky concludes that "in the push for equality, ideology accounts for little unless it is closely meshed with a reorganization of political and economic life" (Wilensky 1968:242).

---

[8]Christianity, in its earliest stages, with its ethic of individual worth, was seen as a radical departure from the explicit patriarchy of Judaism, and therefore attracted a large early female following (Goode 1963). Catholicism's subsequent emphasis upon the father as family head has offset this elevation of the female to equal worth with males.

Crisis and Change

Reorganization of political and economic, as well as family, structures is difficult to effect (Holter 1971). However, at least one condition under which roles—and ultimately social structure, including the stratification system—change, is crisis. Crisis, a condition under which the members of a social system recognize a threat to their sustenance or survival, a threat against which their ordinary coping mechanisms are inadequate, requires reallocation of resources—and ultimately of power (Davis 1963, Lipman-Blumen 1973b). This need for reallocation of resources leads to a breakdown of the stratification system, which focuses more on means (i.e. who is doing what) than on ends (i.e. what is getting done or "goal attainment"). As a result, individuals and groups who can contribute to goal attainment (i.e. crisis resolution) are allowed, even recruited, into roles from which they were previously prohibited because of sex, race, or other stigmata. The fate of women and blacks in the World War II labor market reflects such a pattern (Wool & Pearlman 1947, Killingsworth 1969). The increase in the number of women in national legislatures during and after World War II (Lipman-Blumen 1973b) and the political candidacy of an unprecedented 800 women in the 1974 US elections following the Watergate crisis are further evidence of this phenomenon.

With the resolution of crisis, a new stratification system emerges and begins to rigidify, until the next crisis undermines its stability. The sex stereotyping of occupational roles (Oppenheimer 1968) and other roles that gives way during crisis tends to reappear after the crisis has subsided. However, serious or long-range crises may leave permanent residues of role change in their wakes.

ALTERNATIVES TO STRATIFICATION BY SEX

Rossi examines three models of social equality and their related ideologies (Rossi 1969). The first is a pluralistic model involving a heterogeneous society where many different groups coexist while maintaining their own distinct characteristics. The second equality model—an assimilation model—rests upon female participation in the occupational and political worlds on a par with males. Finally the hybrid, utopian model rejects the present social organization, including traditional sex roles, and projects a new value system based upon creativity, a sense of community, and more meaningful personal relationships.

The companionate marital relationship has been suggested as a structural antidote to sexual stratification, an ideal model in which both men and women can find fulfillment. In this type of unstratified sexual relationship both individuals join in a "mutually supportive and complementary relationship rather than a dominant-subservient one" (Safilios-Rothschild 1972). In a companionate relationship, the spouses are primarily friends and companions, sharing equally in all familial responsibilities and privileges. Social scientists acknowledge the difficulty of developing and sustaining such a relationship (particularly among individuals socialized to be unequal), but they rarely offer means of overcoming these problems (Holmstrom 1972, Safilios-Rothschild 1972). Rapoport & Rapoport (1971) conclude that only when both the wife's commitment to career and her income are as great as her husband's is the companionate relationship a realistic possibility. A relationship of equality is possible only between equal individuals. [The concept of androgyny also has been advanced as a level beyond differentiation toward which role partners might strive (Rossi 1969, Bernard 1975).]

Utopian models of society continue to envision sex roles as ideologically and structurally equalized, rather than stratified. But both macro- and micro-sociological studies report developmental trends that move from egalitarian beginnings to later traditional, stratified sex roles. Recent studies of the Israeli experience note increased differentiation of sex roles along traditional lines. This is in sharp contrast to its early history of official and actual de-differentiation and egalitarianism (Spiro 1956, Talmon 1965).

The reemergence of traditional sex role allocations is attributed to the dynamic interplay of changes in the internal structure of the family and in the external structure of the larger society. Increased numbers of children and greater general affluence are seen as two contributing factors. We would add to these the fact of the underlying, lingering traditional influence of patriarchal ideology that historically characterized both Jewish social structure and the Jewish religious system. Other structural (Blumberg 1974) and psychological (Mednick, 1975) explanations have been developed.

On the micro-sociological level, a similar trend appears among newly married couples who develop an egalitarian relationship during the first year of marriage, but gradually move to a sex segregated model within a few years (Geiken 1960). Men can look both to occupational and family roles for fulfillment, whereas women are socialized to derive their total gratification through family roles. Thus, it is not surprising that women may be reluctant to allow men to encroach upon their sole domain of expertise and satisfaction (Safilios-Rothschild 1972).

SOCIAL MOBILITY

Social mobility is an important component of sexual stratification. And sex as a stratification variable has been at the heart of several studies of intergenerational female mobility [but was noticeably lacking from the benchmark Blau & Duncan (1967) study]. Several of these studies have focused upon mobility through marriage (Rubin 1968, 1969, Scott 1969, Elder 1969).

A more recent study, applying the Blau and Duncan methodology to a female sample, reported no significant differences between male and female intergenerational occupational mobility patterns (De Jong, Brawer & Robin 1971). On the basis of role ambiguity, role conflict, job discrimination, and discontinuity of employment, the authors anticipated that women would experience less occupational inheritance, less upward mobility, and less long distance upward mobility than males. In general, the investigators report that the data did not bear our these expectations. Instead, they report female occupational patterns characterized by greater occupational inheritance than expected, a considerable amount of mobility, more upward than downward mobility, and more short distance than long distance mobility.

Considerable debate has been engendered by the methodology, conceptualization, and analysis of the De Jong et al study (Havens & Tully 1972, Ramsøy 1973, Tyree

& Treas 1974). One critique, which reworks the De Jong et al data, concludes that the finding of "no significant differences" overstates the case. It notes that sufficient discrepancies exist between male and female data to warrant the conclusion that the broad census categories used in the study are inappropriate for the necessary analysis.

A recent study, comparing female mobility through marriage with male mobility through occupational attainment, reported the following: (a) hypergamy (i.e. marriage mobility) essentially explained by the "favorable balance of upward over downward mobility among males," (b) a "weaker relationship of origin to destination among males," (c) a noticeable mobility advantage among males of middle origins, and (d) "substantially more downward mobility into the manual-farm class by females than by males" (Glenn, Ross & Tully 1974:683). The authors conclude that although their data reveal that the "American status structure is more fluid than the male mobility data alone would indicate, there apparently is a condition of relative stasis among middle-origin females" (Glenn et al 1974:683).

Status Inconsistency

Some of the difficulties involved in studying the status of women may stem from the discrepancies women experience as the result of their multiple statuses as wives, mothers, students, employees, and women. These discrepancies, concpetualized as "status inconsistency," can presumably lead to role conflict and ambiguity, as well as to intrapsychic strain.

The concept of status inconsistency may be traced to the work of Weber (1968), who recognized mutiple dimensions of social stratification along which a given individual or group could hold uncorrelated positions. Sorokin (1927) and Benoit-Smullyan (1944) developed variations on this general notion. More recently, Lenski (1954) has developed the notion of status crystallization (i.e. congruence, integration, etc) as a major variant of consistency theory.

Lenski suggests that individuals concurrently occupy statuses in numerous distinct status hierarchies. Status consistency is proposed as an additional "nonvertical dimension" of social status, consisting of the interrelation of an individual's positions on a series of parallel stratification hierarchies. Marked divergence on two or more salient hierarchies produces status consistency.

Gibbs & Martin (1964), influenced by Durkheim and Parsons, propose that the source of status incompatibility is the total social position in which an individual simultaneously occupies unusual or deviant status combinations. Hughes's (1945) discussion of the black physician and the female engineer are cases in point.

Status inconsistency theory suggests that a status-inconsistent individual experiences psychological strain as a result of these discrepant positions. Conflicting role expectations associated with discrepant positions are thought to lead to ambiguous self-definitions and conflicting role directives (Lenski 1954, 1956).

Results of status consistency research have been variable and inconclusive, primarily because of the broad range of methodologies used to study the phenomenon. Problems of sample size and type, measure of inconsistency, and multicollinearity have contributed to past difficulties; however, new approaches are being developed (Hornung 1971).

A regrettably small number of status consistency studies have taken women as their subjects (Jackson 1962, Schmitt 1965, Tickamyer 1973). Jackson, measuring wives' inconsistency by their education, ethnicity, and husband's occupation, found higher rates of stress among women with high education married to men with low occupations. Schmitt's results tend to corroborate this finding.

Despite the shortcomings associated with "operationalizing" the concept of status inconsistency, the concept appears promising in clarifying certain aspects of women's status. Status inconsistency among women should be explored in terms of discrepancies between their education and occupational levels, between their own education, occupation, and income and those of their husbands, and between their own pre- and postmarital occupations, to name just a few variables. This type of approach might provide considerable explanatory power, possibly cutting across the minority-caste-class debate, as well as the intergeneration mobility issue.

CONTRIBUTION OF STRATIFICATION CONCEPT

The concept of stratification, whose roots infiltrate the entire terrain of sociology, has much to contribute to the understanding of sex roles (Acker 1973). Sex differences, sexual behavior, socialization, and sexual segregation of the educational, occupational, political, and legal systems, all stand to be informed by the systematic exploration of sex as a stratification variable. This is so largely because of the intricate relationships among stratification, resources, and power. The concepts of power, influence, resources, and authority, linked in a systematic way, would go far to shed light on women's changing sex role. For example, much of the reviewed literature highlights the impact that women's lack of control over resources (i.e. physiological, economic, and political) has had upon their continuing subordinate position.

One such approach could examine the different types of resources and power available to women in their roles within different institutions of society. In the family, for example, women have access to, and legitimately use, sexual, psychological, interpersonal, and (for children and domestic chores) physical resources. These resources lead to the development of significant power vis à vis children and, more rarely, husbands.

In certain situations, economic, educational, and political resources are less likely to be viewed as viable power bases for women to use within marriage. When this is so, wives and mothers may focus upon personal influence, which rests upon persuasion and forms of manipulation (as opposed to power, with its explicit foundation upon the implied ability to enforce one's will upon a reluctant other). However, when women as family members interact with the external community (i.e. in the role of consumer, employer's wife, volunteer, PTA parent), several of these resources lose their legitimacy.

In the larger economic milieu, education, social class, occupational status, economic surplus, credit, and property are legitimate resources allowed to those few women who possess them. As women move into the economic structure, sexuality, in any explicit sense, is considered largely an illegitimate or covert resource.

Interpersonal skill, as long as it is not overtly manipulative, is regarded as an acceptable medium of exchange and power. When women move—as they do only infrequently—into the political arena, the various resources take on new and mixed coloration of legitimacy. It requires an adept amalgam of these resources to play the political game with any success. The general invisibility of women in the world of politics (Duverger 1955, 1972, Amundsen 1971, Haavio-Mannila 1972) is attributable partly to their inexperience in utilizing these resources. Such inexperience is particularly debilitating within a social structure designed to create external barriers.

Obviously, men's resources work in similar alternately legitimate and illegitimate, overt and covert ways. It is the interplay between these shifting uses of illegitimate and legitimate resources, as well as power, influence, and authority, by both women and men that deserves further exploration within the context of the sexual stratification system.

STRATEGIES FOR FUTURE RESEARCH

To this point, we have focused upon the substantive areas, findings, and methodologies that are current in the literature on sex roles. However, there are serious lacunae in the understanding and knowledge that these provide. In a sense, we are raising the question of where the study of sex roles should go from here. In attempting to address this question, we briefly sketch a set of research strategies that would hopefully enhance future research.[9]

Strategy 1: Critical Syntheses

Although there have been several efforts to develop critical syntheses, each of them, including the present one, suffers at the very least from the areas they have chosen to exclude. Meaningful categories of analysis and in-depth syntheses are necessary to bring coherence to the rapidly expanding literature.

Strategy 2: Process Analyses

Like most scientific disciplines in their early stages, the science of sex roles, at present, appears to be in a taxonomic holding pattern. More work is needed to analyze the processes that underlie and contribute to various forms of sex differences, sex role partitioning, and the formation and perpetuation of women as a group apart. Development and testing of analytic processual models is imperative, before we can begin to develop intervention strategies. Existing work on processes is often contradictory and remains to be tested, refined, and integrated. This emphasis upon delineating process (rather than description) cuts across many of the existing research perspectives. It promises a means of developing a comprehensive picture of sex roles across the entire life cycle.

[9]The first eight strategies are designed to build a systematic knowledge base, while the ninth strategy attempts to implement the knowledge developed in the previous strategies.

Strategy 3: Social System/Personal System Integration

Social system and personal system variables are often analyzed separately, thus ignoring their intrinsic and intricate interdependence. More attention should be given to the complex relationship between individual and/or group differences, and the factors stemming from the larger social system within which the individuals and groups develop. Somehow the laboratory and the real world have to be integrated both conceptually and methodologically. For example, families should be studied more often in situ and less often through detached questionnaires, interviews, and artificial laboratory games.

Sex roles continue to be examined largely within the context of the family, an institution that tends to inhibit change. Sex role research should be conducted within nonfamily settings to develop broader perspectives on how sex roles change.

In addition, there is serious need for comparative research on male sex roles. As noted above, what little work has been done tends to focus on men's occupational roles and needs arising from their work situation. There is virtually total neglect of their roles as fathers, husbands, brothers, colleagues, friends, and lovers.

Strategy 4: Cross-Cultural and Interdisciplinary Analyses

More cross-cultural comparisons of sex role patterns, including comparative studies of sex role learning and expectations, would be illuminating. Studies of this type are invaluable in differentiating those sex role patterns that persist across all cultures, as opposed to those that change their configuration in different cultural settings. Cross-cultural studies offer significant insights into roles considered deviant in some cultures but valuable in others. Such studies can suggest not only *how* roles vary, but *why* they are patterned differently. They deepen understanding of how different patterns operate in social systems that are marked by different levels of development and distinct socio-economic and political systems. Demographic changes, such as later marriage, fewer children, and greater longevity, should be examined cross-culturally to gain perspective on how other societies respond to these trends.

Interdisciplinary research teams, composed of social and natural scientists, can offer the strengths of their individual disciplines in exploring the problems of sex roles. New methodologies must be developed and old ones improved and integrated to nourish the most comprehensive understanding of this area. An interdisciplinary approach is particularly fruitful in cross-national studies, although we do not minimize the substantial difficulties of conducting such research.

Strategy 5: New Theories of the Middle Range

Here we would recommend the development of new theories of the middle range (Merton 1949), which delineate a limited segment of society or social action. Such theories should attempt to break through the confines of previous research, as well as through political and ideological blindfolds.[10] This may be the most difficult strategy of all, in view of human reluctance to relinquish cultural, intellectual, emotional, and political blinders.

[10]Middle-range theories, such as the homosocial view of sex roles, represent a tentative step in this direction (Lipman-Blumen 1974a).

Strategy 6: Mapping Sex Roles onto Sexual Behavior (and vice versa)

The mapping of sex roles onto sexual behavior and vice versa seems such a logical step that it is difficult to believe how rarely it is done. Sexologists tend to study sexual behavior in a vacuum that precludes their understanding of sexual behavior changes, which might be adaptive at different stages in the life cycle.[11]

Sociologists who have been concerned with sex roles per se tend to ignore the sexual behavior of individuals in different social roles.[12] Understanding how sexual behavior is laced into all social roles and how certain sex roles foster or limit different forms of sexual behavior are a critical and currently neglected research area.

Strategy 7: Specification of Conditions for Changing Sex Roles

This strategy would permit us to understand not only how sex roles, but all social roles, change. We often forget that sex roles offer an important theoretical paradigm for understanding the entire spectrum of social roles. Specification of the conditions that permit or encourage sex role alternatives would enable us to design, without chaos, social arrangements through which desired sex role changes could be implemented.

Strategy 8: Multidimensional Methodologies

This strategy calls for developing appropriate, complex multidimensional methodologies to meet the intrinsically complex problems involved in sex role research. In addition to the cross-cultural and interdisciplinary approaches suggested above, social scientists need to design more longitudinal, as well as cross-sectional, studies.

In order to bring the strengths of survey research and ethnomethodology to bear upon these problems, quantitative and qualitative methods must be integrated. Experimental and ethological approaches, interviews, questionnaires, and participant and unobtrusive observation should be developed interdependently to sharpen our research focus. More attention should be given to the perennial problems of sampling, control groups, and replications.[13]

Strategy 9: Intervention and Social Policy Research

This strategy calls for the development of techniques, procedures, and social policy recommendations aimed at changing the traditional sex role patterns that currently limit both females and males in their life situations. The previous eight strategies are directed toward developing knowledge on which to build intervention techniques for transforming utopian plans into realities. The ninth strategy is a natural

[11]For example, homosexuality and autoeroticism might be reexamined as alternative sexual behavior for women as they enter periods in their lives when male companionship is undesirable or unavailable.

[12]For example, the sexual behavior that accompanies work roles often is routinely ignored, as if it were an area of forbidden or invisible knowledge.

[13]Within this strategy we must begin to develop large scale national bases for data on sexual behavior, similar to census data banks, that would permit us to develop an accurate view of the relationship among demographic, sex role, and sexual behavior changes.

outgrowth of those strategies. Resocialization techniques, institutional restructuring, and social policy analyses are crucial research initiatives that social science must undertake. These strategies, building on previous research, will hopefully lead to greater possibilities for understanding and creating more fulfilling alternatives for both women and men.

ACKNOWLEDGMENT

We are indebted to Jessie Bernard, who read and criticized an earlier draft of this paper.

Literature Cited

Acker, J. 1973. Women and social stratification: a case of intellectual sexism. In *Changing Women in a Changing Society,* ed. J. Huber, 174–84. Chicago: Univ. Chicago Press

Acsadi, G. 1961. *Some Factors Affecting Fertility in Hungary.* Presented at Int. Pop. Union Conf., New York.

Aldous, J. 1969. Occupational characteristics and males' role performance in the family. *J. Marriage Fam.* 31:707–12

Aldous, J., Hill, R. 1967. *International Bibliography of Research in Marriage and The Family 1960–64.* Minneapolis: Univ. Minnesota Press

Alper, T. G. 1974. Achievement motivation in college women: a now-you-see-it-now-you-don't phenomenon. *Am. Psychol.* 29:194–203

Altbach, E. H. 1971. *From Feminism to Liberation.* Cambridge, Mass: Schenkman

Amundsen, K. 1971. *The Silenced Majority.* Englewood Cliffs, NJ: Prentice-Hall

Andreas, C. 1971. *Sex and Caste in America.* Englewood Cliffs, NJ: Prentice-Hall

Angrist, S. S. 1969. The study of sex roles. *J. Soc. Issues* 25:215–32

Astin, H. 1969. *The Woman Doctorate in America.* New York: Russell Sage

Astin, H., Parelman, A., Fisher, A. 1974. *Sex Roles: A Research Bibliography.* Nat. Inst. Ment. Health, Dept. HEW Publ. No. ADM 7437

Astin, H., Suniewick, N., Dweck, S. 1971. *Women: A Bibliography on Their Education and Careers.* Washington DC: Hum. Serv. Press

Bakan, D. 1966. *The Duality of Human Existence.* Chicago: Rand McNally

Bardwick, J. M. 1971a. *Psychology of Women.* New York: Harper & Row

Bardwick, J. M., Ed. 1971b. *Readings on the Psychology of Women.* New York: Harper & Row

Bardwick, J. M., Douvan, E. 1971. Ambivalence: the socialization of women. In *Women in a Sexist Society: Studies of Power and Powerlessness,* ed. V. Gornick, B. K. Moran, 225–41. New York: Basic Books

Bart, P. 1970. *Divorced Men and Their Children: a Study of Emerging Roles.* Presented at Ann. Meet. Am. Sociol. Assoc., Washington, DC

Bart, P. 1971. Depression in middle-aged women. In *Women in a Sexist Society: Studies of Power and Powerlessness,* ed. V. Gornick, B. K. Moran, 163–86. New York: Basic Books

Battle-Sister, A. 1971. Conjectures on the female culture. *J. Marriage Fam.* 33: 411–20

Baude, A., Holmberg, P. 1967. The position of men and women in the labour market. In *The Changing Roles of Men and Women,* ed. E. Dahlstrom, 105–34. England: G. Duckworth

Benoit-Smullyan, E. 1944. Status, status types, and status interrelations. *Am. Sociol. Rev.* 9:151–61

Benson, L. 1968. *Fatherhood: A Sociological Perspective.* New York: Random House

Benston, M. 1969. The political economy of women's liberation. *Mon. Rev* 21:13–25

Bernard, J. 1964. *Academic Women.* University Park: Pennsylvania Univ. Press

Bernard, J. 1966. *Marriage and Family Among Negroes.* Englewood Cliffs, NJ: Prentice-Hall

Bernard, J. 1968. *The Sex Game.* Englewood Cliffs, NJ: Prentice-Hall

Bernard, J. 1971. *Women and the Public Interest: An Essay on Policy and Protest.* Chicago: Aldine-Atherton

Bernard, J. 1973. My four revolutions: an autobiographical history of the ASA. In *Changing Women in a Changing World,* ed. J. Huber, 11–29. Chicago: Univ. Chicago Press

Bernard, J. 1975. Sex roles transcendence and sex role transcenders. *Women, Wives, Mothers: Values and Options.* Chicago: Aldine Biddle, B., Thomas, E. J., Eds. 1966. *Role Theory, Concepts and Research.* New York: Wiley

Bird, C. 1968. *The High Cost of Keeping Women Down.* New York: McKay

Blake, J. 1974. The changing status of women in developed countries. *Sci. Am.* 231: 137–47

Blau, P. M., Duncan, O. D. 1967. *The American Occupational Structure.* New York: Wiley

Block, J. H. 1972. *Conceptions of Sex Role: Some Cross-Cultural and Longitudinal Perspectives.* Bernard Moses Memorial Lecture, Univ. Calif., Berkeley, Mimeogr.

Blood, R. O., Hamlin, R. M. 1958. The effect of wife employment on the family power structure. *Soc. Forces* 36:347–52

Blood, R. O. Jr., Wolfe, D. M. 1960. *Husbands and Wives, the Dynamics of Married Living.* New York: Free Press

Blumberg, R. L. 1974. *Structural Factors Affecting Women's Status: A Cross-Cultural Paradigm.* Presented at 8th World Congr. Int. Sociol. Assoc., Toronto, Canada

Boserup, E. 1970. *Woman's Role in Economic Development.* NY: St. Martin's

Bott, E. 1957. *Family and Social Network.* London: Tavistock

Brim, O. G. Jr. 1968. *Adult Socialization and Society,* ed. J. A. Clausen, 182–227. Boston: Little, Brown

Broverman, I. K., Broverman, D. M., Clarkson, F. E., Rosenkrantz, P. S., Vogel, S. R. 1972. Sex role sterotypes and clinical judgements. In *Readings on the Psychology of Women,* ed. J. Bardwick, 320–24. NY: Harper & Row

Brown, D. S. 1957. Masculinity-femininity development in children. *J. Consult. Psychol.* 21:197–202

Carden, M. L. 1974. *The New Feminist Movement.* New York: Russell Sage

Carlson, R. 1971. Sex differences in ego functioning: exploratory studies of agency and communion. *J. Consult. Clin. Psychol.* 374:267–77

Carroll, C. M. 1973. Three's a crowd: the dilemma of the black women in higher education. In *Academic Women on the Move,* Ed. A. Ross, A. Calderwood, 173–86. New York: Russell Sage

Chafetz, J. S. 1974. *Masculine/Feminine or Human?* Itasca, Ill: F. E. Peacock

Chesler, P. 1971. Women as psychiatric and psychotherapeutic patients. *J. Marriage Fam.* 33:746–59

Chesler, P. 1972. *Women and Madness.* New York: Doubleday

Christensen, H. R., Ed. 1964. *Handbook of Marriage and the Family.* Chicago: Rand McNally

Cisler, L. 1971. A selected bibliography on women. In *Rebirth of Feminism,* ed. J. Hole, E. Levine. New York: Quadrangle Books

Coleman, J. S., Chairman. 1973. *Youth: Transition to Adulthood.* Report of the Panel on Youth of the President's Science Advisory Committee. Washington DC: Office Sci. Technol. (Executive Office of the President)

Coleman, J. S. 1961. *The Adolescent Society.* New York: Free Press Glencoe

Collins, R. 1971. A conflict theory of sexual stratification. *Soc. Prob.* 19:3–20

Connell, D. M., Johnson, J. C. 1970. Relationship between sex-role identification and self-esteem in early adolescents. *Develop. Psychol.* 3:268

Crandall, K. 1962. Motivational and ability determinants of your children's intellectual behaviors. *Child Develop.* 33: 643–61

Crandall, V. J., Dewey, R., Katkovsky, W., Preston, A. 1964. Parents' attitudes and behaviors and grade school children's academic achievements. *J. Genet. Psychol.* 104:53–66

Dahlstrom, E., Ed. 1967. *The Changing Roles of Men and Women.* Boston: Beacon

D'Andrade, R. G. 1966. Sex differences and cultural institutions. In *The Development of Sex Differences,* ed. E. E. Maccoby, 173–203. Stanford, Calif: Stanford Univ. Press

Daniels, A. 1974–1975. Feminist perspectives in sociological research. In *Sex and Social Inquiry: Toward a Non-Sexist Sociology,* ed. M. Millman, R. Kanter. To appear in a forthcoming issue of *Sociol. Inq.*

Davis, F. 1963. *Passage Through Crisis.* Indianapolis: Bobbs-Merrill

Davis, K., Moore, W. E. 1942. Some principles of stratification. *Am. Sociol. Rev.* 7:309–321

de Beauvoir, S. 1953. *The Second Sex.* Transl. H. M. Parshley. New York: Knopf

Degler, C. N. 1964. Revolution without ideology; the changing place of women in America. *Daedalus* 93:653–70

DeJong, P. Y., Brawer, M. J., Robin, S. S. 1971. Patterns of female intergenerational mobility: a comparison with male patterns of intergenerational occupational mobility. *Am. Sociol. Rev.* 36: 1033–42

de Tocqueville, A. 1947. *Democracy in America.* Transl. H. Reeves. New York: Oxford Univ.

Dixon, M. 1971–1972. Public ideology and the class composition of women's liberation (1966–1969). *Berkeley J. Sociol.* 16:149–67

Dodge, N. 1966. *Women in the Soviet Economy.* Baltimore: Johns Hopkins

Douvan, E., Adelson, J. 1966. *The Adolescent Experience.* New York: Wiley

Durkheim, E. 1933. *On the Division of Labor in Society.* Transl. G. Simpson. New York: Macmillan

Duverger, M. 1955. *The Political Role of Women.* Paris: UNESCO

Duverger, M. 1972. *The Study of Politics.* Transl. R. Wagoner. New York: Crowell

Ehrlich, C. 1971. The male sociologist's burden: the place of women in marriage and family texts. *J. Marriage Fam.* 33:421–30

Eichler, M. 1973. Women as personal dependents. In *Women in Canada,* ed. M. Stephenson, 36–55. Toronto: New Press

Eichler, M. 1974. *The Double Standard as an Indicator of Sex-Status Differentials.* Presented at 69th Ann. Meet. Am. Sociol. Assoc. Montreal, Canada

Eisenstadt, S. N. 1971. *Social Differentiation & Stratification.* Glenview, Ill: Scott Foresman

Elder, G. H. 1969. Appearance and education in marriage mobility. *Am. Sociol. Rev.* 34:519–32

Engels, F. 1942. *The Origin of the Family, Private Property, and the State.* New York: Int. Publ.

Epstein, C. F. 1970. Encountering the male establishment: sex-status limits on women's careers in the professions. *Am. J. Sociol.* 75:965–82

Epstein, C. F. 1971a. *Woman's Place: Options and Limits in Professional Careers.* Berkeley: Univ. Calif.

Epstein, C. F. 1971b. Women lawyers and their profession: inconsistency of social controls and their consequence for professional performance. *The Professional Woman,* ed. A. Theodore, 669–84. Cambridge, Mass: Schenkman

Epstein, C. F. 1973a. *Memo on Research Developments and Needs Pertaining to Changing Sex Roles.* Prepared for Dr. Saleem H. Shah, Chief, Center for Stud-

ies of Crime and Delinquency. Washington DC: NIMH Task Force

Epstein, C. F. 1973b. Positive effects of the multiple negative: explaining the success of black professional women. In *Changing Women in a Changing Society,* ed. J. Huber, 150–73. Chicago: Univ. Chicago

Erikson, E. 1964. Inner and outer space: reflection on womanhood. *Daedalus* 93:1–25

Etkowitz, H. 1971. The male sister:sexual separation of labor in society. *J. Marriage Fam.* 33:431–34

Etzioni, A., Ed. 1969. *The Semi-Professions and Their Organization.* New York: Free Press

Featherman, D. L., Hauser, R. M. 1974. *Trends in Occupational Mobility by Race and Sex in the United States, 1962–1972.* Presented at 8th Ann. Int. Sociol. Assoc. Meet., Toronto, Canada

Fidell, L., De Lamater, J., Eds. 1971. *Women in the Professions: What's All the Fuss About.* Beverly Hills: Sage

Firestone, S. 1970. *The Dialectic of Sex.* New York: Morrow

Flexner, E. 1959. *Century of Struggle.* Cambridge: Belknap Press, Harvard Univ.

Fogarty, M. P., Rapoport, R., Rapoport, R. N. 1972. *Sex, Career, and Family.* Beverly Hills: Sage

Fougeyrollas, P. 1951. Prédominance du mari ou de la femme dans le ménage. *Population* 6:83–102

Fourier, C. 1841. Théorie des Quatre Mouvements. Paris: Éditions Anthropos in *Oeuvres Complètes* I, 195; cited in Marx, K. 1845. *The Holy Family.* Transl. 1956

Frazier, E. 1949. *The Negro Family in the United States.* New York: Holt, Rhinehart & Winston

Frazier, E. F. 1962. *Black Bourgeoisie.* New York: Crowell-Collier

Frazier, N., Sadker, M. 1973. *Sexism in School and Society.* New York: Harper & Row

Freeman, J. 1973. The origins of the women's movement. In *Changing Women in a Changing Society,* ed. J. Huber, 30–49. Chicago: Univ. Chicago

Freedman, R., Baumert, G., Bolte, M. 1959. Expected family size and family values in West Germany. *Pop. Studies Vol. 2*

Freedman, R., Whelpton, P. K., Campbell, A. 1959. *Family Planning, Sterility and Population Growth.* New York: McGraw-Hill

Friedan, B. 1963. *The Feminine Mystique.* New York: Norton

Fuchs, V. R. 1971. Differences in hourly earning between men and women. *Mon. Lab. Rev.* 94:9–15

Gagnon, J. H., Simon, W. 1967. *Sexual Deviance.* New York: Harper & Row

Galenson, M. 1973. *Women and Work: An International Comparison.* Ithaca, NY: Cornell Univ.

Gans, H. 1962. *The Urban Villagers.* New York: Free Press

Garai, J. E., Scheinfeld, A. 1968. Sex Differences in mental and behavioral traits. *Genet. Psychol. Monogr.* 77:169–299

Garland, T. N. 1972. The better half? The male in the dual profession family. In *Toward a Sociology of Women,* ed. C. Safilios-Rothschild, 199–215. Lexington, Mass. Xerox Coll.

Gaskof, M. 1971. *Roles Women Play: Readings Toward Women's Lib.* Belmont, Calif: Brooks, Cole

Geertz, C. 1964. Ideology as a cultural system. In *Ideology and Discontent,* ed. D. Apter, 47–67. New York: Free Press Glencoe

Geiken, K. F. 1960. Expectations concerning husband-wife responsibilities in the home. *J. Marriage Fam. Living* 22: 122–28

Gerth, H. H., Mills, C. W., Eds. 1946. *From Max Weber: Essays in Sociology.* New York: Oxford Univ.

Gibbs, J. P., Martin, W. T. 1964. *Status Integration and Suicide.* Eugene: Univ. Oregon

Gillespie, D. 1971. Who has the power? the marital struggle. *J. Marriage Fam.* 33:445–58

Ginzberg, E. et al 1966. *Life Styles of Educated Women.* New York: Columbia Univ.

Girard, A., Bastide, H. 1959. Le budget-temps de la femme mariée à la campagne. *Population* 14:281–84

Glass, D. V. March 1968. Fertility trends in europe since the second world war. *Pop. Stud.* 22(1):103–46

Glenn, N. D., Ross, A. A., Tully, J. C. 1974. Patterns of intergenerational mobility of females through marriage. *Am. Sociol. Rev.* 39:683–99

Goldberg, P. 1968. Are women prejudiced against women? *Transaction* 5:28–30

Goldman, N. 1973. The changing role of women in the armed forces. In *Changing Women in a Changing Society,* ed. J. Huber, 130–49. Chicago: Univ. Chicago

Goode, W. J. 1963. *World Revolution and Family Patterns.* New York: Free Press

Goode, W. J. 1964. *The Family.* Englewood Cliffs, NJ: Prentice-Hall

Gordon, M., Shankweiler, P. J. 1971. Different equals less: female sexuality in recent marriage manuals. *J. Marriage Fam.* 33:459–66

Gornick, V., Moran, B. K., Eds. 1971. *Women in Sexist Society: Studies in Power and Powerlessness.* New York: Basic Books

Goslin, D. A., Ed. 1969. *Handbook of Socialization Theory and Research.* Chicago: Rand McNally

Gouldner, A. 1970. *The Coming Crisis of Western Sociology.* New York: Avon

Gove, R., Tudor, J. F. 1973. Adult sex roles and mental illness. *Changing Women in a Changing Society,* ed. J. Huber, 50–73 Chicago: Univ. Chicago

Green, R. 1974. *Sexual Identity Conflict in Children and Adults.* New York: Basic Books

Green, R., Money, J., Eds. 1969. *Transsexualism and Sex Reassignment.* Baltimore: Johns Hopkins

Greer, G. 1971. *The Female Eunuch.* New York: McGraw-Hill

Grønseth, E. 1971–1972. The husband provider role and its dysfunctional consequences. *Sociol. Focus* 5:10–18

Gross, E. 1968. Plus ça change ...? the sexual structure of occupations over time. *Soc. Probl.* 16:198–208

Gross, N., Mason, W. S., McEachern, A. W. 1958. *Explorations in Role Analysis.* New York: Wiley

Haavio-Mannila, E. 1972. Sex roles in politics. In *Toward a Sociology of Women,* ed. C. Safilios-Rothschild, 154–72. Lexington, Mass:Xerox Coll.

Hacker, H. M. 1951. Women as a minority group. *Soc. Forces* 30:60–69

Haden, P., Middleton, D., Robinson, P. 1971. A historical and critical essay for black women. In *From Feminism to Liberation,* ed. E. Altback, 125–42. Cambridge, Mass: Schenkman

Hare, N., Hare, J. 1970. Black women 1970. *Transaction* 8:65–68, 90

Harrington, A. 1974. *Maintaining the Ascriptive Order: The Professional Mystique.* MA thesis. Univ. Maryland, College Park

Hartley, R. E. 1959–1960. Children's concepts of male and female roles. *Merrill-Palmer Quart.* 6:83–92

Hartley, R. E. 1964. A developmental view of female sex-role definition and identification. *Merrill-Palmer Quart.* 10:3–17

Hartley, R. E., Hardesty, F., Gorfein, D. S. 1962. Children's perception and expression of sex preferences. *Child Develop.* 33:221–27

Hartley, R. E., Hardesty, F. 1964. Children's perceptions of sex-roles in childhood. *J. Genet. Psychol.* 105:43–51

Havens, E. M., Tully, J. C. 1972. Female intergenerational occupational mobility; comparison of patterns? *Am. Sociol. Rev.* 37:774–77

Heer, D. M. 1958. Dominance and the working wife. *Soc. Forces* 36:341–47

Heller, C. S. 1969. *Structured Social Inequality.* London: Collier-Macmillan

Hochschild, A. R. 1973. A review of sex role research. In *Changing Women in a Changing Society,* ed. J. Huber, 249–67. Chicago: Univ. Chicago

Hodges, H. M. Jr., Lane W. C. 1968. *Social Stratification.* Cambridge, Mass: Schenkman

Hoffman, L. W. 1963. Parental power relations and the division of household tasks. *The Employed Mother in America,* ed F. I. Nye, L. W. Hoffman, 680–733. Chicago: Rand McNally

Hole, J., Levine, E. 1971. *Rebirth of Feminism.* New York: Quadrangle

Holmstrom, L. L. 1972. *The Two Career Family.* Cambridge, Mass: Schenkman

Holter, H. 1970. *Sex Roles and Social Structure.* Oslo, Norway: Universitetsforlaget

Holter, H. 1971. Sex roles and social change. *Acta Sociol.* 14:2–12

Horner, M. 1968. *Sex Differences in Achievement Motivation and Performance in Competitive and Non-Competitive Situations.* PhD dissertation. Univ. Michigan, Ann Arbor

Horner, M. 1970. Femininity and successful achievement: a basic inconsistency. In *Feminine Personality and Conflict,* ed. J. Bardwick, E. Douvan, M. Horner, D. Gutman, 45–74. Belmont, Calif: Brooks Cole

Horney, K. 1969. Distrust between the sexes. In *Masculine Feminine: Readings in Sexual Mythology and the Liberation of Women,* ed. T. Roszak, B. Roszak, 107–15. New York: Harper Colophon

Hornung, C. A. 1971. *Status Consistency and Status Integration: A New Methodology and Preliminary Analysis.* Presented at Ann. Meet. East. Sociol. Soc., New York

Huber, J., Ed. 1973. *Changing Women in a Changing Society.* Chicago: Univ. Chicago

Hughes, E. C. 1945. Dilemmas and contradictions of status. *Am. J. Sociol.* 50:353–59

Hughes, H. M. 1973. Maid of all work or departmental sister-in-law? The faculty wife employed on campus. In *Changing Women in a Changing Society,* ed. J. Huber, 5–11. Chicago: Univ. Chicago

Inkeles, A. 1968. Society, social structure, and child socialization. In *Socialization and Society,* ed. J. Clausen, 73–130. Boston: Little, Brown

Jackson, E. F. 1962. Status consistency and symptoms of stress. *Am. Sociol. Rev.* 27:469–80

Jacobs, S. 1971. *Women in Cross-Cultural Perspective: A Preliminary Sourcebook.* Urbana: Univ. Illinois, Dept. Urban Reg. Plann.

James, J. 1973. *Law and Commercialized Sex.* Presented at SIECUS Conf., Sex: the Law and the Citizen, New York

Jencks, C., Riseman, D. 1968. *The Academic Revolution.* Garden City, NY: Doubleday

Johnson, M. 1963. Sex role learning in the nuclear family. *Child Develop.* 34: 319–33

Kagan, J., Moss, R. 1962. *Birth to Maturity.* New York: Wiley

Kanowitz, L. 1969. *Women and the Law: The Unfinished Revolution.* Albuquerque: Univ. New Mexico

Kanter, R. 1972. *Commitment and Utopia: Communes and Utopias in Sociological Perspective.* Cambridge, Mass: Harvard Univ.

Killingsworth, C. 1969. Jobs and income for negroes. In *Race and the Social Sciences,* ed. I. Katz, P. Gurin, 194–273. New York: Basic Books

Kinsey, A. B., Pomeroy, W. B., Martin, C. E. 1953. *Sexual Behavior in the Human Female.* Philadelphia: Saunders

Kiser, C. V., Whelpton, P. K. 1949–1954. *Social and Psychological Factors Affecting Fertility.* New York: Milbank Mem. Fund

Knudsen, D. D. 1969. The declining status of women, popular myths and the failure of functionalist thought. *Soc. Forces* 48:183–93

Kohlberg, L. 1966. A cognitive-developmental analysis of children's sex-role concepts and attitudes. *The Development of Sex Differences,* ed. E. E. Maccoby, 82–172. Stanford, Calif: Stanford Univ.

Komarovsky, M. 1946. Cultural contradictions and sex roles. *Am. J. Sociol.* 52:184–90

Komarovsky, M. 1962. *Blue-Collar Marriage.* New York: Vintage

Komarovsky, M. 1973a. Cultural contradictions and sex roles: the masculine case.

In *Changing Women in a Changing Society*, ed. J. Huber, 111–23. Chicago: Univ. Chicago

Komarovsky, M. 1973b. Presidential address: some problems in role analysis. *Am. Sociol. Rev.* 38:649–62

Kraditor, A. 1971. *The Ideas of the Woman Suffrage Movement 1890–1920*. Garden City, NY: Anchor

Kreps, J. 1971. *Sex in the Marketplace: American Women at Work*. Baltimore: Johns Hopkins

Lenski, G. 1954. Status crystallization: a nonvertical dimension of status. *Am. Sociol. Rev.* 19:405–15

Lenski, G. 1956. Social participation and status crystallization. *Am. Sociol. Rev.* 21:458–64

Lenski, G. 1966. *Power and Privilege: A Theory of Social Stratification*. New York: McGraw-Hill

Lesser, G. S. 1973. Achievement motivation in women. In *Human Motivation*, ed. D. C. McClelland, R. S. Steele, 202–21. Morristown, NJ: Gen. Learning

Levi-Strauss, C. 1949. *Les Structures Élémentaires de la Parente*. Paris: Presses Universit. France

Lewis, M. May 1972. Culture and gender roles: there's no unisex in the nursery. *Psychol. Today*, pp. 54–57

Liebow, E. 1967. *Tally's Corner*. Boston: Little, Brown

Liljeström, R. 1966. Konsroller i ungdomsboker och massmedia (sex roles in literature for adolescents and in mass media). In *Kynne Eller Kon? (Talent or Sex?)* Stockholm, Sweden

Linton, R. 1942. Age and sex categories. *Am. Sociol. Rev.* 7:589–603

Lipman-Blumen, J. 1972. How ideology shapes women's lives. *Sci. Am.* 226: 34–42

Lipman-Blumen, J. 1973a. *The Vicarious Achievement Ethic and Non-Traditional Roles for Women*. Presented at Ann. Meet. East. Sociol. Soc., New York

Lipman-Blumen, J. 1973b. Role de-differentiation as a system response to crisis: occupational and political roles of women. *Sociol. Inq.* 43:105–29

Lipman-Blumen, J. 1974a. *Changing Sex Roles in American Culture: Future Directions for Research*. Presented at Nat. Inst. Mental Health workshop on Future Dir. in Hum. Sexuality, State Univ. of New York at Stony Brook, Sch. Med. Stony Brook, NY. Forthcoming in *Ann. Sexual Behav.* 1974–1975

Lipman-Blumen, J. 1974b. *The Relationship between Social Structure, Ideology, and*

Crisis. Presented at 69th Ann. Meet. Am. Sociol. Assoc., Montreal, Canada

Lopata, H. 1966. The life cycle of the social role of housewife. *Sociol & Soc. Res.* 51:1, 5–22

Lopata, H. 1973. *Widowhood in an American City*. Cambridge, Mass: Schenkman

Lynn, D. B. 1962. Sex-role and parental identification. *Child Develop.* 33:555–64

Lynn, D. B. 1969. *Parental and Sex Role Identification: A Theoretical Formulation*. Berkeley, Calif: McCutchan

Maccoby, E. E., Ed. 1966a. *The Development of Sex Differences*. Stanford, Calif: Stanford Univ.

Maccoby, E. E. 1966b. Sex differences in intellectual functioning. In *The Development of Sex Differences*, ed. E. E. Maccoby, 25–55. Stanford, Calif: Stanford Univ.

Maccoby, E. E., Jacklin, C. N. 1974. *Sex Differences Revisited: Myth and Reality*. Presented at Ann. Meet. Am. Educ. Res. Assoc., Chicago

Mack, D. 1971. Stimulus/response: where the black matriarchy theorists went wrong. *Psychol. Today* 4:24, 86, 87

Marx, K. 1959. *Capital, The Communist Manifesto and Other Writings*. New York: Mod. Libr.

Marx, K. 1970. *The German Ideology*, ed. C. S. Arthur. New York: International

Marx, K., Engels, F. 1956. *The Holy Family*. Transl. R. Dixon. Moscow: Foreign Lang.

Masters, W. H., Johnson, V. E. 1966. *Human Sexual Response*. Boston: Little, Brown

Mayer, K. B., Buckley, W. 1970. *Class and Society*. New York: Random House

Mead, M. 1935. *Sex & Temperament in Three Primitive Societies*. New York: Mentor

Mead, M. 1967. The life cycle and its variations: the division of roles. *Daedalus* 96:871–5

Mednick, M. 1975. Social change and sex role inertia: the case of the kibbutz. In *Women and Achievement: Social and Motivational Analyses*, ed. M. Mednick, S. Tangri, L. W. Hoffman. Washington DC: Hemisphere Press

Mednick, M., Tangri, S., Eds. 1972. New Perspectives on Women. *J. Soc. Issues* Vol. 28

Merton, R. K. 1949. *Social Theory and Social Structure*. Glencoe, Ill: Free Press

Merton, R. K. 1957. The role-set: problems in sociological theory. *Brit. J. Sociol.* 8:106–20

Michel, A. 1960. La Femme dans la famille française. *Cah Int.* 12:61–76

Millet, K. 1970. *Sexual Politics.* Garden City, NY: Doubleday

Mincer, J. 1962. Labor force participation of married women: a study of labor supply. In *Aspects of Labor Economics.* Princeton, NJ: Princeton Univ.

Mincer, J. March 1970. The distribution of labor incomes: a survey with special reference to the human capital approach. *J. Econ. Lit.* 8(1):1–26

Mischel, W. 1966. A social learning view of sex differences. In *The Development of Sex Differences* ed. E. E. Maccoby, 56–81. Stanford, Calif: Stanford Univ.

Mitchell, J. 1966. Women: the longest revolution. *New Left Rev.* 40:11–37

Money, J., Hampson, J., Hampson, J. 1955. *Bull. Johns Hopkins Hosp.* 97:301–19

Montagu, A. 1970. *The Natural Superiority of Women.* New York: Collier

Mooney, J. D. 1968. Attrition among Ph.D. candidates: an analysis of a cohort of recent Woodrow Wilson fellows. *J. Hum. Resour.* 3:47–62

Morgan, J. N. David, M., Cohen, W., Brazer, H. 1966. *Income and Welfare in the United States.* Ann Arbor: Univ. Michigan Surv. Res. Center

Morgan, R. 1970. *Sisterhood is Powerful.* New York: Random House

Morrison, D. E., Henkel, R. E. 1970. *The Significance Test Controversy.* Chicago: Aldine

Moss, H. 1967. Sex, age and state as determinants of mother-infant interaction. *Merrill-Palmer Quart.* 13:19–36

Myrdal, G. 1944. Appendix 5. a parallel to the Negro problem. In *An American Dilemma.* New York: Harper

Myrdal, A., Klein, V. 1956. *Women's Two Roles: Home and Work.* London: Routledge & Kegan Paul

Neugarten, B. 1963. Personality changes during the adult years. In *Psychological Backgrounds of Adult Education,* ed. R. G. Kuhlen, 43–76. Chicago: Center for the Study Liberal Educ. Adults

Nixon, R. M. 1973. *Economic Report of the President.* Transmitted to Congress, Jan. 1973. Washington DC: GPO

Nye, F. I., Hoffman, L. W., Eds. 1963. *The Employed Mother in America.* Chicago: Rand McNally

Oetzel, R. M. 1966. Annotated bibliography. *The Development of Sex Differences,* ed. E. E. Maccoby, 223–322. Stanford, Calif: Stanford Univ.

Oltman, P., Goodenough, D., Witkin, H. 1973. *Psychological differentiation as a Factor in Conflict Resolution.* Princeton, NJ: Educ. Test. Serv.

O'Neill, W. L. 1971. *The Woman Movement.* Chicago: Quadrangle Paperbacks

Oppenheimer, V. K. 1968. The sex-labelling of jobs. *Ind. Relat.* 7:219–34

Oppenheimer, V. K. 1973. Demographic influence on female employment and the status of women. In *Changing Women in a Changing Society,* ed. J. Huber, 184–200. Chicago: Univ. Chicago

Orden, S. R., Bradburn, N. M. 1969. Working wives and marriage happiness. *Am. J. Sociol.* 74:392–407

Papanek, H. 1973. Men, women, and work: reflections on the two-person career. In *Changing Women in a Changing Society,* ed. J. Huber, 90–110. Chicago: Univ. Chicago

Parrish, J. B. 1962. Top level training of women in the United States, 1900–1960. *J. Nat. Assoc. Women Deans & Couns.* 25:76–83

Parsons, T. 1942. Age and sex in the social structure of the United States. *Am. Sociol. Rev.* 7:604–16

Parsons, T. 1949. An analytical approach to the theory of social stratification. In *Essays in Sociological Theory Pure and Applied,* 166–84. Glencoe, Ill: Free Press

Parsons, T. 1959. The social structure of the family. In *The Family: Its Function and Destiny,* ed. R. N. Anshen, 241–74. New York: Harper

Parsons, T., Bales, R. F. 1955. *Family Socialization and Interaction Process.* Glencoe, Ill: Free Press

Pavela, T. H. 1964. An exploratory study of Negro-white intermarriage in Indiana. *J. Marriage Fam.* 26:209–11

Pearlin, L. I. 1974. Sex roles and depression. In *Normative Life Crises,* ed. N. Daton, L. Ginsberg. New York: Academic

Pheterson, G. I., Kresler, S. B., Goldberg, P. A. 1971. Evaluation of the performance of women as a function of their sex, achievement, and personal history. *J. Personality Soc. Psychol.* 19:114–18

Pietrofesa, J. K., Schlossberg, N. K. 1972. Counselor bias and the female occupational role. In *Counselor Bias and the Female Occupational Role,* ed. N. Glazer-Malbin, H. Y. Waehrer, 219–21. Chicago: Rand McNally

Pinnelli, A. 1971. Female labor and fertility in relationship to contrasting social and economic conditions. *Human Relat.* 24:603–10

Poloma, M. 1972. Role conflict and the married professional woman. In *Toward a Sociology of Women,* ed. C. Safilios-Rothschild, 189–98. Lexington, Mass: Xerox Coll.

Puryear, G. R., Mednick, M. S. 1974. Black militancy, affective attachment, and the fear of success in black college women. *J. Consult. Clin. Psychol.* 42:263–6

Rainwater, L., Coleman, R. P., Handel, G. 1959. *Workingman's Wife.* New York: Macfadden-Bartell

Ramsøy, N. R. 1973. Patterns of female intergenerational occupational mobility: a comment. *Am. Sociol. Rev.* 38:806–7

Rapoport, R., Rapoport, R. N. 1971. *Dual Career Families.* Harmondsworth, Engl: Penguin

Rapoport, R., Rapoport, R. N. 1972. The dual career family: a variant pattern and social change. In *Toward A Sociology of Women,* ed. C. Safilios-Rothschild, 216–44. Lexington, Mass: Xerox Coll.

Reeves, N. 1971. *Womankind.* Chicago: Aldine-Atherton

Reiss, I. L. 1960. *Premarital Sexual Standards in America.* Illinois: Free Press Glencoe

Reiss, I. L. 1964. Premarital sexual permissiveness among Negroes and whites. *Am. Sociol. Rev.* 29:688–98

Riley, M. W., Foner, A., Hess, B., Toby, M. L. 1969. Socialization for middle and later years. In *Handbook of Socialization Theory and Research,* ed. D. A. Goslin, 951–82. Chicago: Rand McNally

Roby, P. 1972. Structural and internalized barriers to women in higher education. In *Toward a Sociology of Women,* ed. C. Safilios-Rothschild, 121–40. Lexington, Mass: Xerox Coll.

Rosen, B. C. 1959. Race, ethnicity, and the achievement syndrome. *Am. Sociol. Rev.* 24:47–60

Rosenberg, M. 1956. *Society and the Adolescent Self-Image.* Princeton, NJ: Princeton Univ. Press

Ross, H. L., Sawhill, I. V. 1975. *Time of Transition: The Growth of Families Headed by Women.* Washington DC: Urban Inst. In press

Rossi, A. S. 1964. Equality between the sexes: an immodest proposal. *Daedalus* 94:607–52

Rossi, A. S. 1969. Sex equality: the beginning of ideology. In *Masculine/Feminine,* ed. B. Roszak, T. Roszak, 173–86. New York: Harper Colophon

Rossi, A. S. 1972. Women in science: why so few? In *Toward a Sociology of Women,* ed. C. Safilios-Rothschild, 141–53. Lexington, Mass: Xerox Coll.

Rossi, A. S. 1973a. Maternalism, sexuality and the new feminism. In *Contemporary Sexual Behavior: Critical Issues in the 1970's,* ed. J. Zubin, J. Money, 145–74. Baltimore: Johns Hopkins Univ. Press

Rossi, A. S., Ed. 1973b. *The Feminist Papers.* New York: Columbia Univ. Press

Rossi, A. S., Calderwood, A., Eds. 1973. *Academic Women on the Move.* New York: Russell Sage Founda.

Roszak, B., Roszak, T., Eds. 1969. *Masculine/Feminine.* New York: Harper Colophon

Rubin, Z. 1968. Do American women marry up? *Am. Sociol. Rev.* 33:750–60

Rubin, Z. 1969. Reply to Scott. *Am. Sociol. Rev.* 34:727–28

Saario, T. N., Jacklin, C. N., Title, C. K. 1973. Sex role stereotyping in the public schools. *Harvard Educ. Rev.* 8:386–416

Safilios-Rothschild, C. 1971. A cross-national examination of women's marital, educational and occupational options. *Acta Sociol.* 14:96–113

Safilios-Rothschild, C., Ed. 1972. *Towards a Sociology of Women.* Lexington, Mass: Xerox Coll.

Safilios-Rothschild, C. 1974. *Women and Social Policy:* Englewood Cliffs, NJ: Prentice-Hall

Sarbin, T. R. 1954. Role theory. In *Handbook of Social Psychology,* ed. G. Lindsey, 223–58. Cambridge, Mass: Addison-Wesley

Sassower, D. 1970. Women in the professions. In *Women's Role in Contemporary Society,* Rep. New York Comm. Hum. Rights, 350–57. New York: Avon

Sawhill, I. V. 1974. Perspectives on Women and Work in America. In *Work and the Quality of Life,* ed. J. O'Toole, 88–105. Cambridge, Mass: MIT Press

Scanzoni, J. 1972. *Sexual Bargaining.* Englewood Cliffs, NJ: Prentice-Hall

Schmidt, G., Sigusch, V. 1973. Women's sexual arousal. *Contemporary Sexual Behavior Critical Issue in the 1970's,* ed. J. Zubin, J. Money, 117–44. Baltimore: Johns Hopkins Univ. Press

Schmitt, D. R. 1965. An attitudinal correlate of the status congruency of married women. *Soc. Forces* 44:190–95

Schulder, D. 1970. Does the law oppress women? In *Sisterhood is Powerful,* ed. R. Morgan, 139–57. New York: Vintage

Scott, J. F. 1969. A comment on do American women marry up? *Am. Sociol. Rev.* 84:725–27

Scully, D., Bart, P. 1973. A funny thing happened on the way to the orifile: women in gynecology textbooks. In *Changing Women in a Changing Society,* ed. J.

Huber., 283–88. Chicago: Univ. Chicago Press

Siegel, A., Haas, M. 1963. The working mother: a review of research. *Child Develop.* 34:513–42

Silver, C. B. 1973. Salon, foyer, bureau: woman and the professions in France. In *Changing Women in a Changing Society,* ed. J. Huber, 74–90. Chicago: Univ. Chicago Press

Simon, R. J., Clark, S. M., Galway, K. 1967. The women Ph.D.: a recent profile. *Soc. Probl.* 15:221–36

Sklar, J., Berkov, B. 1974. Abortion, illegitimacy, and the American birth rate. *Science* 185:909–15

Smelser, N.J. 1959. *Social Change in the Industrial Revolution.* Chicago: Univ. Chicago Press

Sochen, J. 1972. *The New Feminism in Twentieth-Century America.* Lexington, Mass: D.C. Heath

Sorokin, P. 1927. *Social Mobility.* New York: Harper

Spiro, M. E. 1956. *Kibbutz, Venture in Utopia.* New York: Schocken

Stoller, R. J. 1968. *Sex and Gender, on the Development of Masculinity and Femininity.* New York: Sci. House

Sullerot, E. 1971. *Woman, Society and Change.* Transl. M. S. Archer. New York: McGraw-Hill

Szalai, A. 1966. Differential evaluation of time budgets for comparative purposes. In *Comparing Nations: The Use of Quantitative Data in Cross National Research,* ed. R. Merritt, S. Rokkan, 239–58. New Haven, Conn: Yale Univ. Press

Szalai, A. 1968. Trends in contemporary time budget research. In *The Social Science: Problems and Orientation,* 242–51. Mouton: UNESCO

Talmon, Y., 1965. Sex-role differentiation in an equalitarian society. In *Life in Society,* ed. T. E. Lasswell, J. H. Burma, S. H. Aronson, 144–55. Chicago: Scott Foresman

Theodore, A., ed. 1971. *The Professional Woman.* Cambridge, Mass: Schenkman

Tickamyer, A. 1973. *Status inconsistency of married women: absolute, relational and comparative models.* MA thesis. Univ. Maryland, College Park

Tiger, L. 1970. *Men in Groups.* New York: Vintage–Random House

Toren, N. 1972. *Social Work: The Case of a Semi-Profession.* Beverly Hills: Sage

Treiman, D. J., Terrell, K. 1973. Sex and the Process of Status Attainment: A Comparison of Working Women and Men.

Presented at Ann. Meet. Am. Sociol. Assoc., New York

Tresemer, D. 1974. Fear of success: popular but unproven. *Psychol. Today* 7:82–85

Tresemer, D., Pleck, J. 1972. *Maintaining and Changing Sex-Role Boundaries in Men (and Women).* Presented at Radcliffe Inst. Conf. Women: Resources for Changing World, Cambridge, Mass.

Tumin, M. H. 1953. Some principles of stratification: a critical analysis. *Am. Sociol. Rev.* 18:387–94

Turner, R. H. 1956. Role taking, role standpoint, and reference-group behavior. *Am. J. Sociol.* 61:316–28

Turner, R. H. 1970. *Family Interaction.* New York: Wiley

Tyree, A., Treas, J. 1974. The occupational and marital mobility of women. *Am. Sociol. Rev.* 39:293–302

US Dept. of Commerce. 1971a. Fertility variations by ethnic origin: Nov. 1969. *Pop. Char. Ser.* P-20,226. Washington DC: GPO

US Dept. of Commerce. 1971b. Fertility indicators: 1970. *Curr. Pop. Rep. Ser.* P-23, 36. Washington DC: GPO

US Dept. of Commerce. 1972. *Curr. Pop. Rep. Ser.* P-20, 240. Washington DC: GPO

US Dept. of Labor. 1969. *Handbook of Women Workers.* Women's Bur. Bull. No. 294. Washington DC: GPO

US Dept. of Labor. 1973. *Manpower Report of the President. Report on Manpower and Requirements, Resources, Utilization and Training.* Washington DC: GPO

US Dept. of Labor. 1974. *Manpower Report of the President.* Washington DC: GPO

Valparaiso Law Review. 1971. *Symposium: Women and the Law;* Vol. 5, No. 2

Veblen, T. 1899. *The Theory of the Leisure Class.* New York: Mentor

Vroegh, K. 1971. Masculinity and femininity in the elementary and junior high school years. *Develop. Psychol.* 4:254–61

Walster, E., Aronson, V., Abrahams, D., Rotterman, L. 1966. Importance of physical attractiveness in dating behavior. *J. Personality Soc. Psychol.* 4:508–16

Warshay, D. W. 1972. Sex differences in language style. In *Toward a Sociology of Women,* ed. C. Safilios-Rothschild, 3–9. Lexington, Mass: Xerox Coll.

Weber, M. 1946. Class, status, party. In *From Max Weber: Essays in Sociology,* ed. H. H. Gerth, C. W. Mills, 180–95. New York: Oxford Univ. Press

Weber, M. 1968. Class, status, party. *Economy and Society*, ed. G. Roth. New York: Bedminster

Weil, M. 1961. An analysis of the factors influencing married women's actual or planned work participation. *Am. Sociol. Rev.* 26:91–6

Weiss, R. S. 1973. *Loneliness: The Experience of Emotional and Social Isolation*. Cambridge, Mass: MIT Press

Weissman, M. M., Nelson, K., Hackman, J., Pincus, C., Prusoff, B. 1973. The faculty wife: her academic interests and qualifications. In *Academic Women on the Move*, ed. A. Rossi, A. Calderwood, 187–95. New York: Russell Sage

Weitzman, L., Eifles, D., Hodaka, E., Ross, C. 1972. Sex role socialization in picture books for preschool children. *Am. J. Sociol.* 72:1125–50

Weller, R. H. 1968. *The Employment of Wives, Dominance, and Fertility*. Presented at 63rd Ann. Meet. Amer. Sociol. Assoc.

Weston, P. J., Mednick, M. T. 1970. Race, social class and the motive to avoid success in women. *J. Cross-Cult. Psychol.* 1:284–91

Whelpton, P. K., Campbell, A., Patterson, J. E. 1966. *Fertility and Family Planning in the United States*. Princeton, NJ: Princeton Univ. Press

White, M. S. 1970. Psychological and social barriers to women in science. *Science* 170:413–16

Wilensky, H. L. 1968. Women's work: economic growth, ideology, structure. *Ind. Relat.* 7:235–48

Witkin, H. A. 1973. *The Role of Cognitive Style in Academic Performance and in Teacher-Student Relations*. Presented at Symp. on Cognitive Styles, Creativity and Higher Education, Montreal, Canada, 1972. Princeton, NJ: Educ. Test. Serv.

Wolfe, D. M. 1959. Power and authority in the family. In *Studies in Social Power*, ed. D. Cartwright. Ann Arbor, Mich: Inst. Soc. Res.

Wool, H., Pearlman, L. M. 1947. Recent occupational trends. *Mon. Labor Rev.* 65:139–47

Yorburg, B. 1974. *Sexual Identity*. New York: Wiley

Zelditch, M. 1955. Role Differentiation in the nuclear family: a comparative study. In *Family, Socialization and Interaction Process*, ed. T. Parsons, R. F. Bales, 307–52. New York: Free Press

Zelditch, M. 1964a. Cross-cultural analyses of family structure. In *Handbook of Marriage and the Family*, ed. H. T. Christensen, 462–500. Chicago: Rand McNally

Zelditch, M. 1964b. Family, marriage and kinship. In *Handbook of Modern Sociology*, ed. R. E. L. Faris, 680–733. Chicago: Rand McNally

EVALUATION RESEARCH   ❖10513

Gerald Gordon
New York State School of Industrial and Labor Relations and Department of Sociology, Cornell University, Ithaca, New York 14853

Edward V. Morse
Department of Sociology, Tulane University, New Orleans, Louisiana 70118

Though a wide variety of activities have been included under the label evaluation research (e.g. Suchman 1967, Weiss 1972, Wholey et al 1970), we will limit our review to research aimed at assessing social action or intervention programs. Our intent in this review will not only be to describe current practice but also to try to understand the social factors that have shaped and determined the present state of evaluation research.

At the most elemental level, evaluation research is aimed at determining whether a program was actually carried out. At a more complex level, research is concerned with the effectiveness and/or the economic attributes of a program. Ideally such information should contribute to decisions about whether to expand, curtail, or modify a program. The extent to which the quality of information generated by the bulk of evaluation studies is rigorous enough to be used for this purpose is one of our central concerns. To examine this question in a systematic fashion, in addition to a general review of the literature, we undertook a survey of evaluation articles found in *Sociological Abstracts* for the years 1969, 1971, and 1973.

Before reporting on our survey findings we feel it is important to identify and discuss methodological factors that affect the quality of evaluation research. We have organized this discussion in terms of goal definition, population identification, research, design, time constraints, and measurement problems.

GOAL DEFINITION

A prerequisite to evaluating social action programs is an explicit determination of what a particular program is designed to accomplish. Without a clear understanding of a program's goals, there is no basis upon which to construct testable hypotheses regarding goal attainment. Further, since measurable criteria must be derived from goals, lack of clarity will likely lead to other serious problems in research design.

Unfortunately, as Orlans (1973) notes, the wording in the legislation for most programs is written in vague terms to gain a sufficient amount of backing from legislators. In addition, program goals are often stated in a nebulous manner, as Wholey (1970) suggests, to minimize the number of restrictions put on the local agencies who will be carrying out the program. It has also been argued pro and con that program goals be stated ambiguously because efficacious knowledge is lacking (Freeman & Sherwood 1970; Lazarsfeld, Sewell & Wilensky 1967; Reiss 1970; Wheeler & Cottrell 1966).

Carol Weiss (1972) suggests that evaluators refrain from undertaking evaluation of programs lacking explicitly stated goals. As if to underline this position, Weiss & Rein (1969) report that the conflicts between program administrators and evaluators, resulting from initial goal vagueness, have led evaluators to leave a project before completing their task. Hyman et al (1962) and Freeman & Sherwood (1970), however, view the absence of specific goals as offering the evaluator an opportunity to apply his creativity and ingenuity to figure out what purposes the program has and measure them. The hazards of taking such an orientation are clearly exemplified by the Westinghouse Learning Corporation-Ohio University Study (1969) of the impact of Head Start.

As a multiphasic compensatory education program, Head Start's strategy was designed to upgrade underprivileged children's chances of succeeding in school by altering their health, nutrition, and educational environments. Legislation establishing Head Start, however, offered no delineation of goal priority or concrete objectives. Due to congressional pressure for rapid evaluation, the evaluators assessed only one portion of the educational phase of the program and concluded that Head Start was having little effect. Program administrators protested vigorously that the evaluation carried out was of too narrow a scope to be considered a valid assessment of the total program. This is probably true (Williams & Evans 1969). But lacking any specific guidelines as to how all the various phases were supposed to interact or how they were to articulate with one another, consensus on more inclusive evaluation strategies would have been difficult.

POPULATION IDENTIFICATION

Related to the goal question is the determination of the target population.

This involves identification of an appropriate unit of analysis when assessing the impact of a program on a population. All too often, the unit dealt with in programs is a small, relatively undefined dimension of a very complex phenomenon. That such a strategy for programatic amelioration of social problems is questionable has been noted by Carol Weiss (1970) in her discussion of the bankruptcy of piecemeal programs. Nevertheless, this tendency toward atomization of efforts is unlikely to soon abate given the present federal funding structure.

Whether due to difficulties in goal determination or ambiguities about the intended target population, information on the socioeconomic characteristics of target populations is absent or rudimentary in many evaluation studies. Not only does this absence lead to questions about the adequacy of a given study, but as Breadlove (1973) points out, the lack of such data realistically precludes replications of studies and prevents comparative analysis. This inability to replicate, while of less immediate relevance to program administration, is of importance to the long-run development of evaluation research. If knowledge is to accumulate, as McDill et al (1972) point out, there is an overriding necessity for replication of the program evaluations. Lacking such replication, findings are less than persuasive.

RESEARCH DESIGN

Evaluation research requires that, at a minimum, comparison be made between one group that has been exposed to a program (the experimental group) and another that has not (the control group). Failure to make such comparison logically preempts the researcher from attributing any change observed in the target population to exposure to the program. The use of control groups, randomized placement of individuals in control and experimental groups, and various strategies of pre- and post-testing of subjects are the basic components of experimental and quasi-experimental research designs (Campbell & Stanley 1967).

Madge (1953), Fairweather (1967), Dunnette & Campbell (1968), Becker (1970), Stanley (in Rossi and Williams 1972), and Houston (1972) have strongly argued for the use of experimental design in evaluation research. Fairweather even goes so far as to argue that the evaluation of programs can best be done when the program is carried out on a target population that has been completely isolated from the larger society. Such a stringent strategy is more ideal than practical, and obviously runs into questions of ethical treatment of human subjects, not to mention the costs of such a strategy. In addition to cost, Borus & Buntz (1972) raise the question of whether we know that much about the contamination effect that results from the use of nonrandom samples.

Obviously, as stated earlier, in order to construct a control group it is necessary that the program have well specified goals and a clear delineation of the characteristics of the target population. Even then one is faced with major issues of whether one can ethically withhold a program's services from a group of people for purposes of control. To qualify as a potential member of the control group, one must qualify for participation in the program. To deny a person access to the program because of methodological reasons could be viewed as unethical. The ethical question is complex for it concerns not only the denial of potentially desirable interventions but also the subjecting of persons to programs, the effects of which have never been verified.

Besides the ethical questions surrounding the use of various research designs, there is the matter of practicality. The more extensive the experimental or quasi-experimental design used, the greater the sample size required, the greater the number of better trained personnel who must be employed, and the longer it will take to gather, digest, and write up a report of findings. Increasing the quality of the evaluation designs tends to eat up money and time, two items of which most programs are very short (Weiss 1970). Compounding the problem of utilizing experimental designs is the fact that administrators of programs often envision their projects as flexible or in a continuous state of progression toward the ideal. To the evaluator, however, this means that exposure to the program is not a constant over time. Thus even if the evaluator detects a significant positive impact on the experimental group, he has no way of knowing what caused it. Evaluators and administrators thus face a dilemma. To evaluate a program using an experimental design means that the program must remain stable for a time, possibly to the detriment of the program's clients. On the other hand, if the program tries to learn from past mistakes and improve its services, the results of the experiment are questionable.

Further complicating the problem of designing evaluation research is the relationship between program content and the form in which it is delivered. Over thirty years ago, Roethlisberger & Dickson (1939) noted that (the Hawthorne effect) the behavior elicited by a subject in an experiment could be accounted for simply as a function of having attention paid to him as a subject. The effect of being in an experiment is normally not random but in the direction attempting to be induced. To the extent that participation in a program is comparable to participating in an experiment, we should expect effects both from the form and the content of a program.

There is little need to dwell on the importance of studying both the direct and indirect effects of program form and content. To do both would add to expenses, but considering the Hawthorne effect such effort appears necessary (Rosenthal 1966).

Given the problem inherent in experimental designs, a number of alternatives to the experimental design have been suggested (Suchman 1967, Stufflebeam 1968a, b, Guba 1969, Hyman et al 1962, Weiss & Rein 1970, Trice & Roman 1974). The most viable of these alternatives, in our opinion, involves the exploitation of natural conditions that enable the evaluators to approximate the controlled situation. These include the use of persons who must wait to gain entry to the program, or the identification of persons who are part of, or who have characteristics similar to the target population, but who are not a part of the intervention program. Any attempt to take advantage of naturally occurring phenomena as part of an evaluation program has risks of comparability but, with appropriate care, the risks may be minimized.

TIME CONSIDERATIONS

In designing evaluation research for the evaluator facing the task of assessing a program, time constraints pose important problems. The first is the matter of lag time, or the expected time that must pass after exposure to a program before measurable effects can be reasonably expected (Freeman & Sherwood 1965). Coupled with this is the question of how long a change in behavior or attitudes can reasonably be expected to last (Harris 1963).

Lacking conceptual or empirical guidelines, it would appear that evaluators have often failed to consider these matters or have allowed external exigencies, such as the due date of the final report (e.g. Westinghouse 1969) to determine their time frame. An assumption implicitly used by some evaluators is that measurable effects are present as soon as the program is over. Such an assumption in most cases would seem to be based on expediency rather than knowledge.

On the other hand, there is the matter of deterioration of an effect over time. The absence of effect is usually taken as evidence that a program had no impact and the possibility of a deteriorated effect more often than not is ignored. The detection of a deteriorated effect would suggest the possibility of modifying the program to sustain the initial impact. Unless a series of tests has been administered periodically after exposure to a program, we really do not know whether there was an initial effect that has diminished over time or whether, in fact, there was no effect at all. Lacking such periodic testing, programs that are potentially viable may be cancelled. Such a series of tests would obviously be costly as well as introduce problems of testing effect on the data (Campbell & Stanley 1967, Harris 1963). The questions of contamination of the data might at this point be considered of secondary priority until something is learned of the lag time and permanency of a program's induced change.

MEASUREMENT

Measuring change, according to Harris (1963) remains problematic for the field. Locating and/or developing reliable, validated testing instruments robust enough to single out the behavior desired from a whole configuration of behaviors takes time and money. All too often evaluation studies contain no suggestion of the quality of measures (i.e. reliability and validity) being used to assess a program's impact. Absence of such information truncates the process of refinement which could lead to an accumulation of readily available instruments with known characteristics.

The lack of sensitive, validated, and reliable measurement instruments limits current attempts at evaluation. This lack will be particularly costly if, as appears likely, many programs encounter ceiling effects with regard to how much change can be induced with a given level of resource. With limited resources the impact of a program may be rather small; though, on a larger scale, its impact on behavior and life styles would be meaningful. Without measuring instruments capable of making fine distinctions among isolated behaviors, it is likely the potential impact of such programs will not be correctly assessed. Related to the question of how to measure variables is the question of which variables should be measured. The social science literature offers less in the way of guidelines of which variables to measure than might be hoped for.

The social sciences have primarily concerned themselves with identification of the correlates of a particular behavior within a natural setting and, as Reiss (1970) suggests, the sociologist in particular has emphasized the study of social problems and deviant behavior patterns and has excluded the study of valued behavior. This presents a serious gap in our knowledge, for it is socially valued behavior that social action programs are trying to induce. The attitude change literature would appear of some relevance for evaluation research. But, as Festinger (1964) points out, attitudinal changes often do not lead to changes in behavior patterns.

In attempting to deal with the problem of which variables to measure, Scott & Shore (1974) suggest that stress should be placed on examining what they call tractable or manipulable variables. Unfortunately, the degree to which a variable is manipulable is not constant across social settings. Most often, sex of subject would be treated as an untractable variable. But in many instances, laws can be written so as to include or exclude persons of particular ages, races, and sexes from the scope of a program. Taking a different position than Scott & Shore, Coleman (1970) suggests that the evaluator may have to use or introduce unmanipulable variables because they have important intervening effects. Given the inadequacies of the theoretical base, selection of relevant manipulable or unmanipulable variables is an extremely difficult process. The rather limited knowledge in regard to the identification of relevant variables is a cause for concern—a concern which will continue until viable analytic and theoretical frameworks in regard to evaluation and behavior change are developed.

This discussion was aimed at the identification of some of the major methodological and analytical factors affecting the nature and quality of evaluation research. Our purpose was to develop a framework for our survey of evaluation research.

A SURVEY OF EVALUATION RESEARCH

The survey is based upon a sample of evaluation studies listed in the *Sociological Abstracts* during the years 1969, 1971, and 1973. It is our belief that the abstracts reflect a major core of relevant sociological literature on evaluation. One hesitancy in using the abstracts was that given the selective process of journal publication the studies in our sample would reflect the better evaluation studies. Seven issues of the abstracts are published annually. Two issues each year were selected at random for a total of six issues. Since evaluation studies are as likely to be found either under the specific category being evaluated or the categorical listing for evaluation, all abstracts in an issue were read to determine inclusion in the sample. This meant that we reviewed almost one out of every three articles abstracted in a given year. The criterion for sample inclusion was any statement that intervention was being assessed. Ninety-three of the studies met our criterion. The publications referred to in the abstracts were obtained. The survey of the research is based on these publications.

In analyzing the studies three main questions were asked:

1. Is the study methodologically rigorous?
2. Does the study contribute to cumulative development of the field?
3. What factors relate to favorable and unfavorable evaluation of the programs?

In addition to examining these questions, information on the contextual and institutional base of the investigation was obtained. The studies were categorized on the basis of the coding sheet in Table A–1 of the appendix. Inter-reviewer agreement based on a 10% sample was 85%.

DESCRIPTIVE CHARACTERISTICS

The evaluation research reviewed was conducted primarily by academicians (78%). The great majority of evaluation research (65%) was a single as opposed to a continuous or multistaged research effort. As can be seen in Table 1 the studies in the sample reflect a broad spectrum of social problem areas. The majority of evaluators were interested in program effectiveness (76%). Program cost and/or efficiency were investigated by only 18% of the evaluators.

Thirty-seven percent of the studies evaluate treatment technique, 32% evaluate delivery and organizational aspects of the intervention, and 27% are concerned with both the delivery and treatment system. Overall, the intervention is evaluated as a success by 35% of the studies. A qualified assessment of the intervention (the assessment reflects both some success and failure) is given by 41% of the studies and 23% report failure. This finding is different from the impression obtained from our review of the major works on evaluation research. Our impression was that most evaluation studies tended towards negative judgement of the intervention programs. Could it be the studies with less rigor tend to yield positive results and the more rigorous studies tend toward negative results?

Many of the studies, indeed, can be faulted for their methodology. For example, in 41% of the studies either the target population is not defined or if defined is defined in the most global sense. Similar problems occur in regard to definition of variables. The intervention is not defined except in the most general sense in 31% of the samples and only in 25% of the cases is the intervention sufficiently defined to permit replication. In regard to other independent variables, 19% of the studies have no independent variables other than the intervention, 27% refer to other independent variables but fail to define them, and 17% specify some aspects of the independent variable leaving only 34% of the studies with the variables operationalized in a manner permitting even an approximate replication. The picture in regard to the dependent variables is brighter. Seventy percent of the studies contain defini-

Table 1   Content areas covered by evaluation studies $(N = 93)$

Content Area	Percentage of Studies
Education	15
Mental Health	9
Community Development Programs	13
Social Control (delinquency prisons, etc)	13
Health and Social Service	18
Manpower (includes on the job training, training development)	9
Professional and Paraprofessional Training	14
Miscellaneous	9

tions permitting replication. However, it should be noted that in 11% of the studies, the dependent variable was lacking or seems to bear little or no relationship to the stated purposes of the intervention, and in a quarter of the studies the conclusions drawn by the evaluator do not appear to be in accord with his findings. Moreover, only 29% of the studies had experimental or quasi-experimental designs and over half of the studies lack either controls or sampling designs. Tests of significance and/or measures of association were employed by less than half the studies (44%).

We expected that weakness in one aspect of methodology would be associated with weaknesses in other methodological areas. Therefore, an itemization of areas of methodological weakness and strength might give an exaggerated impression of lack of rigor. To control for this we categorized the studies in terms of whether a study met minimal methodological criteria. To meet these criteria a study must: (a) specify or operationally define at least one of its independent and one of its dependent variables, (b) have control groups or a sampling design and, (c) where appropriate employ tests of significance or measures of association. Twenty-one of the ninety-three studies met these criteria. Our review of the factors affecting quality led us to the conclusion that one of the more important problems facing the field of evaluation research is the development of viable analytic guidelines. The lack of an analytic base is indicated by the fact that only one third of the studies cited the literature in regard to related evaluations. Only a minority of the studies, however, appear concerned with the development of an analytic framework. For example, 75% of the studies do not have formally derived hypotheses (excludes testing of null hypotheses), 63% do not examine the assumptions underlying the intervention, and 84% do not test theory.

RESEARCH QUALITY AND PROGRAM SUCCESS

To test the hypothesis that studies with less rigor tend to assess interventions more positively than studies with more rigor, we combined our methodological standard criteria with an assessment of the appropriateness of the use of given techniques. Though this involved some subjective judgement we felt it necessary to do this because research quality is dependent upon appropriate use of technique rather than simply the presence or absence of a given technique. For instance, the use of tests of significance and measures of association are indicators of good research only when they are properly employed and interpreted. To minimize subjective interpretations of appropriate technique usage we only defined a usage as inappropriate where an obvious and gross error occurred. The correlation of the items used in determining minimal methodological standards and the overall research quality assessment was .69.

On the basis of this quality assessment, projects were divided into four groups.
1. Good = meeting standards of rigor ($N = 7$).
2. Adequate = some sophistication in research design, but some methodological weaknesses ($N = 20$).

3. Questionable = some awareness of methodology and design displayed; but overall methodological weakness and/or grossly misemployed research technique ($N = 30$).
4. Poor = missing even the semblance of design ($N = 34$).

Because there were relatively few good studies, they were combined in later analyses with the adequate studies into an adequate+ category.

Comparing our quality measure with assessment of program success seems to support the hypothesis that as research quality decreases, programs are increasingly evaluated as successful. As can be seen from Table 2, 52% of the poor studies rated the programs they assessed as successful compared to 22% of the adequate+ studies. However, complicating the interpretation of these findings is the fact that organizational affiliation of the evaluator with the program being evaluated also seems to be related to assessments of program success as can be seen in Table 3. Researchers with affiliations to the programs evaluated report 58% success compared to 14% for the evaluators without affiliation. This perhaps could be accounted for by the greater proportion of adequate+ studies conducted by the nonaffiliated evaluators. Nonaffiliated evaluators account for 54% of all evaluation studies conducted and 70% of the studies rated adequate+. We therefore felt it important to examine the combined effect of research quality and affiliation. To simplify the discussion of the effect of research quality and rigor upon assessment we shall first discuss the less

Table 2 The relationship between quality and assessment[a]

| Quality | Assessment | | | |
	Success (%)	Qualified (%)	Failure (%)	N
Poor	52	28	21	29
Questionable	35	38	27	34
Adequate +	22	59	18	27

[a]Chi-square = 7.34231, 4 df, $p = 0.12$.

Table 3 Relationship between affiliation of investigator to the program evaluated and his assessment[a]

| | Assessment | | | |
	Success (%)	Qualified (%)	Failure (%)	N[c]
Affiliated[b]	58	28	14	36
Nonaffiliated	14	57	29	42

[a]Chi-square = 16.6171, df = 2, $p = .0002$.

[b]Includes experimentors who evaluated their own experiment.

[c]N is less than 93 because 15 studies that gave no information about the affiliation of the investigator were excluded.

rigorous studies (poor and questionable research). Where research is less rigorous, as can be seen in Table 4, if the investigator has an organizational affiliation with the program being evaluated, the tendency is toward positive findings (62%), while the reverse appears to be the case for nonaffiliated investigators (18%). There is a greater tendency for nonaffiliated investigators to report program failure. The nonaffiliated investigators report more than twice as many negative evaluations (32%) than do the affiliated investigators (14%). This tendency toward negative assessment among the nonaffiliated, less rigorous investigators appears limited to the studies we labeled questionable (having a semblance of research design). For those studies we labeled poor, there were no negative assessments; though we are hesitant to attach much significance to this finding due to the small number of cases which were nonaffiliated and the research labeled poor ($n=6$).

Turning our attention to the more rigorous studies (adequate+), we find that the nonaffiliated researchers report the highest percentage of qualified assessments (63%) of any of the groups. The nonaffiliated adequate+ studies also contain the lowest percentage of positive assessments in the sample (11%), and while negative assessments (25%) are higher than the less rigorous affiliated studies, they are lower than the less rigorous nonaffiliated studies. Unfortunately, due to the small number of cases ($n=6$), we were unable to viably compare the adequate+ affiliated and nonaffiliated groups.

The pattern of findings, we think to some extent, can be explained by unconscious bias and experimenter effect (Rosenthal 1966). If one assumes, as Rosenthal (1966) does, that as research rigor decreases the affect of unconscious researchers' bias and experimenter effect increases, we have a possible explanation for the pattern of our findings. We hypothesize that researchers with program affiliations have a pro-program bias, and that researchers who are not affiliated with the program and who have some discipline identity as evidenced by attempts at research design (questionable and adequate + studies) have some tendency toward an anti-program bias.

Table 4 The relationship between quality of research, affiliation of evaluator, and his assessment of the program[a]

| | Assessment | | | |
	Success (%)	Qualified (%)	Failure (%)	N
Questionable and Poor Research				
Affiliated	62	24	14	29
Nonaffiliated	18	50	32	22
Adequate + Research				
Affiliated	50	50	0	6
Nonaffiliated	11	63	26	19

[a]Chi-square = 25.5313, 6 df, p = .004.

Improving the rigor of evaluations appears to act as a constraint upon both types of biases. This tendency, we feel, can be seen in a comparison of the extreme types —the "affiliated poor" and the "nonaffiliated adequate+" studies (Table 5). The affiliated poor studies assess projects positively almost seven times as often as do the poor nonaffiliated adequate+ studies (71% to 11%). The nonaffiliated poor studies report 14% failure compared to 26% for the nonaffiliated adequate+ group. A major difference between these two groups occurs in regard to qualified assessments. The affiliated poor group reports qualified assessment only 17% of the time compared to 63% for the nonaffiliated adequate+ group.

Unfortunately the limited number of cases in the nonaffiliated poor category ($N = 6$) and affiliated adequate category ($N = 6$) did not enable us to fully test our hypothesis. Our interpretation, while tenable in terms of our finding, remain unproven. We think the findings however do indicate that the question of possible bias is a matter of field concern and that further investigation is warranted. Investigation of possible biases, however, is difficult, due to lack of information in most articles on the independence of the evaluation. Information on organizational affiliation is routinely given but as can be seen in Table 6, there is a dearth of information relating to sources of funding and budgetary control—two factors that appear related to possible biases. Well over half of the studies do not contain information on source of funding or independence of budget. Where such information is given, in almost all cases it reflects budgetary or funding independence. We raise the possiblity that where independence of funding and budget occurs, it tends to be reported and the

Table 5 Comparison of poor affiliated research with adequate + nonaffiliated research[a]

| | Assessment | | | |
	Success (%)	Qualified (%)	Failure (%)	N
Poor Affiliated	71	14	14	14
Adequate + Nonaffiliated	11	63	26	19

[a]Chi-square = 13.3098, 2 df, p = .001.

Table 6 Financial independence[a]

Budgetary Control:	Budgetary Independence (%)	No Budgetary Independence (%)	No Information (%)
	31	1	68
Source of Funding:	Independent (%)	Related to Program (%)	No Information (%)
	35	10	54

[a]N = 93.

lack of independence tends to be ignored. In any case, if the question of evaluators' independence is to be studied, it would be helpful if information on source of funding and independence of budget were routinely reported in articles.

In conclusion, whether due to bias or not, the fact that a relationship appears to exist between the affiliation of the evaluators to the program evaluated and assessment of program success lends emphasis to the methodological concerns expressed by Suchman (1967), Weiss (1972), Fairweather (1967), Wholey et al (1970), Martinson (1974), Hyman et al (1962), Houston (in Rossi & Williams 1972), etc.

EVALUATION RESEARCH AND SOCIOLOGY

Thus far we have viewed evaluation research as a more or less self-contained subfield. In concluding the survey of the literature, we think it important to relate evaluation research to sociology and the social sciences. Barber (1962:37–38), in evaluating the social sciences, said: "They tend to be still in quite an empiricist tradition, with few if any general conceptual schemes that are widely accepted. . . . The fundamental cause of the difficulty is the high degree of indeterminancy in most social science knowledge." Barber made this statement in 1952, and again in 1962. Others have made similar comments about social science progress.

In Kuhn's (1970) terms sociology lacks a paradigm. According to Kuhn, a paradigm is an implicit body of law, theory application, and instrumentation that is learned through example and practice. Paradigms gain status through their promise of success in directing the search for solutions to acute problems. Normal science is (Kuhn 1970:24) the "actualization of that promise, an actualization achieved by extending the knowledge of those facts that the paradigm displays as particularly revealing by increasing the extent of the match between those facts and the paradigm's predictions, and, by furthering the articulation of the paradigm itself." A paradigm, according to Kuhn, guides scientific research by encouraging expert consensus on what problems and facts are important, what methods and techniques are appropriate, and what scientific standards determine proof of findings.

Studying the structure of scientific fields and the functioning of university graduate departments, Lodahl & Gordon (1972:57–72) investigated the assumed differences in paradigm development between the physical and social sciences. This was done in two ways: 1. members of major departments of physics, chemistry, political science, and sociology were asked to rank seven fields in regard to consensus and; 2. within their respective fields, the department members were asked questions about consensus in regard to curriculum, research, and leadership. In terms of overall consensus, physics and chemistry were ranked at the head of the list and sociology and political science at the bottom. Intrafield consensus also was much higher in physics and chemistry than in sociology and political science.

Why has social science in general and sociology in particular remained in a preparadigm stage? We suggest that along with such factors as the complexity of social phenomenon, resource limitation, social norms, etc, the tendency of social scientists to rely primarily upon internal referents or field-centered criteria in assessing research has hindered paradigm development. We believe that failure to stress both internal and external criteria, of which evaluation research is a prime example, can inhibit the development of emerging sciences such as sociology.

The importance of external criteria to the development of emerging fields can be seen in Ben-David's studies of the early development of medicine. Ben-David (1964:475) found that not only were growth and innovation in medicine stimulated by science systems that were open and free of "defenses against an external influence," but that the major breakthroughs occurred through problem-oriented research. The fact of more effective cure and more predictable prognosis resulting from the work of men such as Pasteur and Lister changed the nature of the medical sciences (Ben-David 1960).

In contrasting disciplinary criteria with problem-solving criteria Coleman (1973:6) states "The criteria of parsimony and elegance that apply in discipline research are not important [in applied or policy-oriented research]; and correctness of the predictions or results is important [in applied research], and redundancy is valuable." Internal criteria appear to reinforce the status quo and protect against theoretical fads. External criteria provide an impetus to change and innovation. Weinberg (1964) suggests that internal criteria reflect the competence of scientists in terms of the standards of a given field, whereas external criteria measure a field's social relevance. He believes that internal criteria constitute a necessary condition for scientific growth and external criteria constitute a sufficient condition.

To the extent that this is true, evaluation research is not just a subfield relating to social engineering, but is directly related to the development of the social sciences in general and sociology in particular. Yet when we examine the relevant sociological journals, we find that in terms of publication patterns, evaluation research seemed to have relatively little impact.

Our sample includes ninety articles published in journals and represents approximately 29% of all evaluation articles published in *Sociological Abstracts* in the three-year period studied. Extrapolating from our sample: 105 evaluation articles were published in a given year; of these 13 would have appeared in what we consider the 22 major sociological journals (see Table A-2 of appendix) and 93 would have appeared in minor journals. On an average a major journal published .6 evaluation articles a year. The publication of evaluation articles appears to have remained relatively constant over the five-year period we studied. Thirty-five percent of the articles were abstracted in 1969, 30% in 1971, and 34% in 1973. Clearly, if our extrapolation from the sample reflects a true picture of evaluation research, in terms of frequency of publication in major journals, evaluation research is not receiving widespread attention in sociology.

Whether this lack of impact is due to limited interest by most sociologists in applied research or the poor quality of the research is debatable. We think it is important to note, however, that one quarter of the adequate+ studies were published in major journals, indicating some receptiveness to rigorous evaluation research by the editors of the major journals. But the fact that three quarters of the adequate + studies did not appear in major journals makes one wary about the degree of that receptivity. We feel that more persuasive evaluation research coupled with greater exposure in major journals would provide an important stimulus toward the development of a sociological paradigm.

CONCLUSIONS

Before going further, an attempt must be made to understand why an academic subfield in which there is a stress upon necessity of following rigorous scientific methodologies should be characterized by poor and questionable research quality. The weakness of the theoretical base in regard to designing and evaluating social action programs contributes to research problems. Lack of replicated knowledge in regard to intervention and assessment lead to difficulties in measurement, variable identification, definition, etc (Reiss 1970). This should not be taken to suggest that the social sciences have generated no conceptual models of human behavior, nor that they lack any empirical data regarding the interrelations among various factors and patterns of human behavior and attitudes. However, as Duncan (1970) posits, where theory exists it tends to be cast in abstract terms that are often too imprecise for practical application. Contributing to the weakness of the knowledge base is the sociopolitical environment in which such research takes place (Reissman 1972). As Weiss notes, "evaluation is now becoming increasingly political" (Weiss 1970). She states that this politicalization has lead to a parochialism in evaluation research. In response to political pressures for quick evaluations, researchers have concentrated on immediate concerns rather than on broader questions relating to underlying assumptions and system perspectives. Evaluation studies stress discrepancies between initial and accomplished goals in a single program, rather than emphasizing the differences among programs. This limited perspective mitigates against the development of generalizable knowledge and theory necessary to effective intervention and evaluation. Our finding that only 16% of the evaluations in our survey were concerned with testing theory and only 37% underlying assumptions lend tenability to her observation.

The pressure toward parochial studies inhibits the development of a cummulative and replicable body of knowledge. Such a body of knowledge can greatly increase the meaningfulness of individual studies by providing design guidelines as well as a contextual framework for interpretation of findings. The constraints of a weak conceptual base affect all evaluation research. For example, a number of more rigorous studies such as Corwin (1973) on Teacher Corps; McDill, McDill & Sprehe (1969) on compensatory education program; Coleman et al (1966) on equality of educational opportunity; Meyer & Borgatta (1959) on mental health rehabilitation; and Westinghouse Learning Corporation (1969) on Head Start, and Lampam (1974) on welfare etc suggest that social programs in a variety of areas have been failures. Unfortunately, lacking a conceptual framework, we have little idea of why the programs fail. Even worse in many instances, we do not know specifically what failed. Thus, in contradiction to the suggestion of Williams & Evans (1969) that we may at least learn from studies that fail, there is often little to be gleaned from previous attempts at evaluation, due to lack of a conceptual framework. The agencies funding evaluation research, it seems to us, can assist in the development of conceptual frameworks by permitting and encouraging researchers to test the theory and assumptions underlying intervention and evaluation. In addition to its affect upon the development of a conceptual base, sociopolitical pressure directly impinges upon the execution of evaluation research (Suchman 1967). Unlike most social science research, evaluation research has the potential of relatively immediate consequences. In a very real sense the evaluator has a margin of fate control over the livelihood and credibility of a program's administrative staff. As Eaton's (1962) research suggests, administrators are not very enthusiastic about public evaluations. This could be a factor toward the use of in house evaluations or cooptation of evaluators. For example, 70% of the evaluators in our survey have some affiliations with the organization they were evaluating. This tendency in terms of obtaining positive evaluations does appear to have *beneficial* consequences. As noted earlier, 58% of the studies by evaluators with such affiliations reported the programs they evaluated were successful, as compared to 14% by the unaffiliated evaluators. We are not implying any deliberateness, but are suggesting that unconscious biases akin to those occurring when investigators examine their own theoretical beliefs may be occurring (Rosenthal 1966).

In any case the variation in success patterns observed between evaluators with an organizational affiliation to the program they are evaluating and evaluators lacking such affiliation indicates that the independence of the evaluator is a matter of concern, a concern that is increased when we note that the quality of research conducted by evaluators with program affiliation tended to be less rigorous than research conducted by researchers without such affiliations. However, where the evaluator lacks programatic affiliation, he is often viewed as a threat, and as a consequence is frequently met with resistance and hinderances to his activities (Baker 1968, Ferman 1969, Rossi 1962). Improving the quality of evaluation research by applying better methodological techniques and by the development of more stringent evaluation criteria will in all probability exacerbate the problem. Since methodological rigor can appear to increase the likelihood of qualified or negative assessments, increase in rigor would increase the threat of evaluations. Some suspicion is perhaps inevitable in any rigorous evaluation. But the resistances engendered by such suspicion can hinder evaluators. It is therefore important to minimize suspicion without sacrificing the evaluators' independence. Suspicion might be reduced if punitive connotations of evaluation were counterbalanced by viable suggestions for improving program performance—suggestions that facilitate rather than threaten administrators. The potential of providing such imput, to some extent, depends upon a systemic perspective as envisioned by Weiss rather than the limited goal perspective often mandated by funding agencies. This approach, however, requires broader and more extensive evaluation studies than currently appears to be the norm.

Though the term evaluation research may conjure up images of large studies (i.e. Head Start, Teacher Corps, Equality of Education, etc), in fact most evaluation is carried out on relatively small pilot and demonstration projects of short duration. These projects usually suffer from underfunding (Weiss 1972). In addition, given the changing winds of fortune in Washington, it is not uncommon for a project to be facing termination regardless of what the evaluator finds.

More than likely the evaluator comes on the program scene only as it nears completion, a period when most of the budget has been spent and there is little time to really develop and execute an adequate evaluation research design. Unlike reports that are required as part of contracted basis research, the deadlines imposed on the evaluator may be very real. After it passes, the decision making processes go on whether the report has been filed or not. Thus there is a political constraint to produce a report, but not necessarily a viable report.

A further force shaping the evaluator's end product is the audience who will read it. Often the reader is untrained in either scientific methodology or the field of sociology. As a result, it is suggested (American City Corp. 1971) that the evaluator present his findings in the simplest, most nonjargonistic, most direct manner possible. Such an approach we hold can result in the type of oversimplication that distorts rather than illuminates findings.

But while lack of knowledge and sociopolitical pressures create problems for the evaluator, they do not in and of themselves lead to bad research. Nor is bad research necessarily the result of lack of research knowledge. For instance, over 50% of the articles that we called questionable contained one or another reason as to why the research was not more rigorous, while none of the adequate+ studies contained references to factors limiting research quality. Thus there is reason to believe that some of the researchers of the less rigorous studies were aware of the limitations in their work. We believe that a major reason that most of the evaluations we reviewed were not methodologically more rigorous is due to the readiness of researchers to compromise with methodological standards. Many research texts reinforce the belief that, while sophisticated research is desirable, if circumstances do not permit a fully rigorous investigation, less rigorous investigation is preferable to no investigation at all. It seems to us that research that does not meet minimal standards of rigor is not only questionable, but often is counterproductive. Further, given the situational and personal biases that occur in all research situations, lack of rigor often leads to findings that may reflect such biases. Research texts for the most part do not provide discussion or guides for conditions under which research should not be undertaken. To our minds, an important step in improving the quality of evaluation research is to make increasingly salient, as Weiss does (1972), the research and methodological factors one should consider in deciding to undertake or not undertake a particular evaluation study. In concluding, we would like to cite the following seven studies: Brechman 1972, Cramer 1970–1971, Jacobi 1968, Klein 1969, Lieberman 1972, Lowe 1972, and Wolfe 1968. These studies, which were included in our sample, demonstrate the type of quality evaluation research suggested by many of the authors we cited. We feel that they ought to be the norm rather than the exception.

ACKNOWLEDGMENTS

We would like to acknowledge the following who helped with the preparation of this paper: Judith A. Stewart, Richard Hardin, and Sue Marquis Gordon.

APPENDIX

Table A-1   Codes used in analysis

Organizational type of senior author
    academic . . . .
    miscellaneous . . . .
    not given . . . .

Source of funding for the evaluation
    organization implementing intervention . . . .
    agency(s) funding organization implementing the intervention . . . .
    agency independent of both . . . .
    other . . . .
    don't know . . . .
    no information . . . .

Evaluator has independent budget
    yes . . . .
    no . . . .
    don't know . . . .
    not given . . . .

Relation of evaluator to project evaluated
    member of target population . . . .
    member of agency funding intervention . . . .
    independent individual/group . . . .
    staff member of evaluatee . . . .
    originator of intervention, experimenter . . . .
    other . . . .
    don't know . . . .
    no information . . . .

Presence of statement that purpose is to evaluate
    yes . . . .
    no . . . .

Is the evaluation
    a single effort . . . .
    multiple staged (fixed # of times) . . . .
    a continuous effort . . . .
    evaluation is an experiment . . . .
    other, miscellaneous . . . .
    don't know . . . .
    no information . . . .

Aspects of organization which evaluator states that he intends to evaluate
    organizational aspects . . . .
    intervention (treatment & delivery) . . . .
    treatment . . . .
    delivery . . . .
    other . . . .
    don't know . . . .
    no information . . . .

Table A-1   (Continued)

Does author state that he intends to evaluate the assumptions underlying the program (at any level)?

    no . . . .

    yes. . . . .

Does author operationalize the assumptions that he intends to evaluate?

    no . . . .

    yes. . . . .

    is not evaluating assumptions . . . .

Does author state that he intends to evaluate the theoretical framework underlying the program (in whole or in part)?

    no . . . .

    yes. . . . .

Does author operationalize the theoretical concepts that he intends to evaluate?

    no . . . .

    yes. . . . .

    is not evaluating theoretical framework. . . . .

METHODOLOGICAL CHARACTERISTICS OF THE EVALUATION ITSELF

Criteria used to select population

    not specified . . . .

    global (single socio-demographic characteristic) . . . .

    multiple socio-demographic characteristics. . . . .

    don't know . . . .

    no information. . . . .

Author presents logically derived hypothesis as occuring prior to data analysis

    no . . . .

    yes, specified . . . .

    yes, operationalized . . . .

    other . . . .

    don't know. . . . .

    no information. . . . .

Hypothesis tested

    no . . . .

    yes. . . . .

    no hypothesis . . . .

    don't know. . . . .

    no information. . . . .

Definition of independent variables other than the intervention

    none. . . . .

    general—discussed without being specified . . . .

    specified, defined . . . .

    operationalized, translated into measures. . . . .

    other . . . .

    don't know. . . . .

    no information. . . . .

Table A-1 (Continued)

Definition of intervention as independent variable
 none. . . . .
 general—discussed without being specified . . . .
 specified, defined . . . .
 operationalized, translated into measures. . . . .
 other . . . .
 don't know . . . .
 no information. . . . .

Definition of dependent variables
 none. . . . .
 general . . . .
 specified . . . .
 operationalized . . . .
 other . . . .
 don't know . . . .
 no information. . . . .

Judgmental criteria
 efficiency—costs. . . . .
 effectiveness—what is getting done . . . .
 discipline—testing a theoretical perspective . . . .
 morale—happiness of target population. . . . .
 other, miscellaneous. . . . .
 don't know . . . .
 no information. . . . .

Nonsampling designs
 no design; random; discussion . . . .
 case study . . . .
 cross sectional . . . .
 longitudinal . . . .
 quasi-experimental (natural e. which includes a control group) . . . .
 experimental . . . .
 other . . . .
 don't know . . . .
 no information. . . . .

Sampling designs
 cross-sectional . . . .
 longitudinal . . . .
 quasi-experimental . . . .
 experimental . . . .
 other . . . .
 don't know . . . .
 no information. . . . .

Table A-1 (Continued)

Conclusions drawn by evaluator
 absent. . . . .
 data presented for major points are strongly contrary to conclusions drawn . . . .
 data presented for minor points are contrary to conclusions drawn . . . .
 "neutral"—data does not support conclusions drawn . . . .
 some support for conclusions drawn (some attempt to rule out
  alternative explanations) . . . .
 good support for conclusions drawn (strong attempt to rule out
  alternative explanations) . . . .
 other . . . .
 don't know. . . . .
 no information. . . . .

Is level of generalization drawn appropriate to level of organization studied?
 in general, no. . . . .
 in general, yes . . . .
 don't know. . . . .
 no information. . . . .

Are there other articles about the same intervention referred to in article by same author
or team member?
 no . . . .
 yes. . . . .

Evaluator's appraisal of success of intervention
 success . . . .
 partial success . . . .
 failure. . . . .

Two sentence description of nature of intervention:

MYTHOLOGY—Reasons why things did not get done.
     "0" means reason was not stated. "1" means reason was
     explicitly mentioned.
 None . . . .
 Underfunded. . . . .
 Conflict between evaluator and program personnel . . . .
 Could not operationalize variables adequately . . . .
 Program failure due to administration of intervention . . . .
 Program always changing (evolving). . . . .
 Phenomenon is too complex in nature . . . .
 Need to evaluate minor (finer) differences . . . .
 Cannot measure program's impact on affective dimension . . . .
 You can't really determine if this type of program really works. . . . .
 Statistics cover up more than they reveal . . . .
 Miscellaneous mythologies (list details of all on miscellaneous sheets) . . . .

Table A-1   (Continued)

Publication date—19
Journal type
   major . . . .
   minor . . . .
   other . . . .
Source
   Soc Abstracts 2/69 . . . .
   Soc Abstracts /69 . . . .
   Soc Abstracts 6/71 . . . .
   Soc Abstracts /71 . . . .
   Soc Abstracts 5/73 . . . .
   Soc Abstracts /73 . . . .
   ERIC . . . .
   Index Medicus . . . .

Table A-2   Major sociological journals

American Sociological Review
American Journal of Sociology
Social Forces
Sociometry
British Journal of Sociology
American Anthropologist
Social Problems
American Political Science Review
Demography
Annals of the American Academy of Political and Social Science
Public Opinion Quarterly
American Economic Review
Journal of Personality and Social Psychology
European Journal of Sociology
Behavioral Science
Rural Sociology
Human Organization
Journal of Social Psychology
Administrative Science Quarterly
Milbank Memorial Fund Quarterly
International Journal of Comparative Sociology

Literature Cited

The American City Corp. 1971. *Making Evaluation Research Useful.* Columbia, Md.: The Urban Life Center

Baker, F. 1968. Program evaluation models and the implementation of research findings. *Am. J. Public Health* 58: 1248–55

Barber, B. 1962. *Science and the Social Order.* New York: Collier

Becker, S. W. 1970. The parable of the pill. *Admin. Sci. Quart.* 15:94–96

Ben-David, J. 1960. Roles and innovations in medicine. *Am. J. Sociol.* 65:828–43

Ben-David, J. 1964. Scientific growth: a sociological view. *Minerva* 2:475

Borus, M., Buntz, C. G. 1972. Problems and issues in the evaluation of manpower programs. *Ind. Labor Relat. Rev.* 25:234–45

Brechman, B. N. January 1972. The impact of Israel's reprisals on behavior of the Arab Nations directed at Israel. *J. Conflict Resolut.,* Vol. 16, No. 2:155–81

Breedlove, J. L. 1972. Theory development as a task for the evaluator. In *Evaluation of Social Intervention,* ed. E. J. Mullen, J. R. Dumpson, 55–70. San Francisco: Jossey Bass

Campbell, D. T., Stanley, J. C. 1967. *Experimental and Quasi-Experimental Designs for Research.* Chicago: Rand McNally

Coleman, J. S. et al 1966. *Equality of Educational Opportunity.* Washington, DC: GPO

Coleman, J. S. 1970. Reply to Cain and Watts. *Am. Sociol. Rev.* 35:42–9

Coleman, J. S. February 1973. Ten principles governing policy research. *APA Monitor,* p. 6

Corwin, R. G. 1973. *Reform and Organizational Survival.* New York: Wiley

Cramer, G. H. Winter 1970–71. The effects of precinct-level canvassing on voter behavior. *Public Opin. Quart.,* Vol. 34, No. 4: 560–72

Duncan, O. D. 1970. *Toward Social Reporting: Next Steps.* New York: Russell Sage Foundation

Dunnette, M. D., Campbell, J. P. 1968. Laboratory education: impact on people and organizations. *Ind. Relat.* 8:1–27

Eaton, J. W. 1962. Symbolic and substantive evaluation research. *Admin. Sci. Quart.* 6:421–42

Fairweather, G. W. 1967. *Methods for Experimental Social Innovation.* New York: Wiley

Ferman, L. A. 1969. Some perspectives on evaluating social welfare programs. *Ann. Am. Acad. Polit. Soc. Sci.* 385:143–56

Festinger, L. 1964. Behavioral support for opinion change. *Public Opin. Quart.* 28:404–17

Freeman, H. E., Sherwood, C. C. 1965. Research in large-scale intervention programs. *J. Soc. Issues* 21:11–28

Freeman, H. E., Sherwood, C. C. 1970. *Social Research and Social Policy.* Englewood Cliffs, NJ: Prentice-Hall

Guba, E. G. 1969. The failure of educational evaluation. *Educ. Technol.* 9:29–38

Harris, C. W. 1963. *Problems in Measuring Change.* Madison, Wis.: Univ. Wisconsin Press

Houston, T. R. Jr. 1972. The behavioral sciences impact-effectiveness model. In Rossi, P. H., Williams, W. 1972. *Evaluating Social Problems: Theory, Practice and Politics,* 51–65. New York: Seminar Press

Hyman, H. H., Wright, C. R., Hopkins, T. K. 1962. *Applications of Methods of Evaluation: Four Studies of the Encampment for Citizenship.* Berkeley: Univ. Calif. Press

Hyman, H., Wright, C. R. 1967. Evaluating social action programs. In *Uses of Sociology,* ed. P. F. Lazarfield, W. H. Sewell H. L. Wilensky, 741–82. New York: Basic Books

Jacobi, J. 1968. Meeting the needs of children and youth in a regional area: the local area study and demonstration projects in the central Berkshire area of Massachusetts, Massachusetts Committee on Children and Youth, Monogr. No.s 4, 5, & 6.

Klein, E. M. W. July 1969. Gang cohesiveness, delinquency and a street-work program. *J. Res. in Crime and Delinquency* Vol. 6, No. 2: 135–66

Kuhn, T. 1970. *The Structure of Scientific Revolutions.* Chicago: Univ. Chicago Press. 2nd ed.

Lampman, R. J. 1974. What does it do for the poor? A new test for national policy. *Public Interest* 34:66–82

Lazarsfeld, P. F., Sewell, W. H., Wilensky, H. L., Eds. 1967. *The Uses of Sociology.* New York: Basic Books

Lieberman, G. M. A., Yalom, I. D., Miles, M. B. January–February 1972. The impact of encounter groups on participation, some preliminary findings. *J. Appl. Behav. Sci.* 8(1):29–50

Lodahl, J. B., Gordon, G. 1972. The structure of scientific fields and the functioning of university graduate departments. *Am. Social Rev.* 37:57–72

Lowe, G. D., Hodges, H. E. Fall 1972. Race and the treatment of alcoholism in a Southern state. *Soc. Probl.* 20(2): 240–52

Madge, J. 1953. *The Tools of Social Science.* London: Longmans Green

Martinson, R. 1974. What works?—Questions and answers about prison reform. *Public Interest* 35:22–54

McDill, E. L., McDill, M. S., Sprehe, J. T. 1969. *Strategies for Success in Compensatory Education.* Baltimore, Md.: Johns Hopkins Press

McDill, E. L., McDill, M. S., Sprehe, J. T. 1972. Evaluation in practice: compensatory education. In Rossi, P. H., Williams, W. *Evaluating Social Problems Theory, Practice and Politics,* 141–85. New York: Seminar Press

Meyer, H. J., Borgatta, E. F. 1959. *An Experiment in Mental Patient Rehabilitation.* New York: Russell Sage Foundation

Orlans, H. 1973. *Contracting for Knowledge.* San Francisco: Jossey Bass

Rein, M. 1969. Choice and change in the American welfare system, *Ann. Am. Acad. Polit. Soc. Sci.* 385:89–109

Reiss, A. J. 1970. Putting sociology into policy. *Soc. Probl.* 17:289–94

Reissman, L. 1972. The solution cycle of social problems. *Am. Sociol.* 17:7–9

Roethlisberger, F. J., Dickson, W. J. 1939. *Management and the Worker.* Cambridge, Mass.: Harvard Univ. Press

Rosenthal, R. 1966. *Experimenter Effects in Behavioral Research.* New York: Appleton

Rossi, P. H. 1962. *Researchers, Scholars and Policy-Makers.* Presented at the Survey Research Center, Univ. Mich., July 1962. Mimeographed

Scott, R. A., Shore, A. 1974. Sociology and policy analysis. *Am. Sociol.* 9:51–59

Stanley, J. C. 1972. Controlled field experiments as a model for evaluation. In Rossi, P. H., Williams, W. *Evaluating Social Problems Theory, Practice and Politics,* 67–71. New York: Seminar Press

Stufflebeam, D. L. 1968a. *Evaluation as Enlightenment for Decision Making.* Presented at Working Conference on Educational Outcomes. The Assoc. for Supervisors and Curriculum Development, Sarasota, Fla., Jan. 1968

Stufflebeam, D. L. 1968b. Toward a science of educational evaluation. *Educ. Technol.* 8:5–12

Suchman, E. A. 1967. *Evaluation Research: Principles and Practice in Public Service and Social Action Programs.* New York: Russell Sage Foundation

Trice, H. M., Roman, P. M. 1974. Evaluation of Training: Strategy, Tactics, and Problems. Training Information Sources. 3. Compiled by Eric Clearinghouse on Adult Education, Washington, DC

Weinberg, Alvin M. 1964. Criteria for scientific choice. *Phys. Today* 17:44

Weiss, C. H. 1970. The politicalization of evaluation research. *J. Soc. Issues* 26:57–68

Weiss, C. H. 1972. *Evaluation Research. Methods of Assessing Program Effectiveness.* Englewood Cliffs, NJ: Prentice-Hall

Weiss, R. S., Rein, M. 1969. The evaluation of broad-aim programs: a cautionary case and a moral. *Ann. Am. Acad. Polit. Soc. Sci.* 385:133–45

Weiss, R. S., Rein, M. 1970. The evaluation of broad-aim programs, experimental design, its difficulties and an alternative. *Admin. Sci. Quart.* 15:97–109

Westinghouse Learning Corp.—Ohio Univ. 1969. *The Impact of Head Start: on Children's Cognitive and Affective Development*

Wheeler, S., Cottrell, L. S. 1966. *Juvenile Delinquency, Its Prevention and Control.* New York: Russell Sage Foundation

Wholey, J. S., Scanlon, J. W., Duffy, H. G., Fukumoto, J. S., Vogt, L. M. 1970. *Federal Evaluation Policy.* Washington, DC: The Urban Inst.

Williams, W., Evans, J. W. 1969. The politics of evaluation. The case of head start. *Ann. Am. Acad. Polit. Soc. Sci.* 385: 118–32

Wolfe, F. S., Badgley, R. F., Kasius, R., Garson, J., Gold, R. J. M. January 1968. The work of a group of doctors in Saskatchewan. *Millbank Mem. Fund Quart.* Vol. 46, No. 1, Part I:103–30

STRANDS OF THEORY AND RESEARCH IN COLLECTIVE BEHAVIOR

❖10514

Gary T. Marx

Department of Urban Studies and Planning, Massachusetts Institute of Technology, Cambridge, Massachusetts 02139

James L. Wood

Department of Sociology, University of California, Riverside, Riverside, California 92502

INTRODUCTION

A recent survey indicated that relatively few sociologists identify "collective behavior" as one of their two areas of specialization, or teach courses with this title (Quarantelli & Weller 1974). Nevertheless, there has been a large amount of research in this and related areas over the last decade or so. National and international events have heightened awareness of social movements, riots, and protests, and have offered rich data to be analyzed. Increased funding for research, advances in quantitative methodology, and larger numbers of people working in the field have all helped make collective behavior one of the more vigorous areas of sociology in the last 15 years.

There have been important theoretical and empirical contributions. Indeed, at least 24 books dealing directly with general collective behavior topics have appeared since 1969 (McLaughlin 1969, Evans 1969, 1973, Gerlach & Hine 1970, 1973, Gusfield 1970b, Rush & Denisoff 1971, Wilkinson 1971, Ash 1972, Turner & Killian 1972, Hughes 1972, Klapp 1972, Short & Wolfgang 1972, Brown & Goldin 1973, Oberschall 1973, Shibutani 1973, Weinstein & Platt 1973, Wilson 1973, Berk 1974b, Howard 1974, Denisoff 1974, Roberts & Kloss 1974, Blumer, forthcoming, and Mauss 1975). In contrast, far less than half this number of books were published over the previous 25 years.

There has also been a great amount of work on more specialized topics such as particular social movements and riots. A large part of the nearly 4000 items listed in a collective behavior bibliography of Hornback & Morrison (1974) are of recent origin. Two newsletters, *The Critical Mass Bulletin,* from the Department of Sociology, University of Tennessee, Knoxville, and *Unscheduled Events,* from the Disaster Research Center at Ohio State University, circulate among many of those interested in the area. And there seems to be increased interest in forming a section on collective behavior in the American Sociological Association. Collective behavior topics have been stressed at numerous scholarly meetings.

The emphasis of the field has changed. At the turn of the century it was dominated by higher status theorists threatened by social change. In the 1950s its spokesmen were more or less detached researchers. These have given way to an increasing number of more activist researchers, who view the study of collective behavior as a way to encourage social change.

Given the abundance and diversity of works that touch the area of collective behavior, the word "strands" in our title is aptly chosen. In this abbreviated essay we cannot begin to review all the literature falling broadly within the area of collective behavior. We are concerned mainly with developments since the early 1960s, especially since the publication of the major works by Turner & Killian (1957), the Langs (1961), and Smelser (1963). Our focus follows the thrust of recent research, which has centered much more on contemporary American social movements than on the "emergent," less organized, elementary forms of collective behavior such as crazes, panics, fashion, rumor, and behavior in disasters.

Even within the area of social movements, our emphasis is primarily on movements of a protest and "rights-seeking" nature, rather than those of a more expressive, personal, or other-worldly orientation. Our purpose is to offer a broad review and analysis of selected developments in the field rather than a polemical evaluation inspired by a particular theoretical perspective. We seek to answer the question, "What's new in the study of collective behavior," particularly with reference to social movements.

Our concern is primarily with theoretical developments in the field and with efforts to test theory, rather than with specific movements as such. For those interested in specific social movements there are extensive bibliographies such as Altbach & Kelly (1973) and Keniston (1973) on student movements, Meier & Rudwick (1973) on the Civil Rights Movement, Lipset & Raab (1970) on the radical right, and Ehrlich (1973) and Hochschild (1973) on the Women's Liberation Movement. A bibliography by Pfautz (1969) lists a large number of social movement case studies, as does the Literature Cited section of this article.

In developing the key analytic and temporal aspects of collective behavior, our discussion is organized around the following topics:

1. Some New Approaches to Conceptualizing and Studying Collective Behavior
2. Strains Underlying Collective Behavior
3. Ideology
4. Mobilization
5. Recruitment
6. Dynamics, Development, and Consequences
7. Smelser's Theory in Light of a Decade's Research
8. Conclusion

SOME NEW APPROACHES TO CONCEPTUALIZING AND STUDYING COLLECTIVE BEHAVIOR

In this section we consider some broad efforts to conceptualize the field of collective behavior, new ways of classifying crowds and social movements, and new empirical approaches to the study of crowds. In contrast to our general emphasis on social movements, this section emphasizes less organized forms of collective behavior.

Because of the large number of dimensions that can be brought into play, the disappearance of old forms and the appearance of new ones, shifts within the same collective behavior event, and lack of clear boundaries between collective and conventional behavior, there is no widely agreed upon generic classification scheme for collective behavior phenomena. Yet progress has been made in the last decade in defining both collective and conventional behavior in light of common frameworks, and in more clearly delineating types and major dimensions of collective behavior. We now have a greater number of better nominal concepts than a decade ago.

Collective and Conventional Behavior: A Vanishing Distinction?

The major collective behavior works published over a decade ago by Turner & Killian, the Langs, and Smelser moved the study of collective behavior more toward the mainstream of sociological analysis. This trend has continued and accelerated to a point where important aspects of collective and conventional behavior can be conceptualized within common frameworks. The areas of collective behavior and social organization are no longer so distinct.

Most writers on short-term episodes of collective behavior (e.g. panics, lynch mobs) and longer-term social movements (e.g. revolutions, religious cults) have regarded these phenomena as noninstitutionalized group behavior, and, as such, to be contrasted with conventional group behavior. Recently, however, this distinction between collective and institutionalized behavior has been challenged, and their fundamental similarities have been identified.

Weller & Quarantelli (1973) offer a thoughtful discussion of traditional approaches and definitions, and suggest a parsimonious typology which helps link collective and conventional behavior. They argue that sociologists have tended to conceptualize collective behavior in individual rather than collective terms, even when they claim to be doing the opposite. The social consequences and social sources of collective behavior have been dealt with, but not the social nature of collective behavior itself. Collective behavior tends to be analyzed in terms of the psychological states of the participants, or as atypical forms of interaction. When the focus is on individual participants, attention is drawn away from the social properties of the behavior as such, which they feel are "comparable but not identical" to those of institutionalized behavior. They argue that both kinds of behavior are ". . . contained within and predicated on social organization." They suggest a "social organizational conception of collective behavior" based on two major aspects of social organization: norms and social relationships. For them, collective behavior is associated with new norms, new relationships, or both.

The first factor follows Turner's emphasis on emergent norms as the essence of collective behavior (1964a,b). Noting that the difference between collective behavior and other forms of human behavior is less clear cut than previously believed, he argued that collective behavior should be analyzed with the same model of interactive and individual behavior as is found in institutionalized behavior. In crowd situations the individual acts not because he or she is automatically infected by group emotion, but rather because certain lines of behavior are seen as appropriate. New norms appear in an undefined context. The norms are there, as in any complex human endeavor, but the differentiating factor is whether or not they are new.

To the dimension of whether or not new norms exist, Weller & Quarantelli add the dimension of whether or not new relationships are present. When these two dimensions (norms and relationships) are combined, four types of collectivity emerge: three representing forms of collective behavior, and a fourth referring to routine patterns of action in existing organizations.

One type of collective behavior involves both emerging norms and emerging relationships—such as those characterizing search and rescue groups in disasters, mass hysteria and delusion episodes, and some crowds. A second type involves emerging norms among those with enduring social relationships—as can be seen in hospital responses to disaster, rioting in police units, and many episodes of fad and fashion. A third type involves emergent social relationships with enduring norms —as is often the case with lynchings, coups d'etat, and looting groups in civil disturbances. The confluence of previously disassociated norms and relationships, as when a well-established professional association becomes a militant social movement, gives rise to a fourth type of collective behavior, though one not as logically derived.

For Weller & Quarantelli, collective behavior is defined as social action by one of the above four types of collectivity. It is defined from a perspective of social organization that also applies to institutionalized behavior. Such an approach focuses attention away from the crowd as the prototype of collective behavior, and considerably broadens the scope of the field. It is more parsimonious than many past schemes, and does not use the same variable to classify and to explain, as does Smelser's use of generalized beliefs. Such an approach can help link the study of collective and more conventional behavior. It offers a way of defining collective behavior in relation to organizational characteristics, rather than by their absence.

Zald & Ash (1966), McCarthy & Zald (1973), and Wilson (1973), among others, have similarly shown the usefulness of approaching social movements through an organizational perspective. There is probably a greater natural affinity between social movements and organizations than among other forms of collective behavior. But lately even the most spontaneous forms of collective behavior, such as riots, are described and analyzed in organizational terms.

Carl Couch (1970), from an interactionist perspective, argues for the need to see the crowd as an organized social system. He argues against traditional taxonomies of collective behavior, and against the use of unique concepts for understanding collective behavior. There are "no activities, relationships, or beliefs unique to collective behavior"; instead, instances of such behavior "simply represent associations within which particular combinations of relationships predominate." Crowds differ from other units not because of the absence of "aligned conduct," but in the way such alignment occurs. He argues that the emphasis should be on how people taking coordinated actions relate to each other.

Couch suggests seven dimensions that characterize how persons mutually align themselves in instances of concerted behavior. The dimensions are: monitoring, acknowledgment, parallel and reciprocal alignment, parallel and reciprocal role taking, identifying, directing, and evaluating. These dimensions are seen to represent a continuum of "bondness" between participants. The bondness or unity of a group within which collective behavior occurs is seen to "rest primarily upon parallel role-taking, whereas in other situations it is based upon the reciprocal acknowledgment, differentiated identities and accountability to the directives and evaluations of others" (Couch 1970:468). Hopefully these concepts can be operationalized and propositions using them developed.

Pfautz (1975:19), however, has questioned this blurring of the distinction between collective and traditional behavior. He argues that the acting crowd is not a social system, if by social system we mean the existence of a persistent, normatively governed social structure. He calls attention to the difference between traditional and collective behavior norms. The latter are concrete and behavioral. The power of a behavioral-situational norm is seen to lie in ". . . the heightened socialized excitement and the close physical proximity of large numbers of others." The process of mutual influence is seen to be "uniquely direct, immediate, visual, and thus, highly involving" relative to the influence of traditional norms that are "indirect, mediate, conceptualized and thus, relatively dissociating." Although he raises salient issues, Pfautz is in the minority among those who have recently tried to conceptualize collective and conventional behavior.

While not yielding concepts as specific as Couch's, others in the interactionist or phenomenological tradition have argued for the need to focus on the social situation. Brissett (1968) notes the close affiliation of "collective behavior" subject matter to that of dramaturgical approaches and feels that the former concept should be dropped. Both are concerned with the transitory and concrete aspects of social relations, with interpersonal relations and interactional careers, and with elements beyond traditional roles. This is in contrast to the sociologist's usual concern with norms that go across situations.

In a somewhat similar vein, Brown & Goldin (1973) offer a useful review of the field and then suggest viewing collective behavior as situated social action. They draw on ideas from the sociology of knowledge and the work of Garfinkle and Goffman, which are applicable to noncollective behavior situations as well. For Brown & Goldin, collective behavior occurs when there are competing collective constructions of the social situation.

In this connection, a recent literature has focused on *rational* motivation underlying collective behavior (e.g. Oberschall 1973, Berk 1974a,b). This is a response to the presumed irrationality of collective behavior participants depicted by theorists such as Le Bon (1895). Elaborating on Freud's (1914) early insights, Couch (1968) notes that there are rational and irrational motivations behind both collective and conventional behavior. Thus collective behavior is not so distinct from conventional behavior in terms of the rational or irrational motivations leading to the behavior.

A dominant theme in the last decade has thus been to show that collective behavior may be approached with the same set of categories as those applying to more traditional behavior. This is a healthy corrective to past tendencies to compartmentalize collective behavior, to define it as a negative residual category, to focus on its more exotic or atypical characteristics, and to focus excessively on the individual. Yet it is well to keep in mind that sociological analysis requires the identification of variation. The excesses of those who saw collective behavior as totally unlike conventional behavior, whether at the social or psychological level, should not now be counterbalanced by seeing it as exactly the same. The important thing is to be able to analyze whatever differences or similarities are present within a common theoretical and conceptual framework.

In sum, the literature in collective behavior still singles out particular kinds of noninstitutionalized behavior for investigation. But common theoretical frameworks are now used to analyze both types of behavior (e.g. symbolic interactionism, Marxist theory, structural-functional analysis, and even cost-benefit analysis). Also, social organization is a part of collective behavior as well as conventional behavior; collective behavior is thus not as spontaneous as previously characterized (e.g. Lang & Lang 1968). Finally, similar types of motivation can be seen to underlie both types of behavior. As a result the boundaries are clearly breaking down between collective and conventional behavior.

Continuing the Taxonomic Tradition

From Le Bon (1895) to Park & Burgess (1924) through Blumer (1951) and Brown (1954) a major concern of collective behavior theorists has been the delineation of types of crowds or social movements. Until recently most energy at the theoretical level went into forming concepts rather than developing propositions about how concepts interrelate.

The taxonomic tradition has continued, but not without difficulties. Chief among these difficulties are the frequent failure to indicate how definitions can be operationalized, the analytic level at which they apply, how they relate to a body of theory, and the failure to develop categories that are logically derived, mutually exclusive, and that can be specified on a continuum. In addition, the formulation of typologies tends to be abstract and not well related to systematic analysis of empirical data.

Another problem in classification of events involving fluidity is the time- and culture-bound nature of most concepts. Our taxonomies tend to be static, whereas collective behavior is not. Roger Brown gave the lynch mob a prominent place in his scheme, yet this form has practically disappeared. New forms such as sit-ins, kneel-ins, park-ins, and swim-ins have emerged. Dramatic newsworthy events have helped focus attention on forms such as "unresponsive bystander crowds." People bound together as victims of terror or highjacking at public transportation routes are an increasingly common type of collectivity that could be analyzed in collective behavior terms. The increased availability of resources from foundations and the government may be making social movements with a minimal mass base more common. A focus on the more analytic elements (some of which we consider in the next subsection) that can characterize any crowd or movement helps avoid this problem, but also misses the richness and even the essence of given forms of collective behavior.

In his early ground-breaking essay Blumer (1939) distinguishes between general and specific social movements, and among reform, revolutionary, and expressive movements. Similarly Gusfield (1968) distinguishes "directed" from "undirected" movements, or segments of a movement. A directed movement consists of an organized group with formal leadership, specific programs, ideology, and members of the organization. The undirected phase calls attention to the reshaping of partisans' perspectives, norms, and values distinct from a specific associational context. Heberle (1968) distinguishes between classical social movements that become "true" mass movements of historical significance, and more limited protest movements that never attract more than small groups of people. He further distinguishes three types of movements in light of the prevailing motivation of members: the value-rational spiritual community, or fellowship of believers; the emotional-affectual inspired by a charismatic leader; and the purposive or utilitarian association in pursuit of private interests.

Turner (1969b) suggests two types of contemporary general movements by reference to the ends sought. In a liberal humanitarian tradition the first is concerned with themes of freedom of speech, assembly, and press. The second, in a socialist tradition, is concerned with demands from society for material needs.

Smelser (1963) uses the nature of the generalized beliefs to classify movements as value- or norm-oriented. The latter is concerned with more limited normative changes, whereas the former attempts to change broad social values.

In analyzing the peyote cult of the Navaho Indians, Aberle (1966) suggests a useful and comprehensive typology of social movements based on two dimensions: the locus of the change desired (the individual or the social structure) and the amount of change desired (partial or total). Combining these two dimensions yields four types of movement:

1. *transformative* movements seeking total change in the social structure;
2. *reformative* movements seeking partial change in the social structure;
3. *redemptive* movements seeking total change in individuals; and
4. *alternative* movements seeking partial changes in individuals.

This is developed out of a concern with theories of relative deprivation and change.

Zald & Ash (1966) refer to "social movement organizations" as one type of complex organization. Two important dimensions of movement organization are: (a) the extent of membership requirements (inclusive organizations require minimum levels of commitment, and exclusive organizations hold the recruit in a long novitiate period, require submission to organizational discipline, and draw from those with strongest commitments); and (b) whether the emphasis is on changing the individual or changing society.

McCarthy & Zald (1973) argue that the increased funding available for social movements from foundations, churches, and the government has facilitated the emergence of a professional class whose careers involve social movement leadership. As a result they argue that the "professional social movement" has lately become much more widespread. Such a movement is characterized by a full time leadership, a large proportion of resources coming from outside the aggrieved group that the movement claims to represent, a very small mass membership base, attempts to speak for a potential constituency, and efforts to affect policy on its behalf. The War on Poverty is an example (Moynihan 1969).

Turner (1974:849–51) distinguishes among: (a) primitive and millenarian movements (b) movements of the spirit (c) interest-group movements (d) revolutionary movements, and (e) nationalist movements. Earlier Turner & Killian (1957, 1972) suggested three inductively obtained types of movement: value-, power-, and participation-oriented movements, with the last subdivided into passive reform, personal status, and limited personal movements. Finally, Turner & Killian distinguish four types of social movements based on varying public definitions of the movements: (a) respectable-nonfactional, (b) respectable-factional, (c) peculiar and (d) revolutionary.

In the case of crowds, Park & Burgess (1924) differentiated between passive and active crowds. Blumer (1951) made a distinction between the casual, conventionalized expressive crowd and the "acting," aggressive crowd. Turner & Killian differentiate among the individualistic/solidaristic, focused/volatile, and active/expressive dimensions of crowds. Roger Brown (1954) makes a distinction between audiences and mobs, and sees four types of the latter: aggressive, escape, acquisitive, and expressive.

Ghetto violence in the 1960s resulted in increased attention on types of mass violence. Tilly (1969) uses the nature of the organizational base (communal or associational) and its relation to the structure of power (acquiring, maintaining, or losing position) to trace the historical development from "primitive" to "reactionary" to "modern" forms of collective violence. Gurr (1970) differentiates among turmoil, conspiracy, and internal war.

Recent ghetto violence has been characterized in various ways. The twentieth century has seen a shift from white-dominated riots, where the primary objects of attack were blacks, to biracial rioting, to black-dominated property-oriented rioting (Masotti et al 1969). Janowitz (1968) distinguishes between earlier "communal" and more recent "commodity" riots. Louis Goldberg (1968) classifies riots as general upheavals, political confrontations, expressive rampages, fulfillment of anticipations, and riots that didn't happen but were reported by the media. Mattick (1968) considers five types of riot: rational, expressive, reified, irrational, and interracial.

Marx (1970b) suggests a typology of riots based on whether or not a generalized belief is present and whether or not the riot is instrumental. This calls attention to the varying relations of riots to ideology and social change. Marx offers some hypotheses and discusses three types of riot: instrumental riots in which a generalized belief is present, as in the eighteenth and nineteenth century European food and industrial riots studied by Rudé and Hobsbawm; riots in which a generalized belief is present, but which are not instrumental in resolving a group's problems, such as most pogroms and communal riots; and issueless riots, such as those occurring in victory or when social control is weakened, which lack a generalized protest belief and have slight implications for social movements and change.

Quarantelli (1973) notes that collective behavior has traditionally been concerned with the emergence of new groups. Yet it has focused primarily on conflict groups at odds with, or engaged in a struggle with, the dominant order, and has tended to ignore another common type of emergent group—that of an accommodative nature. Such a group shows highly cooperative internal relations, and its external behavior seeks to be integrative. The many informal groups that arise to help during emergencies or disasters are good examples. By combining the dimensions of situational context (consensus or dissensus) and involvement (primary or secondary participation) Quarantelli suggests four ideal types of accommodation groups. One type involves primary participants in a consensus situation, such as the new groups formed in the wake of a community disaster; another involves primary participants in a dissensus situation, as with the citizen anti-crime patrols and youth patrol groups that emerged during many recent racial disturbances (Marx & Archer 1971).

While not offering rigorous conceptual definitions, several empirical studies have called attention to previously neglected collective behavior phenomena. Hobsbawm (1959), using historical data on "archaic" or incipient social movements, analyzes the following forms: social banditry, mafia, millenarian movements, urban "mobs," and labor sects. In addition, Hobsbawm has pointed to the distinction between "prepolitical" and political protests.

Leon Mann (1970, 1974b) has considered two generally neglected types of group: the queue and the baiting crowd. The former is among the most ordered forms of collective behavior. It can be short term (waiting at a bus stop) or longer term (lining up to buy season's tickets a day before the sale starts). Strangers come together and norms emerge to regulate butting-in, peace-keeping, and brief absences from the queue. Canetti (1962), though seemingly oblivious to the work of social scientists on collective behavior, has produced an imaginative, if unsystematic and not carefully documented, book on crowds. He suggests a number of types according to their "prevailing emotion." These are the flight, prohibition, reversal, feast, and baiting crowds. Mann (1974b) has considered one form of the baiting crowd (which taunts and torments a victim) in analyzing the morbid gatherings at the foot of a building or bridge who urge a would-be suicide to actually jump. Also, Latané & Darley (1970) have studied bystander crowds.

Thus we have seen a proliferation of taxonomies of collective behavior phenomena. The eventual utility of this work will depend on how the taxonomies are used. In many cases the concepts must be further operationalized. But even with improved indicators, such taxonomies must eventually be more closely tied to efforts at explanation.

Recent Empirical Approaches to the Study of Crowds

New concepts and methods are also present in the increased number of systematic micro-empirical studies of crowd behavior. Such studies are a reaction against past research that has de-emphasized crowd behavior, and focused instead on the often nonobservable, static prior conditions of collective behavior or ideology, or that has focused on the consequences of crowd action.

Collective behavior, unlike many other areas of sociology, emphasizes a type of behavior. It is therefore ironic that crowd behavior as such has been so little directly studied. Of course, there are exceptions. Among the few studies of the actual crowd, Seidler, Meyer & MacGillivray (1974) divided crowds at several political rallies into aerial segments by zones and sectors, then sampled within each. They note variation in degree of commitment to the cause according to zone and sector, with central sectors and front zones having the most committed participants. In another example, Peele & Morse (1969) interviewed participants on the bus ride to a demonstration. Similarly, Heirich (1971) taped interviews of crowd discussions during the Free Speech Movement at Berkeley. In general, however, data used to study crowds are gathered before or after the crowd behavior occurs. This is all the more striking when one considers that theories stressing convergence, emergent norms, contagion, or generalized beliefs depend on data acquired during the occurrence of the collective behavior.

In their thoughtful review, written less than a decade ago, Milgram & Toch (1969) wrote, ". . . a field that consists only of scholars contradicting each other from the armchair can easily degenerate into sterile scholasticism. The most important need in the study of crowds is to get the main questions off the debating rostrum and move them to a level at which measurement, controlled observation, and imaginative experiment can begin to play some part in choosing among competing views." Past efforts have helped frame the right questions and have offered potentially useful theories and concepts. But systematic empirical research during instances of crowd behavior has been significantly lacking.

Unfortunately even the recent emphasis on studying actual crowds has not generally helped link them to the study of social movements. In looking for observable and measurable features of emergent groups that have general applicability, attention has not been focused on symbols, meanings, or the larger context in which the behavior occurs. Instead attention has been given to neglected factors such as size, density, structure, spatial features, duration, and entrance and exit from the crowd. Variables of an ecological and physical nature have been emphasized in the effort to discover underlying principles and structures that characterize humans when they gather together.

In arguing for a quantitative approach to the study of crowd behavior, Milgram & Toch (1969) discuss regularities in the properties of the crowd such as shape, internal structure, rates of growth, dispersion, and boundary conditions. Noting that "nature abhors a square crowd," they consider the tendency of crowds to form a ring around a common object, and to expand in the form of accretions around the initial core (Milgram & Toch 1969:520). They hypothesize that those who are most intensely motivated will be disproportionately at the crowd's core. Over time a "distillation effect" may occur, where reduced crowd size results in a purer concentration of the most ardent supporters, who are most ready for action. They suggest the concept of "laminated crowds" composed of antagonistic subgroups. Here a circle of supporters may surround their leader and be encircled by a hostile group. Boundaries, which set the limit of a crowd, are seen to have two major characteristics: permeability and sharpness of definition.

Milgram & Toch suggest that observation and experimentation with crowds of mental patients, children, the deaf, and those not speaking the same language could be used to explore ideas about the supposed irrationality and childlike nature of crowds, and the importance of language and symbolic meaning.

In an effort to deal with the unpredictability of events, some fire-brigade-type research teams, ready to attend any event, have been established. The Disaster Research Center at Ohio State University and the riot-ready researchers at several universities are examples. The former has significantly advanced our understanding of behavior in disaster and has helped shatter myths about widespread mass panic during community disasters (Quarantelli & Dynes 1970a; see also Brown & Goldin 1973:34–105). However, there have been no published evaluations of such research-ready approaches. There are likely problems: cost; keeping morale up when nothing happens for a long period of time; the fact that when something does happen, the dispersion of collective behavior and its occurrence at a large number of locales may make comprehensive studies impossible; and, as outsiders, the researchers lack familiarity with the local situation. Yet in the absence of efforts such as these one must wait for the rare and happy coincidence of collective behavior occurring in a setting where collective behavior researchers are available to study it, as in Kerckhoff & Back's (1968) very useful analysis of an instance of hysterical contagion.

The unpredictability of collective behavior, and the practical and ethical difficulties of doing research in the middle of it, suggest the need for an experimental approach, where the researcher sets up conditions and manipulates the variables thought to be important. Short of this, hypothesis testing must wait upon when, and what, the natural world chooses to yield. There are limitations to the experimental approach however, including the artificiality of experiments; the inability to create the genuine conditions of spontaneity, indignation, or fear that are often involved in "real" collective behavior; the moral problems involved in even attempting to create such conditions; and the fact that experiments do not deal with the historical events that are at the crux of much sociological interest in collective behavior.

There have been scattered efforts at laboratory and field experiments. For example, Swanson (1953) made an early attempt at laboratory experimentation. Much of the social psychological work on group processes, social influences, communication, and perception has relevance to collective behavior.

A number of studies on panic have been done. Conditions conducive to a form of panic can more easily be created than those making for revolution (Mintz 1951, Kelley et al 1965, Gross et al 1972). These laboratory studies suggest that both a rational appraisal of one's chances, and emotional interference due to fear, may be associated with panic.

Harrel & Schmitt (1972) used a laboratory setting to test the expression of aggression in light of contagion, social facilitation, and emergent norm approaches. Contrary to what Le Bon might have predicted, the expression of aggression was greater under low rather than high anonymity conditions.

The murder of Kitty Genovese while a large number of witnesses looked on has led to research on the bystander crowd. Latané & Darley (1970) simulated a medical emergency (an epileptic seizure) and varied the conditions under which subjects in a laboratory saw this. Their data suggest that the larger the bystander crowd, the less the likelihood of intervention. This is explained in terms of the diffusion of responsibility in larger groups. Piliavin, Rodin & Piliavin (1969), in staging an emergency on the Eighth Avenue Subway in New York City, however, found the reverse.

Other field experiments have also shown size to be an important factor for various outcomes. Milgram, Bickman & Berkowitz (1969) have shown that up to a point, as the number of people involved in nonverbal gestures in a common direction increases, so does the number of passersby who will look in that direction. Elsewhere Milgram & Toch (1969) suggest that rates of crowd aggregation be studied by playing records of crowd noises and that aerial photography be used. Other field experiments in this tradition include Knowles (1973) and Mann (1970), who has affected waiting line behavior at bus stops and libraries.

Beyond experiments as such we have seen more precise field observation procedures. Several studies have employed film. Smith, McPhail & Pickens (1972) found film to be more advantageous than trained observers working with conventional pencil and paper techniques. Film records which can be repeated and decelerated offer a unique means of analyzing the complex and changing patterns of crowd action. Mann (1974a) had judges rate behavior in 27 television news films of riots from four countries. The troubles, of course, are that one must know what to look for, and that the camera can "lie," or at least distort (e.g. Lang & Lang 1953).

In a provocative call-to-battle paper McPhail (1972) argues that the concept of the crowd should be abandoned "as a useless tool in establishing or slicing up behavior sequences into manageable units for systematic description and analysis." He maintains that the observer now lacks criteria for knowing and recording the "existence, continuation, or termination of the crowd". The interest in types and attributes of crowds is seen to have focused attention on the substantive content of crowd events, or on their unique and idiosyncratic features, rather than on precise observation of "the formal and recurrent behavior sequences which are observable wherever human beings are co-present." These behavior sequences include the physical movements and vocal utterances of "co-present collections of individuals" regardless of whether they are in a hotel lobby, a shopping center, or a riot. "Alterations in the direction, frequency and velocity of behavior sequences" should be specified.

McPhail argues that concepts which break the crowd up into smaller units more conducive to systematic observation are needed. Among the concepts McPhail suggests are the following: assembling and dispersing of the group, focusing (convergence of body or gaze orientation), and alignment of behaviors such as cheering, clapping, chanting, gesturing, or throwing. Using such an approach, an elementary but fundamental question for students of collective behavior arises: "does the commonality of gaze orientation increase or diminish when chanting, clapping or singing affect the continuity of gaze orientation?"

In an empirical study of one assembling process, McPhail & Miller (1973) call systematic attention to communication processes and ecological factors. Rather than looking at people's "reason" for being there, they discuss some of the ways people may learn about events, may be directed toward or away from them, and may have access to them. In their study of an unplanned sports rally at an airport, they show that indices of "space-time proximity" to the assembly location are more strongly related to presence at the event than is usually the case with background and attitude variables. Indices of social density, assembling instructions, transportation access, and relative availability were used to analyze this crowd activity.

The above work represents an important departure from traditional approaches. It calls attention to, and helps systematize, some of the behavior that can be observed in crowd situations. Such factors have occasionally been alluded to, but have rarely been developed in a systematic way. Beliefs and motivations can tell us only so much about collective behavior—they are hard to measure accurately, and their link to concrete behavior is often problematic.

Ecological factors of size and space have effects on crowd behavior. To participate people must learn that collective behavior is going to occur or is occurring; they must be available to participate; and they must have some means of getting to the location. Even when a crowd has already formed, it is true we do not have very adequate concepts to describe what people do in relation to each other in the crowd. A number of regularities and ideal-typical patterns are present, however, regardless of the type of gathering. Using the same categories to analyze collective and conventional behavior is a step forward. It offers parsimony in theory construction, and helps to deflate the mystique that has surrounded the study of crowds.

Such research should certainly be encouraged. Yet it is well to note that thus far we have only a bare beginning. This emphasis has not produced any counter-intuitive or very surprising results. Even when it does, the level of abstraction involved and the kind of nonsubstantive phenomena usually focused on may not be of interest to those who are drawn to the study of collective behavior in order to understand social change. For many observers the truly important questions have to do with the consequences of collective behavior, the meaning people give to their behavior, and the kinds of ideology involved. The micro-emphasis discussed above, while needed as a corrective and balance, can lead one to miss the symphony for concentrating on the instruments. To know that common focusing and assembling characterize both the Watts riot and the Rose Bowl parade is not sufficient. With regard to the broader picture, much attention within the area of collective behavior has been paid to social movements, and this occupies most of the remaining discussion.

STRAINS UNDERLYING COLLECTIVE BEHAVIOR

Most recent analysts agree that social movements have their origins in social conditions perceived to be problematical. In reacting against the excessively individualistic approaches of earlier theorists, sociologists with quite divergent theoretical perspectives look to difficulties in social organization for conditions leading to social movements.

Collective behavior has often been associated with strains resulting from economic crises, war, domination, mass migration, catastrophes, and technological change. When a group's traditional or anticipated way of life is disrupted, the likelihood of collective behavior is increased. As expectations that previously guided actions fail, pressure for change is exerted.

Smelser (1963) referred to structural strain as the existence of ambiguities, deprivations, tensions, conflicts, and discrepancies in the social order. From the standpoint of the individual, strain refers to the existence of *perceived* ambiguities, deprivations, tensions, conflicts, and discrepancies. Thus the concept of strain—at the social or psychological levels—is a broad concept encompassing many types of problems.

Social movements are often linked to social change and are seen as efforts at collective problem-solving. In fact, social movements can be defined as noninstitutionalized group attempts to produce or prevent social change. There is disagreement, however, as to the type of strain that should be emphasized, the ways in which different types of strain relate to different types of movements, the link between strain and people's perception of it, and the utility of social movements as mechanisms to solve problems.

Various types of strain have been shown to be associated with social movements. Thus it is difficult to make general statements beyond ones such as "social movements are more likely to appear when strains occur in a conducive context, when an ideology interpreting the strain develops, when people are available for mobilization, and when social control is not unduly repressive." Still, we do know that when only strain exists—apart from ideology, a conducive context, mobilization, and weak social control—social movements are not likely to emerge.

The 1960s witnessed the development of a large literature on the role of strain in producing protests and social movements. The concept received much theoretical and empirical elaboration. A central issue has been whether or not a more specific type of strain, such as relative deprivation, should be substituted for the more general category of strain. In the following discussion we review some of the major contributors to the literature on strain.

Davies (1962, 1969, 1974) has advanced the "J-Curve" hypothesis of revolutions and rebellions which seeks to integrate Karl Marx's observation that revolutions would occur as conditions became worse, and Tocqueville's observation that revolutions were likely after conditions improved. Davies (1962:6) argues, "Revolutions are most likely to occur when a prolonged period of objective economic and social development is followed by a short period of sharp reversal."

Davies selectively illustrates the J-Curve idea by reference to events as varied as Dorr's Rebellion of 1842, the Pullman Strike of 1894, the Russian Revolution, and recent black and student protest movements. He concludes that the J-Curve is a necessary condition of many rebellions and revolutions. His analysis is phrased at such a general level, however, that he can pick and choose examples consistent with the theory and omit inconsistent examples. Nevertheless, the data favorable to his thesis are suggestive of the role of the J-Curve in helping to explain at least some rebellions and revolutions.

Gurr (1970) calls this pattern of success and then failure "progressive relative deprivation." It is one of a number of patterns he considers in an elaborate theoretical and integrative work which greatly extends the concept of relative deprivation. He is concerned with explaining forms of political violence—turmoil, conspiracy, and internal war—rather than only explaining social movements. His analysis is relevant, nevertheless, to understanding strains underlying social movements.

Political violence is explained by the politicization of discontents, and the ensuing reaction of authorities. These are not just any discontents, but discontents derived from relative deprivation. Gurr (1970:13) states: "Discontent arising from the perception of relative deprivation is the basic, instigating condition for participants in collective violence." Relative deprivation, in turn, is defined as "a perceived discrepancy between men's value expectations and their value capabilities" (Gurr 1970:13). Social conditions which increase expectations without increasing capabilities to realize them, or which reduce capabilities without reducing expectations, thereby increase the intensity of discontent.

Among factors responsible for a drop in value capabilities or a rise in value expectations are conditions such as declines in production, increased taxes, loss of social status, exposure to new beliefs about what a group is due, and knowledge about gains of other groups. What people perceive is the important factor, rather than objective relationships, though there is obviously a relation between them. Social forces such as the extent of cultural sanctions for overt aggression, the degree of success of past political violence, the legitimacy of the regime, and the kinds of responses the regime makes to those who feel relatively deprived, affect the focusing of discontent on political objects.

An emphasis on the J-Curve and relative deprivation unfortunately can focus attention away from analyzing the specific class, ethnic, status, and power factors that may underlie conflicts and the synchronization of discontents among different groups (Snyder & Tilly 1972). In contrast, the important work of Rudé (1960, 1964), Hobsbawm (1959), Tilly (1964), and Moore (1966) focuses on specific antagonisms underlying specific conflicts.

Differing from most earlier discussions of strain, Gurr's work offers instructions for operationalizing the concept of relative deprivation. He suggests two ways that this can be calculated, although he does not offer us guidelines for choosing between them. Neither does he tell us how much relative deprivation is required to help generate political violence; nor does he use these operational definitions consistently throughout the book. In spite of these problems, Gurr's attempts at operationalization should be a guide for future research.

His first operational definition of relative deprivation (RD) is

$$RD = (Ve - Vc)/Ve,$$

where Ve = expected value position and Vc = value position perceived to be attainable (Gurr 1970:64). This is illustrated by an example of Italian workers who made $80 a month but who think they should have made $176 a month. This amounts to a "degree of RD" of .55 [i.e. ($176–$80 = $96)/$176 = .55]. Similarly, French workers made $114 a month but they think they should have made $170 a month, which is a "degree of RD" of .33 [i.e. ($170 – $114 = $56)/$170 = .33]. Also, Gurr says that an unemployed worker with no prospects of other income or future employment "would experience the maximum possible degree of RD, 1.00" (Gurr 1970: 64–66). Presumably the Italian workers would be more likely to protest than the French workers, but Gurr does not actually use this operational definition to analyze differential rates of rebellion between the two groups.

Furthermore, Gurr does not often cite relevant data about people's perceptions when he discusses relative deprivation, even though perceptual data are implied by his general definition and appear in his operational definitions. Instead he frequently uses "objective" data, such as employment rates, to infer the psychological state of relative deprivation, which is a methodological problem also plaguing other similar recent analyses (e.g. by Davies 1962, 1969, 1974, Feierabend, Feierabend & Nesvold 1969), as well as a classic discussion by Tocqueville (1955; see Smelser, forthcoming). Others, however, have used subjective data to indicate a contribution of relative deprivation to protests (Pettigrew 1971:chapter 7, Caplan 1971, Searles & Williams 1962, Matthews & Prothro 1966, and Forward & Williams 1970). But these studies have primarily indicated that relative deprivation is a contributing condition of protests, not a necessary or sufficient condition (Sellitz et al 1959:80–87). That is, these studies indicate that relative deprivation contributes to the occurrence of protests, but is neither required nor fully determinative of protests.

Gurr's second operational definition involves use of an ordinal scale to examine the level of political participation a person engages in, compared to what a person expects to engage in. A person who expected to attain a fifth-ranked position but attained only the third rank would have a relative deprivation score of two (Gurr 1970:66).

In drawing upon a vast amount of data to support his numerous propositions, Gurr uses the term *relative deprivation* in many different ways. At times Gurr argues for the importance of relative deprivation, but he actually seems to be talking about *absolute* deprivation. For example, he notes that high wheat prices and high unemployment corresponded with severity of mass protests in England from 1790 to 1850; that variations in bread prices were associated with mob violence in revolutionary France; that lynchings in the American South were inversely associated with indices of economic well-being; and that a strong correlation of $-.93$ existed between per capita income and Communist vote in sixteen Western democracies in the late 1940s. These could easily be examples of more extreme, or absolute, deprivations underlying the protests rather than relative deprivation.

In fact, it should be pointed out that the literature on relative deprivation has emphasized forms of deprivation less extreme than those emphasized by the literature on absolute deprivation. Though there is some overlap between treatments of absolute and relative deprivation, as in Gurr's (1970:46–50) discussion of decremental relative deprivation, and in his previously discussed measure of the maximum degree of relative deprivation (Gurr 1970:64–66), many who stress relative deprivation wish to set it off from more extreme deprivations underlying protests. Theorists such as Tocqueville (1955) and Brinton (1952) have indicated the role of less extreme deprivations underlying even the most extreme protests. Furthermore, they often argue that improving conditions are associated with relative deprivation and protests.

If the relative deprivation theorists were correct, then it would be possible to agree with the basic implication of Gurr's work: to replace the general concept of strain with the more specific term, relative deprivation (or the J-Curve or another similar concept). But the weight of the evidence does not warrant this. Underlying various protests are other types of strain that cannot be reduced to relative deprivation.

Various theorists have emphasized the importance of absolute rather than relative deprivation as the crucial precondition for protests. For example, in his discussion of the "cargo cults," Toch (1965) points to extreme deprivations underlying these protests. In his discussion of the revolutionary crowds in France, Rudé (1960) focuses on rising bread prices and hunger, which reflect the most extreme form of absolute deprivation—minimum human survival. In his analysis of the *lumpen-proletariat* in colonial society, Fanon (1968) clearly emphasizes the role of extreme deprivations in generating their revolutionary protests. In analyzing various protests, Oberschall (1973) focuses on fundamental political and economic discontents while explicitly rejecting the importance of relative deprivation. He argues for the importance of a combination of widespread and fundamental economic and political grievances, which affect different groups and strata. Movements are most likely to arise and produce changes when institutions of conflict regulation are unable to handle these multiple severe strains.

Blumer (forthcoming) suggests another type of perceived strain underlying protests: social unrest. He is critical of the idea of "objective strains" underlying collective protests, as well as of the idea of relative deprivation. He does agree that social inequities can generate discontents. But conditions must not only be perceived as difficult for the affected group; the group must also go the next step and change its views about the legitimacy of the existing order. Those who are discontented and view the existing social order as illegitimate are said to be in a state of unrest.

Because social unrest involves a widespread feeling of the illegitimacy of the social order, social unrest can be a revolutionary state of mind. Blumer stresses, nevertheless, that collective or revolutionary protest is only one of several possible outcomes of social unrest (e.g. the aggrieved population can withdraw to hedonistic satisfactions).

Blumer clearly sets off his analysis of protests from a relative deprivation approach. Relative deprivation emphasizes the importance of perceived inequities in protests. But Blumer argues that people can perceive inequities between themselves and other groups and still not engage in protests. It is when discontented people begin to perceive the social order as illegitimate—a condition not stressed by relative deprivation theory—that their likelihood of protesting significantly increases.

Johnson (1966), offering a somewhat different emphasis than relative deprivation, sees strain, in the form of a "disequilibrated social system," as being the crucial precondition for revolution. This occurs when a society's value system and its environment are out of harmony. Economic and technical changes (among others) can introduce the process of "dissynchronization." The disequilibrium of the system will create demands for change that, if unmet, will lead to a revolutionary situation. Johnson does not offer a clear operational definition of "disequilibrium," but argues that such a condition can be inferred from factors such as rising suicide and crime rates and the expansion of social control forces.

Finally there are those who argue that for certain kinds of collective behavior no strain at all may be necessary. McCarthy & Zald's (1973) discussion of the role of career professionals in generating social movements, and Marx's (1970b, 1974) discussions of riots in victory and the contributions of "agents provocateurs" to particular protest actions, suggest this. Similarly, recent work by Tilly and his associates has deemphasized the importance of discontents in protests, emphasizing instead the importance of power struggles underlying collective violence and protests (Tilly 1969; Snyder & Tilly 1972, 1974; Shorter & Tilly 1974). Also, some discussions have explicitly rejected the importance of relative deprivation in protests (Muller 1972; Oberschall 1973:3; Blumer, forthcoming; Ransford 1968; Wilson 1973:68–69). Once again we see situations where collective episodes—even violent collective episodes—do not require relative deprivation.

In summary, theorists such as Gurr and Davies have clearly made important contributions about specific types of strains underlying various protests. Yet the many kinds of strains underlying different protests cannot all be reduced.to concepts such as relative deprivation and the J-Curve. The J-Curve and relative deprivation are contributing conditions of protest, but not necessary or sufficient conditions. Hence the more general term *strain* should be retained as the basic analytical category.

There is disagreement over the link between a given type of strain and a given type of collective behavior. Smelser sees this relationship as indeterminant. For example, norm-oriented movements can be triggered by strains in values. Lipset & Raab (1970:23–24), however, argue that strains involving social status are likely to be associated with right-wing movements. In contrast, strains involving economics are more likely to be associated with left-wing movements. Others, such as Useem (forthcoming), Aberle (1966), Gurr (1970), and Worsley (1968) have also discussed the relationship between strains and outcomes, and the issue is yet to be resolved.

There are at least two broad ways of testing ideas about strain. One is to take a sample of places and time periods, and then assess the relationship between strains and the appearance of social movements (or more commonly, the appearance of emergent forms of collective behavior, such as riots or demonstrations, from which the presence of a social movement is then inferred). Another method is to look within a given place and time period at the relationship between individuals' perceptions of strain and the extent and type of their social movement participation. The latter is considered in the section on recruitment; here let us briefly look at some of the place and time-period studies.

To provide quantitative support for his deprivation thesis, Gurr (1969) analyzed political violence and deprivation, measured by conditions such as new limitations on political activity and rapid inflation, for over 100 countries. He reports that internal conflict was highest in countries where deprivation was highest.

In contrast, Snyder & Tilly (1972) found that over a 130-year period in France, deprivation (as measured by changes in prices and productivity) was a poor predictor of collective violence. Rather than stressing the gap between expectations and achievements, as do analysts such as Gurr and Davies, Snyder & Tilly emphasize struggles for power as a main source of French collective violence. However, differing from either position, at least one recent analysis has attempted to synthesize the grievance and power struggle approaches, which is a potentially fruitful development (Korpi 1974). Those who are aggrieved periodically engage in struggles for power, although there are varying levels and types of grievances that can lead to power struggles.

A common form for aggregate studies of American urban riots and college protests has been to link social structure, strains, and protest. Spilerman (1970–1972), in analyzing characteristics of riot cities, found that the objective characteristics of cities, such as nonwhite unemployment rates or ratio of white to nonwhite income, were poor predictors of riots. Size of nonwhite population and region were the best predictors. This and other work sheds doubts on direct links between structural characteristics of cities, specific strains, and riots. Among many riot studies with varying findings, but using a similar logic of inquiry, are Downes (1968), Lieberson & Silverman (1965), Bloombaum (1968), Wanderer (1969), and Morgan & Clark (1973). Stark et al (1974), using an interesting array of data, have analyzed temporal and spatial patterns of riot activity within a given city.

A number of studies have examined the characteristics of colleges and universities that experience protests. Some have indicated that structural characteristics generating strains on students are important causes of protests. For example, Scott & El-Assal (1969) focused on large size and bureaucratic structure as conditions leading to protests. But Astin (1968:158–61) and Somers (1965, 1969) are critical of this approach. Furthermore, other research indicates that university *quality* is a stronger determinant of protests than size or bureaucratic structure (Bowers & Pierce 1974). An emphasis on university quality does not point to severe strains on students as sources of protests. Some structural characteristics may generate strains that underlie specific protests. But there are also many negative cases. Relationships among social structure, perceptions, strains, and protests are complex, and research thus far has not been very effective at sorting them out.

Unfortunately what we can do with our methods at hand is not necessarily what is most conducive to testing ideas about strain. We see after-the-fact interpretations of particular cases, where strain is either inferred from a movement's ideology or imputed to exist as a result of the analyst's personal observations. Or at the aggregate level, we see studies of strain dealing with the more emergent and ephemeral forms of collective behavior such as sit-ins and riots. There may also be the problem of the quality of data, which are often drawn from newspaper accounts. Indeed one study suggests that most of the correlations between riots and prior city characteristics disappear when one controls for whether or not a national news wire service is present in the city (Danzger 1974).

Rarely do we see studies at the aggregate level concerned with strain as related to the development of social movements. Incidents such as riots, demonstrations, and sit-ins are easier to identify in the aggregate than are social movements. Many movements do not engage in dramatic outbursts, and even the occurrences of such outbursts do not necessarily imply the presence of a specific movement organization.

Ideas about the social movement-strain linkage could be more appropriately tested if we had more effective operational measures both for strain and for various dimensions of the social movement dependent variable, such as the presence or absence of a movement (which necessitates a broad and representative sample of time periods and places beyond the purposive samples now usually drawn), as well as the size, resources, and number of social movement organizations. Greater specification of the strain-social movement link is thus clearly needed.

IDEOLOGY

Ideology is a crucial component of social movements. Beliefs focus and interpret the strains people feel. They guide participants' and leaders' actions, and justify the purposes of the movement. When there are profound strains in a society and many movements are seeking supporters, some movements will be more effective in recruitment than others. Ideology can be an important differentiating factor between movements that attract, or fail to attract, mass support.

Various empirical studies have explicitly shown the importance of beliefs in social movements. These include Lipset & Raab's (1970) focus on conspiratorial beliefs underlying right-wing movements; studies of radical feminist, Marxist, or reformist beliefs underlying different branches of the Women's Liberation Movement (Firestone 1970, Koedt 1973: 318–21, Hole & Levine 1971: 108–9, Morgan 1970a: xiv–xvi, xxxv); Wood's (1974b) analysis of radical, reformist, and radical-reformist ideologies underlying different phases of the student movement; Bell's (1968), and Pinkney's (1968) analyses of nonviolent protest beliefs underlying the Civil Rights Movement; Somers's (1965) analysis of civil libertarian beliefs underlying the Free Speech Movement; Gerlach & Hine's (1970: 174–75) discussion of the anti-system beliefs in the Black Power Movement; and Ash's (1972) analysis of the class ideology underlying various American labor movements.

Yet in comparison with other areas, the study of ideology has been relatively neglected by sociologists, who generally feel more comfortable studying social structure and behavior than studying symbols and belief systems. As indicated by our earlier discussion of taxonomies, however, this has not stopped sociologists from emphasizing ideas (defined broadly as generalized beliefs, emergent norms, ideologies, or espoused purposes) more than any other single factor in classifying social movements. Ideological distinctions have been useful in distinguishing movements, in pointing out the rational or purposive nature of much collective behavior, and in linking the study of social movements to social change.

Nevertheless, ideology has not been nearly as useful in helping understand the actual dynamics of collective behavior. As researchers move out of the library and into the streets, ideology, as a static concept, is much less helpful. There are difficulties in examining the role of ideology, especially when it is assumed that: (a) ideology is the main factor explaining the type of movement an individual joins; (b) there is a strong fit between official ideology, beliefs of leaders, and beliefs of followers; and (c) the rank and file all have similar beliefs.

The increase in the quantitative attitude studies of activists and of mass constituencies has called attention to the *heterogeneity* of beliefs and motivations among those in the same social movement. Tilly (1964), for example, in his analysis of the

Vendée, is very critical of the notion of similar motives underlying the counterrevolution in France. Stallings (1973), in a study of environmental groups, found it
difficult to classify them as either value- or norm-oriented because of the existence
of participants with both types of orientation. Similarly, Wood (1974b) found that
the Student Movement of the 1960s had members attached to radical, reformist, and
radical-reformist ideologies. In her analysis of the Women's Liberation Movement,
Firestone (1970) indicated the existence of women attached to Marxist ideology and
to radical feminist ideology, as well as to more moderate reform views. Jacobs (1970)
discusses the dramatic ideological split between the Weatherman and Progressive
Labor factions of SDS. Finally, Marx (1974) shows that "agents provocateurs" in
a movement may actually reject movement ideology while appearing to be committed members. In general, the variation in movement ideology partly explains the
tendency of movements to splinter.

Others have stressed homogeneity in beliefs and motivations. Rudé (1960: 22, 43,
199, 208–9) argues that high bread prices and high costs in general were *unifying*
motives of the revolutionary crowds in France at the time of the revolution, although the motives of the *sans-culotte* masses were different from those of the
bourgeois leaders. Also, Heirich (1971:429) and Somers (1965) tend to argue that
the common motives of the desire for free speech and political liberties in general
underlay much Free Speech Movement agitation at Berkeley in 1964. Similarly,
Flacks (1967) emphasizes the role of left-wing beliefs among student activists.

Heterogeneity versus homogeneity in beliefs among protestors often depends on
the level of abstraction involved, type of protest, and stage of the movement. In
addition, Smelser's (1963: 289–301, 356–58) distinction between a "real" and
"derived" phase of collective behavior—wherein the participants' motivation in the
"real" phase is closer to "official" movement ideology, but in the "derived" phase
begins to vary from official ideology—suggests one type of distinction needed to deal
with this issue. Also an analytical separation between beliefs and motivation may
be useful. Thus, most collective protests probably attract, at least eventually, people
who have varying personal motivations, but who may nevertheless share some
common political goals and values.

Aside from the diversity of attitudes among the rank and file, there is often a
discrepancy between the beliefs of the leaders of a movement and the beliefs of the
followers. Marx (1969:233–37) summarizes a number of studies that result in this
finding. The ideas of the leaders of a movement are usually more sophisticated and
complex than those of the followers, and one cannot automatically equate the two
belief systems. Pinard (1971:231–33) shows that there was little relationship between
a right-wing Canadian movement's official ideology and the beliefs of its mass base.
Similarly, Wikler (1973) found a difference between the official ideology of groups
such as the Vietnam Veterans Against the War, and the mixed, often confused
ideology of various rank and file antiwar Vietnam veterans. Even the term "antiwar"
had diverse and contradictory meanings for the various veterans studied. On the
other hand, some studies have reported stronger correlations between leaders' ideas
and those of the rank and file (Wood 1974a,b, forthcoming a). Yet even when participants indicate agreement with an ideology, the actions they take may be for other
reasons. Research on the relationship between leaders' ideology and the masses'

ideology could be more developed by quantifying the ideology of the movement (e.g. by content analysis of speeches, pamphlets, and other movement literature), and correlating it with the members' ideology and motivation.

Finally, we know relatively little about the conditions associated with a greater or lesser congruence between attitudes of leaders and followers, about congruence among attitudes of followers, or to which aspects of a belief system activists with varying characteristics will respond positively or negatively. These are important topics and deserve attention.

As with so many other variables important to collective behavior, we are left in the ambiguous position of having to say that ideology is important, but isn't the only important factor, and for some purposes isn't important at all. Furthermore, we cannot say much in propositional form about the conditions under which it is important. Smelser's position is probably the most cogent in this regard. He argues that for generalized beliefs to affect the occurrence of collective behavior, they must fit within existing strains and precipitating factors—i.e. for the beliefs to contribute to collective behavior, they must help explain and translate the strains for the aggrieved population, and must be given concrete substance by precipitating factors.

Beyond empirical issues such as the above, the analytical interest of some researchers contains at least an implicit critique of ideology. Thus, in looking for similarities among left- and right-wing antidemocratic movements, pluralists have tended to blur, or play down, ideological differences while focusing on such factors as social alienation, the absence of secondary groups, low education or sophistication, and authoritarianism (Lipset 1960, Bell 1962, Kornhauser 1959). Similarly, Bittner (1963) discusses a number of organizational solutions that both left- and right-wing radical movements may impose on members to insure ideological purity in the face of a heterogeneous and potentially disconfirming external environment.

In an important empirical monograph, however, Rogin (1967) has shown that, at least in the case of some specific American movements, the practice of collapsing radical-left and radical-right movements is unwarranted. His work indicates that the right-wing McCarthyist movement had a very different social base of support than the left-wing agrarian Populist movement. Their different goals (for the farmers, economic justice; for the McCarthyites, conservative control of Communists and other "left-wingers") were intimately related to basic ideological differences between the two groups. Although we should be sensitive to commonalities in social and psychological characteristics across ideological groups, ideology is important in understanding social movements and should be recognized as such.

MOBILIZATION

Movements come into being through a process of mobilization. Although there are strains, conducive social arrangements, beliefs, and precipitating factors, a social movement has not yet arisen until the affected group is actually organized to obtain collective goals.

The literature on mobilization has a paradoxical quality to it. On one hand, the concept of mobilization has received elaborate theoretical development. A major contribution of Oberschall (1973) is his consideration of the conditions influencing —or inhibiting—the mobilization of social movements. Yet the literature has not produced much in the way of tested—or even testable—propositions about mobilization.

As a sort of "substitute" for propositions, various discussions have attempted to establish the relative importance of leaders versus masses in transforming a *potential* movement into an *actual* movement. As a polemic directed against a previous emphasis on the role of the masses, recent discussions have strongly emphasized the role of leaders in mobilization. Etzioni (1968:298), in stressing the mobilization of elites, minimizes the importance of mass mobilization—even in crisis situations. He criticizes what he calls the "Cecil B. De Mille version of history." He argues that "the image of the popular uprising as involving 'the' peasants, workers, Negroes, or colonial people is almost invariably inaccurate" (Etzioni 1968:298).

Among the issues which have attracted attention is the role of the professional leader in recent movements. McCarthy & Zald (1973), in an important and suggestive paper, see the rise of the "social movement entrepreneur." They set themselves off from the "classic hearts and minds" model of mobilizing a movement, where money, manpower, and leadership come from the base of the movement—i.e. from the masses. They argue, by way of selective illustration, that "modern movements can increasingly find these resources outside of self-interested (mass) memberships concerned with personally held grievances" (McCarthy & Zald 1973:18). For example, early civil rights organizations had white members and white leaders, as well as white financial support, although the prime beneficiaries were black (Marx & Useem 1971, Rudwick & Meier 1970).

McCarthy & Zald argue that professional movements may even *create* grievances rather than respond to them. In a version of Parkinson's Law, they state: *"we suggest that the definition of grievances will expand to meet the funds and support personnel available ... "* (McCarthy & Zald 1973:23). Therefore, outside funding, from the government or foundations, mobilizes the professional social movement, which is comprised more of the leaders than of the members. Leaders will often give the impression that there are many members of the movement when, in fact, "the membership may be nonexistent or existing only on paper."

Oberschall attempts to analyze conditions under which educated professionals become available for protest activities. When such professionals cannot obtain the jobs they desire, they become more available for protest activities. Oberschall (1973:160–61) finds that this is particularly true in "segmented societies" where mobility is blocked. Using a game theory approach, he suggests that talented and ambitious individuals have little to lose and much to gain by overthrowing the system, or at least by making it more flexible. There are more risks, however,—and hence less active opposition by the talented—in "vertically integrated structures," where there is greater mobility and access to the elite.

Some of the leadership literature focuses specifically on the role of the agitator. This is an unfortunate term, given its popular connotation of a self-interested troublemaker rousing the masses against their ultimate interests. Toch (1965:87), for example, discusses how agitators can exploit the predispositions of the masses in organizing a movement. Turner & Killian (1972:389–91) show the effect of charismatic leaders in generating support, although the leaders' protection from criticism can also eventually lead to serious blunders that can destroy the movement. Blumer (forthcoming), on the other hand, tends to de-emphasize the role of the agitator while stressing the role of social interaction among those in a state of social unrest.

Analytical and empirical work is needed in this area. There are different types of leaders, just as there are different types of followers. For example, a study of leaders in the Russian Revolution from 1905 to 1917 identified six role types: rebel, striker, propagandist, intelligentsia, party organizer, and upper-level politicians (Strauss 1973). Some specific questions which could be addressed in future research are: in what ways do agitators differ from other types of leaders such as professional leaders; what techniques do they employ to mobilize movements, spread beliefs, etc; and how do they maintain power?

This emphasis on the role of leaders in the recent mobilization literature tends to minimize existing evidence on mobilization of the masses. Of course, the importance of mass mobilization depends on the context involved, on the type of movement, and even on one's definition of mobilization. Also the importance given mass mobilization is partly related to the politics of the observer. Those with anti-elitist, populist positions are more likely to emphasize the role of the masses, whereas those with more heirarchical views tend to down-play it.

It is true that most people do not devote their lives to social movements. Yet during exceptional periods large numbers of people are in some way involved in, and supportive of, social movements.

While less than a thousand people stormed the Bastille, thousands were involved in the French Revolution in 1789. In the 1968 version of the French Revolution, according to two estimates, between 7 and 8 million workers and students participated (Adam 1970, Wall 1973:14). Estimates of participation in American ghetto riots suggest that up to 20% or more of the ghetto population was involved, with many others offering passive support. In 1967–1968, an estimated 10% of the American college population (over 500,000 students) had taken part in demonstrations [Peterson 1970:63 (Table 1), 78]. And by 1970 literally millions of American students had taken part in some form of protest (Wood 1974b:145–46, Lipset & Ladd 1971:103–4, Lipset 1972:45, Table 3).

The threat of mass mobilization, even when it is not actually carried out, can be important in negotiations for social change. Those in power sometimes offer concessions in hope of defusing future mass protests. The professional leaders in the antipoverty movement discussed by McCarthy & Zald did have a real constituency "out there" with real grievances, even if it was not highly organized or self-conscious. Its presence made it easier for professionals to raise funds and accomplish goals. There is clearly variation among movements, but some have considerable grass-roots, mass participation.

Mass mobilization is given direct attention in the rationalistic collective decision-making approach. Drawing on the work of economists such as Boulding (1962) and Olson (1965), as well as on the work of Coleman (1966; see also 1973), Oberschall (1973:3) has called attention to the utility of a "game theory" model to analyze mobilization. He applies a "resource management" approach, whereby resources are assembled by a group for purposes of collective goal achievement. In a model stressing cost-benefit analysis by collective actors, people are seen to invest resources to protect their own interests. In doing this, they consider a risk/reward ratio (Oberschall 1973:168–70). The discontented group assembles all the resources at its disposal (from inside and outside the group) to achieve its goals. Forces of social control also assemble their resources to combat the discontented group. This dual mobilization sets up the dynamics of the movement.

Berk (1974b) also argues for the utility of a gaming approach which relies on decision theory and "group problem solving." Ideas such as the mini-max concept are used to understand crowd strategy (i.e. the crowd tries to maximize its advantages and minimize its losses). The crowd is seen as wanting to "win" at the complex "game" and acts accordingly. It is argued that game theory is best used where cooperation is necessary.

In reacting against the idea of the presumed irrationality of crowds, favored by earlier theorists, recent endeavors have stressed the extent to which crowd behavior is a rational means for obtaining goals. Yet there is a danger here in substituting a super-rationalistic model for an irrational model. As Parsons (1949) showed early in his attack on utilitarianism, other considerations than fully economic (or risk/reward) considerations motivate action. The focus on purely means-ends considerations draws attention away from such factors as ideology and social pressure.

Clearly, crowds have rational and irrational aspects. Heirich (1971), in his classic study of the Berkeley Free Speech Movement, has tried to bridge the gap between those theorists emphasizing highly rationalistic decision-making, and those who stress less rational and irrational aspects of collective behavior. He presents much useful data on decision-making in crowds and was much closer to his crowd data than is usually the case.

He argues that the participants saw their actions as rational means for obtaining the goals of free speech. But he also sees a tendency for crowds to simplify the causes and solutions of their problems. The existence of people with common interests in crowds increases the likelihood of a common response to a situation. Yet people in crowds may not have all the information necessary to make a full assessment of the situation. The Langs (1968:564), for example, argue that "the ecology of the crowd is such that persons experience it from different perspectives and no participant can have an overview of all that is going on." Thus, in crowds, participants can be more easily deluded and make decisions they would not necessarily make as isolated individuals. This narrow information available to crowds explains why participants can be deluded in making collective decisions, yet act according to rational decision-making models. Nevertheless, we should note that the extent of crowd delusion depends, case for case, on: (a) what the crowd was told; (b) what the "actual" situation was; and (c) the distribution of beliefs and actions within the crowd. Crowd delusion, like crowd rationality, is variable by context—neither is a universal quality of crowds. And, as abstractions generally applied to what is often a diverse group of people, they will usually be wanting in some degree.

One potentially useful and generally neglected source of data on mass mobilization lies in the role of the "underground" press. The Newspaper Division of the General Library at the University of California, Berkeley has on microfilm an invaluable collection of underground newspapers and journals. It would be interesting, at least retrospectively, to see how mass political consciousness and readiness for mobilization—for antiwar, civil rights, educational reform, and other social movements—were affected by the leftist underground press of the 1960s. This press reached millions of potential social movement adherents. More generally, the role of the mass media in rapidly and widely diffusing protest activities has not received adequate attention.

In assessing the mobilization literature, we have seen a tendency to emphasize either the independent role of leaders or that of masses, and unfortunately to ignore the interaction between them. Future research should focus more explicitly on this interaction. It should focus, for example, on how elites relate to the masses; how they enlist support among masses; how they get the masses to commit resources such as time, money, and energy to the movement; what the elites ask of the masses to help the movement; and what the masses ask of—and get—from the leaders for their participation in the movement. The best discussion of this interaction remains Lenin's (1902) *What is To Be Done?.* Lenin viewed mobilization in terms of a smaller group of leaders consciously interacting with the masses to prepare them for revolution. This analytical focus on leader-mass interaction transcends an undue emphasis on either leaders or masses, and clearly deserves further attention.

RECRUITMENT

Recruitment relates to mobilization (whereby an entire new movement comes into existence) and also to the growth or decline of a movement. Yet our interest here is the issue of *differential recruitment*—i.e. why do some people rather than others join already existing movements? Prior to the 1960s, little systematic attention was usually paid to recruitment, though among the exceptions are Cantril (1941) and Heberle (1951). Classic works such as those of Le Bon (1895) and Brinton (1952:101–33) supplied little in the way of precise data on recruitment. In the first edition of *Collective Behavior* Turner & Killian (1957) included such studies dealing with recruitment as those by Neibhur, Barber, Boisen, McCormack, Messinger, and Binkley, though the level of quantitative evidence was generally low.

In the absence of data, one person's claims about social movement adherents are as acceptable as the claims of the next. People are free to make statements about "true believers" (Hoffer 1951), to offer mental-patient analogies whereby people are attracted to a movement's ideology to reduce their feelings of diffuse terror (Toch 1965), and to suggest "penis envy" or "riff-raff" explanations of racial rioters (Sterba 1947; McCone 1965).

One of the most prominent characteristics of collective behavior research in recent years has been the proliferation of quantitative recruitment studies. Two groups in particular have been the focus of quantitative studies: student political activists and black urban rioters. Other protesters, such as those in the Women's Liberation, ecology, and the earlier nonviolent civil rights movements, did not receive nearly as much attention from quantitative social scientists. Likely it is not accidental that government and foundation money was very available for the study of the two most socially threatening groups of the 1960s: rioters and student activists.

Our discussion focuses primarily on the social and cultural, rather than on the personality characteristics of activists. The former are easier to measure, and better data, having less of an ideological aura are available on them. Still, some recent studies have systematically tried to assess the personality characteristics of activists (Kerpelman 1972, Abramowitz 1973, Haan, Smith & Block 1968).

Indicative of the explosion of information available on the recruitment of students into noninstitutionalized political activities are two recent book-length bibliographies on student politics by Keniston (1973) and by Altbach & Kelly (1973). There are literally hundreds of empirical studies of activists reported, and they do not exhaust the field. Keniston's (1973) work focuses primarily on quantitative empirical research regarding activists since World War II. Altbach & Kelly (1973) report on quantitative and qualitative discussions since 1900, including approximately 200 discussions of the University of California at Berkeley, which probably makes it the most studied campus of all time.

Activism discussions have gone into great detail on the sources of recruitment to the New Left movement. Authors have been concerned with the socio-economic background of activists, their political and ideological background, the activists' own political ideology, the cultural orientations of the activists and of their parents, the nature of their family relations, the impact of the multiversity, the role of social alienation, the impact of permissive childrearing practices, and the effect of the larger society, all as they relate to recruitment to activism.

Some of the main trends of recruitment to activism are as follows. The socio-economic background of activists in the earlier part of the movement (approximately 1960–1964) tended to be upper-middle class (Flacks 1967, Westby & Braungart 1966, Mankoff & Flacks 1971). However, in the later phase of the movement (approximately 1965 to the early 1970s), the social class base of the movement broadened (Mankoff & Flacks 1971, Dunlap 1970b, Lipset 1972:83–87). But the political-cultural base of the movement did not seem to broaden as much as the socioeconomic base. That is, even by the late 1960s, activists were recruited more often from politically left-wing and culturally unconventional families than from politically moderate or conservative families, or from "Protestant Ethic" families (Wood 1974b:83–101; Lipset 1972:93, Table 13, Bowers & Pierce 1974).

The studies showing political or cultural similarity between activists and their families emphasize the importance of *continuity* between the generations as a source of recruitment to activism. Other work, however, has argued for the importance of *conflict* between the generations in the families of activists (Feuer 1969, Block, Haan & Smith 1969).

There have been few, if any, systematic data to support Feuer's argument that unresolved Oedipal crises underlie much student activism. Kensiton (1968) comes closest to getting the in-depth psychoanalytic data needed to test such an idea, but he concludes that there is no evidence for the Oedipal theory of activism (Keniston 1973:xvi) [for an application of the Oedipal theory to a few adult Indian and Russian revolutionary leaders, see Bald (1974) and Wolfenstein (1967)].

Conditions of continuity and conflict between the generations are not necessarily contradictory approaches to activism. Activists may adhere to the political or cultural ideology of their parents, yet come into conflict with parents over the activists' perception that the parents have failed to live up to their own values (Keniston 1967, Wood 1974b:11–20). Thus there is evidence of conflicts in families of activists, but at present this evidence points to political and cultural sources of conflict instead of to unresolved Oedipal complexes.

Although there is empirical support for activists coming from unconventional cultural family backgrounds, there is more doubt about the student's own unconventional cultural values as a source of recruitment to the New Left. Wood (1974b:84–92) systematically examined this cultural theory of activism, primarily derived from the ideas of Roszak (1969), and found it to be weak among Berkeley students. In simplified terms, "hippies" did not usually emerge as political radicals of the 1960s. Other investigators, however, have seen the unconventional cultural values of the student as sources of recruitment to activism (Flacks 1967, Keniston 1971, Roszak 1969). Nevertheless it was argued that those attached to unconventional cultural values, such as romanticism and humanitarianism, could find other outlets for their values than noninstitutionalized politics (e.g. through artistic endeavors or through institutionalized social reform causes). It is likely that a synthesis of the findings would show that the cultural rebels who engaged in activism translated their cultural views into political terms (Flacks 1970). But certainly not all cultural rebels made this translation, and hence many did not emerge as politically conscious activists. In summary, activism is based more on a student's unconventional political values than on his or her unconventional cultural values.

With regard to the intellectualism and high grade point average of activists, hypothesized by some, there are mixed findings. Earlier reports stated that activists were unusually intellectual with high GPAs (Somers 1965:544, Flacks 1967:55–56, Keniston 1967:117–19). Other studies suggest that activists are closer to average students than was previously believed (Lipset 1972:108–9, Lipset & Altbach 1966:333–34). There may have been a higher relationship between GPA and activism in the earlier phase of the movement than in the later phase; this would be similar to other findings indicating a broadening socioeconomic base of the movement by the late 1960s (Robert H. Somers, personal communication). Nevertheless, it is likely that the intellectual stereotype of activists is more accurate for graduate than undergraduate students (Wood 1974b:90–91).

Some have argued that social alienation (Lipset 1965:5–6) is a source of recruitment to activism. That is, those dislocated from solidary social structures, who are faced with problems of isolation and loneliness, have been seen as recruits to the New Left.

Also those who were raised by permissive parents have been seen as likely recruits to the movement (Flacks 1967, Keniston 1967:120–21). The connection between permissive childrearing practices and activism may be partly explained by religion (Liebman 1974, Lipset 1968:49–50). For example, Jewish students disproportionately have had permissive childrearing experiences and have been activists. Although the empirical studies examining permissiveness are complex, recent data have indicated only a limited, if any, role for permissive childrearing as a determinant of activism (Braungart 1971).

Similarly, there is only limited support for the social alienation hypothesis. At Berkeley, for example, the most support regards a condition of "objective" social alienation whereby those who live in isolated living arrangements such as apartments are more likely than others to be recruited to activism (Heirich 1971:62–66, 348, 350–51, 410; Lipset 1965:5–6). But at Berkeley those who felt socially alienated were not especially likely recruits to activism, and the relationship between radical ideology and student activism could not be explained away by either objective or subjective social alienation (Wood 1974b:98).

Finally, the structure of the modern multiversity and the structure of the larger society have been seen to greatly aid recruitment to the New Left. There have been two versions of the impact of education on recruitment to the movement. One focuses on the strictly educational deficiencies of the multiversity, and the other associates educational deficiencies and activism with the larger society.

Much has been written about student discontent over educational problems. Ironically, these problems were described in detail by former University of California President, Clark Kerr (1964). The problems include student dissatisfaction over large class size, bureaucratic and impersonal treatment by multiversities, indifferent, research-oriented professors, poor education in the multiversity, and faculty and administration that cannot be trusted with students' welfare.

Some studies have indicated that students with more educational dissatisfaction were likely recruits to the student movement (Dubin & Beisse 1967, Scott & El-Assal 1969, Schwab 1969). Yet Somers (1965, 1969) and Dunlap (1970a) raised serious criticism of this educational dissatisfaction approach. Somers (1965, 1969) found that a great many students at U.C. Berkeley—the prototype of the modern multiversity—were satisfied with their education. Similarly, Wood (1974b:130, 134–36) found that among U.C. Berkeley students, educational criticisms, apart from more radical criticisms of the social system, were not highly associated with recruitment to activism. Thus, a purely educational approach to activism is about as weak as the cultural, permissive childrearing, and social alienation approaches.

There is another approach to activism that includes educational discontents, but ties these discontents into an analysis of the larger society. The New Working Class theory of activism sees the modern multiversity as attached to and dominated by corporate capitalism. As a result, students are seen as exploited and alienated in a Marxist sense. Therefore, students are seen to develop a class consciousness of their exploitation and alienation, and hence to engage in protests against the university and the larger society (e.g. by opposing university complicity with the Vietnam War). Much discussion on the New Working Class has been theoretical, with only occasional illustrations used to support the main ideas (Gintis 1970, Rowntree, no date).

One attempt to empirically test some of the propositions of the theory indicated that the theory could predict ideological tendencies of activists rather well—i.e. activists were likely to be critical of both the educational system and the larger society (Wood 1974b: 134–35). But various problems with documenting the basic ideas of student alienation and exploitation, as well as dubious assumptions about the fully repressive nature of modern universities, make the New Working Class theory a less convincing theory of activism than the previously discussed theory focusing on the unconventional family backgrounds of activists.

One consequence of the many recruitment studies has been a *lack* of empirical support for Kornhauser's influential mass society theory. Kornhauser (1959) argued that large-scale processes such as urbanization and industrialization loosened many individuals from solidary social groupings, and that this social alienation and isolation made them available for recruitment to mass movements. Recent literature has generally shown, however, that membership in secondary or even primary groups can *facilitate* recruitment to political movements that are radical or reformist in nature. Thus Oberschall (1973:106–7, 112–13, 135), Gerlach & Hine (1970:79–97), Pinard (1971:195–219), Freeman (1973: 794–95, 803), Marx (1969), and Orum (1972) reject Kornhauser's position.

The bulk of recent research points to the *positive* role of secondary organizations in recruitment to radical (or reformist) movements. It is not the absence of these organizations that produces such recruitment. Although Rogin & Shover's (1970) mass society analysis of right-wing movements in Southern California is an exception, mass movements do not seem to usually originate among those who are most socially isolated. Instead members of stable organizations—who experience some discontent—are likely to be early recruits. The sophisticated organizer can use existing organizations to build a movement which, only later, appeals to the socially disinherited.

In contrasting rates and types of protests across societies, Kornhauser's argument is more persuasive. He argued that in societies where few secondary organizations mediated between the state and the family or individual, mass and totalitarian movements (i.e. value-oriented movements) were more likely to arise. In comparison, societies like the United States, which have strong networks of secondary organizations such as trade unions, business associations, and recreational groups, were less likely to generate such movements. Instead, protest would be of a more limited (i.e. normative) variety. This is related to Smelser's discussion of societal differentiation as a factor conditioning the type of social movement that emerges.

With regard to the characteristics of black rioters, beyond the obvious finding that they are disproportionately young and male, research suggests that they tend to be representative of the community in which the riot occurs. They are not disproportionately recent migrants, outsiders, or criminals (Fogelson & Hill 1968). It is difficult to generalize beyond this point, given different settings, different types of riot participation, changes in characteristics as the riot develops, and the varied measures that researchers have used (e.g. self reports vs arrest records). A large number of these studies are summarized by Caplan (1970), and the strength of the relationships is generally rather weak (McPhail 1971).

Finally, there have been some outstanding historical studies of recruitment to protest movements. These include works by Rudé (1960, 1964), Tilly (1964), Hobsbawm (1959), Smelser (1959), and Thompson (1964). Although the historical and political context varies from the French Revolution to the French Counterrevolution to English working class protests to "prepolitical" protests, all of these studies document the role of grievances in recruiting people to social movements. The grievances vary from rising bread prices in France to worker exploitation and the breakup of the traditional family structure in England. As such, they can be considered well-documented examples of real grievances that move people to seek redress through social protest. Hence these social historians emphasize the rational aspects of recruitment to crowd behavior instead of the irrational (in this connection, see Rudé 1964:10–11).

In the above section we have tried to review some of the recent research on recruitment in light of theories of protest. Yet, broad generalizations must be made with care. We usually have studies done on one campus or in one city at one point in time, taking unvalidated reports of protest or attitudes, and using different definitions and operational indicators of protest. Or we have broad national or regional samples devoid of a specific context, considering protest in the abstract. There are different types of protesters [e.g. Lipset & Raab's (1970) "Joiners, Supporters, Approvers"] protests (e.g. institutionalized and noninstitutionalized forms), and movements. What is true at one stage in a movement's career may not be true later. For example much of our empirical review of students referred to noninstitutionalized protests. By the time of the Cambodian invasion, literally millions of students were involved in protests—both institutionalized and noninstitutionalized. As a result, the differentials in recruitment patterns were less accentuated during Cambodia.

It would be foolish to look for a Rossetta stone of recruitment that could account for all or most of the variation in differential recruitment. Yet such limitations aside, the field has at least begun quantitative testing of theories of recruitment. This emphasis on quantitative research on recruitment clearly distinguishes the 1960s from prior decades of research on collective behavior.

While we have significantly increased our knowledge about recruitment to social movements, this knowledge has been selective, especially in relation to black rioters and student activists, and appears to be at a point of diminishing returns. The work also has not been as cumulative as possible. Partly because of the wide array of places in which people publish research, partly because of variation in historical contexts and methods, and perhaps partly out of a failure to review much prior research, or because of a narrow commitment to one perspective, all too many recruitment studies do not demonstrate thorough familiarity with past research, nor do they sufficiently develop the implications of their findings for a general body of knowledge.

Beyond becoming more cumulative, future research on recruitment might also try to:

1. Test Klapp's (1969) argument that social movements represent a "collective search for identity."
2. Understand differences between those drawn to norm-versus value-oriented movements.
3. Understand differences between those drawn to movements open to everyone, such as the Pentecostals, versus more restricted groups such as the Birch Society.

4. Deal more explicitly with differential appeals for activists in the same group, and see changes over time among types of people recruited to the same movement.

5. Understand differential recruitment to different social movements such as the Women's Liberation Movement, the Civil Rights Movement, the Black Power Movement, and the New Left: all social movements do *not* draw on a common base of, say, the socially alienated; and we know little about differential recruitment patterns to different branches of the same movement [e.g. the younger women in the Women's Liberation Movement tend to be in more radical women's groups than the older women (Freeman, 1973:795–97)].

6. Further test Lipset & Raab's (1970:23–24) proposition that recruitment to right-wing movements is especially likely among those who feel status strains.

7. Test Gamson's (1968:154–57) idea that, for some groups, those high on political trust and those high on political alienation are likely recruits to social movements.

DYNAMICS, DEVELOPMENT, AND CONSEQUENCES

Work on the internal processes, dynamics, and development of social movements has of necessity been less quantitative, and more speculative, with fewer propositions, than work dealing with static cross-sectional questions such as the characteristics of activists, cities, or universities with protest activities.

Social movements are more dynamic than most other social forms. As such, generalizations are more difficult to make because over a period of time, movements are likely to change significantly. Sects become churches. Successful revolutionaries can become the old guard. A highly solidary movement may split into factions, whose hatred of each other far exceeds their dislike of those the movement initially saw as the enemy. Reform movements may become increasingly radical as they fail to obtain their goals, and then become reform-oriented again as they face repression and the threat of extinction, or as they get new opportunities for social reform. Spontaneous uprisings may give rise to more planned and organized forms of protest, or occur simultaneously with them. A movement with a strong beginning may simply collapse.

To what extent do movements go through predictable, or at least identifiable, stages of development? The literature is rather better at identifying various stages and possible outcomes that different movements may experience, than at predicting them. In this regard, the natural or life-history approach to social movement phenomena, particularly to revolutions, is one of the oldest (Edwards 1927, Hopper 1950, Brinton 1952).

Hopper, for example, identified four phases of revolutionary movements: 1. the preliminary stage of mass (individual) excitement; 2. the popular stage of crowd (collective) excitement and unrest; 3. the formal stage of formulation of issues and formation of publics; and 4. the institutional stage of legalization and societal organization. He argued that each phase was a prerequisite to the next.

Turner & Killian (1972) suggest that the life-cycle approach can be used to analyze social movements in general, beyond just revolutionary movements. But they do not argue that any given categorization of the life cycle of social movements, such as Hopper's, is applicable to all movements. Still, an interesting example of this approach is Lammers' (1969) comparison of two types of natural history in the development of strikes and mutinies.

Zald & Ash (1966) list three general possibilities of movement development: growth, decay, and change. The first two concepts refer primarily to increases or decreases in membership, but the bulk of their analysis focuses on "change." Among hypotheses they suggest are:

1. "movements created by other organizations are more likely to go out of existence following success than movements with their own linkages to individual supporters";
2. "movements with relatively specific goals are more likely to vanish following success than movements with broad general goals";
3. "movements which aim to change individuals and employ solidary incentives are less likely to vanish than are movements with goals aimed at changing society and employing mainly purposive incentives";
4. "inclusive organizations are more likely to fade away faster than exclusive organizations; the latter are more likely to take on new goals."

These are interesting hypotheses and deserve operational specification and empirical testing.

Wilson (1973:359–60), in stressing the dynamic character of social movements, argues that they "cannot therefore continue as such indefinitely." He suggests that movements either succeed (without disbanding), or reach a "stalemate" (keeping the organizational structure, but not achieving goals), or fail (disband or become a sect).

Wilson uses Parsons' functional systems-problems of adaptation, goal-attainment, integration, and latency to analyze the development of social movements. From his analysis, propositions can be derived about the success, or about the less studied decline, of movements. In general, the less the movement (treated as a system of action) meets these four functional exigencies, the more it is likely to decline. As an example, the less a movement can retain member commitment to ideology, the more likely it is to lose membership; in this case, the movement would have difficulty with the latency system-problem.

Jackson et al (1960), in an analysis of an incipient tax protest movement that collapsed after an impressive beginning, cite conditions that are the obverse of Parsons' four conditions of social system survival. They indicate specific circumstances that led to the demise of the movement: a failure of communication, leadership, ideology, and public image. These would be parallel to the systems-problems of integration (communication and public image), goal attainment (leadership), and latency (ideology).

Similarly, Brill (1971) shows how ineffective leadership was important in the failure of a rent strike. In another study, Useem (1973) has shown how strategic failures in recruitment and amorphous membership criteria contributed to the downfall of the draft resistance movement. Finney & McGranahan (1973) show how various failures led to goal displacement in a poor people's cooperative farm.

Though Smelser rejects a temporally based life-history approach in favor of analytical determinants, his variables can be used to predict movement development and changes. Thus we would predict movement failure when some or all of Smelser's six conditions leading to movement origin are significantly reduced. It has been argued, for example, that the end of the American student movement of the 1960s, as well as of movements of the 1930s, was due to a significant reduction in structural strains, precipitating factors, and mobilization efforts (Wood 1974b:148–50, Messinger 1955). In a similar vein, Statera (1975) argues that a reduction in utopian beliefs was associated with the decline of the European student movement of the 1960s.

Conversely, it is reasonable to argue that movements can be renewed, even after a major decline, as these conditions come to operate at increased levels. The topic of social movement renewal has hardly been studied and is a topic well worthy of research attention. If economic strains increase in the United States, or if there is another war such as Vietnam, it is possible that the student, minority, and working class movements will be rejuvenated.

Beyond decline from repression, from the inability to mobilize, or from inappropriate strategies, movements may change form so as to be almost unrecognizable, as they become institutionalized. One form of institutionalization involves the incorporation of a movement into the existing political and social system. For example, Roth (1963) has analyzed processes by which the Social Democrats of Imperial Germany moved from a smaller Marxist fringe party to an institutionalized member of the German party system. Institutionalization can also refer to the routinization of a movement's activities and to its acceptance by the larger society, as in the change from sect to church.

Organizational and Ideological Changes

Two broad changes that movements may experience over time involve changes of an internal organizational and ideological nature. Whether or not movements go through predictable sequences, they tend to undergo many of the same social processes related to organizational and ideological issues.

Zald & Ash (1966) discuss various internal changes that movements may undergo. Their discussion considerably extends the traditional models of social movement transformation inspired by Weber and Michels, which focused on shifts to more conservative goals, organizational maintenance, and oligarchy. Zald & Ash consider these, but in addition they consider factional splits, increased radicalism, and relations with other social movements. They seek to specify some of the conditions under which alternative movement transformations occur. Among hypotheses offered are:

1. "routinization of charisma is likely to conservatize the dominant core of the movement while simultaneously producing increasingly radical splinter groups";
2. "the more insulated an organization is by exclusive membership requirements and goals aimed at changing individuals, the less susceptible it is to pressure for organizational maintenance or general goal transformation";

3. "the more the ideology of the movement leads to a questioning of the bases of authority, the greater the likelihood of factions and splitting";
4. "exclusive organizations are more likely than inclusive organizations to be beset by schisms."

Zurcher & Curtis (1973), in a study of two local antipornography crusades, found data generally consistent with the Zald-Ash hypotheses. They suggest, however, that in small or emerging movements, organizational leadership orientation, goal specificity, and incentive structure are likely to be particularly important variables. They hypothesize that in such social movements, where the leadership is oriented toward goal diffuseness and solidary incentives, the movement will show the following characteristics: an expressive orientation; charisma; radical tactics; inclusive membership criteria; mergers and coalitions with other social movements; longer duration; susceptibility to pressures for organizational maintenance; goal transformation; an emphasis on person-changing goals; and the lack of a parent organization. In contrast, similar movements, where the leadership is oriented toward goal specificity and purposive incentives, should show opposite characteristics.

Rather than stressing a movement's internal dynamics or relation to its environment as sources of movement transformation, Nelson (1974) notes that the activation of previously latent "premovement factors" can have a divisive effect. He suggests that such factors are most likely to emerge at critical "junctures" in a movement's career. A juncture represents the point at which a movement, having achieved one goal, begins planning to pursue the next goal. He hypothesizes that at this time a movement's receptivity to the effect of premovement factors is increased: if it is characterized more by inclusive than by exclusive membership; the heterogeneity of the membership is greater; the stress is more on societal than on individual transformation; the tendency is more toward group than toward individual recruitment; and the centralization of the leadership and authority structure is less.

In a useful study of the impact of organizational structure on movement dynamics, Rudwick & Meier (1970) have analyzed why, when both CORE and NAACP came under pressure from black power advocates to reorient themselves away from integrationist goals, only the former changed. The NAACP, having a much more formalized and centralized bureaucratic structure and less direct member participation than CORE, was able to resist pressures to adopt a separatist position.

Often related to organizational changes, though analytically distinct, are the ideological changes that movements may undergo. Zald & Ash (1966) hypothesize, contrary to Michels' linking of oligarchy with increased conservatism, that "if a leadership cadre are committed to radical goals to a greater extent than the membership-at-large, member apathy and oligarchial tendencies lead to greater rather than less radicalism."

The Zald & Ash article offers the kind of testable middle-range propositions that the field of collective behavior has generally lacked. It is an interesting commentary on the field that, although the article was published nine years ago and is well known, there has been little in the way of quantitative efforts, using aggregate data across movements, that seek to test the propositions put forth.

Among the most dramatic of ideological shifts are those from a norm- to a value-oriented belief system, or the reverse. Smelser (1963:307–10) argues that when norm-oriented movements are prevented from pursuing normative changes, then a switch to a value-oriented movement can occur. The recent history of segments of major American social movements clearly bears this out. The United States, in spite of its relatively differentiated and democratic social structure, saw the emergence of strident value-oriented movements among a proportion of blacks, students, and women. The general social movements of the New Left, the Black and Third World Movements, and the Women's Liberation Movement all came to have their radical factions, which called for overthrowing such social systems as capitalism, racism, imperialism, and the family.

Movement literature seeks to explain ideological change in terms of such phenomena as the "cultural crisis of capitalism," "the role of reactionary male chauvinism," and "the racism built into all American institutions." Yet such structural characteristics have existed for a long time, and therefore cannot easily interpret the change from a norm-oriented to a value-oriented focus.

The source of change in each of these movements was the view that authorities had closed off avenues of normative change. Segments of the New Left, the Women's Liberation Movement, and the Black and Third World Movements at least eventually perceived that avenues for normative change were blocked in American society. Though each movement began as reformist, the movements later developed radical factions opposed to the entirety of American society, or to some major aspect of it.

For example, the New Left initially hoped that major changes in poverty and race relations, and an end to the Vietnam War, would come about rather quickly after organized protest; but they were, of course, disappointed. This was repeated in the Civil Rights Movement, even to the extent that Martin Luther King (1967:1–22) began to wonder if American society would ever achieve racial justice. In the Black Movement there is the interesting case of the Black Panthers, or at least of their founding segment, moving from a reform to a revolutionary to a reform movement in less than a decade. Many Panthers remain committed to revolution, although the group is now engaged in reform activities. Similarly, in the Women's Liberation Movement many younger women, previously involved in New Left activities, felt that men in the New Left would never give up their positions of power (Thorne 1972, Freeman 1973:800–2, Congressional Quarterly Inc. 1973:8–10). Such women went beyond the moderate reformism of the National Organization for Women (NOW) to positions such as radical feminism (Hole & Levine 1971:143, Koedt, Levine, & Rapone 1973, Carden 1974:47–56, Deckard, forthcoming).

Our discussion thus far has enumerated some of the broad stages and specific changes that movements may experience. To an important extent these are determined by factors such as social control, tactics and recruitment, relation to other movements, interest groups and publics, and effectiveness in attaining goals. These factors are of course often highly interrelated in complex ways. It is to these issues that we now turn.

Social Control

One of the most important issues stressed in collective behavior research in the last decade has been the need to view social movements in their environmental contexts. An important part of this environment has to do with the social control apparatus of the state. As has often been noted, the state can be a crucial determinant of the type, and even of the occurrence, of social movements. But here our concern is with the effect of social control on social movement development, size, and conse-quences. Agents of social control can serve to contain, prolong, alter, or repress movements.

There have been an increased number of studies focusing explicitly on social control in collective behavior contexts. Among these are Shellow & Roemer (1966), Walker (1968), Skolnick (1969), Marx (1970a), Gollin (1971), Donner (1971), Stark (1969, 1972), Rudwick & Meier (1972), Lewis (1972), Smelser (1972), Balbus (1973), O'Toole (1973), Adamek & Lewis (1973), Marx (1974), Wilson (1974), and Turk (forthcoming). More generally, Oberschall (1973) analyzes the complex relationship between social control and mobilization for social movements.

In an interesting study, Smith (1968) has shown how police response to adolescent beach crowds contributed to crowd conventionalization. The crowd is permitted to put up expressive resistance, which police accept, in exchange for a minimum degree of public order. He hypothesizes that crowd conventionalization is most probable when there is a strong public reaction to the expression of unrest and when unrest has very generalized sources.

The career of a social movement can often be usefully approached from a standpoint of social control interactions. The Black Panthers are a good example. They started as a local reform-oriented, self-defense group, but became increasingly radical. The movement's radical development was in part a function of the personality and attitudes of leaders and members, and of the general position of blacks in American society. But more importantly, the police helped make true their original assessment of the Panthers as a violent revolutionary group. The killing of Panthers by police, raids on their offices, surveillance, denial of basic civil liberties, general harrassment, stigmatization by political leaders, and use of undercover agents (the FBI, with agents on both sides, apparently played an important role in the split between the Huey Newton and Eldridge Cleaver factions of the Panthers) gave the Panthers little choice but to become what they were labeled. Helmreich (1973) offers a case study of the short unhappy life of another black group which started with broad reformist goals, but could not get beyond police definitions and actions that treated them as violent revolutionaries.

Studies of police behavior in riots have shown how police may be subject to the same crowd processes as rioters (Marx 1970a, Stark 1972). The particular twists and turns of a given crowd incident have an emergent quality which cannot be very well predicted by a consideration of static structural variables such as the income gap between two groups. Rather, interaction within and between protesters and social control agents must be considered.

An examination of police behavior in American racial riots from 1900 to 1967 indicates a number of ways that police behavior helped to create collective behavior rather than to control it. Such behavior could be organized into categories of (a) inappropriate control strategies, (b) lack of coordination among and within various control units, and (c) the breakdown of police organization. It is hypothesized that the breakdown of police organization, the excessive use of force, and the "police riot" were related to such factors as the extent to which police disagreed with or were threatened and offended by the issues raised by protesters, how organizationally removed the control force was, the use of police officers who did not share the religious, racial, ethnic and/or regional origins of the rioting community, the extent of injuries and provocation faced by the police, the size and stage of the riot, the strength of leadership from civil authorities, the clarity of orders stressing restraint, the tightness of the command structure and whether or not high level officers were on the scene, whether or not it was made clear to police that they would be punished for misbehavior, and whether or not police expected disturbance participants to be sufficiently punished by the legal system (Marx 1970a).

One facet of social control about which little is known is the role that "agents provocateurs" and informants may play. There has been some work of an ethnographic nature, but for obvious reasons of access, little systematic data collection (Donner 1971; Marx 1974; Karmen, forthcoming).

The range of consequences which a theory of the agent provocateur must account for can be suggested, even if such a theory is now lacking. Agents provocateurs can have varied consequences: they may help perpetuate or strengthen a movement by offering resources and moral support; organizations may profit from dramatic protests that agents inspire; the discovery of an agent may help to reduce the legitimacy of the government; the repression that the agent helps produce may create martyrs and call attention to the group.

Yet the negative effects of agents are likely to be more damaging. Perpetuation of the myth of the agent and the discovery of agents can lead to feelings of demoralization and paranoia. The agent, if not discovered, can create internal divisiveness and self-defeating lines of action. A democratic form of organization may be impossible. Agents can help stigmatize a movement as being violent, alienate it from its potential constituency, and focus attention away from the basic issues. The agent can entrap or frame a movement's leaders, and can produce a reorientation of a movement's resources into security, self-defense, and legal needs, even when activists are not convicted.

Wilson (1974) argues that criminalization (the labeling and treating of protest actions as deviant by formal agents of social control) can have an important effect on the bargaining, persuasion, and coercion that goes on between a social movement and its target group (the group it is trying to defeat or win over). He suggests a number of hypotheses regarding the effects of social control on individual attitudes, mobilization, and changes in movement goals and organization. For example: 1. violence of social control agents is likely to increase support of the movement by both activists and by sympathetic bystanders; 2. the more completely criminalization separates political goals from deviant acts, the less the likelihood of mobilization; 3. the closer the identification of target group and social control agents during criminalization, the more radicalization is increased; 4. the more criminalization, the less moderate support and/or potentially supportive elites; 5. the greater the criminalization, the lower the integration of the movement; 6. the more movements are open, and lacking in centralized policy-making machinery, formal structure, and opportunities for the release of emotional tensions, the more damaging the effects of social control efforts. These are interesting hypotheses that should be empirically tested.

Thus the relationship between social control and social movement development and decline is indeed complex. What is clear, nevertheless, is that no linear relation exists between social control and social movement development or decline. Under certain conditions, agents of control can successfully dissipate a movement. But we have also seen where social control agents obviously contributed to movement growth and even to attainment of goals. As such, this crucial relationship between social control and social movement development or decline should be the focus of future research.

Strategies of Movement Growth and Development

Recruitment of new members is the most visible and commonly treated indicator of movement growth. However, growth should probably be defined more broadly in terms of a movement's strength as measured in various ways—such as number of adherents, degree of their commitment, power and prestige of adherents, financial resources of the movement, support (or at least lack of opposition) of various noninvolved publics, interest groups and other movements, ability to influence key decision-makers or media, and quality of the organizational structure. The strength of a movement at any given point in time is a composite of variables such as the above, and they do not necessarily all move simultaneously in the same direction (e.g. mass membership could be in opposition to tightness of organizational structure). Thus many other factors besides recruitment indicate movement growth.

Nevertheless, recruitment of members is important to movement growth and development. Among recruitment strategies considered by Wilson (1973: 167–93) are involvement via friends or relatives, attendance at public meetings, approaches at the doorstep or place of work, uses of the mass media, and circulation of movement literature. These can be aimed at selective audiences or they can be broad appeals to the larger society in general. Wilson, in using a classification scheme similar to Etzioni's (1968:369), sees three general types of recruitment: normative (relying on moral obligations), utilitarian (payments), and coercive (physical force). He hypothesizes that only the development of commitment can keep a member's long-term involvement in the movement. Kanter (1972), in a study of utopian communities, has enumerated a number of commitment mechanisms that can be applied to other types of movements.

There are few hypotheses from the social movement literature about the relative impact of different recruitment strategies in different contexts, on different kinds of people, and for the many kinds of possible movement participation. Yet as movements become more "professional" it is likely that techniques from marketing research and mass persuasion will be increasingly drawn upon, as they are now in political campaigns. The same techniques that have sold deodorant may also sell social movements, if other conducive factors are present.

The way the larger society responds to a social movement influences its choice of strategies. Turner (1969a:827) suggests that the response of the dominant public will partly be conditioned by whether the social movement's activities are seen as legitimate protest or illegal disruption. He lists five possible reactions of the dominant group to the protest group: 1. to ignore or depreciate the conflict; 2. to suppress it; 3. to join the protest, at least symbolically; 4. to conciliate 5. to surrender (which he omits as a viable choice) (Turner 1969a:819).

With respect to conditions that produce—or fail to produce—the social perception of *protest* when disturbances occur, Turner hypothesizes that 1. the more a disturbance is credible as a protest, the more it will be perceived as a protest; 2. the more a disturbance has elements both of appeal and of threat, the more it will be viewed as a protest; 3. the more a disturbance is an aspect of conciliation, the more it will be viewed as a protest; 4. when groups are trying to form coalitions, a protest definition is likely; 5. when official agencies wish to bargain, they are likely to view disturbances as protests and validate a public definition of protests. Altheide & Gilmore (1972) derived and tested propositions related to the credibility of protest, and found support for all but one derived proposition.

One relatively unstudied issue in a movement's development is its relation to other movements, interest groups, and counter-movements (Heberle 1951, Turner & Killian 1972, Cameron 1966). The Civil Rights Movement, for example, was able at times to form effective coalitions (such as COFO) among its various branches, as well as to gain the support of many labor unions and religious groups. Future research might well focus on the different organizations' goals, tactics, material resources, broader values, and political styles as they affect attempts at coalition formation, mergers, cooperation, competition, and factionalism. There is a relevant literature from political science and economics that could be usefully drawn upon, such as work by Olson (1965), Riker (1962), Schattschneider (1960), Downs (1957), Boulding (1962), and Tullock & Buchanan (1962).

One interesting hypothesis is that a synchronization among the more and less radical factions of the same general social movement is conducive to gaining limited reforms (Walker 1963). The extreme statements and actions of the radical factions may make the demands of the moderate groups more acceptable. Yet there is likely to be a delicate balance involved. Too strident, or powerful, a radical group may lead to backlash and repression by the dominant group, and to attention being focused away from the normative changes sought by the moderates.

On the other hand, factions within a general social movement may have to compete with each other for a limited, or contracting membership base. Hypotheses drawing on an ecological perspective might be developed about the size of the potential membership pool required to sustain a given number of movements or factions.

Turner (1973) has discussed determinants of movement strategies, classified as bargaining, coercion, and persuasion. At this point in the development of collective behavior theory, we are in a better position to classify such strategies and discuss their determinants than to predict their consequences. Movement strategies as related to movement growth and success are rather indeterminant. This results partly from a lack of systematic study, partly from the historical uniqueness of each situation, and partly from the fact that what happens to a social movement may be only slightly related to its strategies (political shifts at a higher level may operate to favor or disfavor it, crucial tactical errors by authorities may aide it, etc).

While it can be costly and requires courage, the effort to nonviolently provoke attack on one's group by authorities has often been an effective tactic, when the group is seeking goals consistent with broader societal values. A major factor in the seemingly greater effectiveness of the black civil rights protest in the South than in the North lies in the fact that nonviolent protest strategies were used in the South in such a manner as to implicate police as the aggressors and to create martyrs (Hubbard 1968, King 1958). More generally, Sharp (1973) has examined the effects of nonviolent protest in a wide variety of contexts, and indicates various benefits to the protesters.

There is often an inherent changeability of tactics and strategies as movements develop over time. Some movements seem guided by a trial and error method rather than by a fixed set of principles. There are few studies that try to link types of strategies with types of outcomes, although Safilios-Rothschild (1974) has attempted to do so for the women's movement. But there remains a clear need for organizing principles and hypotheses concerning the impact of general types of strategies on various dimensions of social movement growth and success.

Consequences

Given the variety of places that one can look, the extreme difficulty in most cases in determining causal relations, and the long time periods that may be involved, most statements about the consequences of social movements are primarily descriptive or taxonomic. The systematic study of social movement consequences is much less developed than that of the prior conditions that give rise to movements.

Although he had less than eight years to assess the effects of the Russian Revolution, Sorokin's *The Sociology of Revolution* (1925) offers a classic model for research on the impact of social movements on change. Sorokin attempts to see the effect that revolutionary movements have on a wide variety of social and personal phenomena. He attempts to assess the impact of revolutions on factors such as patterns of speech, property ownership, poverty and wealth, sexual activity, work activity, authority relationships, crime rates, execution rates, religious activity and belief, economic, psychological, and demographic patterns, family relationships and structure, political relations between social classes, relations between political parties, civil and political liberties, education, valuation of the dollar, productiveness of the food supply, and the nature of ideology. In short, he tries to assess the impact of revolution on essentially all important phases of life in a society.

Sorokin examines various impacts in light of two phases of the revolution. The first corresponds to the initial period of revolutionary take-over; the second refers to a phase of "reaction" whereby the revolutionary government stabilizes its control.

These distinctions, as well as Sorokin's attempt to get quantitative data on various changes, make it a study worth repeating on other populations.

Greer (1949) has examined the specific demands of a number of American social movements, and the extent to which the demands were institutionalized over a long period of time. For example, the National Labor Union called for an eight-hour day in 1866 and two years later this was instituted for government employees; but it was not until 72 years later (1938) that the eight-hour day became federal law.

In 1867 the National Grange demanded railway regulation, a Department of Agriculture, and cooperative farm marketing associations (Greer, 1949:282). Railway regulation actually came about in 1887, the Department of Agriculture was created in 1889, and cooperatives received exemption from antitrust laws in 1922.

He also considers movement demands that were not met, such as the International Workingmen's Association's call for the overthrow of capitalism. In addition, he discusses reforms that took place independently of social movements, such as the Gold Reserve Act of 1934.

In successful cases, Greer does not argue that movements as such necessarily were the main causal factors, but he feels they have at least hastened many changes. Causal problems aside, his approach is useful, and points out the need for a long-range perspective in considering the consequences of social movements.

Ash (1972) has summarized the goals of various movements and discusses their successes and failures. For example, she shows that the American Federation of Labor, consciously working within the capitalist system, achieved better hours, wages, and collective bargaining for skilled workmen. Her analysis is imaginative in its attempt to specify the social class factors influencing the success and failure of many American movements.

Marx (1970d), in analyzing riot consequences in cities studied by the Kerner Commission, uses a typology that emerges from combining two dimensions: degree of racial polarization and degree of change beneficial to blacks. Where a city fell on the typology is related to the size of the disturbance and the preriot racial climate. Cities with a maximum of change and a minimum of polarization were those with medium-sized riots and a relatively liberal racial climate. In addition, Anderson (1973) has shown how riots triggered internal changes in black communities.

Gamson (1974) discusses various American reform movements from 1800 to 1945 in terms of their success or failure, with particular concern for the consequences of violent tactics. He drew a sample of movements and provided operational definitions. He notes that violence users (with the exception of revolutionary groups that aim to displace their opposition) were successful in winning new advantages, and that violence recipients were unsuccessful. He also notes, however, that most successful groups had no violence in their history. In a recently published book, Gamson (1975) develops these and related themes.

Finally, Jackson (1973) examines the impact of a specific social movement strategy—that of Affirmative Action—on occupational mobility rates in sociology. Affirmative Action has been backed by women's and Third World groups. Jackson finds only modest gains for women and few for ethnic minorities. This type of study should be expanded to other occupations to gauge social movement impact on occupational changes.

Among some hypotheses that could be tested are:

1. Reform movements are more likely to succeed when they gain the support of political and economic elites (Ash 1972:231, Turner & Killian 1972, Oberschall 1973:206–7).
2. A reform movement will affect lasting changes to the extent that (*a*) vested interests are involved in the changes, and (*b*) it can offer society something to bargain with (Turner & Killian 1972).
3. The less a movement challenges basic political-economic values and interests, the more likely it will be to succeed (Ash 1972:12).
4. At the level of the individual, social movements can (*a*) satisfy the need for security, (*b*) offer an identity, (*c*) help individuals find meaning in their lives (Milgram & Toch 1969, Klapp 1969, 1972).
5. When no movement for the discontented exists, the likelihood of riots increases.
6. For angry crowds to produce lasting effects on society, in contrast to extracting only short-term concessions, the groups must develop an ideology (Turner & Killian 1972:420).
7. The less formally organized a radical or conspiratorial social movement is, the more likely it is to survive (Gerlach 1971:834).

In considering the consequences of protest actions by American racial minorities, Marx (1971) suggests a number of factors which may have more general applicability. He suggests that the challenges of relatively powerless groups are more likely to meet with success to the extent that:

1. Their demands can be seen as consistent with the broader values of the society.
2. They can gain the support of more powerful third parties and/or show how their demands will benefit other groups as well.
3. Their demands are concrete and focused.
4. They can clearly fix responsibility for the situation they are protesting (e.g. protesting against an urban renewal project as compared to protesting over inadequate housing).
5. Pressure is brought to bear on the responsible party, and there is minimum discomfort to those not responsible.
6. They adopt new techniques which authorities have not had experience in dealing with.
7. Neutral third parties are present who have an interest in restoring harmony.
8. The powerless group is willing to negotiate, and its demands do not have a zero-sum quality.
9. Their demands involve a request for acceptance of social diversity, equal treatment, or inclusion, rather than domination over, or change in the practices of, the dominant group towards itself, or fundamental redistributions of income and power.
10. The powerless group seeks to veto a proposed policy rather than to see a new policy implemented.
11. The minority population is large enough to organize itself for conflict but not large enough to be perceived as a serious threat to the dominant group.

A number of other topics could profit from systematic study. One broad problem noted in the literature concerns when social movements can be viewed as causes of social change and when they can be viewed as effects of social change. It can be argued both ways (e.g. Gusfield 1970a, Smelser 1959, 1974, Oberschall 1973). Jackson (1969) offers a useful summary of diverse views on the topic, and he indicates that there is little agreement.

There is no necessary incompatibility between seeing social movements as causes and effects of change. At one point in time broad change can give rise to social movements, which may then help generate additional specific changes (e.g. the change from feudalism to capitalism—i.e. the industrial revolution—could be seen as a cause of the working class movement, but this social movement has generated various changes in the structure of industrial society such as improving wages and working conditions for laborers).

Another unstudied consequence of social movements is the diffusion of protest models. There are spin-off effects where one movement that gains prominence sets an example and serves to inspire others. For instance, the effect that the labor movement of the 1930s and the Indian Independence movement had on the Civil Rights Movement could be studied, as could the latter's effect on the more recent anti-civil rights, student, antiwar, feminist, gay liberation, and ecology movements. Howard (1974) discusses this topic to some extent.

Another idea, from Durkheim and Simmel, could, with imagination, be quantitatively assessed: collective behavior, by permitting tensions to be released and by testing the group's commitment to the value system, can unify and stabilize a group by attacking—and defending—the values of the system or attacking other values (Turner & Killian 1972:424–25).

In summary, the topics of dynamics and effects of social movements are surprisingly understudied. Yet their significance calls for more empirical studies, which could draw upon a few classic models discussed here, as well as on the many theoretical propositions we have enumerated.

SMELSER'S THEORY IN LIGHT OF A DECADE'S RESEARCH

Any assessment of the field of collective behavior must consider the theory put forth and elaborated by Smelser (1963). His work has probably inspired more research in the last decade than any other single approach. Into a loosely organized field which was dominated by social-psychological and even psychological theories, Smelser introduced a more sociological approach to collective behavior. Where there was previously little systematic analysis, Smelser introduced a highly systematic and broad, yet parsimonious, schema, in between middle-range theories and entire systems analysis. A perspective on collective behavior over the last decade may be achieved by considering the current state of Smelser's theory in light of some of the empirical and theoretical developments of recent years.

There have been various attempts to empirically apply and test Smelser's approach. In a very impressive study, Pinard (1971) used much of Smelser's framework to help analyze the rise of a right-wing political party in Canada. Overall,

Pinard's study shows the usefulness of Smelser's theory, although Pinard also brought in supplemental concepts. Quarantelli & Hundley (1969), in analyzing a riot, found four of Smelser's six conditions present, although they did not find evidence of the type of belief and mobilization that Smelser would predict.

Furthermore, in analyzing an antipornography movement, Zurcher et al (1971) used, and tended to verify, Smelser's theory. Smelser (1974) himself used part of his theory to explain conflict in California higher education. Also, in an intriguing study, Kerckhoff & Back (1968) used the theory to analyze an example of hysterical contagion—the widespread imagining of being bitten by an insect in June when no such poisonous insect existed. Similarly to Pinard, they used quantitative data with regard to many of the basic concepts. Also, two analyses of the Kent State crisis tend to verify the approach (Rudwick & Meier 1972, Lewis 1972). Finally, Smelser's theory has been used to analyze the development, decline, and possible renewal of the New Left in general (Wood 1974a:22–48, 1974b:143–51).

While most of the above represent efforts to apply the theory rather than to rigidly test it, the theory has clearly been useful in ordering and helping to understand collective behavior phenomena. It calls attention to six crucial variables, hypothesizes that they must be present if collective behavior is to occur, and states that when they are present, collective behavior will occur (i.e. Smelser's six conditions are necessary conditions of collective behavior, that when combined, constitute a sufficient condition of collective behavior). Finally, there have been a few conscious tests of the theory, which indicated possible modifications in such categories as generalized beliefs (Stallings 1973, Quarantelli & Hundley 1969).

Generalized Beliefs

In fact, among the most prominent criticisms of Smelser's theory are those related to generalized beliefs. Smelser has been accused of focusing on exaggerated, irrational, and unrealistic beliefs (Currie & Skolnick 1970, Oberschall 1973:22–23, Brown & Goldin 1973:21–24), and he has responded to such criticisms (Smelser 1970). The issue of rationality of beliefs aside, collective behavior in the form of a hostile outburst is defined by Smelser in terms of a generalized belief, which is one of the very factors then drawn upon to explain the existence of collective behavior. Yet it has been argued that certain types of expressive crowd behavior such as riots in victory can occur without a generalized belief (Marx 1970b).

Smelser's discussion of generalized beliefs has also been criticized for insufficiently dealing with heterogeneity of beliefs among, and within, the rank and file and the leaders. He argues that generalized beliefs "create a 'common culture' within which leadership, mobilization, and concerted action can take place" (Smelser 1963:82). Furthermore, he suggests that "this principle (is) readily observable in the ideological indoctrination of political and religious movements . . ." (Smelser 1963:82). When citing beliefs of specific movements, such as the Townsend or Technocracy movements, Smelser cites studies of movement ideologies, or statements from the movement's literature, rather than data on the beliefs of the rank and file. The use of general statements of movement ideologies seems to imply that most, if not all, of the participants share these generalized beliefs.

Yet as we have noted there is usually appreciable variation among and between the rank and file and the leaders. There is a need to more carefully analyze the interrelations of beliefs. The variation of beliefs also makes more problematic the immediate classification of a movement as value- or norm-oriented.

A number of modifications of the concept of generalized belief might usefully be made:

1. The norm-value distinction must be applied separately to different factions within a general social movement, to the extent that such factions exist.
2. The norm-value distinction must be supplemented by the recognition that a given movement, or even a faction in the movement, can be simultaneously character- ized by its desire to change norms and values.
3. Recognition must be given to the fact that certain kinds of collective behavior can occur without the presence of a generalized belief that interprets strains; attention must be given to analyzing situations where beliefs play a more or less important role.
4. Generalized beliefs can be classified with respect to the degree to which they are exaggerated and irrational, as against realistic and rational, and the correlates of various types of beliefs should be examined.

Structural Conduciveness

Smelser argues that societies whose institutions are highly differentiated are likely to experience norm-oriented movements, whereas societies whose institutions are less differentiated are likely to experience value-oriented movements. In differen- tiated societies there is the "structural possibility of demanding normative change alone" (Smelser 1963:278). In contrast, in less differentiated societies, normative change is discouraged; therefore if a movement emerges, it is likely to be a more basic, value-oriented movement.

What has the literature said about the condition of structural conduciveness? By and large the literature has agreed with Smelser on the role of differentiation in producing norm-versus value-oriented movements. For example, Oberschall (1973:47–48) and Gurr (1970:274) argue that authoritarian (i.e. less differentiated) societies are more likely than democratic societies to generate radical movements. (For our purposes, an authoritarian regime does not permit political protests, whereas a democratic regime does.) Oberschall (1973:47–48) points out that Hun- gary experienced an attempted revolution because more moderate civil liberties gains were difficult to obtain within the existing system. In authoritarian regimes conflict is less likely to occur than in democratic regimes, but the conflict will be more intense when it occurs (Coser 1956, 1967).

The concept of a social structure permissive of collective behavior is potentially useful but also ambiguous. On one hand, the term points to situations where collective behavior is possible as opposed to impossible (or highly unlikely). For example, it is necessary to have a fluid money market for there to be an "economic crash" like the 1929 depression; traditional societies where barter is the main mode of exchange would be most unlikely to have a depression.

However, the term *permissiveness* can also be tautological when used to analyze collective behavior. Smelser offers somewhat different examples of social arrangements that are similarly conducive to collective behavior. For example, strong governmental control against protests is seen to facilitate value-oriented movements (Smelser 1963:324–37). However, strong governmental control plus governmental ineffectiveness is also seen to facilitate value-oriented movements (Smelser 1963:364–79). Although both conditions may well be conducive to value-oriented movements, the concept of a permissive social structure does not guide us to choose between the two situations of governmental control—or indicate that both situations are of equal importance to value-oriented movements.

Clearly, the concept must be better operationalized if it is to help predict collective behavior. A good operational definition for structural conduciveness regarding social movements must empirically indicate the extent of independence or differentiation among major social institutions. This is certainly consistent with Smelser's usage of the term.

Precipitating Factors

The literature has produced various examples that serve to illustrate Smelser's (1963) initial formulation of the role of precipitating factors in collective behavior. Tilly (1964:4) has shown how the French revolutionary government's call for 300,000 men "to meet the menace on France's frontiers" was a focal issue for the developing tension in the Vendée region of France and that it triggered the counter-revolution. Similarly, Rudé (1960:21–26) showed how the sudden increase in bread prices in France just prior to the revolution ignited popular riots. Heirich (1971:91–186) shows the arrest of Jack Weinberg as the focal point crystallizing the tension that arose between students and the Berkeley administration, and that culminated in the Free Speech Movement of 1964. In her analysis of the Women's Liberation Movement, Freeman (1973:794–95) shows how a crisis, or leaders using rudimentary organizations, can serve as precipitants to develop a group actively fighting for women's rights.

There have also been some elaborations of the concept. Milgram & Toch (1969:602) suggest that precipitating factors for crowds may differ from those for social movements. Precipitants for crowds are specific, whereas precipitants for social movements may be more gradual. Oberschall notes that once precipitating incidents occur, or once a protest movement has shown signs of initial success, protest actions may break out in other parts of the social system; hence a protest at one point in the system could be a precipitating factor for protests in other parts of the system (Oberschall 1973:298). As the topic of precipitating factors did not receive great conceptual attention in the past decade, there is a need for more systematic study and classification of types of precipitants and their consequences.

In giving "additional thoughts" to the study of collective behavior with respect to the Kent State crisis, Smelser suggests that precipitating factors should be eliminated from the analysis of collective behavior. He argues that "many of the instances of 'precipitating factors' I gave were nothing more than sudden intensification of one of the other determinants" (e.g. "the sudden imposition of strain") (Smelser

1972:101). He feels that this determinant was a way of "re-introducing the variable of 'time' into an essentially analytic model" (Smelser 1972:101). Yet in eliminating this factor to strengthen the nontemporal nature of the model, something is clearly sacrificed. Some concept is needed to deal with "the occurrence of a dramatic incident that represents 'evidence' that the forces posited in the generalized belief system are in fact at work . . ." (Smelser 1972:101). In addition, the mere fact that Smelser discusses precipitating factors in terms of other determinants of collective behavior does not necessarily reduce it to the other determinants. Brown & Goldin (1973:15) point out that Smelser often discusses determinants in terms of each other (e.g. a given strain must be within the realm of a given conducive structure in order for the strain to be implicated in collective behavior). Thus we suggest retaining the concept of the precipitating factor.

The Psychological Level

In developing a sociological theory of collective behavior Smelser tended to ignore the psychological level. It was not clear how the more or less "objective" external social structural conditions (strain, conduciveness, social control) related to the perceptions of the individual. This problem of bridging the gap between social conditions and individual perceptions haunts sociological inquiry in general. This is particularly true for the study of social movements where oppressive social conditions are thought to generate individual indignation. This certainly does happen, but not automatically.

Psychological conditions parallel to Smelser's social conditions of collective behavior may also be noted (Brown 1965). Stating parallel psychological conditions, however, does not show *how* social conditions get translated into psychological perceptions.

In a later essay Smelser (1968) added a psychological dimension to his sociological conditions of collective behavior. While this expansion of the theory makes it inclusive of a crucial level of analysis that had been more or less neglected before, it also makes the theory more complex and less determinate. Hopefully we see the beginning of greater integration between structural and social psychological approaches. Wood (1974a) offers an attempt to use this synthesis.

With the addition of the psychological determinants the necessary and sufficient conditions of collective behavior now are:

1. *Structural conduciveness,* or the permissiveness of social arrangements and personality systems to generate collective behavior.
2. *Structural strain,* or the existence of ambiguities, deprivations, tensions, conflicts, and discrepancies in the social order. From the standpoint of the individual, structural strain refers to perceived ambiguities, deprivations, tensions, conflicts, and discrepancies.
3. *Growth and spread of generalized beliefs,* or the existence in the population of beliefs that identify the source of strain, attribute certain characteristics to the source, and specify certain responses to the potential participants. From the standpoint of the individual, this determinant refers to the person being readied for action by attachment to these social beliefs.

4. *Precipitating factors,* or the occurrence of some type of specific event that gives the generalized beliefs concrete substance. From the standpoint of the individual, this determinant refers to the individual perceiving this event as a threat to cherished norms or values.
5. *Mobilization of participants for action,* or the organization of the effected group into action. From the standpoint of the individual, this determinant refers to the availability of the individual for recruitment into the activity.
6. *The ineffective operation of control,* or the ineffectiveness of the social counter-determinants that prevent, interrupt, or inhibit the accumulation of the other five determinants of collective behavior. From the standpoint of the individual, this determinant refers to the lessening of personal controls, for example, because the actions are viewed as "morally correct." In addition, the combination of harshness and weakness by authorities aggravates instances of collective behavior.

Although the six conditions of collective behavior have stimulated much discussion and research, these conditions are not well operationalized. For example, how are we to know when a given strain will influence an occurrence of collective behavior? All societies always have a certain amount of strain, but collective behavior is not continually in existence. Smelser would argue that for a given strain to influence collective behavior, it must fit within the realm of a conducive social structure, and it must combine with the other determinants of collective behavior. Even when these arguments are granted, however, we are still left with the problem of specifying how much strain needs to exist before it helps generate collective behavior. Thus future work on Smelser's theory should develop better operational definitions of the social and psychological dimensions of the six determinants of collective behavior.

Methods and Concepts

The methodology in *Theory of Collective Behavior,* that of systematic comparative illustration, did not emphasize quantitative scales to measure the main concepts. Smelser relied on others' studies, and most results cited are not quantitative. Furthermore, the range of studies cited precludes using the same units for easy quantitative comparisons. Hence, Smelser could point to the existence of some level of strain (or of beliefs, precipitating factors, etc), but could not easily say how much strain, etc, existed. He showed cases where several of the six conditions occurred together, but where there was no collective behavior, because the other necessary conditions were lacking. His illustrations all support his ideas. We are offered no negative cases where all the determinants were present yet no collective behavior occurred, or where only a few determinants were present and collective behavior occurred.

Were quantitative scales developed for the concepts, more specific testing, rather than citation of illustrations, would be possible. Such scales would help meet a persisting criticism of Smelser's theory: that it is not predictive or falsifiable.

There is a conceptual problem in Smelser's deriving a typology of collective behavior from the components of social action. One of his major arguments is that four components of action generate five types of collective behavior. That is, when there is strain with regard to a specific component of action, we can predict a specific type of collective behavior, provided the other determinants of collective behavior are also operative. The four components of action are:

1. values, or the desirable ends which guide any human endeavor;
2. norms, or the more specific rules of conduct which guide action;
3. mobilization of motivation into organized action, or motivation of the agents who will pursue the desired ends and follow the rules;
4. situational facilities, or "the means and obstacles which facilitate or hinder the attainment of concrete goals in the role or organizational context" (Smelser 1963:28). The main types of collective behavior are the panic, the craze, the hostile outburst, the norm-oriented movement, and the value-oriented movement.

Although Smelser (1963:9) says that the types of collective behavior are derived from the components of action, only two of the types of collective behavior clearly correspond to the components of action—the norm-oriented movement and the value-oriented movement. Smelser stretches his argument when he says the panic or craze is generated from the component of situational facilities. There are two types of collective behavior derived here, but only one type in the other cases. Furthermore, other forms of collective behavior also involve facilities. Similarly, Smelser stretches the point when he says that the hostile outburst comes from "action mobilized on the basis of a belief . . . assigning the responsibility for an undesirable state of affairs to some agent" (Smelser 1963:9). Here Smelser is trying to include the term *mobilization for action* in both the component and the type of collective behavior. But the notion of action mobilized against some agent could also include norm-oriented movements and value-oriented movements, rather than just the hostile outburst.

Also questions can be raised about how distinct the types of collective behavior necessarily are. For example, Smelser analyzes hostile outbursts (such as racial violence) as distinct from either norm- or value-oriented movements. For some purposes this is adequate, but for others, riots can be very much a part of social movements.

There is also inconsistency in Smelser's treatment of the time-ordering of the six conditions of collective behavior. At some points he suggests that a definite time-ordering of the conditions must occur, with the time-order being: structural conduciveness, strain, growth and spread of generalized beliefs, precipitating factors, mobilization of participants for action, and breakdown of social control (Smelser 1963:15–16). At other points, however, he says that there must only be analytical time-ordering, not empirical time-ordering. Thus strain could actually appear before conduciveness in the latter formulation. Analytical time-ordering seems to represent Smelser's basic position, and it is the stronger formulation.

Finally, Smelser is not entirely clear about which of the six conditions of collective behavior are involved in producing norm-oriented versus value-oriented movements. On one hand, there is the implication that differences exist for each of the six conditions as they relate to norm- versus value-oriented movements. But on closer inspection, only three of Smelser's six conditions distinguish between the movements.

The three conditions that distinguish norm- from value-oriented movements are structural conduciveness, generalized beliefs, and social control.

With respect to structural conduciveness, the more the structural differentiation, the greater the chance of a norm-oriented movement. Normative and value-oriented beliefs are associated with their respective types of movement. Finally, social control distinguishes the movements because authorities can influence the type of movement likely to ensue (i.e. when authorities permit norm-oriented movements to exist, the movements tend to remain norm-oriented and not to become value-oriented—and vice-versa).

But the other three conditions—structural strain, precipitating factors, and mobilization for action—do not distinguish the movements, and therefore cannot be used to predict the occurrence of a norm-oriented movement as opposed to value-oriented movement. All the conditions are necessary for some kind of movement to occur, but only three of the six conditions predict one movement rather than the other.

In spite of these criticisms, Smelser offers a comprehensive and systematic approach to collective behavior, and his theory clearly remains a useful guide for understanding collective episodes. He has located the key conditions leading to the development of collective behavior, and he has put these conditions into a perspective that transcends previous middle-range theorizing. Smelser's theory—and the various empirical studies supporting it—shows that just discontents, or just radical beliefs, or just sophisticated leaders, etc, are not sufficient circumstances to generate collective behavior. All six conditions in his value-added theory must be simultaneously operating at high levels of intensity for collective behavior to occur. This insight is probably Smelser's single most important theoretical contribution to understanding collective behavior.

CONCLUSION

Where does the field of collective behavior stand today, relative to where it stood 10 or 15 years ago? Taking earlier reviews as a point of departure—Blumer (1939, 1951, 1957), Brown (1954), Killian (1964), Turner (1964a), Gusfield (1968), Heberle (1968), Lang & Lang (1968), and Milgram & Toch (1969)—continuity, as well as a number of changes, can be seen.

With respect to the sheer quantity and diversity of material, we have had much more to choose from than other reviewers. The field is richer with respect to case studies and descriptions. For example, there is a great deal of factual and interpretive material available on the civil rights and student movements. Sociologists do not have to rely, to the extent they once did, on journalists, historians, or anthropologists for their case study materials. We know more now about historical and comparative instances of collective behavior. Much more quantitative data is available on the characteristics of people and places involved in collective behavior, if not often on the behavior as such. The field has continued in its eclectic nature and has more explicitly incorporated ideas from other disciplines. In addition, there has been, if not a breakdown in roles between activist and scholar, at least greater self-consciousness about the kinds of questions chosen for study and the possible uses of the scholar's work.

We are now better at classification and definition of collective behavior phenomena, and at identifying ideal-typical sequences and crucial variables than we were in the 1950s. There is an extensive body of work that elaborates and documents empirical possibilities and selectively illustrates theories after the fact. (Religion can inspire protest or can inhibit it; absolute deprivation can trigger protest or increase mere concerns for survival; police use of violence can mean effective repression or the spread of a movement as martyrs are created; some movements go through a life cycle model from unrest to organized protest to institutionalization, while others never get beyond unrest; social movements can lead to change or be a result of change, etc.) To be sure, laying out such possibilities is only an important first step. Trying to figure out under which conditions one or another outcome is likely is the crucial next step, and we have seen discussions in this direction.

We have also seen an elaboration of concepts and a proliferation of ways of thinking about collective behavior that go beyond the somewhat amorphous social psychological tradition that predominated until the early 1960s. The student seeking to understand collective behavior has a number of perspectives and methods to choose from, and can now draw more easily upon general social science concepts. The artificial intellectual boundary between collective and "noncollective," or conventional, behavior is breaking down. The incorporation of concepts and approaches from the study of organizations, interaction, coalition formation, decision-making, and social psychology is reducing the area's estrangement from general sociology. Conversely, efforts to understand social change and conflict draw heavily on the research traditions in the field of collective behavior.

We are seeing the development and use of improved methods for gathering and analyzing collective behavior data, whether in the historical archives or on the streets. For example, there is increased use of films, field experiments, controlled observation, research teams poised and waiting for an instance of collective behavior to occur, the coding of newspaper accounts and arrest records, and the use of mathematical models to plot the diffusion and patterning of multiple instances of collective behavior. In addition, the excellent historical studies by Tilly (1964), Rudé (1960, 1964), etc, using archival data, have shown the possibility of more systematic analysis of historical instances of collective behavior. All of these methods have helped bring new insights and vitality to the field.

Videotaping is a potentially fruitful method which should be used more extensively. A vast amount of primary data are available in the form of news filmed for television. The problem, of course, lies in figuring out how to systematically and theoretically approach videotaping. Martínez (forthcoming) explains how to use film and videotape for purposes of sociological teaching and research.

Archives on various social movements, particularly of the last decade, are developing, and loose networks exist among those collecting such material. *The Critical Mass Bulletin* newsletter of December 1974 lists various archives throughout the United States. Many of the surveys done on participation in collective behavior activities are in data archives such as those found at the University of North Carolina and the University of California at Berkeley's Survey Research Center. The creation of something along the line of a Human Relations Area File for collective behavior could greatly facilitate research.

We have seen the development of many testable propositions in the recent litera-ture. Most of the propositions, however, remain to be tested, or at least to be more thoroughly tested. Yet the formulation—as well as some testing—of propositions has been a central aspect of the advancement of the field of collective behavior in recent years.

In spite of clear progress in the last decade, one can question whether a cathedral-building image of science applies as clearly here as it does to some other areas of sociological inquiry. We are wiser now about social movements than in the early 1960s, but the increased wisdom may not be commensurate with all the time and energy that has gone into studying them. We know more and we know more where to look, and we have seen some useful integrative and theoretical efforts. Still, the field has done a better job of developing nominal concepts than of developing theories, and it has been better at refuting old ideas than at establishing the truth of new ones.

Why should this be the case, at least to a greater extent in this area of sociology than in many others? There is no single answer, but among important factors would seem to be:

1. Our theories and methods for studying static structures are much more devel-oped than those for studying change and process.
2. There is a lack of clear definition of, and agreement on, what collective behavior is and how it differs from conventional behavior; it has tended to be a residual, often negatively defined category, with diverse phenomena lumped together, to the exclusion of conventional phenomena with which it may share important characteristics.
3. Collective behavior phenomena tend to be vast, diffuse, and complex, and may go on unpredictably and simultaneously in many geographical areas, involving very large numbers of diverse people, and changing over time.
4. Probably to a greater extent than in most other areas of sociology, those drawn to the study of social movements have a personal interest in understanding or telling the story of a particular movement, and are less interested in theory as such.
5. Trying to understand a particular historic event such as the Watts riot or the Free Speech Movement is different from seeking to understand more enduring general group properties such as the division of labor or inequality.
6. We can say what is likely to occur given certain conditions, but we are usually not able to say *when* these conditions will occur.
7. The political and value-laden nature of the topic may make it harder to see clearly, ask the relevant questions, and accept answers contrary to what we would like the truth to be.

Finally, in light of the millenarian and spiritual quality of many social move-ments, it may be appropriate to close with twenty-two categorical imperatives along the line of the Ten Commandments for those who would study social movements and collective behavior:

I   Thou shalt be mindful of general theories in sociology and not treat collec-tive behavior as a negatively defined residual category.

II Thou shalt study social movements in their organizational and environmental contexts.

III Thou shalt continue to make efforts to quantify, but thou shalt not be seduced by numbers unbounded by theory, nor necessarily associate wisdom with quantitative sophistication.

IV Thou shalt be mindful of prior research on the question studied.

V Thou shalt cease doing unvalidated attitude studies when they have the quality of abstracted empiricism, devoid of context, and lacking of implications for theory.

VI Thou shalt bring a compassionate skepticism to publicly available data on any given movement.

VII Thou shalt ground statements about social movements in careful empirical observations.

VIII Thou shalt seek to make and test statements about the relations among variables that can be falsified.

IX Thou shalt move from observed behavior or official ideology to presumed motives and attitudes with great hesistancy, and preferably only with data from known participants.

X Thou shalt not use the concept of strain unless it is operationalized, and thou shalt look for the ways in which various types of strains are related to types of collective behavior.

XI Thou shalt try to relate conditions of social strain to people's perceptions of strain and to their participation—or lack of participation—in collective behavior activities.

XII Thou shalt not confuse leaders with followers.

XIII Thou shalt be more sensitive to types of social movement participation, and thou shalt not confuse followers with sympathetic bystanders.

XIV Thou shalt be aware of the possible uses and misuses of research on social movements.

XV Thou shalt seek to more systematically link the study of social movements with the study of crowds.

XVI Thou shalt focus more research attention on the actual behavior of people in crowd situations.

XVII Thou shalt take insights where they can be found, and not assume that because approaches have been misused and unfruitful in the past—as have the focus on physiological changes among crowd members, or parallels to animal behavior—that they must continue to be so in the future.

XVIII Thou shalt seek to move from static cross-sectional to dynamic interactive models of social movement development.

XIX Thou shalt walk an intellectual tight rope that permits collective and conventional behavior to be viewed in light of common theoretical and conceptual frameworks, but that does not claim that no differences exist between them.

XX Thou shalt not restrict the study of crowds to those of an acting, aggressive, and ideological nature, nor treat the crowd as the only prototype of collective behavior.

XXI Thou shalt appreciate the interactive and emergent character of much collective behavior beyond the causal impact of history, of broad social structural conditions, and of the personality of participants.

XXII Thou shalt not be too optimistic about building a science of collective behavior but thou shalt try anyway.

Acknowledgments

We are grateful to Neil J. Smelser, Robert H. Somers, Ralph H. Turner, and Patricia A. Wood for their very helpful comments on an earlier draft of this manuscript, and to Susan Schuller Friedman, Wing-Cheung Ng, Royce Singleton, and Patricia A. Wood for helpful assistance. Finally, we gratefully acknowledge Kay Pratt's conscientious typing of the manuscript.

Literature Cited

Abel, T. 1937. The pattern of a successful political movement. *Am. Sociol. Rev.* 2:347–52

Aberle, D. F. 1966. *The Peyote Religion Among the Navaho.* Chicago: Aldine. 454 pp.

Abramowitz, S. I. 1973. The comparative competence-adjustment of student left social-political activists. *J. Personality* 41 (June):244–60

Adam, G. 1970. Étude statistique des grèves de Mai-Juin 1968. *Rev. Fr. Sci. Polit.* XX [1 (Février)]:105–19

Adamek, R. J., Lewis, J. M. 1973. Social control violence and radicalization: the Kent State case. *Soc. Forces* 51 (March):342–47

Altbach, P. G. 1967. Students and politics. In *Student Politics,* ed. S. M. Lipset, 74–93. New York: Basic Books. 403 pp.

Altbach, P. G., Kelly, D. H. 1973. *American Students: A Selected Bibliography on Student Activism and Related Topics.* Lexington, Mass: Lexington Books, Heath. 537 pp.

Altheide, D. L., Gilmore, R. P. 1972. The credibility of protest. *Am. Sociol. Rev.* 37 (Feb.):99–108

Anderson, W. A. 1973. The reorganization of protest *Am. Behav. Sci.* 16 (Jan./Feb.):426–39

Ash, R. 1972. *Social Movements in America.* Chicago: Markham. 274 pp.

Astin, A. W. 1968. Personal and environmental determinants of student activism. *Meas. Eval. Guid.* 1 (Fall):149–62

Bacciocco, E. J. Jr. 1974. *The New Left in America: Reform to Revolution 1956 to 1970.* Stanford, Calif: Hoover Inst. Press, Stanford Univ. 300 pp.

Balbus, I. 1973. *The Dialectics of Legal Repression: Black Rebels Before the American Criminal Courts.* New York: Russell Sage. 269 pp.

Bald, S. R. 1974. Politics of a revolutionary elite: a study of Mulk Raj Anand's novels. *Mod. Asian Stud.* 8:473–89

Bay, C. 1967. Political and apolitical students: facts in search of theory. *J. Soc. Issues* XXIII (July):76–91

Bell, D. 1962. *The End of Ideology: On the Exhaustion of Political Ideas in the Fifties.* New York: Free Press. 474 pp. Revised ed. Originally published in 1960.

Bell, I. 1968. *CORE and the Strategy of Non-Violence.* New York: Random House. 192 pp.

Berk, R. A. 1974a. A gaming approach to crowd behavior. *Am. Sociol. Rev.* 39 (June):355–73

Berk, R. A. 1974b. *Collective Behavior.* Dubuque, Iowa: Brown. 80 pp.

Berk, R. A., Aldrich, H. E. 1972. Patterns of vandalism during civil disorders as an indicator of selection of targets. *Am. Sociol. Rev.* 37 (Oct.):533–47

Berkeley Daily Gazette. 1974. Police end UC campus protest. Thursday, May 30, pp. 1–2

Bittner, E. 1963. Radicalism and the organization of radical movements. *Am. Sociol. Rev.* 28(Dec.):928–40

Block, J. H., Haan, N., Smith, M. B. 1969. Socialization correlates of student activism. *J. Soc. Issues* XXV:143–77

Bloombaum, M. 1968. The conditions underlying race riots as portrayed by multidimensional scalogram analysis: a reanalysis of Lieberson and Silverman's data. *Am. Sociol. Rev.* 33(Feb.):76–91

Blumer, H. 1939. Collective behavior. In *An Outline of the Principles of Sociology,* ed. R. E. Park, Pt. IV:221–80. New York: Barnes & Noble. 353 pp.

Blumer, H. 1951. Collective behavior. In *New Outline of the Principles of Sociology,* ed. A. M. Lee, 166–222. New York: Barnes & Noble. 356 pp.

Blumer, H. 1957. Collective behavior. In *Review of Sociology: Analysis of a Decade,* ed. J. B. Gittler, 127–58. New York: Wiley. 588 pp.

Blumer, H., forthcoming. Social unrest and collective protest. In a book on Collective Behavior by H. Blumer. Chicago: Univ. Chicago Press

Boesel, D., Rossi, P. H., eds. 1971. *Cities Under Siege.* New York: Basic Books. 436 pp.

Boulding, K. 1962. *Conflict and Defense.* New York: Harper Torchbooks. 349 pp.

Bowers, W. J., Pierce, G. L. 1974. *Student Unrest and the Impact of Extra-Institutional Contexts.* Washington DC: U.S. Dept. HEW, Office Educ., Bureau Res. (August). 159 pp.

Braungart, R. G. 1971. Family status, socialization, and student politics: a multivariate analysis. *Am. J. Sociol.* 77 (July): 108–30

Brecher, J. 1974. *Strike!* Greenwich, Conn: Fawcett. 416 pp. Originally published in 1972.

Brill, H. 1971. *Why Organizers Fail: The Story of a Rent Strike.* Berkeley: Univ. Calif. Press. 192 pp.

Brinton, C. 1952. *The Anatomy of Revolution.* New York: Prentice-Hall. 324 pp. Revised ed. Originally published in 1938.

Brissett, D. 1968. Collective behavior: the sense of a rubric. *Am. J. Sociol.* 74 (July):70–78

Brown, M., Goldin, A. 1973. *Collective Behavior: A Review and Reinterpretation of the Literature.* Pacific Palisades, Calif.: Goodyear. 349 pp.

Brown, R. 1954. Mass phenomena. In *Handbook of Social Psychology,* ed. G. Lindzey, 2:833–76. Cambridge, Mass.: Addison-Wesley. Two volumes, 1226 pp.

Brown, R. 1965. *Social Psychology.* New York: Free Press. 785 pp.

Cameron, W. B. 1966. *Modern Social Movements.* New York: Random House. 183 pp.

Campbell, A., Schuman, H. 1968. Racial attitudes in 15 American cities. In *Supplemental Studies for The National Advisory Commission on Civil Disorders,* O. Kerner, Chairman. Washington DC:GPO. 248 pp.

Canetti, E. 1962. *Crowds and Power.* Transl. C. Stewart. New York: Viking Press. 495 pp.

Cantril, H. 1941. *The Social Psychology of Social Movements.* New York: Wiley. 274 pp.

Caplan, N. 1970. The new ghetto man: a review of recent empirical studies. *J. Soc. Issues* 26:59–73

Caplan, N. 1971. Identity in transition: a theory of black militancy. In *The New American Revolution,* ed. R. Aya, N. Miller, 143–65. New York: Free Press. 342 pp.

Caplan, N., Paige, J. M. 1968. A study of ghetto rioters. *Sci. Am.* 219 (2):15–21

Carden, M. L. 1974. *The New Feminist Movement.* New York: Russell Sage. 234 pp.

Cockburn, A., Blackburn, R., eds. 1969. *Student Power: Problems, Diagnosis, Action.* Baltimore: Penguin Books, in association with New Left Review. 378 pp.

Cohn-Bendit, D., Cohn-Bendit, G. 1968. *Obsolete Communism: The Left-Wing Alternative.* Transl. Andre Deutsch Ltd. New York: McGraw-Hill. 255 pp.

Coleman, J. S. 1966. Foundations for a theory of collective decisions. *Am. J. Sociol.* 71:615–27

Coleman, J. S. 1973. *The Mathematics of Collective Action.* Chicago: Aldine. 191 pp.

Congressional Quarterly Inc. 1973. Editorial Research Reports on the Women's Movement. 1735 K Street NW, Washington DC 20006: Congressional Quarterly Inc. 184 pp.

Coser, L. A. 1956. *The Functions of Social Conflict.* Glencoe, Ill: Free Press. 188 pp.

Coser, L. A. 1967. *Continuities in the Study of Social Conflict.* New York: Free Press. 272 pp.

Coser, L. A. 1972. Introduction to collective violence and civil conflict. *J. Soc. Issues* 28:1–10

Couch, C. J. 1968. Collective behavior: an examination of some stereotypes. *Soc. Probl.* 15:310–22

Couch, C. J. 1970. Dimensions of association in collective behavior episodes. *Sociometry* 33:457–71

Currie, E., Skolnick, J. 1970. A critical note on conceptions of collective behavior. *Ann. Am. Acad. Polit. Soc. Sci.* 391 (September):34–45

Danzger, H. 1974. Validating Conflict Data. Unpublished paper, Lehman College, City Univ. New York, Bronx, NY

Davies, J. C. 1962. Toward a theory of revolution. *Am. Sociol. Rev.* 27 (February):5–19

Davies, J. C. 1969. The J-Curve of rising and declining satisfactions as a cause of some great revolutions and a contained rebellion. In *The History of Violence in America,* ed. H. D. Graham, T. R. Gurr, 690–730. New York: Praeger. 822 pp.

Davies, J. C., ed. 1971. *When Men Revolt and Why.* New York: Free Press. 357 pp.

Davies, J. C. 1974. The J-curve and power-struggle theories of collective violence. *Am. Sociol. Rev.* 39 (August):607–10

Deckard, B., forthcoming. *The Women's Movement: Political, Socio-Economic and Psychological Issues.* New York: Harper & Row

Denisoff, R. S., ed. 1974. *The Sociology of Dissent.* New York: Harcourt Brace Jovanovich. 398 pp.

Dixon, M. 1971–1972. Public ideology and the class composition of women's liberation (1966–69). *Berkeley J. Sociol.: Critical Rev.* XVI:149–67

Donald, D. 1956. *Lincoln Reconsidered, Essays on the Civil War Era.* New York: Knopf. 200 pp.

Downs, A. 1957. *An Economic Theory of Democracy.* New York: Harper. 310 pp.

Downes, B. T. 1968. Social and political characteristics of riot cities: a comparative study. *Soc. Sci. Quart.* 49 (December):504–20

Donner, F. 1971. The theory and practice of American political intelligence. *NY Rev. Books* XVI (April 22):27–39

Dubin, R., Beisse, F. 1967. The assistant: academic subaltern. *Admin Sci. Quart.* 11 (March):521–47

Dunlap, R. 1970a. A comment on "multiversity, university size, university quality, and student protest: an empirical study." *Am. Sociol. Rev.* 35 (June):525–28

Dunlap, R. 1970b. Radical and conservative student activists: a comparison of family backgrounds. *Pacific Sociol. Rev.* 13 (Summer):171–81

Eckstein, H. 1964. Introduction: Toward the theoretical study of internal war. In *Internal War: Problems and Approaches,* ed. H. Eckstein, 1–32. New York: Free Press Glencoe. 339 pp.

Edwards, L. P. 1927. *The Natural History of Revolution.* Chicago: Univ. Chicago Press. 229 pp. Reprinted in 1970.

Ehrlich, C. 1973. The woman book industry. *Am. J. Sociol.* 78 (Jan.):1030–44

Elsner, H. Jr., ed. 1972. *Robert E. Park: The Crowd and the Public and other Essays.* Chicago: Univ. Chicago Press

Etzioni, A. 1968. *The Active Society.* New York: Free Press. 698 pp.

Evans, R. R., Ed. 1969. *Readings in Collective Behavior.* Chicago: Rand McNally. 660 pp. 1970. 2d ed.

Evans, R. R., Ed. 1973. *Social Movements: A Reader and Source Book.* Chicago: Rand McNally. 605 pp.

Fanon, F. 1968. *The Wretched of the Earth.* Transl. C. Farrington. New York: Grove. 316 pp. Originally published in 1961.

Feagin, J. R., Hahn, H. 1973. *Ghetto Revolts.* New York: Macmillan. 338 pp.

Feierabend, I. K., Feierabend, R. L., Nesvold, B. A. 1969. Social change and political violence: cross-national patterns. In *The History of Violence in America,* ed. H. D. Graham, T. R. Gurr, 632–689. New York: Praeger 822 pp.

Feuer, L. S. 1969. *The Conflict of Generations.* New York: Basic Books. 543 pp.

Finney, H. C., McGranahan, D. 1973. *Community Support and Goal Displacement in a Poor People's Cooperative Farm,* Discussion Paper 152–73. Madison, Wisc: Univ. Wisc. Inst. for Res. on Poverty

Firestone, S. 1970. *The Dialectic of Sex: The Case for Feminist Revolution.* New York: Morrow. 274 pp.

Fisher, C. 1972. Observing a crowd. In *Research on Deviance,* ed. J. Douglas. New York: Random House

Flacks, R. 1967. The liberated generation: an exploration of the roots of student protest. *J. Soc. Issues* 23 (July):52–75

Flacks, R. 1970. Social and cultural meanings of student revolt: some informal comparative observations. *Soc. Probl.* 17 (Winter):340–57

Flacks, R. 1971. *Youth and Social Change.* Chicago: Markham. 147 pp.

Fogelson, R. M., Hill, R. B. 1968. Who riots? a study of participation in the 1967 riots. In *Supplemental Studies for the National Advisory Commission on Civil Disorders.* Washington DC: GPO. 248 pp.

Forward, J. R., Williams, J. R. 1970. Internal-external control and black militancy. *J. Soc. Issues* 26:75–92

Foster, J., Long, D., eds. 1970. *Protest!: Student Activism in America.* New York: Morrow. 596 pp.

Freeman, J. 1973. The origins of the women's liberation movement. *Am. J. Sociol.* 78 (January):792–811

Freire, P. 1970. *Pedagogy of the Oppressed.* Transl. M. B. Ramos. New York: Herder & Herder. 186 pp.

Freud, S. 1914. *Psychopathology of Everyday Life.* London: Ernest Benn. Authorized Engl. ed. 341 pp.

Gamson, W. A. 1968. *Power and Discontent.* Homewood, Ill: Dorsey. 208 pp.

Gamson, W. A. 1974. Violence and political power: the meek don't make it. *Psychol. Today* 8 (July):35–41

Gamson, W. A. 1975. *The Strategy of Social Protest.* Homewood, Ill: Dorsey. 217 pp.

Gerlach, L. P. 1971. Movements of revolutionary change: some structural characteristics. *Am. Behav. Sci.* 14 (July–August):812–36

Gerlach, L. P., Hine, V. H. 1970. *People, Power, Change: Movements of Social Transformation.* Indianapolis: Bobbs-Merrill. 257 pp.

Gerlach, L. P., Hine, V. H. 1973. *Lifeway Leap: The Dynamics of Change in America.* Minneapolis: Univ. Minneapolis Press. 332 pp.

Geschwender, J. A. 1964. Social structure and the Negro revolt: an examination of some hypotheses. *Soc. Forces* 43:248–56

Geschwender, J. A., Singer, B. D., Harrington, J. 1969. *Status Inconsistency, Relative Deprivation, and the Detroit Riot.* Presented at 64th Ann. Meet. Am. Sociol. Assoc. San Francisco. Mimeo

Gintis, H. 1970. The new working class and revolutionary youth. *Continuum* 8 (Spring–Summer):151–74

Glock, C. Y., Stark, R. 1965. *Religion and Society in Tension.* Chicago: Rand McNally. 316 pp.

Goldberg, L. C. 1968. Ghetto riots and others: the faces of civil disorder in 1967. *J. Peace Res.* 2:116–32

Gollin, A. 1969. *Mass Protest and Action for Change: Black and White Views.* Presented at 19th Ann. Meet. Soc. Stud. Soc. Probl., San Francisco (Bureau Soc. Sci. Res. Inc., 1200 17th St. NW, Washington DC 20036)

Gollin, A. 1971. *Social Control in Non-Violent Protest.* Presented at 66th Ann. Meet. Am. Sociol. Assoc. Denver

Gornick, V., Moran, B. K., eds. 1971. *Woman in Sexist Society.* New York: Basic Books. 515 pp.

Graham, H. D., Gurr, T. R., eds. 1969. *The History of Violence in America.* New York: Praeger. 822 pp.

Greer, T. H. 1949. *American Social Reform Movements: Their Pattern Since 1865.* New York: Prentice-Hall. 313 pp.

Gross, D. E. Kelley, H. H., Kruglanski, A. W., Patch, M. E. 1972. Contingency of consequences and type of incentive in interdependent escape. *J. Exp. Soc. Psychol.* 8:360–77

Gusfield, J. R. 1963. *Symbolic Crusade: Status Politics and the American Temperance Movement.* Urbana, Ill: Univ. Illinois Press. 198 pp.

Gusfield, J. R. 1968. The Study of Social Movements. In *International Encyclopedia of the Social Sciences,* ed. D. L. Sills. 14:445–52. New York: MacMillan & Free Press

Gusfield, J. R. 1970a. Differential Responses to Social Change. In *Protest, Reform, and Revolt: A Reader in Social Movements,* ed. J. R. Gusfield, 9–12. New York: Wiley. 576 pp.

Gusfield, J. R., ed. 1970b. *Protest, Reform, and Revolt: A Reader in Social Movements.* New York: Wiley. 576 pp.

Gurr, T. R. 1968. A causal model of civil strife: A comparative analysis using new indices. *Am. Polit. Sci. Rev.* 62 (December): 1104–24.

Gurr, T. R. 1969. A comparative study of civil strife. In *The History of Violence in America,* ed. H. D. Graham, T. R. Gurr, 572–632. New York: Praeger. 822 pp.

Gurr, T. R. 1970. *Why Men Rebel.* Princeton, NJ: Princeton Univ. Press. 421 pp.

Haan, N., Smith, M. B., Block, J. H. 1968. Moral reasoning of young adults: political-social behavior, family backgrounds, and personality correlates. *J. Personality Soc. Psychol.* 10:183–201

Hamilton, R. F. 1972. *Class and Politics in the United States.* New York: Wiley. 589 pp.

Harrell, W. A., Schmitt, D. R. 1972. *The Social Facilitation of Physical Aggression: A Lab Study of Different Theories of Collective Behavior.* Presented at 67th Ann. Meet. Am. Sociol. Assoc., New Orleans

Heberle, R. 1951. *Social Movements: An Introduction to Political Sociology.* New York: Appleton-Century-Crofts. 478 pp.

Heberle, R. 1968. Types and functions of social movements. In *International Encyclopedia of the Social Sciences,* ed. D. L. Sills, 14:438–44. New York: MacMillan & Free Press

Heirich, M. 1964. The use of time in the study of social change. *Am. Sociol. Rev.* 29 (June):386–97

Heirich, M. 1971. *The Spiral of Conflict: Berkeley, 1964.* New York: Columbia

Univ. Press. 502 pp. Originally published in 1968.

Helmreich, W. B. 1973. *The Black Crusaders.* New York: Harper & Row. 186 pp.

Hobsbawm, E. 1959. *Primitive Rebels.* Manchester, England: Manchester Univ. Press. 208 pp.

Hochschild, A. R. 1973. A review of sex role research. *Am. J. Sociol.* 78(Jan.):1011–29

Hoffer, E. 1951. *The True Believer: Thoughts on the Nature of Mass Movements.* New York: Harper. 176 pp.

Hole, J., Levine, E. 1971. *Rebirth of Feminism.* New York: Quadrangle Books. 488 pp.

Hopper, R. D. 1950. The revolutionary process: a frame of reference for the study of revolutionary movements. *Soc. Forces* 28:270–79

Hornback, K., Morrison, D. 1974. *Collective Behavior: A Draft Bibliography.* Dept. Sociol., Michigan State Univ. East Lansing. 267 pp. Mimeo

Horowitz, D. 1962. *Student: the Political Activities of the Berkeley Students.* New York: Ballantine. 160 pp.

Howard, J. R. 1974. *The Cutting Edge: Social Movements and Social Change in America.* Philadelphia: Lippincott. 276 pp.

Hubbard, H. 1968. Five long hot summers and how they grew. *Publ. Interest* 12 (Summer):3–24

Hughes, H. 1972. *Crowds and Mass Behavior.* Boston: Allyn & Bacon. 227 pp.

Jackson, M. 1969. The Civil Rights Movement and social change. *Am. Behav. Sci.* 12, (March–April):8–17

Jackson, M. 1973. Affirmative action—affirmative results? In *Am. Sociol. Assoc. Footnotes* 1: [9 (December)]:3–4, 6

Jackson, M., Petersen, E., Bull, J., Monsen, S., Richmond, P. 1960. The failure of an incipient social movement. *Pac. Sociol. Rev.* 3 (Spring):35–40

Jacobs, H., ed. 1970. *Weatherman.* Berkeley: Ramparts Press. 519 pp.

Jacobs, P., Landau, S. 1966. *The New Radicals.* New York: Random House. 333 pp.

Janowitz, M. 1968. *Social Control of Escalated Riots.* Chicago: Univ. Chicago Center for Policy Studies. 44 pp.

Johnson, C. 1966. *Revolutionary Change.* Boston: Little, Brown. 191 pp.

Kanter, R. M. 1972. *Commitment and Community: Communes and Utopias in Sociological Perspective.* Cambridge, Mass: Harvard Univ. Press. 303 pp.

Karmen, A., forthcoming. Agents provocateurs in the contemporary U.S. New

Left Movement. In *Criminology: A Radical Perspective,* ed. C. Reasons. Pacific Palisades, Calif.: Goodyear

Kelley, H. H., Condry, J. C. Jr., Dahlke, A. E., Hill, A. H. 1965. Collective behavior in a simulated panic situation. *J. Exp. Soc. Psychol.* 1:20–54

Keniston, K. 1967. The sources of student dissent. *J. Soc. Issues* XXIII (July):108–37

Keniston, K. 1968. *Young Radicals.* New York: Harcourt, Brace & World. 368 pp.

Keniston, K. 1971. *Youth and Dissent.* New York: Harcourt Brace Jovanovich. 403 pp.

Keniston, K., in collaboration with Duffield, M. K., Martinek, S. 1973. *Radicals and Militants: An Annotated Bibliography of Empirical Research on Campus Unrest.* Lexington, Mass: Lexington Books, Heath. 219 pp.

Kerckhoff, A. C., Back, K. W. 1968. *The June Bug: A Study of Hysterical Contagion.* New York: Appleton-Century-Crofts. 239 pp.

Kerner, O., chairman. 1968. Report of the National Advisory Commission on Civil Disorders. New York: Bantam Books. 608 pp.

Kerpelman, L. C. 1972. *Activists and Nonactivists.* New York: Behavioral Publ. 162 pp.

Kerr, C. 1964. *The Uses of the University.* Cambridge, Mass: Harvard Univ. Press. 140 pp.

Killian, L. M. 1964. Social movements. In *Handbook of Modern Sociology,* ed. R. E. L. Faris, 426–55. Chicago: Rand McNally. 1088 pp.

King, M. L. 1958. *Stride Toward Freedom: The Montgomery Story.* New York: Harper & Brothers. 230 pp.

King, M. L. 1967. *Where Do We Go From Here: Chaos or Community?.* New York: Harper & Row. 209 pp.

Klapp, O. E. 1969. *Collective Search for Identity.* New York: Holt, Rinehart & Winston. 383 pp.

Klapp, O. E. 1972. *Currents of Unrest: An Introduction to Collective Behavior.* New York: Holt, Rinehart & Winston. 420 pp.

Knowles, E. 1973. Boundaries around group interaction: the effect of group size and member status on boundary permeability. *J. Personality Soc. Psychol.* 26 (June):327–31

Koedt, A. 1973. Women and the radical movement. In *Radical Feminism,* ed. A. Koedt, E. Levine, A. Rapone,

318–21. New York: Quadrangle Books. 424 pp.

Koedt, A., Levine, E., Rapone, A., eds. 1973. *Radical Feminism.* New York: Quadrangle Books. 424 pp.

Kornhauser, W. 1959. *The Politics of Mass Society.* Free Press Glencoe. 256 pp.

Korpi, W. 1974. Conflict, power and relative deprivation. *Am. Polit. Sci. Rev.* 68 (Dec.):1569–78

Kriesberg, L. 1973. *The Sociology of Social Conflicts.* Englewood Cliffs, NJ: Prentice-Hall. 300 pp.

Kuhn, T. S. 1970. *The Structure of Scientific Revolutions. Int. Encycl. Unified Sci.* Vol. 2, No. 2. Chicago: Univ. Chicago Press. 210 pp. Originally published in 1962.

Lammers, C. J. 1969. Strikes and mutinies. *Admin. Sci. Quart.* 14 (Dec.):558–72

Lang, K., Lang, G. 1953. The unique perspective of television and its effect: a pilot study. *Am. Sociol. Rev.* 18 (February):3–12

Lang, K., Lang, G. 1961. *Collective Dynamics.* New York: Crowell. 563 pp.

Lang, K., Lang, G. 1968. Collective behavior. In *International Encyclopedia of the Social Sciences,* ed. D. L. Sills, 2:556–65. New York: MacMillan & Free Press

Lao, R. C. 1970. Internal-external control and competent and innovative behavior among negro college students. *J. Personality Soc. Psychol.* 14:263–70

Latané, B., Darley, J. M. 1970. *The Unresponsive Bystander.* New York: Appleton-Century-Crofts. 131 pp.

Le Bon, G. 1895. *Psychologie des Foules.* Transl. as *The Crowd* or similar title. English editions 1903. London: Unwin; 1952. London: Ernest Benn. 239 pp.; 1968. Sellanraa, Dunwoody, Ga: Norman S. Berg. 219 pp.; 1974. New York: Arno; 1960. New York: Viking

Leffler, A., Gillespie, D. L. 1971–1972. A feminist reply: we deny the allegations and defy the allegator. *Berkeley J. Sociol.: Crit. Rev.* XVI:168–79

Leggett, J. C. 1973. *Taking State Power: The Sources and Consequences of Political Challenge.* New York: Harper & Row. 533 pp.

Lenin, V. I. 1969. *What Is To Be Done?.* New York: Int. Publ. 199 pp. Originally published in 1902.

Lewis, J. M. 1972. A study of the Kent State incident using Smelser's theory of collective behavior. *Sociol. Inq.* 42:87–96

Lieberson, S., Silverman, A. R. 1965. The precipitants and underlying conditions of race riots. *Am. Sociol. Rev.* 30 (December):887–98

Liebman, A. 1974. *The Jews and the Left.* Dept. Sociol., State Univ. NY at Binghamton. 103 pp. Unpublished

Lipset, S. M. 1960. *Political Man.* Garden City, NY: Doubleday. 432 pp. Originally published in 1959.

Lipset, S. M. 1965. University student politics. In *The Berkeley Student Revolt,* ed. S. M. Lipset, S. S. Wolin, 1–9. Garden City, NY: Anchor Books. 585 pp.

Lipset, S. M. 1968. The activists: a profile. *Public Interest* Fall: 39–51

Lipset, S. M. 1972. *Rebellion in the University.* Boston: Little, Brown. 310 pp.

Lipset, S. M., Altbach, P. G. 1966. Student politics and higher education in the United States. *Comp. Educ. Rev.* 10 (June):320–49

Lipset, S. M., Ladd, E. C. Jr. 1971. College generations—from the 1930s to the 1960s. *Public Interest* 25 (Fall):99–113

Lipset, S. M., Raab, E. 1970. *The Politics of Unreason: Right-Wing Extremism in America, 1790–1970.* New York: Harper & Row. 547 pp.

Lipset, S. M., Wolin, S. S., eds. 1965. *The Berkeley Student Revolt.* Garden City, NY: Anchor Books. 585 pp.

Mankoff, M. L. 1969. *The political socialization of radicals and militants in the Wisconsin student movement during the 1960's.* PhD dissertation. Dept. Sociol., Univ. Wisconsin, Madison

Mankoff, M., Flacks, R. 1971. The changing social base of the American student movement. *Ann. Am. Acad. Polit. Soc. Sci.* 395 (May):54–67

Mann, L. 1970. The social psychology of waiting lines. *Am. Sci.* 58:390–98

Mann, L. 1974a. Cross national aspects of riot behavior. In *Readings in Cross Cultural Psychology,* ed. J. Dawson, W. Lonner. Hong Kong: Univ. Hong Kong Press

Mann, L. 1974b. Flinders, Univ. South Australia. Unpublished

Manning, R. 1973. Fifteen years of collective behavior. *Sociol. Quart.* 14:279–86

Martínez, T., forthcoming. Becoming a film maker. In T. Martínez, *Media Mystique.* Berkeley: Quinto-Sol

Marx, G. T. 1962. *The Social Basis of Support of a Depression Era Extremist: Father Coughlin.* Monogr. 7, Surv. Res. Center, Univ. Calif., Berkeley

Marx, G. T. 1969. *Protest and Prejudice: A Study of Belief in the Black Community.* New York: Harper Torchbooks. 256 pp. Originally published in 1967.

Marx, G. T. 1970a. Civil disorder and the agents of social control. *J. Soc. Issues* 26:19–57

Marx, G. T. 1970b. Issueless Riots. *Ann. Am. Acad. Polit. Soc. Sci.* 391 (September):21–33

Marx, G. T. 1970c. Riot. *Encycl. Brit.* 19:349–50c. Chicago: Benton

Marx, G. T. 1970d. Two cheers for the Riot Commission report. In *Black America,* ed. J. F. Szwed, 78–96. New York: Basic Books. 303 pp.

Marx, G. T., ed. 1971. *Racial Conflict.* Boston: Little, Brown. 489 pp.

Marx, G. T. 1972. Perspectives on violence. *Contemp. Psychol.* 17 (March):128–31

Marx, G. T. 1974. Thoughts on a neglected category of social movement participant: the agent provocateur and the informant. *Am. J. Sociol.* 80 (September):402–42

Marx, G. T., Archer, D. 1971. Citizen involvement in the law enforcement process: the case of community police patrols. *Am. Behav. Sci.* 15:52–72

Marx, G. T., Useem, M. 1971. Majority involvement in minority movements: civil rights, abolition, untouchability. *J. Soc. Issues* 27:81–104

Marx, K. 1952. *Wage Labour and Capital.* Moscow: Foreign Language Pub. House. 51 pp. Originally published in 1849

Masotti, L. H., Bowen, D. R., eds. 1968. *Riots and Rebellions.* Beverly Hills, Calif.: Sage. 459 pp.

Masotti, L. H., Hadden, J., Seminatou, K., Corsi, J. 1969. *A Time to Burn?* Chicago: Rand McNally. 187 pp.

Matthews, D. R., Prothro, J. W. 1966. *Negroes and the New Southern Politics.* New York: Harcourt, Brace & World. 551 pp.

Mattick, H. W. 1968. The form and content of recent riots. *Midway* 9 (Summer): 3–32

Mauss, A. L. 1971. On being strangled by the stars and stripes: the new left, the old left, and the natural history of American radical movements. *J. Soc. Issues* 27:183–202

Mauss, A. L., 1975. *Social Problems as Social Movements.* Philadelphia: Lippincott. 718 pp.

McCarthy, J. D., Zald, M. N. 1973. *The Trends of Social Movements in America: Professionalization and Resource Mobilization.* Morristown, NJ: General Learning Press. 30 pp.

McCone, J. A., chairman. 1965. *Violence in the City—An End or a Beginning? A* Report by the Governor's Commission on the Los Angeles Riots (December 2). State of California, PO Box 54708. Los Angeles, California 90054. 101 pp.

McEvoy, J., Miller, A., eds. 1969. *Black Power and Student Rebellion.* Belmont, Calif.: Wadsworth. 440 pp.

McLaughlin, B., ed. 1969. *Studies in Social Movements: A Social Psychological Perspective.* New York: Free Press. 497 pp.

McPhail, C. 1969. Student walkout: a fortuitous examination of elementary collective behavior. *Soc. Probl.* 16 (Spring):441–55.

McPhail, C. 1971. Civil disorder participation: a critical examination of recent research. *Am. Sociol. Rev.* 36 (December):1058–73

McPhail, C. 1972. *Theoretical and Methodological Strategies for the Study of Individual and Collective Behavior Sequences.* Presented at 67th Ann. Meet. Am. Sociol. Assoc., New Orleans

McPhail, C., Miller, D. 1973. The assembling process: a theoretical and empirical examination. *Am. Sociol. Rev.* 38 (December):721–35

Meier, A., Rudwick, E. 1973. *CORE: A Study in the Civil Rights Movement, 1942–1968.* New York: Oxford Univ. Press. 563 pp.

Merton, R. K. 1957. *Social Theory and Social Structure.* London: Free Press Glencoe. 645 pp. Revised and enlarged ed. Originally published in 1949.

Merton, R. K., Rossi, A. K. 1957. Contributions to the theory of reference group behavior. In R. K. Merton, *Social Theory and Social Structure,* London: Free Press Glencoe. 645 pp. Revised and enlarged ed.

Messinger, S. L. 1955. Organizational transformation: a case study of a declining social movement. *Am. Sociol. Rev.* 20:3–10

Michels, R. 1962. *Political Parties.* Transl. E. Paul, C. Paul. New York: Free Press. 379 pp. Originally published in 1911.

Milgram, S., Bickman, L., Berkowitz, L. 1969. Note on the drawing power of crowds of different size. *J. Personality Soc. Psychol.* 13:79–82

Milgram, S., Toch, H. 1969. Collective Behavior: Crowds and Social Movements. In *The Handbook of Social Psychology,* ed. G. Lindzey, E. Aronson, 4:507–610. Reading, Mass: Addison-Wesley. 694 pp. 2d ed.

Mintz, A. 1951. Non-adaptive group behavior. *J. Abnorm. Soc. Psychol.* 46:150–59

Moore, B. 1966. *Social Origins of Dictatorship and Democracy: Lord and Peasant in the Making of the Modern World.* Boston: Beacon Press. 559 pp.

Morgan, R. 1970a. Introduction: the women's revolution. In *Sisterhood is Powerful: An Anthology of Writings from the Women's Liberation Movement,* ed. R. Morgan, xiii–xl. New York: Vintage Books, A Division of Random House. 602 pp.

Morgan, R., ed. 1970b. *Sisterhood is Powerful: An Anthology of Writings from the Women's Liberation Movement.* New York: Vintage Books, A Division of Random House. 602 pp.

Morgan, W. R., Clark, T. N. 1973. The causes of racial disorders: a grievance-level explanation. *Am. Sociol. Rev.* 38:611–24

Morris, M. B. 1973. The public definition of a social movement: women's liberation. *Sociol. Soc. Res.* 57 (July):526–43

Morrison, D. E. 1971. Some notes toward theory on relative deprivation, social movements, and social change. *Am. Behav. Sci.* 14 (May/June):675–90

Moynihan, D. P. 1969. *Maximum Feasible Misunderstanding.* New York: Free Press. 218 pp.

Muller, E. N. 1972. A test of a partial theory of potential for political violence. *Am. Polit. Sci. Rev.* 66 (September):928–59

Murphy, R. J., Watson, J. M. 1969. *Level of Aspiration, Discontent, and Support for Violence: A Test of the Expectation Hypothesis.* Presented at 64th Ann. Meet. Am. Sociol. Assoc., San Francisco

Nelson, H. A. 1974. Social movement transformation and pre-movement factor effect: a preliminary inquiry. *Sociol. Quart.* 15 (Winter):127–42

Newton, H. P. 1972. *To Die For The People.* New York: Random House. 232 pp.

Oberschall, A. 1968. The Los Angeles riot of August 1965. *Soc. Probl.* 15 (Winter):322–41

Oberschall, A. 1973. *Social Conflict and Social Movements.* Englewood Cliffs, NJ: Prentice-Hall. 371 pp.

Oglesby, C., ed. 1969. *The New Left Reader.* New York: Grove. 312 pp.

Olson, M. Jr. 1965. *The Logic of Collective Action.* Cambridge, Mass.: Harvard Univ. Press. 176 pp.

Omvedt, G., forthcoming. *Cultural Revolt in Colonial Society: The Non-Brahman Movement in Western India, 1870–1930.* Poona, India: Sci. Soc. Educ. Trust

Oppenheimer, M. 1969. *The Urban Guerrilla.* Chicago: Quadrangle Books. 188 pp.

Orbell, J. M. 1967. Protest participation among Southern Negro college students. *Am. Polit. Sci. Rev.* 61 (June): 446–56

Orum, A. M. 1972. *Black Students in Protest: A Study of the Origins of the Black Student Movement.* Washington DC: Arnold M. & Caroline Rose Monogr. Ser., Am. Sociol. Assoc. 89 pp.

O'Toole, R. 1973. Aspects of conspiracy theory in social movements: the case of the political sect. In *Social Movements: A Reader and Source Book,* ed. R. R. Evans, 452–60. Chicago: Rand McNally. 605 pp.

Palmer, S., Linsky, A. S., eds. 1972. *Rebellion and Retreat.* Columbus, Ohio: Merrill. 524 pp.

Park, R. E., Burgess, E. W. 1924. *Introduction to the Science of Sociology.* Chicago: Univ. Chicago Press. 1040 pp.

Parsons, T. 1949. *The Structure of Social Action.* New York: Free Press Glencoe. 817 pp. Originally published in 1937.

Parsons, T. 1974. Epilogue: the university "bundle." In *Public Higher Education in California,* ed. N. J. Smelser, G. Almond, 275–99. Berkeley: Univ. Calif. Press. 312 pp.

Peele, S., Morse, S. 1969. On studying a social movement. *Publ. Opin. Quart.* 33 (Fall):409–11

Peterson, R. E. 1970. The scope of organized student protest. In *Protest!: Student Activism in America,* ed. J. Foster, D. Long, 59–80. New York: Morrow. 596 pp.

Pettigrew, T. F. 1964. *A Profile of the Negro American.* Princeton NJ: Van Nostrand. 250 pp.

Pettigrew, T. F. 1971. *Racially Separate or Together?.* New York: McGraw-Hill. 371 pp.

Pfautz, H. W. 1961. Near-group theory and collective behavior: a critical reformulation. *Soc. Probl.* 9:167–74

Pfautz, H. W. 1963. Review of Neil J. Smelser, *Theory of Collective Behavior. Soc. Res.* 30 (Winter): 541–46

Pfautz, H. W. 1969. *Collective Behavior Bibliography.* Brown Univ., Providence, RI. Unpublished mimeo

Pfautz, H. W. 1975. *Collective Behavior and Its Critics: an Uncritical Mass.* Brown Univ., Providence, RI. Unpublished xerox

Piliavin, I. M., Rodin, J., Piliavin, J. A. 1969. Good Samaritanism: an underground phenomenon? *J. Personality Soc. Psychol.* 13 (December):289–99

Pinard, M. 1971. *The Rise of a Third Party: A Study in Crisis Politics.* Englewood Cliffs, NJ: Prentice-Hall. 285 pp.

Pinkney, A. 1968. *The Committed: White Activists in the Civil Rights Movement.* New Haven: Coll. & Univ. Press. 239 pp.

Portes, A. 1971. On the logic of post-factum explanations: the hypothesis of lower-class frustration as the cause of leftist radicalism. *Soc. Forces* 50 (September):26–44

Quarantelli, E. L. 1973. Emergent accommodation groups: beyond current collective behavior typologies. In *Human Nature and Collective Behavior: Papers in Honor of Herbert Blumer,* ed. T. Shibutani, 111–23. New Brunswick, NJ: Transaction Books. 404 pp. Originally published in 1970.

Quarantelli, E. L., Dynes, R. D. 1970a. Editors' introduction: organizational and group behavior in disasters. *Am. Behav. Sci.* 13 (January/February):325–30

Quarantelli, E. L., Dynes, R. D. 1970b. Property norms and looting: their patterns in community crises. *Phylon* 31(Summer):168–82

Quarantelli, E. L., Hundley, J. R. Jr. 1969. A test of some propositions about crowd formation and behavior. In *Readings in Collective Behavior,* ed. R. R. Evans, 538–54. Chicago: Rand McNally. 660 pp.

Quarantelli, E. L., Weller, J. M. 1974. The structural problem of a sociological specialty: collective behavior's lack of a critical mass. *Am. Sociol.* 9 (May): 59–68

Ransford, H. E. 1968. Isolation, powerlessness, and violence: a study of attitudes and participation in the Watts riot. *Am. J. Sociol.* 73 (March):581–91

Riker, W. H. 1962. *The Theory of Political Coalitions.* New Haven: Yale Univ. Press. 300 pp.

Roberts, R. E., Kloss, R. M. 1974. *Social Movements: Between the Balcony and the Barricade.* Saint Louis: Mosby. 200 pp.

Rogin, M. P. 1967. *The Intellectuals and McCarthy: The Radical Specter.* Cambridge, Mass: MIT Press. 372 pp.

Rogin, M. P., Shover, J. L. 1970. *Political Change in California: Critical Elections and Social Movements, 1890–1966.* Westport, Conn: Greenwood. 231 pp.

Roszak, T. 1969. *The Making of a Counter Culture.* Garden City, NY: Anchor Books. 303 pp.

Roth, G. 1963. *The Social Democrats in Imperial Germany.* Totowa, NJ: Bedminster. 352 pp.

Rowntree, J., Rowntree, M. No date. The political economy of youth: youth as class. *The Radical Education Project,* pp. 1–36. Box 625, Ann Arbor, Michigan 48107. Also in *Our Generation,* Vol. 6, Nos. 1–2

Rubenstein, R. E. 1970. *Rebels in Eden.* Boston: Little, Brown. 201 pp.

Rudé, G. 1960. *The Crowd in the French Revolution.* Great Britain: Oxford, Clarendon Press. 267 pp.

Rudé, G. 1964. *The Crowd in History: A Study of Popular Disturbances in France and England 1730–1848.* New York: Wiley. 281 pp.

Rudwick, E., Meier, A. 1970. Organizational structure and goal succession: a comparative analysis of the NAACP and CORE, 1964–1968. *Soc. Sci. Quart.* 51 (June):9–24

Rudwick, E., Meier, A. 1972. The Kent State affair: social control of a putative value-oriented movement. *Sociol. Inq.* 42:81–86

Runciman, W. G. 1961. Problems of research on relative deprivation. *Eur. J. Sociol.* 2:315–23

Runciman, W. G. 1966. *Relative Deprivation and Social Justice.* Berkeley: Univ. Calif. Press. 338 pp.

Rush, G. B., Denisoff, R. S., eds. 1971. *Social and Political Movements.* New York: Appleton-Century-Crofts. 520 pp.

Safilios-Rothschild, C. 1974. *Women and Social Policy.* Englewood Cliffs, NJ: Prentice-Hall. 197 pp.

Schattschneider, E. E. 1960. *The Semisovereign People.* New York: Holt, Rinehart & Winston. 147 pp.

Schwab, J. J. 1969. *College Curriculum and Student Protest.* Chicago: Univ. Chicago Press. 303 pp.

Schwartz, D. C. 1973. *Political Alienation and Political Behavior.* Chicago: Aldine. 286 pp.

Scott, J. W., El-Assal, M. 1969. Multiversity, university size, university quality and student protest: an empirical study. *Am. Sociol. Rev.* 34 (October):702–9

Seale, B. 1970. *Seize the Time: The Story of the Black Panther Party and Huey P. Newton.* New York: Random House. 429 pp.

Searles, R., Williams, J. A. 1962. Negro college students' participation in sit-ins. *Soc. Forces* 40:215–20

Sears, D. O. 1969. Black attitudes toward the political system in the aftermath of the Watts insurrection. *Midwest J. Polit. Sci.* XIII:515–44

Seidler, J., Meyer, K., MacGillivray, L. 1974. *Crowd Structure and Data Collection at Political Rallies.* Ohio State Univ. Unpublished

Sellitz, C., Jahoda, M., Deutsch, M., Cook, S. W. 1959. *Research Methods in Social Relations.* New York: Holt, Rinehart & Winston. 622 pp. Revised one-volume ed. Originally published in 1951.

Sharp, G. 1973. *The Politics of Nonviolent Action.* Boston: Porter Sargent. 902 pp.

Shellow, R., Roemer, D. V. 1966. The riot that didn't happen. *Soc. Probl.* 14:221–33

Shibutani, T. 1966. *Improvised News: A Sociological Study of Rumor.* Indianapolis, Ind: Bobbs-Merrill. 262 pp.

Shibutani, T., ed. 1973. *Human Nature and Collective Behavior: Papers in Honor of Herbert Blumer.* New Brunswick, NJ: Transaction Books. 404 pp. Originally published in 1970.

Short, J. F. Jr., Wolfgang, M. E., eds. 1972. *Collective Violence.* Chicago: Aldine-Atherton. 387 pp.

Shorter, E., Tilly, C. 1974. *Strikes in France 1830–1968.* New York: Cambridge Univ. Press. 428 pp.

Skolnick, J. H. 1969. *The Politics of Protest.* New York: Ballantine. 419 pp.

Smelser, N. J. 1959. *Social Change in the Industrial Revolution.* Chicago: Univ. Chicago Press. 440 pp.

Smelser, N. J. 1963. *Theory of Collective Behavior.* New York: Free Press Glencoe. 436 pp. Originally published in 1962.

Smelser, N. J. 1968. Social and psychological dimensions of collective behavior. In *Essays in Sociological Explanation,* 92–121. Englewood Cliffs, NJ: Prentice-Hall. 280 pp.

Smelser, N. J. 1970. Two critics in search of a bias: a response to Currie and Skolnick. *Ann. Am. Acad. Polit. Soc. Sci.* 391 (September):46–55

Smelser, N. J. 1972. Some additional thoughts on collective behavior. *Sociol. Inq.* 42:97–101

Smelser, N. J. 1974. Growth, structural change, and conflict in California public higher education, 1950–1970. In *Public Higher Education in California,* ed. N. J. Smelser, G. Almond, 9–141. Berkeley: Univ. Calif. Press. 312 pp.

Smelser, N. J., forthcoming. *Comparisons in the Social Sciences.* Englewood Cliffs, NJ: Prentice-Hall

Smith, R., McPhail, C., Pickens, R. 1972. *Obtrusiveness in Systematic Observation: A Field Experiment With Two Observation-Recording Procedures.* Presented at 67th Ann. Meet. Am. Sociol. Assoc., New Orleans

Smith, T. S. 1968. Conventionalization and control: an examination of adolescent crowds. *Am. J. Sociol.* 74:172–83

Snyder, D., Tilly, C. 1972. Hardship and collective violence in France, 1830 to 1960. *Am. Sociol. Rev.* 37 (Oct.):520–32

Snyder, D. R., Tilly, C. H. 1974. On debating and falsifying theories of collective violence. *Am. Sociol. Rev.* 39 (Aug.): 610–13

Somers, R. H. 1965. The mainsprings of the rebellion: a survey of Berkeley students in November, 1964. In *The Berkeley Student Revolt,* ed. S. M. Lipset, S. S. Wolin, 530–57. New York: Anchor Books. 585 pp.

Somers, R. H. 1969. The Berkeley Campus in the Twilight of the Free Speech Movement: Hope or Futility? In *Black Power and Student Rebellion,* ed. J. McEvoy, A. Miller, 419–40. Belmont, Calif: Wadsworth. 440 pp.

Sorokin, P. 1925. *The Sociology of Revolution.* Philadelphia: Lippincott. 428 pp.

Spilerman, S. 1970. The causes of racial disturbances: a comparison of alternative explanations. *Am. Sociol. Rev.* 35(August):627–49

Spilerman, S. 1971. The causes of racial disturbances: tests of an explanation. *Am. Sociol. Rev.* 36:427–42

Spilerman, S. 1972. Strategic considerations in analyzing the distribution of racial disturbances. *Am. Sociol. Rev.* 37:493–99

Stallings, R. 1973. Patterns of belief in social movements: clarifications from an analysis of environmental groups. *Sociol. Quart.* 14 (Autumn):465–80

Stark, M. J. A., Raine, W. J., Burbeck, S. L., Davison, K. K. 1974. Some empirical patterns in a riot process. *Am. Sociol. Rev.* 39 (December):865–76

Stark, R. 1969. Protest + police = riot. In *Black Power and Student Rebellion,* ed. J. McEvoy, A. Miller, 167–96. Belmont, Calif: Wadsworth. 440 pp.

Stark, R. 1972. *Police Riots: Collective Violence and Law Enforcement.* Belmont, Calif: Wadsworth. 250 pp.

Statera, G. 1975. *Death of a Utopia: the Development and Decline of Student Movements in Europe.* New York: Oxford. 294 pp.

Sterba, R. 1947. Some psychological factors in Negro race hatred and in anti-Negro riots. In *Psychoanalysis and the Social Sciences,* ed. G. Roheim, 1:411–26. New York: Int. Univ. Press

Stinchcombe, A. L. 1968. *Constructing Social Theories.* New York: Harcourt, Brace & World. 303 pp.

Stouffer, S. A. et al 1949. *The American Soldier.* Princeton: Princeton Univ. Press

Strauss, H. J. 1973. Revolutionary types: Russia in 1905. *J. Conflict Resolut.* 17 (June):297–316

Swanson, G. E. 1953. A preliminary laboratory study of the acting crowd. *Am. Sociol. Rev.* 18:522–33

Swanson, G. E. 1971. *Social Change.* Glenview, Ill: Scott, Foresman. 185 pp.

Swanson, G. E. 1973. Toward corporate action: a reconstruction of elementary collective processes. In *Human Nature and Collective Behavior: Papers in Honor of Herbert Blumer,* ed. T. Shibutani, 124–44. New Brunswick, NJ: Transaction Books. 404 pp. Originally published in 1970.

The Critical Mass Bulletin. 1974. Dept. Sociol., Univ. Tennessee, Knoxville. 1[4(Dec.)]:1–10

Thompson, E. P. 1964. *The Making of the English Working Class.* New York: Pantheon. 848 pp. Originally published in 1963.

Thorne, B. 1972. *Girls Say Yes to Guys Who Say No: Women in the Draft Resistance Movement.* Presented at 67th Ann. Meet. Am. Sociol. Assoc., New Orleans

Tilly, C. 1964. The *Vendée.* Cambridge, Mass: Harvard Univ. Press. 373 pp.

Tilly, C. 1969. Collective violence in European perspective. In *The History of Violence in America,* ed. H. G. Davis, T. R. Gurr, 4–45. New York: Praeger, 822 pp.

Toch, H. 1965. *The Social Psychology of Social Movements.* Indianapolis: Bobbs-Merrill. 257 pp.

Tocqueville, A. de. 1955. *The Old Régime and the French Revolution.* Transl. S. Gilbert. Garden City, NY: Doubleday. 300 pp. 1st ed. Originally published in 1856.

Tomlinson, T. M. 1968. The development of a riot ideology among urban Negroes. *Am. Behav. Sci.* 11 (March–April): 27–31

Touraine, A. 1971a. *The May Movement: Revolt and Reform.* Transl. L. F. X. Mayhew. New York: Random House. 373 pp. Originally published in 1968.

Touraine, A. 1971b. *The Post-Industrial Society.* New York: Random House. 244 pp.

Trautwein, M. 1974. UC's "Crim" protest growing. *Berkeley Daily Gazette,* Friday, May 31:1–2

Trotsky, L. 1957. *The History of the Russian Revolution,* Vol. 1–3. Transl. M. Eastman. Ann Arbor: Univ. Michigan Press. 483 pp., 349 pp., 504 pp.

Trow, M. 1958. Small businessmen, political tolerance, and support for McCarthy. *Am. J. Sociol.* 64:270–81

Tullock, G., Buchanan, J. M. 1962. *The Calculus of Consent.* Ann Arbor: Univ. Michigan Press. 361 pp.

Turk, A., forthcoming. *Political Criminality and Political Policing.* New York: MSS Modular Publ.

Turner, R. H. 1964a. Collective behavior. In *Handbook of Modern Sociology,* ed. R. E. L. Faris, 382–455. Chicago: Rand McNally. 1088 pp.

Turner, R. H. 1964b. New theoretical frameworks. *Sociol. Quart.* 5 (Spring):122–32

Turner, R. H. 1969a. The public perception of protest. *Am. Sociol. Rev.* 34 (December):815–31

Turner, R. H. 1969b. The theme of contemporary social movements. *Brit. J. Sociol.* 20:390–405

Turner, R. H. 1973. Determinants of social movement strategies. In *Human Nature and Collective Behavior: Papers in Honor of Herbert Blumer,* ed. T. Shibutani, 145–64. New Brunswick, NJ: Transaction Books. 404 pp. Originally published in 1970.

Turner, R. H. 1974. Collective Behavior. *Encycl. Brit. Macropaedia.* 4:842–53. Chicago: Benton

Turner, R. H., Killian, L. M. 1957. *Collective Behavior.* Englewood Cliffs, NJ: Prentice-Hall. 547 pp.

Turner, R. H., Killian, L. M. 1972. *Collective Behavior.* Englewood Cliffs, NJ: Prentice-Hall. 435 pp. 2d ed.

Useem M. 1973. *Conscription, Protest, and Social Conflict: The Life and Death of a Draft Resistance Movement.* New York: Wiley Interscience. 329 pp.

Useem, M., forthcoming. *Protest Movements in America.* Indianapolis, Ind: Bobbs-Merrill

Vander Zanden, J. W. 1959. Resistance and social movements. *Soc. Forces* 37:312–15

Walker, D. 1968. *Rights in Conflict.* New York: Grosset & Dunlap. 233 pp.

Walker, J. L. 1963. Protest and negotiation: a case study of negro leadership in Atlanta, Georgia. *Midwest J. Polit. Sci.* 7:99–124

Wall, I. 1973. May 1968: when students spoke for France. In *The Highlander* (Univ. Calif., Riverside newspaper), Thursday, January 18: 11, 14–16

Wanderer, J. J. 1968. 1967 riots: a test of the congruity of events. *Soc. Probl.* 16 (Fall): 193–98

Wanderer, J. J. 1969. An index of riot severity and some correlates. *Am. J. Sociol.* 74 (March):500–5

Weinstein, F., Platt, G. M. 1973. *Psychoanalytic Sociology: An Essay on the Interpretation of Historical Data and the Phenomena of Collective Behavior.* Baltimore: Johns Hopkins Univ. Press. 124 pp.

Weller, J., Quarantelli, E. L. 1973. Neglected characteristics of collective behavior. *Am. J. Sociol.* 79 (November):665–85

Westby, D. L., Braungart, R. G. 1966. Class and politics in the family backgrounds of student political activists. *Am. Sociol. Rev.* 31 (October):690–92

Wikler, N. J. 1973. *Vietnam and the veterans' consciousness: pre-political thinking among American soldiers.* PhD dissertation. Univ. Calif., Berkeley, Calif. 346 pp.

Wilkinson, P. 1971. *Social Movement.* London: Pall Mall. 176 pp.

Wilson, J. 1973. *Introduction to Social Movements.* New York: Basic Books. 369 pp.

Wilson, J. 1974. *The Effects of Social Control on Social Movements.* Presented at 69th Ann. Meet. Am. Sociol. Assoc., Montreal, Canada

Wilson, W. 1973. *Power, Racism, and Privilege.* New York: MacMillan. 224 pp.

Wolf, E. R. 1969. *Peasant Wars of the Twentieth Century.* New York: Harper & Row. 328 pp.

Wolfenstein, E. V. 1967. *The Revolutionary Personality: Lenin, Trotsky, Gandhi.* Princeton, NJ: Princeton Univ. Press. 330 pp.

Wong, P, forthcoming. *China's Higher Leadership in the Socialist Transition.* New York: Free Press

Wood, J. L. 1974a. *Political Consciousness and Student Activism.* Sage Prof. Papers in Am. Polit., Vol. 2, Ser. No. 04–015. Beverly Hills & London: Sage. 55 pp.

Wood, J. L. 1974b. *The Sources of American Student Activism.* Lexington, Mass: Lexington Books, Heath. 187 pp.

Wood, J. L., forthcoming a. *New Left Ideology: Its Dimensions and Development.* Sage Professional Papers in American Politics. Beverly Hills and London: Sage

Wood, J. L., forthcoming b. Student political activism. In *American Education: a Sociological View,* ed. D. W. Swift. Boston: Houghton Mifflin

Worsley, P. 1968. *The Trumpet Shall Sound.* New York: Schocken Books. 300 pp. 2d augmented ed.

Zald, M. N., Ash, R. 1966. Social movement organizations: growth, decay and change. *Soc. Forces* 44 (March):327–41

Zurcher, L. A. Jr., Curtis, R. L. 1973. A comparative analysis of propositions describing social movement organizations. *Sociol. Quart.* 14:175–88

Zurcher, L. A. Jr. et al, forthcoming. *Citizens for Decency: A Study of Anti-Pornography Crusades.* Univ. Texas Press

Zurcher, L. A. Jr., Kirkpatrick, R. G., Cushing, R. G., Bowman, C. K. 1971. The anti-pornography campaign: a symbolic crusade. *Soc. Probl.* 19:217–38

POLITICAL PARTICIPATION AND PUBLIC POLICY[1]

❖10515

Robert R. Alford
Board of Studies in Sociology, University of California, Santa Cruz, California 95064

Roger Friedland
Department of Sociology, University of Wisconsin, Madison, Wisconsin 53706

INTRODUCTION

Most major studies of political participation have focused upon one of two types of problems: (*a*) "historical comparisons of the processes of decision-making which led to the expansion of the electorate and the standardization of registration and voting procedures" and (*b*) "statistical comparisons of trends in political reactions of the masses of lower class citizens and of women after their entry into the electorate" (Rokkan 1970:30).

A third type of studies has barely begun:

> *institutional and structural* comparisons of the different ways in which the pressures of the mass electorate, the parties and the elective bodies are dovetailed into a broader system of decision-making among interest organizations and private and public corporate units. [p. 30]

In this chapter we try to develop links between studies of trends and social correlates of participation and the emerging institutional and organizational structures in which participation occurs, considering as problematic the relations between participation and power. Consequently, hypotheses that are implicitly assumed in conventional definitions of political participation, namely that participation leads to power and that power requires participation, become analytically problematic. The traditional definition of participation must be both broadened—

[1] We are indebted to many friends and colleagues for helpful comments—Jillian Dean, Alex Hicks, Edwin Johnson, and Jon Minkoff—and for bibliographic suggestions—William Gamson, M. Lal Goel, Lester Milbrath, Dorothy Nelkin, Sidney Tarrow, and Sidney Verba. Participants in several seminars in Madison and Santa Cruz where our hypotheses were presented were extremely helpful. Although some of our critics are responsible in an important sense for some of the argument, they must not be blamed for our formulations.

to include not only individual but also private or public "corporate units" as agents or beneficiaries of participation—and narrowed—to avoid the assumption that participation actually influences public policy making.

We thus do not deal with several important lines of research on voting behavior and individual participation, and the literature cited is limited by time and space mainly to studies of political participation in the United States from 1960 to 1975. For recent reviews of the data and literature bearing on turnout and representation in presidential primary elections, see Ranney (1972); for an analysis of the changing American electorate, see Converse (1972) and Burnham (1970); for an analysis of the complexity of measuring voting, see Kelley & Mirer (1974).

For the most recent general inventory of the literature on political participation, see Milbrath (1965). Milbrath defines participation as individual acts intended to influence the political system in some way, and he develops a set of dimensions of participation and a hierarchy of involvement ranging from merely exposing oneself to political stimuli to holding public and party office (p. 18). The major correlates of these types of participation form the major chapters: stimuli, personal factors, political setting, and social position. (See also in this volume a 23-page bibliography through 1964.)

PARTICIPATION AND POWER

Our definition of political participation is broader than that of Milbrath and also that of another recent major work on the subject. We regard political participation as those present *or past* activities by private citizens and *private or public organizations and groups,* that are more or less directly aimed at influencing the selection of governmental *structures and* personnel, and the actions they take *or do not take.* Except for the italicized words, this is Verba & Nie's (1972:2) definition of political participation. The added words are intended to stress that historically created structures condition and limit the ranges of action possible not only by individual citizens but also by organizations and groups. We believe that the more limited definition has the following inadequacies: 1. It assumes that the structure of political authority is given. 2. It regards as theoretically residual the historical origins of that structure in past conflicts, and its continual impact on political participation and current conflicts. 3. It neglects those actions of the state ("public organizations") that significantly affect the possibility of participation by private citizens. 4. It ignores the way in which the structures of the state constrain both the ranges of possible action by their personnel and the political issues likely to be raised.

The conventional concept of participation takes as given the differentiation between the private and the public, the economy and the state. The ways in which economic activity impinges upon the state, government, and public sectors, without political participation by elites and dominant classes, are thus difficult to understand. Our broadened definition is intended to encourage systematic research into these complex interconnections.

Our definition does not include the consequences of such processes as ecological change, firm location, migration, and inflation, which differentially benefit various groups, but which are not specific activities intended to influence governmental structures, personnel, and policies. In the context of a market society, such processes may differentially benefit particular groups, but they do not constitute political participation per se. Nor does our expanded definition include the consequences of participation. We believe that the consequences are problematic and should not be definitionally assumed.

Both Verba & Nie (1972) and McClosky (1968) included direct or indirect consequences of political participation as part of its definition. McClosky referred to "sharing . . . in the formation of public policy" (p. 252) and Verba & Nie to "influencing . . . the actions . . . governmental personnel . . . take" (p. 2). Verba & Nie qualified this somewhat by restricting the definition to the intent of participation ("aiming" at influence), but McClosky did not. However, neither Verba & Nie nor McClosky referred to any literature that analyzed the actual consequences of political participation for public policy, and the data Verba & Nie analyzed (surveys of leaders and citizens in 64 United States cities) did not directly bear on the issue. Although Verba & Nie stated their fundamental theoretical concern to be with "attempts to influence the authoritative allocations of values for a society, which may or may not take place through governmental decisions" (p. 2), their data allowed them to study only individual attempts to influence governmental decisions, a far narrower empirical problem. An analytically differentiated conception of the relations of participation and power restores their initial theoretical concern to a central place. Unfortunately, "the effect of the franchise on the fortunes of groups and the operation of the state has not been empirically investigated," a rather striking gap (Huber & Form 1973:120; see also Greer & Orleans 1964:822).

Thus, power is held by those who benefit over time from the operation of social, economic, and political structures. Power is not held by those who win in a given electoral battle or attempt to influence a decision; we would call that "influence." Important as influence is in specific political situations and conflicts (see March 1966), this definition of power does not focus on the structural context in which influence is or is not exerted. Nor is power a capacity to control; that suggests a negative or passive approach to power that has properly been criticized by the pluralists as an empty empirical cell. If a capacity is not used, then there is no way of knowing what would happen if it were used. Our definition has the advantage of referring to concrete behavior—not the behavior of those seeking benefits, but of those who, consciously or unconsciously, intentionally or unintentionally, act in such a way as to confer benefits upon one group rather than another.

Therefore, we argue that power should not be assumed to follow from participation. Power and participation are independent although causally related phenomena, and their various relationships allow us to reexamine the literature of the past 15 years. Participation may be associated with power, but power can exist without participation, e.g. social groups may benefit from the operation of structures without any participation on their part. Participation may occur without power—*symbolic participation* (Edelman 1964)—and powerlessness can exist without participation when particular social groups withdraw or are excluded. We call power without participation *systemic* power. Finally, the ways in which the organization of the state affects the exercise of all modes of power is *structural* power. While the creation of such structural power requires participation, its effects are often to reduce the need for participation by dominant groups.

This broadened perspective makes it possible to link the research literature on political participation to a classic question: what accounts for the disproportionate political participation of the upper classes and the wealthy? In the next section we summarize and evaluate a recent major study showing that social class remains the strongest correlate of political participation. Our concern is not, however, to summarize the latest batch of studies demonstrating this relationship, but rather to consider how the recent literature bears on alternative explanations for this relationship. We believe that the explanation should be sought in (*a*) antecedent structural factors, (*b*) the historical origins of those structures, and (*c*) the success of dominant interests in the society in making those structures serve their interests. These assumptions differ sharply from those of the dominant pluralist model (see McFarland 1969, Pateman 1970), but provide a better starting point, in our opinion, for a theory of political participation.

Our emphasis upon the importance of social class is consistent with the bulk of the literature, but we do not wish to suggest that it is the only important factor related to political participation. See Greeley (1974) for a recent demonstration of the continuing importance of ethnicity in the political behavior of United States citizens, over and above social class. Also, for recent compilations of cross-national studies and data, see Bruhns, Cazzola & Wiatr (1974) and Di Palma (1970).

The conventional definition of participation assumes that the object of participation is control over popular instruments of representation such as legislatures and parties. As the next section shows, however, the major thrust of the empirical literature is that voting turnout and party competition are very slightly related to policy outputs, mainly to public expenditures. We conclude from this literature that the absence of any impact of variations in legislative and party politics indicates that the presumably most responsive sections of the state are not significantly influenced by variations in voting turnout and party competition. Unfortunately, electoral participation is not highly correlated with power as measured by public expenditures and other measures of state responsiveness.

Rather than political factors, the level of industrialization or economic development is the main predictor of public expenditures. In societies like the United States where major decisions about capital investment, plant location, land use, technological innovation and application, and uses of alternative energy sources are made by private groups or by nominally public agencies essentially under private control, this finding can be interpreted to mean that a lack of public control over public expenditures is due to private control over public expenditures. In its effect, this is power *without* participation; not only legislative and party structures, but also the administrative structures of the state, function to maximize the political impact of economic power.

However, these findings only redefine the question. If legislative and party politics are not significant foci of political participation, at least in terms of substantive consequences for public expenditures, perhaps there are other channels of access.

Perhaps the growth of the administrative agencies of government has been a tangible response to the inability of legislatures and parties to transform political demands into political outputs. On the contrary, as the next section shows, the major finding of the studies of the growth of state bureaucratic structures is that government agencies serve to insulate dominant interests from political challenge. Through control of regulatory agencies, through special access to officials, and through involvement at the point of origin of these agencies to limit or shape their jurisdictions, dominant interests maintain the responsiveness of the agencies to themselves. We conclude from this literature that a major consequence of the growth of state agencies has been that the structure of the state itself has incorporated a continuous response to certain interests and a systematic exclusion of other interests from representation. This pattern constitutes power *with* participation.

These structures of the state also function to minimize the impact of political participation upon the power of nondominant groups, those who need the power the most. Empirically, as the literature summarized in the next section shows, the forms of participation in nonparty, nonlegislative institutions by the poor and working classes have very little impact on the structure and policies of those institutions and ultimately little effect upon the conditions of their lives. We conclude from this literature that the political participation by the poor has had the effect of siphoning off political leadership into ineffective channels, thus preventing political challenge of the dominant economic institutions of the society. The function, if not the intention, of those forms of participation is to control or limit the consequences of that participation. This is participation *without* power.

Participation without power is thus characteristic of the poor and working classes, and power with or without participation is characteristic of the rich and upper classes. If the processes that generate these patterns are stable, then one has explained class differences in political participation as a way to reproduce a stratification system. However, our broadened definition of political participation also leads us to consider the endemic origins of cyclic patterns of noninstitutionalized and illegitimate forms of political participation. There is considerable evidence, treated in the next section, that political violence and protest are normal and rational forms of political participation. If this is the case, then the image produced by the studies already summarized—an image of the stable, institutionalized representation of some interests and the exclusion of others by the operation of state legislative, party, and bureaucratic agencies—is an incomplete snapshot of the historical development of the state in relation to society. The recent literature on political protest indicates that the seemingly stable forms of representation that uphold the interests of the rich, and the forms of "unrepresentation" that affect the interests of the poor (Gamson 1968)—as manifested by private control over public expenditures, incorporation of bureaucratic agencies into dominant interests, and the symbolic forms of participation offered to the poor—are insufficient under all historical conditions to contain the grievances and repress the protest of the poor. But the reactions of the state are such, in most situations, as to restore political stability. The various techniques of repression, disenfranchisement, territorial dislocation, administrative fiat, and co-optation are all available. In the long run, the effect of state response to riots, disruption, and protest is to remove the poor and working classes even further from the possibility of conjoining participation and power.

Since the focus of this chapter is upon participation and not upon partisanship, we cannot review the literature on changing partisan alignments in detail; but Burnham's thesis that there has been a major "decomposition of the hold of party on the electorate" (1970:170) helps explain both the decline of electoral participation and its severe class bias. The reduction in the proportion of the electorate that identifies with one of the two major parties is one of the major indicators of that decomposition [see Burnham (1970, Chapters 5 and 6 and the literature cited therein) as well as Converse (1972) for a different interpretation of these trends].

Various political reforms adopted after the critical election of 1896 "depoliticized" the electorate: the Australian ballot; the direct-primary system; nonpartisanship, at-large elections, and the council-manager form of local government; and manipulation of voting qualifications and requirements, especially in the South (Burnham 1970:74–77). Another change was the separation of national and state elections into different years. Burnham summarized the effect of this as follows: "Dropoff between presidential and off-year elections in the current period involves between one-fifth and one-quarter of the presidential-year electorate" (Burnham 1970:94; see also Burnham 1965 and Campbell 1966). Burnham presented both national and state data on shifts in voting turnout over the past 100 years and argues that the "cumulative effect of these rules changes was, with few exceptions, heavily depoliticizing and antipartisan" (Burnham 1970:93).

Burnham argued that a "necessary consequence of the realities of incremental bargaining politics in the United States [is] that they will tend to produce crises which lead to nonincremental change" (p. 137). That is, it is the very pluralism of interest-group politics that makes it impossible for political elites, even if they wanted to, to take a long-term view and represent the interests of excluded groups. Unless and until such groups become themselves organized, they are ignored by the political system (see Wolff 1965).

With this overview we turn to an examination of the various studies of political participation that have been conducted in the last 15 years, starting with the relationship of social class to participation, using the Verba-Nie definition.

SOCIAL CLASS AND POLITICAL PARTICIPATION

A recent important study based on a 1967 United States survey confirmed a

generalization that is already well established in the literature: Citizens of higher social and economic status participate more in politics. This generalization has been confirmed many times in many nations. And it generally holds true whether one uses level of education, income, or occupation, as the measure of social status. [Verba & Nie 1972:125; see also Lipset 1960; Nie, Powell & Prewitt 1969, and Dahl 1961:282–83 for a sampling of other references on this point.]

Not only is the class-participation relationship pervasive, it is constant. A reanalysis of the seven election surveys done by the Survey Research Center at the

University of Michigan found that "the relationship has been remarkably stable" over the period from 1952 to 1970 (Verba & Nie 1972:254). And a comprehensive review of the surveys on partisanship and voting turnout up to 1967 concluded that the "social composition of voters and non-voters does not change significantly from one election to the next" (Flanigan 1968:20). This stability is all the more remarkable in that it occurred in the midst of increasing campaign activity, which might have been expected to mobilize the previously nonparticipatory segments of the population.

The Verba-Nie volume is part of a series of works based on cross-national surveys, beginning with a five-nation (United States, United Kingdom, Germany, Italy, and Mexico) study reported by Almond & Verba (1963) and continuing with a new cross-national study, much of which remains unpublished. [See Verba, Nie & Kim (1971) for a preliminary report of surveys in the United States, Austria, India, Japan, and Nigeria between 1966 and 1969, and Verba & Nie (1972) for a detailed analysis of the same United States data. A reanalysis of the Almond & Verba (1963) data is contained in two articles by Nie, Powell & Prewitt (1969).] To summarize their basic finding,

> Participants come disproportionately from upper-status groups. This is clearest if one compares the inactives [those who do not participate at all] with the complete activists [those who engage in all forms of participation: electoral campaigning, joining various community organizations, contacting officials both for broad social issues and for personal benefits]. Aside from the complete activists, . . . the more difficult activities are engaged in heavily by upper-status citizens. [Verba & Nie 1972:100]

Verba & Nie then define what they call a "standard model" of participation that compares all factors except social status to the importance of status for participation. Status-based participation is regarded as primary, and other factors potentially affecting participation—age, sex, race, religion, type of community, party membership—are analyzed in relation to and as they affect the primary importance of social class.

We use the term *class* rather than *status,* however, because status refers either to social honor (prestige) or to multivariate hierarchies of rewards (prestige, income, education, social power, wealth, desirable occupations) and the correlations and causal links among them, usually summarized as socioeconomic status (SES). Where these stratification characteristics are correlated and combined into a single index (as in Verba & Nie), the implicit theoretical assumption is that institutionalized allocations of privileges and rewards produce a high correlation among all indices of stratification. We believe such a system is more appropriately described by the term class. Verba & Nie's usage of the term status would be appropriate if they had maintained separate indices of all forms of stratification and tested for their separate effects, an analysis they did not report in the book (see p. 130: they did "not decompose the components of socioeconomic status"). In effect, they tried to straddle this distinction, because frequently they refer to "upper status" and "lower status" citizens (and even to the "class basis of politics," p. 340) as if a dichotomous description were accurate. Although this usage may have been for shorthand convenience, their image of the stratification system is clearly not one of a diversity of hierarchies of various rewards.

Testing for the effect of organizational participation upon the relationship between social status and political participation, the authors found that

> on the individual level organizational affiliation has a greater impact on the political participation rate of those lowest in the socioeconomic hierarchy, and thereby works in the direction of lowering the participation gap between upper- and lower-status citizens. [p. 203]

This conclusion is problematic for several reasons. 1. There were too few cases of lower-status individuals active in more than two organizations to allow comparisons with higher-status persons. This seemingly minor empirical detail is testimony to the initial high correlation between status and organizational activity, which renders the attempt to control for status problematic. 2. The authors did not examine the possibility of other differences between their trichotomy of status groups that might interpret the relationship in a way consistent with the primary hypothesis about the importance of status. That is, low-status (by their measure, which combined income, occupation, and education) persons active in organizations may have differed from low-status persons not active in organizations in significant ways having to do with their status and class, and the crude trichotomy could not deal with those differences. 3. In relation to the above point, the authors could have used the continuous component variables comprising their SES index (and this would have been more consistent with their theoretical interpretation using the term status rather than class), and looked for empirical thresholds or "break points" in the correlations with other variables, which would have indicated the impact of those variables empirically, without having to assume that the cutting points arbitrarily chosen were correct.

At the individual level, they argued that organizational participation reduces status-group disparity in political participation. At the group level, however, the reverse is true.

> So many more upper-status individuals are organizationally active, particularly in the multiple active category, that their gain in participation as a group far exceeds that of the lower-status group. . . . In short, organizations increase the disparity in participation between upper- and lower-status groups because upper-status individuals are more likely to take advantage of that gain. [p. 205]

Thus, to the extent that organizations are the instruments through which political influence over public policies is brought to bear, participation in them is still another mechanism for reinforcing class advantages.

Partisan identification was found to have the same effect as organizational activity.

> Citizens from all status levels receive a boost in participation if they are partisans, but . . . upper-status individuals receive more of a boost when it comes to difficult modes of participation—campaigning and communal activity—while lower-status individuals receive more of a boost in voting participation. [p. 220]

Political ideology also "modifies the workings of the standard socioeconomic model. But the modification is to accelerate the workings of that model" (p. 228). That is, conservative beliefs among Republicans heightened their political participation considerably, but liberal beliefs among Democrats did not have the same effect. Thus, liberal ideology did not offset "normal" status differences in participation. Also participants were more conservative than the population as a whole.

> Our data show that participants are less aware of serious welfare problems than the population as a whole, less concerned about the income gap between rich and poor, less interested in government support for welfare programs, and less concerned with equal opportunities for black Americans. [p. 298]

To the extent that leaders pay attention to participants and not to public opinion in general (through polls), conservative opinions will thus carry greater weight in policy making. But this inference assumed that leaders were watching and responding either to participants or to public opinion. Was that true?

Verba & Nie attempted to answer this question by looking at leader responsiveness. They computed an index of *concurrence*—the degree to which leaders and voters agree on the most important problems facing their community—and attempted to infer from this measure the degree of responsiveness of leaders to the citizenry. As the authors said, "responsiveness . . . has . . . never been related to participation" before, at least empirically (p. 300). Given our concern in this chapter with the various relations between participation and power, their recent attempt to specify the impact of participation upon leader responsiveness must be treated in some detail.

The concurrence score for an individual respondent was measured by the number of community leaders mentioning a community problem that was also mentioned by the individual respondent, divided by the total number of leaders interviewed (between three and seven). [See Appendixes H and I in Verba & Nie, and also Hansen (1973) for more details.] These individual scores were aggregated to form concurrence scores for a community or for any subgroup within it. Controlling for four social characteristics—status, race, age, and sex—Verba & Nie also computed aggregate participation scores for communities and related these scores to the level of concurrence between leaders and citizens, to the level of "consensus" between activists and nonactivists among the citizenry (consensus was simply the concurrence measure applied to subgroups within the citizenry), and to actual voting turnout (Chapters 17–20).

The basic finding was that individual participation scores correlated with concurrence, even when social characteristics were controlled (p. 307). In all communities, regardless of the aggregate level of participation, leaders were more likely to agree with activists than with less active citizens (p. 317). Where activists agreed with nonactivists on priority community problems (a "consensual" community), concurrence was more consistently associated with participation than in nonconsensual communities (p. 321). When various modes of participation were examined separately (voting, campaign activity, communal activity, and particularized contacting), the relationship of each mode to concurrence remained the same in consensual communities, but differed sharply among nonconsensual communities (p. 325). Finally, Verba & Nie showed that concurrence was highest between leaders and high-status high participants, lowest for low-status citizens, regardless of their level of participation (p. 337).

Verba & Nie summarized their basic findings as follows: "The close relationship among social status, participation, and responsiveness is our major conclusion about American politics" (p. 339). They argued that it is the very absence of class-based parties and political movements that "makes, paradoxically, such status a more potent force in American politics" (p. 340). They cited in addition the finding from their various cross-national studies in eleven countries that the United States exhibits a stronger relationship between status and participation than all but one (the United Kingdom) (Verba & Nie 1972:340, Nie, Powell & Prewitt 1969, Verba, Nie & Kim 1971).

Their explanation in terms of the absence of class-based ideologies and organizations is a plausible and often-mentioned one. What are the institutional mechanisms that maintain class-based inequalities, despite the existence of instruments of political democracy? Verba & Nie came to an essentially optimistic conclusion because of a crucial assumption. They believe that citizen preferences influence leader preferences and behavior, not the other way around. Unfortunately, every finding they presented can be interpreted as causally opposite from the way they did. First, they did not have measures of the actual degree of responsiveness of leaders, but only of their perceptions of citizen priorities for community problems, their agreement with citizens, and their degree of political and organizational activity. No measures of individual leader behavior were available, nor were there any objective measures of what the community actually did with reference to a high-priority problem.

Second, although Verba & Nie were aware of the theoretical possibility that leaders can shape citizen perceptions and preferences, they assumed throughout almost all of their analysis that the reverse is true, and in fact said that their data are consistent with either interpretation (p. 304). Given the heavy stress laid upon status or class factors in participation, however, it would seem equally as justified for them to have interpreted the data in terms of leadership influence over citizens rather than citizen influence over leaders.

Two findings were cited to support their assumption. First, a higher correlation was found between citizen activity and concurrence than between leader activity and concurrence (p. 332). Their assumption was that citizen activity is the significant causal factor leading to concurrence because of the higher correlation. This interpretation has two problems: 1. It assumes that a high correlation is evidence of time order. 2. The correlations cannot be compared in that way, because the leaders were selected initially for their high activity. The procedure used to reach this finding converted a characteristic (activity), which had already been used to stratify the sample, into a variable, and then measured internal differences in the values of that variable. The two levels of "activeness" (leaders and citizens) thus cannot be compared, and the lower correlations of leader activity and concurrence may be an artifact of the lower variance in activity among the leaders when placed on the same range of comparison with citizens.

A second finding was cited to support the interpretation that citizens influence leaders.

> The leadership characteristic that relates most strongly to concurrence is a measure of how positively leaders evaluate *citizen* interest and concern with community affairs—a result consistent with our emphasis on the positive impact of participation. [p. 332]

This interpretation is simply a gesture of confidence in the good faith and sincerity of leaders. An opposing and equally plausible interpretation is that those leaders who positively evaluated citizen interest were the persons most successful in winning over supporters to their own position.

All of those findings can be interpreted consistently with Verba & Nie's own major findings if participation is regarded as a mechanism of social control over the electorate, rather than as a form of influence over leadership. Concurrence may be a result of the penetration of ideologies of dominant interests into the electorate. If so, concurrence would indeed be highest in communities where participation in conventional political institutions (elections, campaigns, voting) is highest. Where activists among the electorate agree with nonactivists, the correlation of participation and concurrence was found to be highest, which may mean, contrary to Verba & Nie, that activist opinions are channels of influence of leader opinion to the electorate, not vice versa. If there is no intervening layer of activists who agree with leaders (i.e. if consensus is low), there is little such penetration of leader ideologies to citizens, regardless of the level of participation. It would be interesting to know how much actual political conflict there is in such nonconcurrent, nonconsensual, but highly active communities, and over what issues. But in any case empirical measures of the degree of agreement (concurrence) between leaders and citizens on issues have not been shown to be adequate measures of the responsiveness of leaders to citizens, and thus the importance of political participation as an instrument of power for citizens is still not shown.

The poor, the less educated, and those in working-class occupations are those who are most affected by state policies (they pay higher proportions of their income in taxes, are most likely to be on welfare or in prison, are subject to sanctions by various agencies, and pay most for the education of their children); they also are most dependent on the state (for unemployment insurance, health insurance, public transportation, home loans at reasonable rates, and so forth). They should be the most active in attempts to influence public policy and the structure of government, but in fact are the least active.

It is interesting that the correlation of class and participation is not really a problem for the dominant pluralist view of American democracy. Some assume that political participation is an individual decision and that most individuals, regardless of their social status, are not political animals (Dahl 1961:225). Or there are explanations that rely on the distinctive properties of a lower-class culture. Almond & Verba, summarizing the results of their comparative study of the United States, Great Britain, Italy, West Germany, and Mexico, said that "in all five countries the less educated strata of the population tend to constitute subject and parochial subcultures," rather than participant ones (1963:386). Dahl added that in the subculture of the wage earner and others of lower social standing, familiarity with politics and people who move in political circles is decidedly less than it is among higher social strata, even when differences in education are taken into account. [1961:233]

Inkeles, in a study of six developing countries (Argentina, Chile, India, Israel, Nigeria, and East Pakistan), referred to the lower "modernity" of the less educated (1969:1132).

We cannot here review all of the explanations offered in terms of individual, subcultural, or class characteristics, but can only observe that the unit of analysis is the individual, and that the explanatory variables are either at the individual level or in terms of group or class characteristics. In contrast, we argue that at least as fruitful an explanation can be sought in the structuring of the political institutions in which participation occurs and in the functioning of those institutions to limit challenges to class inequalities.

To summarize, a nearly universal although varying relationship between individual status or class, however measured, and political participation, however measured, has been found. The leading question is now why? The rest of this chapter is devoted to an analysis of the empirical literature on political participation that bears on the answers to this question.

ELECTORAL PARTICIPATION WITHOUT POWER

While various analysts have noted the relatively low level of electoral participation in the United States, particularly among lower-status individuals, this has been taken to be nonproblematic for democratic values. It has been variously argued that low political participation is functionally necessary to insulate leaders and insure system capacities for action (Berelson, Lazarsfeld & McPhee 1954, Kornhauser 1959) or that high participation is democratically unnecessary where there is party competition for votes combined with procedural norms that permit potential mass participation (Dahl 1961:164, Almond & Verba 1963: Chapter 15).

Such views, however, are inconsistent with an assumption implicit in most studies of class and racial voting (Alford 1963, Lipset 1960, Hamilton 1972, Verba & Nie 1972), in most studies of political development (Rokkan 1970, Kahl 1968, Lipset & Rokkan 1967), and in most analyses of American power structure (Dahl 1961, Rose 1967, Polsby 1963, Aiken & Alford 1974). This assumption is that partisan party competition and high levels of electoral participation would increase the extent of popular control over public policy and contribute to policy innovation.

Comparative case studies of state politics in particular suggested that partisan party competition and voter participation compelled the elected elites to show higher levels of responsiveness to the populace, and in particular to lower-status groups (Key 1949, 1956, Fenton 1966, Lockard 1959). However, a later series of quantitative comparative studies of state and city politics indicated that electoral and legislative politics did not effectively control public policy. When controls were made for relevant economic variables such as industrialization, income levels, and urbanization, electoral variables such as turnout and party competition were rarely significant or powerful predictors of (a) the level of spending, whether the total, broad functional categories, or specific programs, (b) the progressiveness of the tax structure, or (c) the level of policy innovation. A recent review of comparative urban politics research provides the basis for a similar conclusion for Western Europe (Fried 1975).

In *Understanding Public Policy* (1972) Dye analyzed the impact of electoral and environmental economic variables on a series of taxation and expenditure-based output measures. In general, he found that voter turnout, Democratic control of the state government, interparty competition, and the extent of malapportionment had little effect compared to that of such economic variables as urbanization, industrialization, levels of wealth, and education. Using partial correlations, he found that controls for economic variables eliminated the moderate bivariate correlations between electoral characteristics and state outputs (p. 263) such as per capita welfare expenditures, unemployment benefits, and level of taxation.

However, comparative research on the extent of electoral control of public policy has been methodologically and theoretically deficient in a variety of ways. First, comparative studies have not used available methodologies that allow appropriate statistical representation of their theoretical models. For example, some investigations have used partial correlations based on symmetrical associations to "test" causal models, where asymmetrical techniques such as regression analysis allowing estimation of causal effects would have been more appropriate [for examples of correlational estimation of causal effects, see Dawson & Robinson (1963), Cnudde & McCrone (1969)]. Further, such research has confined itself to single-equation models to estimate coefficients for models that theoretically require multiequation model specification, in order that both direct and indirect effects on outputs can be estimated. This point is particularly relevant to the ongoing discussion about whether or not political development mediates the effects of economic development (Jackman 1974, Dawson 1967, Cnudde & McCrone 1969, Dye 1972). The assignment of partial correlation coefficients to causal paths is a misrepresentation of the path analytic schema (except in the two-variable case). The comparison of relative reductions in regression coefficients by alternative stepwise ordering of variable entry (Dye 1972, Cnudde & McCrone 1969) is incorrect, considering that the implicit assumption of orthogonality among regressors is highly dubious. Given the availability of causal modeling techniques that use structural equations to model both recursive and nonrecursive processes, a tighter fit between technique and theory is possible [for models with reciprocal causation, see Blalock (1971) and Goldberger & Duncan (1973)].

Second, the prediction of disaggregated program expenditures by electoral characteristics assumes the "systems" framework within which much comparative state and urban politics research has been carried out. Analyzing programs separately assumes that the state aggregates interests and responds relatively equally to all social groups, that expenditures are substantive responses to the needs or demands of specific social groups, and that the state as a totality is the aggregate of differentiated responses to a series of politically unconnected interests. The separate analysis of the determinants of different categories of expenditure (e.g. welfare, health, highways, industrial development) assumes their analytic equivalence as well as their analytic independence.

In our view the particular aggregation of interests in the structure of the state should not be assumed to be either functionally necessary or politically neutral. If the state mediates the political relationships between different interests, then the particular way in which the state aggregates those interests is an important component of the power relationships between interests. The "political system" (see Easton 1965) as an interacting set of subsystems must be analyzed as a totality in order to assess the possible substitutabilities among different categories of expenditure (e.g. military and welfare programs nationally, highways versus school expenditures at the state level), the potential opportunity costs of increased expenditures in any given direction, or the possible mutually stimulative effects of spending in different areas (e.g. FHA housing loans, highway expenditures, urban renewal). In a world of scarce fiscal resources, the ability of interests to secure expenditure increases in one area may constrain expenditures on programs critical to other interests.

A third problem with the comparative politics literature lies in the interpretation of the findings that levels of electoral participation rarely have strong or significant effects on redistributive expenditure levels. The empirical findings that nonvoters tend to be working-class poor (Verba & Nie 1972, Hamilton 1972:208) and that the poor favor governmental intervention in the economy to solve their personal economic problems (Verba & Nie 1972:273–277, Huber & Form 1973: Chapter 8) are quite clear. These findings suggest *not* that participation has no effect on welfare expenditure levels, for example, but that the participation of lower-income people who are more likely to hold liberal, pro-welfare state, pro-state redistribution views does not affect such expenditure levels.

A fourth problem is with the use of gross expenditure data to operationalize outputs or policy. Not only have a variety of empirical studies shown the absence of a relationship between level of expenditure and the nature or impact of services, but rarely has there been any substantive analysis of the consequences of particular program expenditures for different interests (Sharkansky 1967b). Dye (1966) found no relationship between educational expenditures and drop-out or mental failure rates. Forrester (1972) found a low relationship between urban performance and expenditures (see also Bahl 1969a, Boaden 1971, Davies 1968). In a time-series analysis attempting to specify empirically the existence of feedback in a state political system, Grumm (1972) found no impact of outputs on the environment and therefore no feedback effects.

> In the normal course of events, the slight effects of outputs on the environment are not,
> fed back as information about increased or reduced tensions to the legislature. In effect,
> the feedback process appears to be inoperative most of the time. [p. 285]

Most literature in comparative state and urban politics is deficient in this respect. For example, the seminal work on "public regarding ethos" by Wilson & Banfield (1964) gives us no criteria by which expenditure categories can be judged to serve public as opposed to particularistic interests. Comparative urban research on the decision-making structure (Clark 1974, Aiken 1970) or on community mobilization

(Aiken & Alford 1974) is almost devoid of any reference to the impact a given program might have on particular interests, and thus to what participants in the decision-making process might stand to lose or gain from a particular decision.

Edelman's (1964, 1971) work on symbolic politics and Alford's (1975) on health planning both suggest that the level of spending may indicate only the power of dominant interests to prevent effective government responses to social needs. There have been two types of attempts to overcome these difficulties: comparative studies using sophisticated redistributive effect measures and studies of the congruence between electoral preferences and legislative attitudes and behavior.

First is the actual redistributional effect of state spending on low-income families. Fry & Winters (1970) first attempted to assess the political impact of mass political variables (e.g. participation, Democratic vote, and interparty competition) on the net redistributive effect of revenues and expenditures. They used the ratio of expenditure benefits to revenue burdens for the three lowest-income deciles in each state. However, as Booms & Halldorson (1973) later pointed out, Fry & Winters used bases of allocation for state expenditures and revenues based on a national distribution of families by income class. Booms & Halldorson reformulated the redistribution index based on state-specific class structures and found that while interparty competition and Democratic vote did not have an appreciable independent effect, political participation did, but that socioeconomic variables had a greater independent effect.

Such measures of redistribution are biased in a progressive direction, however. For example, the basis of allocation used for highway expenditure and motor vehicle tax revenue by income class was the percentage of all automobile expenditures in the state accounted for by that income class. Thus, if an income class accounted for ten percent of all expenditures on automobile operation, they were allocated ten percent of the burden for motor vehicle taxation. However, the relative progressiveness or regressiveness of different tax forms does not enter the redistributive index, and we know that the degree of regressiveness of taxation varies from state to state. In addition, the bases of allocation assume existing inequalities in access to material goods that are reflected in class inequalities in expenditure patterns: many lower-income families do not have cars at all, and expenditures for highways restrict the ability of the state or city to build public transportation systems. It is assumed that expenditures are allocated equitably in terms of access and quality by class. Thus the basis of allocation for elementary and secondary education expenditures in the state is the number of children under 18 in a given income class. Educational expenditures vary by municipality, and these variations are associated with the class composition of city residents (Hill 1974). Further, even within a given state or city there are inequalities in the distributional impact of expenditures or income transfers. The differential impact of highway expenditures on the fiscal burdens of middle-class suburbanites as opposed to poorer central city residents is not reflected in the redistributional index (Bowles 1972, Bonnen 1969). Consequent patterns of metropolitan locations may impose high levels of social cost expenditures on the central city that must be generated from a lower fiscal capacity, which means higher tax rates for lower-income families.

Second is legislative responsiveness to electoral preferences. Considerable legislator autonomy, if not explicit opposition to popular pressures, has been found. In an analysis of the roll call votes of 116 Representatives and a sample of their constituents' policy preferences, Miller & Stokes (1963) found that the correlation was only .4. Analyzing the extent of congruence between electoral opinion and state policy in the area of state lotteries, capital punishment, right-to-work laws, public accommodation laws, and gun control, Munger & Mezey (1968) found that electoral competition and participation had no effect on opinion-policy congruence. Munger (1969) later found that in such redistributive policy areas as antidiscrimination laws and right-to-work laws, 34 and 31 states respectively had majorities favoring these policies, yet only 2 and 17 states respectively had such statutes. Rose (1973:1168) reanalyzed the same data to find cases in which state opinion differed from national opinion. He found that contra-national state opinions agreed with state law only 37 percent of the time. Shaffer & Weber (1972) found that changes in policy preferences had no effect on policy responsiveness, if not a negative effect (in the areas of firearms control, police and teacher unionization, and right-to-work laws). Further, they found that changes in opinion were more likely to be due to accommodation to an existent law than vice versa ("greater responsiveness was produced by the citizenry changing its opinion to conform with existing public policy," p. 40). Finally, Jones (1973) analyzed Texas state legislator roll call behavior and concluded that

> the over-all impression one gets from the data is that there is little connection between the policy activity of the typical Texas representative and the policy attitudes of his constituency through the mechanism of responsiveness. [p. 933]

In fact, Jones found that party competition in a legislative district was associated with legislative opposition to constituent preferences. This is particularly so in the area of consumer taxation.

> The finding that legislators from competitive districts are least responsive ... on the intense, salient issue of taxing the consumer is most ironic. The electoral accountability model would predict most responsiveness on issues which are salient and which tend to mobilize large groups of constituents such as consumers. That legislators from marginal districts not only ignore their constituents' policy attitudes but actually consciously vote in opposition to them is difficult to accept. It is more likely that some unidentified factor is distorting the relations in the model. [p. 938]

Jones noted that "the leadership was often in agreement with business-interest groups, and such groups were especially active on the issue of taxation" (p. 938). Similar findings for the Congressional level are analyzed by Miller (1964).

If elected officials are not responsive to their mass constituencies, there is evidence of responsiveness to dominant economic interests. Wahlke et al (1960:190), in a study of state legislators in four states, identified a "facilitative role orientation" toward interest groups. Further, there were over six times (81 to 13) more pro-business "facilitators" than pro-labor "facilitators" (p. 197).

Data on Congressional roll-call voting and committee assignment suggest that state dependence on military spending is a strong predictor of Senator support for large military budgets and of Congressional committee assignment (Clotfelter 1970, Lieberson 1971). The policy success of dominant economic interests in legislative politics has been suggested by a variety of studies. Francis (1967), in his comparative study of state legislatures, found that interest-group conflict was common (p. 71) and that it was negatively associated with partisan conflict (p. 46). While organized labor and business were important interest groups in most issue areas (e.g. p. 43) and both business and labor issues involved high levels of pressure-group conflict (p. 49), policies vis-à-vis organized labor were more likely to be dealt with in partisan conflict (p. 24) whereas policies vis-à-vis business were more likely to be factional conflicts. That the partisan politicization on an issue indicates the relative powerlessness of an interest group is suggested by the high level of policy success (as measured by legislator perceptions) by business interests, and the low level of policy success by labor interests (p. 70). Zeigler (1965), reviewing the structure of lobbying, observed that "no matter what kind of economy enjoyed by the state, the businesses dominate the *numerical* structure of lobbying" (p. 109).

If electoral politics does not control the structure of expenditures and taxation, legislator voting patterns, or legislative policy, and if dominant economic interests do exercise control, then political participation by lower-status individuals may be an effective form of social control, not a cause of political power. Here we must again take up the recent major study by Verba & Nie (1972). In contrast to other work on elected officials' responsiveness to their electoral constituencies, they provide seemingly optimistic conclusions (see also Hansen 1973).

Using 1967 survey data for 65 communities with populations under 50,000 on elected and nonelected leader and citizen issues, priorities, and policy preferences, Verba & Nie found that increased aggregate political participation increased leader-citizen concurrence (pp. 313, 317). When high voting levels created generalized pressure for responsiveness, other forms of electoral and nonelectoral participation were particularly effective in securing high levels of leader-citizen concurrence (p. 327). For lower-status persons the frequency of contested elections, electoral competition, partisanship of elections, and strength of political parties are all positively correlated with low-status citizen/leader concurrence (Hansen 1973: Table 7). Little statistical association was found for the high-status citizens. Given previously mentioned class differences in policy positions and issue priorities, this suggests that electoral politics depoliticizes class conflict and brings lower-status individuals into the American ideological consensus (Lipset 1963). For if there is ideological class conflict, then increases in working-class concurrence should be associated with decreases in upper-class concurrence, or at least upper-class concurrence should not be independent of the extent of electoral competition.

Further evidence for this proposition is that people who confine their political activity to voting ("voting specialists") have higher than average partisanship (Verba & Nie 1972:88), yet are much less likely to be involved in community conflict (people were asked if there was conflict in the community and whether or not they took a side in such conflicts). This suggests that, contrary to Lipset's theory of the "democratic class struggle" (Lipset 1960: Chapter 7), electoral politics does not necessarily politicize actual or potential conflict.

Verba & Nie also developed a "consensus" measure for the policy preferences of the politically active and nonactive citizenry; given the high association of class and participation, this measure can be used as an indicator of "interclass consensus." They found that in low-consensus communities, the association of class status and participation was particularly high (pp. 320–22). In such low-consensus communities, the level of political participation had no effect on the level of citizen-leader concurrence (pp. 320–22). They came to this conclusion:

> Where there is a high level of agreement among citizens, the segment of the population that participates can speak for the entire community, and concurrence goes up monotonically. Where the active segment of the community does not speak for the whole community—where there is little agreement between the activists and the rest of the citizenry—participation does not lead to greater leader concurrence with the citizenry. [pp. 320–21]

And with respect to the lower participation of low-status persons in low-consensus communities,

> The point is that where the socioeconomic model works most strongly, the largest differences in preferences between the participants and the rest of the population appear *simply because the former come more heavily from upper-status groups.* [p. 322, italics added]

Given the finding that interclass consensus is highest in partisan communities with frequently contested elections (Hansen 1973:24) and that partisan electoral politics does not politicize community conflict (Verba & Nie 1972:88), the particularly low participation of lower-class people under conditions of low consensus should not be regarded as a cause of low concurrence, but as a rational adaptation and thus a consequence of the inability of electoral politics to represent cleavages in the community.

This is also supported by the lack of a sense of efficacy felt by those lower-class individuals who do vote, the "voting specialists" (p. 88). Another interpretation of the particularly low participation of low-status people under conditions of low consensus is that political elites will mobilize lower-status persons only where major cleavages are not manifest, because they would otherwise threaten consensual two-party electoral strategies or politically important dominant interests. Reviewing an attempt at community organization in Newark, Parenti (1970) notes the following:

> Many "non-decisions" are really decisions of a sort, specifically to avoid or prevent the emergence of a particular course of action. Much of the behavior of Newark's officials can be seen as a kind of "politics of prevention," to use Harold Lasswell's term, a series of decisions designed to limit the area of issue conflict. More extensive study of the attitudes, actions, and inactions of municipal authorities toward lower-strata claims might reveal a startling number of instances in which office-holders avoid politically difficult responses to lower-class pressures. [p. 521]

A social control interpretation of electoral politics also suggests itself because one would expect low-status individuals to participate *more* under conditions of low consensus. This would seem to be the assumption of those who assume the potential power of a normally quiescent and nonparticipant electorate (Dahl 1961, Almond & Verba 1963). The important findings of the Verba & Nie study, when linked to those summarized in this section, cast doubt on the significance of electoral politics as a powerful form of political participation.

POWER WITHOUT PARTICIPATION

If the character of electoral politics has rarely been found to be strongly associated with the structure of public expenditures, studies have found "environmental" economic characteristics to be a consistent correlate of city, state, and national variations in expenditure patterns. Besides the already-cited studies that found electoral factors to be weak predictors, see Fabricant (1952), Hofferbert (1971, 1972), Schumaker (1974), Sacks & Harris (1964), and Dye (1972). The dominant tendency has been to treat the level of economic development as an exogenous, nonpolitical determinant of political development through its resource or technocratic constraints. The statement by Hollingsworth (1973) is typical:

> While there were considerable variations in public policy, the substance of policy over time . . . was moving in the same direction—especially in the areas of education and public health. As technology became increasingly complex, the range of problems confronting elected officials, particularly in these two policy areas, required such specialized training that decision making slowly became removed from the electorate and concentrated in the hands of professionals with appointments in municipal bureaucracies. For the most part it was similarity in economic growth that underlay such policy likeness. [pp. 31–32]

The relationship between economic development and the structure of expenditures and revenues should, we believe, be regarded as a political relationship by which dominant economic interests are able to use their economic power to constrain the structure of state outputs. The fiscal capacity of all units of government is contingent upon the locational, production, and investment decisions of increasingly concentrated corporations. Given their frequently superior financial resources, especially when compared to cities and states, and their locational flexibility, corporations present a constant constraint on city, state, and even national attempts to increase tax rates, to change the tax structure, or to cut back on the subsidies available to corporations in other political units. Thus the absence of corporate participation in political decision making does not indicate the extent of corporate systemic power.

The debate regarding the "bifurcation of power" (Schulze 1961) in urban communities, a debate that relied exclusively on participational indicators of corporate political power, thus only scratched the surface. Since both fiscal capacity and public spending are contingent upon corporate growth and reinvestment, governments encourage the political participation of owners and executives in order to assure the development of policies favorable to a "good business climate" (Dahl 1961:131). Thus Dahl pointed out that New Haven's big businessmen controlled the Board of Finance over the past three-fourths of a century despite their declining direct representation on the Board of Aldermen (pp. 81–83).

Given that the fiscal viability of state programs is contingent upon their impact on the dominant economic interests and because the power of those interests is not necessarily contingent upon their political participation, it is not surprising to find that the state often organizes their political participation. Thus the participation of those interests in the state can be interpreted as a consequence, not a cause of their power.

The considerable autonomy of local and state governments in the United States to raise and allocate their own fiscal resources, in particular via the fragmentation of municipal political units, has increased the power of nationally organized corporate interests. The inability of fragmented political units to control the locational decisions of corporate capital or high-income residences, the absence of uniform urban or state policies, and heavy reliance on property taxation (Netzer 1966:12) have produced intercity and interstate competition to attract high tax yield businesses and residences (see Alyea 1967).

Dominant economic interests have consequently been able to prevent any change in the tax structure and insulate local and state (and federal; see below) tax systems from electoral challenge. Penniman (1965) demonstrated that state political characteristics were not related to the progressiveness of the tax structure. Thus Democratic strength and party competition were not related to the extent of reliance on a more regressive sales tax or a less regressive personal income tax. As she noted, "major economic interests usually have the political strength to influence legislators to withstand proposals of heavy taxation" (p. 320). The active political participation of corporate elites in preventing more progressive taxation has also been found by Fisher (1969:178–79) and Lockard (1959:79).

Thus, state and local expenditures, where the financing of the most general public services and of the most direct forms of collective consumption (Castells 1972) is concentrated, have been increasingly financed out of regressive forms of taxation. State and local expenditures rely on property, income, and sales taxes that studies have found to be variably regressive (Penniman 1965, Barlow 1974). At the state and local levels, Penniman has argued that the income tax is the only potentially progressive element in the tax structure. Yet she argues that

> where states closely follow the federal pattern of deductions, exemptions, and special provisions and further allow deductions of the federal income tax, the net impact of the income tax is likely to be low. [p. 306]

Thus the relationship between economic development and expenditure can be regarded as the political consequence of the high level of systemic power accorded to dominant economic interests in a decentralized, fragmented, and tax-dependent federal government structure.

The fiscal relationship between the state and economy is an aspect of state structure that maximizes the systemic power of dominant economic interests. As long as state revenues depend on taxes, the autonomy of the state is limited by the necessity to avoid any policies that impinge upon capital accumulation and growth. And to the extent that growth and thus fiscal capacity depend on continued private control of investment, production, and location decisions, issues will not be raised nor policies legislated that impinge upon that control. Crenson's (1971) important study of urban air pollution has empirically demonstrated the nondecisional power exercised by a single corporation.

Economist James O'Connor, from whose recent work on state finance (1973) the following points are derived, has argued that dominant economic interests want to assure the continued dependency of the state on tax revenues and debt financing, "to reduce the possibility that a popular government would reorder the allocation of material resources" (p. 180). While there are few technical barriers to nationalization as an alternative to state debt and nonprogressive taxation, this development has not occurred in the United States, and its effectiveness has been limited in Europe. The means used have included legal prohibitions on the use of equity financing of state enterprise, and confinement of state enterprise to backward infrastructural industries (the postal service and—potentially—the railroads in the United States) or to temporary support for technologically or competitively uncertain industries (e.g. nuclear fuel production).

During the nineteenth century, United States courts prohibited the use of tax revenues for state enterprise. While city governments could increase their fiscal capacity through utility ownership, "powerful forces seek to keep the utilities in private hands or to prevent them from generating surpluses should they fall to the state" (O'Connor 1973:182).

The political consequences of the systemic power of capital, reinforced through capital control of state debt financing, are manifold, and only a few examples can be given. At the national level the unwillingness of capital under inflationary conditions to increase its holdings in long-term federal bonds has forced the Treasury to rely on short-term bills and special-issue internal financing (the average length of bill was eight years in 1950 and was down to five years in 1963). Such short-term and special-issue financing of federal debt is more liquid and thus more inflationary. Inflationary state finance pushes up interest rates and thus increases the state debt servicing costs.

At the state and local levels, capital control of finance and budget is more stringent. Banks and other financial institutions control state and municipal securities. The relatively small number of institutional government securities buyers and bond underwriters are able to exact high interest rates and impose restrictive conditions on the use of state revenues. Bond financing is thus biased in the direction of those social capital projects that are self-liquidating and that expand the tax base by stimulating or subsidizing private investment (e.g. airport bonds, industrial revenue bonds, urban renewal). Controls are exercised by investors who avoid bond investments that they consider beyond the proper scope of government, by controls over the state or city credit ratings, or by screening of major capital projects by ad hoc business committees before bond referenda. Popular control over state and local finance is potentially exercised through referenda on general obligation bond requirements. However, such popular controls have increasingly been limited by the increase in self-financing revenue bonds that do not require such electoral ratification (Bollens & Schmandt 1970).

These few examples illustrate the ways in which economic processes not under the control of the state limit the impact of "normal" forms of political participation upon state outputs. If political participation is regarded as an end in itself or as an object of analysis without regard for its societal context, the critical importance of power without participation will not be apparent. The ability to shape issues and constrain policy by determining the conditions of functioning for a nominally representative state apparatus is the essence of systemic power: power without participation.

POWER WITH PARTICIPATION

The comparative "outputs" literature has shown that various measures of legislative and electoral politics rarely influence public expenditures and thus, as we interpret the findings, that the state is not accessible to these mechanisms of political participation. Also, the state maximizes the political impact of economic power, as inferred from the impact of economic development on public expenditures. None of these studies, however, deals with the intervening causal mechanisms or with the historical processes that lead to different levels and types of public expenditures. Several studies of budgeting at city, state, and federal levels have shown the incremental way in which such expenditures grow. This growth is apparently a result of the increasing autonomy of bureaucratic agencies to assure their continued funding, thereby preventing political reordering of expenditure priorities. The implicit assumption of the comparative state and city output literature was that increased spending was a substantive response to the level of electoral or popular demand. If in fact the best predictor of an agency's budget this year is its budget last year, across all agencies, then one must assume either an historical invariance in the preferences of the electorate, or the insulation of agency growth and spending from electoral control.

Levels of previous expenditure for a given agency or program have been found to be the strongest predictor of current expenditures, even controlling for economic and political characteristics. Thus Sharkansky's (1967a) study of state programs found that the expenditure level five years earlier eliminates the effect of current income levels, population size, level of federal aid, and revenue levels. Similar findings have been generated from city, state, and national data (Cowart 1969, Davis, Dempster & Wildavsky 1966, Fenno 1966, Meltsner 1971, Peacock & Wiseman 1961, Sharkansky 1970, Wildavsky 1964). The same is true even though periods of political and social cataclysm intervene. Fried (1974), reacting to the fact that fifty percent of the variance in West German cities can be predicted by city spending level in 1928, noted the following:

> While it is perhaps not so surprising to find evidence for the incrementalist theory of budgeting in the politically stable American states, it is surprising to find it in urban institutions that have undergone the upheavals of totalitarianism, mass terror, war, and foreign occupation. [p. 55]

If, as Domhoff (1967:42) has argued, the tax structure is a highly sensitive indicator of the power structure, then the barely incremental changes in the tax structure are an important indicator of a static balance of power between major class interests in the United States polity. In the area of taxation Dye (1972) argued that since the 1913 adoption of the Sixteenth Amendment permitting the use of federal income tax, there have been no comprehensive changes in federal tax laws, despite frequent political demands for "tax reform."

> Instead, tax policy has been characterized by a gradual accretion of decisions, most of which have resulted in a reduction in progressivity. . . . Almost ritualistically, Congressmen and Presidents have pledged to eliminate "loopholes" and "reform" the tax structure. Yet every major effort to do so has failed. [pp. 221–23]

Such incremental budget processes have been explained mainly by the conservative decision-making rules used by governmental officials, rules that are nonideological and nonprogrammatic given the politically and the fiscally complex and uncertain nature of budgeting. Decision makers have limited knowledge and time to consider the budget as a whole, and thus use simplifying rules that accept the previous structure of expenditures as a framework by which to judge current appropriations requests.

The incrementalist literature has made methodological errors, however, in failing to work with structural equations with relevant independent variables at all time points under consideration. These methodological deficiencies have potential theoretical implications. The extent of correlation of error across time in the dependent variable (the residual correlation across time) represents the extent to which variables related to the residual at different points in time have been left out of the model. Thus the supposedly incrementalist relationship between present and past expenditure levels may be inflated because of the omission of important variables that may account for the probable correlation of error across time (Hibbs 1974). Further, there are possibilities of lagged direct effects between relevant independent or dependent variables across time.

These incrementalist models have thus been specified in a way that omits important structural and political aspects of the American polity. "Habits" or "decision-making rules" are, we believe, only proximate causes of a phenomenon rooted deeply in the structure of the American political economy. Control over both policy formation and expenditures has increasingly devolved to nonlegislative agencies independent of electoral control, which has allowed dominant interests continuously privileged access to the state and the process of political allocation. Insulated, bureaucratized politics have continuously reproduced a highly limited structure of expenditure and revenue.

Both in the United States and in Europe, the parliamentary determination of policy has declined as policy making has devolved to increasingly autonomous bureaucratic agencies. In the United States the conditions for agency autonomy at the federal level include the absence of cohesive, nationally organized political parties, particularized political support by congressmen through the committee system, and the relatively superior professional expertise and long tenure of the congressional committees and elites relative to the executive when compared to other Western parliamentary-executive relationships. The increasingly complex and technical nature of government policy, due in part to the increasing interpenetration of the state and the economy, also helps to account for bureaucratic autonomy. This devolution of power has been treated by most pluralist analyses with a lack of alarm. A number of democratic benefits are said to flow from such a restructuring of political authority: interest-group elites are not cohesive, multiple points of access block gross injustice, and agency competition substitutes for political party competition.

Yet there have been few studies of the impact of bureaucratic elites on decision making. Jacob & Lipsky (1968), in a review of the comparative state politics literature, wrote that such studies have been confined to

case studies of isolated incidents and investigations of the social backgrounds of key personnel in state agencies. Even though it is generally recognized that most key decisions are initiated or made within executive agencies, the conditions under which they operate . . . remain unmapped. [p. 523]

Similarly there have been few studies of bureaucratic implementation (Pressman & Wildavsky 1973: Appendix 2), of the impact of agencies on effective policy making, or of the participation of interest groups at the point of implementation. In general the study of group and organizational participation has been underdeveloped.

Sharpe (1973), in an incisive essay comparing American and British theoretical traditions, characterized the dominant perspective.

The tradition also sees divided government always as a positive good as well. Thus a federal system is more democratic than a unitary system. Divided government is not only preferable as between horizontal levels, but also within each level; and not only does division itself promote democracy but it also promotes competition between the divided elements of each level. This competition also safeguards democracy by never allowing one agency to dominate, each checking and balancing the other. [p. 135]

Sharpe goes on to argue that this American "populist" or "interest group liberal" tradition has simply assumed the responsiveness of government, while failing to consider the ways in which the fragmentation of political authority impedes government's capacity to act. The consequence is a structural bias against large, heterogeneous social groups with limited political resources. Fragmentation of policy making encourages policies favorable to particularized private interests rather than socialized collective interests.

Accordingly, the devolution of political power into autonomous bureaucratic agencies has increased the penetration of specialized dominant interests into the state, facilitating the private control of public power in a manner that has depoliticized decision making and allocation and has insulated it from partisan electoral controls.

Private enterprise has had some striking successes in actually capturing a number of enclaves inside the structure of the Federal government. . . . The combination of Congressional pressures and the spontaneous desire of Bureau and Agency chiefs to live on terms of amity with their "constituents" has secured for a number of important interest groups a powerful influence over the decisions taken by the authorities charged with the supervision of their affairs. [Shonfield 1965:334–35]

McConnell adds the following:

What emerges as the most important reality is an array of relatively separated political systems, each with a number of elements. These typically include: (1) a federal administrative agency within the executive branch; (2) a heavily committed group of Congressmen and Senators, usually members of a particular committee or subcommittee; (3) a private (or quasi-private) association representing the agency clientele; (4) a quite homogeneous constituency usually composed of local elites. Where dramatic conflicts over policy have occurred, they have appeared as rivalries among public administrative agencies, but the conflicts are more conspicuous and less important than the agreements among these systems. The most frequent solution to conflict is jurisdictional demarcation and establishment of spheres of influence. Logrolling, rather than compromise, is the normal pattern of relationship. [1966:244]

The independence of bureaucratic agencies at all levels of government, their penetration by dominant interests, and the consequent inability of either executives or legislatures to control budgetary priorities, have been recurrently discussed (Anton 1966, O'Connor 1973). Sharkansky pointed to a lack of legislative control over appropriations due to agency autonomy and made the following argument:

Chief executives and legislators have surrendered much of their potential for innovation for a more limited role as reviewers of administrators' requests. [1969:111]

The ability of interests to institutionalize expenditure priorities and insulate them from political challenge through "earmarking" has also been documented. In 20 states over half of all state taxes are earmarked (O'Connor 1973:88).

As the economy has become dependent on state intervention, policy making has been decentralized into autonomous state bureaucracies. But precisely because of this increased reciprocal dependency of state and economy, economic elite participation has been relatively noncontentious and, from the point of view of the bureaucratic elite, politically and functionally necessary. As state agencies have become more autonomous, they have become more dependent on the interest groups to whom their policy is directed. Such interests become major political constituents, in the agency competition for limited fiscal resources and for legislative renewal. Agency competition has increased interest-group power. Direct agency access to the interest groups that control those strategic resources upon which the nature and success of their programs are dependent is a source of agency autonomy from "political control."

Although elitist analyses have stressed the similar social class and ideological origins of interest-group and agency elites, the reverse is also true, assuming that the interest groups organize and use state power. The state organizes or reinforces the political participation of dominant interests because of their systemic power. Ehrmann in the following quotation refers to France, but we believe the process is very similar in the United States.

Either on their own initiative or prodded by the Ministry with which they have dealings, the groups will shape their organizational structure so as to resemble the institutions they wish to influence. The resulting parallelism between the structure of public administration and of interest groups does much to facilitate informal and continuous group access. [1971:336]

Similarly where no political organization of critical interest groups is available, the state will often create one.

> Where organs of consultation and cooperation are lacking, the administration will frequently create them. In all countries, especially in the wake of war-time or emergency controls, the need of the bureaucracy for contacts with groups has been stimulus for the organization of interests. Some of the large confederations . . . owe their existence to the initiative of the government. [p. 336]

The interest groups provide the agency with information, technical expertise, a career ladder for agency employees, and channels for the communication of policy. Further, dominant interest groups offer certain organizational characteristics that make them particularly attractive to bureaucratic elites. The specialized and intense nature of their interests, the magnitude of their politically relevant material and organizational resources, and the usually concentrated organizational field in which they operate, make dominant interest groups easily organized and a relatively reliable source of political support. "Economies of scale" influencing the agency search for a predictable political environment insure that those interests that are already or can most effectively be organized into a constituency will be structurally dominant.

Thus the bureaucratic structure reinforces the political power of those interests most easily or best organized, further militating against the possible access of those interests that are difficult to organize. While those social aggregates not located in the production process (e.g. consumers and patients) are difficult to organize politically, those social groups that are larger, more heterogeneous, with less specialized and thus less intense interests, and few resources, are not likely to secure effective access to agency decision making (Offe 1972). Certain groups and issues are thereby organized *out* of the political structure. Further, there are probably structural disincentives for political participation by all those groups who want to transform political priorities and allocation.

> The administration cannot fulfill its function as a mediating authority in regard to groups which give expression to fundamental discontents. Where the disruption of the consensus divides the community into armed camps, the bureaucracy risks being transformed into a battalion of one of the armies. [Ehrmann 1971:348]

The political domination of depoliticized agencies by specialized interest groups has meant that legislation is usually drafted with their active collaboration, thus reducing general partisan legislative conflict to reactive choices: passage, veto, or marginal amendment. Agencies do not regulate industry in the public interest, but mediate between the particularistic claims within the industry (Haveman & Hamrin 1973). Finally, even more generalized policy is delimited in its origins through research, specification of the politically relevant dimensions of "social problems," and drafting of actual model legislation, all carried out by corporate-controlled policy research groups such as the Committee on Economic Development, the Council on Foreign Relations, National Civic Federation, and Resources for the Future (Domhoff 1970). The explanation for the dominance of these groups lies in the poverty of party politics in the United States, the increasing independence and power of the executive vis-à-vis Congress, and the depoliticized nature of the symbiotic connections among interest groups, congressional committees, and federal agencies [for further case studies, see Haveman & Hamrin (1973)].

Pluralist analyses, in focusing on the point of legislative conflict (as the point where political elites respond to mass political participation), typically do not gauge the ways in which policy origins, initiation, legislative approval, administration, and implementation are structured so that different interests have differential power in the whole process of political production. The studies of lawmaking (Redman 1973, Rose 1967: Chapter 12) or of legislator-constituency attitudinal congruence (Miller & Stokes 1963) implicitly assume the point of legislative initiation and debate to be the point at which the most important decisions are made, political power can be best observed, and democratic responsiveness can be measured. Choosing this point of political production as the unit of analysis results in a pluralistic view of politics. Legislative battles are fought. Policies are introduced, defeated, passed, and amended. Party candidates point to their legislative records when wooing the voter. The League of Women Voters, the American Civil Liberties Union, and a host of interest groups collect roll-call vote records. The power and caliber of political elites is judged in this realm of normal pluralist politics.

As the historiography of "corporate liberalism" has argued, however, social groups are differentially powerful in the development and delimitation of policy and programmatic responses (Kolko 1963, Weinstein 1968, Radosh & Rothbard 1972). It is argued that preemptive policy development by these "corporate liberal" groups has thwarted the development of autonomously organized mass participation around issues that could otherwise lead to working-class challenges to political and economic domination by the interests of capital. Even if legislative voting and the structure of outcomes were responsive to constituency opinion (and the literature we have summarized calls this into question), analysis of participation at the point of policy origin and development suggests that policy alternatives were generated by a sharply delimited set of organized dominant interest groups. Although the legislative vote may sometimes be responsive within these confines, the development of policy is dominated by a few elites and is relatively impermeable to public or partisan accountability. Mass publics can participate only at those points of political production where the power of dominant interests is *not* located.

BUREAUCRATIC PARTICIPATION WITHOUT POWER

The major effort to develop federally sponsored instruments for the participation of the poor in new bureaucratic agencies independent of local government, although established with the machinery of elections, was the War on Poverty established by the Economic Opportunity Act of 1964. The various programs initiated under this Act, especially the Community Action Programs (CAPs), attempted to develop "maximum feasible participation" of the poor. These programs are the best recent example of bureaucratic participation *without* power: the political incorporation of leaders of the poor into administrative instruments using the ideology of "citizen participation" (Krause 1968). We cannot do justice to the enormous literature describing and analyzing the consequences of these programs, and have selected a few works reflecting different methodologies and theoretical perspectives. For histories and analyses of such programs at both national and local levels, as well as fuller bibliographies on this special topic, see Levitan (1969), Greenstone & Peterson (1973), Kramer (1969), Marshall (1971), and Piven & Cloward (1971).

Although these programs created representative bodies elected by poor neighborhoods, the level of voting participation was extremely low, ranging in the first year (which might be expected to be a period of relative optimism and thus participation) from one to five percent of those eligible. An analysis of Community Action Agency elections during OEOs first 18 months concluded that

> the lack of participation stemmed from absence of issues or constituencies, from the fact that there were few contestants with charisma to inspire a large turnout, and from general skepticism of the poor that the new program would be more successful than previous efforts had been. [summarized in Levitan 1969:114]

That such skepticism was warranted is indicated by the few studies of the impact of the participation of the poor in these programs in Chicago, New York, Philadelphia, Los Angeles, Baltimore, and Detroit. Most found little or no substantive impact of such participation, other than short-term benefits for the participants in the form of jobs and social mobility. The major effect was to integrate the poor—mainly black—communities into the political system.

Perhaps just as important, however, is the lack of serious comparative studies of the actual impact of such bureaucratic participation. The most recent empirical study of participants in such programs (Cole 1974) found, after a review of the literature, that

> despite the extensive number and variety of citizen participation programs which have been adopted in the past ten years, no study is available which attempts to systematically determine how effective these programs are in achieving either or both of these objectives [i.e. to improve the image of government and to improve services]. [p. 10]

Cole's data were derived from questionnaires filled out by 396 participants in 26 Midwest urban CAPs, Model Cities, or urban renewal programs; and from data given by city officials in 227 United States cities of over 50,000 population, regarding the presence, functions, and powers of neighborhood councils, "little city halls," and multiservice centers in their cities. These dimensions (number and powers) were collapsed into a single scale of citizen participation for each city.

Cole found that the SES of his 396 participant respondents was higher than that of their constituents in the community, and, in addition, that the more participatory the program, the more likely the active persons were to be of higher social class than their community (p. 97).

Using his respondents' own reports of the degree of their satisfaction "with the program's ability to achieve more satisfactory distribution of goods and services . . . from city hall" (p. 103), Cole found that most of the participants rated "their overall program and specific project attempts as successful" (p. 104). However, a curvilinear relation was found between the level of participation in the program and the degree of satisfaction. Programs in the middle of the participation scale were judged the most successful. Unfortunately, Cole had no data on the actual impact of the program on the "material rewards" to the community; but he postulated that such rewards actually produced the program satisfaction and improved trust in political leaders found by his interviews. If few material rewards in fact resulted, an hypothesis consistent with the findings of the other city case studies cited in this section, then participant trust probably derives from the symbolic gratification of participation itself (Lipsky 1970) or the selective bias of such programs for less disaffected community members. Thus, Cole's optimistic conclusions about the consequences of participation in such programs may not be warranted by his own data.

A few studies attempting to evaluate the impact of attempts to implement the "maximum feasible participation" clauses in the poverty program legislation began almost immediately after its passage in 1964. Five California communities (Berkeley, Contra Costa County, Oakland, San Francisco, and Santa Clara County) were studied from 1964 to 1968. Kramer (1969) summarized the impact of the programs on four "target systems": social service agencies, minority groups, the poor, and local government. Generally, participation was found to have had very little impact. With respect to the social service agencies,

> if one starts with the most ambitious goals of the CAP . . . one finds relatively little change in the basic orientation of health, education, and welfare agencies. . . . One of the very few instances of what might be described as a major shift in organizational mission as well as methodology occurred in the Legal Aid Society in Oakland and to a much lesser extent in the state department of employment, but in both cases, the changes were due less to the participation of the poor than to . . . persuasion through financial incentives. [p. 240]

With respect to the impact on local government,

> the effects on city politics of resident participation were . . . minimal. Although a new center of minority influence was established in each community, the CAP did not appear to disrupt the prevailing structure and balance of power in any significant way. [p. 257]

With respect to the impact on the poor,

> those who were employed in the CAP gained experience and skills and many of the CAP participants improved their understanding, but there was widespread recognition among both groups in all communities that the hard-core and unaffiliated poor had really not been reached, nor did they benefit in any substantial way from the programs and services of the war on poverty. [p. 256]

With respect to the impact of the CAPs upon minority groups, Kramer concluded that

> resident participation in the CAP may have provided the first major foothold for Negro and Mexican-American groups to gain control of an urban community decision-making center and the use of some social service and economic resources. [However,] so far it is an unexploited and underdeveloped political resource. [p. 250]

The conclusion, at least for these California cities, has to be that the mechanisms of citizen participation may have created a potential for future power; but this is an expression of the analyst's faith, not a prediction yet justified by evidence.

Summarizing the results of over 700 interviews with participants in economic development programs in communities within 13 states in 1967 and 1969, Sundquist (1969) dealt with the reasons that Community Action Agencies (CAAs) could not in fact mobilize and coordinate community activities on behalf of the poor, regardless of the level of their militancy or the quality of their leadership. "The federal government could not, and did not, confer any significant coordinating *power* upon the CAAs" (p. 47). Sundquist divided the CAAs into three types. The "respected" ones were "aggressive, even militant, but with a quality of leadership and administrative competence to match . . . their political strength, which rested upon the mobilization of the poor" (pp. 46–47). The "innocuous" ones and the "outcasts" were those that "had not been able to match their militancy with a leadership and competence that compelled respect. They were effectively contained, left to administer the programs financed from Washington but otherwise ignored or even shunned" (p. 47).

Sundquist emphasized that "*none* of these three types had potential as the community mobilizers and coordinators that were envisioned when the Economic Opportunity Act was passed" in 1964 (p. 47, italics added). He cited a number of examples of CAA-led or -encouraged citizen protests against official actions and even citizen initiatives. Sundquist added, however, that the community's "power structure" does have power, and "the force of its retaliation has been sufficient to cripple a number of community action agencies or, in at least a few rural cases, to disband them" (p. 65). In any case, they could not carry out any coordinating functions in the services to the poor.

One study of OEO-sponsored neighborhood centers concluded that "with a few exceptions the centers had not attempted to organize the poor and had failed to alter the political structure of their communities" (cited in Levitan 1969:130). Levitan, commenting on the absence of any serious studies of the impact of these participatory programs, concluded that "no meaningful summary judgment can be made about their effectiveness" (p. 131). He commented that "it is not at all surprising that OEO's modest efforts at involving the poor in the CAA's have brought more condemnation than praise" (p. 131).

Another study of a CAA in Los Angeles [the Economic and Youth Opportunities Agencies (EYOA) of Greater Los Angeles] in 1968 focused on the consequences of membership on the board for the attitudes of members, and did not deal with the impact of the agency's programs on the target population. The main conclusion, based on interviews with 32 members, poor and nonpoor, was that "community representatives on the EYOA were co-opted. They did not gain power over the decisions made by the board, or diminish the public agencies' predominant influence on the board" (p. 141). The effect on individuals was "somewhat different": their "level of participation in the political system was raised" (Marshall 1971:141). Marshall found that poor participants learned greater self-confidence as leaders and greater organizational skills and information without losing their "dissatisfaction with established patterns of dealing with poverty and their interest in faster change" (p. 141). "Experience on the board gives the community representatives more skill, confidence, and involvement without eliminating their poverty perspective" (p. 142). Increases in feelings of efficacy were accompanied not by more positive feelings by the community representatives toward the CAA, but by more negative ones (p. 144). Based on this consequence, Marshall argued that "some participation is better than no participation," because leadership is being created for future struggles (p. 142). This political evaluation is not inconsistent with her substantive conclusion that the presence of the poor on the CAA board had basically no effect.

Another major study of CAPs in five large cities (Chicago, Philadelphia, Los Angeles, Detroit, and New York) was begun in June 1965; field interviews with over 300 participants in the five cities and in Washington DC were concluded by August 1968 (Greenstone & Peterson 1973). Although the research may have been conducted too soon really to assess the impact of the programs, the authors came to fairly definite conclusions.

> At the most apparent level, OEO was hardly more successful in attacking political poverty [lack of channels of political participation for the poor] than it was in alleviating economic poverty. To be sure, in two of our five cities some power redistribution occurred as low-income and minority groups gained representation on city and neighborhood poverty councils and managed to influence the operations of various governmental bureaucracies. Yet in most places OEO had to settle for little more than formal representation of the poor on local boards and agencies. In the decentralized American political system, the impact of federal policy can be blunted by established local elites, political, economic, and bureaucratic, unless the latter are themselves committed to its program. OEO's own grass roots rhetoric of community action only provided these elites with a federal mandate for shaping the program to their own needs (which were not necessarily the same as those of the poor). [p. 5]

Even those power redistributions that did take place were mainly jurisdictional conflicts within and between organizations; they did not constitute substantive policy changes. In the most participatory city, New York, examples were given of serious conflict, but they were always over internal organizational politics and procedures, organizational relations with other agencies, or battles between the neighborhood council and its staff; none were about substantive policy issues. The authors assumed that the conflicts and the high level of participation must have had some consequences, but little evidence was given. They said that "community conflict functioned to generate the articulation of *demands* for broad changes in governmental services to the poor" (p. 185, italics added).

Demands, but not broad changes, is probably accurate. The internal battles for participation and representation of different groups among the poverty communities consumed almost all of their political energies, and procedural and organizational battles became ends in themselves. This illustrates the point that bureaucratic participation, as in Community Action Programs and Model Cities, serves to divert political participation from concern with substantive issues to concern with organizational ones.

One study by May (1971) described the consequences of community participation in West Oakland as substantial.

> The immediate consequence was the creation of a second government for the West Oakland community. West Oakland residents, in effect, declared their independence from the authority of the local government and established new institutions which they vested with legitimacy. [p. 58; see also Hayes 1972]

Left at that, the consequences of participation for the redistribution of power seem rather great. But May immediately added the following:

> Their negotiated victory may prove short lived; a small change in federal administrative or legislative policy could have an enormous effect on the viability of the West Oakland "government." [p. 58]

This undoubtedly accurate prediction underlines a neglected aspect of the recently developed forms of bureaucratic participation by the poor: its almost total dependence on vacillating and undependable federal financial support. State action created the conditions under which various forms of participation are possible, and limited the potential range of their consequences for either the redistribution of power or for substantive policy changes.

A similar conclusion was reached by another study of 54 "community decision organizations" in nine cities conducted from 1967 to 1972, analyzing the impact of citizen participation upon various degrees of responsiveness to the poor (Warren, Rose & Bergunder 1974). The organizations were of several types: Model Cities agencies, Community Action Agencies, public school systems, urban renewal agencies, mental health planning agencies, and health and welfare planning councils. While "gross responsiveness" was fairly great—provision of formal positions on boards, employment of poor residents, formal relationships with organized groups, and informal program review—the impact of actual substantive participation was slight and, more important, was blocked whenever it attempted institutional change. Warren and his collaborators classified the defensive reactions of institutions as "preventing" (effective socialization blocking even initial attempts at change), "blunting," and "repelling" (p. 128 ff). The major example of a significant attempt at change singled out for detailed study was the Oakland Economic Development Council, which ultimately was "destroyed through cutting off its vital resources" (p. 65). Their general conclusion concerning the impact of citizen participation through these bureaucratic agencies was that the usual pattern of participation

> clearly reinforced existing rationales, intervention strategies, and organizational maintenance needs. Where citizen action pressed beyond such insubstantial involvement it encountered—and was usually contained by—... the exercise of various types of co-optation and the exercise of governmental authority. [p. 128]

This interpretation is supported by another recent major work on the origins of various programs which include participation by the poor (Piven & Cloward 1971). The authors stressed the social control functions of such programs.

> Over a period of time ... federal intervention had the effect of absorbing and directing many of the agitational elements in the black population. ... From the perspective of integrating blacks into the political system, the Great Society was a startling success. [pp. 275–76]

Militants became mayors or directors of programs, or Model Cities directors, or community action executives; that is, "they became government employees or contractors, subject to the constraints of federal funding and federal guidelines" (p. 274). This study described not only the origins of the programs in the political requirements of rebuilding the Democratic Party coalition and of quieting black protest, but also the course of concrete program developments in the 1960s. They emphasized the remarkable impact of these programs on the swelling of relief rolls in the 1960s and the place of militant demonstrations and mass actions in producing concrete benefits. "Taken as a whole, there is little reason to doubt that the many-faceted welfare rights movement had a crucial impact on [expanding] the rolls" (p. 331). Thus, the bureaucratic (nonelectoral) participation of the poor can produce temporary and immediate benefits in the form of changes in the practices of bureaucratic agencies, even though permanent structural or institutional change does not take place. Welfare programs are a result of mass demands for government benefits, given the failure of the private sector to provide enough jobs. Piven & Cloward documented the continuous but shifting response of the state to this form of political participation, as first coping with the demands by immediately offering money to prevent continuation or broadening of mass protests (special emergency grants in New York reached an annual rate of 100 million dollars in 1968 following militant mass actions). Then, when protests receded, benefits were reduced, criteria were raised, or people were shifted into low-paying jobs. More generally, the establishment of these federal programs simultaneously provided an organizational target for demands for material benefits—an immediate and tangible goal which precipitated widespread community organization—but also undercut independent political organizations by co-opting community leaders onto the staffs and boards of a wide variety of federally funded agencies. In this way, political participation was channeled into specific forms and against specific types of targets.

The forms of bureaucratic participation just described bear at least some resemblance to traditional politics: elections are held, meetings are attended, officials are petitioned. Not so with the next case of bureaucratic participation: the relations of individuals and groups to the courts, which express "depoliticized" political relations between groups. The example is drawn from a study of garnishments and bankruptcies (Jacob 1969). These actions by creditors (to force employers to turn over a proportion of an employee's wages to them) and by debtors (to be released from their debts) are both instances of Verba & Nie's definition of political participation: actions by private parties aimed at influencing government personnel to do something. That is, courts are petitioned to act either on behalf of the creditor or on behalf of the debtor. As Jacob said, these actions are not normally perceived as "political involvement." However,

> the increasing use of government services, grants, and regulations . . . involves people in the political system in intricate and extensive ways. . . . Such involvement embraces people in the political system more comprehensively than voting. [p. 4]

"Demands articulated through voting, interest group activity, or the media . . . are generally perceived as distinctively *political* acts; consumption [of government services] is rarely perceived as a political act," although as Jacob pointed out, such "consumption activities constitute an important way of expressing political demands" (p. 5).

Jacob's systematic study of a sample of garnishments and bankruptcies in four Wisconsin cities (Madison, Racine, Kenosha, and Green Bay) is a rare example of a study of political participation through nonelectoral institutions, although the form of participation itself is not rare. [See Alford (1969) for another study of the same cities, using leader and citizen interviews. The same data were analyzed by Alford & Scoble (1968).]

Several examples of the class bias of the courts in allowing differential access can be cited. Court action is less readily available to low-income groups.

> The imposition of sanctions in civil suits through the borrowing of state power is usually directed at disadvantaged groups. Low socio-economic status is likely to be associated with the consumption of court sanctions because of the services available and the conditions governing the requisitioning of these services. Eviction orders, wage garnishments, and mortgage closures are readily obtainable; their counterparts which might be directed at landlords, creditors, and banks are not as easily imposed. [Jacob 1969:22]

Even legal institutions originally established to serve the interests of the poor are converted to serve the interests of business:

> The special courts [small claims courts] established to handle these cases—although designed to make justice more accessible to the poor—have become the instruments of businessmen who are their most regular clients. [p. 22]

Among debtors, the incidence of bankruptcy is also class related. The poor do not become bankrupt; the program has been "co-opted by working and lower middle-class credit users." This is so because "the poor do not use credit to the same extent that more prosperous members of the society do, and a portion of the credit they do use comes from loan sharks who would not recognize the cancellation of the debt by bankruptcy" (p. 72). Less than half of those debtors who were garnished used the bankruptcy right, although most were in a legal position to do so.

The findings of this study have been given in some detail to illustrate the point that courts are the objects of political participation and that they, like electoral and bureaucratic institutions, are structured in ways that favor the wealthy and those organized to take advantage of political institutions: finance companies, hospitals, large retailers. These economic institutions are organizationally able to make routine use of court procedures. On the other hand, debtors do not "form the traditional kind of interest group which might operate in the electoral, legislative, or administrative arenas" (p. 53) and are therefore unable to act politically to restructure those legal institutions.

In conclusion, the 1960s witnessed a flurry of attempts to institutionalize the participation of electorally unrepresented, legislatively ineffective, and bureaucratically unincorporated interests: the poor, consumers, blacks, and other minorities. To some extent the very appearance of these mechanisms of bureaucratic participation through a wide variety of programs is testimony to the inability of these sections of the population to use electoral and legislative channels to control the quality and character of public services to them, and also the incapacity of traditional representative institutions to attack the causes of unemployment, low-income jobs, and housing and job discrimination. As the importance and scope of legislative politics has declined, the bureaucratic incorporation of the poor has become critical precisely because of their increasing organization and ability to engage in enormously costly forms of noninstitutionalized participation (see the next section).

The overall structure of participation is critical. Just as the central city is increasingly composed of poor families, and just as blacks are gaining substantial electoral representation as mayors and councilmen, federal urban program grants since World War II locate the origins of urban policy and thus the substantive limitations on urban expenditure *outside* the urban political system. This structure of urban policy formation thus favors those interest groups best able to organize politically at supra-local levels of government. The blacks and the poor have been able to organize politically only at the local level and have been able to mount electoral and nonelectoral political challenges at the local level (riots, New York teachers' strike, minimal blockage of urban renewal programs, election of many black councilmen and mayors). At the national level black groups have been loose, ineffectual federations of local groups. Their efforts have been confined to legislative lobbying in terms of "citizen participation" and reactions at the local implementation stage, once the limits of substantive policy variation have already been set, rather than at the point of policy origin and development. Wolman & Thomas (1970) argue that

at those stages certain actions can be prevented and marginal changes in policy outputs affected, but the major thrust of policies cannot substantially be altered, for they have been shaped in the earlier innovative and formulative stages when the basic agenda is set. [p. 883]

Thus the use of federal and state grants aids local urban policy formation, but the substantive limitations on urban spending are set outside the urban political system. Policy formation and control over the uses of severely limited city fiscal resources are thus made less accessible to local electoral political elites and community groups. Local political elites are reduced to choosing whether or not to participate in federal programs. The impotence of urban electoral power, rather than "revolutions of rising expectations," might explain the observed relationship between black electoral representation and the incidence and intensity of black political protest in cities (Eisinger 1973).

The central city is not a closed system, nor is it a subsystem sufficiently differentiated to permit a theory of urban politics devoid of reference to the relationship between the city and the national political economy. The city is a location for a multitude of class relationships and for the contradictions and social problems these engender. As Katznelson (1975) writes,

America's largest cities can be seen as territories where the most basic class and racial contradictions of American society get expressed as "social problems." [manuscript p. 13]

A recent series of Rand studies on Seattle, St. Louis, and San Jose (Rainey et al 1973, Levine 1972, Morrison 1973, Williams 1973) concluded that the very structure and viability of the central city was outside the control of urban political elites. Economic interests whose economic and political organization as well as the agency and legislative supports for their power are located outside the city (e.g. federal legislation pertaining to FHA financing, prime lending rates, federal legislation on uses of urban renewal, and metropolitan transportation) increasingly determine the quality of life and the viability of our central cities.

Thus the decentralization to the cities of social programs dealing with such problems as poverty, unemployment, lack of social services, and so forth, for lower-income families encourages political participation at a level of government where the political and economic power of those interests that control resources critical to the solution of such problems is not located. It is by no means inevitable that the city should be the point of political participation (e.g. Model Cities, CAP) to deal with the social consequences of contradictions that are experienced locally but that originate and are politically and economically structured elsewhere. The decentralization of funds, policy, and implementation discretion to the city level of government thus reinforces the urban polity as the unit of political participation for response to problems whose causes lie outside the urban system; this insulates from any kind of political challenge dominant interests whose political power and economic organization are located elsewhere. The structure of federal urban programs has been instrumental in minimizing the political organization and power of the poor, while insulating dominant interests from political challenge and thereby minimizing their need for political organization and participation. The structure of the state thereby severs the politics of wealth from the politics of poverty.

The general inference that can be drawn from most of the studies of bureaucratic participation is that these programs are still another example of the way in which participation by the poor is encouraged at the points in the political system where policy making does *not* take place, thus limiting the potential effects of participation to spasmodic challenges of the ways public policies are conventionally implemented. OEO-sponsored bureaucratic participation of the poor was a form of what Edelman (1964) has called "symbolic politics." Participation of this kind functions to produce political quiescence while societal institutions continue to reproduce inequality and injustice.

THE POWER OF VIOLENCE AS PARTICIPATION

The forms of electoral and bureaucratic participation summarized above, whether caused by or producing power, might seem to constitute a stable system of co-optation. Yet the past decade also witnessed considerable turbulence—ghetto revolts, student strikes, antiwar protests, antibusing demonstrations, and the desegregation movement. If these noninstitutionalized and illegitimate types of participation, sometimes taking violent and disruptive forms, can be regarded as temporary, unique, abnormal, or engaged in by pathological personalities, then they do not have to be analyzed within the same theoretical frame of reference as such orderly forms as voting, or even serving on the board of a community action program. The evidence seems to show that this is not the case.

Given the thrust of our interpretation of the literature—namely that institutionalized political participation does not have the power to reshape political priorities, i.e. the power of dominant interests without participation—the system may be a stable one, if in fact votes compensate for wealth, and if serious deprivations and grievances are ultimately responded to. On the other hand, if institutionalized inequalities are reinforced and reproduced by societal institutions, and if these inequalities are not effectively and permanently legitimated by the existence of formal civil, political, and social rights [see Marshall (1964) for this argument], then we might expect periodic outbursts of noninstitutionalized political protest. Such protest might either be sporadic, random, and spontaneous—the result of enormous frustration simply exploding into vandalism and senseless violence—or be directed toward specific objects related to the source of oppression and producing tangible responses from the state. Our argument leads us to hypothesize that such protest is a normal and rational aspect of the political process in the United States, but in addition that repression and co-optation will also operate simultaneously to restore order and maintain the legitimacy of the society and its political institutions.

Research on the ghetto revolts of the 1960s constitutes the main literature in the last decade bearing on this question. It focused largely on the characteristics of riot participants (Paige 1971) or on the correlates of riot or protest location and intensity with community characteristics (Spilerman 1971, Morgan & Clark 1973, Eisinger 1973), but very little on the consequences of riot or protest participation for policy change or for the conditions of life for ghetto residents. It is thus difficult to assess the relative effectiveness of institutionalized versus noninstitutionalized forms of political participation.

Summarizing a wide variety of studies of the ghetto riots of the 1960s, Fogelson (1971) says that

> a substantial minority of the ghetto population, ranging from roughly 10 to 20 per cent, actively participated in the riots. Second, that the rioters, far from being primarily the riffraff and outside agitators, were fairly representative of the ghetto residents. And third, that a sizable minority (or, in some cases, a majority) of blacks who did not riot sympathized with the rioters. [p. 29]

As Fogelson said, these findings have important implications. They suggest that the "violent acts were articulate protests against ghetto conditions" [(p. 30); see also Grimshaw (1969) for a broad collection of both historical and contemporary readings].

The latest published study (Eisinger 1974) reported on a 1970 Milwaukee study that was one of the first to compare white and black samples in a major city. Black protestors were higher than nonprotestors in occupation, income, education, and home ownership. Eisinger interpreted this to mean that protestors were "drawn disproportionately from its more integrated stable elements" (p. 599). For similar findings, see Orbell (1967:450), Matthews & Prothro (1966:418), and Ladd (1966). A majority of blacks in the 1970 Milwaukee survey believed that protest was a device to gain certain ends, either access to decision makers or substantive goals. Forty-three percent of all blacks (71 percent of persons who had engaged in protests) would like to see more protests. Since this survey was taken after the major black protests were over, one might assume that a fairly stable pattern was located. Thus, majority support was found in the black community for those protests regarded as instrumental behavior (see also Marx 1967:15–17).

A survey of 237 black males between 14 and 35 conducted six weeks after the July 1967 revolt in Newark, New Jersey, found that those who reported having participated (over one-third of the respondents) matched the age characteristics of arrested persons in Newark, and also that the blocks used in the sample had reported participant rates roughly corresponding to arrest rates. The author (Paige 1971) concluded that the sample had some validity.

The basic finding relevant here is that those blacks with *highest* political information (knowledge of the race of local and national political figures) and lowest trust in the government were most likely—nearly two-thirds of the group—to have participated in the revolts, rather than the poorly informed (p. 815). Participants were "much *less* likely to be found among the alienated (low information, low trust), the subordinate (low information, high trust), or the allegiant (high information and high trust)" (p. 819, italics added).

A survey of 312 black male heads of households in three Los Angeles areas (Watts, Crenshaw, South Central) immediately after the Watts riot of 1967 found that over one-quarter were "willing to use violence to get Negro rights," although only five percent admitted to having participated in any violent acts (Ransford 1968: recomputed from Table 1, p. 586). Low social contact with whites, a sense of powerlessness (as measured by beliefs that a few people in power run things and that the average citizen has little influence on government decisions), and a belief that blacks were treated no better in Los Angeles than in the South, were all related to willingness to use violence. Among those high on all three, 65 percent were willing to use violence; among those low on all three, 12 percent. Among blacks with some college or more as well as any one of the predisposing conditions, the proportion willing to use violence ranged from one in ten to nearly one in five. Over half of all blacks with less than college education and, in addition, any one of the predisposing conditions, were willing to use violence.

These are highly significant findings, indicating that political violence has a remarkably high degree of support among the black community. These were relatively stable black families: all respondents were male heads of households between 18 and 65. One in ten, even among the best educated, was the lowest proportion found supporting violence in any subgroup analyzed. Ten percent is small only if one is making an analogy to an election. The fact that one-third of the entire sample had low social contact, one-third exhibited high racial dissatisfaction, and nearly one-half felt powerless (recomputed from Table 1, p. 586) indicates that the major preconditions for approval of violence are widespread and likely to increase if conditions do not change. That the proportion approving of violence rose to two-thirds among those with low social contact, high dissatisfaction, and a sense of powerlessness indicates the pervasive if only potential support for political violence among the black community.

These findings that the participants were high status and that participation was widespread and enjoyed wide support in the community are important to stress, because they indicate that political protests and violence must be regarded as an endemic form of political participation to be taken seriously, not only in the midst of or in the aftermath of a disorder.

Individualized forms of violence against property may be proto-political forms of noninstitutionalized participation. Rossi, Berk & Eidson (1974) and Berk & Aldrich (1972) suggested that the probability of a retail store being vandalized in 1967 and 1968—the period of most frequent and most intense riots—was higher if the race of the owner or manager was white or if he had negative attitudes toward customers or civil rights. Further, stores located in residential areas were less likely to be hit than were stores located in specifically commercial zones. The violence seemed thus neither mindless nor random since it was directed against those institutions experienced as directly oppressing the residents.

The connection between "normal" and "protest" politics is exhibited clearly by a case study of Baltimore. Baltimore's city government, up to the riots in April 1968, was able to contain the black community by various political and organizational devices. The Community Action Agency was formed as a city department rather than as a private agency, which gave the Mayor and City Council considerable control over it, enabling them, for example, to deny it the right to hold a voter-registration drive in 1966. Although

militants labored throughout 1966 and 1967 . . . the rewards were meager by almost any standard: a few concessions were wrung from the Establishment, and several previously covert grievances were made overt; but far from having built a solid political base, [the major militant organizations] were reduced at the end of 1967 to little more than paper organizations. [Bachrach & Baratz 1970:76–77]

Bachrach & Baratz offered as a main reason the desire of "probably a clear majority of Baltimore's Negroes . . . to *avoid* conflict" (p. 78). As we have argued earlier in analyzing Verba & Nie's study, such "concurrence" is probably a consequence of the political success of the dominant interests in Baltimore, and not a cause of the absence of conflict. Technically speaking, it is an intervening, not an independent, variable.

Another device for reducing the significance of the federal requirement of community (poor) representation was the exclusion of militants from appointment to the Community Action Commission (p. 82). The staff of the Community Action Agency was also "expressly forbidden to take part, individually or collectively, in demonstrations, protest marches, and the like" (p. 83).

These successful control techniques failed in April 1968 when Baltimore rioted for several days following the assassination of Martin Luther King. Moderates were encouraged to raise their demands. As Bachrach & Baratz put it,

where previously, moderate black leaders sought their objectives within established political channels and in accordance with accepted values and procedures, many of them now were prepared, if necessary, to operate *outside* established channels and in defiance of accepted rules. [p. 88]

Baltimore illustrates the effectiveness of violence in changing the effectiveness of political participation. Bachrach & Baratz said that "in the wake of the riots, long-standing covert grievances became overt and erupted into political conflict in a number of arenas" (p. 88). They coupled this interpretation of the consequences of the riots with an interpretation of the consequences of the various federal programs—Model Cities, the Community Action Agency, Model Urban Neighborhood Demonstration—as having produced access to an integration into the Baltimore political system.

> The programs and money have helped directly by enforcing the administrative guidelines on citizen participation in planning and distributing services. They have helped indirectly in that the poor are increasingly being enlisted to support different local welfare agencies in their competition for a larger share of the city's available funds. [p. 99]

We interpret this consequence as successful incorporation of the demands of the poor, and often of their representatives, into the bureaucratic agencies that utilize the formality of participation to further the organizational and professional interests of the staff.

Rent strikes are a type of political participation intermediate between fully legitimate political activity, such as voting, and violent riots. They illustrate the continuity between various types of political participation and the varying degrees of reliance upon established political institutions by social groups under different conditions. A study of rent strikes in 1963–1964 in New York illustrates these points (Lipsky 1970). The Community Council on Housing, led by Jesse Gray, organized and led rent strikes in between 150 and 200 buildings in the city, mainly in Harlem and the Lower East Side, although relatively few families in each building were on strike. Lipsky gave a detailed analysis of the course of events in 20 buildings.

Central to the protests were high rents, no repairs, and rat infestation. The ambiguous legitimacy of the rent strikes derives from the fact that although the legality of the strikes themselves was problematic, the city in fact possessed, but had never used, many legal powers to force landlords to repair their buildings (p. 94). Lipsky documented the ease with which landlords could use such legal machinery as evictions, and the extreme difficulty that tenants had in using the law for their interests (Chapter 5). Even when the tenants did go on strike, the benefits were few. Even in buildings under court supervision, although some in which many rent strike participants live were repaired,

> just as many continued to live in substandard conditions, were forced to move because of continued disrepair, and/or suffered the paste and putty jobs which pass for workmanship in the slums. [p. 154]

Lipsky concluded that

> when one considers the extraordinary energy required for mounting a rent strike campaign . . . it cannot be said that the payoffs for rent strike participants were commensurate with the effort involved. [pp. 154–56]

However, the protest organization coordinating the rent strikes "was able to obtain extraordinary responsiveness from city agencies in specific instances of complaint" (p. 199). In this respect the strikes were successful.

Eisinger (1974) has pointed out that the routinization of protest may reduce its potential as a form of participation for achieving power.

Escalation ultimately leads to the necessity to consider violence, a step which most practitioners of protest do not wish to take. So they are caught in a dilemma, the resolution of which is not at all clear. [p. 606]

This illustrates the dynamics of shifts from one strategy to another, as a group or class attempts to give one form of political participation or another some tangible consequences in the form of power. For nondominant interests, alteration of both institutionalized and noninstitutionalized bases of participation may be the only secure long-range strategy.

Up to this point, we have primarily treated only studies dealing with the characteristics of protests and protestors, and not at all those concerning the character of the immediate state response to collective violence. Our broadened definition of political participation allows us to consider the mobilization of various components of the state as the ghetto revolts occurred—the police, the courts, the legislature— in their attempt to restore order following the revolts. One recent study has treated this question (Balbus 1973).

Balbus' study focused upon three major black revolts in Los Angeles (1965), Detroit (1966), and Chicago (1968) following Martin Luther King's assassination, including "minor" revolts in each city. The four-day revolt in Detroit was the "single largest instance of collective violence witnessed in this country in our time" (p. 114), since 44 persons were killed (mostly blacks by the police and National Guard), 6000 ghetto residents were arrested, and $40 million in property was damaged. While the revolts in the other two cities were somewhat smaller, in all three cities the legal system was overburdened at every stage, from arrest to charging to arraignment to detention to trial. The submission of participants to the procedures and penalties evoked from the various components of the legal system constituted an important instance of political participation in addition to the participation that constituted the revolt itself.

Balbus found that in all three cities

the processes of arrest, charging, and bail-setting were characterized by serious and widespread abrogations of the dictates of formal rationality and organizational maintenance whose interplay ordinarily determines the nature of these processes. [p. 232]

Arrests were characterized by "dragnets" and an absence of the normal rules of prima facie evidence and witnesses. The normal screening of charges was not carried out, and police requests for prosecution were routinely accepted, not the normal procedure. Except in Chicago, bail was much higher than normal, and normal screening procedures were not exercised; thus releases before trial were much lower than usual. After the revolts were over, the opposite deviations from "legal rationality" were found: releases before trial were sharply higher after the first week, even for felony charges, and the proportion convicted and sentenced to further time in prison was much lower than for equivalent behavior in "normal" times. Balbus emphasized that every component of the legal system strove for normality, however; many more participants could have been killed, held without charges, charged with extraordinary crimes, and tried on trumped-up evidence.

Despite sharp differences among the cities in the proportion of nonwhites, the cohesion of the political authority, and the cohesion of legal defense for the participants, these differences were related to the way the courts treated participants only in the minor revolts, not in the major ones. For the major revolts, the three cities demonstrated remarkably similar curves describing the proportions of cases that went through the various stages from arrest through imprisonment (p. 241). The minor revolts were treated quite differently, however:

> In machine cities [Chicago, less so Detroit] court authorities were more able to overlook the constraints of formal rationality and organizational maintenance than were court authorities in reform cities. [p. 249]

This difference indicated that under conditions of extreme provocation, general factors common to all cities—i.e. the general similarity among the legal and political systems of American cities—prevailed, rather than the internal structural differences among cities.

Balbus' analysis showed how the level of political consciousness of riot participants interacted with the necessity of managing the contradictions among three important functions: the simultaneous maintenance of civil order, the legitimating principle of legal rationality, and the integrity of the organizations comprising the legal system. That is, order could not be restored without both violating due process and overloading the court process. The overall success in minimizing the challenge to legal rationality, despite the sharp deviations from due process summarized above, was possible because neither the defendants nor their legal defense treated the trials as political in character (thus calling for amnesty, or organizing demonstrations in jail or in the courts). Balbus treats this success as evidence of the legal system's effectiveness in the liberal state as an instrument of legal repression that functions by successfully transforming mass protests into "ordinary" criminal behavior, thus treating mass protest with the normal instruments available for individual acts. The political consequence of relying upon legal rationality was to depoliticize violence by subsuming it under normal criminal categories. The liberal response reinforced the repression by seeking only to maintain the rights of "criminals" to due process within the legal system. The balance between the contradictory imperatives could be maintained by political elites because they "encountered no sustained effort to prevent them from doing so on the part of the 'rioters' and/or their political and legal spokesmen" (p. 258).

This case is important for our general argument because, as Balbus said, the revolts were "without organization, leaderless, and generally unaccompanied by far-reaching political demands" (p. 260). Precisely for that reason, the reactions of the state to the revolts could depoliticize the behavior for both participants and liberal publics, although not for political elites who planned future riot controls and instituted various programs responsive to the riots.

The ghetto revolts of the 1960s are only the latest in a long series of challenges to the established order in the United States. A recent study sampled groups in United States history from 1800 to 1945 that have challenged some aspect of the status quo. From about 500 or 600 groups that met the classifying criteria—that the group must have sought to mobilize an unorganized constituency and that the group's antagonists were outside that constituency—53 were chosen for detailed analysis (Gamson 1975: Chapter 2). Gamson summarized a major result of this analysis as follows:

> Those who are unruly have the most notable success. A willingness to use constraints, including violence in some cases, is associated with gaining membership and benefits, not with its opposite. This is only true for groups with certain kinds of goals, but it cannot be said that, in general, violation of the rules of pluralist politics is self-defeating for challengers. [p. 141]

Eight of the 53 groups unequivocally used violence in pursuit of their goals (for one more the evidence was unclear): the Amalgamated Association of Street and Electrical Railway Workers, the Native American Party, the International Longshoremen's Association (on the West coast), the Packinghouse Workers Organizing Committee, the United Hebrew Trades, the Tobacco Night Riders, the Steel Workers Organizing Committee, and the Christian Front Against Communism. Another 13 used some form of "constraint" (strikes, boycotts, personal attacks, or violence). Groups using violence were more likely to gain acceptance from their antagonists (consultation, negotiations, formal recognition, or inclusion) than were violence recipients, and were far more likely to gain new advantages (75 percent) than were either violence recipients (zero percent) or groups that used no violence (53 percent) (p. 79).

Gamson interpreted the data as undermining the hypothesis that "violence is the product of frustration, desperation, and weakness" (p. 81). Instead, "violence should be viewed as an instrumental act, aimed at furthering the purposes of the group that uses it when they have some reason to think it will help their cause" (p. 81). He rejected the distinction between extremist, irrational politics—the viewpoint held by theorists who hold that riots and violence are instances of pathological collective behavior—and normal, pluralist politics (p. 138).

In conclusion, according to Charles Tilly,

> collective violence is one of the commonest forms of political participation. . . . Rather than treating collective violence as an unwholesome deviation from normality, we might do better to ask under what conditions (if any) violence disappears from ordinary political life. [quoted in Gamson 1975:139]

He adds that one should hesitate to

> assume that collective violence is a sort of witless release of tension divorced from workaday politics: [consider] its frequent success as a tactic, its effectiveness in establishing or maintaining a group's political identity, its normative order, its frequent recruitment of ordinary people, and its tendency to evolve in cadence with peaceful political action. [p. 139]

CONCLUSIONS

Many studies of political participation have aggregated bits of individual behavior —voting, contacting public officials, working for a candidate, attending meetings—

into a composite index. Such methodological procedures conceal theoretical premises that allow research to proceed without attention to the "environment" within which such behavior occurs. One such premise is that each bit of behavior is a significant type of participation, neither fictitious, misleading, nor pathological. If, in fact, much of such behavior is purely symbolic with no consequences except personal gratification, or if much of it has the opposite consequences from those intended by the participants, one would have to reconsider the operationalization of the concept. By comparing the rates and aggregate levels of individual participation of different groups, such studies implicitly assume either that participation is the major source of power or that participation can be analytically severed from other bases of power. Our perspective suggests that groups have access to different types of power that affect the level and consequences of their members' participation. Thus the participation of different groups is unlikely to be analytically equivalent.

At the institutional level, an analogous methodological choice is usually made. Participation is analyzed within a single unit of analysis: a legislature, a court, a political party, a program, a decision, or a policy area. This procedure assumes that the process of inputs to and outputs from that unit can be analytically isolated and that a larger historical state-system need not be taken into account. Our perspective on the varied relationships between participation and power has allowed us to treat the literature in a way that links institutions to each other and relates participation in different locations in the state, although few of the studies summarized have done so explicitly.

We briefly summarize the overall findings of this literature, placing them within a theoretical sketch of the relationship among components of the state and class structures that shape the forms and consequences of political participation, and suggest some major lines for future research.

The state structure in the United States has (a) bureaucratically insulated dominant interests from political challenge, (b) politically fragmented and neutralized nondominant interests, (c) supported fiscal and policy dependence on private economic power, and (d) therefore resulted in a lack of legislative or electoral control over the structure of expenditures and revenues. Participation through normal institutionalized channels has little impact on the substance of government policies. Ineffective symbolic responses to the demands of nondominant interests have resulted in cycles of noninstitutionalized participation, co-optation, and repression, and have institutionalized participation as a form of social control. If the structuring of the state has thus prevented the effective political organization of nondominant interests, and if programs designed to meet their needs have been symbolic and ineffectual, then the particularly low level of participation by lower-income individuals is neither analytically surprising nor politically irrational. For pluralist theories of participation and power it is paradoxical that those interests receiving fewest benefits from the society are least likely to participate politically, although they have the most to gain and although political channels are the only ones available to them to achieve power.

The theoretical and methodological implications of our general perspective are several.

1. The structure of the state should be seen neither as a neutral political marketplace nor as a pliable instrument. Rather the structure of the state is the historically specific outcome of conflict among interests over the reorganization of the formerly nonpolitical relationships of domination (Dahrendorf 1959) and processes not previously requiring political legitimation or control. Thus state structure should be seen as the political mediation of relationships among interests—class as well as others. Methodologically this means that one cannot study a particular agency, a particular legislative act, or the attempts of a particular interest to create or control state power, without a serious theoretical bias towards pluralist analysis, in which power is conceived of as expanding with the system's capacity to attain goals or as adhering to the winners of overt political battles. Rather, one must start with a particular social problem and the relationships among different interests that bear upon the creation and solution of that problem. Then one must analyze the way in which the state structure has developed as a result of conflict (or its absence) within the manifest political relationships of interests as well as within the various nonpolitical processes those interests control. One must compare where the capacity to control different processes is located in the state, both in relation to each other and in relation to the level of political organization and bureaucratic incorporation of the different interests.

2. The structure of the state should also be seen as a powerful cause of political organization, political consciousness, and the kinds of demands raised by different interests. The scope of any agency and its structural position vis-à-vis other agencies will vitally affect the nature of demands likely to be raised, the extent to which other interests are likely to be challenged or insulated from political challenge, and the cohesiveness and comprehensiveness of the political organization of different interests.

3. Our analysis leads us to suggest that further research on the causes and consequences of political participation should include a theoretical distinction between structural and systemic power. *Structural* power refers to the ways in which the particular organization of political authority (itself the outcome of historical struggles among interests) differentially affects the level and effectiveness of political participation of different social groups. The structure of the state intervenes between participation and power. The state is an historically structured battleground on which some interests are strategically placed, whereas others are incorporated in locations far from the real centers of power. *Systemic* power refers to the ability of dominant interests to control the material conditions of the legitimacy and effectiveness of the state. To the extent that dominant interests control those economic processes that determine the nature of social problems and delimit the extent and type of state interventions dealing with these social problems, dominant interests wield systemic power.

Political participation by dominant interests is thus not a cause but a consequence of power and is analytically not equivalent to participation by nondominant interests. For dominant interests, participation communicates and reproduces power. For nondominant interests, participation has been a symbolic substitute for power, a means of reproducing the *absence* of political power. Where the participation of nondominant interests, often through noninstitutionalized forms, threatens to become powerful, this is reflected in attempts to restructure the state. The state is reorganized to create locations for the challenging interests that preserve the systemic and structural power of dominant interests, and to thereby minimize the necessity for future participation by the dominant interests.

An analysis that does not take as problematic the historical reproduction of institutional relationships will explain them as resulting from habit, from political culture, or from the individual irrationalities of decision makers faced with a complex, uncertain world. Structural changes appear as genetic developmental sequences. History is analytically depoliticized, just when emerging political and economic conflicts in contemporary Western societies have begun to challenge the adequacy and even the legitimacy of welfare state forms of social policies. This picture of the "normal" process of political participation is obviously not the same interpretation as many of the authors of the studies cited would draw. But we believe that it is sufficiently plausible to serve as a source of hypotheses for research on the economic and political conditions under which political participation can become a genuine and valid contribution to the life of the society, instead of a fictitious and manipulated symbol.

Literature Cited

Aiken, M. 1970. The distribution of community power: structural basis and social consequences. In *The Structure of Community Power*, ed. M. Aiken, P. E. Mott, 487–525. New York: Random House

Aiken, M., Alford, R. R. 1974. Community structure and innovation: public housing, urban renewal, and the War on Poverty. In *Comparative Community Politics*, ed. T. N. Clark, 231–87. New York: Halsted Press Division, Wiley

Alford, R. R. 1963. *Party and Society: The Anglo-American Democracies.* Chicago: Rand McNally

Alford, R. R., in collaboration with Scoble, H. M. 1969. *Bureaucracy and Participation: Political Cultures in Four Wisconsin Cities.* Chicago: Rand McNally

Alford, R. R. 1975. *Health Care Politics: Ideological and Interest Group Barriers to Reform.* Univ. Chicago Press

Alford, R. R., Friedland, R. 1974. Nations, parties, and participation: a critique of political sociology. *Theory Soc.* 1: 307–28

Alford, R. R., Scoble, H. M. 1968. Sources of local political involvement. *Am. Polit. Sci. Rev.* 62:1192–1206

Almond, G. A., Verba, S. 1963. *The Civic Culture: Political Attitudes and Democracy in Five Nations.* Princeton: Princeton Univ. Press

Alyea, P. E. 1967. Property-tax inducements to attract industry. *Property Taxation–USA*, ed. R. W. Lindholm, 139–58. Madison: Univ. Wisconsin Press

Anton, T. J. 1966. *The Politics of State Expenditure in Illinois.* Urbana: Univ. Illinois Press

Bachrach, P., Baratz, M. S. 1970. *Power and Poverty: Theory and Practice.* New York: Oxford Univ. Press

Bahl, R. W. 1969a. *Metropolitan City Expenditures: A Comparative Analysis.* Lexington: Univ. Kentucky Press

Bahl, R. W. 1969b. Studies on determinants of public expenditures: a review. In *Sharing Federal Funds for State and Local Needs: Grants-in-Aid and PPB Systems*, ed. S. J. Mushkin, J. F. Cotton, 184–203, Append. 6. New York: Praeger

Balbus, I. D. 1973. *The Dialectics of Legal Repression: Black Rebels before the American Criminal Courts.* New York: Russell Sage

Barlow, R. 1974. The incidence of selected taxes by income classes. In *Five Thousand Families: Patterns of Economic Plagues,* ed. J. N. Morgan, 2:213–45. Ann Arbor: Univ. Michigan Inst. for Soc. Res.

Berelson, B. R., Lazarsfeld, P. F., McPhee, W. N. 1954. *Voting: A Study of Opinion Formation in a Presidential Campaign.* Chicago: Univ. Chicago Press

Berk, R. A., Aldrich, H. E. 1972. Patterns of vandalism during civil disorders as an indicator of selection of targets. *Am. Sociol. Rev.* 37:533–47

Blalock, H. M. Jr., ed. 1971. *Causal Models in the Social Sciences.* Chicago: Aldine

Boaden, N. 1971. *Urban Policy-Making: Influences on County Boroughs in England and Wales.* Cambridge: Cambridge Univ. Press

Bollens, J. C., Schmandt, H. J. 1970. *The Metropolis: Its People, Politics, and Economic Life.* New York: Harper & Row. 2d ed.

Bonnen, J. T. 1969. The absence of knowledge of distributional impacts: an obstacle to effective public program analysis and decisions. From *The Analysis and Evaluation of Public Expenditures: The PPB System,* a compendium of papers prepared for Subcomm. Econ. Govt. Joint Econ. Comm. US Congr., 91st Congr., 1st Sess. Washington DC: GPO

Booms, B. H., Halldorson, J. R. 1973. The politics of redistribution: a reformulation. *Am. Polit. Sci. Rev.* 67:924–33

Bowles, S. 1972. Unequal education and the reproduction of the social division of labor. In *Schooling in a Corporate Society: The Political Economy of Education in America and the Alternatives Before Us,* ed. M. Carney. New York: McKay

Bruhns, F. C., Cazzola, F., Wiatr, J., eds. 1974. *Local Politics, Development, and Participation: A Cross-National Study of Interrelationships.* Pittsburgh: Univ. Pittsburgh Center Int. Stud.

Burnham, W. D. 1965. The changing shape of the American political universe. *Am. Polit. Sci. Rev.* 59:7–28

Burnham, W. D. 1970. *Critical Elections and the Mainsprings of American Politics.* New York: Norton

Campbell, A. 1966. Surge and decline: a study of electoral change. In *Elections and the Political Order,* A. Campbell, P. E. Converse, W. E. Miller, D. E. Stokes, 40–62. New York: Wiley

Castells, M. 1972. *La Question Urbaine.* Paris: Francois Maspero

Clark, T. N., ed. 1974. *Comparative Community Politics.* New York: Halsted Press Div., Wiley

Clotfelter, J. 1970. Senate voting and constituency stake in defense spending. *J. Polit.* 32:979–83

Cnudde, C. F., McCrone, D. J. 1969. Party competition and welfare policies in the American states. *Am. Polit. Sci. Rev.* 63:858–66

Cole, R. L. 1974. *Citizen Participation and the Urban Policy Process.* Lexington, Mass: Lexington Books

Converse, P. E. 1972. Change in the American electorate. In *The Human Meaning of Social Change,* ed. A. Campbell, P. E. Converse, 263–337. New York: Russell Sage

Cowart, A. T. 1969. Anti-poverty expenditures in the American states: a comparative analysis. *Midwest J. Polit. Sci.* 13:219–36

Crenson, M. A. 1971. *The Un-Politics of Air Pollution: A Study of Non-Decisionmaking in the Cities.* Baltimore: Johns Hopkins Press

Dahl, R. A. 1961. *Who Governs? Democracy and Power in an American City.* New Haven: Yale Univ. Press

Dahrendorf, R. 1959. *Class and Class Conflict in Industrial Society.* Stanford: Stanford Univ. Press

Davies, B. 1968. *Social Needs and Resources in Local Services: A Study of Variations in Standards of Provision in Personal Social Services Between Local Authority Areas.* London: Michael Joseph

Davis, O. A., Dempster, M. A. H., Wildavsky, A. 1966. A theory of the budgetary process. *Am. Polit. Sci. Rev.* 60:529–47

Dawson, R. E. 1967. Social development, party competition, and policy. In *The American Party System: Stages of Political Development,* ed. W. N. Chambers, W. D. Burnham, 203–37. New York: Oxford Univ. Press

Dawson, R. E., Robinson, J. A. 1963. Interparty competition, economic variables, and welfare policies in the American states. *J. Polit.* 25:265–89

Di Palma, G. 1970. *Apathy and Participation: Mass Politics in Western Societies.* New York: Free Press

Domhoff, G. W. 1967. *Who Rules America?* Englewood Cliffs: Prentice-Hall

Domhoff, G. W. 1970. *The Higher Circles: The Governing Class in America.* New York: Random House

Dye, T. R. 1966. *Politics, Economics, and the*

Public: Policy Outcomes in the American States. Chicago: Rand McNally

Dye, T. R. 1972. *Understanding Public Policy.* Englewood Cliffs: Prentice-Hall

Easton, D. 1965. *A Systems Analysis of Political Life.* New York: Wiley

Edelman, M. 1964. *The Symbolic Uses of Politics.* Urbana: Univ. Illinois Press

Edelman, M. 1971. *Politics as Symbolic Action: Mass Arousal and Quiescence.* Chicago: Markham

Ehrmann, H. W. 1971. Interest groups and the bureaucracy in Western democracies. In *European Politics: A Reader,* ed. M. Dogan, R. Rose, 333–53. Boston: Little, Brown. Originally published in French in 1961: *Rev. Fr. de Sci. Polit.* 11:541–68

Eisinger, P. K. 1973. The conditions of protest behavior in American cities. *Am. Polit. Sci. Rev.* 67:11–28

Eisinger, P. K. 1974. Racial differences in protest participation. *Am. Polit. Sci. Rev.* 68:592–606

Fabricant, S. 1952. *The Trend of Government Activity in the United States since 1900.* New York: Nat. Bur. Econ. Res.

Fenno, R. F. Jr. 1966. *The Power of the Purse: Appropriations Politics in Congress.* Boston: Little, Brown

Fenton, J. H. 1966. *People and Parties in Politics: Unofficial Makers of Public Policy.* Glenview, Ill: Scott, Foresman

Fisher, G. W. 1969. *Taxes and Politics: A Study of Illinois Public Finance.* Urbana: Univ. Illinois Press

Flanigan, W. H. 1968. *Political Behavior of the American Electorate.* Boston: Allyn & Bacon

Fogelson, R. M. 1971. *Violence as Protest: A Study of Riots and Ghettos.* Garden City, NY: Anchor Books

Forrester, J. W. 1972. Urban goals and national objectives. *Stud. Comp. Local Govt.* 6:18–26

Francis, W. L. 1967. *Legislative Issues in the Fifty States: A Comparative Analysis.* Chicago: Rand McNally

Fried, R. C. 1975. Comparative urban performance. In *Handbook of Political Science,* ed. F. I. Greenstein, N. W. Polsby, Vol. 6. Reading, Mass.: Addison-Wesley

Fry, B. R., Winters, R. F. 1970. The politics of redistribution. *Am. Polit. Sci. Rev.* 64:508–22

Gamson, W. A. 1968. Stable unrepresentation in American society. *Am. Behav. Sci.* 12:15–21

Gamson, W. A. 1975. *The Strategy of Social Protest.* Homewood, Ill: Dorsey Press

Goldberger, A. S., Duncan, O. D., eds. 1973. *Structural Equation Models in the Social Sciences.* New York: Seminar Press

Greeley, A. M. 1974. Political participation among ethnic groups in the United States: a preliminary reconnaissance. *Am. J. Sociol.* 80:170–204

Greenstone, J. D., Peterson, P. E. 1973. *Race and Authority in Urban Politics: Community Participation and the War on Poverty.* New York: Russell Sage

Greer, S., Orleans, P. 1964. Political sociology. In *Handbook of Modern Sociology,* ed. R. E. L. Faris, 808–51. Chicago: Rand McNally

Grimshaw, A. D., ed. 1969. *Racial Violence in the United States.* Chicago: Aldine

Grumm, J. G. 1972. A test for the existence of feedback in state legislative systems. In *Comparative Legislative Behavior: Frontiers of Research,* ed. S. C. Patterson, J. C. Wahlke, 267–85. New York: Wiley-Intersci.

Hamilton, R. F. 1972. *Class and Politics in the United States.* New York: Wiley

Hansen, S. B. 1973. Participation, political structure, and concurrence. Unpublished paper, Univ. Illinois

Haveman, R. H., Hamrin, R. D., eds. 1973. *The Political Economy of Federal Policy.* New York: Harper & Row

Hayes, E. C. 1972. *Power Structure and Urban Policy: Who Rules in Oakland?* New York: McGraw-Hill

Hibbs, D. A. Jr. 1974. Problems of statistical estimation and causal inference in time-series regression models. In *Sociological Methodology 1973–1974,* ed. H. L. Costner, 252–308. San Francisco: Jossey-Bass

Hill, R. C. 1974. Unionization and racial income inequality in the metropolis. *Am. Sociol. Rev.* 39:507–22

Hofferbert, R. I. 1971. The nationalization of state politics. In *State and Urban Politics: Readings in Comparative Public Policy,* ed. R. I. Hofferbert, I. Sharkansky, 463–74. Boston: Little, Brown

Hofferbert, R. I. 1972. State and community policy studies: a review of comparative input-output analyses. In *Political Science Annual: An International Review,* ed. J. A. Robinson, 3:3–72. Indianapolis: Bobbs-Merrill

Hollingsworth, J. R. 1973. The impact of electoral behavior on public policy. Unpublished paper, Univ. Wisconsin

Huber, J., Form, W. H. 1973. *Income and Ideology: An Analysis of the American Political Formula.* New York: Free Press

Inkeles, A. 1969. Participant citizenship in six developing countries. *Am. Polit. Sci. Rev.* 63:1120–41

Jackman, R. W. 1974. Political democracy and social equality: a comparative analysis. *Am. Sociol. Rev.* 39:29–45

Jacob, H. 1969. *Debtors in Court: The Consumption of Government Services.* Chicago: Rand McNally

Jacob, H., Lipsky, M. 1968. Outputs, structure, and power: an assessment of changes in the study of state and local politics. *J. Polit.* 30:510–38

Jones, B. D. 1973. Competitiveness, role orientations, and legislative responsiveness. *J. Polit.* 35:924–47

Kahl, J. A. 1968. *The Measurement of Modernism: A Study of Values in Brazil and Mexico.* Austin: Univ. Texas Press Inst. Lat. Am. Stud.

Katznelson, I. 1975. The crisis of the capitalist city: urban politics and social control. In *Theoretical Perspectives on Urban Politics,* ed. W. Hawley, M. Lipsky. Englewood Cliffs, NJ: Prentice-Hall

Kelley, S. Jr., Mirer, T. W. 1974. The simple act of voting. *Am. Polit. Sci. Rev.* 68:572–91

Key, V. O. Jr. 1949. *Southern Politics in State and Nation.* New York: Knopf

Key, V. O. Jr. 1956. *American State Politics: An Introduction.* New York: Knopf

Kolko, G. 1963. *The Triumph of Conservatism: A Reinterpretation of American History 1900–1916.* New York: Free Press Glencoe

Kornhauser, W. 1959. *The Politics of Mass Society.* New York: Free Press Glencoe

Kramer, R. M. 1969. *Participation of the Poor: Comparative Community Case Studies in the War on Poverty.* Englewood Cliffs: Prentice-Hall

Krause, E. A. 1968. Functions of a bureaucratic ideology: "citizen participation." *Soc. Probl.* 16:129–43

Ladd, E. C. Jr. 1966. *Negro Political Leadership in the South.* Ithaca, NY: Cornell Univ. Press

Levine, R. A. 1972. *San Jose: The Urban Crisis and the Feds.* Santa Monica, Cal: Rand Corp. Research Paper, p. 4839

Levitan, S. A. 1969. *The Great Society's Poor Law: A New Approach to Poverty.* Baltimore: Johns Hopkins Press

Lieberson, S. 1971. An empirical study of military-industrial linkages. *Am. J. Sociol.* 76:562–84

Lipset, S. M. 1960. *Political Man: The Social Bases of Politics.* Garden City, NY: Doubleday

Lipset, S. M. 1963. *The First New Nation: The United States in Historical and Comparative Perspective.* New York: Basic Books

Lipset, S. M., Rokkan, S. 1967. Cleavage structures, party systems, and voter alignments: an introduction. In *Party Systems and Voter Alignments: Cross-National Perspectives,* S. M. Lipset, S. Rokkan, 1–64. New York: Free Press

Lipsky, M. 1970. *Protest in City Politics: Rent Strikes, Housing and the Power of the Poor.* Chicago: Rand McNally

Lockard, D. 1959. *New England State Politics.* Princeton, NJ: Princeton Univ. Press

March, J. G. 1966. The power of power. *Varieties of Political Theory,* ed. D. Easton, 39–70. Englewood Cliffs, NJ: Prentice-Hall

Marshall, D. R. 1971. *The Politics of Participation in Poverty: A Case Study of the Board of Economic and Youth Opportunities Agency of Greater Los Angeles.* Berkeley: Univ. Calif. Press

Marshall, T. H. 1964. *Class, Citizenship, and Social Development.* Garden City, NY: Doubleday

Marx, G. T. 1967. *Protest and Prejudice: A Study of Belief in the Black Community.* New York: Harper & Row

Matthews, D. R., Prothro, J. W. 1966. *Negroes and the New Southern Politics.* New York: Harcourt, Brace & World

May, J. V. 1971. Two model cities: negotiations in Oakland. *Polit. Soc.* 2:57–88

McClosky, H. 1968. Political participation. *Int. Encycl. Soc. Sci.* 12:252–65

McConnell, G. 1966. *Private Power and American Democracy.* New York: Knopf

McFarland, A. S. 1969. *Power and Leadership in Pluralist Systems.* Stanford: Stanford Univ. Press

Meltsner, A. J. 1971. *The Politics of City Revenue.* Berkeley: Univ. Calif. Press

Milbrath, L. W. 1965. *Political Participation: How and Why Do People Get Involved in Politics?* Chicago: Rand McNally

Miller, W. E. 1964. Majority rule and the representative system of government. In *Cleavages, Ideologies and Party Systems: Contributions to Comparative Political Sociology,* ed. E. Allardt, Y. Littunen, X: 343–76. Helsinki: Trans. Westermark Soc.

Miller, W. E., Stokes, D. E. 1963. Constituency influence in Congress. *Am. Polit. Sci. Rev.* 57:45–56

Morgan, W. R., Clark, T. N. 1973. The causes of racial disorders: a grievance-level explanation. *Am. Sociol. Rev.* 38:611–24

Morrison, P. 1973. *San Jose and St. Louis in the 1960's: A Case Study of Changing Urban Populations.* Santa Monica, Calif.: Rand Corp. Rep. R-1313 NSF

Munger, F. 1969. *Opinions, Elections, Parties, and Policies: A Cross State Analysis.* Presented at Ann. Meet. Am. Polit. Sci. Assoc., New York

Munger, F., Mezey, M. 1968. *Participation and Party Competition as Determinants of State Policy: The Old Politics and the New.* Presented at Ann. Meet. NY State Polit. Sci. Assoc., Poughkeepsie

Netzer, D. 1966. *Economics of the Property Tax.* Washington DC: Brookings Inst.

Nie, N. H., Powell, G. B. Jr., Prewitt, K. 1969. Social structure and political participation: developmental relationships. *Am. Polit. Sci. Rev.* 63:361–78, 808–32

O'Connor, J. 1973. *The Fiscal Crisis of the State.* New York: St. Martin's Press

Offe, C. 1972. Political authority and class structures—an analysis of late capitalist societies. *Int. J. Sociol.* 2:73–108

Orbell, J. M. 1967. Protest participation among Southern Negro college students. *Am. Polit. Sci. Rev.* 61:446–56

Paige, J. M. 1971. Political orientation and riot participation. *Am. Sociol. Rev.* 36:810–20

Parenti, M. 1970. Power and pluralism: a view from the bottom. *J. Polit.* 32:501–30

Pateman, C. 1970. *Participation and Democratic Theory.* Cambridge: Cambridge Univ. Press

Peacock, A. T., Wiseman, J. 1961. *The Growth of Public Expenditure in the United Kingdom.* Princeton: Princeton Univ. Press

Penniman, C. 1965. The politics of taxation. In *Politics in the American States: A Comparative Analysis,* ed. H. Jacob, K. N. Vines, 291–329. Boston: Little, Brown

Piven, F. F., Cloward, R. A. 1971. *Regulating the Poor: The Functions of Public Welfare.* New York: Pantheon Books

Polsby, N. W. 1963. *Community Power and Political Theory.* New Haven: Yale Univ. Press

Pressman, J. L., Wildavsky, A. B. 1973. *Implementation: How Great Expectations in Washington Are Dashed in Oakland; Or, Why It's Amazing that Federal Programs Work at All, This Being a Saga of the Economic Development Administration as Told by Two Sympathetic Observers Who Seek to Build Morals on a*

Foundation of Ruined Hopes. Berkeley: Univ. Calif. Press

Radosh, R., Rothbard, M. N., eds. 1972. *A New History of Leviathan: Essays on the Rise of the American Corporate State.* New York: Dutton

Rainey, R. B. Jr. et al 1973. *Seattle's Adaptation to Recession.* Santa Monica, Calif: Rand Corp. Rep. R-1352 NSF

Ranney, A. 1972. Turnout and representation in presidential primary elections. *Am. Polit. Sci. Rev.* 66:21–37

Ransford, H. E. 1968. Isolation, powerlessness, and violence: a study of attitudes and participation in the Watts riot. *Am. J. Sociol.* 73:581–91

Redman, E. 1973. *The Dance of Legislation.* New York: Simon & Schuster

Rokkan, S. 1970. *Citizens, Elections, Parties: Approaches to the Comparative Study of the Processes of Development.* New York: McKay

Rose, A. M. 1967. *The Power Structure: Political Process in American Society.* New York: Oxford Univ. Press

Rose, D. D. 1973. National and local forces in state politics: the implications of multi-level policy analysis. *Am. Polit. Sci. Rev.* 67:1162–73

Rossi, P. H., Berk, R. A., Eidson, B. K. 1974. *The Roots of Urban Discontent: Public Policy, Municipal Institutions, and the Ghetto.* New York: Wiley

Sacks, S., Harris, R. 1964. The determinants of state and local government expenditures and intergovernmental flows of funds. *Nat. Tax J.* 17:78–85

Schulze, R. O. 1961. The bifurcation of power in a satellite city. In *Community Political Systems,* ed. M. Janowitz, 19–80. Glencoe: Free Press

Schumaker, P. 1974. *Protest Groups, Environmental Characteristics and Policy-Responsiveness.* Presented at Ann. Meet. Midwest Polit. Sci. Assoc., Chicago

Shaffer, W. R., Weber, R. E. 1972. *Political Responsiveness in the American States.* Presented at Ann. Meet. Am. Polit. Sci. Assoc., Washington DC

Sharkansky, I. 1967a. Economic and political correlates of state government expenditures: general tendencies and deviant cases. *Midwest J. Polit. Sci.* 11:173–92

Sharkansky, I. 1967b. Government expenditures and public services in the American states. *Am. Polit. Sci. Rev.* 61:1066–77

Sharkansky, I. 1969. *The Politics of Taxing and Spending.* Indianapolis: Bobbs-Merrill

Sharkansky, I. 1970. *The Routines of Politics.* New York: Van Nostrand Reinhold

Sharpe, L. J. 1973. American democracy reconsidered: part II and conclusions. *Brit. J. Polit. Sci.* 3:129–67

Shonfield, A. 1965. *Modern Capitalism: The Changing Balance of Public and Private Power.* New York: Oxford Univ. Press

Spilerman, S. 1971. The causes of racial disturbances: tests of an explanation. *Am. Sociol. Rev.* 36:427–42

Sundquist, J. L. 1969. *Making Federalism Work: A Study of Program Coordination at the Community Level.* Washington DC: Brookings Inst.

Verba, S., Nie, N. H. 1972. *Participation in America: Political Democracy and Social Equality.* New York: Harper & Row

Verba, S., Nie, N. H., Kim, J. 1971. *The Modes of Democratic Participation: A Cross-National Comparison.* Beverly Hills, Calif: Sage Publ.

Wahlke, J. C., Buchanan, W., Eulau, H., Ferguson, L. C. 1960. American state legislators' role orientations toward pressure groups. *J. Polit.* 22:203–27

Warren, R. L., Rose, S. M., Bergunder, A. F.

1974. *The Structure of Urban Reform.* Lexington, Mass: Lexington Books

Weinstein, J. 1968. *The Corporate Ideal in the Liberal State: 1900–1918.* Boston: Beacon Press

Wildavsky, A. 1964. *The Politics of the Budgetary Process.* Boston: Little, Brown

Williams, B. 1973. *St. Louis: A City and Its Suburbs.* Santa Monica, Calif: Rand Corp. Rep. R-1353 NSF

Wilson, J. Q., Banfield, E. C. 1964. Public-regardingness as a value premise in voting behavior. *Am. Polit. Sci. Rev.* 58:876–87

Wolff, R. P. 1965. Beyond tolerance. In *A Critique of Pure Tolerance,* R. P. Wolff, B. Moore Jr., H. Marcuse, 3–52. Boston: Beacon

Wolman, H. L., Thomas, N. C. 1970. Black interests, black groups, and black influence in the federal policy process: the cases of housing and education. *J. Polit.* 32:875–97

Zeigler, H. 1965. Interest groups in the states. In *Politics in the American States: A Comparative Analysis,* ed. H. Jacob, K. N. Vines, 101–47. Boston: Little, Brown